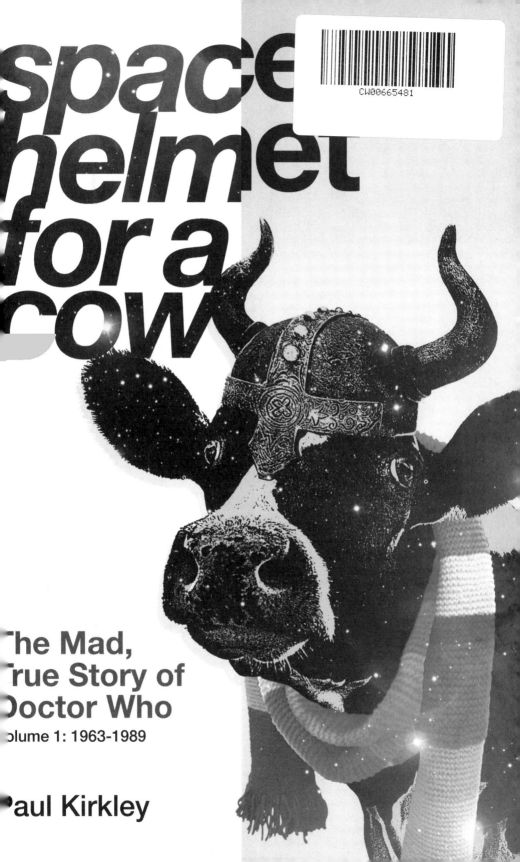

space helmet for a cow

The Mad, True Story of Doctor Who

Volume 1: 1963-1989

Paul Kirkley

Introduction

The celebrated screenwriter Nigel Kneale once described *Doctor Who* as the sort of terrible idea you might have in the bath, and then forget about. But he was just bitter because no-one ever offered to market a Quatermass talking doll or a Year of the Sex Olympics ice lolly.

Fortunately for us, the people who created *Doctor Who* – and the programme is a rare example of successful design by committee – managed to remember the idea long enough to get out of the tub and find a pen. Not that I'm suggesting they were all in the bath together. Though they might have been, I suppose: it *was* the 60s, and they did work in television.

But I digress. Frequently. In fact, that's one of the things you'll notice that's a bit different about this book. Because there have been millions upon millions of words written on the subject of *Doctor Who* – surely a contender for the most analysed television programme of all time. And many of these millions of words are by people who actually worked on the show, as opposed to just watched it.

But for a programme that is, at heart, an entertainment – and perhaps more frequently than we would care to admit, slightly *silly* entertainment at that – it's surprising how seriously many writers have chosen to treat the subject. And that's just the straight-down-the-line histories: don't even get me *started* on the avalanche of academic texts in which earnest media studies lecturers – the sort of people who "read" television, while the rest of us merely watch it – ruminate on discourses of authorship and metatextual signifiers in a Doctor Who duvet set, or stretch to depict the jelly monsters from *The Three Doctors* as a metaphor for fluctuations in 1970s international... um, jelly tariffs.

Actually, I'm fortunate enough to call several such authors friends, and they're not really that earnest at all. In fact, most of them could drink me under the table. Also, you'd be surprised how metatextual a duvet set can be. But, as someone who thought Todorov was the

bloke from *Fiddler on the Roof*, I don't really feel qualified to sit at that particular table so, instead, I set out with the simple aim of writing as entertaining a history of *Doctor Who* as possible.

Because here's another thing: despite whole forests laying down their lives for the *Doctor Who* publishing industry, there are surprisingly few books available telling the story of how the show was actually *made*, and the incredible, colourful and occasionally downright crazy people who made it. In fact, I'm going to stick my brass neck out and say this may well be the most in-depth history of *Doctor Who* ever published as a single, unfolding narrative. And if it isn't, it's certainly the most in-depth history of *Doctor Who* ever published as a single, unfolding narrative with lots of stupid jokes.

An important note on fact vs. fiction: This is the true story of *Doctor Who* but, along the way, I have had a little fun imagining the conversations that *might* have happened between certain parties. (It's very hard to avoid doing this, if you're made – like myself – to repeatedly stop and ponder the bizarre situations so many of the prime movers behind *Doctor Who* found themselves in.) Hopefully, it will be blindingly obvious which quotes are real and which are flights of fancy.

That said, this is a story where truth is occasionally stranger – and certainly sillier – than fiction. So, just to remove any doubt, this book adheres to the following system: If it's a real quote, it will be outside parentheses and have an Arabic numeral after it, and the source of that quote will be appropriately credited in the Sourcing Notations section. If there's no such number and it's within parentheses, then it's just my little joke. If there's a Roman numeral, that refers to additional information in the End Notes section (where I give a quick summation of the Hartnell titles debate, the UNIT dating controversy, etc and so on). Try not to get over-stimulated.

What you have in your hands, then, is not a spoof or a pastiche: for newcomers, or people who only know the bare bones of the story, my ambition is to provide a genuinely useful, highly readable guide to the evolution of the world's greatest TV series, crammed with as many fascinating facts and as much behind-the-scenes gossip as I could a) find and b) get past the lawyers.

But I also want the book to appeal to those fans, like me, who can (and quite possibly do) recite story production codes in their sleep, who toss out phrases like "pseudo-historical", "cosmic hobo" and "Edwardian roadster" (stay with me newbies – all will become clear) like it's the most natural thing in the world, and for whom burgundy is neither a region of France nor a fine-bodied Pinot noir but the colour of Tom Baker's fetching Season 18 scarf-and-coat combo.

This is a book, then, that will tell you which Doctor is which (and even in which order – I told you it was a proper history and every-thing) and which of their adventures, in the author's humble opinion, are most worthy of your time. (I'm not sure at which point I decided I would also review every story – all 241 of the buggers – though I strongly suspect alcohol must have been involved.) But it's also a book which asks the questions others were too afraid – or possibly just too sensible – to ask. Questions like: Where does a Yeti keep change for the loo? How does a talking cab-bage get an Equity card? Who is Fiachra Trench, if not a cabaret drag act? What would have been in William Hartnell's Glastonbury set? Is Begonia Pope a Catholic? And what the hell is a "roundel" anyway?

I hope, in short, that I have found a fresh, engaging way of telling this fascinating, thrill-ing, hilarious, heroic, poignant and frequently ridiculous story, whether you are familiar with that story or not. If the result has even a frac-tion of the wit and warmth and joie de vivre of the series itself, then I will consider it a job well done.

Adventures in Time and Spain... in Space!

1963: BBC dragged kicking and screaming into the 50s

Sydney Newman was once described – by the Controller of BBC Television, no less – as "a Canadian who looked like a Mexican." This is both racist and wrong. With his bow tie, bushy black eyebrows, slicked back hair and comedy moustache, Newman looked like a cross between Groucho Marx, a travelling showman and the Joker's jollier, less psychotic uncle.

What he decisively didn't look like, when he joined the British Broadcasting Corporation in 1963, was any of his colleagues. It's often said Britain was psychologically still stuck in the Fifties until The Beatles came along; if that's true, many at the BBC were still struggling to let go of the Forties. Run by people who'd cut their teeth in radio – the wireless was still very much the respectable medium back then – BBC Television existed in a world of Harris tweed and Windsor knots, the air thick with pipe smoke and the tang of dry sherry. You've seen *Mad Men*? Well, it was absolutely nothing like that.

Since arriving in Britain in 1958, Newman had been working as a senior drama producer at independent television franchise ABC, where he had successfully launched stylish espionage caper *The Avengers* and the ground-breaking anthology series *Armchair Theatre*.

The latter had created a stir by broadcasting plays about "real people" – some of whom didn't even have servants or a separate parlour for Sundays. *I know!* Newman recognised that, while television was a mass medium, its drama output was largely aimed at an educated elite. "Damn the upper classes," he said. "They don't even *own* televisions."[1] (Some of them did, of course, but they kept them discreetly hidden behind tasteful antique tapestries and only wheeled them out for coronations and state funerals.)

The BBC's diet of classic serials and drawing room dramas looked particularly dated in the face of the new breed of "kitchen sink" realism that had swept through theatre, literature and film: by 1963, John Osborne's *Look Back in Anger* was already seven years old, and social realist writers like Alan Sillitoe and Shelagh Delaney had seen their books and plays adapted for the big screen. Some of them were even set in the North. *I know!*

But the Beeb's phalanx of ex-wing commanders and recalled foreign bureau correspondents weren't ready for the kitchen sink quite yet. (Indeed, what would a sink even be *doing* in a kitchen – it ought to be in the scullery, surely?) So it came as quite a shock when this brash, no-nonsense Canadian was brought in as the new Head of Drama Series and Serials. (Readers in the US might like to ponder just how conservative the Corporation must have been at the time for a Canadian to be considered "brash".)

One of the first conversations between Newman and his new boss Donald Baverstock – after the awkward one about the best place to buy tortillas and sombreros in Shepherd's Bush – concerned the need for a new programme to fill a gap in the schedules between Saturday afternoon sports mainstay *Grandstand* and *Juke Box Jury*, a sort of musical crown court, in which groovy hep cats like Pete Murray, Alma Cogan and Thora Hird passed sentence on the latest single releases.

Newman, who had previously produced the children's serials *Pathfinders in Space* and its sequels, asked Donald Wilson, his pipe-smoking Head of Serials, to convene a meeting to discuss ideas for a new science fiction series. Wilson invited input from Alice Frick and John Braybon, two of three story editors who had authored reports on the potential for a sci-fi series the previous year. (The third was Donald Bull: basically, if you wanted to work for the BBC in the early 60s, it helped to be called Donald; even Frick must have considered changing her name and investing in a briar pipe and a tin of Ready Rub.) Also present was staff writer Cecil Edwin Webber – known to all as Bunny. Probably best not to ask.

It was Wilson who first floated the idea of a time-space machine, while Braybon favoured the idea of a group of scientific troubleshooters. Webber was tasked with developing some of the ideas further, and his proposal, delivered at the end of March, included the following character suggestions: A "handsome young hero (to appeal to teenagers)"; a "handsome, well-dressed heroine (appealing to older women)" and a "maturer man, 35-40, with some 'character twist' (appeal to fathers)". It says a lot about the era that 35-year-old men were considered "mature": this was in the days when they had to look and act like grown-ups, instead of dressing like teenagers and spending all day playing *Angry Birds* on their iPads.

Newman liked the characters, and the time travel concept (he had previously tried to launch a time travel show at ABC), but vetoed the "troubleshooters" notion in favour of his own idea of a senile old man who had fled his own planet in a time machine. He would be accompanied by a teenage girl, while an older couple would provide the romance. In other words, being a typical manager, he ignored nearly everything his staff had said and told them to do it his way instead.

Newman also insisted he wanted the programme as "rooted in reality" as possible and to avoid science fiction clichés, while early paperwork pointed out the series should be classified as "neither fantasy nor space travel nor science fiction".

Webber came back with a revised proposal for a series, to be split into serials of six or seven 25-minute episodes, about four people travelling through space and time in an unreliable invisible spaceship. The foursome were identified as: Bridget, or Biddy, a "with it" 15-year-old girl; a 24-year-old school teacher called Lola McGovern (who would be slightly "timid" – despite the porn star name); athletic schoolmaster Cliff; and, finally, Dr Who, "a frail old man lost in space and time". According to Webber, "they give him this name because they don't know who he is". (Note the lack of a question mark, though: we might have

expected better punctuation from two teachers, but that's inner-city schools for you.)

Webber also had a curious notion about Dr. Who having "a hatred of scientists, inventors, improvers" and "malignantly" trying to stop progress wherever he finds it, while searching for some personal panacea in the past. Newman carefully annotated this suggestion by writing "NUTS!" next to it in great big letters. He also rejected the invisible spaceship idea, but numerous elements of Webber's proposed opening episode, "Nothing at the End of the Lane", would eventually make it to the screen. (One of them, the idea that the Doctor's own people were concerned with him "monkeying around with time", would take years to come to fruition – and, disappointingly, even when it did, the charge of "monkeying" would never formally be laid.)

Newman had approached Rex Tucker, one of BBC drama's six staff directors, to produce the show, which was now slated to be recorded in early July for broadcast later that month, with a budget of £2,300 per episode. Tucker and Newman had several meetings with another staff director, Richard Martin, who was in line to helm the first episodes, and it was from these sessions that the name Dr. Who appears to have emerged. (Some accounts have Tucker scribbling himself a footnote in TV history, while Martin recalled that Newman wrote "Dr who?" on a piece of paper, and the title of the show was arrived at when no-one in the room could think of a proper answer, but this sounds suspiciously more like a convention anecdote than an actual fact.)

In discussion with Newman and Wilson, Bunny Webber created a further document with various ideas for future stories, including an adventure in Roman Britain and something set, rather vaguely, on "Mars or Venus" ("Which is the red one again?"). By now, Bridget had become Sue, Dr. Who's age was given as 650 (though casting would probably need to look for someone younger) and his time ship originated in the year 5733. Webber also included a synopsis for a debut serial called *The Giants*, in which our heroes would be accidentally miniaturised in Cliff's lab, and suggested that the ship could be disguised as a police telephone box. Perhaps to Webber's surprise,

Newman did not write NUTS! next to this latter, somewhat out-of-left-field idea.

Newman and Wilson made further revisions to the format for the show, which was now scheduled for an August launch. Meanwhile, Tucker approached Welsh actor Hugh David – then in his late 30s – about playing the lead, but he had recently starred in a Granada adventure series called *Knight Errant*, and wasn't interested in another potentially long-running TV role.

In May, Webber handed in his completed synopsis for *The Giants*. Newman wasn't happy: he said it was low on action, character and drama, and the visual effects were too ambitious. He also disliked the idea of a giant spider, as he was obsessed by the idea of the show not featuring what he called BEMs: Bug Eyed Monsters. ("Okay, but *apart* from that, what did you think?")

Possibly alone at the BBC at that time, Newman was a science fiction fan, and knew exactly what he wanted from his new show. "*Doctor Who* was really the culmination of almost all my interests in life," he recalled in later years. "I wanted to reflect contemporary society; I was curious about the outer-space stuff and, of course, being a children's programme, it had to have a high educational content.

"I wrote in my memo that the outer-space stories must be based on factual knowledge. Also, by going back in time, we could bring history alive for the young, having Dr. Who on the shores of Britain when Caesar landed – that sort of thing."[1]

In June, Tucker was taken off the job – apparently much to his relief, as he wasn't really interested in the show (though he was still slated to direct some episodes) – and Newman offered it to another director, Don Taylor, who turned it down. ("Really though, Sydney, everyone at the BBC is very excited and totally behind this new show of yours. And of course, I'd *love* to do it, but I'm, erm, busy that month. Whichever month it is.")

When he received a phone call from a former ABC colleague – a "fiery" production assistant called Verity Lambert – Newman advised her to apply for the job of *Dr Who* producer, deliberately goading her into giving it her best shot by saying she probably wouldn't

get it. It worked. The Roedean-educated daughter of a Jewish London accountant, Lambert was just 27 when she arrived at the BBC, where no producer had previously had the audacity to be both a woman and below 30. Naturally, feathers were ruffled.

"There were rumblings because Verity was a girl," said Newman. "She was tough, good looking and stubborn. If she didn't like something, she came out honestly and said so."[2] (To which BBC managers most likely responded: "Calm down dear – let's not spoil that pretty face with a frown, shall we?")

"All of a sudden, this woman arrived on the scene," Lambert recalled. "Not just a woman, but a very young woman, comparatively, and the only one in the department. I had never produced anything. I hadn't got a university degree. I was not a BBC-type person. I was aware that I was an oddity. People were not particularly rude to my face, but they were obviously quite shocked when they met me for the first time."[2]

Lambert had to put up with a lot of gossip and innuendo about how she might have got the job, but the challenge of launching what was potentially a year-round show with just three months' set-up time was enough to focus her mind on the job ahead. As a precaution, Wilson brought in Mervyn Pinfield – a technically accomplished producer and director, who had experience of science fiction – to hold her hand. Not literally, of course – she'd probably have bitten it off.

David Whitaker, a staffer in the BBC Script Department, had also been recruited as story editor. He'd commissioned a script from Australian staff writer James Anthony Coburn about prehistoric man's quest for fire circa 100,000 BC; when Bunny Webber's "Nothing at the End of the Lane" went down with a terminal case of myxomatosis, this serial was moved into pole position, Coburn taking Webber's opening episode outline and grafting it onto the front of his caveman caper, giving a name – TARDIS – to Dr Who's ship (though it's not clear if this was Coburn's invention or something he was told to include) and making it clear, for decency's sake, that his teenage travelling companion was actually his granddaughter. And just to make extra sure no-one could ever perceive her as a sex object, her name was changed to Susan.

When they arrived, Coburn's scripts – in which much of the dialogue consisted of people going "uuuggh" and "aaagghh" – were not exactly what Lambert and Whitaker had been hoping for to launch this shiny new series. "I can honestly say, had I had the choice, I would not have commissioned the first serial on cavemen," admitted Lambert. "I thought it was extremely difficult to do with a straight face."[3] Especially if you were made up as a caveman at the time.

Writer Terence Dudley was asked to provide a different script at short notice, but that didn't work out either, and no-one else was available, *Quatermass* creator Nigel Kneale being among the growing number of people who had passed on the project.

In the end, Whitaker was forced to rely heavily on Associated London Scripts, which had been founded as a not-for-profit writers' co-operative in the 1950s by Eric Sykes, Spike Milligan and *Hancock's Half Hour/Steptoe and Son* writers Ray Galton and Alan Simpson. Fortunately for Whitaker, it wasn't a particularly radical workers' collective, so he wasn't faced with too many scripts in which our heroes visit the planet of the Greedy Space Capitalists and set about implementing a programme of agrarian reform based on shared land ownership.

When Newman returned from holiday in June, he was furious to find the production still in a state of disarray. Broadcast was put back again, this time to early November, while Tucker and Martin were joined on the director's roster by a young Anglo-Indian director called Waris Hussein. Cue more spluttering into sherry glasses: first women, now colonials – what kind of a bloody ship did Newman think he was running here?

"I'll never forget the first drama directors meeting," recalled Hussein. "We all sat around this table and I could feel myself being stared at. It was like going back to school."[2] They were probably waiting for him to serve the drinks.

By now, the show's target audience had been identified as eight to 14-year-olds. Traditionally, anything for that age group had been produced by the BBC's Children's Department, but

Newman was keen to give it to the Drama Department. This managed to upset just about everyone, as the Children's Department wanted it and couldn't have it, and the Drama Department got it and didn't want it.

And they weren't the only ones who thought this new kids' show was beneath them. "I didn't feel I was taken seriously by the servicing departments," Lambert complained. "Design in particular was absolutely horrendous and behaved abominably. They gave me a designer, Peter Brachacki, who wasn't available most of the time and was basically incredibly patronising.

"The attitude of his bosses was equally disgraceful: they tried to scupper the entire series by taking the cost of the TARDIS set and averaging it over 13 rather than 52 episodes, then saying it wasn't going to be done for the money. They did everything they possibly could to try and make it not work."[2]

In fact, official BBC paperwork shows the head of the design department made a formal complaint about the show, claiming it would put both his staff and their colleagues in the Scenic Services Department in an "untenable" position, adding: "This is the kind of crazy enterprise which both departments could well do without."

Design's bit of creative accounting over the cost of the TARDIS prompted Donald Baverstock to send a memo to Donald Wilson kicking off about the budget overspend. "Such a costly serial is not one that I can afford for this space in this financial year," he wrote. "You should not therefore proceed any further with the production of more than 4 episodes." He finished by demanding ideas for a replacement show at "a reliable economic price".[1]

Lambert was hauled into the office of Joanna Spicer, Assistant Controller of Planning for Television ("a terrifying woman"[1] according to the producer), where she explained the design department's bit of mischief-making. Spicer agreed to fix the budget of future episodes at £2,500 each, and Baverstock agreed to an initial batch of 13 episodes, dependent on the outcome of the pilot. Not long after, Barry Newbery was appointed as *Dr Who's* new designer after Brachacki fell ill – presumably having worked really hard on his phoning-in-sick voice.

The various delays to production meant Hussein, not Tucker, was now scheduled to direct the pilot. He had found Brachacki equally un-cooperative: "Quite frankly, he didn't care a jot for *Doctor Who*. He thought the show was a load of bollocks. The TARDIS interior was just a hexagonal control panel, which he literally threw together in an afternoon. He then gave me three walls with circles in them and said 'That's your ship'. He couldn't be bothered thinking about it."[5] Though, to be fair, he was probably quite a busy man who didn't have time to sit around staring at the three walls. Besides, if they thought *he* was grumpy, irritable and difficult to work with, they hadn't seen anything yet. It's time to meet the star of our show.

Don't Carry On, Sergeant

Born in St Pancras in 1908 to an unmarried mother, and partly raised by family members and a foster mother, William "Billy" Hartnell had fallen into petty crime after leaving school, before being introduced to acting by a mentor he'd met at a boys' boxing club.

By the early 60s, he had appeared in more than 60 films (and spectacularly failed to appear in one more: after Hartnell turned up late on the first day of shooting for Noel Coward's *In Which We Serve*, Coward made him personally apologise to every member of the cast and crew, and then fired him). He specialised in hard case roles like policemen, soldiers and heavies, and was best known to television audiences from his recent turn as Sergeant Major Bullimore in National Service comedy *The Army Game*. (He had also played the titular – oooh matron, stop messin' about, etc – Sergeant in the first Carry On film, i.e. the one without any of the regular Carry On actors. Or any jokes, come to that.)

Tiring of these tough guy parts, Hartnell had jumped at the chance to appear in the more sensitive role of an ageing talent scout in Lindsay Anderson's 1963 film adaptation of David Storey's *This Sporting Life*, which was about an angry young Yorkshire coal miner who takes out his aggression on the rugby pitch. Television executives of a sensitive disposition should be warned that it contains several kitchen sinks.

For the crucial lead part in *Dr Who*, Verity Lambert had initially approached the distinguished Shakespearean actor Leslie French. He turned it down, as did the Irish stage and screen veteran Cyril Cusack and a younger actor called Geoffrey Bayldon, who decided the role of the eccentric, time-travelling Doctor wasn't for him, before going on to find fame as the eccentric, time-travelling wizard Catweazle.

As the search continued, Lambert remembered William Hartnell's performance in *This Sporting Life*. On July 11th, Hartnell received a call at his home in Mayfield, East Sussex, from his son-in-law, who was also his agent (and obviously a canny operator – not many people can get away with taking a man's daughter *and* 10% of his earnings), inviting him to lunch with Lambert and Waris Hussein the next day.

It's fair to say Hartnell didn't go on many dinner dates with young Jewish women or Indians. He was a bit – how to put this? – set in his ways like that. "I felt terrible," said Hussein. "He was a very opinionated man – that is, prejudiced. He kept sort of looking at me sideways as if to say, 'Who the hell is this guy?' First of all, I was a kid. Second, I was Asian. None of this was spoken, but I was hardly getting through the meal."[5]

Hartnell also had concerns about the part, wondering if he was cut out to play this ancient eccentric. (Incredibly, Hartnell was only 55 at the time – that's younger than Kevin Bacon, Madonna and Ice-T are now – but he looked much older. Though admittedly not 600 years older.) But after some persuasion, he began to see the potential of the role, and agreed to do it. Though he still couldn't understand why the waiter was sitting at the table with them.

If the production team were pleased to have got their man, it was nothing compared to Hartnell's wife Heather. "I was delighted, because it got him away from his sergeants and that sort of thing," she recalled in later years. "When you are playing the same part day in, day out, it begins to rub off. When he was playing Doctor Who, he was delightful to live with."[6] No more square-bashing around the kitchen for Mrs H, then.

The role of Susan was offered to actress Jackie Lane, who – you guessed it – turned it down. Though, as it turned out, we haven't heard the last of her. Then Hussein spotted a young girl called Carole Ann Ford screaming on a studio monitor; at least, he thought she was a young girl: Ford was actually a 23-year-old mother but, because she was five feet tall and looked like a teenager, was actively trying to break away from being cast as juveniles. Susan, of course, *was* a juvenile – but the production team managed to sell the part to her as a sort of cross between the synthetic alien in ponderous sci-fi drama *A For Andromeda* and Honor Blackman's high-kicking judo expert Cathy Gale in *The Avengers*. So Ford signed up thinking she was going to play a kick-ass action heroine with telepathic powers. (Perhaps alarm bells should have rung when they started measuring her up for her school uniform and saying, "Let's just have a listen to that girlie scream one more time.")

Sunderland-born William Russell – real name Russell Enoch (he'd changed his name at the suggestion of Norman Wisdom, no less) – had found fame as the lead in ITV's *The Adventures of Sir Lancelot* (the first British TV series to be shot in colour, should you ever find yourself in need of an interesting fact with which to impress a date). He was 38 when he signed on as Ian Chesterton – the new, slightly less hip name for schoolteacher Cliff – though, with his matinee idol looks, could have passed for a decade younger.

Jacqueline Hill was married to a friend of Lambert's, the director Alvin Rakoff, and the producer sounded her out about playing Barbara Wright – the disappointing new name for Miss Lola McGovern – at a party. In hiring the 33-year-old, the show had finally cast someone who looked somewhere round about their actual age. A RADA graduate with an impressive list of stage and screen credits under belt, Hill had once recommended her husband cast a former Edinburgh milkman-turned-walk-on actor called Sean Connery as the lead in one of his television plays, telling him he'd be popular with women. In 1963, Waris Hussein invited his friend Diane Cilento and her new boyfriend – the self same Sean Connery – to dinner at his mother's flat. When Connery mentioned he had recently played Ian Fleming's James Bond in a film called *Dr No*, Hussein said he hoped it wouldn't cause confusion with his own current project, *Dr*

Who. I hope I'm not spoiling it for anyone when I say that both went on to do kind of okay.

Not that you'd have known it from the sticky combination of chaos, inter-departmental bad blood and management commitment issues that continued to dog Lambert and her team as they attempted to get the show on the air. Whitaker now had two scripts from Coburn – his Paleolithic opener, called *The Tribe of Gum* (and no, it wasn't about a bunch of Yorkshire cavemen) and a second story with the in-no-way pulpy title of *Dr Who and the Robots*. He had also commissioned a third serial – a historical adventure in which the TARDIS team meet Marco Polo, called *Journey to Cathay* – from John Lucarotti, who had moved back to Britain after a successful stint scripting Canadian TV shows, and had a storyline in from a Welsh comedy writer called Terry Nation.

At the time, Nation was writing for Tony Hancock[1], and not hugely interested in *Dr Who*. Then Hancock fired him after a row, at which point he became noticeably more interested. ("Dear David. I take your point about my original story idea – 'the travellers land on a planet of some description, and have an adventure of some sort' – being a bit vague. I'll try to sketch in some more details later. Yours, Terry. p.s. What was the name of the show again?")

In July, a meeting was held with *Radio Times*, the BBC's long-running (hence the name) listings magazine, to discuss promotional opportunities for the new show. The same month also saw the series being threatened with its first legal action, as a production company called Zenith Films claimed the format had been stolen from an idea for a puppet film they had submitted to the BBC. It was absolute nonsense, of course – though William Hartnell did wonder why he was being measured up for strings.

Hair and make-up trials took place in August, with Lambert stipulating Hartnell should wear a long white wig. Carole Ann Ford, meanwhile, had her long hair cut and styled into something more "experimental" – we've all had those sorts of visits to the hairdresser – by London's hottest stylist, Vidal Sassoon. It could have been a real trendsetter, except of course no Carnaby Street hipster was ever going go into a salon and ask for a "Susan".

"An Unearthly Child": so good, they made it twice

For the series' theme tune, Lambert wanted something spooky, futuristic and avant-garde, so she contacted a Parisian ensemble called Les Structures Sonores, who used glass rods set in steel to make experimental music. They submitted a sample, but ultimately proved too expensive, so Lionel Salter, the Corporation's head of music, suggested Lambert try the BBC Radiophonic Workshop. Despite sounding like a CIA experiment in industrial noise terror, the RW had been set up in 1958 by Desmond Briscoe and Daphne Oram to provide innovative new music and sounds for radio.

Based at the Beeb's Maida Vale studios, they specialised in forms of musique concrète and tape manipulation not normally heard on *Family Favourites* or *Friday Night is Music Night* – unless the BBC Concert Orchestra was considering swapping their string section for a man hitting a car battery while repeatedly flushing a toilet. Briscoe suggested Ron Grainer – the Australian composer behind such iconic signature tunes as *Maigret*, *Steptoe and Son* and *That was the Week That Was* (and, a short while later, *The Prisoner*) – to write the theme, which would then be realised by the Workshop's Delia Derbyshire. A working class girl from Coventry, Derbyshire had received offers from both Oxford and Cambridge – doubly impressive in an age when only one in ten Oxbridge students was female – and had graduated from the latter with an MA in mathematics and music in 1959. ("That's really splendid," said the BBC bosses when she arrived for her interview, while secretly wondering how fast she could type.)

Grainer's instructions included such abstract requests as "wind bubbles" (it's probably best not to ask how exactly the Workshop was expected to produce these – but Delia did seem to be spending an awful lot of time in the bathroom these days). Even Grainer, though, couldn't have envisaged the nature of the groundbreaking, eerie, truly otherworldly sound Derbyshire would eventually come up

with. "Did I really write that?" he asked, when she played it back to him. "Most of it," she replied. Grainer was so impressed, he asked for Derbyshire to get a co-writers' credit and half the royalties, but was told that this was against the rules for BBC staffers (and she *was* a woman, for goodness' sake).

Briscoe had also recommended a young engineer and composer called Brian Hodgson to create the show's sound effects. One of his first tasks was to devise the sound of the TARDIS engines as the police box ship arrived at and departed its various locations. He achieved this by scraping his mother's front door key along the bass string of a gutted Steinway piano and electronically treating the recording. The result was so genuinely strange, people have struggled to describe it ever since, with efforts ranging from the popular "wheezing, groaning sound"[7] to "a screeching, grinding roar, somewhere between a raging elephant and a protesting asthmatic".[8] It is one of the most iconic pieces of sound design of the past 50 years – though, on the down side, Mrs Hodgson has been struggling to lock her front door ever since. Let's just hope it wasn't her piano as well.

Elements for the opening title sequence were recorded over two days in August by Mervyn Pinfield, his colleague Ben Palmer and graphic designer Bernard Lodge. They used a video feedback process called "howlaround", achieved by pointing an electronic camera at a monitor showing its own output. When Lou Reed tried something similar with guitars a decade later, the result was one of the most unlistenable records of all time. But the living Rorschach pattern created by Lodge and company was highly evocative, especially when overlaid with Grainer and Derbyshire's music and the words DOCTOR OHO slowly emerging through the electronic fog. The fact this wasn't the name of the programme was a mere detail. (The OHO was a product of the symmetrical image generated by the split-screen process; after a few seconds, it was overlayed with correct title, which it had now been decided would feature the full form of the word "Doctor", partly to suit the title sequence, but mainly to annoy pedantic fans whenever the abbreviated "Dr" was used at any point over the following half-century.)

September saw test recordings take place for the TARDIS dematerialisation effect – although the police box prop itself was too tall to get through the studio doors, which meant other props had to be used in its place. No-one knows what these were, but if you should ever stumble across a piece of cine film featuring a vanishing mop and bucket marked "property of the BBC", chances are you've found the first ever footage recorded for *Doctor Who*.

On the 19th of that month, a stand-in actor called Leslie Bates earned himself a small footnote in history when he became the first person ever captured on camera for *Doctor Who* – albeit just his shadow cast across a prehistoric landscape for what would be the opening episode's only pre-filmed insert. The following day, the regular cast were brought together for the first time for publicity photos at Television Centre. By now, Hartnell was already very enthused by the character, and was confident the show would be a hit. Russell was less convinced it had legs, and Ford predicted it wouldn't run beyond eight weeks. (Spoiler alert: it did.)

In fact, despite none of them having met before, the four regulars quickly formed a strong bond: even Hartnell, with his reputation for being prickly and irritable, was well liked by his colleagues. Carole Ann Ford admitted he "wasn't backward in coming forward" – a euphemism if ever we've heard one – but insisted that, "Basically, he was as soft as butter. Like a lot of people who are like that, he gave the appearance of being quite crusty and hard, so that you didn't get the better of him, I suppose."[9]

"He wasn't difficult in any serious sense at all," concurred William Russell. "I wouldn't agree at all that he was crusty or particularly difficult. He wasn't to me, anyway."[10]

Rehearsals began the following day in the glamorous location of a freezing Territorial Army drill hall with a leaking roof on the Uxbridge Road. When Hartnell had said he wanted to stop playing army officers, joining the TAs probably wasn't what he had in mind. Claiming not to like fancy hotels or hanging out with other actors, he took digs in Ealing, where he preferred to spend his evenings down the pub.

Back in the office, Whitaker was still struggling with endless script issues. A serial set in Roman Britain was briefly on the cards, but was dropped because there were too many historical stories; the Robots adventure was also scrapped, and Terry Nation's story, *The Mutants*, bumped up to second in the run.

Unfortunately, Newman hated Nation's script, claiming its main adversaries – a bunch of post-apocalyptic mutations driving around in metal casings called the Daleks – were exactly the sort of BEM he'd specifically wanted to avoid. Donald Wilson was even more damning: he called Lambert and Whitaker into his office and, according to Lambert, told them: "This is one of the worst things I've ever read. It's utterly appalling. It can't go out."[11]

Lambert mounted a robust defence of the story based around Nation's feel for character, his singular vision of a society struggling to adapt to the long nuclear winter following a devastating holocaust and the fact that, now you mention it, they didn't have anything else. At all. So, basically, we have a combination of production chaos and Tony Hancock's temper to thank for the creation of British television's most iconic (and definitely, definitely not bug-eyed, okay?) monsters.

Studio recording on *Doctor Who* finally began on Friday, September 27th, 1963, when "An Unearthly Child" – the opening episode of *The Tribe of Gum* – was committed to tape between 8.30 and 9.45 in the evening. The production team had hoped to record the show at Television Centre; instead, their groundbreaking futuristic series went before the cameras in the BBC's creaky, cramped, stuffy, outdated and generally unfit-for-purpose Studio D at Lime Grove. The TARDIS set filled most of the tiny, corridor-shaped studio space and the hulking, antiquated cameras were so difficult and heavy to manoeuvre, the cameramen occasionally got stuck in a corner of the set and couldn't get out. "It was horrendous," recalled Lambert. "If it got too hot, the sprinklers would come on!"[1]

After the recording, a screening of the episode was arranged for Newman and the cast and crew. The drama boss's verdict was as short as it was sharp: "Bullshit!" he shouted. "Do it again!"

Afterwards, Newman took Lambert and Hussein to a Chinese restaurant, where he told them he was thinking of firing them both. Hussein must have been wondering if he would ever enjoy eating out again. In the end, Newman said he was going to give them another chance, and the go-ahead was given to re-make the episode.

By any reading of that pilot – which now serves as a fascinating insight into the development of *Doctor Who* in utero – "bullshit" is clearly very harsh. Sure, there are some serious technical problems: those elephantine Lime Grove cameras occasionally clang into the set, and Barbara and Ian's iconic first entrance into the TARDIS is followed by a good two minutes of the doors flapping about uselessly behind them as stagehands struggle to get some sort of grip. But the story itself – in which the two teachers follow their mysterious pupil Susan Foreman home to what turns out to be a giant spaceship packed away inside a tiny police box, and are then kidnapped by her sinister grandfather, who they know only as the Doctor – is strange, dark and utterly compelling. Newman thought it was *too* dark: he wanted the Doctor to be "more funny and cute" (Cute?! Had he *seen* who they'd cast?), and Susan more cheeky. Hartnell agreed – he thought the character was too bad-tempered, and was allowed to be a bit more playful in the re-mounted version. But only a bit: he was still more into the whole sinister skulking and kidnapping shtick than, say, party games and jazz dance.

As late as October, Lambert was still budgeting for the series to end after the initial four episodes, but the regulars were then contracted for seven more, plus the pilot re-mount. ("I can't believe they're re-making 'An Unearthly Child'," said their BBC colleagues. "I know – is nothing sacred? It's bound to be a travesty of the original.")

Pre-filmed inserts for *The Tribe of Gum* began filming on October 9th and, nine days later, "An Unearthly Child" went before the cameras again. And this time, the results would actually make it to air. *Doctor Who*'s journey had begun.

"This will run and run! (for 13 weeks)"

And it began largely as it would continue: teetering on the brink of total collapse in a state of barely-controlled chaos. Here's how the ever-cheery Waris Hussein summed up production on *The Tribe of Gum*:

"It turned out Anthony Coburn had said 'Oh sod this, I don't want to work on it any more. This is a load of rubbish!' Verity was faced with a writer who didn't want anything to do with cavemen, and a director who didn't want anything to do with cavemen. I don't think David Whitaker reckoned those first episodes very much either. We had appalling studio facilities, a designer who didn't care a hang, and a writer who didn't want to do rewrites and disappeared."[5] And just when they thought things couldn't get any worse, the cast started getting eaten alive.

Keen to depict the Paleolithic era as realistically as possible – or at least as realistically as you can in a glorified corridor just off the Goldhawk Road – Hussein had a load of sand dumped in the studio, which turned out to be crawling with fleas; under the hot studio lights, the critters woke up and set about biting the actors – most of them dressed only in skimpy furs – from head to toe (but mainly the bits in between). During auditions, Hussein had asked the actors to undo their shirts to see if they were hairy enough, as it would have proved too costly and time-consuming to apply synthetic body hair. The result was the most hirsute cast since *101 Dalmatians* (and the men were no better). And just to add that final extra touch of authenticity, real animal bones were provided by a local abattoir, and soon started smelling in the heat. All in all, it's fair to say working on the story was no picnic. Unless you were a flea.

For William Russell, it didn't exactly feel like the birth of a TV legend: "We all fell about," he said, "and thought we'd be out of work and back on the dole queue in six weeks!"[12] ("And have you looked for work since the year 100,000 BC, Mr Russell?")

Meanwhile, the *Doctor Who* publicity machine was shifting into gear. The first ever article on the show had appeared in September in trade paper *Television Mail*, and the following month the series was the subject of a feature in another trade sheet, *Kinematograph Weekly*. To give you some idea of how long that particular paper had been in circulation, its original title was *Optical Magic Lantern and*

Photographic Enlarger. Not exactly *Rolling Stone*, then, but it was a start.

Back in the office, budget wrangles continued, while in late October pre-filming got underway on Terry Nation's *The Mutants*. By this time, the rest of the initial run was shaping up as: *Marco Polo* (formerly *Journey to Cathay*); *The Miniscule Story* (formerly *The Giants* – clearly it was all a matter of perspective); *The Masters of Luxor* (the new name for *The Robots*, which had worked its way out of the bin and back onto Whitaker's desk); a Whitaker-penned historical; *The Hidden Planet*, a new story from a writer called Malcolm Hulke about a world just like Earth where women are in charge (so a planet just like Earth, basically); *The Red Fort*, Terry Nation's take on the Indian Mutiny; and a futuristic four-parter to be confirmed. On November 1st, however, the BBC issued a promotional document listing just *Dr Who and a 100,000 BC* (sic)[II], *Dr Who and the Mutants* and *Dr Who Inside the Spaceship*; the latter was a two-parter written by Whitaker making use of just the regular cast and standing sets, designed to allow the show to come off the air if Donald Baverstock decided not to extend it beyond the 13 episodes already (sort of) agreed.

Donald Wilson was annoyed to learn that a plan to feature *Doctor Who* on the cover of *Radio Times* during its launch week had been dropped in favour of the return of Kenneth Horne's radio comedy *Beyond Our Ken*. In a letter to the editor, Wilson wrote: "I myself believe that we have an absolute knock-out in this show, and that there will be no question that it will run and run." ("What's that? You'd heard we'd written a story to wrap the whole thing up after 13 weeks? Oh, you don't want to go reading anything into *that*.")

At Lime Grove, filming of *The Mutants* ran into trouble when it was discovered talkback from the gallery was audible on the soundtrack. It's not known exactly what could be heard – let's hope it wasn't Sydney Newman shouting "These BEMs are bullshit – do it again!". As a result, the whole episode had to be re-recorded: five episodes in, and they'd already had to do two of them twice. It was all going terribly well.

In the run-up to the first episode – now scheduled (really, this time) to be broadcast on Saturday, November 23rd – Hartnell appeared as himself in a series of radio ads promoting the series ("Hi, I'm William Hartnell – you might remember me from such films as *I'm An Explosive*, *The Goose Steps Out* and *The Night We Dropped A Clanger!*"[III]), and, on November 16th, the British public got their first glimpse of *Doctor Who* when a trailer was shown on BBC1.

Five days later, as the *Radio Times* went on sale with a half-page feature on the show, Hartnell and his co-stars met the press as part of a major publicity push; resulting items included a piece on the series' "space music" on the Home Service's *Today* programme and the show making its first splash in the popular press with a feature in *Tit-Bits* magazine. (Note to younger and non-UK readers: this weekly mag, which ran from 1881 until 1984, wasn't nearly as exciting as it sounds.)

Buoyed by the press interest, on Friday, November 22nd, Baverstock gave the green light for a further 13 episodes, likely to be followed by 13 more (perhaps it was his lucky number). After all the disasters, rows, recriminations and setbacks, *Doctor Who* was finally launching with a fair wind behind it, and the omens for the future looked good. And that's when, in a book depository in Dallas, a disgruntled ex-marine called Lee Harvey Oswald decided he didn't like the sound of this new teatime sci-fi serial at all, and was damn well going to do something about it.

Head of BBC Design sighted on grassy knoll

On Saturday, November 23rd, 1963, the sun came up on a world still reeling in shock from the assassination of John F Kennedy. For *Doctor Who*'s production team, that Kenneth Horne magazine cover suddenly didn't seem like such a big deal. Nevertheless, at 5.16pm that evening, while the world was looking the other way, television history sneaked in under the radar, as Ron Grainer and Delia Derbyshire's unearthly howl of a theme and the swirling vapours of Bernard Lodge's title sequence announced, to those still paying attention, that something new and wonderful and strange had arrived in the British cultural landscape.

As if the murder of the leader of the free

world wasn't enough to dampen the mood, a power outage meant some regions weren't able to see the first episode of *Doctor Who* even if they'd wanted to. Under the circumstances, the episode's audience of 4.4 million wasn't too shabby at all. Indeed, a few days later, Donald Wilson sent a telegram to Sydney Newman, who was in America, stating: DOCTOR WHO OFF TO A GREAT START. EVERYBODY HERE DELIGHTED. Even so, the numbers were less than the BBC had hoped for, and so the Corporation's Programme Review board took the unprecedented step of scheduling a re-run immediately before the following week's episode. This time around, "An Unearthly Child" pulled in a healthier six million viewers – though obviously some people still grumbled about bloody repeats ("I mean, that's one this year!").

In the decades that followed, conventional wisdom held for a long time that *Doctor Who*'s first story was a game of two halves – or, more accurately, a game of one and three quarters, with the taut, creepy, atmospheric opener giving way to three episodes of cavemen running around grunting and hitting each other with bones. And it's true that those first 25 minutes are astonishingly good television. But the rest of it isn't half bad either. Okay, it's not exactly the sexiest period of history to kick off with but, now that they were stuck with it, both Coburn and Hussein deliver the goods with a quite shockingly bleak and claustrophobic script, skilfully directed to give a tangible sense of peril and dislocation. There is some terrific dialogue (the Doctor's "fear makes companions of us all" pretty much encapsulates the edgy, paranoid feel of this whole first season) and Coburn pulls no punches in presenting the Doctor as a scheming, selfish, unpredictable alien, not least in the scene where he is clearly intent on dashing an unconscious caveman's brains in until Ian – at this point very much the hero of the hour – steps in to stop him.

After just two episodes, viewers of kids' feedback show *Junior Points of View* voted *Doctor Who* their second favourite programme, after the police procedural *Z-Cars* (also produced by the Drama Dept – poor old Muffin the Mule would be in for a kicking when the head of the Children's Dept got wind of this). Some eagle-eyed *JPoV* viewers also wrote to say

that, in certain scenes, you could see the cavemen's underpants. The little darlings took great delight in pointing out that cavemen, of course, didn't wear underpants – but the alternative would probably have left them psychologically scarred for years to come.

The BBC's own Audience Research department, meanwhile, reported a largely favourable reaction, with one viewer describing the programme as "a cross between Wells' *The Time Machine* and a space-age *Old Curiosity Shop*" – which is actually a much better description than anything all those BBC working groups had come up with.

Another sign of the new show's success came in early December when ex-Goon Michael Bentine recorded the first *Doctor Who* spoof for his sketch show *It's A Square World*. The skit featured Wilfred Bramble, Patrick Moore and Clive Dunn – then in his early 40s, but already playing older characters even than Hartnell – as Dr Fotheringown, dressed in Hartnell's actual costume. There was even a hilarious gag riffing on the name "Doctor Who?" ("No, not Doctor Who – Dr Fotheringown!") – making it precisely 50 years since that joke stopped being funny.

But if *Doctor Who*'s opening story, which had peaked at almost seven million viewers, was cautiously being welcomed as a hit, it was nothing compared to what happened next. Broadcast two days before Christmas, "The Dead Planet", the first episode of Nation's Mutants story, was watched by 6.9 million people. On New Year's Eve, Donald Baverstock agreed to a further ten episodes while at the same time asking the production team to "brighten up the inventiveness and logic of the scripts" and focus "more on historical and scientific hokum". At which everyone nodded and went "uh-huh, sure thing boss – brighter logic, more hokum, not a problem" before going away to try to work out what the hell he actually wanted them to do.

Then, on January 4th, "The Escape" – the first episode shown after viewers had got a proper look at the Daleks the previous week – saw a sudden climb to 8.9 million viewers. Seven days later, it added another million to that; by the sixth and seventh instalments, 10.4 million were tuning in. And what they all wanted to see was not the Doctor or his companions – or even how bright the inventiveness and logic of the scripts was. They wanted to see the Daleks.

The central concept of a race of twisted genetic mutations scheming to visit genocide upon the local peaceniks isn't, on the face of it, the most tea-time friendly subject matter – and certainly not the sort of idea that naturally translates into duvet sets and novelty shampoo bottles. That's because the real genius of the Daleks is their iconic design – often likened to a pepperpot or, in particularly unfunny newspaper cartoons, a dustbin. Terry Nation can, it seems, take some credit for this: he claimed to have formulated the basic shape of the Daleks after seeing a performance by the Georgian State Dancers on television, and being struck how the combination of tiny steps and floor-length skirts gave the illusion of gliding across the stage. If you ever want to wind a Dalek up, you could do worse than point out they were inspired by female ballet dancers prancing about on their tippy-toes: it's a stage of their evolution they'd really rather forget. There's evidence to suggest we should accept this story as true, unlike Nation's famous claim to have made up the word Dalek from the letters DAL-LEK on the spine of an encyclopaedia; for *that* to be true, the authors would have to have dedicated at least one volume to the letters A-C, before dashing through the next nine letters in a single edition. Maybe they had a deadline looming.

The designer tasked with turning the Daleks into a physical reality was one Ridley Scott. But when he went off to be a big-shot Hollywood director ("Yeah, good luck with *that*," said his colleagues), the job went to a BBC staffer called Ray Cusick instead.

"Mervyn Pinfield suggested that I got cardboard tubes," Cusick recalled of his initial design brief. "[He said] first of all get a large cardboard tube for the body and then other cardboard tubes for the arms and legs – and paint them all silver. Well, I said no."[13]

Looking for a more informed steer, Cusick phoned Nation up one Sunday, but found him "totally disinterested": "He'd written it and that was it; he didn't really want to talk about it."[14] Christopher Barry, one of the two directors allocated to helm the second serial, found the writer equally unresponsive. "I only met

Nation once," he said. "He seemed to have as little time for me – or the programme – as I came to have for him."[15]

It's true that, since sending off his script for *The Mutants*, Nation had been pursuing more comedy work, and had declined to progress his Indian Mutiny story, claiming he wasn't interested in writing for kids. But, once again, he was about to get very interested, very quickly, when it became apparent what a hit he had on his hands.

"Everyone tried to examine what it was about these things, these mobile pepperpots, which appealed to the audience," said Verity Lambert. "And of course you can't dissect that. If you could, you'd be right every time. They were sort of vaguely comic as well as being frightening."[13]

The Dalek props were built by Shawcraft Models, a freelance company operating out of a couple of sheds near Uxbridge ("where dreams are made!"). A number of cardboard cut-outs were also used to bulk out their numbers in later episodes, while the iconic first appearance by a Dalek – menacing Barbara in the episode one cliffhanger – was just floor manager Michael Ferguson waving a sink plunger. Ferguson, who later went on to direct several stories, was chosen because he had an Equity card, though it wasn't the most demanding of acting jobs ("I'm just not sure what this plunger's *motivation* is supposed to be").

As it became clear just how popular the Daleks were, Donald Wilson was no doubt feeling a little abashed about his previous antipathy. ("Did I say worst thing I'd ever read? I meant *best* thing I've ever read. The acoustics in here are terrible.") In truth, *The Mutants* – now almost universally known as *The Daleks*, though there's a militant faction that still holds out for *The Dead Planet* – really is a game of two halves: the opening four episodes, in which our heroes try to escape from the Dalek city on the holocaust-ravaged world of Skaro, work hard to create an atmosphere of clammy tension and, in many ways, serve as the template for *Doctor Who*'s first year, when the show was less about righting galactic wrongs than getting the hell out of there before that crazy Doctor dude got everyone killed. But things fall off a cliff quite dramatically in later episodes as Nation struggles to sustain the narrative across seven weeks and director Richard Martin takes over from Chris Barry, with hilarious consequences. The sixth episode, in particular, is a real doozy, with a Dalek crashing into the set, William Russell caught red-handed with a fistful of polystyrene wall, and a control panel exploding before the Doctor's actually got round to sabotaging it. The name of this masterpiece? "The Ordeal".

The Daleks also features the first fully-fledged example of what are now popularly known as Billyfluffs – those moments when William Hartnell heroically grasps at something approaching the actual line, but can't quite make the leap. In this instance, anti-radiation drugs comes out as "anti-radiation gloves". With hindsight, it's likely these memory lapses were at least partly the result of vascular dementia stemming from arteriosclerosis – a hardening of the arteries that would eventually contribute to Hartnell's death. In that sense, it's hardly a laughing matter, but these comic deviations from the script have become such a part of this era's charm, we shouldn't feel too bad about celebrating them. Bad, but not *too* bad.

By now, Hartnell was becoming something of a Pied Piper figure in his village, with 20 or 30 children regularly following him home from the train or down to the shops. The actor was delighted with the response he was getting: "Although I portray a mixed-up old man, I have discovered I can hypnotise children," he told the *Daily Mirror* in 1965. "Hypnosis goes with fear of the unknown. I communicate fear to the children because they don't know where I'm going to lead them. This frightens them and is the attraction of the series."

He also received letters addressed to Mr Who and even Uncle Who – and one four-and-a-half-year-old girl wrote to him with a proposal of marriage. So much for playing a scary, sinister alien.

Carole Ann Ford, meanwhile, likened playing Susan to being "a pop star": "I could not go out of my front door without being mobbed. Some places I went, like a fete or something, I'd have to have the soldiers called in to give me an armed guard!"[9] (Never mind being sent off to deal with the Aden Emergency, grumbled the squaddies – these village fete jobs were lethal.) Despite, or possibly because of, all the

adulation, Ford was unhappy with the way her character had diverged from the vision she'd been sold, and was already looking to move on.

Back at the Beeb, Sydney Newman was thrilled with his new hit – though, as Verity Lambert recalled, "other people at the BBC were a bit shocked; they thought 'How did this little children's show get into the ratings? It's not the sort of thing we do'."[11]

By now, *Doctor Who* was becoming a regular fixture on *Junior Points of View*, one edition of which featured a short Nation-scripted piece featuring both Hartnell and the Daleks. The metal meanies also popped up on Rolf Harris' show *Hi There*, and Nation and the BBC received their first tentative enquiry about licensing a range of Dalek products. With the canny commercial nous the Corporation was known for, they replied that the Daleks were over and done with.

Meanwhile, David Whitaker continued to wrestle the script octopus: with so many stories running into trouble, he commissioned an emergency serial from Terry Nation, and entered into discussions with actor and writer Moris Farhi about a romantic little number called *The Fragile Yellow Arc of Fragrance*. Yes, you read that right. ("What do you think, David – not too pretentious is it?" "No, no – it's lovely. Restful. Though I might just need to tweak it a *tiny* bit. How does *Dr Who and the Space Monsters* strike you?") In the end, Whitaker wrote back and told him "love, as a subject for *Doctor Who*, is very difficult", but invited him to submit further ideas; Farhi took this encouragement a bit far and sent in an entire six-part script about Alexander the Great called *Farewell, Great Macedon!* Whitaker's reply roughly translated as: Farewell, Moris Farhi!

TV history is made, then lost

In February, William Hartnell was taken ill and his role in one episode of the upcoming Marco Polo adventure had to be reduced to a single line. Before that, viewers had time to come down from the thrill of all that Dalek action with Whitaker's zero-budget *The Edge of Destruction*. Contained entirely within the TARDIS set, this taut two-parter – in which a malevolent force prompts the crewmates to turn on each other – boasts some surprisingly strong psychological horror (a scene in which Susan goes gonzo and tries to stab Ian with a pair of scissors earned the series its first slapped wrist from BBC management). It's a pity, then, that it doesn't make a *great* deal of sense, the revelation it was all down to a faulty spring is prosaic to say the least, and poor old Hartnell is all over the place: he says one line, "It's not very likely", twice and omits another, really quite important one – an explanation for why the ship's clocks have melted – altogether. Though it could have been worse: in rehearsals, he had a habit of referring to the fault locator as the fornicator.

By contrast, *Marco Polo* is almost insanely ambitious, recreating landscapes as diverse as the Himalayas, the snowy wastes of the Plain of Pamir, the Gobi desert, a bamboo forest and the Summer Palace at Shang-Tu within Lime Grove Studio D. Waris Hussein, who directed six of the serial's seven episodes, had originally wanted to cast a dwarf to sit on one of the actors' shoulders (surely it would have been cheaper just to hire a taller actor?), but eventually settled for a spider-monkey instead. During recording, the creature escaped into the gallery, where it did what any frightened spider-monkey lost in a hot television studio would do. The cleaners who had only just managed to get rid of all the fleas from Hussein's last story must have been delighted.

As far as we can tell from photographs taken during production, the team rose to the script's challenges magnificently. But we can't be entirely sure how well it translated to the screen because, sadly, *Marco Polo* is the earliest example of a *Doctor Who* story that no longer exists. At time of writing, a total of 97 episodes from the programme's first six years are missing from the archives – a result of the BBC's official policy of wiping material for economic and space-saving reasons that continued until as late as 1978. (At least, they *said* it was official policy – though it's possible the exec in charge of archiving came home one day to find his wife had taped over hundreds of hours of classic broadcasts with episodes of *The Golden Shot*. "Well how was I supposed to know? You should have written on them!")

Many *Doctor Who* episodes that were previously missing have since been recovered from film copies sold to TV stations across the world, from Australia to Zambia. It's sobering to note that a country like Nigeria, which has endured back-to-back military coups, a devastating civil war and widespread ethnic violence in the Niger Delta, still managed to hang on to its copies of early *Doctor Who* stories longer than the BBC; in the absence of democracy, human rights or enough to eat, the bountiful abundance of Hartnell episodes must have been a source of great comfort to the populace.

What we *can* judge *Marco Polo* on is its intelligent, lyrical script and fine performances, as evidenced in the off-air audio recordings. (The soundtracks of all missing episodes are available to listen to, mainly thanks to enthusiastic fans recording them at the time of broadcast. And, thankfully, there's at least one copy of each story without any bits where someone's mum tells them to turn off that rubbish and come and eat their tea.)

The third episode, "Five Hundred Eyes", turns *Doctor Who*'s educational remit up to 11 with tutorials on everything from etymology and art history to condensation and traditional national dance. None of which were quite as exciting as the Daleks, but the serial held its own in terms of audience numbers, never dropping below nine million and finishing on a high of 10.4m.

Despite this, all the buzz was still focused on the Skaro salt-shakers, who had started popping up everywhere in the press and on TV shows like *Crackerjack* and *Blue Peter*. Finally waking up to the merchandising possibilities of the characters, BBC Enterprises, the Corporation's commercial arm, started casually asking the production office if any further Dalek stories were in the pipeline. They said there were no plans as yet – but how did they fancy making action figures of Tegana, the Chinese peace emissary who travelled through Central Asia with Marco Polo? Or Ping-Cho, the charming 16-year-old daughter of a government official in Samarhand? No? How about this charming, if slightly soiled, spider-monkey? Please yourselves.

David Whitaker had now commissioned two further scripts: another historical from John Lucarotti, this time about the Aztecs, and a futuristic space opera by Peter R Newman called *The Sensorites*, while asking Malcolm Hulke to undertake a heavy rewrite of his Hidden Planet story. Hulke's agent took umbrage at this, and so *The Hidden Planet* was hidden away for good, at the back of a filing cabinet.

In early February, the first letter about *Doctor Who* had been published in the *Radio Times*, with Mrs Janet Harris of Leeds praising the show as "extremely good and very realistic". At the end of the month, Lilian Roberts of Chorley responded by suggesting Mrs Harris "needs her head examining" if she found any value in the programme's "silly Daleks and hammy acting". In March, Jean Glazebrook from Cornwall weighed in to propose Mrs Roberts "needs *her* head examining" because *Doctor Who* is "very clever". In a sense, these frank exchanges of views were the pioneering precursor to today's internet fan forums – except neither Mrs Glazebrook nor Mrs Roberts were in the habit of writing ROFLMAO.

On March 13th, the *Daily Mail* announced the news excitable boys and girls everywhere – especially at BBC Enterprises – had been waiting for: the Daleks were set to return in a second adventure. Before that, though, viewers got the chance to see if Terry Nation could bottle lightning twice with his latest creations. For the answer to how well he succeeded, you may want to take a moment to consider the last time you saw a Voord plushie, pencil case or lunchbox.

To be fair, if the villains of *The Keys of Marinus* didn't exactly become household names – even in the Nation household – it wasn't entirely the writer's fault. Having been brilliantly served by the design department with the Daleks, the Voord were realised by some men in wetsuits and gimp masks. You could argue Nation's story – in which our heroes have to retrieve the keys to a special thingummy hidden at various locations about the planet – is an ambitious portmanteau script without the budget to realise it. Or you could argue it's just a load of random scenes slung together, lacking any sense of urgency or momentum. Either way, the production is unforgivably – or perhaps forgivably, under the circumstances – amateurish, with any number of cast members and technicians wandering in and out of shot, and Hartnell delivering an all-

time great Billyfluff when he tells Ian: "And if you'd had your shoes on, my boy, you could have lent her hers." Guest actor George Colouris had been in *Citizen Kane*, but as he watched an "alien" frogman tripping over his own flippers, he must have known that he'd truly arrived.

Still, *The Keys of Marinus* didn't entirely sink without trace: one actor later wrote about his experience in the Voord's skintight rubber for a fetish publication – and I don't mean *Doctor Who Magazine* – while the title of episode two, "The Velvet Web", was later appropriated as the title of a gay erotica novel. William Hartnell would have been so proud.

Dr Who is away

With the cast now contracted for the remainder of the initial run, the writers were asked to start incorporating their holidays into the script. Not literally, of course: the Doctor doesn't suddenly abandon the quest on Marinus for a fortnight in Magaluf, but the serial does mark the first time he mysteriously disappears for a couple of episodes, going on ahead to find the final key (but in reality more likely to come back with a sombrero, a wicker donkey and 500 duty free fags).

At Easter, the Daleks officially opened Fareham Easter Market, proving that, while they weren't yet officially bigger than Jesus, they *were* starting to muscle in on his act. Meanwhile, *Doctor Who* went international when Australia's ABC network bought the first three serials.

When the BBC announced Lime Grove Studio D would be out of action over the summer and production on *Doctor Who* would be moved to the even pokier Studio G, Sydney Newman flexed his muscles and threatened to abandon the new Dalek serial if it couldn't be done justice. Donald Baverstock agreed it could be recorded at the Beeb's Riverside studios, though some episodes of other serials would still have to shove up and squeeze into Lime Grove's box room.

By now, it had been decided Susan would be written out at the end of the Dalek story, Carole Ann Ford having officially handed her notice in. There is a taste of life without Susan when she vanishes for two episodes of *The*

Aztecs, which instead serves as a terrific show-case for Jacqueline Hill, as Barbara is mistaken for an Aztec goddess and attempts to use her power to end the practice of human sacrifice. The Doctor furiously tells her "you can't rewrite history, not one line" (even though that's exactly what they do every week) and busies himself accidentally getting engaged to a local pensioner. Hartnell is at the top of his game in these scenes – in fact he's terrific in this story generally; there's even a certain inge-nuity to his memory lapses as he tells his granddaughter, "Susan my child, how glad... I'll tell you how glad I am to see you later."

Though the action and fight scenes are often clunky (stunt arranger Derek Ware has described director John Crockett as "terrible", claiming he didn't even own a telly), *The Aztecs* – like John Lucarotti's previous effort – is a wonderful, poetic testament to what *Doctor Who* was capable of achieving even as it took its first baby steps.

Wonderful and poetic are not words nor-mally associated with *The Sensorites* although, in many ways, this is the first truly typical *Doctor Who* adventure; what we might call the series' ur-text, if we hadn't already agreed not to do that sort of thing. Crucially, it's the first story in which the Doctor's motive is to save the day, rather than his own skin.

After a strong, impressively sinister opening episode, this tale of emnity between the epon-ymous bulb-headed aliens and the human crew of a twenty-eighth century spaceship starts to trip itself up – literally, in the case of at least two of the plate-footed Sensorites – with cameras clonking into the furniture, talkback from the gallery audible on the soundtrack and almost the entire cast showing solidarity with William Hartnell by fumbling their lines. As dullard astronaut Maitland, Lorne "blank" Cossette gives possibly the worst performance in *Doctor Who* history (and believe me, there will be serious competition) and, for those following the holiday rota, Barbara spends two episodes in orbit aboard a spaceship and then returns with a tan.

As well as a guest role for Peter Glaze – an icon to a generation of kids from his hundreds of appearances on Friday night slapstick-fest *Crackerjack* (if you're not currently shouting "Crackerjack!" back at this page, you obviously

didn't grow up in Britain in the 60s and 70s) – *The Sensorites* sees Mervyn Pinfield turning his hand to directing. Away from *Doctor Who*, Pinfield's most lasting contribution to human progress was inventing the autocue – or, as he failed to persuade the world to call it, the Piniprompter. Maybe if he'd brought one into the studio, the cast would have managed to stick to something approaching the script.

In June, the Daleks opened the Barnardos Fair and the East Ham Show (they might not have conquered the Earth quite yet, but they certainly had the summer fetes sewn up), and made a cameo in Roy Kinnear's sitcom *A World of His Own*. The end of the month saw the publication of *The Dalek Book* – the first official piece of *Doctor Who* merchandise – while in July there were rumblings that the much-anticipated Dalek toys might not be ready in time for Christmas.

Around this time, the BBC were contacted by Disney with a view to remaking a *Doctor Who* serial as a film: surprisingly, the story in the frame wasn't *The Daleks* but *Marco Polo*, which the House of Mouse promised would be a faithful adaptation (give or take the odd tweak, one presumes, such as making the spi-der-monkey the lead and turning Kublai Khan into a wisecracking beagle).

By now, a document had been drawn up called The Proposed Elimination of Susan – which was either a discussion of ways to write the character out, or evidence they didn't take kindly to defectors in this firm. Meanwhile, Carole Ann Ford made her third appearance on *Juke Box Jury*, this time alongside George Harrison. If it was in any way intimidating sharing the limelight with one quarter of the hippest group on the planet, Harrison didn't show it.

In August, rehearsals moved to the less than salubrious London Transport Assembly Rooms, where Hartnell endeared himself by making racist remarks about the immigrant workers. On the plus side, he had to admit it was handy for the bus.

On screen, French revolution caper *The Reign of Terror* saw evidence of the series' first ever location filming. Okay, so it was only in Denham, and featured a stand-in pretending to be William Hartnell, but it was a start, and surely only a matter of time before the regulars were able to start topping up their St Tropez tans.

The script marked the debut of Dennis Spooner, a comedy writer and veteran of Gerry Anderson's *Fireball XL5* and, true to his idiosyncratic style, is more of a light farce than a bloody history lesson, with the time travellers in and out of jail more times than Pete Doherty as they get embroiled in a Scarlet Pimpernel-riffing plan to topple Citizen Robespierre. Spooner delights in playing with (or nicking, depending on how generous you're feeling) the well-worn tropes of the genre – yes, there's even an old crone knitting next to the guillotine – and the final episode, "Prisoners of Conciergerie", is the first example of a pun in a *Doctor Who* episode title. But you've got to *really* want to see it[IV]. Unfortunately, director Henrich Hirsch didn't see the funny side: he found the whole production so stressful, he collapsed outside the studio gallery.

The three remaining cast members had now been contracted for a further 13 episodes, and a decision had been made to hold the final two stories of the first production block – *Planet of Giants* (finally, a usable take on the endlessly rehashed "Miniscule Story"), plus the Dalek rematch – over to the start of the second run, a policy that would become standard practise over the next few years. Despite this, the BBC was still dragging its feet over the future of the show, and it was only when Verity Lambert said Hartnell had received an offer elsewhere that Donald Baverstock guaranteed another 13 episodes with an option for – you've guessed it – 13 more. Because Whitaker had already committed himself to another project, it was announced the script editor's chair would be taken by Dennis Spooner, who provided a fitting soliloquy to close the first series as the Doctor tells his companions at the end of *The Reign of Terror*: "Our lives are important – at least to us – and as we see, so we learn. Our destiny is in the stars, so let's go and search for it..."

It's a shame about Ray

With a successful year under their belts, the cast and crew celebrated at a housewarming party thrown by Terry Nation at the luxurious country pile he had bought in Kent, partly on the proceeds of his lucrative Dalek licensing deals. If you spotted someone at that party staring glumly into the bottom of a whisky bottle, it was probably Raymond Cusick: because he was a salaried BBC employee, Cusick was not entitled to any royalties from any commercial exploitation of his design. So whereas Nation would go on to make millions, Cusick had to make do with around £500 and a modest ex-gratia payment.

The designer recalled standing next to his boss in the BBC toilets one day. "I said, 'It all smells of merchandise [the Daleks, not the BBC toilets – they smelled of something far worse] – is any of this money coming my way?' I got an answer the following week, and that was: no."[16] Not that he was bitter, of course: why would he want to live in a mansion and race speedboats around Monte Carlo with a bevy of bikinied beauties when he could be knocking up plywood sets in Shepherd's Bush?

As the new Dalek tale took shape, 14-year-old Pamela Franklin was chosen to play Jenny, Susan's replacement. But then a schedule change meant the new companion wouldn't be in the Dalek story after all, so the actress was never formally contracted.

On August 20th, an iconic photocall saw the Daleks in action at major London landmarks as the cameras started rolling on what was now called *The Dalek Invasion of Earth*. For the first time, the regulars were involved in a large amount of location work, including the first use of what would become a *Doctor Who* staple, the quarry (in this case, doubling as... a quarry).

With the papers full of Dalek pictures, Donald Baverstock finally agreed to Verity Lambert's request for a guaranteed six-month commitment. ("Are you *sure* you wouldn't prefer 13 weeks instead? Sort of has a nice round feel to it, don't you think?")

In September, camera tests got underway for Susan's replacement (no, really this time), while Dennis Spooner explored ideas for the following season's scripts. William Hartnell suggested a story called *The Son of Dr Who*, in which he would also play the Doctor's evil offspring – for double the fee, no doubt – but Spooner politely declined, possibly reasoning that, if there's one thing William Hartnell wasn't cut out for, it was playing spunky juvenile versions of himself.

The Dalek scripts had to be amended after Hartnell suffered a bad fall in rehearsals, and was given a week off to recover. Meanwhile, Maureen O'Brien, a 21-year-old actress in rep at the Liverpool Playhouse, was cast as the new companion, at this point going under the less-than imaginative name of "Susan". Seems like someone was having trouble moving on.

William Hartnell definitely was: over the past year, the regular cast had become very close – on recording days, they gave BBC catering a miss and shared picnics together in the dressing room – and Hartnell simply couldn't understand why Carole Ann Ford was bailing on such a success. He even wrote a letter asking her to stay, and was visibly upset when she recorded her final scenes on October 23rd. That sort of took the shine off the series wrap party, where the team also celebrated further overseas sales to Australia, New Zealand and Canada. But Ford was adamant and, several decades later, was still claiming *Doctor Who* was "absolutely the kiss of death" on her career".[9] That's a bit harsh: she went on to appear with Frankie Howard, Reg Varney, Terry Scott and Arthur Mullard in celluloid masterpiece *The Great St Trinian's Train Robbery* – and who can forget her stunning performance in 1975's *The Hiding Place* as "Woman"?

Yeah, maybe she had a point.

Daleks "biggest thing since the Daleks"

At Hallowe'en 1964, eight million people tuned in for the start of *Doctor Who's* second season, as the time travellers finally visited the *Planet of Giants* (actually a house in England – it was the regular characters who were shrunk down small enough to be terrorised by such fearsome monsters as an ant, a household cat and, um, a kitchen sink). Appropriately, the story itself was cut down to size when the production team took the decision to lop off the fourth episode, "The Urge To Live", for fear the audience might lose theirs. (All concerned knew the serial wasn't really strong enough for a season opener, but, being Carole Ann Ford's penultimate adventure, they weren't left with any choice.)

In a notable reversal of *Doctor Who's* usual shortcomings, *Planet of Giants* is an accomplished realisation of a weak script: while the oversized props and sets look fantastic, it's the banal plotting that lets it down. The giant ant, incidentally, was from stock: what a fabulous place the BBC must have been in those days of in-house productions. ("Giant insects? Down that corridor, third door on the left, just past oversized fruit and the Pyramids of Giza – if you end up in the Cretaceous Age, you've gone too far.")

As well as kicking off the show's sophomore season, the serial marked two other significant firsts: episode three was the first credited to Douglas Camfield, who would become one of the series' most prolific and well-loved directors; a former Lieutenant in the Territorial Army, he was famous for running his shoots like military operations. Also making his debut was Australian composer Dudley Simpson, who would go on to score almost 300 episodes of *Doctor Who*. According to many, Simpson's soundtracks – with their heavy use of bass clarinet and the occasional marimba – provide a "cheeky counterpoint" to the on-screen action, often underplaying dramatic moments while giving the full bells and whistles treatment to, say, someone picking up a cup. His many admirers argue he was allowing the action to do the talking with the former, while playing with audience expectations on the latter. At no point has it ever been suggested he simply wasn't looking at the screen.

But perhaps a more significant event than even those debuts occurred on November 1st when the first *Doctor Who* novelisation was published by Frederick Muller. Written by David Whitaker, the presumptuously titled *Doctor Who in an Exciting Adventure With the Daleks* was a reworking of Terry Nation's first Dalek script, though Whitaker took certain liberties with established continuity by introducing Ian and Barbara in a totally different way at the start of the book, thus prompting the first ever use of the *Doctor Who* fan's all-time favourite question: "Yes – but is it *canon*?"

Though they couldn't have known it at the time, this was to prove the start of a publishing phenomenon as impressive as the parent show itself: with around 150 novelisations of TV serials and, in later years, hundreds more original works of fiction, *Doctor Who* holds the Guinness World Record for the most works of fiction based around one principal character. More significantly, in the pre-video and DVD age, it was the novels which made the most lasting impression on many fans, to the extent it was not uncommon to be sorely disappointed when you finally got the chance to see the original and realised that rampaging sea monster you'd pictured so vividly in your head was actually a man with a green rubber glove splashing about in a washing-up bowl.

Also in November, it was announced that film producer Milton Subotsky had secured the rights to a big screen re-make of the Dalek story. Yes, said the fans. But is it *canon*? And in the same month, *TV Comic* started running a cartoon strip chronicling the adventures of siblings John and Gillian and their mysterious time-travelling grandfather, Doctor Who. But was it *canon*? Also, proving that satire wasn't dead – just very unwell – the *Daily Mirror* ran a feature on a schoolboy who had written his own spoof *Doctor Who* script. And no, before you ask, it definitely wasn't canon.

In the week of the series' first anniversary, *Doctor Who* threw a birthday party to remember as the Daleks returned to TV screens in an avalanche of publicity, appearing in TV trailers, hogging the cover of the *Radio Times* and muscling in on popular and/or racist music hall throwback *The Black and White Minstrel Show*, where they shuffled about in the background while white men dressed as cartoon plantation slaves performed tap routines to such wholesome numbers as Sweet Muchacha. Quite why anyone thought such evil, racist creatures were suitable for a light entertainment show was anyone's guess, but the Daleks didn't seem too bothered.

Dalek merchandise on the shelves for Christmas 1964 included a fantastically unconvincing – but massively popular – dressing-up costume, greetings cards and packets of sweet cigarettes. Quite why anyone thought such a poisonous, deadly design was suitable for a line of children's confectionary... oh, fill in the rest yourself.

Skaro's finest also invaded the hit parade when songwriter Johnny Worth recorded the novelty song "I'm Going to Spend My Christmas With a Dalek" with The Go-Gos

(not the one with Belinda Carlise – this was a "semi-professional" group from Newcastle who we can safely say didn't trouble the charts again).

Over the festive period, the Daleks were the star attraction at the *Daily Mail* Boys and Girls Exhibition at London's Olympia. Quite why anyone would want to align themselves with such a fascist, rabidly right wing... etc. Even Carole Ann Ford got in on the act: the actress took time out from appearing in *Sleeping Beauty* at Bromley New Theatre to sign books at a London toy shop – dressed as a Dalek. Seriously, I don't know what she means when she says her career was in ruins.

Terry Nation and Raymond Cusick also appeared together on the TV show *Late Night Line-up*. At the end of the interview, Nation promised the designer he would be "looked after" in terms of the Daleks' commercial exploitation. After that night, Cusick never heard from him again. Of course, Nation was happy to take the money – but only if it didn't compromise the integrity of his creation, and the universe's most merciless genocide machines were allowed to keep their dignity. In other news, a Dalek appeared in panto in Liverpool alongside Dick Emery[V].

Not surprisingly, *The Dalek Invasion of Earth* – the fictional one, as opposed to the one being played out in toyshops and schoolyards across the land – attracted between 11.4 and 12.4 million viewers across its six episodes. And there can't have been many left disappointed by the serial's pyrotechnic mix of action and adventure: the early sequences of a ruined, deserted London in the year 2150 see *Doctor Who* showcasing a new cinematic confidence, and there's no shortage of whizzes and bangs to keep the kids happy. By the time the final credits rolled, Nation had already been commissioned to deliver a third Dalek serial.

That said, when looked at objectively – divorced from the heady rush of what was already being called Dalekmania – the story is actually a bit of a mess. The plot – basically to strip down the Earth and put an engine in it, like you might with a knackered MG – is beyond bonkers, and the "science" (the Daleks' claim that they chose the Earth because it's the only planet with a magnetic core) would be ridiculous even if they *weren't* going to chuck it out anyway and steer the planet about the cosmos like a massive dodgem car) must have had physics teachers (not to mention Sydney Newman) spitting their tea across the staff-room.

This being a Richard Martin production, there are the usual unscheduled appearances by various studio technicians and boom-mic shadows, the Daleks' saucer – yes, an actual flying saucer – has the most visible wires this side of *Thunderbirds*, and one of the nasal Daleks famously trundles around repeating (or so it sounds) "we are the bastards of Earth" like he's auditioning for a Guy Ritchie movie.

On the plus side, the episode one cliffhanger featuring a Dalek slowly rising from the Thames is one of the show's most enduring visuals (though you can't help wondering what it was doing in the river in the first place – perhaps it just fell in?). But the real standout moment is Susan's departure, as she becomes both the first companion to leave the show – and the first to impulsively decide to get married to a man she's just met. Unlikely as it all seems, it's very well written and played, with Susan claiming there has never been "any time or place I belonged to; I've never had any identity" to which the Doctor responds with a genuinely moving farewell speech, telling her: "One day I shall come back... Until then, just go forward in all your beliefs, and prove to me that I am not mistaken in mine." If you'll excuse me, I have something in my eye.

A Funny Thing Happened to Dr Who on the Way to the Forum

A new year brought a new occupant to the TARDIS and, by the time she made her screen debut in the David Whitaker-penned two-parter *The Rescue*, Maureen O'Brien's character – a twenty-fifth century Earth girl orphaned in a spaceship crash on the planet Dido – had been through several name changes, starting out as Tanni and Lukki before settling on the slightly less exotic Vicki.

O'Brien wasn't quite prepared for the attention the role brought her way: she got a rude awakening when journalists besieged her house and she had to escape through a back window – an experience she later described as

"terrifying" (which seems a bit strong – unless she lived in a top-floor flat, in which case fair enough).

The Rescue is a slight piece in which the monster of the week turns out to be nothing more than a man in a silly suit; nothing unusual about that, of course – except this time it's *meant* to be a man in a silly suit. To hide the actor's identity, the fake monster in question, Koquillian, is credited to Sydney Wilson – a nice nod to two of the series' driving forces. Or shameless toadying to the bosses, if you prefer.

At the end of the day the story, like the ship, is really a vehicle for Vicki, and in that regard it does its job well. And, with more than 13 million viewers, the second instalment took *Doctor Who* into the TV Top 10 for the first time.

There was more positive affirmation when *The Daily Telegraph* hailed the show as the best children's programme of 1964. But EC Cole of Birmingham begged to differ: he wrote to the *Radio Times* to complain that, while *Doctor Who* was "acceptable adult entertainment", it shouldn't really be classed as science fiction alongside the likes of *Quatermass* and *A for Andromeda*. Get him.

Now that Verity Lambert had proved herself more than capable of running a hit show, Mervyn Pinfield relinquished his associate producer title in order to spend more time with his autoc... sorry, Piniprompter. Meanwhile, the Daleks conquered new territory by starring in their own comic strip in *TV Century 21*, a comic purporting to be from 100 years in the future, albeit a future where publishers were still using Letraset.

On screen, Vicki's maiden TARDIS flight took her to ancient Rome, where viewers got their first real taste of Dennis Spooner's vision for the programme. Inspired by a visit to the set of *Carry On Cleo*, Spooner's script is a shameless romp in which William Hartnell demonstrates a surprising gift for knockabout comedy, especially when he's trying to compete with Derek Francis' showboating turn as Emperor Nero. While the other episodes show a certain restraint, episode three is the closest *Doctor Who* would ever come to a Whitehall farce – it's just a pity it was broadcast on the day of Winston Churchill's funeral, when Benny Hill-style scenes of Nero chasing

Barbara around the palace didn't exactly chime with the solemn national mood.

From the sublime to the utterly ridiculous, *The Web Planet* was – and very possibly still is – *Doctor Who*'s most outré experiment to date. The only serial in the show's 50-year history not to feature any humans or humanoids beyond the regulars, there are still people convinced they suffered a very bad acid trip in the 60s when, in reality, they were just watching this. Sample dialogue: "A silent wall. We must make mouths in it with our weapons, then it will speak more light." Woah – far *out*, man. The soundtrack, meanwhile, featured stock music from our old friends Le Structure Sonore – and even they probably thought it was a bit "weird".

Really, you can't help but admire the vaulting ambition of Bill Strutton's script, in which the insect-like Menoptera wage war on the planet Vortis with a race of giant ants called the Zarbi. But it was clearly never going to work for a series with the budget of the average sitcom, recorded as live on a Friday evening in a tiny TV studio. In possibly the show's most overtly Acorn Antiques moment, a Zarbi headbutts the camera and knocks it over, revealing the studio ceiling. Episode three, in particular, was beset by disasters, recording going ahead even though half the set was stuck in traffic, and they hadn't had time to finish painting the other half. Not that you could see that – or much of anything else – on screen, as Richard Martin had decided it would help the otherworldly vibe if he smeared all the camera lenses with more Vaseline than a Led Zeppelin tour bus.

Another thing you couldn't see on screen was Martin Jarvis, playing one of the Menoptera. Verity Lambert had secured the rising stage and screen star after pitching the role as a troubled prince avenging the overthrow of his father, like a sort of alien Hamlet. What she failed to mention was he'd be dressed as a giant bee and strung up in a flying harness. To perfect his movements, Jarvis had lessons from choreographer Roslyn de Winter. "I don't think she thought I was particularly good," he recalled. "She kept asking me to stay behind for extra Menoptera practice."[17] It was widely agreed their chances of being crowned *Strictly Come Dancing* champions 1965 were poor.

The BBC were keen to push the Zarbi as "the new Daleks", and arranged a photocall featuring the oversized ants queueing for a bus and dropping in for lunch at a café ("hold the salt"). But it was clearly never going to work: though *The Web Planet*'s opening episode audience of 13.5 million would be the highest ever achieved by *Doctor Who* in the 60s, by its end the story had shed two million viewers and the Audience Appreciation (AI) index had tumbled to a miserly 42%.

In the *Daily Mail*, Peter Black lamented the serial's "inaction", adding: "The heroes are the dullest quartet in fiction, and so remarkably incompetent it would take their combined intellectual resources to toast a slice of bread." For all that, *The Web Planet* remains a noble attempt to create something genuinely alien and avant-garde. Unwatchable, but noble.

The Crusade is arguably even more noble, as it's essentially David Whitaker sneaking a Shakespeare history play in under the *Doctor Who* banner. Even RSC veteran Julian Glover, playing Richard the Lionheart, was impressed by the quality of the script, parts of which were in actual iambic pantameter (though, along with the rest of the cast, he was less impressed when director Douglas Camfield managed to trump Waris Hussein by dumping a decomposing cow under the hot studio lights). Some dodgy boot polish make-up jobs aside, the story is also surprisingly enlightened, admirably resisting the prevailing view – still being preached in Sunday sermons across the land – of the Crusades as a just Holy War against the Saracen infidels.

Some of the adult themes proved a bit strong for Verity Lambert, who wisely requested the suggestion of an incestuous relationship between Richard and his sister Joanna be dropped. Nevertheless, Whitaker cited the serial as his proudest achievement on the series. "I relished the dialogue the story allowed me to write, and it became almost a labour of love to produce a script worthy of the depth of drama that had inspired it,"[18] he said. "It was the best *Doctor Who* script I've ever worked on," concurred Douglas Camfield. "It was beautifully written and meticulously researched, and I don't remember having to alter a single line."[19] All in all, everyone agreed the production was the sort of quality drama that justified the BBC's licence fee. The kids hated it, obviously, with ratings slipping back below the ten million mark. And if they thought *that* was boring, they must have been thrilled to learn next episode was set in a *museum*.

The Space Museum is an odd fish. The first episode, in which the TARDIS jumps a time track and the travellers arrive in their own future to find they've been stuffed and mounted in display cases, is brilliantly bizarre, and the time-warp element throws up some surprisingly complex existential questions for 5 o'clock on a Saturday afternoon. But it soon degenerates into an extremely tedious rebels vs. dictators skirmish that's as dull as every other museum your parents used to drag you round (and it doesn't even have a shop).

Tosh – a byword for quality

With the Daleks about to hit screens large and small, Terry Nation told the *Daily Mail* the rights to the creatures were worth around £300,000 – that's almost £5 million in today's money. Somewhere in a pub in White City, Ray Cusick folded his paper, looked thoughtfully out of the window, and considered switching to the *Daily Mirror* instead.

For William Hartnell, April 1965 was to prove the cruellest month, as William Russell, Jacqueline Hill and Verity Lambert all signalled their intention to leave, the latter being rewarded for her stewardship of *Doctor Who* with a new twice-weekly soap called *The Newcomers*. Dennis Spooner also announced he was moving on to join Terry Nation supervising the scripts for new ITV show *The Baron*. Lambert and Spooner's replacements were announced as John Wiles, a former writer and story editor turned "reluctant" producer, and the in-no-way worryingly named Donald Tosh, formerly of the soap *Compact*. ("How's the script, Tosh?" "Not at all – it's pretty good actually." And so on.)

It may only have been four months into the year, but Christmas was already facing cancellation when a fire at one manufacturers wiped out the entire stock of Dalek playsuits. Fortunately, Terry Nation was already looking to double his money by introducing a new race of robot enemies for his metal cash cows in the form of the Mechanoids, giant spherical robots who were introduced to the public at a photocall shortly before the Daleks returned to menace our heroes in their most exciting adventure yet (it said in the press release).

If *The Keys of Marinus'* "quest" storyline seemed a bit thrown together, *The Chase* feels like Nation forgot to take his script out of his jeans before putting them through a fast spincycle, its back-of-a-fag-packet premise – the Daleks invent a time machine and pursue the Doctor across the universe – used as an excuse for all manner of high concept wheezes, like an episode set in a haunted house and a horror movie team-up between Dracula and Frankenstein's monster. In Africa. And as if all that weren't enough, the Doctor introduces the TARDIS' in-house entertainment system, a "time television" (yes, really) that allows the regulars to stand around watching Abraham Lincoln give the Gettysburg Address and Shakespeare hanging with Elizabeth I, for no obviously apparent reason. (When Vicki gets hold of the remote, she chooses to watch The Beatles. The producers approached Brian Epstein with an idea for the Fab Four to appear made up as old men, but he said it wouldn't be good for their image. Perhaps in honour of his late manager's wishes, Paul McCartney still refuses to appear as an old man today.)

The Chase also marks the first time the Daleks have been used for what we must assume is meant to be comic effect. For a measure of how funny the results are, let's just say it's not hard to see why Nation and Tony Hancock were no longer on speaking terms.

Still, at least there's always something to look at: mainly stray cameras, boom mics, bemused crew members wandering into shot... Other highlights include a robot "duplicate" of the Doctor played by an actor with an uncanny resemblance to a man who looks nothing like William Hartnell, an eye-opening scene in which Ian gets his hands down Barbara's pants and an attempt to recreate last year's "Dalek rising from the Thames" shot, only this time using sand. Unfortunately, it proved impossible to pull the bloody thing out, and the sequence had to be recreated using a model.

Adventures in Time and Spain... in Space!

For all we know, the original is still buried under Camber Sands to this day. As for the Mechanoids, you can't help thinking someone in the design department read the instructions wrong, as they're so impractically large they struggle to get through the doors of their own city. Even Terry Nation must have known these oversized spinning tops were unlikely to challenge his prized pepperpots in children's hearts.

In *The Daily Telegraph*, TV critic Philip Purser was among the first to suggest the novelty might be wearing thin: "The Daleks, recalled with increasing frequency and increasing desperation, are fast losing their ancient menace," he wrote, adding: "One of them has acquired a South London accent, and another is undoubtedly queer." Excuse me? Just because he's spent six weeks chasing the Doctor around the galaxy, there's no need to go jumping to conclusions.

As with the previous Dalek story, the best thing about *The Chase* by a country mile is the moving farewell scene. As Ian and Barbara elect to use the Daleks' time-ship to return home, the Doctor launches into a heartfelt tirade, the power of which is only slightly lessened by a classic Billyfluff ("You'll end up as a couple of burned cinders flying around in Spain... in space!"). We are then treated to a wonderful montage of stills of Ian and Barbara goofing around in 60s London (directed by Douglas Camfield as part of pre-filming for the following serial) that serves as a fitting tribute to two tireless troupers whose contribution to *Doctor Who* as it found its feet simply can't be overestimated.

"I was quite relieved when Jackie said 'I'm thinking about [leaving] too'," Russell recalled. "And then we had to face Bill. I thought Bill would be upset and cross – and he was – and wouldn't understand. And the scene that takes place at the end of *The Chase* when he really gets angry, you can see he is very angry and very disappointed. That was very much like what had happened. He couldn't understand. 'I don't understand you', he said. 'Here we are, we've got a wonderful job, a great team, everything's going well – why do you want to leave it?' It was difficult to explain to him that I felt I had other things to do, in the theatre, in life, and everything."[20]

According to Richard Martin, Russell and Hill were "very supportive of Bill Hartnell, who by the end of *The Chase* didn't know whether he was chased or chasing. He was a very tired man, and he was already beginning to show signs of the illness that would kill him, unfortunately. He knew the overall pattern, he knew where he had to be and what he had to do. Sometimes, he would fluff his way through the text. But Bill and Jackie were able to support him and never make him look foolish. They did that with consumate love, and they did it all the way through."[20]

As Russell and Hill departed (to tour together, rather sweetly, in a production of *Separate Tables*), the TARDIS' revolving door flung out a new fellow traveller in the shape of Peter Purves' dashing astronaut Steven Taylor. Purves had been given the gig after impressing the producers with his performance in an earlier episode of *The Chase*, in which he played a hillbilly American tourist indulging in some crassly unfunny comic business with the Daleks at the top of the Empire State Building. Quite *why* this impressed the producers is a mystery but, to their credit, Purves does a pretty good job when he gets to use his own accent, and isn't forced to chew his way through a comedy routine that would shame a school panto. Crucially, he also got on well with Hartnell, which helped soften the blow of the last of the original line-up leaving, though by now it was clear Maureen O'Brien already had itchy feet.

The last episode of *The Chase* on Saturday, June 26th was watched by 9.5 million people – a respectable figure by any estimation, but a clear three million down on the finale of *The Dalek Invasion of Earth*. Nevertheless, the previous day had seen Dalekmania step up a gear with the release of the scourge of Skaro's much-anticipated big screen debut.

Dr Who and the Daleks had been sold to audiences with the promise that, in the words of the trailer: "Now you can see them in colour on the big screen, closer than ever before! So close you can feel their fire! So thrilling you must be there!" For good measure, it also warned audiences to "beware these men of steel!", which was just wrong in every way.

Adapted from Terry Nation's original Dalek serial by producer Milton Subotsky, there's no danger of a "but is it canon?" debate ever troubling this particular production, which rewrites every bit of established continuity it can think of: in place of William Hartnell's mysterious, nameless alien, we have Brit horror legend Peter Cushing as doddery old English inventor Dr Who, who has somehow managed to knock up a time machine inside a police box in his garden. While showing off, he accidentally whisks his two granddaughters – foxy Barbara (Jennie Linden) and precocious pre-pubescent Susan (Roberta Tovey) – off to the planet Skaro, along with Barbara's hapless, pratfalling boyfriend Ian (indefatigable, record breakin' song and dance man Roy Castle – Tovey recalls trying to do her schoolwork in her dressing room while he played the trumpet next door, which is exactly what you would hope Roy Castle did in his breaks).

After that, things stick vaguely to the original plot, while making full use of the fact it's In! Colour! with a rainbow-coloured army of different liveried Daleks, and even the blonde, Aryan-syle Thals getting a pink rinse.

To publicise the film, the Daleks had made an appearance at that year's Cannes Film Festival, where they'd met John Lennon, undoubtedly staying up late into the night drinking and swapping stories about the pressures of life during Beatle/Dalekmania ("YOU-KNOW-JOHN, IT'S-REALL-Y-GOOD-TO-BE-A-BLE-TO-TALK-TO-SOME-ONE-WHO-UN-DER-STANDS"). They had failed to win the Palme d'Or, despite threatening to exterminate the jury but, nevertheless, the film opened to positive reviews and a strong box office performance. It also spawned two cash-in singles: "Dance of the Daleks" by Jack Dorsey and his Orchestra and "Who's Who" by 12-year-old Tovey, which couldn't have been more grating if the Daleks had recorded it themselves.

Just in case anyone felt the Daleks were in danger of being under-exploited, the BBC had asked for their next appearance to be expanded into a whopping 12-parter. Verity Lambert agreed – though it would be her successor who actually got lumbered with making the thing. The corporation also showed its faith in a third series by contracting William Hartnell for a further 30 episodes. Which was good news for him and his wife: in a *Daily Mail* interview in July, the actor revealed he had given Heather a

solid gold TARDIS topped with a sapphire, painting a charming picture of the Hartnells as the Jay-Z and Beyonce of their day.

That month, the second series drew to a close with *The Time Meddler*, the first example of what many fans like to call a "pseudo-historical" – i.e. it's set in the past (1066, in fact – and yes, it is about all *that*), but features a non-contemporaneous sci-fi element. In this case, that turns out to be (drum roll please)... *one of the Doctor's own people*. With his own TARDIS. At this stage in the series' history, there's still no indication of who the Doctor's people might *be*, but if I tell you the Meddling Monk – he's not a real monk, but he is a real meddler – is played for laughs by Carry On stalwart Peter Butterworth, you won't be surprised to learn it's Dennis Spooner's name on the credits.

For all its larky nature, *The Time Meddler* features perhaps the most shocking incident in the whole of *Doctor Who's* first half-century when the Saxon villager Edith is raped by the marauding Vikings. It's "tastefully" done several miles off camera, of course, but would still feel jarring in any *Doctor Who* adventure, let alone a knockabout one like this. Still, it's a strong end to the season, boasting some typically memorable Spooner dialogue. The Doctor, in particular, is on unusually witty form, condensing Steven's TARDIS tour down to: "That is the dematerialising control, and that over yonder is the horizontal hold. Up there is the scanner, those are the doors, that is a chair with a panda on it. Sheer poetry, dear boy. Now please stop bothering me." Shortly afterwards, when they stumble across a Viking helmet on the beach, but Steven still refuses to believe they have travelled in time, the Doctor asks him sarkily: "What do you think it is, a space helmet for a cow?" And suddenly, the title of the rash impulse purchase you're holding starts to make a little more sense.

The Dalek Invasion of Woolworths

With *Doctor Who* off the air for another six weeks, disappointed viewer Timothy Ward wrote to *Junior Points of View* offering to loan the BBC his granddad to fill the gap. Presumably his granddad would have had quite a shock if the BBC had taken him up on his offer (though he couldn't have looked any more confused than Peter Cushing).

In August, the first *Dr Who Annual* appeared on the shelves, and William Hartnell was the guest on BBC Radio 4's *Desert Island Discs*, where he surprised listeners with his love of reggae and Jamaican dancehall. Not really – though he did plump for some Paul Robeson and Louis Armstrong, along with Charlie Chaplin, Flanagan and Allen, Rachmaninov, Beethoven and Borodin. His book of choice was *English Social History* by GM Trevelyan, and his luxury item was cigarettes. And a lighter, presumably.

Also that month, *Doctor Who* fandom was born as the William (Doctor Who) Hartnell Fan Club was established in Stoke-on-Trent, bringing members all the latest news and views on the series and its leading man – sort of like Twitter, only with a four month delay and a free badge.

To kill time between skirmishes with their mortal enemy, the Daleks were present at Jersey's Battle of the Flowers, where they were inevitably disappointed by the scale of the battle in question. Meanwhile, Terry Nation – who appeared to talk to the press more than he did his wife and children these days – suggested the Daleks might be in line to get their own series. Whether that was a realistic prospect or not, Britain's toy, confectionary and clothing manufacturers were in no doubt who was already the star of the show, with more than 50 Dalek product lines in the shops between summer and Christmas 1965, including Dalek jigsaws, money boxes, playsuits, slippers, board games, masks, glove puppets, stationery, balloons, transfers, candles, wallpaper, soap, crockery and even a nursery toy for terrifying small babies in their cots.

Verity Lambert recalled meeting Walter Tucker, whose company held a manufacturing licence for Dalek toys, in a restaurant one lunchtime. "When I said my name, he said, 'You have made me a millionaire'. I was earning £1600 a year, and this man had been made a millionaire."[15]

But the prize for most shameless marketing trick has to go to Lincoln International, whose extensive range included Dr Who's Anti-Dalek Jet Immobiliser, Dr Who's Anti-Dalek Fluid Neutraliser and Dr Who's Anti-Dalek Neutron Exterminator. Or, as they'd been known in their previous packaging, guns.

Also in the re-packaging business that August were the satirists at radio comedy *I'm Sorry I'll Read That Again*, who lived up to their name by hastily turning a *Quatermass* spoof into a *Doctor Who* one, recasting Graeme Garden from Professor Thunderblast to Dr Why. How we laughed, etc.

But the most significant event of the summer of 1965 occurred on August 6th with the recording of *Mission to the Unknown*, the final episode overseen by Verity Lambert as producer. A photocall saw Lambert being menaced by numerous alien critters, and there were glowing profiles in the *Mail* and the *Express* – possibly the last time either of those organs would look kindly on a female professional making a successful career for herself when she could have been at home having babies and baking cakes like a normal woman.

A few months earlier, Lambert had talked about her vision for the show in another piece for the *Mail*. "I have strong views on the level of intelligence we should be aiming at," she told the paper. "*Doctor Who* goes out at a time when there is a large child audience, but it is intended more as a story for the whole family. And anyway children today are very sophisticated and I don't allow scripts which seem to talk down to them."

If you're looking for reasons why the series she launched on a wing and a prayer in 1963 is still going strong 50 years later, that's as good a place to start as any.

"It's not me, it's you"

On September 11th, *Doctor Who* returned to BBC1 with a story about a planet run by women – a wheeze first mooted way back in the days of Bunny Webber and company. In this case, steely blondes the Drahvins are locked in a war with the Rills and their robot servants the Chumbleys. Asked why he'd devised the main villains as females, writer William Emms admitted, "I wanted to work with four beautiful blondes", before clarifying: "No, I actually liked the concept. All I did was the simple trick of inverting the logic so that the beautiful blondes were the evil ones and the monsters were the goodies. It was a morality play."[21] Yeah right. From all the available evidence, it appears whatever slight qualities *Galaxy 4* possesses were the result of frantic stool-polishing by the producer and the director. But even their best efforts couldn't distract from the fact the robots – who are supposed to appear threatening in order for the whole reverse morality thing to work – look like Henry vacuum cleaners (a case of being dragged down by the Chumbleys, which always brings a tear to the eye). The robots were controlled by a group of dwarves who, off camera, were prone to getting involved in punch-ups over women – though Drahvin-Chumbley relationships were strictly off limits. Well there is a war on, you know.

Despite the new series still attracting more than nine million viewers, there was a vague sense in the air that *Doctor Who* was last year's news: viewer comments on *Junior Points of View* became noticeably more disparaging, and ITV purchased the glossy US import *Lost in Space* in a bid to dangle something new and shiny in front of the kids.

Mission to the Unknown is unique in the *Doctor Who* canon in that it doesn't feature any of the regular cast. A bottle episode serving as a teaser to the upcoming Dalek 12-parter, it was commissioned from Terry Nation to fill the gap left when the fourth episode of *Planet of Giants* was dropped. The notional star of the episode is Edward de Souza as Earth secret agent Marc Cory, who uncovers a Dalek plan to conquer the Solar System. But for Nation, of course, it's basically a dry run for a Dalek TV series, free of that annoying bloke with the police box. In the end, the series never came off, but British kids at least had 12 solid weeks of Dalek action to look forward to after Agent Cory and company got them all worked up. All they had to do first was sit patiently through four weeks of the Doctor and company fannying about in ancient Greece, which had somehow managed to work its way into the schedules between the Dalek prequel and the main event.

With Verity Lambert gone, *The Myth Makers* was John Wiles' first serial as producer. By now, William Hartnell was become increasingly irascible – at least, that's usually the favoured euphemism – and, from the get-go,

the new boss was at loggerheads with his star. In fact, it seemed there was only one thing the two of them *could* agree on, and that was that neither of them wanted Wiles to be there.

"I was never happy with the role of producer," said Wiles, interviewed by *Doctor Who Magazine* in 1983. "A producer is really a desk person, deriving satisfaction from battles in the office. This was very frustrating for me, as I am much more a writer and a director. I was constantly pestering Donald Wilson to put me on a director's course but Donald decided, for reasons I will never fully understand, to make me into a producer."[22]

Wiles and Tosh both felt *Doctor Who* was stuck in a "childish rut", and wanted to push it more towards "adult science fiction" – to touch subjects, according to Wiles, their predecessors hadn't wanted to touch. That much is clear from the fact the new producer's first suggestion for a *Doctor Who* story was based on the in-no-way controversial premise of the TARDIS being hi-jacked by God. There would, it's fair to say, have been letters.

Wiles and Hartnell's relationship got off to a disastrous start when, at an early script meeting, the actor insisted on having his trademark oohs, hahs and hmms inserted into all his lines. When this blew up into a stand-up row with the writer, William Emms, Wiles intervened and, according to Emms, told Hartnell to "do it the way it is or I'll sack you"[23]. And things went rapidly downhill from there.

"He [Hartnell] wasn't as old as he thought he was," said Wiles. "When he was with me, Bill treated himself almost as a 75-year-old. It may well have been that he was physically not in the best of health and so could not learn lines, but studio days could be absolutely purgatory for everybody. If Bill was in a terrible state, it put everybody into a terrible state."[22]

"They fought like cats and dogs whenever they met," said Tosh. "There was an electric current between those two, always."[24]

According to Wiles, the increasing number of studio "incidents" (on one occasion, Hartnell managed to offend a dresser enough for the entire department to walk out in protest) led to directors devising a secret code, where "you'd better phone the designer" actually meant "you'd better get the producer down here now".

Of course, that's just one side of the story. For his part, Hartnell was unsettled by all the changes, and was unhappy that the new team envisaged returning to a harsher interpretation of the Doctor than the more avuncular figure he had gradually evolved. It was also becoming obvious that his health and memory were getting worse and, amidst all this strain, his Aunt Bessie – the nearest thing in his life to a mother – died, and Wiles refused to release him for the funeral. After this, the actor started going over his producer's head, which didn't exactly earn him many Employee of the Month certificates.

"He was past the zenith of his skills," admitted Peter Purves. "There were directors he didn't get on with, actors he didn't get on with..."[24]

Despite this, relations were still good between the three regulars. "My job was to laugh Bill out of his five or six tempers a day," said Maureen O'Brien. "And that's what I did. And I did it very happily all the time I was there. I can't explain what he was like – he was a charming creature in spite of his irascibility, and those terrible teeth he used to bear when he was angry."[24]

Unfortunately, Hartnell was about to lose this vital ally: if Wiles wasn't taking any nonsense from his leading man, O'Brien got even shorter shrift. Having grumbled endlessly about how much she hated the scripts and her character, the actress was nevertheless shocked when she returned from her (unfortunately rather expensive) summer holiday to be told she was being written out.

"We went off on our six week break and when I came back, I expected to find the next four scripts waiting for me. And there weren't any scripts. I was desperate to leave. If they had offered me another contract, I might have been torn because 50 quid a week wasn't a great fortune even in those days, but it was a great fortune to me. I suppose I was angry I'd gone and holiday and I'd rather have been looking for work. So that was the end of me in *Doctor Who*."[24]

According to Purves, "Bill was furious. He said, 'This is outrageous – I'm not going to have this'."[24]

Sadly, the die was cast – though Donald Tosh later admitted to deep regrets about how

badly the situation had been handled. "I understood that Maureen wanted to go. Then we get to the first read-through and Maureen arrives, absolutely furious, 'cos no-one had told her. She said, 'You've written me out.' I said, 'Yes I have, I thought you wanted to go.' 'I never said I wanted to go.' Oh god, it was now deeply, deeply embarrassing."[24]

And so it is that, at the end of *The Myth Makers*, Vicki becomes the second TARDIS teenager to make an impulse husband purchase. In this case, her intended, Troilus, declares his intention to re-name his bride Cressida. If Vicki had brushed up on her Shakespeare recently, she might have guessed this wasn't going to end well. Still, there's a pleasing symmetry to a character first encountered on the planet Dido ending up in Greek mythology. And, of course, myth is the operative word, with *Who*'s take on the Trojan War the first to plonk the TARDIS down in the middle of Homeric legend, as opposed to actual history.

The script by newcomer Donald (well, of course) Cotton is played for laughs (he even wanted to call the third instalment "Is There a Doctor in the Horse?", until some spoilsport intervened in favour of the infinitely more boring "Death of a Spy") right up to the final episode, when there's a sudden, entirely inappropriate lurch into wholesale violence and slaughter.

One of the biggest liberties taken with the tales of Troy is the absence of Helen – she of the face that would launch a thousand ships – after the production team decided they wouldn't be able to afford anyone attractive enough. ("None taken," said the rest of the female cast.)

Kids raised on Ray Harryhausen's version of Greek mythology may also have been disappointed when the fearsome Cyclops turned out to be nothing more spectacular than *Who* regular Tutte Lemkow, here making his third appearance, and the second in an eyepatch – although this one was worn over the other eye to the one in *Marco Polo*; as an actor, he was nothing if not versatile.

Troy itself was recreated at Frensham Ponds, an area of heathland near Farnham in Surrey, which was chosen for its striking similarity to twelfth-century Asia Minor, and not in any way because it was right next door to director Michael Leeson-Smith's house.

Katarina and the waves hello, says goodbye

Of course, as one companion departs, so another must arrive, and so we welcome – briefly – Adrienne Hill as Trojan handmaiden Katarina, who is saved from certain doom at the end of the story and whisked away aboard the TARDIS. Unfortunately, no sooner had she been cast than Wiles and Tosh decided it was too difficult to write for a "historical" companion so, having snatched her from the jaws of death in one story, they resolved to deliver her back into them in the next one. And just to make sure she didn't get too comfortable in the role, her death scene was the first thing Hill actually filmed.

Katarina makes it a third of the way into marathon 12-parter *The Daleks' Master Plan* before being sucked out into space while saving her new friends. The extant second episode and a brief clip of her final scenes is all that now remains of Hill's contribution to the series, and even this latter TV treasure cuts off just before her noble sacrifice – a source of some regret to the actress in later years.

Though it has to sustain twice the material, *The Daleks' Master Plan* is actually a huge improvement on *The Chase*, thanks in large part to Douglas Camfield's direction, and Wiles and Tosh having the cojones to put our heroes in real peril; in addition to Katarina's early exit, the Doctor and Steven are given a new ally in the form of Special Security Services agent Brett Vyon (played by Nicholas Courtney – you might want to make a note of that name), only for him to be shot dead by his sister, fellow SSS gunslinger Sara Kingdom (Jean Marsh in a role clearly inspired by Honor Blackman's kick-ass judo expert Cathy Gale in *The Avengers*); no sooner has *she* seen sense and thrown her lot in with the Doctor than she is aged to death in a quite horrifically graphic way. Marsh recalls that, at one point, she had to retrieve some maguffin or other from her "space box" – steady – at which point she remembered she also had her sandwiches and dressing room key in there. She eventually managed to open the box without revealing its

contents and hand over the item in question. ("CAN AN-Y-ONE SMELL EGG MAY-O-NNAISE?" asked the Daleks, suspiciously.)

Debate still rages among fans as to whether Katarina and Sara Kingdom count as official "companions" or not; clearly there's a stronger case to be made for Katarina, as she travels by TARDIS and appears in more than one story, but we won't really have closure on the issue until the United Nations does the decent thing and sends in a special mediator. As a further aside, Stanley Kubrick was so impressed by Katarina's exit, he contacted the BBC to ask how it had been done. You can't help thinking he must have been a little disappointed by the somewhat prosaic answer, "with a trampoline".

Peter Purves was less than impressed with the story, declaring "the big 12-parter was tosh".[11] ("Yes?" said Donald Tosh – honestly, it never gets old.) In fact, much of the script *was* Tosh: the workload was supposed to have been divided up evenly between Terry Nation and Dennis Spooner – both of who were also busy writing scripts for ITC – but Nation pulled up outside Tosh's house in a taxi late one night and hastily handed over his "scripts" before driving on to the airport to catch a flight to New York. "He left me standing on the pavement holding an envelope containing barely enough pages for one episode, let alone six," said Tosh.[29] Douglas Camfield had no choice but to start filming without a script, resorting to writing scenes himself and then shooting them.

Under the circumstances, it's a surprise the story – in which the Doctor has to stop the Daleks from developing a Time Destructor, while also finding time for a rematch with Peter Butterworth's Meddling Monk – is as coherent as it is. And at least episode seven's dubbing speed version of *The Chase*, in which the Daleks pursue the time travellers through the Oval cricket ground and spoof versions of *Z-Cars* and silent-era Hollywood (complete with captions) is *meant* as a joke: a bit of light relief to mark the fact it was being broadcast on December 25th. At the end of the episode, "The Feast of Steven", the Doctor brings out a tray of drinks, turns to the camera and offers "a Happy Christmas to all of you at home." Yes, said all the fans watching. But are we *canon*?

Despite a full three months of Dalek action,

Adventures in Time and Spain... in Space!

there was no noticeable bump in the ratings, and *Doctor Who* was no longer a fixture in the TV Top 20. The death of Katarina also came under fire, with one mum telling the *Daily Mirror* the programme was now banned in her home. By now, regular arguments were raging about whether the show had become too violent, with the *Radio Times* letters page reading like an early version of Mumsnet.

By all other measures, though, Dalekmania appeared to still be in full swing, with a raft of new books, products and TV appearances, including one as a butler serving tea to Dick Emery and another threatening to exterminate Max Bygraves. Just goes to show there's a bit of good in everyone. A second feature film was announced, there was talk of a Dalek radio serial, and, over Christmas, the nation's favourite bits of skirt made their stage debut when *The Curse of the Daleks* opened in the West End (not a bad production, by any means, but everyone agreed that, in hindsight, the Daleks' tap routine had been an ask too far).

The Massacre:
not as much fun as it sounds

In an interview with the *Manchester Evening News* in early December, William Hartnell had announced he would probably be leaving *Doctor Who* – which was news to his agent. It was clearly intended as a shot across John Wiles and Donald Tosh's bows, but they responded with enthusiasm, making plans to have the Doctor disappear in upcoming story *The Celestial Toymaker* and reappear with a new face.

Hartnell quickly backtracked, saying he still had faith in the show and was looking forward to it eventually being made in colour. But by now Wiles had decided he didn't care either way, and informed the BBC he was going back to his typewriter, telling Donald Tosh he'd "had it up to here".

When the Corporation approached Welshman Innes Lloyd to take over, the conversation went something like this:

BBC: "Do you want to produce *Doctor Who*?"

IL: "No thanks – I've come here to be a director and, anyway, I don't like science fiction."[22]

He started the job a few weeks later.

Donald Tosh had initially planned to carry on. "And then I met Innes, and his ideas and mine were miles and miles apart." According to Tosh, Lloyd wanted to go down the "pure science fiction" route, which the story editor thought was "dead wrong for the programme".[24] So he too decided to move on, to be replaced by Gerry Davis, who had worked with Lloyd on twice-weekly football soap *United!* The new team's gameplan was to make the show pacier and more contemporary, with more of an emphasis on real science. (What, more real than the Time Destructor?) With Hartnell finding the scripts increasingly difficult to memorise, and getting more upset and bad-tempered as a result, Lloyd also decided from the outset to treat his star with kid gloves in order to avoid a Wiles-style rift.

One consequence of Hartnell's deteriorating health was an increasing tendency to try to offload chunks of his dialogue on to other actors. For the next televised adventure, *The Massacre*, Tosh had written a big speech for the Doctor which he wanted to keep intact, so he made a point of telling Hartnell in rehearsals how well he'd read the piece, successfully flattering him into not junking it.

Set on the eve of the 1572 Massacre of St Bartholomew – when Catholics plotted to murder all French protestants – the story has its origins in a behind-the-scenes gentleman's agreement: David Whitaker had verbally consented to commission a story from John Lucarotti on Eric the Red, but the incoming production team rejected the script, and offered Lucarotti the chance to write something else instead.

Hartnell had long been requesting the chance to play someone else in the show (remember *Son of Doctor Who*?), which is why he spends much of this serial portraying the Abbot of Amboise who, rather conveniently, just happens to be the spitting image of the Doctor. What's remarkable about this is the utter transformation Hartnell affects to play the abbot, suggesting his approach to the Doctor was also more of a performance than he often gets credit for, and that much of the endless hemming and hawing really was *acting*, as opposed to him just trying to remember his lines.

The Massacre caps a hat-trick of first-rate

33

space helmet for a cow

scripts from the show's original go-to history guy. Or at least, it would have done, if Lucarotti had actually written it. In fact, in contrast to his previous successes, *The Massacre* proved to be a miserable experience for the writer. "What he delivered," claimed Tosh, "was a bad Hollywood version which someone who'd never set foot outside Wisconsin thinks might have happened."[24] This seems like an overly generous view of the average Wisconsinite's grasp of sixteenth-century French politics, but we'll let it go. The point is, Lucarotti was paid off and Tosh wrote the story himself. Lucarotti hated the results, and asked for his name to be taken off the credits, until his agent persuaded him otherwise.

Whatever bad blood might have been poured into it, there's little denying the quality of what eventually appeared on screen: the story is grim, downbeat, fatalistic and about as adult as *Doctor Who* gets; if anything, it treats its audience with *too* much intelligence – or certainly too much knowledge of history – but if that's the worst criticism that can be levelled, it says a lot about this smart, sophisticated, beautifully written piece of television.

In fact, the only thing that really spoils *The Massacre* – unless you're a French Huguenot, in which case the whole thing was pretty much a downer from the start – is the clunking coda tacked on to introduce the new companion. Played by Jackie Lane – those who've been paying attention will recall she was originally offered the part of Susan – Dorothea Chaplet, known as Dodo, is a 60s teenager who literally stumbles into the TARDIS thinking it's a real police box. In a remarkable coincidence, it's strongly intimated she is a descendant of Anne Chaplet, who the Doctor and Steven have just been hanging out with in sixteenth-century Paris. Basically, a giraffe on roller skates would have made a more elegant entrance and, from the moment she arrives, it seems Dodo's chances of being considered a classic companion are as dead as a... well, you get the idea.

Not that she doesn't know how to make an impression: Dodo's first act as a member of the TARDIS team in her debut adventure, *The Ark*, is to almost wipe out what's left of the human race by passing on her cold. The humans in question are travelling on board a giant spacecraft ten million years in the future, en route to

a colonise a new planet while everyone else back home rides the Earth straight into the Sun. Also on board the ship is a menagerie of Earth animals – hence the name – and the humans' servants, a race of one-eyed, Beatle-mopped aliens called the Monoids. At least, they *start out* as servants – in a neat twist, the second half of *The Ark* sees the Doctor and company returning to the spaceship 700 years later to find the Monoids have risen up and enslaved the humans – mainly because the latter were so weakened by Dodo's snotty germs.

Paul Erikson's thoughtful script – the first to really force the Doctor to question the consequences of his itinerant existence – is well served by director Michael Imison, who really pushes the envelope of what could be achieved in a television studio in 1966. He pushed it so far, in fact, that he spent half the budget for the following story – though clearly he still couldn't stretch to a proper prison set as, in one memorable scene, our heroes are ordered to be held in the ship's "security kitchen". ("Is everyone alright with file-in-a-cake?")

For those keeping score, Imison outdid both Waris Hussein and Douglas Camfield by turning the Ealing sound stage into a veritable zoo, with guest artists including an elephant, monitor lizards and even a boa constrictor. The elephant, Monica, arrived in a van to find the BBC hadn't arranged a parking permit; Imison subsequently spent the night on babysitting duty, while the van driver checked into a hotel. Or was it the driver who spent the night babysitting Imison, and the elephant checked into a hotel? Something like that, anyway.

In the end, the director was fired in the gallery just before recording commenced on the final episode (for going over budget, we assume – or possibly the elephant disgraced itself over the new reception carpet).

By this point in the season, *Doctor Who* had been moved back – or brought forward, technically – to its original 5.15 slot, swapping places with *Juke Box Jury*. As a result, audiences slipped to around six million, leaving the show languishing at the business end of the Top 100, and taking a weekly pummelling from ITV's *Thank Your Lucky Stars*. Communist Party propaganda sheet the *Daily Worker* also proffered its opinion that the show was going into decline, which was surprising during a

34

Labour government. Nevertheless, Hartnell was contracted in February for 19 more episodes; Purves, on the other hand, was offered just a dozen more, with no option to extend beyond that. The actor was "very upset", which unsettled Hartnell even further.

Clearly, John Wiles hadn't gone through with his plan to replace Hartnell during *The Celestial Toymaker* – not that he'd have been able to afford a new actor anyway, now that Michael Imison had spent all the cash. But the Toymaker – a powerful immortal who kidnaps innocent victims and forces them to play deadly games for his amusement (we've all been to parties like that) – does get rid of the Doctor for two whole episodes because he's irritating him. Not that Hartnell should go reading anything into that, of course.

Donald Tosh and writer Brian Hayles had originally envisaged the story as a sort of sequel to Gerald Savory's absurdist 1937 play *George and Margaret*. Which obviously the kids were pretty psyched about. It just so happened that, by 1966, Savory was the BBC's head of drama – not that that had anything to do with it, of course. But when Tosh rewrote large chunks of the script for practical and budget reasons, Savory got cold feet and withdrew permission for the use of his characters, so that particular piece of toadying backfired spectacularly. And there were more rights issues when the BBC was forced to issue a disclaimer that fat, sniggering schoolboy Cyril was in no-way based on fat, sniggering schoolboy Billy Bunter, even though he quite obviously was.

Despite these teething troubles, Tosh was quite pleased with the results – until he returned from holiday and found Gerry Davis had pretty much scrapped his efforts and started again, dismissing the script as "a sort of pseudo-smart Noel Coward comedy". *That'll teach you to completely rewrite someone else's work*, thought John Lucarotti. *That'll teach you to take a holiday on this show*, thought Maureen O'Brien.

For many years, *The Celestial Toymaker* was presumed to be one of *Doctor Who's* great lost treasures, until episode four actually turned up, at which point everyone realised it was basically Peter Purves and Jackie Lane playing hopscotch on a very cheap set. *The Gunfighters*, on the other hand, went through the same process in reverse: for a long time, Donald Cotton's comic take on the shoot out at the OK Corral was widely considered to be the worst *Doctor Who* story ever made – a reputation largely based on its historically low Audience Appreciation index of just 30%. But when the serial – which sees Rex Tucker (remember him?) finally earning a *Doctor Who* credit as director – started to appear in wider circulation on video and then DVD, everyone felt able to lighten up and admit that, actually, it's rather good fun. Okay, so the fake American accents are appalling and, like Cotton's previous script, there's a sudden, jarring switch to serious and deadly in the final reel but, otherwise, what's not to love about Wild Billy Hartnell whooping it up in Tombstone? As a bonus, the entire story is accompanied by narration in the form of a saloon bar ballad sung by an unseen Lynda Baron.

Off screen, Hartnell was still busy talking himself out of a job, telling the *Daily Mail* he needed a change in conditions if he was to continue beyond October. He admitted he was becoming increasingly argumentative with directors, and was needing more time off. Separately, Innes Lloyd had come to the conclusion that the actor's health was simply no longer up to the demands of carrying a series like *Doctor Who*. As the producer began formulating plans to topple the head of state, his story editor was looking to push their agenda of beefing up the show's science content. Somewhat radically, Gerry Davis did this by sounding out actual scientists, figuring they probably knew more about this sort of thing than the unemployed comedy writers the series usually relied on. He was particularly pleased when ophthalmologist Dr Christopher "Kit" Pedler responded positively to his request for story ideas about the totemic new GPO Tower taking over London (with something slightly more dramatic, thankfully, than "Perhaps it could broadcast city-wide reminders to book an eye test?"). Davis also had meetings with legendary stargazing curmudgeon Patrick Moore and Dr Alex Comfort, who was later to find fame as the author of seminal (so to speak) rumpo manual *The Joy of Sex*. We can only speculate what ideas *he* might have come up with: *Missionary Position to the Unknown*? *Galaxy 4play*? Whatever it was, it would no doubt have involved some very generous beards.

As, indeed, did the next televised adventure. Set on a planet where a so-called civilised elite literally drain the life-force from a safari park full of fright-wigged primitives, *The Savages* finds writer Ian Stuart Black sticking it to The Man with a right-on parable about slavery and exploitation, nature versus technology, capitalism, racism and several other isms, while mounting a very 60s challenge to the idea that age automatically confers moral authority over youth. John Wiles had been very impressed by the idea, telling Donald Tosh it was a "very exciting synopsis" – though he probably just liked it because he thought it would wind William Hartnell up.

The serial breaks new ground in several ways: it is the first story to feature neither "monsters" (though you wouldn't exactly hire the Elders to babysit) nor famous historical figures, the first to be transmitted under a single umbrella title (and hence the first in this book you can reliably trust) and the first time a quarry (Shire Lane Quarry in Chalfont St Peter, if you fancy a day out) doubles as an alien planet. It also sees Steven making a very hasty exit, staying behind to unite the Elders and the Savages as their new leader – a role he doesn't appear to particularly want, but is willing to accept until something better comes along. Purves himself was out of work for the best part of 18 months afterwards, and became convinced he must be a "lousy" actor. Talk about blue Peter.

Dr Who is required to leave

Having been promoted back into a stronger slot for *The Celestial Toymaker* – and attracting an audience of eight million for its troubles – the poor reaction to *The Gunfighters* saw *Doctor Who* back on the early shift, up against ITV's *The Adventures of Robin Hood* and the popular ATV soap *Weaver's Green* (no, me neither), with ratings slumping to five million. Meanwhile, Michael Craze and Anneke Wills, two actors in their early 20s, had been contracted for four serials as new TARDIS crew members Ben and Polly (it was Wills' husband, Michael Gough – recently seen as the Toymaker – who suggested she go for the part, though

she had in fact been asked to audition for Susan). From the moment they make their debut in *The War Machines*, it's clear these two swinging Carnaby Street hipsters have been drafted in as the public face (and, in Polly's case, legs) of Lloyd and Davis' more contemporary vision for the series. In fact, Michael Craze is on record as saying they wanted him to be "*Doctor Who*'s Alfie" – though with less shagging, presumably. All of which is bad news for Jackie Lane's Dodo, who disappears half way through the story – all we're told is she has "gone to the country" to convalesce after a nasty hypnotism incident – and is never mentioned again. In fact, Lane had been told she was being written out while her debut story was being broadcast; according to Gerry Davis, part of the problem was the camera picked up the fact she was an older woman. ("Well since you put it like that, that's fine," said Lane.)

Everything about *The War Machines* – in which a supercomputer called WOTAN tries to brainwash the population into submission from the top of the Post Office Tower, years before Noel Edmonds tried something similar – screams of the new regime's desire to be seen as hip and of the moment. It even features a scene in which the Doctor – *William Hartnell's Doctor* – goes to a groovy nightclub, where he wins approval for his "fab gear" and gets mistaken for Jimmy Savile. Weirdly, that last bit isn't a joke.

The idea that we will all somehow become slaves to a powerful, interconnected artificial intelligence is, of course, frighteningly prescient – though, in this reality, WOTAN uses its power to persuade the populace to build deadly robots, rather than check Facebook and upload funny cat videos.

In addition to a truly heroic Billyfluff – in which Hartnell begins "I wonder, Sir Charles, do you suppose..." then wanders over to a table and faffs about with some papers, before concluding "No, I don't suppose you would" – *The War Machines* contains perhaps the most controversial line ever spoken in the series (don't worry, it's not a William Hartnell ad-lib), as WOTAN declares that "Doctor Who is required".

Now, you can read this in one of two ways: either the world's most advanced super-computer has simply got it wrong – perhaps it was accessing an early version of Wikipedia – or the name of the show's lead character really *is* Doctor Who, and the reason he's been keeping it a secret all this time is because... well, wouldn't you? Or maybe he just really hates knock-knock jokes. And if he really *is* called Doctor Who, what's his first name – Alan Who? Geoff Who? Given he's a BBC employee, my money's on Donald.

From the start, it was apparent the generation gap and differences in attitude between Hartnell and his new young co-stars was going to be a problem. "He was amazingly short-tempered," recalled Wills. "At the drop of a hat, he would completely lose his temper, over the most ridiculous things. I couldn't handle the lead player being so irascible – we were on our tippy-toes around him, and that doesn't make for a very creative atmosphere, does it? We were all terrified of him."[25]

Early on, Wills made the mistake of sitting in the star's "special chair", which had Bill Hartnell written across it. He got someone else to tell her off, after which she got her own chair and wrote "Anneke Wills – and anybody else who would like to sit down" on the back. Being a self-confessed "total leftie", Wills also found it hard to stomach some of Hartnell's more extreme views. "He was less than tolerant towards most people, actually," she said, but added: "When I first came on the *Doctor Who* circuit, I was the first person to readily admit that he was, let's face it, a miserable bugger. But over time, I've decided there's enough negativism in the world without me contributing, especially as Bill Hartnell is... well, first of all he's dead. And, at the time, he wasn't a well man. So I don't think it's fair for me to bring out my racist stories. We'll let him rest in peace. He was welcome to his chair."[25]

In June, the cast and crew – jolly, united little company that they were – headed to Cornwall for the series' most extensive location shoot to date (they even got to stay in a hotel, though probably not a very good one). Three months later, the results of this week in the West Country would see *Doctor Who's* fourth season get underway in swashbuckling style with *The Smugglers*, a rum seventeenth-century romp in which the Doctor unwittingly becomes the only man on Earth with a clue to the location of the famous pirate Captain Avery's loot-ed booty. Whereas most previous historicals had taken great pains to avoid the obvious clichés, this one goes all out for a full-on Moonfleet/Dr Syn pastiche, complete with scurvy sea dogs (one of them even has a hook), secret passages, clues to hidden treeeeaaysure hidden in riddles and lashings of grog. It's good fun for what it is, but perhaps indicative of a show that was in danger of forgetting what it was created to do. The fact some episodes struggled to scrape four million viewers – disastrous for a season opener – suggests the viewing (or, more accurately, not viewing) public were minded to agree.

On the plus side, after three years, the programme finally found a speaking role for a black actor (Elroy Josephs as pirate called, um, Jamaica), and the stunt work is impressive, thanks to the debut of Derek Ware's HAVOC stunt team – who might sound like *Britain's Got Talent* semi-finalists, but will go on to provide years of sterling service crashing vehicles, getting blown up and generally falling off things. (During filming, someone moved the mattress Ware was supposed to land on, causing him to break his thumb and damage his arm. He went straight from this job to John Schlesinger's *Far From the Madding Crowd*, where he carried out duties as the film's swordmaster, despite having one arm in a sling and the other in a cast. Told you he was a trouper.)

While filming on board a boat, director Julia Smith – who in later years would go on to find fame as the co-creator of *EastEnders*, and infamy as the woman behind *Eldorado* – managed to throw up over the side in between saying the words "Get ready" and "Action!". That's a professional for you. But that challenge was nothing compared to trying to direct William Hartnell, who exploded into a rage when she tried to get him to press the wrong button on the TARDIS console. And quite right, too: it might have had terrible consequences for the space-time continuum or, at the very least, put too much sugar in his tea.

Once Innes Lloyd had decided that it was impossible for Hartnell to carry on, there was a certain amount of "hard thinking", in Gerry Davis' words, at the BBC about whether *Doctor Who* should continue at all. In the end, head of serials Shaun Sutton gave Lloyd the go-ahead to find a new leading man and so, while

Hartnell was filming in Cornwall, the producer put in a call to a film unit in Ireland where the company included the actor Patrick Troughton.

The 46-year-old – already a familiar face on British television – was sounded out about the possibility of taking over from Hartnell. Troughton wasn't convinced: he thought the series had run its course, and had serious doubts about whether it could survive the loss of its leading man. On the other hand, he did have two families to feed (more on *that* later).

Originally, the plan appears to have been to find a like-for-like replacement for Hartnell, with Michael Horden the favourite at one time. (Jimmy Savile, thankfully, was never in the frame.) Then Lloyd and Davis hit upon the concept of "rejuvenation" – a canny wheeze that allowed them to cast a younger man better able to cope with the demands of the show.

When Hartnell learned that discussions about his successor had been taking place, he was devastated. Now 58, he was determined to see through his original plan to do five years on the show. At the same time, he knew he was getting more ill – even if he didn't yet know why – and his wife Heather was very keen for him to leave, even though, she later admitted, it "broke his heart".

On Saturday, July 16th, Hartnell came to a decision: he would leave *Doctor Who* in October. Heather noted in her diary that her husband felt "too much evil had entered into the spirit of things", though Hartnell would later put this paranoia down to a combination of pleurisy and a nervous breakdown.

According to Lloyd, while there were other names on the shortlist – including Patrick Wymark and Ron Moody – Troughton was pretty much everybody's first choice, including Shaun Sutton and, crucially, Sydney Newman. "So I went to Billy and told him who we'd got. 'The only man in England who could take over from me!', he said. So we got it right for him as well."[26] (How much of a face-saving gesture this was, we don't know – but some accounts have Hartnell actually *suggesting* Troughton in the first place.)

Patrick Troughton was officially contracted on August 2nd and, four days later, Hartnell's departure was announced in *The Times* and the *Daily Mail*. "I think that three years in the part is a good innings and it's time for a change," he said. Shortly afterwards, the William (Doctor Who) Hartnell Fan Club changed its name to The Official Doctor Who Fan Club. There's loyalty for you.

Welcome to Earth, twinned with Mondas

In cinemas, audiences were being reminded of exactly what *Doctor Who* without William Hartnell was like when Peter Cushing returned in *Daleks – Invasion Earth: 2150AD*, a block-busting (relatively speaking – it cost around £50,000) Technicolor re-make of... oh you work it out. The film had been launched in July with a big tie-in through Sugar Puffs cereal – as well as giving away a full-size Dalek prop (in a competition, not in the actual box), Sugar Puffs signs and products can be seen throughout the movie – though, sadly, there was no role for the Honey Monster.

With Jennie Linden and Roy Castle both unavailable, Castle's friend Bernard Cribbins stepped in to play klutzy Special Constable Tom Campbell, while former shooting champ Jill Curzon played Dr Who's niece, Louise. Despite some decent set-pieces (and, indeed, some decent sets), box office returns were nowhere near as impressive as the first film, and a plan to adapt *The Chase* was abandoned – so at least something good came out of it in the end. As an interesting aside, Cushing also recorded a pilot for a proposed 52-week radio series based on his version of the Doct... sorry, of Dr Who. Nothing ever came of it, but it remains a fascinating curio.

With the Doctor on the way out and the appeal of his most reliable adversaries on the wane, it was clear some fresh ideas were needed – and Gerry Davis and Kit Pedler thought they might have the very thing. Arising from their discussions about hot scientific talking points, Davis had commissioned Pedler to write a story inspired by the increasing use of artificial limbs and organs in surgery, and the two had become quite excited by where their brainstorming had led them: a race of humanoids who have gradually replaced most of their organic matter with mechanical parts to the point where they are more machine than man, with their capacity for compassion and empathy replaced with cold, calculating logic. The first Doctor may have been about to take his bow, but he had one last fight left in him – with the Cybermen.

Unfortunately, if *The Tenth Planet* demonstrates one thing it's that, as a physicist, Kit Pedler makes a very good eye doctor. It's amazing to think something so fundamentally... *wrong* as the basic plot mechanics here should have occurred in a series that was, for the first time, retaining the services of a so-called "scientific adviser". The Cybermen's basic plan is to drain the Earth of its energy and transfer it to their own planet, Mondas, which has somehow managed to "creep up" on the Earth (its lost twin, apparently, though no-one can recall a twinning ceremony) without anyone noticing, before Mondas goes ka-boom – even though it's only in danger of going ka-boom because they brought it back near the Earth's orbit in the first place. Chuck in an embarrassing inability grasp such basic concepts as radiation, supernovas and even the weather, and it's not much of an advert for the show's newfound academic credentials.

But it hardly matters because, at the end of the day – and an era – all that really counts here are William Hartnell and the Cybermen. Of the two, the Cybes come off best. Just about. For a race whose big shtick is that emotions are a weakness, they're terribly excitable at times, but the central premise is strong, and they're well realised by costume designer Sheila Reid. Not that the cast saw it that way: Anneke Wills remembers laughing at how "cheap and shabby" they looked (though she was more impressed when she saw them out of costume: "They were these six-foot hunks... tall and gorgeous"[25]) while Michael Craze thought they were "a bit of a joke – the designers thought they could just spray it all silver and get away with it."[27]

Craze, incidentally, has good reason to recall the serial with mixed feelings: he'd just come out of hospital where a procedure to have a channel in his nose cleared had gone wrong, bursting a blood vessel in his head that nearly killed him. When he arrived on the Antarctic set at Ealing – the bulk of the action is set in a remote South Pole space tracking station, thus declaring the programme's Base Under Siege Era officially open – he asked the production assistant to be careful with the polystyrene

snow blower, as it could be quite dangerous to get some stuck up his nose. She promptly blasted him with a face-full of the stuff, and they married three years later.

The design may have been primitive – with what appeared to be giant socks over their faces, a Davey lamp on their heads and an accordion-like chest unit that made them look like they might break into a sea shanty at any moment – but there's an argument to be made that this is the most scary iteration of the Cybermen there would ever be: far from being just metal monsters, there's something disturbingly *surgical* about them. Their sing-song voices, delivered through an immobile, gaping hole of a mouth, are also strangely unnerving.

For William Hartnell, sadly, *The Tenth Planet* would prove a less than fitting epitaph. Midway through filming, the actor contracted bronchitis, and Davis had to hurriedly write him out of the penultimate episode, while he concentrated on getting well enough for the last hurrah. When the moment came to film his final moments on Saturday, October 8th, Patrick Troughton – waiting in the wings to make his debut – could see how upset he was, and modified his approach accordingly.

Scandalously, Hartnell is denied a grandstanding final speech. His line "It's all over, that's what you said. No, but it isn't – it's far from being all over" has a pleasing sense of defiance about it, but his actual last words, as he's handed a cloak – "Ah yes, thank you. It's good. Keep warm." – aren't the sort of thing you're likely to see on a blue plaque any time soon.

The rejuvenation itself was filmed on the TARDIS set using a faulty mixing desk to create a flaring, overexposed picture, causing Hartnell's features to dissolve into a sea of white, to be replaced moments later by Troughton's. It was a moment of genuine TV history – but it would have been asking a lot for William Hartnell to see it that way at the time. At a leaving party at Innes Lloyd's flat after the recording, Hartnell was emotional, but put on a brave face to the press, telling some he wanted to return to the stage, and had had offers from Australia, while admitting to others he would have stayed if they'd offered to renew his contract.

The final episode of *The Tenth Planet*, broadcast on Saturday, October 29th, 1966, was watched by 7.5 million people – a rise of two million from the start of the serial. If you were one of those 7.5 million, consider yourself lucky as, though the rejuvenation sequence itself still remains, *The Tenth Planet* episode four is among the most sorely-missed from the BBC archives. It also means that fate conspired to remove William Hartnell from the last surviving episode of his tenure – though, thankfully, it's not *quite* the last we've heard of him.

Hartnell's first job after *Doctor Who* was appearing, apparently somewhat reluctantly, in pantomime as Buskin the Cobbler in a touring production of *Puss in Boots* which, when it arrived at the Southend Odeon, was utterly trashed by the local paper under the headline "Town Deserves Better Than This" (quite something when you consider this is Southend we're talking about). Afterwards, he mainly worked on stage (though did appear in an episode of *Z-Cars*) and, in later years, became increasingly bitter about what he saw as his ill-treatment by the BBC, even claiming he had provided his own coat for *Doctor Who* and not been paid for it.

But these sour grapes – and Hartnell's battles with his health and his bosses in later years – shouldn't be allowed to overshadow the enormous achievements of the man whose commitment, dedication and enthusiasm helped forge a television legend. From the shifty, mercurial, morally dubious figure of *An Unearthly Child*, Hartnell's Doctor had gradually morphed into the heroic, avuncular eccentric still adored by millions around the world today. And, perhaps more than any other actor since, he considered it his very great privilege to do it – especially for the kids.

"I think he took the part seriously, he loved the character, he owned it and he was very proud of it," his granddaughter, Jessica Carney, said recently. "I think he'd be so thrilled how successful it is now."[28]

Maureen O'Brien recalled Hartnell telling her that, when he'd received the script for *Doctor Who*, he had decided "this was my chance: I was going to make it mine – and I do make it mine and I make this show mine".

"And that's why he insisted on everything being right," said O'Brien. "It was his. It was his reward after a lifetime of slogging away at

things he didn't respect. So you could forgive him an awful lot of the irascibility and the standing on principle and all that, because it was so important to him."[24]

For William Hartnell, the Pied Piper of East Sussex, *Doctor Who* was not merely a job, it was a calling.

② Run for Your Wives

"Show me the money! (Oh, you already have.)"

Having agreed to become the new *Doctor Who*, Patrick Troughton's first task was to make sure no-one ever found out about it. His early ideas for the character included a stuttering, monocled aristo toff ('cos who doesn't love those guys, right?), a crazy-haired, Einstein-style mad professor, a Victorian windjammer (it's a type of ship, apparently) captain and a blacked-up Arab in the style of *1001 Nights*. ("That's terrific, really terrific," said Innes Lloyd when he heard. "Are you absolutely *sure* Michael Horden wasn't interested?") In short, Troughton was looking for anything to ensure nobody would recognise him off-camera. Not that he wasn't terribly proud of his new role, of course. It's just that... you know, people who knew him might be watching.

"I was reluctant at first," Troughton later admitted. "It had been going on about three years and I had a feeling that, in a way, the joke was over, that it had gone on too long. I didn't know know how long the BBC were really thinking of keeping it."[1]

So he turned it down – several times. And then, "After about a week of better and better offers, I thought, 'Well, I'm crazy. This is ridiculous. Even if it only lasts six weeks, it's worth doing it'."[1]

As well as the money, it helped that his two young sons, David and Michael, were fans of the show. In fact, Troughton claimed to have watched just about every Hartnell episode with them, and even turned to them for advice about how to approach the part. Though, being fans, they probably told him it had all gone downhill since the last guy left anyway.

As previously intimated, Troughton's personal life was *complicated*. Having fathered three children – David, Michael and Joanna – with his wife Margaret, he upped sticks to live with his girlfriend, Ethel "Bunny" (no relation) Nuens. By the time he joined *Doctor Who*, he was supporting his original family in a house in Mill Hill, north London, as well as Bunny

and their children Jane, Peter and Mark in a bungalow in Kew. ("That's disgusting," said his shocked Mill Hill neighbours when they found out. "Why on Earth would anyone choose to live in *south London*?")

Every Christmas and Easter, Troughton would go round to his mother's house and play happy families with Margaret and the kids, and Mrs T Sr went to her grave knowing nothing about her son's secret second brood. On the plus side, it saved her a fortune in Christmas presents. When, in later years, Michael asked his father why he had left them, he told him: "Things have to change all the time for me I'm afraid, that's the way I am made. I am sorry if I hurt you."[2]

This restlessness had also been reflected, somewhat less damagingly, in Troughton's career. Born and educated in Mill Hill (at school, his brother Robin had shared the 1933 Walter Knox Prize for Chemistry with fellow pupil Francis Crick), Troughton attended the Embassy School of Acting in Swiss Cottage – or was it the Cottage School of Acting in the Swiss Embassy? – before winning a scholarship to study his craft at the John Drew Memorial Theatre on Long Island, New York.

Returning home after the outbreak of the Second World War, Troughton's ship was sunk by a mine. He escaped in a lifeboat and, undeterred, signed up with the Royal Navy, where he saw action off the British coast, and was awarded the 1939-45 Star and the Atlantic Star. During service, he routinely wore a tea cosy on his head – he claimed it was to keep warm but, given his predilection for disguises, it's just as likely he was trying to pass himself off as a teapot.

After the war, Troughton spent a number of years in rep, but admitted he preferred television and film to theatre, which he described, not inaccurately, as "shouting in the evening". As well as being the small screen's first Robin Hood, his roles included Kettle (see? It's all starting to make sense now) in *Chance of a Lifetime*, Sir Andrew Ffoulkes in *The Scarlet*

Pimpernel, the title role in *Paul of Tarsus*, semi-regular appearances in *Dr Finlay's Casebook* and guest spots in all the TV big hitters of the day, including *Maigret, Danger Man, The Saint, Sherlock Holmes, Ivanhoe, Compact, Armchair Theatre, The Wednesday Play, Adam Adamant Lives!* and *Z-Cars*.

By the time Troughton had been contracted for an initial five *Doctor Who* serials, David Whitaker had already been commissioned to write his debut adventure, *The Destiny of Dr Who*, and a deal had been struck with Terry Nation to use the Daleks. A second story had also been accepted from comedy writer Geoffrey Orme called *Doctor Who Under the Sea*. No, it wasn't a musical. And there were discussions with Donald Cotton about a Loch Ness monster story – this despite Cotton's previous effort having signalled the death-knell for one of *Doctor Who's* staple ingredients: in the light of *The Gunfighters'* poor ratings and audience scores – or possibly because he just didn't like them – Innes Lloyd had resolved to phase out historical stories as soon as possible. Though not before he'd reluctantly commissioned one about the Battle of Culloden from writer Elwyn Jones. (It's not hard to imagine how this conversation went: "I'm sorry, we don't do historicals any more." "But I'm the outgoing Head of Drama Series – and a very influential man in the BBC." "Since you put it like that, I've always loved history.")

Actor threatens to sue over "new Doctor Who" smear

Troughton's casting was officially announced in the press on Friday, September 2nd. Privately, though, the actor was growing increasingly jittery about the fact no-one seemed able to agree on how he should play the part. Even the costume was a source of conflict: Troughton was now favouring a gentleman fop look, complete with a tottering stovepipe hat, and a curly Harpo Marx wig was briefly in the mix. But Sydney Newman – who had come back to the floor to take a more hands-on approach to the show during the transition – came up with the idea, apparently on the spot, that he should dress like a "cosmic hobo". In the end, they opted for something not dissimilar to how William Hartnell's Doctor

might have looked if he'd been reduced to sleeping in his car.

Days before filming on Troughton's debut serial – now called The *Power of the Daleks* – was due to begin, Whitaker's scripts were again revised to re-tool the new Doctor's character. But Newman still wasn't happy, claiming he was too much like Sherlock Holmes. One discussion document had proposed the new Doctor should ape the "sardonic humour" of the famously frosty detective; it also said, in reference to the transformation from one body to another: "It is as if he had had the LSD drug and, instead of experiencing the kicks, he has the hell and dank horror which can be its effects." Clearly the Summer of Love was going to be a long time coming to the BBC.

One idea Troughton responded positively to was the notion that his Doctor should be more of a listener than a talker – mainly because it meant fewer lines to learn and also because, as a man with two wives, pretending to listen was something he had down to a fine art.

A writers' guide issued around this time stated: "The new Doctor is younger than the former characterisation. He is more of an enigma, using humour to gain his ends rather than direct confrontation. His clowning tends to make his enemies underestimate him and his obsession with apparent trivialities, clothes, novelties of all kinds etc, is usually a device merely to give him time to examine a newly-discovered clue."

Despite this on-the-money description of how Troughton's Doctor would eventually pan out, recording on his first episode was delayed by a week to allow yet more refinement of his character. Gerry Davis recalled one meeting going on for more than two hours, with Troughton becoming increasingly confused by the crossfire of ideas; in the end, Davis slammed his fist on the table and told everyone else to get out – his bosses included – and leave him and Troughton to thrash it out between themselves. (Senior executives *love* this sort of spunky behaviour – why not give it a try at the next monthly team meeting?)

Concerned that Whitaker's scripts weren't quite right, Davis drafted in Dennis Spooner to do some rewrites while he himself wrestled with the Culloden story, Elwyn Jones having pulled out shortly after starting work. In other words, it was brand new Doctor, same old chaos. (If you want to be so vulgar as to talk money, incidentally, Whitaker got £300 per episode, Spooner got £75, Nation got £15 and Ray Cusick got slaughtered in the BBC bar.)

A week or so after making his studio debut at the end of *The Tenth Planet*, Troughton walked into his first rehearsal in St Helen's Church Hall in north London – only to find Michael Craze and Anneke Wills sporting t-shirts declaring "Come Back Bill Hartnell – All Is Forgiven". Troughton, already on edge, found this a bit upsetting (though it could have been worse – at least they weren't on sale at the BBC Shop), but it quickly became clear the trio were going to get on well, with Craze and Wills particularly relieved to be working with a leading man who was, in Wills' words, "completely sweet, and absolutely adorable, and totally friendly – we fell in love with him on the spot."[3]

Troughton's first full episode was recorded on October 22nd at the show's new home of Riverside, the actor improvising at times by throwing in ad-libs and bits of comic business which the director either liked or failed to notice. The second Doctor's trademark haircut – a sort of distressed Beatlemop – was only arrived at moments before the cameras started recording, the actor having mussed it up at the last minute using Michael Craze's comb.

Meanwhile, Terry Nation – who didn't rate Whitaker's/Spooner's new scripts – was trying to interest the BBC in co-producing a Dalek film series in which the pepperpots would do battle with Jean Marsh as Sara Kingdom (the fact she was dead was a mere detail) and her Special Space Service chums. He proposed filming a pilot, called *The Destroyers*, on December 12th – an unusually specific request; possibly he'd already promised an order of Sara Kingdom dolls in time for Christmas.

With *The Highlanders*, as the Culloden story was now called, having swapped places with *Under the Sea* owing to – what else? – script problems, head of serials Shaun Sutton recommended Frazer Hines for the role of plucky young Jacobite piper Jamie McCrimmon, with an option to keep him on for further episodes if he proved popular – which it appears they'd already kind of decided he would.

In the first week of November, publicity for the launch of the new series kicked in with the Daleks on a *Radio Times* cover and a TV trailer promising more red-hot Dalek action. Of the new Doctor, strangely, there was not a word – much to the delight of the series' new marketing manager, a Mr Tatrick Proughton.

On the day his full screen debut as the Doctor was broadcast – November 5th, 1969 – Troughton was busy recording episode three of the same story. He was extremely anxious about going public, and refused to watch the finished broadcast, but was cheered – literally – when he walked into the BBC bar that evening to an enthusiastic reception from colleagues. In fact some of them were as enthusiastic as newts.

Set on an Earth colony on the planet Vulcan – no, not *that* one, though the two were devised at around the same time[1] – *The Power of the Daleks* delights in confounding expectations. We might have expected the BBC to have wheeled on the show's most reliable warhorses to help provide some reassurance for viewers befuddled by the change at the top, but in fact the Daleks only add to the confusion by being uncharacteristically nice and touchy-feely and offering everyone biscuits and foot-rubs. Of course, it's really just a clever ruse: they're actually buying time in order to regain enough strength to expand their army and resume their busy exterminating schedule. By the end, new Daleks are rolling off the production lines with such efficiency, it must have doubled Britain's manufacturing output overnight.

The new Doctor is a puckish, sly, somewhat shadowy figure who remains at a slight remove and doesn't exactly put himself out to win our – or his companions' – trust until, in a piece of inspired scripting, the Daleks do the job for him: the moment they clock him as their mortal enemy is the moment everyone breathes a sigh of relief and realises that, yes, this is the Doctor, and everything is going to be okay. Before that, he spends a fair bit of time tootling on his recorder (that's not a euphemism – just a bit of business suggested by Troughton before he had anything more solid to work with) and leafing through his new 500 Year Diary. ("I can do lunch on March 23rd, 2331, but can't hang about as I've got the dentist at 2.30.")

Idiot makes refreshing change, say viewers

In the story editor's office, it was business as usual: William Emms had been taken ill while writing a serial set aboard a sailing ship in space, forcing Gerry Davis to forge ahead with *The Fish People* – the new, only marginally less silly name for *Doctor Who Under the Sea* – despite serious reservations from everyone concerned. One of the most concerned was the director assigned to it, Hugh David. He phoned up a contact at Pinewood Studios who had co-ordinated the underwater sequences for the recent Bond film *Thunderball*. When asked how much he had to spend, David told him he had £3,500 for the whole show. His contact then revealed they'd spent £3 million on the water tank sequence alone, and it still hadn't been enough – at which point David put the phone down, phoned up Innes Lloyd and asked if he could direct *The Highlanders* instead.

Actor and director Barry Letts also sent in several story proposals around this time, including one about a sinister alien organisation using an amusement park as a front to try to take over the world ("Get your own plan," complained a Mr M Mouse of California), and Malcolm Hulke's latest attempt to get commissioned saw him teaming up with David Ellis for a story called *The Big Store*, about faceless aliens disguised as shop dummies (or Saturday assistants – whichever had the blankest expressions). Meanwhile, the success of the Cybermen prompted Davis to commission Kit Pedler to write a second story called – wait for it – *Return of the Cybermen*. It was less good news for the Daleks though: in November, the BBC wrote to Terry Nation to tell him they weren't interested in his proposed film series, so he took it to America to try to flog it to NBC instead. (We can only wonder at what the network execs made of them: "Sure, the Daleks, we love those guys! Though they seem a little on the slow side – have you ever thought about giving them legs? And those voices: is it just me or are they a bit grating? I'm thinking more of a wisecracking, Mr Ed-type deal might be funnier? Also, is it weird we can't see their faces? Cos if we could move on that, I'm think-

ing this would be just perfect for Jimmy Garner.")

As the first reactions came in, Troughton was concerned he might be subject to a backlash from viewers. A BBC audience research report for *The Power of the Daleks* stated:

"Most of the comment centred round Patrick Troughton as Dr Who. Much of this took a critical form, some viewers saying that, although an excellent actor whom they much admired as a rule, he seemed miscast, not to say 'wasted', hero [sic], although according to a Teacher he 'seemed to be struggling manfully with the idiotic new character that Dr Who has taken on since his change'. Others criticised him for overdoing the part, 'playing for laughs', making the Doctor into 'something of a Pantomime character' – 'I'm not sure that I really like his portrayal. I feel the part is over-exaggerated – whimsical even – I keep expecting him to take a great watch out of his pocket and mutter about being late like Alice's White Rabbit'. Frankly, some said, they preferred William Hartnell in the part. However, there was also comment to the effect that Patrick Troughton had not yet settled down as Dr Who, there was still time for him to become fully accepted, and there was praise in some quarters for his portrayal as excellent; he had made 'a refreshing change', and 'brought a new dimension to the character'."

In the *Radio Times*, meanwhile, Troughton appeared to have lost the previously solid Cornish housewife vote, as a Mrs Estelle Hawken of that parish complained about the Doctor being turned into "Coco the Clown". But G Howard of Leeds declared: "Patrick Troughton and the superb character he has created has dragged the programme out of the unfortunate mess it had degenerated into."

Ratings for the serial held steady around the eight million mark, but the show was being bounced out of the ring by *Professional Wrestling* on ITV. Maybe they should have made the new Doctor a 32-stone ex-welder in a spangly leotard.

In December, Innes Lloyd decided the series' opening titles needed refreshing, and a new sequence was recorded by Bernard Lodge and Ben Palmer, this time incorporating the

Doctor's face into the feedback patterns. Speaking of faces, in *TV Comic*, John and Gillian's granddad suddenly got a new one, without any explanation whatsoever. But they didn't seem to mind; the message appeared to be: Kids, if a complete stranger turns up claiming to be your grandfather and tries to bundle you into a box, just go with it.

As *The Highlanders* went into the studio, Troughton found himself working for the man who had been offered his job even before William Hartnell. If Hugh David had been worried about the budget constraints of *The Fish People*, he must have been pleased to see this one was conveniently set slightly *after* the Battle of Culloden, thus avoiding having to re-stage the massacre of 4,000 Jacobites by 9,000 English soldiers in a small television studio on a Saturday evening. The queue for the canteen alone would have been a nightmare.

The Doctor sides with the Jacobite rebellion as much to cause a bit of mischief as through any commitment to being a revolutionary firebrand, and the story lets Troughton loose in the dressing-up box by disguising himself as a cockney Redcoat, a German physician called Dr Von Wer (see what they did there?) and a Scottish grandmother, years before Robin Williams made millions from the same idea.

Despite being dashed off in a hurry, *The Highlanders* is an engaging enough Robert Louis Stevenson pastiche, (though it doesn't help when Polly points out its similarity to season opener *The Smugglers*; honestly – everyone's a critic). But Innes Lloyd was determined to make these historical capers a thing of the past, declaring: "*The Highlanders* had a certain charm – but only to us, I think."[4] And viewers in Scotland, of course, but since when had anyone worried about what they thought?

Frazer Hines – who, despite the convincing Caledonian name, is actually from Leeds – had appeared with Charlie Chaplin in *A King in New York*, and worked well enough alongside this Chaplinesque new Doctor to be offered an extended contract. What upcoming scripts were available were rewritten to accommodate him, and he was welcomed warmly into the fold by the existing cast, who by now were becoming good friends, regularly stopping off for drinks together on the way home from the studio.[II]

By the time the serial finished recording on Christmas Eve, everyone was in fine spirits, and Troughton was feeling more optimistic – or as optimistic as he could be for a man who had to spend the next day at his mother's praying the kids wouldn't blurt anything out about Daddy's other family. Encouraged by Lloyd, he also felt confident enough to start toning down the comedy showboating.

Continuing problems with the scripts for *The Underwater Menace* – the absolutely final, still slightly rubbish name for *Doctor Who Under the Sea/The Fish People* – forced the cancellation of the New Year's Eve recording session, meaning that, in little over a month, the show had gone from having a three-week window between recording and transmission, to just one. Still, as long as they didn't try anything too ambitious – like, say, recreating the lost City of Atlantis – what was the worst that could happen?

Fish story tanks

If director Julia Smith's New Year's resolutions had included staying calm, not losing her temper and not crying, they weren't going to last very long. As Hugh David had predicted, everything about *The Underwater Menace* was a nightmare – starting with the script.

"You just knew it was a dodo," recalled Michael Craze. ("Did someone call?" asked Jackie Lane, who was still in the dressing room waiting to be called for her leaving scene.) "The whole thing was badly conceived – tatty old scripts and costumes and everything. It ended up as pantomime. Julia Smith was so emotionally charged that she'd burst into tears at anything."[5]

According to Anneke Wills, the more uptight and shouty Smith got, the more rebellious the regulars became. "We would mess around, and she would get more and more like a schoolteacher, so we got naughtier and naughtier. Pat would call her a 'miserable old bitch', but that's what we were like. We had power, we were the main actors. Otherwise, most of the directors we got on really well with. Only Julia had a bad time with us. We made her life a misery."[3] Of course, Smith would get her own back in later years by inventing *EastEnders*, and making *everyone's* life a misery.

It's hard to know where to start the post-mortem on *The Underwater Menace*, but let's begin with the villain of the piece, Professor Zaroff – a beyond-mad scientist (he's a plankton expert with a pet octopus, dontcha know) played with eye-rolling Germanic gusto by Joseph Furst (Austrian-born Furst was actually using his real accent – it's just unfortunate his real accent is so unconvincing).

Zaroff's plan is to boil the Earth's oceans away – with a plunger, no less – until the whole planet cracks open, and everyone dies. Why? For a laugh, apparently. Atlantean slaves the Fish People, meanwhile, flap about like confused ballerinas trying to untangle themselves from some net curtains, and the sequence of them staging an insurrection is like a display by the world's worst synchronised swimming team, complete with visible fishing lines. But just because they look ridiculous doesn't mean they don't have rights, which is why part of the plot concerns the Fish People's attempts to unionise. You can imagine the meetings:

"What do we want?"

"Equal rights for Fish People!"

"When do we want it?"

"When do we want what?"

Unbelievably, despite the fact this is the closest to an all-out Ed Wood production *Doctor Who* had ever come, episode three – the one with the unsynchronised swimming gala – was one of the few the BBC chose to save from the incinerator. Possibly just to serve as a lesson to all involved.

The serial started out with 8.3 million viewers, and shed more than a million of them along the way. Still, at least Joe Orton enjoyed it – the playwright wrote admiringly in his diary about Frazer Hines dressed head-to-toe in rubber "like a Victorian masher" – which must have doubled the story's AI average.

By now, Ellis and Hulke's *The Big Store* had been renamed *Dr Who and The Chameleons* and the action had shifted from a department store to an airport (this was in the days when you could still tell the difference). Lloyd and Davis had also decided to conclude the season with an epic "final battle" between the Doctor and the Daleks – removing the latter from *Doctor*

Who so they could pursue their solo career in the US. Quite why the BBC would willingly pass on the Daleks while continuing with the Doctor – who, let's face it, was never going to win a playground popularity contest between the two – isn't clear, but there were rumblings from some at the corporation about Nation using Ray Cusick's designs in a non-BBC show.

With Hines now contracted for the next two serials, a decision was taken to drop Ben from the show. It can't have been lost on Michael Craze that everyone from the producer to the viewers seemed more excited about Jamie these days, with the young groover brought in to give the show a hipper, more contemporary edge now being outshone by an eighteenth-century Scotsman. Maybe it was the kilt. Anneke Wills was initially asked to stay on, but opted to go at the same time as her friend in a show of solidarity.

On January 17th, as his successor was signed up for a further 23 episodes, William Hartnell talked about his reasons for leaving the show in a heroically bad-tempered interview – "I'm a legitimate character actor!", he scolds the interviewer – for regional news programme *Points West*; clearly the Piers Morgan's *Life Stories* of its day. It was only a matter of time before a Dalek popped up, talking tearfully about being dropped from *Doctor Who*. ("I-DON'T-KNOW-WHAT-I'M-SUPP-OSED-TO-HAVE-DONE, NO-ONE'S-TOLD-ME-ANY-THING.") In the meantime, the creatures were still regular fixtures on everything from *Blue Peter* to comedy sketch shows and, in February, part of the score for the second Dalek movie was issued as a single called "Fugue for Thought", though no-one for the life of them knows why.

Daft side of the moon

There was a gratifying amount of press interest in the return of the Cybermen, helped by photocall in which the silver giants queued for a bus in Ealing (being London, everyone else in the queue just kept their eyes down and pretended not to notice), contributing to an upswing in ratings for *The Moonbase*, which outperformed ITV's offerings – even in the Midlands, where it was up against ABC's candy-coloured kerpow-caper *Batman*. (That's assuming anyone in the Midlands had a colour TV, which is a stretch.)

It's perhaps surprising it took *Doctor Who* more than three years to reach the moon but, on February 11th, 1967 the show beat Neil Armstrong and company to the punch by a good 29 months as the Cybes invaded a lunar base to mess with the Earth's weather systems and destroy the population. Or, at the very least, ruin their summer ("picnics are a weakness!").

In other words, it's *The Tenth Planet* on the moon, complete with crew of international stereotypes and a wanton disregard for basic scientific principles – though *Space Helmet's* scientific adviser insists a tea-tray being used to successfully plug a hole in the dome of the lunar base *is* perfectly feasible (providing you take the biscuits off first). The tray in question had recently been wielded by Polly, who was now being pressed into service as a char lady on almost a weekly basis. So much for the counter-culture. Though it's not all quite so appallingly sexist – when she's not living up to her name by putting the kettle on, Polly does get to wipe out some Cybermen in this story. Using nail polish remover.

The new-look Cybes have now abandoned the fabric look – that was, like, *so* four months ago – in favour of metal helmets and face-masks and silver jumpsuits accessorised with practice golf balls. You can laugh, but you'll all be wearing them next year. Staying with fashion desk, Patrick Troughton had by now lost the stupid hat, which had somehow survived Sydney Newman's impromptu make-over, and his voluminous trousers were being gradually taken in week-by-week by a stealth seamstress, so that he wouldn't notice. The actor nearly had a few inches taken off his head, too, when a very heavy prop crashed to the studio floor, missing him by inches. The prime suspects were believed to be a Mrs J Smith of Shepherd's Bush and a Mr W Hartnell of East Sussex.

The Doctor gets a lovely speech in this story, telling his companions, "There are some corners of the universe which have bred the most terrible things – they must be fought." As a mission statement, it showed how much the the programme's direction had changed since the days of a shifty William Hartnell attempting to leg it to safety at the first sign of trouble.

Unfortunately, *The Moonbase* is riddled with the sort of holes no tea-tray in the galaxy can plug, particularly in the final reel, when the Cybermen – who have basically won by this point – suddenly decide to sabotage their own mission by blowing a massive chunk out of the base just to show off, after which their plan derails spectacularly. Even the serial's money shot – of the silver giants marching across the lunar surface – is undermined by the ludicrous decision to add a comedy "boing!!!" every time one of them jumps in the air. Stanley Kubrick never phoned to ask about that one, strangely.

Back on Earth, production returned to our old friend Lime Grove Studio D for the next story, *The Macra Terror* – an everyday tale of a holiday camp in space run by giant crabs. (They say there are only seven basic stories in the world, but this surely can't be one of them.) The camp is actually a human work colony on an un-named planet, but Ian Stuart Black – one of the series' better ideas men of the era – had obviously had a very unfortunate experience at Butlins (other dreadful British holiday experiences are available, sadly) if this unsettling mix of *Nineteen Eighty-Four* and *Hi-de-Hi* is anything to go by. With its depiction of a brainwashed population constantly assaulted by creepy jingles and tinny musak, *The Macra Terror* also steals a march on Patrick McGoohan's cult head-scratcher *The Prisoner* by a good six months. Did I mention that Ian Stuart Black also created *Danger Man...*?

Director John Davies got a telling off for making the story "too scary" for the kids – which almost certainly means they loved it. Unfortunately, everyone's efforts were somewhat undermined by the Macra itself, which ended up looking less like a giant alien crab and more like a hairy family saloon with pincers and eyes. Eyes on sticks. "That thing cost the price of a Mini, and it was rubbish," complained Frazer Hines. "It couldn't move properly... if it had to grab somebody, that person had to throw themselves at it. You had to stick your hand in and shout, 'Oh, it's got me!'"[6]

The cost and quality of the prop persuaded Innes Lloyd to stop using Shawcraft Models, and an agreement was reached with BBC Visual Effects Department heads Jack Kine and Bernard Wilkie that, from now on, the department would allocate a staffer to each serial.

In April, Lloyd received confirmation that *Doctor Who* would continue at least until the autumn. But time was up for Anneke Wills and Michael Craze, who recorded their final scenes on the 8th of that month. Far from getting a fitting send-off, Ben and Polly are out of action for most of the *The Faceless Ones*, vanishing in episode two and only reappearing for a cursory goodbye at the end. It's not quite as bad as Dodo's unceremonious off-screen bow, but after ten stories and serving as an effective bridgehead between the first and second Doctors, the characters – and the audience – surely deserved better.

To add insult to injury, the Doctor spends most of the story running round with plucky Scouse newcomer Samantha Briggs (played by a young Pauline Collins), not even waiting until his previous companions have been round to the TARDIS to collect their books and CDs before moving the new girl in. In the event, Innes Lloyd's overtures to Collins fell on deaf ears, and thus Sam Briggs was destined became the first one-shot companion since Sara Kingdom.

Both Wills and Craze were unhappy with the way their exits had been handled. Troughton and Hines were also upset: Troughton credited Wills, in particular, with helping him find his feet in the early days. Though Wills ultimately jumped, it's not clear why Craze was pushed. Some have suggested he was being punished for his part in the Great Underwater Rebellion of 67 – but if that was the case, why single him out for special treatment? After *Doctor Who*, high-profile work eluded him. "He was one of those actors who, I'm afraid, fell through the net," said Wills. "He was so unhappy. He was a marvellous actor. He could have been huge, but he just wasn't given the breaks."[3] When Craze died in a fall in 1998, the *Doctor Who* theme was played at his funeral.

For her part, Wills went on to open a craft shop, moved to Belgium, joined an ashram in India and, more recently, wrote a fabulously indiscreet showbiz autobiography, highlights of which include discussion of her turbulent marriage to Michael Gough, her love affair with Anthony Newley (who fathered her first child, before leaving her for Joan Collins) among other memorable swinging 60s tales.

The final end (until the next one)

Ben and Polly weren't the only ones having trouble with departures in *The Faceless Ones*. David Ellis and Malcolm Hulke's story concerns a group of aliens operating a scheduled air service out of Gatwick (how they got the permits is anyone's guess) and then secretly spiriting them away to an orbiting space station in order to steal their identities, having apparently lost their own in – and this is verbatim – "a gigantic explosion". This unusually metaphysical response to a big bang is just one of the flaws in a daft plot that had been unnaturally stretched out to six episodes in order to help pay for *The Underwater Debacle*. On the plus side, the central conceit of aliens stealing bodies out of a desperate survival instinct is a bit more mature than the usual galactic conquest phooey, and there's some disturbing psychological horror about identity loss, if you look hard enough for it.

Innes Lloyd and Gerry Davis were clearly still keen to push *Doctor Who* down a more contemporary thriller route – though it's unfortunate the James Bond element they choose to emulate here is one of those "I could kill you, but instead I'm going to leave you at the mercy of this very slow-moving laser" moments. Still, Gatwick does look suitably shiny and new (the BBC had bought the co-operation of staff by offering them tickets to *The Rolf Harris Show* – yes, really) and, at the end of the day, there aren't many alien invasion stories where the aliens have gone to the effort of obtaining valid British passports.

With Pauline Collins having given him the brush-off, Lloyd started the search for a new female companion, to be introduced in season finale *The Evil of the Daleks*. Six actresses auditioned for the role of Victorian teenager, er, Victoria, including Gabrielle Drake, future star of Gerry Anderson's *UFO* and, later, *Crossroads*. ("Aren't you Nick Drake's[III] sister?" "Yes." "Never heard of him.") The role was initially offered to Denise Buckley, then they changed course and gave it to 19-year-old Deborah Watling, who Lloyd had seen playing Lewis Carroll's *Alice*, and who didn't even have to audition.

Another new face on the team was Peter

Bryant, an actor-turned-radio script supervisor who had been helping Gerry Davis with his workload, and was now offered the more permanent role of assistant producer. A crib sheet was available in the form of a new production document issued by Lloyd, which stated that the average budget was now £2,570 per episode and stipulated that, owing to the cost of tape-editing, each recording could only be allowed a maximum of five breaks. Directors were also instructed to include a five-second fade-to-black midway through each episode to allow for ad breaks on overseas broadcasts.

Then, on April 13th, BBC One controller Michael Peacock announced a more permanent fade-to-black when he commissioned *Doctor Who* for a fifth run – but said he wanted it replaced the following year with a new series called *Bonaventure*. It probably wasn't as rude as it sounds.

Gerry Davis wasn't hanging round to find out – he'd accepted a job on high-profile new drama *The First Lady*, so Peter Bryant took over as story editor, where his first commission was a script called *Doctor Who and the Abominable Snowman*. Meanwhile, production had started on the first story of the fifth series, *Tomb of the Cybermen*, which Bryant was overseeing as holiday cover for Lloyd. ("Just pop in from time to time to pick up the post and water the plants, that sort of thing. Oh, and if you could produce the season opener, that would be terrific.") During this time, story editing duties were handled by Bryant's assistant, Victor Pemberton, who had previously appeared in a non-speaking role as a scientist in *The Moonbase*. Are you following all this, or should I draw a diagram?

Before his next re-match with his arch enemies, though, there was the small business of a final showdown with his even archer-er enemies. *The Evil of the Daleks* owes a heavy debt to writer David Whitaker's *TV Century 21* comic strips, most obviously in the introduction of the 12-ft high Emperor Dalek – the most badass Dalek of the lot, even if he does have somewhat restricted movement on account of being plumbed into the walls like a dishwasher. The story also sees the Doctor taking his first trip to Victorian England – surprisingly tardy given the show's HG Wells/*Old Curiosity Shop* roots – where a mad scientist's

home-made time machine has accidentally made the Daleks appear in his cupboard. Don't you hate it when that happens?

Despite reckoning themselves to be the supreme beings of the universe and all that (they don't really do humility), the Daleks are looking to augment themselves by isolating something called The Human Factor – nothing to do with Simon Cowell (he's not human, obviously). By the time the action moves to Skaro, the Doctor has managed to affect a switcheroo that sees "humanised" Daleks – now capable of such qualities as courage, pity, chivalry, friendship and compassion (and presumably whingeing, grumbling, moping and heavy sarcasm) – taking on the purebloods in an almighty civil war.

The Evil of the Daleks is big, ambitious, confident and epic. Sure, there are the usual plot holes and scientific hooey – mad Prof Maxtible's time travel kit is *literally* all done with mirrors – but it hardly matters: if this is indeed what the Doctor calls "the final end" of the auld enemy, then it's a fitting one. Ironically, the one person who cautioned against writing them out entirely was Sydney "BEM" Newman, offering one of his final pieces of advice before leaving the BBC for an ill-fated spell with the ailing Associated British Picture Corporation.

Two people who weren't that happy with the story were Deborah Watling and Terry Nation. Like any teenager, Watling was mortified to wake up on her first day of recording with "a giant spot" on her face (Lord knows why she was so worried – the BBC's HD service was rubbish in those days), while someone forgot to include Nation's name in the credits, forcing the continuity announcer to make a grovelling on-air clarification.

From a strong start of 8.1 million, *The Evil of the Daleks* managed to shed two million viewers over its run, but that was probably more down to the time of year – the final episode went out on July 1st – than any disaffection on the part of viewers. In fact, ratings for Troughton's first run had brought much-needed stability after the rollercoaster ride of Season Three, and the audience appreciation figures had also been climbing. This was partly thanks to Frazer Hines, who was rapidly establishing himself as the series' first real heartthrob. ("I think he's the best-looking actor on television!" gushed a breathless *Junior Points of View* correspondent – though bear in mind the big TV stars of the day included Robert Robinson, Marty Feldman and Frank Muir.) Hines even fancied a crack at a pop career, recording a song, "The Time Traveller" (written by his brother), that was tragically never released.

But the new Doctor himself had also been judged a success. In fact, the new-look show was such hit with some viewers, *Junior Points of View* received a letter from a group of young fans during the series' summer break, demanding the BBC bring it back NOW "or we will kill you all". And people say TV is a bad influence.

It's lucky this paramilitary wing of the *Doctor Who Fan Club* didn't get wind of what was happening at the BBC that summer: on August 17th, clearance was given to wipe the master tapes of the first 79 *Doctor Who* episodes, starting with the pilot. But they held on to the 16mm film copies for overseas sales so, just as long as no idiot ever lost *those*, there was nothing to worry about. Phew!

Croeso i Tibet (Welcome to Tibet, look you)

Doctor Who eventually returned to BBC1 in its own good time on September 2nd, with no loss of lives as far as we know. Helped by a big publicity push (including another *Radio Times* cover), *The Tomb of the Cybermen* got the fifth series off to a strong start with solid ratings – the final episode was watched by 7.4 million people – and positive audience feedback. It even got a glowing review in *The Times* – though three schoolgirls from Wiltshire tried to spoil the party by telling *Junior Points of View* the story was "stupendously stupid". The success of the serial gave Kit Pedler, who had already rejected a 40/60 split on ownership of the Cybermen, leverage to hold out for 50/50 – though whether he got the top or the bottom half isn't recorded.

The Tomb of the Cybermen opens with a bunch of archaeologists – shifty foreign types, mainly, this being a Kit Pedler script – rocking up at the entrance to a hidden city on the planet Telos at the same time as the TARDIS team. The Doctor is shocked to learn the party has come to excavate the famous lost tombs of

the Cybermen – though he'd have been less shocked if he'd taken more notice of the 15-ft Cyberman stencilled on the wall next to his head. (Say what you like about the Cybes and their ridiculously overcomplicated schemes, the guys from branding didn't miss a trick.) The Doctor warns the expedition about the folly of their plan, while simultaneously doing everything he can to help them progress towards certain death. ("See these levers to open the doors? You definitely don't want to touch those. Though if you did you'd need to do them in a very specific order, like... here, let me show you. See how the doors are open now? I told you that would happen. Didn't I tell you that would happen? Anyway, I definitely wouldn't go through them if I were you. I'd run for your lives if I were... ooh, hang on, is that the button that restores power to the whole complex? I definitely wouldn't touch *that*.") If he's trying to prove a point, it's a very bloody way of doing it.

The early, *Curse of the Mummy's Tomb*-riffing episodes do a good job of ratcheting up the tension. Unfortunately, once the Cybermen are released from their subterranean chiller cabinet, they don't actually *do* much except mooch about until it's time to go back in again. This is particularly bad news for the Cyber Controller – you can tell he's the Controller from his large veiny helmet (oh stop it) – who has spent 500 years squatting uncomfortably in a small cryogenic chamber like the world's most dedicated hide-and-seek champion. ("Guys, in case you hadn't noticed I'm, like, seven feet tall – would it have killed you to make it big enough to stand up in? Or at least put a chair in. Can we really not stretch to a chair? Does this helmet mean *nothing*? You really start to feel it on the quads after the first 150 years or so.")

The Controller was played by Michael Kilgariff – a respected radio actor, so an obvious choice for a non-speaking part. Also in the cast is Shirley Cooklin, AKA Mrs Peter Bryant. That's right: his first story in charge and he's hired the missus. (Perhaps she was the clingy type: "What do you mean you're producing *Doctor Who* this evening? You know it's our bridge night. Well, I hope you don't expect me to sit here on my own twiddling my thumbs: you'd better find me a part as an exotic but deadly beauty plotting to form a power-sharing alliance with the Cybermen – or is that *too much to ask?*") Embarrassingly, Frazer Hines didn't recognise Mrs B out of costume/make-up and tried to hit on her, which must have made things awkward at his next appraisal.

For years, *The Tomb of the Cybermen* enjoyed a reputation as the great lost classic of *Doctor Who*, venerated as the series' *Citizen Kane* – *but with Cybermen*. Then, in 1991, it had the temerity to turn up in Hong Kong and was rush-released on video. At which point everyone realised it wasn't that great after all; not *bad* by any means – we're not talking *Phantom Menace* levels of disappointment here – but not quite the masterpiece we'd been led to believe.

The story also came under fire for being "too violent", a charge levelled on the new BBC1 discussion show *Talkback*. Kit Pedler remained bullish in the face of parents' accusations that the programme was unsuitable for children but, privately, Patrick Troughton – who had just agreed to sign for a further 24 episodes – was concerned by the criticism, and resolved that the Doctor should play down frightening situations in the future. Possibly by rolling his eyes and saying "what*ever*" whenever he was threatened by a monster.

Next up was the Doctor's encounter with the Abominable Snowmen. Except they weren't men or particularly abominable – in fact they looked positively cuddly – and there was no snow, on account of the story being filmed in Wales in early September. The Nat Fracon Pass in Gwynedd is perhaps not a natural substitute for the Himalayas – Tibet has fewer people in orange kagouls drinking Bovril out of tartan flasks for one thing – but the same location had also doubled for Afghanistan a fortnight earlier for the filming of *Carry On Up the Khyber*.

The script – in which a Buddhist abbot under the influence of a formless Intelligence builds some robot Yetis in order to scare people away (and he'd have gotten away with it, too, if it hadn't been for that meddling Doctor) – was written by Mervyn Haisman and a sometime actor called Henry Lincoln. Lincoln would go on to co-author an international bestseller in the form of *The Holy Blood and the Holy Grail* – a ripe slice of conspiracy nonsense about Jesus having French kids and something to do with a secret society of... something or

other (it made the robot Yeti plan look positively credible, frankly) – which in turn inspired *The Da Vinci Code*. So thanks for that.

The part of crusty anthropologist and explorer Professor Travers was played by Deborah Watling's father Jack as part of that year's Bring Your Dad to Work Day. The role of moustachioed monk Ralpachan, meanwhile, was played by Harold Pinter as part of that year's Bring a Nobel Prize-Winning Playwright and Poet to Work Day. Not really, of course – but the rumour of Pinter's involvement has persisted for years based on the fact the part was credited to David Baron, which had previously been Pinter's stage name, and because Baron looks a bit like Pinter might look if you stuck a big moustache on him and sort of squinted a bit.

In Wales, *The Abominable Snowmen* was shown in primetime so everyone could take pride in the local scenery, which must have distracted from the whole Himalayan vibe somewhat; even today, there are probably Welshman who think the world's chief Buddhist is a local bloke called Dai Lama.

Troughton enjoyed the location shoots, but was finding the schedule of filming one story while rehearsing the studio sessions for the previous one punishing. Also juggling two shoots in November 1967 was Bernard Bresslaw, who combined regular duties as the Carry On team's lugubrious giant with playing Varga, leader of the Ice Warriors in Brian Hayles' story of the same name. Set during the second Ice Age in the future – *Daily Mail* readers will be pleased to know global warming *was* a myth after all – the story sees the crew of a scientific research base (yes, another one) accidentally defrosting some big green men from Mars. Director Derek Martinus was so keen to cast people over six feet, he ended up auditioning all sorts of dubious characters with prison records as long as their arms. And they had very long arms. At 6'7", Bresslaw towered over even these lags; his fibreglass costume (which caused the actors to sweat up to a pint of liquid an hour) meant he couldn't sit down during breaks, so had to rest on a shooting stick "rammed" – according to Frazer Hines – "up his backside". To make matters worse, he was virtually blind without his glasses, and ended up stumbling round the set like a green, seven-foot Mr Magoo. Fellow guest stars Peter Sallis – who would later star in 158 identical series of pensioner-in-bathtub caper *Last of the Summer Wine*, before finding a new audience as the speaking half of Wallace and Gromit – and Peter Barkworth had it easy by contrast.

Though the Ice Warriors would come to be seen as one of *Doctor Who's* all-time great monsters, their debut story is repetitive and overlong. It's also hard to see why *Doctor Who* would serve up a morality play where the message is "beware scientific progress" – especially when it's written by someone who doesn't know the difference between oxygen and carbon dioxide (tip: never go deep sea diving with Brian Hayles). Even the Doctor professes to be suspicious of computers (probably just because he keeps getting asked to install Windows updates when he's trying to save the world).

Mere months after killing them off "forever", the BBC were already approaching Terry Nation about the possibility of using the Daleks in a story with the Cybermen, but, mindful of any potential rivals, Nation vetoed the idea. In late November, *Blue Peter* launched a competition to design a new monster for the series. (For *Doctor Who*, that is; I don't mean they were thinking of replacing Valerie Singleton with a nightmarish creature – though Lesley Judd did sport some particularly nasty blouses.) The rules stipulated the monster had to be "strong enough to defeat the Daleks", which suggested the production team's ongoing bid to find a villain to rival their popularity had taken a desperate turn. The competition, judged by Doctor Who himself (Patrick Troughton preferred to make public appearances in costume and in character), attracted an astonishing 250,000 entries. The three winning entries – the Steel Octopus, Hypnotron and Acwa Man – were showcased over Christmas at the *Daily Mail* Boys and Girls Exhibition as part of a menagerie that also included a Yeti, an Ice Warrior, a Cyberman and a Dalek, none of which were quite reactionary enough for the *Daily Mail*.

Innes: I'm out

Viewers settling down to watch the Bond film that Christmas must have wondered why the budget had been so drastically cut – until they realised it was just Innes Lloyd's latest attempt to see if *Doctor Who* could punch its weight alongside 007.

Like any good Bond movie – and, indeed, all the bad ones – *The Enemy of the World* features exotic locations (the story opens with the TARDIS arriving on a sun-kissed Australian beach – or it would have been sun-kissed, if it hadn't been filmed in West Sussex in November) and a dastardly villain with a highly impractical plan for world domination. The twist here is that the mad Mexican dictator Ramon Salamander is an almost exact doppelganger for the Doctor, thus giving Pat Troughton the chance to let rip with his best Speedy Gonzales accent. "Frazer and I were on the floor," admitted Debbie Watling. "We couldn't believe he was really going to do it like that."[7]

David Whitaker's near future-set story has ambitions to be a serious political thriller, as Salamander – who has managed to end famine (yay!) by using GM crops (boo!) – attempts to undermine his enemies in a global power struggle. This being *Doctor Who*, though, he does this by getting some people to live underground and cause earthquakes, thus *literally* destabilising a rival power bloc. You can't help thinking acquiring a few incriminating photographs with a hooker would have been a lot less effort.

Hot on the heels of Peter Bryant's wife and Debbie Watling's dad, this story finds room for Frazer Hines' brother Ian and Pat Troughton's son David as guards; it was only a matter of time before a clerical error at central casting saw Troughton starring alongside both his wives, with hilarious consequences.

The lack of budget is obvious from the fact one character is kept prisoner *in a corridor*, but, to its credit, the story does boast an impressive sequence with an exploding helicopter that wouldn't look out of place in an actual Bond movie. That's because it's a clip from *From Russia With Love*.

The Enemy of the World was the first *Doctor Who* story to be recorded on 625-line videotape, as opposed to the old 405-line system. So what?, you might ask, but this sort of stuff's like hardcore porn to *Doctor Who* fans. More significantly, it was Innes Lloyd's last story as producer. Opinion on Lloyd's tenure is divided: on the one hand, his and Gerry Davis' approach, with its endlessly recycled villains and base-under-siege plots, seems like a highly reductive interpretation of a format created for its limitless boundaries. On the other, he's the man who rescued *Doctor Who* from its vertiginous ratings slide by giving the kids exactly what they wanted: monsters, monsters and more monsters. "Looking back, I suppose *Doctor Who* taught me the sheer wonder of fantasy, and that science fiction has far more potential as a storytelling device than I had ever anticipated," Lloyd recalled a couple of decades later. "Some people I met at the time had a very pompous attitude towards the programme, but I'm sure that the adults were tempted at the odd moment to join their children behind the couch."[4] Particularly during *The Underwater Menace*.

Debbie Watling had also signalled her intention to move on, and it was decided she would be replaced by a new character called Zoe, an astrophysicist and librarian ("In space, no-one can hear you ssshhhh"). Bryant once again approached Pauline Collins, and was once again rebuffed. Frazer Hines suggested his current squeeze Susan George, but it's probably just as well she wasn't cast: the relationship didn't last, and no-one wants to spend half the day trapped in a small blue box with their ex.

For his part, Troughton had been offered another year but wasn't sure he could cope with the workload. Barry Letts, the director of *The Enemy of the World*, suggested he ask for a reduction in the number of stories to allow for a less hectic schedule. Planning for the next series was already too far advanced but, after staging what he called "a sort of sit-down strike",[8] Troughton received an assurance that he would no longer have to work weekends, and would be excused from location filming on the first two serials of the next block. A hefty outstanding tax bill also proved persuasive. After a night down the pub with Hines and Watling weighing up his options, he resolved to sign for one more year.

The actor was also allowed a week's holiday during taping of the next story, *The Web of Fear*, which he spent fishing with his sons. His absence was explained by the Doctor getting caught in a bomb blast and lying unconscious for an episode – not brilliant, but better than hanging "Gone Fishing" on the TARDIS door.

With Bryant now producing, another actor-turned-writer – it was the only hope most of them had of getting any work – called Derrick Sherwin joined the show as story editor, assisted by Terrance Dicks, a former advertising copywriter who had started writing radio and TV scripts in attempt to do something more worthwhile and fulfilling with his life. And had then ended up working on *Crossroads*.

The new team's first venture saw the Yeti making a speedy return to action, this time in a contemporary adventure in which they bring chaos and disruption to the London Underground. Like anyone was going to notice *that*. ("We regret to inform passengers there are currently delays on the District, Circle and Hammersmith and City lines owing to an infestation of Abominable Snowmen at Moorgate." "Typical lack of planning," grumbled the commuters. "Surely they could have anticipated this?")

London Transport wanted to charge £200 an hour to film on the Underground – that's more than Patrick Troughton earned in a day – so designer David Myserscough-Jones (that's his name – I wasn't just clearing my throat) and his team built their own. The result was so convincing the BBC received a letter of from LT complaining about them filming without permission. The trains probably ran better, too.

Now that they were celebrities, the Yeti returned sporting a new slimline look, and their fur was made from genuine Yak hair. The gossip mags were suitably impressed ("How YOU can get a bikini body like the Yeti"), but it was only a matter of time before congratulation turned to concern ("The Yeti: dangerously thin?"). They also boasted a new roar, which was achieved by slowing down the sound of a flushing toilet. It's not hard to guess where the sound designer came up with all his best ideas.

Jack Watling returned for another outing as Professor Travers – well he was giving Debbie a lift into work anyway, so why not? – while Tina Packer played his plucky daughter Anne. The rest of the cast is largely made up of people playing assorted squaddies – Douglas Camfield was in his element – and leading Our Brave Boys into battle is one Colonel Lethbridge-Stewart: Camfield had originally cast sheep farmer-turned-actor David Langton in the role, but when a scheduling conflict forced him to drop out, Nicholas Courtney, previously seen as Bret Vyon in *The Daleks' Master Plan*, was rapidly promoted from his role as Captain Knight. It was a decision that would change the actor's life forever – though forever nearly wasn't very long, as Camfield almost blew him up with a live bazooka; it was only when Courtney asked if he ought to move out of the way that a potential tragedy was averted. (We know Camfield liked to run his shoots like military operations – it's a pity he didn't run his military operations the same way.)

An artful blend of atmosphere and action, *The Web of Fear* had a big impact on the kids who saw it at the time. Camfield lights it like a piece of German Expressionist cinema, as opposed to a monster mash on the Central Line, and it's none the worse for it. The story is docked points for its appalling depiction of wealthy art collector Julius Silverstein – a grasping Jewish stereotype who makes Fagin look like Father Christmas – and a denouement that would be a cop-out even if it wasn't a blatant re-hash of *The Evil of the Daleks*. And there's no getting away from the fact it's the ultimate running-up-and-down-corridors (or tunnels, technically) story. But none of that should be allowed to take away too much from one of the most memorable, slickly executed productions of the era.

Victoria's secret (she's a Cliff Richard fan)

By this stage, the regular cast were such good friends, even Lt Camfield had trouble stopping them goofing about: during the camera rehearsal for *The Web of Fear*, Frazer Hines whipped out a pair of frilly red knickers instead of the handkerchief stipulated in the script and declared "These as Victoria's!". Later, he produced them again and used them to mop his brow. It really was the joke that kept on giving.

Midway through the story's run, cravat-

sporting gentleman journalist Alan Whicker turned his tortoise-shell specs to the subject of *Doctor Who*'s creepier critters in an edition of his documentary series *Whicker's World* called "I Don't Like My Monsters to Have Oedipus Complexes". During the programme, Whicker drops in on Terry Nation at his palatial country retreat, which he appears to share with at least four Daleks – sort of like the Playboy mansion, but with mutant alien fascists instead of nubile young centrefolds. (And no funny business, obviously – with Terry, it's strictly a business arrangement.)

Perhaps Victor Pemberton should have taken some advice from the Dalek deal-maker: years after the broadcast of his serial *Fury from the Deep*, the former script assistant professed to being "pert with rage" – an arresting mental image, to be sure – over his lack of credit for the story's most enduring contribution to *Doctor Who*: the sonic screwdriver. The Doctor's groovy new gadget was surely a shoo-in to be top of every Christmas list come December, especially after a memorably dramatic debut in which the Doctor uses it to vanquish a fearsome enemy in a titanic struggle to the death. Just kidding – he uses it to open the valve on a gas outlet pipe. Still, though – sonic, eh?

Fury from the Deep finds our heroes visiting a North Sea gas refinery and learning for themselves the dangers of too much weed (not *that* sort of weed: this one's alien and has ambitious plans to take over the world – something the other type might talk about, before deciding it couldn't be bothered and falling asleep). The BBC foam machine – which was putting in as many appearances as the regular cast during this era of the show – goes into overdrive in a story that delivers proper scares without a single death. Director Hugh David had also splashed out on a helicopter but, in the hotel bar the night before it was due to be used, the pilot downed a crate of champagne and two bottles of brandy, swung from the chandelier, which came crashing down on top of him, and then walked about on his hands eating – yes, eating – all the empty glasses. Strangely enough, Patrick Troughton refused to take off with this lunatic in charge, so David was forced to simulate the effects of flight by wheeling the cameraman round in a baby's pram.

The serial also marks the departure of Victoria, whose decision to leave is telegraphed by the fact she spends most of the story moaning about everything, including the fact they're "always landing on Earth" (understandable – that's where the show is made) and complaining that "every time we go somewhere, something awful happens". In a twist to the usual pattern, Victoria gets to be adopted, rather than married off. It's not the *most* convincing arrangement, but there is at least a good ten minutes dedicated to her farewell – more than Dodo, Ben and Polly put together.

Debbie Watling was optimistic she'd got out in time to avoid typecasting, but was then out of work for nine months. Having said that, she spent much of the next decade spilling out of bikinis in various saucepot roles, and raised a few eyebrows as promiscuous landlady's daughter "Naughty Nora" in the wartime drama *Danger UXB*, so she sort of got her wish in the end. She also starred alongside Cliff Richard in the 1973 film *Take Me High*, a musical romantic comedy set in Birmingham. At least Una Stubbs got to go to Athens.

In March, the bulk of recording moved back to Friday evenings at BBC Television Centre. Peter Bryant also started contracting out some fx work to a freelance company called Trading Post, which led to a permanent rift between the producer and the BBC's Visual Effects Department. Also that month, the *New Statesman* became possibly the first publication to use the C word in connection with *Doctor Who*. It's so offensive I can't really bring myself to say it. Oh okay then: they called it a cult.

April saw the Daleks make their long-awaited return to the screen in Britain's longest-running space series when they made a guest appearance on *The Sky at Night*, while Troughton departed for a holiday at a new riverside property he'd purchased in Norfolk, where he told his family he thought the *Doctor Who* stories were becoming tired and predictable. They must have been bad to make moving to Norfolk seem an attractive proposition.

On April 27th, new recruit Wendy Padbury made her debut as Zoe Heriot – she of the quantum book-stamping skills – in season finale *The Wheel in Space*. The 20-year-old was another *Crossroads* graduate, having bagged the role of soap doyen Noel Gordon's foster daughter after coming runner-up on the TV talent contest *Search for a Star*. (Incidentally, since production notes give Zoe's age as 15, we must either assume they're more relaxed about child labour in this unspecified part of the twenty-first century, or she's on work experience. Which, as anyone who's ever dealt with a career's officer will know, would explain why an astrophysicist is working in a library.)

The story finds the Cybermen invading *yet another* UN-style base, only this one's shaped like a wheel. And it's in space. This time, the plan is bonkers even by their standards. There isn't enough ink in the world to fully explain it, but suffice to say it comes in six stages, most of them entirely unnecessary, and appears to be largely based on the old Ali Baba trick of hiding in the laundry basket.

Director Tristan DeVere Cole managed to rub Peter Bryant up the wrong way, and was never asked back. Thus his entire *Doctor Who* legacy amounts to a contender for the dullest story ever made – though, in his defence, even Douglas Camfield would have struggled to inject much life into this script. The only really good bit, in fact, comes right at the end when the Doctor decides to give Zoe a crash course in *Doctor Who* by firing up the TARDIS DVD player to show her *The Evil of the Daleks*, thus paving the way for the first ever repeat of a complete story. (It was either that, or show her his holiday slides.)

"I can't come in to work, my face has fallen off"

During that year's summer break, *Junior Points of View* correspondents indicated they'd given up armed struggle in favour of political legitimacy by suggesting Doctor Who should be made Prime Minister. Possibly they thought he'd have made a better job than Harold Wilson at staving off the devaluation of the pound – which, to be fair, would have made for a slightly more exciting story than *The Wheel in Space*. Patrick Troughton would probably have enjoyed playing politics, too – at least you got most of the summer off. As it was, he likened his six-week break to being demobbed, and went to France with his new family before spending some quality time with his old one (and his golf clubs).

space helmet for a cow

In early August, Season Six got underway in time-honoured fashion – with the latest naked attempt to find "the new Daleks". And this time, they managed to get it *really* wrong.

The Quarks were the robot slaves of impractically-collared galactic dictators the Dominators, and Mervyn Haisman and Henry Lincoln claim they were devised in response to a specific request from the production office to create a marketable new villain. They even provided sketches – though the design was subsequently changed – so were somewhat miffed when they discovered a deal had been done behind their backs to license the characters to the Doctor Who *TV Comic* strip. Haisman phoned the comic's publisher direct and threatened them with an injunction if they went ahead with the strip, claiming, "They came back within half an hour and offered us a small bag of gold".[9] The issue was taken up by the BBC's Head of Copyright (the legal issue, I mean – not the issue of *TV Comic*; he was far too busy for that sort of thing) and, according to Haisman, Derrick Sherwin got "the biggest rap over the knuckles that I've ever seen. As we left the office. Sherwin said to me, 'You think you've won, don't you?' That's why we never attempted to do another *Doctor Who*."[9] The duo even applied to trademark the name Quark, which must have been news to the estate of James Joyce – and potentially inconvenient for any quantum physicists thinking of publishing a paper that year – and, for a while, there was a serious possibility that the BBC wouldn't be able to broadcast the season opener at all. Eventually, Haisman and Lincoln came to an agreement with the Corporation, and the serial was back on.

It hardly helped relations that Sherwin had edited Haisman and Lincoln's six scripts down to a five-parter, with the writers so unhappy with the results they asked for their names to be removed from the story in favour of the pseudonym Norman Ashby, a portmanteau name derived from their wives' fathers.

Watching *The Dominators*, you can only assume Haisman and Lincoln didn't get on too well with the in-laws. Even the name of the planet, Dulkis, and its pacifist inhabitants, the Dulcians, is dull. It's unusually hawkish philosophy also feels jarringly at odds with the whole ethos of *Doctor Who*: there's something

sadistic – even borderline fascistic – in its gleeful demolition of peaceniks, intellectuals and other namby-pamby leftie milksops. It's also highly ironic that anyone should ever have fallen out over the ownership of the utterly hopeless Quarks, which look like hotel mini-bars with heads and whose childlike voices were meant to be creepy, like ghosts, but just sound annoying, like children. To make matters worse, viewers were reminded just what a poor relation these giggling fridges were compared to the real deal when the Daleks made an appearance in sci-fi anthology series *Out of the Unknown*, in an episode designed by Ray Cusick, no less. ("Erm, you don't want paying for these *again*, do you?" asked the producer, shortly before Cusick threw him out of an upstairs window.)

Wendy Padbury had settled in well to the show – that is to say, she had accepted being relentlessly teased by Troughton and Hines with stoic good grace. On one memorable occasion, while the cast were rehearsing in a church hall, Hines undid the buckles on her kilt and then made her jump out of her seat. She ended up running out of the room and straight into the vicar, wearing only her knickers (Padbury, not the vicar). Of course, these days you'd never get away with stripping a female colleague down to her pants in the workplace – it's political correctness gone mad, frankly. Luckily, the actress gave as good as she got, even helping Hines debag Troughton during one rehearsal. What with Jamie in his kilt, some days there wasn't a member of the regular cast to be found with their trousers on. To add to the atmosphere of mature professionalism, the trio all had nicknames: Troughton was known as Fluff, because of his tendency to mangle his lines (they clearly hadn't met the last guy – though even *he* never managed a fumble as heroic as Troughton's request in *The Wheel in Space* to turn on the "sexual air supply"); Hines was known as Cough, a reference to his default method of covering his own mistakes; and Padbury was known as Fart... an accusation she denies to this day.

Cougher Hines was now actively looking for his next job, and a new companion called Nik was created to take his place. But Troughton asked his friend to stay on a bit longer so they could both leave together; Hines' agent advised

56

against it[IV], but the actor's father had recently died and, mindful of the fact he was now his family's main breadwinner, he agreed to an extension of his contract. The news wasn't taken well by writer Dick Sharples, who had already delivered his scripts for upcoming story *The Prison in Space*; Sharples argued that rewriting the story to include Jamie amounted to a change of brief ("Did someone mention briefs?" asked Hines, suddenly perking up), and so work on the serial was halted. This caused Troughton to become uneasy about the possibility of script problems resurfacing again – a bit rich, given it was him who'd persuaded Hines to throw a tartan spanner in the works in the first place.

Slicing an episode off *The Dominators* left the production team with a spare 25 minutes to fill, so Derrick Sherwin scripted a prelude to the next serial, *The Mind Robber*. This budget-busting bottle episode utilises just the regular cast, the TARDIS and a mysterious white void – otherwise known as BBC Television Centre Studio 3 – and some robots borrowed from *Out of the Unknown*. Or possibly stolen, given the hasty re-spray job to turn them white.

The result is highly effective, culminating with a brilliantly realised sequence in which the TARDIS explodes and flings its occupants out into the void. Not that the effects designer needed to bother trying so hard, as the camera lingers so long on a close-up of Zoe's lamé catsuit-clad derrière; he could have done the explosion on an Etch-a-Sketch and no-one would have noticed.

Happily, the rest of *The Mind Robber* manages to maintain the momentum in the show's first real pass at a proper fairytale, as the Doctor and company find themselves lost in a strange land peopled by fictional characters. Writer Peter Ling was the co-creator of – you guessed it – *Crossroads*, and set out with the deliberate intention to write a *Doctor Who* story "about literature, not science" (as distinct from *Crossroads*, which was about the hospitality industry in the West Midlands). Hence we have appearances by the likes of Gulliver (who, for most of his screen time, only speaks lines by Jonathan Swift, though he didn't get a fee), Rapunzel, Medusa and the Minotaur, and wonderfully imaginative sequences in which our heroes get lost in a forest of words and, in

one cliffhanger, are trapped in the pages of a giant book (pipe down whoever said just said "we know the feeling"). There's even a trot-on part for a unicorn, which director David Maloney, making his *Doctor Who* debut, filmed on an RAF runway using a horse which had also been in for a re-spray. As if that wasn't bad enough, the poor beast's stick-on horn kept dropping off. ("Don't worry," said Maloney. "It could happen to anyone. Give it a few minutes and we can try again.")

Jamie was also subject to a radical make-over: when Frazer Hines went down with chickenpox, he was replaced by actor Hamish Wilson in an ingenious bit of business that sees the Doctor bungling a challenge to piece his companion's face back together like a jigsaw. (This may also explain Michael Jackson in his later years.)

Lyrical, magical and surreal, *The Mind Robber* is a glowing testament to what could be achieved even on *Doctor Who*'s laughable budget with a bit of care, attention and, above all, imagination. Patrick Troughton considered it to be the high watermark of his tenure; he probably wasn't wrong.

At the story's end, Frazer Hines had got his own face back – just in time, as it happened, to finally make his belated assault on the pop charts. His comedy (it says here) ditty "Who's Doctor Who" was penned by Barry Mason and Les Reed, whose numerous songwriting successes included Tom Jones' "Delilah" and Englebert Humperdinck's "The Last Waltz". Sadly, this particular collaboration managed to break the duo's run of consecutive hits (Hines claimed it was five-time Ivor Novello winner Mason's only chart flop) and plans for a follow-up, a sort of sci-fi "Donald Where's Your Troosers" called "Jamie's Awa' in his Time Machine", written by future glam rock pub belter Alex Harvey, were scrapped. Maybe they should have gone with Hamish Wilson instead.

Producer throws a wobbly over space jellies

While *The Mind Robber* may be the Troughton era's crowning glory, it was the next story, *The Invasion*, that would have the most lasting impact. With Bryant working on his exit strategy and Sherwin the producer in all but name,

Terrance Dicks took over the job of what was now called script editor – only to be told this was probably going to be the show's final season.

"After Patrick announced that he was leaving, there was a general feeling that would most likely be the end of the show," said Dicks. "I used to say it was like getting a job as cabin boy on the *Titanic* – you weren't going to be there very long."[10]

For his part, Sherwin claimed *The Invasion* was always intended as a pilot to re-launch *Doctor Who*, not replace it: buoyed by the success of *The Web of Fear*, the story trialled a new format that would see the Doctor brought down to Earth with a bang for a series of action-packed adventures with his friends Professor Travers and Colonel Lethbridge-Stewart. In the end, Jack Watling indicated he didn't want to appear in the series now his daughter had left, which is why the Doctor ends up throwing his lot in with the in-no-way familiar Professor Watkins and his plucky daughter, Isobel. And Sherwin – who wrote the scripts based on an idea by Kit Pedler – possibly also had half an eye on limiting the royalty payments he'd have to make to his BFFs Haisman and Lincoln. Lethbridge-Stewart still made the final cut, though, now promoted to Brigadier and running a military black ops outfit called UNIT (United Nations Intelligence Taskforce) charged with defending the Earth from extraterrestrial, paranormal and other threats too silly for the rest of the military to bother with. (It was agreed that Haisman and Lincoln would receive £2.10 for every serial the Brigadier appeared in – and, having proved highly popular with viewers over the decades, he would go on to earn his creators in excess of £46.)

Another member of the UNIT team making his debut was John Levene as Corporal Benton. Levene, who had previously played a Cyberman and a Yeti, was originally meant to be donning the silver jug-handles again until Camfield sacked the actor playing Benton – and probably tried to have him court martialled too – for constantly turning up late. Famed for his bafflingly Byzantine pronouncements, Levene would later declare: "I love Benton, because he was what I call the manifestation of the reflection of the other charac-ters."[11] But what everyone else would call a grunt.

Ranged against the Doctor and his boot boys are a new army of Cybermen, with yet another of their infamous cunning plans. This time, they've teamed up with scheming industrialist Tobias Vaughn (a scene-stealing turn from Kevin Stoney) and moved into the consumer electronics business, flooding the market with gadgets containing circuits that, when activated, produce a hypnotic signal that sends humans to sleep. Anyone who's ever accidentally downloaded a Westlife song onto their iPod will know the feeling. They then plan to follow through with – and this is the really subtle bit – a Cyber-Megatron Bomb. It's probably not as dangerous as it sounds.

Sherwin claimed part of the motivation to set more stories on contemporary Earth was a desire to get away from "jellies wobbling around in space"[10] – but it was also clearly designed as a cost-cutting exercise (space is a prohibitively expensive place to set stories – and, indeed, jellies). So it's ironic that, at £25,000, *The Invasion* was actually the most expensive *Doctor Who* story to date. Douglas Camfield certainly puts all the money up there on screen, though: the re-designed Cybermen look fantastic, and the shots of them emerging from the sewers and descending down the steps in front of St Paul's are among the most iconic in the show's history. Having said that, it's painfully obvious that the big UNIT battle sequence takes place off-camera, but Camfield compensates by having Zoe and Isobel constantly flash their knickers to distract us from any shortcomings in the... what was it again? Production assistant Chris D'Oyly-John – who claims to have suggested the St Paul's backdrop to Camfield – recalled getting on famously with the director, even though he was "very right-wing". "He used to talk about 'when the invasion comes' – meaning the Communists."[12] Others said Camfield had an air-raid shelter in his garden stocked with tins of bully beef.

A large of chunk of the story was filmed on location at a Guinness factory, where Troughton and Hines admitted to partaking in a little too much free "falling over water". In December, the factory sent the cast and crew Christmas puddings filled with Guinness, but Troughton's exploded all over his agent's office, so he never got it. At least that's what his agent told him – he was probably just looking for his 10% of the sixpence.

If *The Invasion* sometimes feels like a case of style over substance – but what style – it's probably partly to do with the fact it had to be stretched to fill eight episodes as scripts were falling like dominoes at this point: as well as the loss of *The Prison in Space*, at least five other works-in-progress were written off, including *The Laird of McCrimmon* (AKA Frazer Hines' leaving do, now abandoned for obvious reasons), *Invaders from Mars* by David Whitaker, and something called *The Dream Spinner* by someone called Paul Wheeler. Throw in ongoing problems with Brian Hayles' sequel to *The Ice Warriors*, and it was apparent the production team were on a sticky wicket even *before* the series was suddenly extended by four episodes, with Troughton contracted for an extra serial designed to serve as a set-up for the show's new format.

Into this fray stepped Robert Holmes, a former military officer, policeman and court reporter who had originally submitted his story *The Space Trap* to *Out of the Unknown*, only to find it passed over to – and, indeed, by – Donald Tosh on *Doctor Who*. Holmes had sent the scripts in again after coming across them while moving house (he also had a load of old gramophone records and a set of kitchen knives if anyone could find a home for them) and it had ended up being rushed into production with little more than a month until the cameras turned over.

For a story that had languished in a desk drawer for several years, Holmes' tale of student rebellion turned out to be highly topical for a story that sneaked onto screens in the dying hours of 1968. Granted, it's a very polite, RADA-trained sort of rebellion – scenes of hairy young men in Afghan coats chucking Molotov cocktails to a soundtrack of Jimi Hendrix are in short supply, and there's not a Che Guevara poster in sight – but there's enough peacenik conchie talk like "It is not patriotism to lead people into a war they cannot win" to make you wonder what William Hartnell would have made of it if it *had* been made three years earlier. It's certainly a refreshing counterblast to the reactionary nonsense of *The Dominators*.

The headline villains of *The Krotons*, as it was now called, are crystalline immortals who have literally put down roots on the planet of the Gonds, where they regularly cream off the brightest students – known as High Brains to the Krotons (and class swots to everyone else) – and siphon off their mental energy to help repair their spaceship. In other words, they've introduced selective education to the Gond world. Before you knew it, they'd be setting up their own grammar schools; no wonder the students are angry.

The Krotons themselves have the makings of a good design, but they're played with Brummie accents (no-one knows why, but I suspect the answer might involve the word Crossroads). Also, in a moment of pure Spinal Tap farce, the costumes proved too small, so they added skirts to cover up the actors' hairy wee legs. (Don't worry, though – I'm sure Troughton and Hines soon whipped them off.)

The script boasts some nice ideas which, given more time, might have been worked up into something quite good. As it is, the rushed production is all too evident (half the cast had been contracted for *Prisoner in Space*, which explains why some of the student radicals look more like maths teachers) and it all just feels a bit pedestrian. Episode one's audience of nine million was the highest-rated Patrick Troughton episode, though two million had gone AWOL by the final instalment. According to the BBC's audience research report, viewers found it "generally satisfactory", which seems as good a description as any.

Toys Rn't Us

By now, the BBC had committed itself – if that's the right word – to another year of *Doctor Who* on the basis that no-one had managed to come up with anything better (or, failing that, cheaper). On New Year's Eve, Bryant and Sherwin announced slightly revised plans for their re-tool of the show, which would now see the Earth-bound Doctor teaming up with the Brigadier and Zoe or, if Wendy Padbury chose not to continue, another big-brained, short-skirted boffin identified as "Liz". And anyone who thought it was just going to be a re-tread of *The Invasion* couldn't have been more wrong – this time, it would be in colour.

Serial AAA[V] – the additional story Troughton had signed for – would now be held over to introduce the new Doctor, while the remaining two Season Six scripts – Malcolm Hulke's *The Impersonators* and an untitled story by Sherwin – were scrapped in favour of an epic ten-part season finale that promised finally to fill in some of the Doctor's backstory. Work on this "monster", as Derrick 'Sherwin called it, was divvied up between Hulke and Terrance Dicks, just as soon as the latter had finished completely re-writing Brian Hayles' troubled Ice Warrior re-match from the top down.

"Derrick came into my office and said, Terrance, we need a ten-part *Doctor Who* and we need it tomorrow," recalled Dicks. Though, of course, he didn't mean *literally* tomorrow – next week would be fine. "Being young and naïve, I said okay."[13]

To give Dicks a bit of breathing space, Robert Holmes was hastily commissioned to provide Troughton's penultimate adventure, on the basis that his previous script had been a) not complete rubbish and b) finished, which was more than could be said about anyone else's efforts right now.

Finally making it to air in late January, Hayles-Dicks' *The Seeds of Death* finds the Ice Warriors invading a scientific research station – *on the moon*! Anyone starting to see a pattern here? This time, the plan is to spread oxygen-sucking seeds across the Earth using T-Mat, the worldwide teleportation system that has replaced more traditional methods of transport. (You'd think T-Mat stands for Trans-Mat – as in matter transmission – but it actually stands for TravelMat, which sounds like something you might keep in the boot of your car for picnics.) This proves the cue for some effective nostalgia for the golden age of space travel (the Doctor even flies an old-skool rocket to the moon) – a really rather forward-thinking idea for a piece broadcast six months before Neil Armstrong set foot on the lunar surface.

Director Michael Ferguson pushes the envelope with some imaginative camerawork that's a cut above the usual point-and-shoot approach, helping to disguise the fact this six-parter is another script that's been extended way beyond its natural life. Hence the drawn-out chase sequences – even by the standards of this era, when the closest thing the Doctor had to a catchphrase was "When I say run – run!" – one of which turns into an out-and-out Keystone Cops pursuit, complete with a comedy silent movie score and an actual funfair-style hall of mirrors (no moonbase is complete without one).

There's some decent design work on show, too (though the T-Mat operators' overalls-and-giant-nappy combo is not a great look, even if foxy blonde bombshell assistant controller Gia Kelly carries off what looks like a large pair of incontinence pants as well as anybody can reasonably be expected to). And the BBC foam machine really makes the most of its final appearance, filling the studio like an Ibiza nightclub and even being taken on location to help the Ice Warriors spray their seed all over Hampstead Heath. So to speak. (Incidentally, the Christmas break resulted in an unusually long gap between the location filming and studio taping, during which Troughton obviously decided to get down with the kids and grow some bushy mutton-chop sideburns, which is why he runs over Hampstead Heath looking like Doctor Who and arrives at a weather station a few minutes later looking like one of Slade.)

The Seeds of Death also boasts one of the second Doctor's finest moments when, cornered by the Ice Warriors, he pulls himself up to his full 5'7" and declares: "Your leader will be angry if you kill me – I'm a genius!" It was a sentiment echoed by the *Junior Points of View* audience, who wrote furious letters in response to the news of Troughton's imminent departure. This prompted some children to respond that "the golden age was over" anyway, and it was time the show was put out of its misery, which escalated into a full-scale war of words that was only resolved when guest Cilla Black stepped in to say that it should definitely continue. That proved good enough for Terrance Dicks, who commissioned the first third Doctor story – provisionally entitled *Facsimile* – from Robert Holmes before Dusty Springfield or Sandie Shaw could weigh in with a counter-argument.

Viewers tuning in to Holmes' second Troughton adventure might have been forgiven for wondering why he had suddenly become the production team's new go-to guy. But if *The*

Space Pirates is a disappointment – and most would agree that's putting it mildly – it's often for reasons beyond Holmes' control. For starters, he was asked to write something with no monsters in it, as Peter Bryant was currently attempting to hold BBC Enterprises to ransom by threatening to end the regular supply of alien creatures unless a percentage of merchandise revenues was ploughed back into the show. As it happened, this may have been something of an empty threat, since merchandise was pretty thin on the ground anyway: apart from the *Doctor Who Annual*, which was still coming out every year – hence the name – the most significant tie-in product during the second Doctor's era was Walls' Sky Ray: a vaguely rocket-shaped ice lolly that came with a free *Doctor Who* picture card and, rather thrillingly at the time, was promoted with a colour TV advert in which the Daleks invaded the TARDIS and attacked a man dressed in Patrick Troughton's clothes. A TARDIS climbing frame/playhouse combo also went into production in 1969, but, in a less than wholehearted endorsement of the series' future prospects, they only made 12.

Despite this conspicuous lack of enthusiasm from manufacturers, and continued competition from producer Irwin Allen's stable of glossy US adventure shows such as *Time Tunnel*, *Land of the Giants* and *Voyage to the Bottom of the Sea*, *Doctor Who* continued to hold its audience share, and was still considered a hot enough property to spawn a 13-part Radio 2 spoof, *Professor Prune and the Electric Time Trousers* (yes, really), starring *I'm Sorry I'll Read That Again* stalwarts Graeme Garden, John Cleese and Bill Oddie. Laugh? No, since you ask.

To compensate for the lack of monster action, *The Space Pirates* goes all out for visual spectacle with a *Thunderbirds*-meets-*Buck Rogers*-style space opera in which our heroes join forces with the International Space Corps on the trail of galactic raiders who have been stripping the precious metal from beacons used to aid inter-stellar navigation – a bit like students nicking traffic cones, but on a much more ambitious scale. Unfortunately, it was a bit *too* ambitious for the programme's budget, which is why the spaceships don't look nearly as convincing as the flying lollies in the Sky Ray advert. Also, just as Gene Roddenberry's "wagon train in space" was running out of road in America, Holmes' attempt to reflect the pioneering spirit of the Wild West in the form of grizzled prospector Milo Clancy results in one of the most – ahem – *distinctive* performances in *Doctor Who* history from Gordon Gostelow, whose attempt at an American accent cleared all Dick Van Dyke's debts overnight.

Once again, the story is stretched to breaking point to fill six episodes, which makes it even more baffling that the TARDIS crew are given so little to do: they don't even turn up until the first episode's nearly over – and this was one of those rare stories when none of the cast were on holiday. Then again, while the writers were desperately trying to pad out scripts, Troughton and Hines were constantly looking at ways to reduce the amount of dialogue they had to learn – their favourite trick being to read their lines veeeeeeryyyy slooooowly in the hope the episode would overrun and need to be cut.

By now, an increasingly irritable Troughton was losing patience with the whole being Doctor Who thing, leading to a confrontation with Bryant, Sherwin and director Michael Hart. Michael Troughton recorded in his diaries: "I remember my father arriving at our house after completing a producers' run-through for episode two of *The Space Pirates*. He was angry, but anger born of frustration rather than aggression. I recall him complaining to my mother about how dull and unwatchable *The Space Pirates* was going to be: 'This is episode two and we're still trapped in that bloody awful spaceship set. I told them people will just turn off'."[7]

Was history repeating itself? Not really – though Troughton had clearly had enough, dramas like this were still rare compared to the almost hourly blow-ups of the late Hartnell era. And all three regulars could see the finish line (Padbury had eventually declined the invitation to stay on): all they had to do was get through the shoot for the mammoth saga that would bring the black and white era of *Doctor Who* to a close. Which, for Patrick Troughton, meant spending his 49th birthday on a giant rubbish dump. Where they then tried to blow him up.

The War Games:
like a real war, only longer

The dump in question – Sheepcote Rubbish Tip near Brighton (there was none of your "municipal waste management facility" nonsense back then) – was doubling for the Western Front of the First World War, complete with handy trenches and barbed wire left over from the recent filming of Richard Attenbrough's *Oh! What a Lovely War*. (Film companies usually have a duty to clean up after themselves, but Attenborough's crew had clearly figured no-one was going to worry too much about them spoiling the look of a rubbish dump.) Troughton, who had developed a hatred of rats during his time in the Navy (possibly on account of their reputation for deserting sinking ships), warned he'd quit on the spot if he saw one. Presumably he never did, though Wendy Padbury recalls the place being overrun with them and, to add to the fun, it was so cold she was reduced to concealing a bottle of brandy in her coat.

Things soon warmed up when visual effects designer Michaeljohn Harris arrived with his bag of explosives, but Troughton, Hines and Padbury were unhappy with being told to stand close to a detonation without knowing how big the resulting bang was going to be. Harris sent his explosives expert over to assure them everything would be fine – which might have been more convincing if he hadn't had a badly scarred face and two missing fingers. Troughton insisted on seeing the explosion for himself and, as the charge was blown, a huge boulder came flying out of the ground and landed exactly where the actors had been standing a moment ago. "That," Frazer Hines recalls Patrick Troughton saying, "is why I wanted to see the charge."[13] According to designer Roger Chevely, Harris had brought enough explosives "for a real war" and, at the end of the shooting day, stayed behind to let them all off in the rubbish tip, causing a large cloud of black smoke to drift towards the centre of Brighton.

Troughton also refused to take to the wheel of the vintage WWI field ambulance used on location, leaving all the dangerous driving through artillery fire to guest actress Jane Sherwin. And yes, she is who you think she is

(well if it was good enough for Peter's wife...). Far from tempers fraying, though, Troughton, Hines and Padbury all recalled being "giggly" with tiredness – though "tiredness" may have been a euphemism for "brandy".

History really *does* repeat itself in *The War Games*, which actually takes place on a distant planet where aliens are using brainwashed soldiers to recreate some of humanity's bloodiest conflicts: as well as the 1914-18 slaughter, there are zones featuring Roman centurions, the American, English and Mexican Civil Wars, the Boer, the Crimean and every schoolboy's favourite, the 1905 Russo-Japanese Peninsular War. And they weren't just doing it for kicks, like those historical re-enactment societies where supply teachers from Ruislip spend the weekend faithfully recreating the Battle of Naseby, albeit with a nice pub lunch. Here, the aliens, led by the War Lord (that's what he calls himself anyway – he's probably called Nigel) are using the games in order to create the ultimate army with which to conquer the galaxy. Which would explain why there are no Italians involved.

Terrance Dicks claims he and Mac Hulke knew they had "a good first episode and a good last episode – it was the eight in between that gave us the trouble".[14] In fact, *The War Games* sustains interest surprisingly well across ten weeks: the various different conflicts (most of them suggested by David Maloney's 12-year-old son, so the director could actually start getting on with something while the scripts were being bashed out) offering at least the *impression* of forward momentum, while the power struggle between the War Lord (the quietly menacing Philip Madoc) and his subordinate the War Chief (the noisily menacing Edward Brayshaw) helps ensure that, even at this length, serial ZZ never becomes serial ZZZZZ. In its final story of the decade, it's also pleasing to see *Doctor Who* properly embracing 60s Pop Art with a groovy, *Austin Powers*-style set that makes the aliens' Central Control look like Andy Warhol's Factory. Minus all the drug-fuelled orgies, presumably.

And it is here that, in episode six, bit-part actor Vernon Dobtcheff – playing an unnamed scientist, and with his back to the camera – casually drops a proper noun into his conversation with the War Chief that will redefine the entire future of *Doctor Who*. The words are "Time" and "Lord" and, two weeks later, we learn that the Doctor himself is one of these god-like beings. After that, the revelations pile up thick and fast: Time Lords can "live forever, barring accidents"; the Doctor fled his home planet because he was "bored" – you know what kids in their early 200s are like – and frustrated with his people's reluctance to use their great power as a positive force for good in the universe; and he didn't build his TARDIS – he nicked it.

When the challenge of ending the War Games proves too great (for the Doctor I mean, not the writers, although...), our hero sacrifices his own freedom in order to ask the Time Lords for help, and is taken back to his home planet to stand trial on a charge of meddling in the affairs of other planets, often quite slowly and with an unnecessary amount running about. Though they accept his mitigation that *somebody* has to fight all the monsters, otherwise every week would be just like *The Space Pirates*, he is nevertheless found guilty and, as punishment, is sentenced to be exiled to the planet Earth in the late twentieth century. (Oh well, thought the Doctor. I suppose that's not too bad. "Did we mention it's Britain in the 1970s[VI]? I'd take some candles and a warm coat if I were you.")

They also force him to change his appearance, flashing up potential new faces on a big screen which the Doctor declares "too thin, too fat, too young, too old..." (It was only a matter of time before he asked if they had anything in black – "with a turban perhaps? Or how about a windjammer captain? No, *windjammer* – it's a type of boa... oh never mind".)

Perhaps the most powerful moment, though, is when the Doctor is forced to say goodbye to his friends: Jamie and Zoe's departure is the most affecting since Ian and Barbara four years earlier, as the pair are returned to a point in time just after they'd met the Doctor; they won't forget him completely, but they won't remember anything of their adventures except the first one – particularly unfortunate for Zoe, as it's *The Wheel in Space*.

Patrick Troughton's final recording day took place on Thursday, June 12th, 1969. His successor in the role had been contracted three weeks earlier, but there was no studio hando-

ver – we last see the second Doctor spinning off into the void for an extreme make-over, Time Lord-style.

As he clocked off from his final shift, the actor was sad but relieved. Nine days later, on June 21st, *The War Games* episode ten brought the monochrome era of *Doctor Who* to a close – and with an unprecedented six-month break between series, the Time Lord wouldn't be back on screens until 1970, by which time the world would be in colour and we'd all be wearing silver jumpsuits and whizzing about on jetpacks or something. Or, at the very least, there'd be a new 50p coin.

Troughton started work reasonably quickly on the BBC's lavish production of *The Six Wives of Henry VIII*, in which he played the Duke of Norfolk (not bad going for someone who'd only just bought a holiday house there). He would later liken *Doctor Who* to being in weekly rep, claiming to have loved the part, but not the workload.

Broadcast on the Summer Solstice, Troughton's departure was only witnessed by five million viewers; indeed the whole of *The War Games* struggled in the ratings, with episode eight – the landmark episode in which the series' title question is partly answered – ironically being the least watched episode of the programme's first 25 years. By the time the second Doctor's final moments were repeated on *Junior Points of View*, all the buzz was about this shiny new American import called *Star Trek*. And yet that series had already been cancelled, whereas *Doctor Who* was about to enter a new decade with a new look, a new team and a new leading man.

Clearly, many at the BBC thought the show was already living on borrowed time, drinking at the Last Chance Saloon and generally hanging about like a bad smell. But it was being given one last make or break chance to prove itself – and that wouldn't have happened if the funny, scruffy little man with the Beatlemop and bandy legs hadn't rescued the series from its mid-60s stumble, and proved the show could not only weather change, but positively thrive on it.

For that alone, Patrick Troughton's curatorship of *Doctor Who* must be considered a success. Though if you asked him, of course, he'd still deny ever having being in it.

③ Hai! My Name is...

"At least buy me dinner first"

In the summer of 1969, as Neil Armstrong took one giant leap for mankind, and the human race lifted its face to contemplate a new life among the stars, plans were already well advanced to bring *Doctor Who* crashing back to Earth.

Equally, while the space age promised The Future right here, right now, the touchstone for Peter Bryant and Derek Sherwin's vision of the show was Nigel Kneale's *Quatermass* serials, which had first appeared on the BBC as early as 1953. True, the eponymous Professor Quatermass was a pioneering scientist with the British Experimental Rocket Group, so bang on trend in that sense, but was generally to be found wandering round Wimbledon Common in a raincoat and brogues, as opposed to zipping about the cosmos in a shiny space tunic.

Terrance Dicks recalls that an actual *Quatermass* revival was one of the options discussed for a possible replacement for *Doctor Who* at the end of Patrick Troughton's tenure. Later, when the Doctor had been given a stay of execution, Dicks and his assistant, Trevor Ray, viewed what was left of *The Quatermass Experiment* in the BBC's depleted archives for inspiration, but came to the conclusion it was probably all a bit dry and dusty for half past five on a Saturday night.

Nevertheless, Sherwin was determined, in the post space jelly-age, to give viewers "something they could believe in": "So I said, let's take it down to Earth, let's do it like *Quatermass*, let's make it real. Let's make them really shiver – get behind that sofa and shake."[1]

Of course, such a plan was reliant on finding a leading actor with enough gravitas and moral authority to make this bold new approach work. And Peter Bryant thought he'd spotted just the man in that year's tough, unflinching vision of life on the lawless frontier, *True Grit*. Sorry, my mistake, it was *Carry On Cowboy*.

As inept Sheriff Albert Earp, Jon Pertwee doesn't last too long into 1965's entry into the Carry On canon before being dispatched by Sid James as the Rumpo Kid. But it was enough to secure him second place on Bryant and Sherwin's list of potential new Doctors, behind Ron Moody. (The previous year, Moody had won a Golden Globe and received an Academy Award nomination for his role as Fagin in *Oliver!*; in total, Carol Reed's musical had picked up six Oscars, which is precisely six more than *Carry On Cowboy*. I think you can probably see where this is going.)

Listing the qualities he thought Pertwee could bring to the role, Bryant said: "He can do funny voices, he's a good comic, he can sing, he can play the guitar and he's a tall, authoritative figure".[2] And one of those they'd end up making actual use of, as the third Doctor is, indeed, tall.

Pertwee was in rehearsals for the *The Navy Lark*, the long-running radio sitcom in which he played at least five regular roles, when co-star Tenniel Evans told him Patrick Troughton was quitting *Doctor Who*, and encouraged him to apply for the job. Initially laughing off the suggestion, Pertwee eventually decided it was worth a shot and persuaded his agent, Richard Stone – who thought it was a terrible idea – to phone Peter Bryant. After an awkward pause, Bryant admitted to Stone that his client's name was already near the top of the list. ("It's you they want, Jon!" Stone reported back. "What's that name crossed out above mine?" asked Pertwee suspiciously. "Oh that, that's nothing – it just says, erm, 'list'.")

Head of Drama Shaun Sutton, an old friend of Pertwee's, stepped in to persuade the actor to take on the part. "Shaun rang and said, 'Do you want to do *Doctor Who*?'" recalled Pertwee in a 1995 interview. "I said, 'I'm not sure', so he said, 'Let's have a bit of lunch'. So we had lunch and he said, 'Would you like to do it?' and I said I'd think about it, and the next week he said, 'Do you want to do it?' and I said, 'Can we have another lunch?', and he said, 'Yeah, alright'. At the end of lunch he said, 'So, do you want to do *Doctor Who*?' and I said, 'Well,

I'll think about it'. And the next week I rang up and said, 'Do you dinners?'"[3]

At this juncture, it's worth pointing out that most of Jon Pertwee's stories need to be taken with a pinch of salt. And when I say pinch, I'm talking the sort of pinch you could grit a motorway with. Popular words to describe him include "flamboyant", "larger-than-life" and a "showman", and, while his anecdotes usually contained an essential truth, many of them became so embroidered over the years, you occasionally suspected he was being flamboyant through his teeth.

Unlike Hartnell and Troughton, Pertwee was already a Star (he'd have insisted on the capital). He'd appeared in more than 25 films – albeit three of them Carry Ons – was a familiar face on TV panel shows and, in 1966, had even headlined his own ITV variety showcase, the imaginatively-titled *Jon Pertwee Show*. But he was best known for his work on radio, where he'd made his name on the comedies *Waterlogged Spa* and *Puffney Post Office* before joining *The Navy Lark* in 1959.

John Devon Roland Pertwee had been born into the business in Chelsea in 1919: his father Roland was a respected screenwriter – a trade Jon's older brother Michael also pursued – and his cousin Bill would find fame as Chief Warden Hodges in *Dad's Army*. (In 1968, Pertwee had been forced to turn down the lead as Captain Mainwaring in the same show, owing to a prior commitment; they went with the virtually identical Arthur Lowe instead.) The family were descended from Huguenots, the full, non-Anglicised version of their name being de Perthius de Laillevault (thank God they changed it, as The de Perthius de Laillevault Years would never have fitted on the DVD covers).

Young Pertwee had been expelled from various expensive schools around the Home Counties, and had also been kicked out of RADA for refusing to play a Greek wind in the chorus of Euripides' *Iphigenia*, claiming it was a waste of his father's money. (Ron Moody, no doubt, scooped the prize for Best Element and/or Meteorological Phenomenon in a Classical Tragedy and never looked back.)

Like Patrick Troughton, Pertwee served as a Naval officer during the Second World War, transferring off the HMS *Hood* shortly before she was sunk with the loss of all but three lives. Like any good sailor, he also woke up one morning after a drunken night in port to find a cobra tattooed on his right arm (which must have been nothing compared to the shock the cobra got when it woke up with a tattoo of Jon Pertwee on its back).

After suffering a serious head injury in a bomb attack, Pertwee was posted to Naval Intelligence, where he took orders from Ian Fleming and refreshments from able seaman, tea boy and future Prime Minister Jim Callaghan. The way Pertwee tells it, being a spy was very much like Fleming would go on to describe it in his James Bond novels, complete with compasses hidden in brass buttons, secret maps in cotton handkerchiefs that only showed up when you urinated on them, and tobacco pipes that fired a .22 bullet. He also claimed that, when he attended meetings with Winston Churchill, he used to collect the PM's cigar butts and sell them to the Americans. Let's hope he didn't get them mixed up with that new consignment of exploding cigars from Q branch.

Later, Pertwee was assigned to the Naval Broadcasting Section, which many considered to be a cushy deal, but some of those bon mots could be pretty sharp, let me tell you. Sent to investigate a Services comedy show that Naval chiefs thought was being too critical of the Government, he ended up standing in for an absent performer, and three weeks later joined the cast full-time, which must have made for an interesting report. ("No evidence of sedition, but new cast member shows obvious gift for mimicry and comic timing; recommend immediate pay rise.")

In 1955, Pertwee embarked on a short-lived marriage to Jean Marsh – AKA future space sandwich-eating quasi-companion Sara Kingdom – but by the time he was being sounded out about *Doctor Who*, he was married to German-born Ingeborg Rhosea, with whom he had two children, Sean and Dariel.

In the spring of 1969, Mrs Pertwee found herself dining alone yet again as her husband screwed yet another meal out of Shaun Sutton. Eventually, the actor decided he'd strung his old friend along for long enough and told him that, in answer to his question: yes, he would have pudding. And, what the heck, he might as well play Doctor Who as well.

I've been to Puffney Post Office, but I've never been to me

Having made a commitment to Sutton, Pertwee still had reservations (about the role – and possibly at several restaurants, too). "I said I didn't know how the hell I was going to do it," he admitted. "I didn't know what he wanted. He said, 'I want Jon Pertwee', and I said, 'Who the hell's that? I've never been me'."[3]

Perhaps not but, once the seed had been planted in his head, Pertwee grew increasingly excited by the prospect of throwing off his comedy shackles and showing a new, serious side to his talents. According to Trevor Ray, he had a niggling resentment that no-one had ever taken him seriously as an actor, and saw this as his big chance. By 1971, Pertwee was telling *Saturday Titbits* he had only accepted the part after being "assured I could play the character straight; as I see it, this is the only way Dr Who can be played". Though try telling that to *Junior Points of View* viewers: their shortlist of favourite candidates to replace Troughton had included Rolf Harris, Marty Feldman, Brian Rix and Dick Emery. Oh, and Peter Cushing, but that was just being silly.

Pertwee was contracted for an initial run of 21 episodes on May 21st, 1969. A week later, Nicholas Courtney was also booked to reprise his role as Brigadier Lethbridge-Stewart. By now it had been decided that the new series would run for six months from January (less than two months after the launch of BBC1's colour service), the almost-halved episode count allowing for a less frenetic pace of production (i.e. exactly what Patrick Troughton had been asking for, which must have thrilled him no end when he heard). It had also been agreed that most stories would run to seven episodes, helping to cut costs by reducing the number of stories per season.

The new Doctor was introduced to the press on June 7th, goofing about with a Yeti at his London home. (Pertwee's London home, that is – everyone knows Yetis live in the Himalayas. Or Wales.) A few weeks later, Pertwee did another photoshoot for the *Radio Times*, cutting quite a dash in a frilly shirt, velvet smoking jacket and a black and scarlet cape he'd inherited from his grandfather. The actor had originally hoped to wear a dark Nehru suit for the role but, when costume designer Christine Rawlings came up with a Victorian dandy look, partly inspired by the *RT* shoot, Pertwee was quickly won over. It didn't hurt, of course, that this retro foppery was currently all the rage among Carnaby Street hipsters – even Pertwee's granddad would have looked the part – while Peter Wyngarde had also recently made his debut as Jason King, an extravagantly moustachioed vision in crushed velvet in ITC action series *Department S*.

With Robert Holmes writing the new Doctor's debut adventure, Dicks commissioned *The Carriers of Death*, a suitably topical story about a British space exploration mission, from original story editor David Whitaker, plus a script from his former oppo, Malcolm Hulke, currently going under the somewhat vague title *Doctor Who and the Monsters* (he'd fill in the details later). Hulke had his doubts about the new format, telling Dicks it only left them with "two plots: alien invasion and mad scientist",[4] before coming up with something completely different in a bid to prove himself wrong. For his part, Whitaker was struggling to adapt to the show's more realistic, "adult" brief, prompting Dicks to swap the running order and bring Hulke's script forward.

Meanwhile, actress Caroline "Carry" John was hired as new companion Liz Shaw on the strength of her work with the National Theatre and, just possibly, the bikini shots she had recently sent into the BBC. This may explain why Liz – a Cambridge scientist with degrees in medicine and physics – combined a big brain with skirts so small they could only be identified at a sub-atomic level. (Introducing John to the press, Bryant made much of the fact the new character was very much the Doctor's equal: a strong, smart, sophisticated, modern woman. Sure, she wasn't exactly overburdened with clothes at the time but, honestly, who was to say what went on during Dress Down Fridays at the Cavendish Laboratory these days?)

In August, Pertwee struck various poses for the show's new title sequence, and tests were carried out using the new Colour Separation Overlay (CSO) technique – the early BBC equivalent of today's blue or greenscreen work. The results showed that the process worked, in so far as it allowed you to project one image onto another – albeit with a thick yellow outline that made everyone look like they'd overdosed on Ready Brek.

The following month, cast and crew headed to Surrey for a week's location filming for *Spearhead from Space*, the new name for *Facsimile*. With *Doctor Who's* first colour footage in the can, the studio recordings were scheduled for October – until the studio technicians noticed that it was almost the 1970s, so they really ought to go on strike. With the loss of TC3 – Television Centre's only colour studio – the January launch date was starting to look doubtful, so Sherwin asked the BBC if he could make the whole story on film instead. Naturally, this went down like a bucket of cold sick, so Sherwin came up with a cunning Plan B: he would film all the remaining scenes at the BBC's own engineering training facility at Wood Norton in Evesham – so the Corporation would effectively be hiring facilities from itself. With five days to re-plan the whole shoot, Sherwin and director Derek Martinus had their work cut out, but they ended up bringing the serial in several thousand pounds under budget. To make further savings, Sherwin and Pertwee bunked in together in the same room, which had definitely never happened in William Hartnell and Verity Lambert's day.

While filming inside the main Wood Norton Hall – a Victorian mansion that had formerly belonged to Prince Philippe, Duke of Orleans, the last pretender to the throne of France – Pertwee came across an apparently abandoned antique console table in the attic. His attempts to procure – that is to say, steal – it for himself involved several comedy staircase run-ins with security guards, before it was eventually lowered out of a window, and remained in pride of place chez Pertwee for the rest of the actor's life. The team also discovered an original Victorian shower stall but, without the aid of a good plumber, it would probably have been impractical to take that home, so Pertwee settled for filming a scene in it instead – which is when viewers discovered that, as well as being offered the chance to choose a new face at the end of *The War Games*, the Doctor had also apparently been allowed to browse the catalogue of a Time Lord tattoo parlour.

Nicholas Courtney's problem, by contrast, was what he *hadn't* got: in *The Invasion*, he'd been augmented with a stick-on moustache to make him look older, and subsequent attempts to grow his own had made him look less like a military commander than The Beatles hanging out with the Maharishi Mahesh Yogi, so he was forced to stick – literally – with a synthetic version. And his soup strainer wasn't the only thing bristling on that location shoot: Courtney was also having trouble adapting to the new leading man.

"At the beginning of Jon's era, he and I didn't find it especially easy to rub along with one another," the actor wrote in his 2005 autobiography. "He was working his way into his new role and tentatively sizing me up. He always seemed to be everywhere at the same time: he had a certain mercurial quality and an extraordinary, bubbling energy, which always made him hard to pin down. Since I also happened to be going through a little personal difficulty at the time, in those early days I felt isolated and a little depressed."[5]

Or maybe he was just upset that the producer hadn't wanted to bunk in with *him*.

Windows for dummies

Loyal viewers tuning in to the first episode of *Spearhead from Space* on Saturday, January 3rd, 1970, were in for quite a shock, as nothing about the story resembled the series that had gone off the air six months earlier. The theme tune was broadly the same, the TARDIS still looked like a police box, Nick Courtney was a vaguely familiar face and Jon Pertwee started the episode in Patrick Troughton's clothes but, apart from that, everything was new. And the really striking thing wasn't the change of face – most viewers had lived through that before – but the change of *pace*. Thanks in large part to the enforced decision to make the whole thing on film and on location, *Spearhead from Space* feels spiritually closer to one of ITC's slick, glossy, fast-moving adventure shows like *The Saint* or *Man in a Suitcase* (trust me, that one's more fast-moving than it sounds) than slow, stagey, studio-bound *Doctor Who*.

This was, of course, slightly misleading: by the time it went out, Jon Pertwee had hours of videotaped studio time under his belt, and that year's remaining three serials were all set to unfold over a leisurely seven instalments. But as a way of serving notice that this was a new Doctor for a new decade[1], *Spearhead from Space* couldn't have been more successful.

The stroke of genius at the heart of Robert Holmes' script is that, while amorphous telepathic space entity the Nestene Consciousness wouldn't make much of an action figure, the army of animated shop window dummies it gets to do its dirty work are positively terrifying: the sight of blank-faced plastic zombies smashing their way out of a storefront on Ealing High Street and mowing down innocent passers-by with their built-in weaponry is ingrained in the memory of everyone who saw it at the time. Even if the budget didn't stretch to *actually* smashing the window; instead, we get the sound of breaking glass over a shot of a startled policeman.

This deployment of familiar, everyday objects in a horrific context is one of the lodestones of the Pertwee era – what the actor himself called the "Yeti on a loo in Tooting Bec" effect, the argument being it's much scarier to encounter an Abominable Snowman in a recognisable domestic setting than it would be half-way up the Hindu Kush. (Given how its roar was created, it's possible said Yeti may have stumbled into said loo after mistaking its flush for a mating cry. Or maybe it just fancied a nice sit down and a read of the *Tibetan Times*. Whatever the reason, given the creature's regular diet of raw yak, mountain goat and the occasional distracted monk, I'd definitely recommend giving it five minutes if I were you.)

As well as showing us his tat, *Spearhead from Space* is the first story to reveal that the Doctor has two hearts (either that, or he needs to go to a better hospital) and is capable of putting himself into a coma with "no detectable brain activity", which should come in handy if anyone ever tries to make him sit through *The Wheel in Space* again.

After Troughton's scruffy little rebel, this latest Time Lord appears rather more grand in every way: as well as the flash duds, he has a

haughty, almost supercilious manner, addressing the Brigadier as "my dear fellow" and generally looking like he'd be more at home swigging a fine brandy in a St James' club than inciting a revolution against killer robots. For the first time since the early Hartnell stories, the Doctor's main preoccupation is looking out for number one (or number three, in this case): he only accepts a job as UNIT's scientific adviser because he sees it as his best chance of repairing whatever damage the Time Lords have done to the TARDIS, and is quite prepared to abandon the Earth to a plastic zombie invasion when he thinks he's managed to repair it. At this rate, he'd be lucky to pass his three-month probation at all.

Spearhead also premieres a couple of the era's other popular tropes, namely the comedy yokel with the Mummerset accent (in this case, jibbering cloth-capped poacher Sam Seeley) and Jon Pertwee's talent, if that's the right word, for comedy gurning. Despite his insistence on playing it straight, Pertwee will subsequently embellish every moment of strangulation, asphyxiation and general physical trauma with the sort of boss-eyed boggling Mr Bean might have considered "too broad". Here, he does it while being mauled by a rubber octopus, which isn't perhaps the strongest climax to an otherwise triumphant launch for *Doctor Who*'s dynamic new format.

Elsewhere, a couple of other dynamic new formats were proving noticeably less dynamic. Alongside their *Who* commitments, Peter Bryant and Derrick Sherwin had been developing a new show – partly inspired by their experience of working with the MOD on *The Invasion* – called *Special Project Air*, starring Peter Barkworth as an RAF troubleshooter. A two-episode – ahem – pilot was broadcast in the autumn of 1969, but failed to – oh go on then – take off with viewers. At around the same time, the BBC's much-anticipated TV adaptation of Francis Durbridge's Paul Temple novels – which has proved such an iconic hit on the wireless – had run into trouble, prompting the Corporation to parachute (sorry, force of habit) Bryant and Sherwin in to sort out the mess.

With the *Doctor Who* producer's seat suddenly vacant, the Beeb approached Douglas Camfield, who had experience directing the show and could probably be relied upon to run a tight ship – possibly by forcing under-performing members of staff to run 50 times round the Television Centre car park with a heavy kit bag. When Camfield turned the job down (for reasons that will soon become clear), they turned instead to Barry Letts, the actor-turned-writer/director who had helmed Troughton caper *The Enemy of the World*.

An unassuming figure with a strong moral compass and a long-standing interest in Buddhist teachings, Letts recalled his appointment, with typical modesty, in his autobiography *Who & Me*: "Nobody else would take it on. It was being given a last chance. Part of my brief was to find a replacement for the Saturday slot if the decision was taken to dump it."[6]

Shortly after his appointment, Letts arrived at his new office on Shepherd's Bush Green to find Derrick Sherwin packing a few last odds and ends into his briefcase. "Thank God you're here," said Sherwin. "If you want to know anything, give us a ring at the Centre."[6] And thus concluded the official *Doctor Who* production handover. He could at least have told him where the toilets were.

70s power cuts blamed on unions / lizard men

When Barry Letts sat down at his desk – at least, he hoped it was his desk – the first job in his in-tray was (what else?) sorting out a massive row. Taking advantage of the the the cavernous Television Centre studios that were now *Doctor Who*'s permanent home, designer Barry Newbery had come up with an ambitious schematic for the extensive cave sets required for Malcolm Hulke's story. When Studio Management saw the plans, they threw a hissy fit, claiming *Doctor Who* was categorised as a "small drama" and that they'd have to stick with the amount of scenery they'd used at Lime Grove. Newbery suggested that, instead of recording the story in order, they could do all the cave scenes in one go, reducing the need to strike and rebuild the heavy sets – a solution that seemed to calm the waters for a while. Then, early on the morning of the first studio day, Newbery rang Letts at home to tell him the outside contractor who was supposed to be making the caves had only half-finished

the job – and the bits they *had* supplied looked terrible. Letts threw himself on the mercy of BBC management, who pulled every available builder, chippie, painter and construction crew off all non-essential work and sent them along to the producer like the world's biggest Village People tribute band. In the end, they only lost half a day's recording – a glowing testament to the unrivalled talent pool within the world's largest TV production house. Lord only knows what would happen if a similar circumstance arose in today's outsourced, sub-contracted BBC. ("I haven't got any carpenters, I'm afraid, but I could send you a couple of brand managers, an editorial compliance executive and stakeholder liaison officer, if that's any use?")

Doctor Who and the Silurians (the somewhat unweildy name Hulke chose for his story despite, as we'll see, neither bit of it being correct) is the first serial credited to Letts as producer – though, as he was still tying up contractual loose ends on his previous job, much of the day-to-day showrunning, as no-one called it back then, fell to assistant script editor Trevor Ray. All producers will tell you that half the job is firefighting – but Ray found this truer than most when, during location filming on Hankley Common in Surrey, the ever-enthusiastic Michaeljohn Harris and his team managed to set fire to an entire hillside. Ray and around 60 others managed to beat it all out with shrubs and, when the fire crews turned up, did his best to look innocent (or as innocent as he could manage with a blackened face and gently smouldering eyebrows).

The Surrey location was doubling for Wenley Moor in Derbyshire, home to an atomic research station blighted by a series of power losses. Unlike most 1970s power cuts, this one wasn't caused by industrial action but a bunch of subterranean reptiles (and their pet dinosaur) who had awoken after a 200 million-year hibernation to find the Earth overrun by talking monkeys in lab coats. Everyone in the story refers to these lizard men as "Silurians" (understandably, since it's on the front of the script) but, paleontologically speaking, they're probably closer to Eocenes. (The script also mistakes the Ozone layer with the Van Allen belt – which is a silly schoolboy error, as everyone knows Ozone provides the Earth with protection from ultraviolet light, while Van Allen is an 80s soft metal band.)

Barry Letts likened producing a seven-part *Doctor Who* story to "sprinting across a muddy field with gum boots on"[6], but, for the audience at least, *Doctor Who and the Silurians* manages to keep up a decent pace across its near three-hour running time – even if the Doctor does spend a full two minutes staring at some microscope slides. The location filming continues the new era's more cinematic approach, and the scenes in which the Silurians unleash a deadly virus on London – including a memorable attack at Marylebone Station – inject a welcome change of pace. By presenting the "monsters" as the Earth's original civilisation, and the humans as arrogant latecomers, Hulke had already found a neat way of subverting the "alien invasion" plot he was so wary of. Being the left-wing radical he was (he had previously written for East German state television – whoever just said "perfect training for the BBC then", shut up and get back to your *Daily Mail*), Hulke also takes a moral stand by showing the Doctor's horror at the Brig's decision to blow all the Silurians up – although, ironically, this does provide the writer with a neat way of wrapping the story up, and the Doctor appears to have mostly overcome his objections to his genocidal new friend by the following week.

After *Spearhead*'s gritty film look, *The Silurians* offered the first chance to see what the new *Doctor Who* would *really* look like – including the first use of CSO in the series. As the technology was so new, the crew spent a day filming an extra flailing about in a frankly risible full-size dinosaur costume before realising they could have done it a lot more convincingly (relatively speaking, anyway) with a glove puppet. Luckily, composer Carey Blyton – nephew of Enid, and the creator of baffling fruit/sleepwear hybrid *Bananas in Pyjamas* – is on hand to distract from any visual shortcomings with his frankly deranged musical score. Taking his cue from the ancient nature of the titular creatures, Carey opted to use medieval instruments for added authenticity (or as authentic as he could get given the lack of 200 million year-old alternatives), which is why each appearance by the Silurians is accompanied by the sound of a man playing what

sounds like freeform jazz on a crumhorn. Groovy.

Carey also provides a parping little signature tune for the show's newest star, a canary yellow vintage kit-car which the Brigadier gives the Doctor in lieu of any actual wages. (A fanatical petrolhead, Pertwee had spotted a car by the same maker on TV, and persuaded Letts it would be good for the show.) Nicknamed Bessie, the car – which, for any *Top Gear* fans reading, was built around a Ford Popular chassis, and is often wrongly referred to as a roadster – sports the number plate WHO 1, thus adding more weight to the argument that the Doctor's real name is Donald Who.

By the time they'd started rehearsing *Doctor Who and the Silurians* in a drill hall in Tooting Bec ("Come on, own up – who broke the toilet seat?"), Pertwee and Courtney were getting along better – though the latter was shocked when, having invited his co-star for a lunchtime pint in the pub, Pertwee accused him of having a drink problem. (He didn't have a drink problem, of course – in fact, he was quite the expert at it.)

Barry Letts was also getting to know his leading man. Very early in their working relationship, the producer received a call from Pertwee complaining of a "gammy leg", but insisting he could still make it to rehearsals if Letts sent a BBC car to take him to his osteopath. A few weeks later, the actor requested Letts' help in staging a charity photoshoot at Television Centre, and could he arrange for Bessie to be driven over for the afternoon? The producer not only obliged, he ended up chaperoning one of Pertwee's elderly guests and, when she went to give him a tip, he decided it was probably time he started showing the Doctor who was boss.

In his book, Letts describes Pertwee as "a kind and unselfish man", but says he was also "over-sensitive, worried, manipulative" and "a good performance actor; indeed, he was usually giving a performance even when he was just being Jon."[6] Caroline John also saw the contradictions inherent in her co-star. "Jon was a good leading man in the sense that he encouraged a positive input from the cast, and he would go into every story with gusto and enthusiasm," she said. "If things went wrong, however, the air would turn blue – and woe betide anybody that messed up things during the vital process of recording, for Jon's wrath would be upon them in its full, unabated force."[7]

As well as scoping out his star, Letts was beginning to get a handle on this whole producing lark. "After a while, my wife asked me, 'What does a producer do?' 'I'm not sure,' I said, 'but it seems I sit in an office and every so often somebody comes in and screams, 'You'll never believe what's happened now!'"[8]

Luckily, the producer was not alone, as he had quickly established a firm friendship with Terrance Dicks. By now, Trevor Ray had also decamped to *Paul Temple* (he was briefly replaced by former pop singer Robin Squire, before the assistant script editor post was scrapped) and Dicks had been looking to move on himself. In Letts, however, he found a kindred spirit: both were determined to put an end to the hand-to-mouth days of lurching from one script crisis to another and, partly inspired by research showing that 58% of *Doctor Who* viewers were aged 21 or over, both felt strongly that, rather than just being a straightforward action/adventure serial, the stories should make an effort to be "about" something. "One of the big shifts in policy we've tried to make on *Who*," wrote Dicks in a letter to Terry Nation (whose stories tended to be "about" making money for Terry Nation) "is the development of more adult realistic characters and of a strong human interest theme running through every story, as well as the very necessary fights, action, monsters etc." (Despite its changing audience demographic, *Doctor Who* would continue to be dogged by the label of "children's television" for many years, based on nothing more than prejudice, ignorance and the fact it was about a spaceman fighting robots and aliens and stuff.)

Producer and script editor were also united in their dislike of the UNIT set-up their predecessors had lumbered with them, and began devising ways of launching the Doctor back into space at the earliest opportunity.

As production began on the third serial, the verdict on the the new Doctor's screen debut was starting to come in.

"Reaction to this first episode of the new Dr. Who series can hardly be described as enthu-

siastic," said the BBC's Audience Research report, "but the majority of the reporting sample were clearly quite satisfied with it.... There was little additional comment on either acting or production but both appear to have been considered satisfactory and there was some comment to the effect that Jon Pertwee had made a most acceptable and satisfactory 'new' Dr. Who."

Yeah, cheers for that. The *Daily Mirror's* Matthew Coady was slightly more effusive, claiming Pertwee's Doctor was *wholly* acceptable, while the *Morning Star's* Stewart Lane found him "charming". For *Junior Points of View's* young correspondents, though, it was still all about *Star Trek*, with *Doctor Who* coming under fire for having replaced Kirk, Spock and company in the Saturday night schedules. Whatever happened to children being seen and not heard?

The real test, of course, was the ratings and, with *Spearhead from Space's* audience staying north of eight million across all four episodes, there were encouraging signs that, if *Doctor Who* was still drinking at the Last Chance Saloon, it might at least be invited to stay for a lock-in.

HAVOC: it's lack of health and safety gone mad

If *Doctor Who and the Silurians*, with its themes of race memory and creatures from Earth's pre-history buried beneath the soil, had owed more than a passing debt to 1958's *Quatermass and the Pit*, the connection is even more explicit in *The Ambassadors of Death* which – like Nigel Kneale's original 1953 serial *The Quatermass Experiment* – concerns a group of astronauts returning home with a deadly cargo of serious whoop-ass. In this version, it transpires the crew of Mars Probe 7 have been replaced by radioactive aliens, who are then kidnapped by a xenophobic faction of the British Army in a bid to provoke the Earth authorities to attack the aliens' spaceship. ("As if we didn't have enough of an image problem being called the Ambassadors of Death," they grumbled. "Now that I think about it, I'm really not convinced it sends out the right message.")

In other words, it's another consipracy thriller designed to upset the cosy consensus of the Lloyd/Davis years that humans = good and aliens = bad. So it's no surprise that, while it's David Whitaker's name on the credits, this is really another Mac Hulke show. Whitaker was paid off after delivering the first three episodes, and promptly disappeared to Australia (surely the scripts weren't *that* bad?), leaving Hulke to pen the remaining four and, when he'd done that, re-write the first three for good measure. It's a little sad that David Whitaker's association with *Doctor Who* should have ended this way, and slightly baffling that Derrick Sherwin, in one of his last acts as producer, should have written to one of the show's visionary pioneers telling him the series was aiming to be "somewhat more sophisticated" than previously. This is the man, lest we forget, who wrote *The Crusade*, getting a lesson in sophistication from one of the men responsible for *The Space Pirates*.

With so many fingers in the inkwell, it's perhaps not surprising *The Ambassadors of Death*'s plotting is leakier than a hedhehog's spacesuit; parts of the story are set up like a whodunnit, except it's more of a godonlyknowswhodunnit, as not even the writers appear to know the answer, and one UNIT soldier who gets killed in episode four is back at work by episode six (that's defence cutbacks for you). The pacing is all over the place, too, with endless padding and frequent longueurs suddenly interrupted by random action sequences featuring Derek Ware's HAVOC team – here making their credited debut – trying to write off as many types of transport as they can get their hands on. During one big stunt sequence, a motorbike shed its rider, ploughed through several people and crashed into the director's assistant, gashing her leg so badly she needed hospital treatment. But then, you get what you pay for when you hire a crew named HAVOC. Caroline John, who hadn't told anyone she was four months' pregnant, was understandably nervous about too much physical work; she also had to have her skirts taken out at the waist ("And while you're at it, maybe you could take them down a couple of inches at the hem?").

For all its faults, *The Ambassadors of Death* is another stylish, epic production with an intel-ligent, morally ambiguous storyline that, appropriately for the new-look show, suggests not everything in the universe is as black and white as it might once have seemed. And a story about astronauts in peril could scarcely have been more thrillingly topical, as the world watched the Apollo 13 drama unfolding above them between the serial's fourth and fifth episodes.

To close the third Doctor's debut season, Dicks had commissioned a script from former *Crossroads* colleague Don Houghton with the working title *Operation Mole-Bore*, which was later pimped up to become *The Mo-Hole Project*, before settling on the altogether more sensible *Inferno*. It's set in yet another top secret research establishment, where a project to drill through the Earth's crust accidentally releases a gas that turns people into werewolf zombies. But, to help sustain another seven-week behemoth, it's also a parallel world story, with the Doctor slipping sideways into an alternative reality where "Brigade Leader" Lethbridge-Stewart and Section Leader Elizabeth Show – Caroline John channelling her inner dominatrix – are working for a brutal totalitarian regime that's executed the Royal Family and turned Britain into a fascist Republic. (Finally, a convincing argument that the UNIT stories must have been set in the 1980s.)

Douglas Camfield was an obvious choice to direct, and re-hired *The Invasion*'s John Levene as the newly promoted Sergeant Benton (after which he was hastily added to the cast of *The Ambassadors of Death*, too). Feeling he lacked military bearing, Camfield took Levene to Richmond Park to teach him how to walk, salute and stand to attention; later, to help him with Benton's transformation into a lycan-thropic Primord creature, Camfield took Levene back to the park for some werewolf practice. Whether this involved fetching a stick we can't be sure, but it gave the other dog walkers... sorry, I mean it certainly gave the dog walkers something to talk about.[II]

For someone with a reputation as a bit of an action man, Jon Petwee admitted to being pet-rified filming on top of the giant storage tanks at the Kingsnorth Industrial Estate in Kent – unlike the boys from HAVOC, who couldn't wait to climb up and chuck themselves off the top at the first opportunity. The group continued to live up to their name when, instead of diving out of the way of Pertwee driving Bessie, stuntman Alan Chuntz slipped and fell under the car. He needed 18 stitches in his leg, and walked with a limp for the rest of his life – though it didn't stop him jumping into the sea at the docks three days later, with a plastic bag tied around his leg. ("Do you think," asked Barry Letts, "that maybe we should have hired a stunt team called CAUTIOUS instead?")

The new Doctor also boosts his tough guy credentials by busting some chop socky moves he claims to be "Venusian karate". Later he'll prefer the term Venusian aikido, but it's set to become a permanent fixture of this era, usually accompanied by an enthusiastic cry of "Hai!"; more patient people than me have counted 73 Hais in total. Caroline John, by contrast, proved fighting just wasn't her scene, man, by refusing to fire a prop gun, as she didn't think it was right to use a deadly weapon while carrying a life inside her.

Nick Courtney, meanwhile, relished playing the fascist Brigade Leader, complete with scar and eye-patch. During one sequence, he turned around to find Pertwee, John and Levene had entered the room all wearing eye-patches of their own in an effort to make him corpse; ever the professional, he managed to play the scene totally straight until his tormentors gradually cracked up. (Courtney would go on to tell this story so many times at *Doctor Who* conventions, even the audience started turning up in eye-patches. *Doctor Who* fans don't get out much.)

Inferno is as intense a serial as *Doctor Who* ever attempted, with the relentless ramping up of the stakes reflected by the increasing volume of the ever-present drilling, until even the most perfunctory exchanges have to be conducted at shouting level. Frankly, it's like a seven-week migraine – and there are only so many times you can listen to Olaf Pooley, as maniacal project director Professor Stahlman, insisting THE DRILLING MUST GO ON in a VERY LOUD VOICE before you start to go a bit demented yourself. But, industrial noise terror aside, *Inferno* is one of the most dramatic – and well executed – stories in the *Doctor Who* canon, comfortably giving the lie

to one character's assertion that "there's never been a bore like this one."

Perhaps, though, it was all a bit *too* intense for Douglas Camfield: mid-way through production, the director was hospitalised with tachycardia – a type of cardiac arrythmia which he'd been keeping a secret for fear of losing work.[III] Letts took over for the rest of the story, becoming the first director to benefit from his own revised schedule of rehearsing and recording two episodes a fortnight, instead of one a week. Maths students will already have spotted that this isn't, technically, much of a gain, but apparently it was something of a revolution in television for all sorts of, um, televisiony reasons.

Impressed by the numbers for the first two stories (from a starting high of 8.8 million, *The Silurians* had kept all but a million or so of them hooked over seven long weeks), in March the BBC confirmed *Doctor Who* would indeed be back for an eighth season in 1971. But while Pertwee and Courtney were contracted for further episodes, Letts and Dicks felt the character of Liz Shaw was just too clever by half to properly fulfil the companion's anointed role of looking pretty while asking stupid questions, so it was decided that Carry John would not carry on. It was only after telling her her services would no longer be required that Letts discovered she was pregnant and had been planning to leave anyway, so that's one awkward conversation he could probably have saved himself. Despite this, John – who later admitted she spent years thinking she was "rotten in the part" – was upset by the way her departure was handled, and annoyed that no-one even bothered to write her a leaving scene. Liz's non-appearance the following year, in fact, would be dismissed with a hand-waving explanation that she'd gone back to Cambridge.

"It would have been better had [Barry] said 'I've come in, and I want a change. What you're doing is excellent, it's just that we want a different slant on it'," she said. "As a young girl, I would have appreciated that, because you're very vulnerable when you're young. I thought he didn't like what I did, period."[9]

Pertwee was reassured to learn that the Brig, at least, would be staying on: after their faltering start, he and Courtney had gradually begun to see eye to eyepatch, and were fast forming a firm friendship. Courtney recalled one incident, in particular, during the location shoot for *Inferno*:

"Jon and I were going through lines in his car just before filming started. As he finished, he turned to me and said, 'Brig, you're one of the nicest men I've ever worked with'. I had to get out of the car, my eyes started to smart. They still do when I think back to that day. I remember thinking: 'Now I've got him to trust me, we can do anything and everything.' It's no exaggeration to say we never looked back."[5]

Letts get this party started

As a producer, Barry Letts was occasionally summoned to attend meetings on the BBC's sixth floor – the level of Television Centre where the Corporation's senior management worked. It was distinguished from the rest of the building by the fact it had carpets – which came in useful for the frequent carpetings.

At one such meeting, Letts was astonished to hear one exec claiming the BBC "mustn't be afraid to bore people", the argument being it was better to be dull than common (like – he could barely bring himself to say it – ITV). He was quickly shouted down by his colleagues – if you can call "I say old boy, bit strong, isn't it?" shouting down – which was fortunate for Letts, as he was currently tacking squarely in the opposite direction. Though the seventh season of *Doctor Who* had been a success, the producer was intent on toning down some of the gritty realism – or as close to gritty realism as you could get in a show about plastic zombies, lizard men and werewolves – bequeathed by his predecessors and introducing a bit more, colour, experimentation and razzle-dazzle into proceedings. He also ruled out any more gum boot-bothering seven-parters and, somehow, managed to persuade the Beeb to stump up extra cash for costumes and visual effects by arguing they always overspent on these anyway. (Something to bear in mind at your next budget review. And do let us know how it goes.)

Along with Terrance Dicks, Letts had also hatched a plan whereby each story of the new series would be linked by a common enemy – a "renegade Time Lord" known as the Master.

(Weirdly, despite having clearly come up with this immodest soubriquet himself, the Master succeeds in getting everyone else to call him it too, whereas if you or I suddenly announced at work that, from now on, we would like to be known as Captain Brilliant, everyone would just laugh in our faces. Then again, being an expert hypnotist probably helps.)

The idea for the Master came from Letts and Dicks noting that the Brigadier was something of a Dr Watson to the Doctor's Sherlock Holmes – so perhaps he ought to have a Moriarty as well. Letts approached Roger Delgado, an old friend from his acting days, about playing the role. With a Spanish father and a Belgian mother, Delgado was constantly being cast as swarthy Mediterranean types (he had his father's colouring) though he had, in fact, been born in Whitechapel, so was technically a cockney. Just not a very convincing one.

The replacement for Liz Shaw, meanwhile, was about as far from a Cambridge scientist as you could get: Jo Grant was kooky, klutzy and, by her own admission, "a bit dim". Whether she was always intended to be quite such a contrast is open to question, as some of the shortlisted candidates (Barry Letts saw more than 200 pretty young things for the two female regulars he would cast during his tenure; he was nothing if not thorough) were known for playing more sophisticated roles. On one occasion, Letts and Dicks travelled to Westcliff-on-Sea to see Rula Lenska in William – brother of Alec – Douglas Home's play *The Amorous Prawn*, but concluded she was "too tall and voluptuous". (The chap in the giant prawn costume was terribly good, though.)

The auditions were pretty much done and dusted by the time Letts received a call from an agent asking if he'd see one more girl. "She nearly lost the chance because she went to the wrong building," wrote Letts in his memoir. "She was scatty; so short-sighted as to be almost blind, so tiny that two-shots with Jon would exercise all the director's skill, had enormous rings on all eight fingers; couldn't stop talking, and was completely enchanting. There was one slot left in the schedule. If she could act as well – and if she could scream... Her name was Katy Manning."[4]

"Katy was far and away my favourite girl, and she fitted in perfectly with the way I wanted to do the show," recalled Jon Pertwee. "Katy was by no means conventionally attractive – she was really quite a funny mix – but I still think she was incredibly sexy in the part." [10] I *think* that's meant to be a compliment. John Levene, naturally, had a more spiritual take on the matter: "Too many people desired Katy on a physical level, but I've always thought pure love is better than sex," he declared. "I would never countenance a physical relationship with her – it was her personality, not her body that I fancied."[11] Yeah – especially when her personality wore that mini-skirt with the thigh boots.

Completing the new UNIT family, er, unit was Richard Franklin as the Brig's captain, Mike Yates. The character had originally been conceived as a love interest for Jo, but this idea was never developed – partly, according to Manning, because the Doctor and Jo's "rapport" was such that a boyfriend might have upset the chemistry. (Not that there was anything funny going on – Jo's not that sort of girl and, even if she was, the Doctor's certainly not that kind of man. At least not yet, anyway.)

As the new cast members were being contracted, Dicks was performing the usual script shuffle for the upcoming season. A story called *The Cerebroids* was commissioned from Charlotte and Dennis Plimmer, but scrapped within a week; *Web Planet* writer Bill Strutton re-surfaced with something called *The Mega*; Bristol-based duo Bob Baker and Dave Martin proposed an idea called *The Friendly Invasion* – oooh, *scary* – and even Jon Pertwee tried to get in on the act, teaming up with American actor and writer Reed de Rouen to submit a seven-part story called *Doctor Who and the Spare-Part People*.

Filming for the series opener – now called *Terror of the Autons* – got under way in September with a location shoot in a Bedfordshire quarry, where the myopic Manning got off to a flying start by badly twisting her ankle on the first day. When a member of the crew said they could re-shoot around what she'd done and then "get someone else", the 18-year-old became convinced she was going to be sacked. "The next thing, Jon Pertwee finds me sobbing with my leg up, ready to be taken to hospital," she said. "He was very cross I'd been put through this trau-matic experience of thinking it all started and ended in a day."[12]

And you won't be surprised to hear Manning wasn't the only one to have a little accident: stuntman Terry Walsh missed his footing filming a cliff fall and – you guessed it – had to be taken off for an x-ray.

Just to add to the hilarity, Nick Courtney was also in a bad way: the actor had been battling with depression and, the night before filming began, had, by his own account, "started to shake with fear for no particular reason". A doctor was called but, by the next morning, the actor was in an even worse state. "We arrived at the location and, when it was time for my first piece, I was unable to stop shaking. Jon Pertwee noticed my distress, as indeed did Barry Letts and Roger Delgado. It was soon quite obvious that I was in no state to do any work."[5]

Courtney was duly dispatched to join the queue at the hospital – which by now had started to resemble an early *Doctor Who* convention – and was later signed off, forcing a hasty re-scheduling exercise. One of the few people who wasn't injured, ironically, was visual effects designer Michaeljohn Harris who, as with *The War Games*, stayed behind after hours for another of his personal firework parties; the explosion was so big, it created, acording to Letts, a "mini-mushroom cloud". "Bonkers, the lot of them," the producer concluded.[4]

As Marc Bolan rode a white swan to the top of the charts in January 1971, *Terror of the Autons* saw *Doctor Who* entering the glam-rock era with a retina-scorching explosion of colour in total contrast to the previous year's muted palette. Whereas the Autons (the Nestene's plastic zombie army) in *Spearhead from Space* had been blank-faced assassins in boiler suits, here they wear stripey yellow blazers, big painted smiley faces and jaunty straw boaters. Formally in the director's chair for the first time since *The Enemy of the World*, Barry Letts is also such an enthusiastic evangelist for CSO that, as well as the usual effects sequences, he uses it to show, at various points, the inside of a lab, a kitchen and a scientist's lunchbox. ("How did they *do* that?" gasped viewers. "For a minute there, I thought they must have built a real lunchbox!")

The plot sees the Master stealing a Nestene energy unit which, alarmingly, is on loan from UNIT to a museum (suggesting this top secret military organisation has a frankly hazardous educational outreach programme) and using it to make contact with the consciousness in its physical form as "telepathic octopoid cephalods". That's easy for them to say.

According to the Brigadier, Liz Shaw upped sticks and headed back to Cambridge after realising the Doctor only needs someone to "hand you a test tube and tell you how brilliant you are", which is all a bit meta, and the new girl certainly fits that particular bill: her big entrance sees her blundering into the Doctor's lab and ruining his experiment, prompting him, in the mistaken belief she's the new tea lady, to deliver one of the oddest insults of all time by calling her "a ham-fisted bun vendor". Note that if any Doctor was going to be so rude to the ancillary staff, it's this one – in fact he's starting to be positively insufferable at times: later in this story, he claims that he and Lord "Tubby" Rowlands are members of the same club, which suggests his journey from anarchist revolutionary to establishment patsy is now complete. In other catering-based banter, there's a classic *Acorn Antiques* moment when Richard Franklin tells the Doctor he'd "gone to fetch some cocoa", to which Pertwee replies "gone to fetch a tin of *what*?".

As the Master, Roger Delgado makes an immediate impact, quickly establishing himself in the front rank of *Who* villainy despite the character, as written, being as hackneyed and cliched as his pointy, satanic beard and Bond villain Nehru suit would suggest. He also establishes several of the character's more preposterous traits right off the bat, including a predilection for utterly pointless disguises and a shocking inability to think his plans through properly. Here, he succeeds in establishing the Nestene on Earth, only for the Doctor to casually point out they'll kill him too, at which point he metaphorically slaps his forehead, Jerry Lewis-style, and realises he'd better switch sides pretty sharpish. And the Brigadier isn't much better – faced with a handful of enemy combatants on a knackered old coach, our supposedly unflappable hero panics and authorises an RAF air strike (good luck

explaining *that* one at the next budget meeting).

Despite being a more garish, less adult and less sophisticated re-tread of *Spearhead from Space*, *Terror of the Autons* nevertheless managed to upset viewers more than just about any story that had gone before it – and it wasn't the dodgy CSO or gratuitous bun-vending insults that did it. The problem arose from Robert Holmes ramping up the "Yeti on a loo in Tooting Bec" effect by turning such everyday objects as dolls, telephone wires, plastic daffodils and, in one particularly gruesome scene, an inflatable PVC chair, into weapons of mass destruction. Holmes later admitted that he'd created a whole speaking part specifically so he could finish the character off by suffocating him in the chair. This caused a bit of a hoo-ha among the chattering classes, with one *Daily Express* columnist dashing off a piece titled "Why My Children Will Never Watch *Doctor Who* Again", while Letts received a letter from New Scotland Yard complaining that showing Autons disguised as policemen was undermining their efforts to win children's trust (quite right, too – you really shouldn't start distrusting the police until you're at least 18).

Shortly afterwards, Letts was invited to see his boss. "Take a seat," he said, while the producer eyed the inflatable chair suspiciously. He told him he had overstepped the mark, and a memo from the director general, Huw Wheldon, made it clear the show was under renewed scrutiny. Not that he wasn't watching it anyway – in the same memo, Wheldon admitted *Doctor Who* and *Match of the Day* were the only "musts" in the Wheldon household. Maybe they were more of an ITV family.

Furge-thangering for beginners

From an opening audience of 7.3 million, ratings for *Terror of the Autons* had climbed to 8.4m by the final episode: among viewers who weren't writing strongly worded letters or newspaper columns, the new format was clearly a hit.

Jon Pertwee, though, was worried his new nemesis might be *too* popular – a concern not helped by the fact a close-up of the Master had hogged the front of the New Year issue of the

Radio Times, with Pertwee peering over his shoulder like a man reduced to photobombing his own show. "People keep asking me how I feel about Roger Delgado taking over as the Doctor," he grumbled to his producer.

"There was a time when I began to get a bit jealous of the amount of attention that he was receiving," Pertwee admitted in later years. "I was joking one evening after a studio recording that they were going to re-title the series in his favour – only half-seriously, I might add – and he laughed it off."[10]

Despite this, Pertwee and Delgado were soon as thick as thieves (though not quite as thick as the Master), with the whole cast – Pertwee, Courtney, Manning, Franklin, Levene and Delgado – becoming a very tight-knit company. "It all got very involved very quickly," recalled Manning. "We used to go to each other's parties, drive each other to work, and go for a drink together after recordings, none of which was necessary, it's just that we got on so well."[13] Pertwee used to pick Manning up outside her house and take her either in his car or on his motorbike – and this was years before HOV lanes, so they must have genuinely been close. He also started using her as his personal masseur to help ease his ongoing back problems – thought to be a result of years of comedy pratfalling – claiming, "She had a very light touch – when she left, I really felt it".[10]

In contrast to the sugar-rush confection of the opener, Season Eight's sophomore story, *The Mind of Evil*, is like stepping back in time to the sober, austerity *Who* of 1970, with Don Houghton apparently still working to the Sherwin and Bryant template (pithily summed up by Barry Letts as "*Quatermass* meets James Bond") by delivering scenes of geopolitical intrigue interspersed with flashy helicopter and motorbike stunts.

This one's largely set in a prison – always a laugh-riot – where the Master is using an alien parasite that feeds on fear to recruit hardened cons for his crackpot scheme to hi-jack a missile full of nerve gas and fire it at a world peace conference, thus triggering World War III and destroying the planet. Once again, his lack of forward planning lets him down, as he's failed to take into account that he's currently trapped on said planet himself. Honestly, if he'd just

take the time to sit down and properly work this stuff out – ideally with a spreadsheet, or at least a Post-It note to remember to ask "will I also die?" – he could save himself a lot of wasted time and effort.

Houghton's script isn't too shabby by any means, though it's let down by the reptitive nature of the cliffhangers, in which the parasitic Keller Machine snacks on the fears of its victims – twice, in the case of the Doctor, which means twice the amount of "under attack" mugging by Pertwee. In doing so, the machine summons up a fearsome managerie of the Time Lord's most terrifying adversaries, including the Daleks, the Cybermen, the Ice Warriors and, um, Koquillion from *The Rescue*. Even Koquillion, however, looks scary compared to the indignity visited upon the American Ambassador: instead of the monstrous creature envisaged in the script, the unfortunate official finds himself being menaced by what Barry Letts described as "an eight-foot pink quilted pyjama case", and which Terrance Dicks christened Puff the Magic Dragon.[IV]

The production team somehow persuaded the Army to supply a genuine Bloodhound surface-to-air missile, which presumably arrived with a note stating: "Do not, under any circumstances, let Pertwee play with this." Director Tim Combe filmed the fight to take the missile in one unfolding shot, Robert Altman-style, which cheesed Barry Letts off no end. Combe had been re-hired despite a cock-up during the Silurian story, when he'd failed to get any close-ups of plague victims at Marylebone Station. As luck would have it, that day's rushes had then been lost at Ealing, so they'd been able to re-mount the scene with the film studio footing the bill. But that didn't stop the director making exactly the same mistake again – *twice* – on *The Mind of Evil*. The second instance was a big set-piece battle at the prison, which had been filmed at Dover Castle. According to Letts, Combe's interpretation of the scene boasted "long shots, high angle shots, wide shots, all beautifully planned and executed – but there was hardly a close shot to be seen"[4]. The producer ordered the director and his team back to Dover for half a day, saving money by having members of the crew appear as extras. "Legend has it," said

Letts, "that if you look carefully, you can see Tim Combe shooting himself. Serve him right."[4]

As viewers were admiring the length of Combe's tracking shots, Jon Pertwee found himself being nobbled by Eamonn Andrews for an appearance on long-running televised hagiography *This is Your Life*. Hating to be the centre of attention, Pertwee modestly demurred and told Andrews that "the work was reward enough". (Of course he bloody didn't – he couldn't get into that studio quick enough.) Meanwhile, one of his predecessors was also making headlines, as William Hartnell told the *Daily Sketch* that, in his opinion, *Doctor Who* was "no longer a programme for children".

It is perhaps no coincidence that this interview appeared during transmission of *The Claws of Axos*, which doesn't offer much in the way of adult sophistication either in script or execution, but does feature the Doctor being menaced by an alien phallus – with a blinking eye, no less – housed inside a spaceship entered via what can only be described as a giant sphinctre.

The Claws of Axos – the story that had eventually evolved from *The Friendly Invasion* – was written by Bob Baker and Dave Martin, known in the office as "The Bristol boys" on account of being the only television people in history not to live in North London. (Their West Country location would serve Baker well in later years, when he became Nick Park's chief collaborator on the Oscar-winning scripts for *Wallace and Gromit*.)

The friendly invaders are the Axons – attractive, golden humanoids who offer the British government a miraculous energy source (Axonite, natch) that appears almost too good to be true. Which, of course, it is, as the aliens are eventually revealed to be writhing great blobs of vegetable matter intent on sucking the Earth of all *its* energy.

Much of the action takes place in the Axons' organic spaceship, the interior of which appears to have been designed by members of the Jimi Hendrix Experience doing a bit of painting and decorating between gigs. The ship is supposed to be half-buried in the beach, and filming at Dungeness in Kent took place in conditions so cold that the pebbles stuck together, and Nick Courtney's mous-

tache kept falling off when the glue froze. Katy Manning, meanwhile, came close to getting frostbite, and ended up with blue legs to complete her all-purple ensemble of boots, miniskirt and knickers. (Flashes of Jo's pants will become one of the signatures of the era – though, in the interests of fairness, Benton will go one further by wearing a nappy; watch this space, if you dare.) In fact, the weather was going nuts throughout the whole shoot, changing from snow to sun literally between takes, prompting Dicks to add a hand-waving explanation about the Axons' arrival causing "freak weather conditions".

There are some good ideas in Baker and Martin's script – as well as some very stupid ones, such as the scene where Jo and the Brig escape an exploding nuclear power station by driving down the road a bit, then ducking for cover – but they're fighting for space among the gaudy production design and the shonky effects, and the end result just feels a bit workmanlike. Certainly, Tim Piggot-Smith, playing an Army captain, doesn't recall his TV debut with much fondness: "I always thought of Jon Pertwee as having played comedy all his life," he said. "It was funny that, because he took *Doctor Who* desperately seriously. I found that a little bit risible, because the material doesn't warrant that degree of gravity."[14] Sorry we asked.

These days, *The Claws of Axos* is perhaps best remembered for Derek Ware's immortal appearance as Pigbin Josh, a prince among Pertwee-era comedy yokels, whose insane ramblings – "Furge-thangering muck-witchellers rock-throbblin' this time of o' day" – were apparently scripted to the letter. ("But do you think my character would really *say* furgethangering?", asked Ware anxiously. "I must say, I've always seen him as more of a milchflangerer.") Ever the trouper, the stuntman also had to plunge into a frozen drainage ditch on a child's bicycle. His stoic response? It was warmer in the water anyway.

From April, legendary *Eagle* comic artist Frank Bellamy began furnishing each new *Doctor Who* story with an exciting new strip in the *Radio Times*. For his debut piece, he provided a dynamic interpretation of the opening minutes of the next story, *Colony in Space* – in which our hero blasts back into the stars for the first extraterrestrial adventure of the colour era. The start of this serial also coincided with *Doctor Who* being moved to a new regular timeslot of 6.15pm, and picking up around a million extra viewers into the bargain.

It's a pity, then, that the real *Colony in Space* should turn out to be a boring morality play – about crop rotation and mineral rights, mainly – set on a planet so dull it's probably twinned with the Isle of Wight; even Jo – making her maiden voyage in the TARDIS, and taking her first steps on an alien world – treats it with all the wonder of a trip to the post office.

It's a Malcolm Hulke script, so obviously he has some Issues to work through. This time, it's an eco-parable in which a bunch of human settlers are being harassed by an intergalactic mining company that wants to start drilling on their farmland. As such, it's an effective – and, as it turned out, highly prescient – swipe at corporate land grabs that might serve as an allegory for everything from Nigerian oil to the plight of the Native Americans. But if the story is indeed a Western in reverse, it could do with a few more shoot outs and saloon bar brawls to pep things up a bit. Instead, we get six long weeks of faffing about in a drab china clay pit, populated by drab colonists (if I tell you one of the more interesting ones is *Coronation Street's* hamster-faced tragedy magnet Gail Platt, you'll start to see the scale of the problem) and rubbish monsters. It's a toss-up which is worse: the mining company survey robot that looks like Wall-E with fake lizard hands glued to it, or the Godlike Guardian, a glove puppet with a walnut for a head.

Despite their official policy of non-intervention, the Time Lords are not beyond using the Doctor for the occasional black ops mission when there's a real crisis brewing – in this case, because the Master has stolen their file on something called the Doomsday Weapon. And when they say stolen their file, they mean stolen their *file* – he has literally walked away with one of the bits of paper that serves as a data-store for the universe's most advanced civilisation and, to make things worse, it appears nobody had even bothered to make a photocopy. The Master obviously does a lot of this sort of thing, as our first glimpse inside his TARDIS reveals it to be exactly the same as the

Doctor's, except it has black roundels – 'cos he's evil, see? – *and a filing cabinet*. Once again, though, our criminal genius has forgotten to drop a courtesy email to his proposed new allies asking if they'd be happy to share their super-weapon with him, forcing yet another face-saving team-up with the Doctor. The plank.

Sadly, the one thing that might have made *Colony in Space* vaguely interesting was vetoed by BBC management. For the role of Morgan, the fascistic mining boss, Michael E Briant – who would go on to be one of the decade's most prolific *Who* directors – had the idea of casting a woman; Letts agreed, and Susan Jameson was contracted for the part. But when Ronnie Marsh, the fearsome Head of Serials, found out, he hit the roof, telling Briant: "A sadistic female with a whip striding about the place in kinky boots murdering people? In *Doctor Who*? Change it back!"

Letts was so angry, he marched into Marsh's office, past his secretaries ("That's how grand his role was," he recalled. "Even his secretary had a secretary."[4]) and demanded to know why his authority as producer was being undermined. After a furious row, Letts stormed back out, the actor Tony Caunter – originally cast in a supporting role – got a sudden promotion, and Susan Jameson got paid to sit at home and do nothing. And that is literally the most interesting thing about *Colony in Space*.

Destruction of village church takes shine off pond drainage success

Ask anyone who was working on *Doctor Who* in the early 1970s what their favourite story is, and they'll almost certainly tell you it's *The Daemons*.

The Season Eight finale is credited to Guy Leopold, but was actually the first of several stories written by Barry Letts and his friend Robert Sloman. Letts was desperate to write for *Doctor Who*, but BBC guidelines cautioned against "commissioning down the corridor", so he recruited Sloman – whose day job was circulation manager for *The Sunday Times*, though he'd also written several plays – to help him get round the problem. Sloman's son was called Guy, while Leopold was Letts' middle name. After this, all future collaborations would be credited to Robert Sloman alone, and it was quite a few years later before Letts finally came out as his other half. So to speak.

Tapping into the hippy fad for ley-lines, longbarrows and pagan worship, *The Daemons* is styled as an occult thriller in the Dennis Wheatley mode. (Wheatley's 30s potboiler *The Devil Rides Out* had been a big hit in cinemas a couple of years earlier, and the first Glastonbury Festival in 1970 had seen thousands of new age revellers descending on the vale of Avalon in order to channel the spirit of King Arthur or, failing that, neck vast quantities of cider while watching Jethro Tull.) As such, it offers a welcome change of pace for the series, helped by the extensive location filming – two weeks instead of the usual one – in the picture postcard Wiltshire village of Aldbourne (the parish council received a substantial contribution towards their pond drainage scheme for their troubles). And that's why everyone involved is so fond of it, not because it's an all-time classic – after a strong start, it actually fizzles out pretty spectacularly – but because they had a jolly fortnight's holiday making it. Even Katy Manning enjoyed it, despite running smack bang into a barbed-wire fence when she veered off the trail of white stones that had been carefully laid out for her to follow.

The BBC was so wary of not offending religious sensibilities it banned any references to God in the script – though having the Devil summoned into being in a church crypt was apparently fine, as was having the Master clipping on a dog collar and passing himself off as Reverend Magister (see what he did there?). Of course, Azal – the fella with the cloven hooves and pointy horns – is not really the Devil, but the last of a race of scientists from the planet Daemos who have been influencing the Earth's progress for a hundred thousand years. And the crypt is never referred to as a crypt: it's a "cavern" under a church. Because people can get a bit funny about these things. Apparently.

Nevertheless, at least one viewer was horrified enough to write in to the *Radio Times* complaining that an entire village church had been destroyed in the name of a TV drama. The special effects team took it as a badge of honour that their model shot had been so convincing, though repeated viewing on DVD suggests it may have been more a case of congenital idiocy on the part of the viewer. (These days, of course, it wouldn't be a problem, as there would be a making-of show in which we get to see the church being blown up from 400 different angles to a soundtrack of "Boom! Shake the Room".)

The Daemons is a good story for the UNIT boys: Yates and Benton get to spend the whole thing in their natty, early 70s civvies, while the Brigadier is at his most deathlessly stoic when, confronted by an animated church gargoyle, he tells one of his troops: "Chap with the wings there... five rounds rapid."

It's a pity we can't say the same about the Doctor: this is one of the stories that portrays this particular incarnation at his most insufferable, being horrible to Jo, patronising to the Brigadier and generally punchable to everyone else. First in line to take a swing was director Christopher Barry, though it was more the actor than the character he was annoyed with. Barry had been trying to shoot a sequence in which an invisible heat barrier singes the ground – an effect not helped by Aldbourne being hit by a freak snowstorm (in early May). After a series of delays, Barry announced it might not be possible to get the scenes in the can after all, at which point Jon Pertwee fired up the Doctor's commandeered motorbike and drove off in a huff. "I hit the roof, using the most colourful language at my disposal, and generally behaving in a most unprofessional manner,"[10] the actor later admitted sheepishly – or as sheepish as Jon Pertwee ever got. Relations between director and star were already strained, after plans to film on Sunday were shelved so Pertwee could perform one of his regular cabaret engagements in Portsmouth, despite the fact Barry had missed his sister's wedding to be on set.

Thankfully for the human race, the Doctor acting like a plum doesn't stop Jo stepping in front of the Time Lord to take a metaphorical bullet for him – an act of self-sacrifice that confuses Azal so much, he blows up. At least they'd have been able to identify him by his dental records: Stephen Thorne, who played Azal, asked if he could keep the fanged dentures as a souvenir, but was told they were BBC property, despite being modelled on his own teeth, and thus useless – or, at best, deeply unpleasant – to anyone else.

Many have commented that this "talking the monster to death" shtick is one of the weakest plot resolutions in *Doctor Who* history but, to be fair, being prepared to lay down your life for someone who's acting like such a colossal dick would be enough to confuse *anyone*. And, of course, they couldn't exactly stake Azal through the heart at 5 o'clock on a Saturday teatime: there's only so far down the pagan horror route you can go before *The Wonderful World of Disney* has started. Though it's surprising what they do get away with showing: viewers of a sensitive disposition should be warned that *The Daemons* features several gratuitous scenes of Morris dancing.

Dalek reunion: "I thought *you* were sending the invites?"

After eight full years on the air, in 1971 *Doctor Who* finally found itself being automatically recommissioned for another series without anyone at the BBC trying to replace it with something newer, shinier or cheaper. There was also renewed interest in merchandise opportunities, with Nestle launching a Doctor Who chocolate bar (the wrapper featured a picture story in which the Master unveiled his devastating "Masterplan Q", no doubt as useless as masterplans A-P), and Pertwee appearing on boxes of Kellog's Sugar Smacks promising the cereal would provide "timeless energy" (i.e. sugar, or possibly smack).

But Barry Letts and Terrance Dicks weren't resting on their laurels, or anyone else's: despite the ratings success of the eighth season, they were the first to admit they'd "overdone" the Master, and resolved to limit his appearances to one or two stories a year from now on. Instead, they had started to look to the series' past, making tentative enquiries about bringing *Doctor Who*'s most iconic 60s monster back for a new generation. Or, if Koquillion wasn't available, they'd have to make do with the Daleks.

Terry Nation, now working on jet-setting international playboy caper *The Persuaders!*, couldn't be, um, persuaded to re-join *Who*, but did give his blessing for the Daleks to be used in someone else's script (for a fee of £25 per

episode), so Robert Sloman was "commissioned" – at least that's what the BBC paperwork said – to start work on a ninth series finale called *The Daleks in London*. (This was long before the BBC had to start demonstrating a greater commitment to the regions – today, they'd have to have called it *The Daleks in Salford*.)

Another blast from the past was Louis Marks – writer of second season opener *Planet of Giants*, and not to be confused with Louis Marx, the company which had made a range of popular Dalek toys in the mid 1960s (though it's possible, given the creatures' imminent return, they'd phoned up the wrong one).

Marks had an idea for a script about time-travelling guerillas, broadly inspired by the Six Day War in the middle-east (though that didn't involve time travel, as far as we know). Back then, Israel was still very much viewed as the plucky little nation fighting for survival against the big nasty Arabs ("Values were very different then to now,"[15] Marks observed many years later), which is why all the freedom fighters in his story have Israeli names.

Then Letts and Dicks had a change of heart, and decided they wanted to bring the Daleks forward to start the new season with a bang, so *The Daleks in London* was scrapped and Marks was asked to incoporate them into his story instead. Also that summer, Letts held talks with the Ministry of Defence about involving the Navy in a Malcolm Hulke script called *The Sea Silurians*, which would be a bit like *Doctor Who and the Silurians* except... well, you can probably fill in the blanks.

Jon Pertwee – who continued to juggle his *Doctor Who* commitments with *The Navy Lark* – spent his summer break recording appearances on various TV and radio quizzes, while Nicholas Courtney took a job in a military memorabilia shop to help make ends meet (if nothing else, being a Brigadier must have been useful for pulling rank over the tea rota).

Assigned to direct the new series opener, Paul Bernard made an exploratory trip to the BBC stores and was dismayed to find three-and-a-half mouldering Daleks was all that remained of Skaro's once all-conquering army. With no money in the budget to build any new ones, Bernard was told to do the best he could with what was available.

Late December saw the publication of the first regular Doctor Who fan magazine. With the original organiser of The Official Doctor Who Fan Club having transferred his affections to *Star Trek* – I *know* – the reigns were taken up by a 14-year-old enthusiast called Keith Miller, who established a good enough relationship with the production office to be able to start issuing a newsletter called *Doctor Who Fan Club Monthly*. Unlike later fan publications, it largely confined itself to nuggets of news about upcoming stories, rather than slagging off the producer and moaning that the show wasn't as good as it used to be. The *Radio Times* also helped hype up the new season with a dramatic Frank Bellamy cover declaring The Daleks Are Back! Well, three of them were, anyway.

Whatever its other qualities, there's no getting away from the fact that *Day of the Daleks* – which made its debut on New Year's Day 1972 – is all Day and no Daleks. In fact, the pepperpots appear for an average of just 2.5 minutes per episode, and even then they don't do much except stand around nattering in their weedy, reedy new voices. As the series' first concerted effort to explore the sticky implications of time travel – with a group of twenty-second century guerillas coming back in time to try to prevent World War III (again), and inadvertently *starting* it instead ("D'oh! That's exactly what we *didn't* want to happen," said their frustrated commander at the mission de-brief) – it raises some quite interesting ideas. It also continues this era's newfound enthusiasm for exploiting topical issues: when this first went out – nine months before the Munich Olympic massacre – trendy terrorist units like Black September were all the rage.

The production's shortcomings are never more evident than in the (anti) climactic battle, when the three Daleks stooges stage a particularly ineffective assault on a mansion house hosting a world peace conference (yes, another one) by going in round the back, thus allowing all the delegates to run out of the front. ("I-THOUGHT-YOU-WERE-COV-E-RING-THE FRONT?" "I-THOUGHT-THIS-*WAS*-THE-FRONT?")

The third Doctor continues to defeat all-comers in the Britain's Smuggest Man competition, giving Jo a dressing down about the importance of respect – while showing her precisely none – and, as she points out, "carrying on like a one-man cheese and wine party" by constantly stuffing his face with claret and gorgonzola. (He doesn't even put his drink down during fisticuffs, in a fight sequence which Pertwee himself choreographed after persuading the director he'd done loads of this stuff in his wartime commando days.)

A few months after namedropping Chairman Mao in *The Mind of Evil*, here the Doctor claims to be a good friend of Napoleon ("Boney, I said..."), suggesting he's moved on from "Tubby" Rowlands and now likes to hang out with fully-fledged dictators. Pertwee's love of gadgets also backfires when, having persuaded Letts to write in a new motorised trike he'd spotted, the Doctor and Jo are forced to make a painfully slow escape from the Dalek city, with the ape-like Ogrons clearly trying their best not to catch up with them.

And for those keeping score, this week Jo's knickers are red.

After the giddy thrill of the Daleks, the kids were knocked out to hear the next story would be a topical parable about Britain's entry into the EEC. Well, that was the theory, anyway. As written, *The Curse of Peladon* – in which a conniving high priest murders his political rivals in a bid to stop the eponymous planet joining the Galactic Federation – is clearly *inspired* by that year's controversial UK accession to Europe, without offering much of an opinion on the matter either way. Brian Hayles' story is actually more of an anti-religious polemic, presenting superstitious primitives as the enemies of progress and reason – without using the words God or crypt, of course, or blowing up any churches.

Hayles' intelligent script is well served by Australian director Lennie Mayne, here cutting his *Who* teeth on one of only two studio-only stories in the entire Pertwee canon. And if that's the sort of trivia that floats your boat, you'll also be interested to know this is the first ever *Doctor Who* story to be broadcast out of production order, having been taped after completion of the following serial; it has the production code MMM in honour of this interesting fact.

If the name Brian Hayles rings a bell, it's because he wrote the two Troughton adventures featuring the Ice Warriors (or, technically, wrote one and gave up writing the other). So who should rock up here as the Martian delegates to the Federation summit? (It's not a trick question – it's the Ice Warriors.) It will probably come as no surprise to learn that our favourite Martians are, in fact, green – I know, who knew? – but what *does* come as a surprise is that they're now good guys. The Doctor, in particular, has trouble believing this, which makes for an unusually sophisticated commentary on the nature of prejudice.

Mayne copes well with the limitations of creating a cod-Medieval alien planet – all Bavarian castles and flaming torches – in Television Centre but, alas, even he couldn't do much with the unfortunate delegate from Alpha Centauri, a "hermaphrodite hexapod" who pushes the Eye of Axos into a poor second in the 1971/72 Most Inappropriate Monster competition. Apparently, when the director saw the design – basically a green shaft with a bulbous head and a blinking eye – he declared, with typical Aussie reserve: "It looks like a fucking prick!" A cloak was hastily added to protect what little modesty could be salvaged, after which Mayne observed: "Now it looks like a prick in a cape!" (Actress Ysanne Churchman, who had become a household name as Grace Archer in the BBC's long-running farming soap – famously doing her bit for the Corporation by carking it in a fire on the night ITV launched – had been instructed to play the role as a "prissy, homosexual civil servant". Assuming, of course, such a thing had ever existed.)

The director's potty-mouth was also responsible for one of the serial's more memorable studio moments. Frustrated with his cast's British reserve, Mayne insisted their reaction to the first appearance by the mythical beast Aggedor should be more of a "holy fucking cow!" moment. Before the scene was re-mounted, Jon Pertwee circulated among his fellow players – including Patrick Troughton's son David as the young Prince Peladon – so that, when Mayne called action on the re-take, the entire company responded in unison with "Holy fucking cow!" Legend has it that this happened at the exact moment Barry Letts was showing a party of boy scouts – or possibly a vicar – around the studio, but that's probably

just one of the loftier examples of Pertwee's talent for tall stories.

The Navy lark

If *The Curse of Peladon* was a throwback to *Doctor Who*'s theatrical, even Shakesperean early days, *The Sea Devils* – that's serial LLL, for those who've been paying attention – is perhaps the ultimate example of early 70s *Who*: big, panoramic, action-packed, exciting and just a little bit daft.

After a couple of stories lying low, the Master is back. He's actually in prison, but it's obvious he's not going to be there long as a) he's got the governor in his pocket and b) there's a handy rack of swords placed right outside his cell, which must surely have seen points docked at the next inspection. And this time, he's teaming up with the Silurians' aquatic cousins for bonkers scheme No. 448. His plan is to assist them in taking over the Earth for no other reason than he thinks it will really wind the Doctor up. And yes, before you ask, he completely fails to anticipate his allies' betrayal *again*.

The Sea Devils are never named as such – but the script does go out of its way to clear up the Silurian name gaffe; let's hope they don't retrospectively start trying to tidy up *all* the show's plot holes and lapses in logic, or we could be here for a while. The creatures themselves look like seven-foot walking turtles in string vests (they were originally designed to be naked, but Michael E Briant thought that looked a bit... you know, wrong).

The story's most famous sequence, in which the Sea Devils emerge from the waves onto the beach, proved a nightmare to film, as the heads were so bouyant they kept popping up through the water – apparently, the language from the HAVOC boys would have made even Lennie Mayne blush.

This was to be the accident-prone stunt troupe's last contribution to *Doctor Who*: from now on, Terry Walsh's Profile gang would be doing the honours, Walsh having bagged the gig while still a member of HAVOC, mainly on account of being able to convincingly double for Jon Pertwee. (Though "convincing" is a relative term, given some of the dodgy wig shots over the following years.) Ware – who'd made his debut as a caveman right back in the series' first story – later admitted that assigning Walsh to a stunt on *Terror of the Autons* hadn't been "the best day's work of my career": "Before long, I wasn't doing *Doctor Who* any more – and Terry was. If you can get hold of a stunt co-ordinator who actually looks like the leading man..."[16]

At heart, *The Sea Devils* is a flashier re-tread of *The Silurians*, with a bigger budget but a smaller worldview. (You can't help thinking the Doctor blowing all the Sea Devils up at the end somewhat undermines his – and, indeed, Malcolm Hulke's – moral outrage at the Brigadier doing the same thing at the climax of the former story.) At other times, it feels more like a Royal Navy recruitment film, with the Senior Service chucking as many boys' toys as they can at the production in order to show how exciting it is – though the chase on a pair of Buccaneer sea scooters was a late addition at the request of you know Who.

Despite these shortcoming – and in spite of yet another power cut denting the ratings – *The Sea Devils* remains one of *Doctor Who's* most fondly remembered stories, and it's rather difficult not to get swept along on the tide of the production's sheer enthusiasm. Just as long, that is, as you can ignore the music.

Ah yes, the music: *The Sea Devils'* soundtrack is distinctive, to say the least. In fact, it sounds like nothing on Earth – which they might just have got away with, conceptually speaking, if the whole story hadn't been set on the English south coast. As a money-saving exercise, the BBC Radiophonic Workshop had been producing the music for *Doctor Who* electronically from *Terror of the Autons* onwards, mainly from conventionally-written scores by the nearest thing to an in-house composer, Dudley Simpson. It was something of a laborious process, and the RW had been lobbying to be given the chance to write something from scratch. *The Sea Devils* was that chance, and it's fair to say the Workshop's Malcolm Clarke blew it in spectacular fashion.

The department had recently taken delivery of a cutting-edge Synthi 100 synthesiser and *The Sea Devils*, in the words of one critic, was "Malcolm Clarke fighting with it – and losing". Hence, for example, scenes of the Doctor and Jo running across some fields are accompanied

by a cocophony of parping, squelching and what at one point sounds like a car alarm going off underwater. Director Michael Briant has described the results as "different" and "interesting" – which it is, in the same way that the Ebola virus is different and interesting. Barry Letts insisted a lot of the score was cut out in a bid to limit the damage, and the Radiophonic Workshop wouldn't be asked to contribute their composing skills to the series for another eight years. But apart from that, Clarke was delighted with how it had all gone.

All this was good news for Dudley Simpson, who could now take his marimba back out of storage again. But not before Tristram Cary had made his own, typically idiosyncratic contribution to the next story, *The Mutants*. When he wasn't composing avant-garde musique concrete scores for expos and the like, Cary liked to get his hands dirty with the electonics side of the business, and had helped to design the world's first portable synthesiser. Suffice to say, the fact he was more passionate about valve oscillators and voltage-control than melody isn't entirely lost on viewers of *The Mutants*.

Say what you like about Bob Baker and Dave Martin – and you could, because they lived in Bristol – no-one could accuse them of lacking ideas. Coherency, certainly, but not ideas. The concept for *The Mutants* – a mad Marshal tries to scupper plans to give the exploited indigenous population of an Earth colony independence – started life as a conversation between Martin and his biologist neighbour about the lifecycle of a butterfly. By the time the script was finished, it was also, according to the writers, designed as "a kind of commentary on South Africa at the time" (the indigenous Mutts were originally called Munts – the Boer insult for black people – but this was changed for reasons that ought to be obvious) and "an allegory of the British India situation in 1947"[17], with an allusion to the Nazi gas chambers also thrown in as window dressing.

As with *Colony in Space*, the result should have been powerful and thought-provoking, but is actually an unfortunate combination of boring and silly, with Rick James, as Cotton, crashing into the Top 10 worst all-time *Doctor Who* performances – though, to be fair, he's not helped by the frequently preposterous, over-declamatory dialogue, which gifts characters around him with such immortal lines as "Die, overlord, die!" and "You are a fool, Varan, a fool!".

The production design is a mixture of the garish – say hello to an *actual* tinfoil creature – and the excellent: the Mutants themselves, created by future Oscar-winning costume designer James Acheson and ace mask-maker John Fiedlander, are a triumph of skill and imagination over budget.

Today, though, *The Mutants* is best remembered for its opening scene of a wild, bearded old geezer running up towards the camera in an uncanny – though presumably accidental – recreation of the "It's..." man from *Monty Python's Flying Circus*, and the fact the story warrants a mention in Salman Rushdie's *The Satanic Verses*. For such a supposed poindexter, Rushdie managed to miss the point *entirely* by suggesting the show supported the view that mutation = evil, when that's exactly the stance it was supposed to be satirising. This upset quite a few *Doctor Who* fans and, subsequently, Rushdie had to go into hiding for many years.

Away from the main show, *Doctor Who* faces (those of them who had faces, anyway) were popping up more frequently on other TV shows than at any time since the Hartnell era. On top of his inveterate quizzing, Pertwee made an appearance on *Ask Aspel*, answering questions from young viewers, while Alpha Centauri popped up, so to speak, on *The Black and White Minstrel Show* performing "Walking Down the Road" (I'd like to see him/her try). Katy Manning also recorded an edition of the antiques quiz *Going for a Song* (yes, it was as exciting as it sounds) while a Dalek proved he could still laugh at himself – even if no-one else did – by starring in a sketch about computer dating on *Look, Mike Yarwood!* (exclamation mark sub-standard impressionist's own).

There was more comedy in store – much of it unintentional – as viewers tuned in for the epic Season Nine finale, *The Time Monster*. The story had its genesis in Robert Sloman's fascination with the idea that all time exists concurrently, as espoused by JW Dunne in his essay "An Experiment in Time", which had also proved a strong influence on JB Priestley's

"time plays" such as *An Inspector Calls*. Here, the Master, posing as a Cambridge professor, constructs a machine called TOMTIT (and anyone disappointed that the last three letters stand for "through interstitial time" should hang on until episode five) which he uses to summon Kronos: a creature who devours time, possibly to distract from the fact he looks like a giant paper chicken in a welder's mask. Being the Master, of course, he's unable to keep it on a leash, and all manner of temporal chaos kicks off before everyone legs it to the lost city of Atlantis, where the Doctor encounters the Minotaur and Ingrid Pitt's chest. (As the Queen of Atlantis, the seasoned Hammer Horror screamer boasted, by her own estimation, "one of the biggest expanses of bosom ever seen in *Doctor Who*".[18] After a thorough audit of the situation, I am pleased to report she's probably right.)

Appropriately, this story about time-eaters features more time-wasting faffery than just about any *Doctor Who* serial to date: one whole episode is wasted with the Doctor and the Master effectively Skype-ing each other, while in another the Doctor spends an age knocking up a "time flow analogue" from a wine bottle, some cutlery, keyrings, tea-leaves and a mug; improbably, this saves the entire universe from destruction (for a few seconds, anyway).

As Professor Thascalos (that's Greek for Master – it's almost like he *wants* to be rumbled, isn't it?), Roger Delgado attempts a Hellenic accent for all of two lines, then thinks better of it. There's a rare bit of backstory for the Doctor, meanwhile, as he informs us that, as a boy, he lived halfway up a mountain, behind which sat a hermit under a tree. Chuck in all the Age of Aquarius nonsense – rainbow-coloured voids, floating female dieties – and you'd never guess it's Barry the Buddhist and Bob the Gaia-loving Earth mother at the controls, would you?

This story is also the first to suggest the TARDIS might be more than just a machine: the Doctor refers to her as "she" and mentions her telepathic circuits. She also gets a re-fit, complete with washing-up bowls all over the walls, which was scrapped immediately afterwards because everyone hated it. (Also, no-one at the BBC had been able to do any washing-up for weeks.)

For all its faults – the laboured attempts at humour, the clumsily inserted black and white stock footage, the horrible music, the frequent longueurs and, it bears repeating, the giant paper chicken – *The Time Monster* is kinda fun (and not just because *Doctor Who* fans have turned it into a perilous drinking game). Also, things pick up considerably when the action moves to Atlantis – "all that Cretan jazz," as Jo so succinctly puts it – for the final reel, though Ingrid Pitt was apparently upset that her lines kept being cut. The excuse they came up with to placate her? They'd **cough** "run out of videotape". Apparently.

If you only watch one scene from this story, though, make it the one in episode six where Benton – who had previously been turned into a baby (don't ask) – reverts back to fully-grown Benton who is either butt naked or still wearing a nappy. Mercifully, it's not possible to tell from the broadcast footage, though John Levene claims to have been wearing a nappy at the time: "Every second I was doing that scene, I thought the nappy was going to drop off," he recalled. "I found out after the show the dressers had tried to rig the safety pin! Fortunately, it didn't fall off, but I was still very embarrassed. It's not like I've got this bulging, muscled body and, in those days, I certainly didn't have a tan or anything, so I was very self-conscious about it, and I didn't really want to strip off. I wouldn't mind now," he concluded, in an interview for *Doctor Who Magazine* when he was in his mid-50s, "because I'm a little bit more attractive." Form an orderly queue, ladies.

While BBC1 viewers were enjoying – for want of a better word – *The Time Monster*, location filming was already in progress for the second story of the next season. In the capable hands of the unflappable Barry Letts, *Doctor Who* had finally discovered the principle of forward planning. What's more, Robert Holmes had been asked to write a story with two distinct sets of characters who never meet, thus allowing the actors to be contracted for a fortnight each, rather than the whole month. For a Buddhist, Letts was surprisingly hot with a spreadsheet.

The various production efficiencies also meant a longer summer holiday, freeing up Jon Pertwee to do other things – quiz shows, cabaret, driving very expensive cars very fast –

which the producer thought would help keep him sweet for another year or two. Basically, you had to get up very early in the morning to catch Barry Letts out.

For anyone missing their *Who* fix that summer, there was an unexpected bonus in the form of the two big-screen Dalek films, making their debut on the BBC a full seven years after the first film's release. With around ten million viewers, the films drew a much bigger audience than the TV series had ever managed in a summer timeslot. What's the betting no-one dared point this out to Jon Pertwee? Not that he had a fragile ego – but when a company called Personality Posters put out a Doctor Who pin-up that summer, it had to be withdrawn and replaced with a different picture more to the actor's liking.

Also in the business of resurrecting a slice of 60s *Who* was Richard Henwood, an editor at publisher Universal-Tandem who had stumbled by chance across the three Frederick Muller novelisations from the 60s, and quickly optioned them for his new Target children's book range. He contacted the BBC with a view to repackaging the books with Pertwee's Doctor on the cover. They refused – which is just as well, as the implications for canonicity may well have led to mass fan suicides – but agreed to Henwood's request to expand the range with adaptations of actual Pertwee serials. (Pertwee had already featured on one cover that year, incidentally: published in April, Malcolm Hulke and Terrance Dicks' *The Making of Doctor Who* was the show's very first reference guide, offering background information on the series as well as an in-depth look at production of *The Sea Devils*. It remains one of the most influential works on the series ever published, though it doesn't have nearly as many jokes about pants as this one.)

On the verge of the programme's tenth anniversary year, the 60s nostalgia bug had even reached the production office. After the summer break, shooting had commenced in September on *Frontier in Space*, the first half of a whopping 12-part adventure featuring the Master and the Daleks, which Letts and Dicks had conceived as an update of the epic space operas of the Hartnell era – most notably *The Daleks' Master Plan*. After a break of more than seven years, Terry Nation had also agreed to return to the show and, just to add that extra touch of 60s authenticity, he was bringing all his old scripts with him.

But even that was just a sideshow compared to the *real* celebration Letts and Dicks had planned to kick off the anniversary season: a plan so audaciously brilliant in its simplicity, it's a surprise no-one had thought of it before.

Actually, it turns out *everyone* had thought of it before.

Three's a crowd

According to Barry Letts, "People had often come up to us and said, why don't you have the Doctor meet himself? And we suddenly thought, why are we so against it? It's quite a nice idea."[19]

As such, Letts sounded out William Hartnell and Patrick Troughton about reprising their roles, and also managed to win Jon Perwtee round to the idea by reassuring him he would still be top dog. (There are no further details, but I strongly suspect at least one lunch was involved.)

A script was commissioned from Bob Baker and Dave Martin with the working title of *The Black Hole*, with Letts and Dicks stipulating that it should end with the Time Lords returning the Doctor's TARDIS to full working use, thus effectively drawing a line under the show's three-year Earth exile.

The Bristol Boys' initial proposal arrived in the form of an homage to Ingmar Bergman's *The Seventh Seal*, complete with a cameo by Death. It was pretty grim stuff, prompting Terrance Dicks to write back saying: "The whole atmosphere of mass suicides, corpse filled morgues, lumbering ghastly zombies and man-eating fungus will give our viewers nightmares and our Head of Department apoplexy." Though, to be fair, most of us been to worse 10th birthday parties.

A more suitable storyline was agreed, and work on the script was well advanced when Letts received a phone call from Heather Hartnell. "She said, 'Bill seems to think he's going to be in *Doctor Who*, is that right?'" recalled Letts. "And I said, 'Well yes, I did ask him'."[19]

"She said, 'You must have got him on one of his good days, when he was feeling bright and cheerful'," [19] explained Terrance Dicks. Apparently, Hartnell's arteriosclerosis was now so advanced, there were days when he couldn't recall ever having been Doctor Who at all (on others, he still nursed a grudge at his perceived ill-treatment by the BBC): there was clearly no way he could cope with a return to acting.

Which left them with a big problem. "We were stuck with *The Three Doctors* by this time," said Letts. "It had gone out in all the publicity and all the rest of it."[19]

The producer went back to Heather Hartnell and asked if her husband could handle a very small contribution to the serial; she agreed, so Dicks sat down to redraft Baker and Martin's scripts, limiting the first Doctor's contribution to a handful of brief appearances on the TARDIS monitor (a cameo by Jamie also had to be dropped, as Frazer Hines couldn't be released from buttering barmcakes or whatever it was he got up to on *Emmerdale Farm* these days).

For the filming, Hartnell was taken by car to Ealing, where he was seated in a chair while his dozen or so lines were held up in front of him on cue cards. To help the cast with their reactions, audio from these scenes was played into rehearsals for the story – which, in order to fit in with Patrick Troughton's schedule, finished recording a mere 18 days before broadcast, with the following two stories already in the can.

The three Doctors did convene in the same space-time event – specifically, for reasons no-one can recall, a private garage in Wandsworth – for a *Radio Times* cover shoot. And this time, Jon Pertwee made sure there would be no repeat of the debacle with the Master – which is why, if you can track it down, you'll find that particular issue of the *Radio Times* features the third Doctor literally standing on a box in order to loom large over his predecessors in a very physical show of top doggery.

For anyone who hadn't yet got the message, during the build-up to *The Three Doctors*, Pertwee also attempted an assault on the pop charts with "Who is the Doctor", in which he dramatically blows his own trumpet – actual lyrics: "I cross the void beyond the mind / The empty space that circles time / I see where others stumble blind / To seek a truth they never find / Eternal wisdom is my guide / I am... the

Doctor!" – over a glam rock take on the *Doctor Who* theme. It failed to chart despite being, in a bombastic, vaguely comical sort of way, rather magnificent – and despite the frankly suspicious theft of a Dalek from outside the record company's offices making the news.

As recording commenced on *The Three Doctors*, the rest of the cast were on eggshells, nervous to see how the two leads – not that that's how Pertwee would have termed it, of course – would get along. The answer, initially at least, was not brilliantly.

Eternal wisdom may have been his guide, but the current Doctor also relied on the script to tell him where to go, what to say and who to say it to. Pertwee was a stickler for accuracy: much like Hartnell, his method was to commit his lines to memory early on, and then cling on to them for dear life. Troughton, on the other hand, preferred to freestyle his way through a rough approximation of the scripted scene, adding innumerable quirks and tics and ad-libs as he went along. This infuriated Pertwee, who struggled to perform his own lines without the correct cues. In the end, director Lennie Mayne found a compromise, with Pertwee agreeing to relax a little if Troughton made a concerted effort not to wander off-piste so much. Though he still managed to ruffle Pertwee's peacock feathers by suggesting "It doesn't matter what we do – they're all looking at the monsters".

"The nice thing was," said Terrance Dicks, "in their scenes there was a tension and rivalry between them, and in their actual acting there was a tension and rivalry between them."[19]

For a serial commissioned to mark the show's tenth anniversary on November 23rd, 1973, *The Three Doctors* arrived somewhat prematurely on the last Saturday of 1972. As well as teaming up the Doctors, the story also introduces Omega, the Time Lord "temporal engineer" who created the power source that set his people up among the gods, but got trapped on the wrong side of a black hole in the process, and is now pretty fed up, to say the least. By this stage, Omega is a being of pure anti-matter holding together an anti-matter universe through sheer force of will, which must make it difficult to meet women. He has his eye – or at least he would, if he had an eye – on the third Doctor as his replace-

ment, which is a good choice, as no-one enjoyed being the centre of the universe more than Jon Pertwee.

As usual, the "science" on offer is absolute bunkum ("the light here must be travelling backwards, because I can see" being one quotable example) and some of the dialogue is a bit ripe, to say the least. "Holy Moses, what's *that*?" screams a UNIT troop at one point – though, to be fair, he is under attack from what appears to be a giant fruit salad with crab claws at the time. The Brigadier also seems to have undergone a frontal lobotomy: granted his first look inside the TARDIS, he assumes it's some sort of conjuring trick and, when transported to an alien planet, insists it must be Cromer. The latter is very funny – especially if you've ever been to Cromer – but it's a bit sad to see the intelligent, dynamic action man of the Troughton serials and Season Seven complete his journey to fully paid-up military buffoon. The Brig now also gets a namecheck on the new sign outside UNIT HQ. That's the large sign advertising the headquarters of a *top-secret military organisation*. These days, they'd probably have their own Facebook page, too ("Brigadier Lethbridge Stewart has just checked in to the top-secret UNIT HQ").

This week, Miss Jo Grant is once again dressed head-to-toe in purple – and, yes, that does include her knickers. Leaving those aside, so to speak, the main attraction of this fun but surprisingly functional caper can't help but be the interplay between Doctors Two and Three, with – as Terrance Dicks noted – the rivalry between the two stars translating into some truly classic scenes of one-upmanship: Troughton all twinkly-eyed mischief; Pertwee brisk, businesslike and irritable.

William Hartnell, meanwhile, manages to make his presence felt in just a few very short scenes, to the extent it seems perfectly logical for his other selves to defer to his greater wisdom even though, technically speaking, he's the baby of the group.

Not surprisingly, *The Three Doctors* would prove to be Hartnell's final professional engagement. He died less than three years later, on April 23rd, 1975, aged 67. He is one 24 people commemorated with a plaque at BBC Television Centre, but, of course, his real monument lives in the hearts and minds and imaginations of anyone who ever has loved *Doctor Who*. And for all those people, it is reassuring to know the man who helped create the legend ultimately made his peace with the show. According to Heather Hartnell, being invited to appear in *The Three Doctors*, however fleetingly, put something of the old sparkle back in her husband's eye. "He glowed again," she said, "as if it had taken ten years off his illness."[20]

Draconia: surprisingly nice this time of year

With an average audience of 10.3 million – boosted by various promotional interviews, including Troughton and Pertwee sharing the limelight on Birmingham-based lunchtime chat show *Pebble Mill At One* – *The Three Doctors* was the highest-rating *Doctor Who* story since *The Web Planet*, way back in 1965. Not surprisingly, the BBC were keen to hang on to their hit team, and Pertwee was contracted for a fifth year in early January. Letts and Dicks were both starting to think about an exit strategy, but the BBC put its hands over its ears, said "la la la can't hear you" and told them to get on with making more of that ratings-bustin' *Doctor Who*, thank you kindly. How times had changed.

Not all of the team would be hanging around, though, as Katy Manning had her sights set on a new challenge (just so long as someone held the new challenge up very close to her face): "I decided to prove to myself that I could act in other things," she said. "It was a very hard decision to make. I went to Barry Letts fairly early on in the season and said that I was thinking of leaving, and he said it'd probably be a good idea as Jon would have completed four years, and it was unlikely he'd do it much longer. If I were to leave with Jon, Barry pointed out, any potentially good publicity I might get at announcing my own departure would be swamped in the news of Jon's leaving. It was a career thing, really. I wasn't fed up with it."[13]

Plans were made to write Jo out in the season finale. Before that, *Carnival of Monsters* – the Robert Holmes story that had been made all the way back in May and June the previous year – finally arrived on screens. Holmes was slightly peeved to find the name of the serial

had been changed from its working title of *Peepshow*, Terrance Dicks apparently having decided that might send out the wrong message (particularly as it's one of the few stories of the era where you don't even get to see Katy Manning's underwear).

The story opens with the Doctor and Jo materialising on board a cargo ship in the Indian Ocean in the 1920s – the third Doctor's first trip back into Earth history. Except it's not really, because it turns out our heroes are actually trapped in a miniscope: an entertainment system containing real people and events in miniaturised environments, which people pay for the privilege of watching. In other words, it's reality TV, decades before the phrase had even been invented.

Though Holmes couldn't have foreseen the era of Simon Cowell, *Big Brother* and Rebecca Loos pleasuring a pig (non-UK readers, you'll just have to go with me on this), he clearly did intend *Carnival of Monsters* to serve partly as a commentary on television – and possibly *Doctor Who* itself (monsters-of-the-week the Drashigs are described as "great favourites with the children"). As such, this is a whole new genre of *Doctor Who* story – a witty, playful satire that introduces several classic Holmes motifs, most notably an obsession with petty bureaucracy and a gift for mixing the mundane and the fantastical to maximum comic effect, years before Douglas Adams made millions from the same idea.

This heavily stylised approach covers a multitude of sins in production terms: the scenes on the planet Inter Minor are particularly cheap – gaudy and overlit, with bald caps and wigs coming unstuck all over the place – but you could almost, *almost* argue that the artificiality just adds to the joke. Not that the kids – or, indeed, Barry Letts – would necessarily have seen it that way. The Drashigs (glove puppets with the jaws from real terrier skulls, gruesome fact fans) are more of a qualified success: they work well in the filmed location scenes – shot on the marshes at Burnham-on-Crouch where, inevitably, Katy Manning stumbled off the safety boards and started sinking – but are conspicuously less convincing in the studio. Anyone tuning in late must have thought Basil Brush had had a *very* rough night.

Carnival of Monsters continues to take the third Doctor in a wildly divergent direction from his predecessors: here, he orders a large Scotch, claims to have had boxing lessons, and states it is impossible for him to be wrong about anything. (He's wrong about that, for a start.) Despite this, the story remains one of the most widely admired of this or any other era – and perhaps the first real indication of why Robert Holmes would come to be regarded by many as *Doctor Who's* most accomplished writer.

Viewers in Australia, however, might remember it for less edifying reasons. As part of the tenth anniversary celebrations, a new version of the *Doctor Who* theme had been commissioned from the BBC Radiophonic Workshop. The work was undertaken by Brian Hodgson and Paddy Kingsland, under Delia Derbyshire's supervision, on the Workshop's modular "Delaware" synthesiser. The result sounded like someone pinging the tab of a Coke can while torturing a mouse, and was abandoned after one fleeting appearance on a trailer for *The Three Doctors*. However, some copies of *Carnival of Monsters* found their way out of the building before the original theme could be re-dubbed back on, and later surfaced Down Under – possibly having been shipped there for crimes against music. And that's why we can now all enjoy the Delaware disaster in all its glory on YouTube. Shortly afterwards, Brian Hodgson left the BBC to set up his own company; it's slightly unfortunate this twanging monstrosity should have been his parting gift, but we really shouldn't let it besmirch the record of one of *Doctor Who's* great early innovators.

His replacement as the show's sound effects wiz was Dick Mills, who had in fact helped Delia Derbyshire with the original version of the theme in 1963. According to Mills, Dudley Simpson was keen for the sound boys to avoid anything that might make viewers think he'd written a duff note. To placate him, Mills came up with the apocryphal "option four": "We gave Dudley a knob to twiddle to keep him quiet," he explained. "He thought that it modified what he had heard, changing it in some way. We would turn it a bit, and he would shake his head; we'd turn it some more, and he would say, 'Much better!' What we

didn't dare tell him was that the knob wasn't connected to anything at all. Poor old Dudley."[21]

While Dudley was twiddling his knob, Terry Nation had been twiddling his thumbs since *The Persuaders!* had been canned after just 24 episodes. That's why, when Letts and Dicks approached him about using the Daleks in their *Master Plan*-style intergalactic epic, he exercised his option of first refusal, and took the gig himself.

Mindful of the problems that had beset the 1965 12-parter, the production team had decided to split their space opera into two separate but linked stories, using the first six episodes as the tenth season's sole outing for Roger Delgado's Master. The go-to guy for this sort of thing was, of course, Mac Hulke, who duly delivered an intelligent Cold War parable in which even the Master's latest wheeze feels vaguely plausible: this time, he's teamed up with the Ogrons – the simian grunts from *Day of the Daleks* – to hi-jack space vessels in order to provoke a war between Earth and its auld enemy, Draconia. It says a lot about the Master that employing monkeys as space pirates counts among his more sensible schemes.

Consumed in one go – which, of course, *Doctor Who* stories were never intended to be – *Frontier in Space* tends to repeat on you, with its endless series of captures, escapes and interrogations. But director Paul Bernard succeeds in giving the piece a sense of scale, and the design work is a cut above the average. The spaceships were part of a job lot bought from Gerry Anderson, and the Draconians – reptiles in Japanese Shogun dress – are particularly good, as you might expect from James Acheson and John Friedlander. (Though Paul Bernard claimed to have made "innumerable sketches" of the aliens and was annoyed at Friedlander "taking the credit": "After all, he's just a craftsman contracted by the make-up department."[22] So that told him. Friedlander, for his part, recalled having nothing more than "a vague description in the script"[23] to go on.) Jon Pertwee would later insist that, during one recording break, he forgot there were actors behind the masks, and struck up a conversation with one of them as if he were real. It's hard to imagine how this conversation might have gone – "How was the traffic getting in?

Draconia to Acton must be murder at that time of morning" – so I think we can probably assume this was Pertwee-speak for "the design was very impressive". Though, to Hulke's credit, they didn't just have nice heads: Draconia turns out to be an unusually civilised and nuanced alien society, thus rendering the name mildly inappropriate – a bit like changing Sweden's name to Pitiless.

The slick visuals (slick by early 70s *Doctor Who* standards, anyway – don't go expecting *Avatar*) must have come as a particular relief to Barry Letts and Terrance Dicks, for whom all this space-faring action also served as a dry run for a new project they were developing as a future career option. *Moonbase 3* was designed as a grown-up, grittily realistic alternative to *Doctor Who*, set in an under-funded lunar station where, instead of scary monsters, the crew had to battle with budget cuts and meddling bureaucrats. It probably sounded more exciting when they said it.

Of course, you can't get through six weeks of space opera on a BBC budget without coming apart at the seams somewhere along the line (literally, in Katy Manning's case – she splits her trousers at one point). But *Frontier in Space* really only overreaches itself twice: during the Doctor's spacewalk, where he is very visibly on wires (maybe they bought him off Gerry Anderson, too) and a truly risible monster – apparently the most feared creature in Ogron history – that has variously been described as a duvet, a giant plastic bag and a deflated bouncy castle, all of which flatter to deceive.[V] It was so bad, in fact, that the script had to be re-written to reduce its screen time. This led to a somewhat botched ending – reshot by the following serial's director, David Maloney, to provide a better lead in to the next six episodes – in which the Master simply disappears, apparently swept up in a crowd of panicking Ogrons. A few months later, the true significance of this ignominious exit would become tragically clear.

Before that, though, there were Daleks to deal with. Introduced in a surprise twist in the final episode of *Frontier in Space*, it was the first time the creatures' reappearance had ever been kept a secret. Once the pepperpot was out of the bag, though, the publicity machine cranked into gear, including a *Radio Times* competition

to win a full-size Skarosian by writing a brand new Dalek story. It's just a pity they couldn't persuade Terry Nation to write one as well.

Planet of the Daleks is the Nation equivalent of those comeback tours where the band just go out and play the hits in lieu of any new material. Which is fair enough: in the pre-video and DVD age, half the viewers would never have seen a Terry Nation Dalek story before, and those who had would only be able to recall the haziest details.

And so we get all the old favourites: jungles, invisibility, countdown clocks, people hiding in Dalek casings... Even the Thals make a comeback, only this time they're a crack – well, crack-ish – commando unit who revere the Doctor as the legendary figure who stirred them out of their pacifist torpor. So, inevitably, he does a shameless volt face and starts lecturing them about the evils of war. There's just no pleasing some people.

The Thals have come to the planet Spiridon to destroy a Dalek army who are on the planet picking up tips from the natives on how to turn themselves invisible (seriously – this actually went out, on proper telly and everything). The Doctor is also on the trail of the Daleks, but Nation appears to have forgotten that, so writes in a "oh no, so *that's* what we're up against!" scene anyway. In most other stories, that would be the dumbest moment, but the prize here has to go to the bit where a bunch of plants fire their sap all over the TARDIS exterior (don't even go there), thus cutting off the oxygen supply to the infinite time ship – which, lest we forget, exists in a whole different dimension to its exterior. Did Terry Nation *really* think that's how the TARDIS occupants were able to breathe – because of air coming through cracks in the door? And how would that work in the vacuum of space, incidentally? The ship's control room has also had a make-over, with the introduction of some flat-pack furniture including drawers, a wardrobe and a fold-out bed. Someone's clearly been to the planet Ikea recently.

The Daleks themselves – one of which is a re-dressed prop from the second Peter Cushing film (a Dalek prop, I mean; it's not a coat stand or something) – are shabby, slow and generally useless (in contrast to the Doctor, whose new natty crushed purple velvet pimp suit is without doubt the most superfly thing ever seen on Spiridon), and, when one of them accidentally bumps into a polystyrene rock, it moves along the floor like… well, like a polystyrene rock. And whatever invisibility trick the Spiridons are teaching the Daleks, it clearly doesn't work on the bits of string pulling the futuristic space doors open.

With his long experience of writing for television, Nation should also have guessed that a climax in which thousands of Daleks are consumed in a wave of molten ice was always going to stretch the BBC's resources. In the end, they turned to Louis Marx (not the *Day of the Daleks* writer, the toy manufacturer this time – keep up, do), which is why the finale feels like one of those annoying toy adverts where they always have a really impressive diorama that looks way cooler than your bedroom carpet. Though, let's be honest, most bedroom carpet battles have better scripts.

According to some of the guest actors, Jon Pertwee and Katy Manning set the tone for the studio sessions by performing a haka, and organising a game of hoopla. Pertwee was also famous for his preferred vocal warm-up – leading the entire company in a musical salute to the pre-war dance band leader Harry Roy. It seemed impolite to ask why.

Since joining *Doctor Who*, the star had never made any secret of his dislike of the Daleks – he thought they lacked dramatic potential, and gave him nothing to work against as an actor. But Nation had a different take on it: "I always believed he didn't like them in the same sense that actors don't like playing with children or dogs," he said. "Because they're scene stealers."[24] When it comes to a battle of egos between Jon Pertwee and Terry Nation, it's hard to know who to believe – so let's just assume they were both wrong.

You had me at "spores"

Bringing the curtain down on the tenth season – and, in many ways, signalling the end of an era – *The Green Death* is one of the best-remembered *Doctor Who* stories of the age – though most people recall it by its more common name, The One With the Giant Maggots.

With its themes of pollution and environmental devastation, Barry Letts and Robert Sloman's script was ahead of its time, pre-dating even the British Green Party. Letts had read an article about the damage being wrought upon the Earth's fragile eco-system, and wanted to do something about it. According to Terrance Dicks, it was he who suggested Letts could write a *Doctor Who* story about it – though, in retrospect, it's difficult to see what else Letts might have done, short of walking up and down Oxford Street with a sandwich board proclaiming The End is Nigh.

In *The Green Death*, a company called Global Chemicals – no, honestly, I'm sure they're lovely people really – is dumping pollutants down an abandoned Welsh mine, the charming side effects of which include giant maggots and insects, and certain death for the local population. Clearly it was going to take more than planting a few trees to offset that little PR problem. Unlike his producer, though, the Doctor doesn't give a tupenny toss about the Earth's eco-system – he's more interested in taking a holiday to Metebelis 3, the famed blue planet that this incarnation of the Time Lord is always banging on about visiting. Fortunately for us, it turns out to be rubbish – he's barely had time to nick a blue crystal (it will look perfect on his console table) before he's being attacked by a giant bird – so he legs it back to Earth, and agrees to a Welsh detour after the Brigadier's memorable description of a local victim: "This fellow's bright green, apparently. And dead!"

There he discovers that Global Chemicals is being run by a scheming – though surprisingly chatty – supercomputer called BOSS (with a name like that, he was always destined for promotion), and that the locals are all absurd Welsh stereotypes, look you, who can't so much as cough without adding a "boyo".

Assisting our heroes are the right-on members of the Wholeweal community – a self-sufficient commune known locally as "the Nuthutch". Jo is particularly taken by one of their number, Professor Cliff Jones, who wins her over with his early chat-up line "Shut the blasted door – you'll contaminate my spores!"

Jones is played by Manning's then-real-life boyfriend, Stuart Bevan – a move director Michael E Briant initially resisted (he thought it might get messy if they broke up), before agreeing he was the best candidate for the part.

If you hadn't guessed by now, Jo Grant is about to ditch *Doctor Who* in favour of Professor Mushroom,[VI] in one of the most convincingly portrayed expedient romances in the show's history. In fact, there's an atypically genuine, natural feel to much of this story, in which characters actually sit down and talk and eat together, like real people. Granted, the scenes of bright green miners and giant larvae with fangs are less naturalistic – as are the ones where Jon Pertwee dresses up as a milkman and a cleaning lady – but then this *is* still *Doctor Who*, not a Mike Leigh film.

The giant maggots were created using a mixture of CSO, maggots on strings, balloons, hand puppets and – oh yes – water-filled condoms. No doubt the props buyer got some funny looks when he walked into the chemist and asked for 200 packets of three. ("And a little something for the weekend, sir?" "No, I think that will be enough to be getting on with for now, thanks.") The bombs UNIT drop on them, meanwhile, were actually lavatory ballcocks. I'm pretty sure that contains all the ingredients you need for a truly filthy joke, but we'll move on.

Viewers paying close attention may notice one of *The Green Death*'s principle supporting characters, Global Chemicals PR man Elgin, disappears from the story without explanation at the end of episode four, after which his function is taken by a new character. This was an unscripted substitution after Tony Adams – now best remembered as moustachioed motel boss Adam Chance in *Crossroads* – fell ill, and was hastily replaced by Dalek voice regular Roy Skelton – now best remembered as effeminate pink hippopotamus George and zip-mouthed felt puppet... um, thing Zippy in kids' TV classic *Rainbow*.

If Skelton was tempted to bring some of his other skills to the party – by, for example, turning one of the glove puppet props into a loveable comedy character called Marvin the Maggot – he would probably have judged that it wasn't really the time or the place. The mood during filming was noticeably subdued and, by the time the moment arrived to record Katy Manning's final scenes, had spilled over into an outright blub-fest.

Pertwee was particularly upset to be losing his friend, co-star and personal masseuse (by now, his back problems were really starting to hamper his action man lifestyle, on and off screen) and, according to Briant, having Stewart Bevan as Cliff made it feel like "he was taking Katy from the show in real life, as well as in the story"[25]. "Playing that [final] scene was the most difficult thing in the world for all of us," said Manning. "We were in tears. It was very genuine. After spending three years of my life with these people, I was absolutely lost. It was like leaving home."[15]

The final shot of *The Green Death* sees the Doctor driving off alone, under the setting Welsh sun, following an emotional farewell to his best friend. Forty years on, it remains one of *Doctor Who*'s most affecting moments.

Katy Manning's first job after *Doctor Who* was presenting an arts and crafts series called *Serendipity*. In 1978, she made waves by posing nude with a Dalek for the magazine *Girl Illustrated* ("I-DID-N'T-REC-OG-NISE-YOU-WITH-OUT-YOUR-PANTS-ON," said the Dalek, as Manning straddled its sucker arm in a move that looked distinctly awkward for both of them). She spent many years in Australia – where she was advised the climate would be better for her twins Georgie and Jonathan, who were born two months' prematurely in 1979 – and in 1996 managed the rare feat of silencing TV motormouth Ruby Wax when she and her childhood friend Liza Minelli appeared, clearly – ahem – "refreshed", on Wax's TV show.

It also transpired that *The Green Death* wasn't quite the last we'd see of Jo Grant, but fans would have to wait more than 35 years until her next appearance – by which time she'd be in her 60s, and keeping her knickers firmly under wraps.

You say potato, I say SonTARan

For viewers tuning in on June 23rd, 1973, Jo Grant's departure was rendered even more poignant by the knowledge that, five days before, Roger Delgado had been killed in a car crash while being driven to a film shoot in Turkey. Always keen to be punctual, Delgado and two technicians had taken an unlicensed cab, which had driven off a cliff near Nevishir.

Some time earlier, Delgado had requested to

leave *Doctor Who* – some casting directors believed he was still a full-time cast member, and he thought this was costing him work. In honour of his origins as the Moriarty to the Doctor's Holmes, Barry Letts and Terrance Dicks were planning one last titanic, Reichenbach-style struggle between the two adversaries the following year. Sadly, it wasn't to be, leaving the Master's confused exit from *Frontier in Space* to stand as the great Roger Delgado's wholly unsatisfactory final appearance in the show.

For Jon Pertwee, it felt like the writing was on the wall: Manning had gone, his UNIT chums were making ever more infrequent appearances, and his back was causing him agony. And now this. "When [Roger] was killed, it affected the whole thing – tainted it, and spoiled the pleasure of doing the show," he admitted.[10]

Nevertheless, he got his kicks where he could – including persuading Letts to soup up Bessie with a larger engine. Ride suitably pimped, Pertwee liked to take her out on the North Circular, where he would outgun expensive sports cars just to see the look on the drivers' faces. Hey, everyone needs a hobby.

The star's next request was addressed to the editor of the Doctor Who Fan Club magazine, who he asked to stop running so many articles on his predecessors. But, as it happened, salvation was already at hand in the form of the Jon Pertwee Fan Club, set up by a long-time friend of the actor's, Stu Money. As rivals gangs went, it wasn't exactly the Sharks vs. the Jets – though the pins on those button badges could be quite sharp.

His face also graced the cover of the *Dr Who Colouring Book* and the Doctor Who Space Mission Pad (a notepad with a carbon copy sheet; history doesn't record whether NASA ever put in an order). Target also launched their range of Doctor Who books with the 60s Hartnell re-prints, while Terrance Dicks and Malcolm Hulke agreed to novelise *Spearhead from Space* and *Doctor Who and the Silurians* respectively. It became standard format for the range to use the *Doctor Who and...* prefix, but that didn't solve the problem of the whole Silurian/Eocene hoo-ha, so Hulke eventually played it straight and called his book *Doctor Who and the Cave Monsters*. (This may have

been Hulke deliberately creating a playful ambiguity around the question of who the *real* monsters are – the reptiles or the humans. Or is may have just been because Doctor Who fights some monsters in a cave.)

Already in the can by the time of that summer's tragic events, the first story of the eleventh season would introduce viewers to the Doctor's new companion, investigative reporter Sarah Jane Smith – who, you won't be surprised to learn, was young, female and as plucky as a double-shift in a chicken factory.

"I told everyone that I wanted somebody who was attractive, a very good actress, with a very good personality in her own right – and cheap!"[13] explained Letts. He found all these qualities in a young actress called April Walker, who had appeared in supporting roles in the likes of *Dad's Army*, *Crossroads* and *The Onedin Line*. Unfortunately, once Walker was introduced to Jon Pertwee, it was clear the two just didn't look right together – with Walker too tall, too busty and too assertive to be tucked under the third Doctor's protective cloak. In other words – she was a bit too much like Jon Pertwee. Apart from the busty bit, obviously. Letts – who went to his grave refusing to name the original actress (Walker's name only came to light in 2012) – was left with no choice but to release his new signing, who would be paid in full for the whole series, and start the search again.

Step forward Elisabeth Sladen, 26, who had spent several years at the Playhouse in her home town of Liverpool before joining Manchester's Library Theatre and spending a six-week stint behind the bar of the Rover's Return in *Coronation Street*. Sladen had recently moved to London with her actor husband, Brian Miller, appearing in various TV roles, including *Z-Cars*, whose producer recommended her to Barry Letts. This time, Letts left nothing to chance, introducing Sladen to Pertwee who, she later learned, had been secretly making a thumbs-up sign behind her back. Though, as someone who had spoken with a lisp his whole life, he good-naturedly admonished the production team for saddling him with a sidekick called "Tharah Jane Thmith" in the first place.

Initiation test completed, one of Sladen's first tasks was a shopping trip with James

Acheson to find a suitable look for Sarah, who Letts and Dicks had decided should be more of a feminist than her predecessor. According to Sladen, when she whipped off her clothes in Biba, Acheson didn't know where to look. But then, naked people are probably a costume designer's worst nightmare.

Filming for Robert Holmes' season curtain-raiser, *The Time Warrior*, took place at Peckforton, a mock-medieval castle in Cheshire (even today, this remains the northernmost place *Doctor Who* has ever been filmed). Things got off to a rather disastrous start for the new TARDIS team when, in the hotel bar on the night before shooting commenced, Pertwee accidentally called Sladen "Katy" – and then promptly burst into tears. It was okay, people kept reassuring her: it will just take Jon a bit of time to adjust to Katy not being there. "By the end of the night," Sladen wrote in her autobiography," I was ready to punch the next person who even mentioned that woman's name."[26]

Alongside Sarah Jane, *The Time Warrior* marked the debut of potato-headed clone warriors the Sontarans, who would quickly establish themselves in the top flight of *Who's* major league monsters. What started out as a cheeky Robert Holmes gag – a creature who takes his helmet off, only for the head to be exactly the same shape underneath – was transformed by the crack team of Acheson and Friedlander into the show's most convincing prosthetic to date. (Strangely, it would never be this good again.) Cast as Linx – a Sontaran warrior who crash lands in thirteenth-century England – was Australian actor Kevin Lindsay. According to those on set, it was Lindsay who decided on the distinctive pronunciation of SonTARan. When director Alan Bromly said he thought the emphasis should be on the first syllable instead, Lindsay turned to him and said: "Well I think it's SonTARan – and I come from the fucking place, so I should know."[26]

On the first day of filming, Pertwee invited Sladen to come over and meet some fans who had gathered to watch. Already feeling anxious, she declined, at which point Pertwee grew more insistent. "Suddenly, everything had changed," she said. "This wasn't a request to join him, it was an order. I thought, okay, I'm getting a handle on this operation now.

Someone is going to need to be pleased quite a lot."[26]

In time, Sladen would be as generous to the fans as anyone, but she admitted that, "At that moment, I felt like punching the lot of them – and him".[26]

Reluctantly, she trooped over, at which point Pertwee told his fans, "Look everyone, Lissie's about to do her first scene for us," and promptly unfolded a shooting stick and sat down, arms folded, surrounded by his adoring public, to watch as she took her first steps in her new role.

"Of course Jon, bless him, had only the best of intentions," Sladen reflected later. "All he wanted to do was make me feel special by giving me the honour of him as an audience... I'm sure he thought it would give me confidence but, honestly, I could have kicked him in the teeth."[26] Somehow, the new girl managed to survive the shoot without lamping her leading man, the fans or anyone who happened to mention her predecessor. At the end, Pertwee insisted on giving her a lift back to London in his Lancia, but not before, as navigator, she'd helped him reverse it into the props van.

Then, on Sladen's first studio day, an embarrassed-looking cameraman took her aside and explained she was supposed to wear special underwear to protect her modesty during CSO work – because the monitors had been showing everything she'd got. Sladen rushed over to costume, demanding to be given the CSO underwear – at which point everyone collapsed in hysterics at their little joke. On the Tube home, the actress couldn't help but see the funny side – and decided she might be going to enjoy her time on *Doctor Who* after all...

Ullo Jon! Gotta new motor?

While Sarah Jane was getting her feet under the TARDIS console, Terrance Dicks had decided it really was time to get another job – even if it was unlikely to be on *Moonbase 3*, which had proved a ratings flop during its six-week run that autumn. Instead, Dicks planned to write freelance, including novelising stories for the Target *Doctor Who* range (he would go on to write more than 60 – 60! – of these books, some of the more challenging of which took him the morning *and* the afternoon). With this in mind, his nominated successor – who else but Robert Holmes? – began shadowing the role in October, with a view to taking over full-time in the spring. And, as if to reaffirm his concerns about the increasingly repetitive nature of the job, Dicks found himself turning back the clock five years as he took over from Brian Hayles in order to get an Ice Warrior sequel – this time a follow-up to *The Curse of Peladon* – into usable shape.

In October, Pertwee's biggest fan – okay, second biggest fan – Stu Money wrote to the *Radio Times* asking if they had any plans for a magazine to celebrate the show's tenth anniversary, at all, just out of interest? It's funny you should ask Stu, said the editor, as a special publication was due in the shops in just a few weeks' time. Hitting the streets on November 11th, the glossy magazine boasted exclusive photoshoots, star interviews, detailed plans for building your own Dalek (possibly to stop the originals being stolen – another pair had recently gone walkabout from Television Centre before being found abandoned several miles apart in west and south London), an exclusive Terry Nation Dalek story (in so much as any Terry Nation Dalek story can be said to be exclusive) and information on every serial from *An Unearthly Child* to the end of the upcoming eleventh season. Along with Hulke and Dicks' *The Making of Dr Who*, the *Radio Times* tenth anniversary special remained the only readily available reference source on the series for many years, and continues to influence fan opinion on certain stories to this day.

Among the satisfied customers was a 15-year-old Scottish fan called Peter Capaldi, who wrote to *RT* to lavish praise on the special, singling out the "excellent" Terry Nation story and looking forward to seeing something similar for the twenty-fifth anniversary in 1988. Capaldi was not unknown to the *Doctor Who* production office: such was his ardour, he bombarded them with letters – almost getting himself blacklisted by Barry Letts' secretary – and later tried to stage a coup d'etat for the presidency of The Doctor Who Fan Club. Later still, he went on to win an Oscar... and an even more valuable prize. Watch this space.

The following month, Barry Letts handed in his notice – he planned to return to directing

– and Pertwee decided the time was probably coming to call it a day, too. But he might be persuaded to stay just a *little* longer with the right... you know, incentives. "I said to my old friend Shaun Sutton, 'I will stay on for another season if you pay me a little more money'. And he said, 'I'm terribly sorry to see you go'. I said, 'Surely you're going to discuss this with the rest of your directors, aren't you?' And he said 'No, we have a budget and that's it, and anything more than that we can't do, so bye'. And I left."[3]

Barry Letts disputed this, however. "That's absolute nonsense," he said. "It would be nothing to do with Shaun. It would be my business. He definitely went because the family was breaking up."[27] Whatever the truth – and it's possible Pertwee had made up his mind to go, but thought it was worth a cheeky shot across his old friend's bows – it was now clear that the eleventh series would be the last for *Doctor Who's* longest-serving star, producer and script editor.

In late December, Pertwee was back on the front of the *Radio Times* promoting the new season and, this time, far from playing second fiddle to the Master or sharing the spotlight with his predecessors, our man was firmly centre stage, surrounded by a coterie of adoring lackeys – actually Michael Parkinson, actress Vanessa Miles and Brit blues legend Paul Jones and his son Matthew, who all came out as fans of the show.

Debuting in Christmas week 1973, *The Time Warrior* finds Robert Holmes developing the voice he'd found on *Carnival of Monsters* with a fresh, funny "pseudo-historical" (remember them? – they're like real history, except you don't have to look as many things up) in which Linx the Sontaran abducts a handful of twentieth-century scientists to help him re-build his spaceship, which has crashed in medieval England, while maintaining an uneasy partnership with local robber-baron Irongron (a roaringly good turn from David Daker).

There are obvious echoes of Mark Twain's *A Connecticut Yankee in King Arthur's Court*, and Pertwee's Doctor – "a longshank rascal with a mighty nose", according to Irongron – feels so at home in a historical setting, it's a shame we didn't get to see more of it. (Disguising himself as a monk, Pertwee adopts his standard comedy yokel accent, as used for the Postman in *Waterlogged Spa* and, later, for *Worzel Gummidge*. Not for nothing did they call him the Man of a Thousand Voice. Sorry, I mean Voices.)

History is made when the Doctor's homeworld gets its first namecheck – it's called Gallifrey, if you want to write it down – and there's a lovely, character-defining moment when, asked if he's serious, the Doctor replies: "About what I do, yes – not necessarily about the way I do it."

The new series also boasted a new title sequence: in place of the "howlaround" effect that had survived in one form or another since 1963, Barry Letts commissioned a new piece from Bernard Lodge inspired by – okay, stolen from – the "star gate" sequence in *Stanley Kubrick's 2001: A Space Odyssey*. This was a budget version, naturally, achieved using, among other things, a stretched plastic bag – but the result is rather impressive (though the full body cut-out of the Doctor just looks silly). To complete the make-over, the show also got a new logo, with the words Doctor Who sitting in a heavily stylised diamond that, objectively speaking, ought not to work (it's really more suited to a circus or a funfair), but clearly did, going on to become one of the programme's most iconic pieces of design.

Which is not something that can be said about the stars of *Invasion of the Dinosaurs*. Look, we all know the score by now: if you care more about special effects than characters and storytelling, you're sniffing up the wrong trouser leg with this show. But just occasionally, something goes so badly wrong that even the most forgiving fan would need a crane and a whale harness in order to suspend their disbelief. And it never went more badly wrong than this.

If you're looking for someone to blame, try the Drashigs. Barry Letts was so impressed with the combination of puppets and CSO in *Carnival of Monsters*, he felt emboldened to ask Malcolm Hulke to incorporate dinosaurs in central London into a time-travel storyline he'd already submitted. This late addition is all too obvious in the resulting Jurassic farce, in which the prehistoric pests are nothing more than a giant red herring – actually, a giant red herring would probably have looked more

convincing – being used by the leaders of a wacko cult to scare people away from the capital, *Scooby Doo*-style, so they can get on with their fiendish plan. It's a pity, because what's left of the story Hulke wanted to tell – a group of idealists are tricked into thinking they're en route to colonise another planet, when in fact they're going to be used to populate the Earth once the temporal re-set button has been pressed and the rest of the planet wiped out – is really quite strong. And having Mike Yates turn traitor and throw his lot in with the villains is a nice touch that helps shake up the cosy familiarity of the "UNIT family".

Unfortunately, it takes a supreme effort of goodwill to see beyond the truly risible dinosaurs: lumpen, immobile Chewit monsters that look like they've been fashioned out of plasticine during a junior school wet playtime. (Amazingly, one of the contractors who made the models went on to work on Disney's *One of Our Dinosaurs is Missing*. I can only assume they did the missing one.) The Doctor's mop fight with a pterodactyl on a string also has to be a contender for the most unintentionally hilarious moment in *Doctor Who* history – especially as the poor creature is in serious danger of getting snagged in the towering bouffant Jon Pertwee is sporting by this point.

And that's not the only thing that's different about the Doctor this week: he's also gone and got himself a new car. A shiny, futuristic space car with huge silver fins. Yes, Barry Letts has been the victim of yet more Pertwee pester power. Except, this time, the producer stood firm and said they couldn't afford it – so Pertwee bought it himself, and persuaded Letts to write it into the show.

Based on a Bond Bug chassis, the car – which Pertwee called the Alien, but everyone else seemed to refer to as (wait for it) the Whomobile – had a top speed in excess of 100mph and, despite its bizarre appearance, could legally be driven on British roads. And so cutting up commuters in Bessie was replaced by winding up traffic cops – who took some convincing the vehicle was roadworthy – as Pertwee's favourite new hobby. Lis Sladen, who likened the car to "a silver manta ray", recalled Pertwee driving her to a location shoot in it at rush hour, and having to take evasive action several times as shocked motorists weaved across the road into their path. Eventually, they were flagged down by a policeman, who began his interrogation with a deadpan greeting of "Hello, Doctor – I'm afraid you can't drive this through Kingston High Street." ("I'm sorry officer – I thought this lane was reserved for buses, taxis and ludicrous TV star vanity projects.")

Invasion of the Dinosaurs was director Paddy Russell's first time in charge since *The Massacre* eight years earlier. "I was outraged by Pertwee's beastly Whomobile," she declared. "Suddenly I was told that it had to fit in somewhere, which wasn't easy."[28]

It's fair to say the director and star didn't exactly hit it off. "Jon was so much more interested in what he was going to wear than what he was going to say," she said. "He wasn't very good on lines, and [guest star] John Bennett said to me that it was the only time he's played opposite somebody who never looked at him once over the six episodes. Pertwee's lines were written all over the set!"[28]

To his credit, Jon Pertwee never made any secret of this habit. "I used to write my script on everything," he confessed. "Backs of cupboard doors, on clipboards... I used to open drawers, and there's the script at the bottom!"[29] ("Brigadier, the future of the entire world depends on you inserting the dowling rods into the side panel before affixing the metal bracket... oh hang on, that's the instructions for the drawers. Who's moved my bloody script?")

Without doubt, the most effective scenes in *Invasion of the Dinosaurs* are the early sequences in episode one of an eerily deserted London, which Paddy Russell and her cameraman filmed guerrilla-style – i.e. illegally – in the early hours of one Sunday morning in locations such as Westminster Bridge, Whitehall and Trafalgar Square. This episode was broadcast simply as "Invasion" in a bid not to spoil the big surprise – even though the game had already been blown in both that week's *Radio Times* and the tenth anniversary special (and even though the dinosaurs, when they did turn up, were more than capable of spoiling the moment themselves). Malcolm Hulke wrote to the production office to complain about this, saying he thought they'd probably

lost viewers as a result. Yes, Malcolm – because if there's one glaringly obvious fault with this story, it's the inconsistency in the title.

On February 8th, Jon Pertwee's departure was made public, by which time the ever-efficient Barry Letts had already cast his successor, who took time off from his job as a labourer on a building site – thereby, as you may well imagine, hangs a tale – to greet the gentlemen of the press the following week. Later that month, Pertwee undertook a short tour of the country to sign copies of the two new Target books – which was a bit of a cheek, as he hadn't written them. Meanwhile, BBC1 started showing the story he had made immediately before handing in his resignation. The fact it featured the Daleks, and had been filmed in a freezing quarry in the middle of November, was probably just coincidence though.

If I tell you that *Death to the Daleks* sees the Doctor teaming up with a bunch of Space Marine Corps looking for the cure for a space plague – and that, in the original script, the action took place in a jungle instead of a quarry – you can probably guess who was at the typewriter for this one. Significantly, though, it's also the first story to be edited by Robert Holmes (legend has it Terrance Dicks left him a note stating: "Good luck – the aspirins are in the bottom drawer"), which is why it feels like someone's suddenly turned out the lights. That's literally true – the first episode opens with the TARDIS losing power (well it *was* 1974), and the Doctor and Sarah exploring the quarry planet by candlelight – but it's reflected in the whole tone of the story, which is darker, creepier and more sinister than we've seen in recent years. A scene in which Sarah unwittingly seals herself inside the TARDIS with a hooded creature – seen lurking behind her in the stygian gloom of the console room – is pure horror movie stuff, and a signpost to where things are heading over the next few years.

At the heart of the adventure is a living, breathing, sentient city designed like a Peruvian temple. According to the script, the indigenous population, the Exxilons, once visited the Earth, where they influenced the development of the Inca civilisation – a nice grace note that has Holmes' fingerprints all over it. The Doctor teams up with a friendly native, Bellal – played with such endearing, child-like wonder by future *EastEnders* script-writer Arnold Yarrow, he's the first *Doctor Who* alien you'd seriously consider adopting – to explore the city, playing logic games and avoiding deathtraps as they go. Some of this is highly effective, but it's unfortunate that, owing to a timing cock-up, the episode three cliff-hanger features our heroes coming across a small section of mosaic flooring and... er, that's it. It actually turns out to be quite deadly, as mosaics go, but because we don't know this yet, it just looks like our hero has a serious aversion to mock-Peruvian tiling (fair enough, I suppose).

While the Doctor is trying to avoid death-by-hopscotch, and Sarah's been strung up for sacrifice by the locals (because the Doctor wandered off and left her alone on an alien planet at night, literally *seconds* after promising he wouldn't, the bastard), the Daleks are having a bit of trouble with their, you know, *per-formance*. Unfortunately for them, the same force which drained the TARDIS power cells has rendered our tin chums totally impotent in the firepower department: they can wiggle their whisks all they like, but it's just not hap-pening for them. This raises an interesting philosophical question: if a Dalek can't kill, what is its function? To which Terry Nation's answer is: sod philosophy, we've got a plague bomb to build.

Off camera, the pepperpots were also having a bit of trouble with the sandy terrain – that's why Daleks almost never take beach holidays – but Michael E Briant and his team had come up with an ingenious solution: attach wheels to their casings, and run them along camera dolly-tracks. And ingenious it certainly would have been – if they'd been filming on the flat. Among the dunes, though, it was positively suicidal.

"Each actor had a Dalek assigned, and he had to push the Dalek to get it started," explained Briant. "Jon Pertwee, being Jon, pushed his Dalek hard and, with little John Scott Martin inside, it just took off! We ached with laughter as it roared off along this track, and fell off the end. Little John was screaming 'Help! Help!' as he hurtled along."[30]

Continuing the quiet revolution behind the scenes, *Death to the Daleks* was the first *Doctor Who* story recorded set by set, rather than epi-sode by episode. It's also the first – and last – story to feature the London Saxophone Quartet, Carey Blyton having decided that dark, sinister alien worlds are best accompa-nied by a soundtrack of ambient jazz (the clos-est musical approximation to pure evil, I guess).

No sooner had the Daleks finished brushing sand off their balls (or "hemispheres", techni-cally) than they found themselves back at the beach for the opening of one of two official Doctor Who Exhibitions (the other being at Longleat House in Wiltshire) on Blackpool's Golden Mile. Situated in a basement beneath a café – probably where the toilets used to be – it might not have given the execs at Universal Studios many sleepless nights, but, for a gen-eration of British children, stepping through those TARDIS doors and descending into the monster menagerie below was just about the most exciting – and terrifying – experience imaginable. (Actually, as most trips involved staying in a Blackpool guest house – evening meal included – it was probably the *second* most terrifying experience imaginable.)

Jon Pertwee and Lis Sladen were the guests of honour at the official opening on April 8th. Sladen was shocked to find hundreds of fans besieging their hotel – though not as shocked as Pertwee when he realised his getting undressed for bed had created a silhouetted strip show for the audience gathered outside. (In Blackpool, you normally have to pay at least a pound for that sort of thing.)

The following day, crowds of cheering peo-ple lined the roadside as the Doctor drove Bessie proudly along the Golden Mile to the exhibition. By this time, recording was under way on the third Doctor's final story, during which Pertwee was noticeably withdrawn: instead of taking charge of the company as he had done throughout his tenure, he was often to be found sitting alone at a table, diligently answering his fanmail. Watching him working the crowds and soaking up the adulation in Blackpool, Sladen realised she'd "never seen him happier". "And," she added, "I suddenly realised, *I'll never see him this happy again.*"[26]

Third Doctor confronts own ego, dies

It would be nice to think of Jon Pertwee's penultimate story as a bit of an encore from the old showman. Sadly, *The Monster of Peladon* is more of a dodgy cover version – as if someone had dictated the entire script of *The Curse of Peladon* down a very bad phone line. This time, instead of Britain's wrangles over EC membership, we get *Doctor Who's* take on the 1973 miner's strike (for the record, not that dissimilar to the real thing, except the miners all look like badgers with afros). And – surprise surprise – the Ice Warriors are back, this time helping to stir up a rebellion as an excuse to put the planet under martial law.

All the gains made in the original Peladon story to present the Martian warlords as more a complex, nuanced race are thrown out of the window in a story that sees them returning to the lumbering giants of the Troughton era. (For some reason, a vague effort is also made to keep their presence on Peladon a secret until The Big Reveal – to the extent of "hiding" their big green bulks behind frosted glass – even though it's blindingly obvious to everyone who they are; I mean, it was never going to be the paper chicken from *The Time Monster*, was it?)

With its right-on take on feminism, worker's rights and the exploitation of small nation states, *The Monster of Peladon* is certainly worthy – but boy is it ever dull. Sarah Jane's Girl Power speech to the Peladon Queen ("There's nothing 'only' about being a girl") is particularly clunky – and the irony of male writers getting a male character to order a woman to talk about women's lib wasn't lost on Lis Sladen.

It's likely the story only ended up being so topical because it took so damned long to write: Brian Hayles' first draft preceded the miners' walk-out, and his second pass was also rejected, at which point Dicks took over the job himself. And any notions he had of writing the whole thing off as a bad job were scuppered by the fact the story had been previewed in the *Radio Times* tenth anniversary special, leaving him with no choice but to plough on. By the time it went into production – uncomfortably close to broadcast date, by this regime's

standards – the production was almost too topical for its own good, as it ended up being made during endless power cuts and the three-day working week ordered by the Government as an energy-saving measure. (For non-UK readers, it should be explained that the three-day week applied to the whole country; they didn't hope to solve Britain's energy crisis just by limiting *Doctor Who's* studio time – though they probably could have done if they'd asked Jon Pertwee to make fewer unnecessary journeys in his space car.)

Further hampered by ropy visuals – Terry Walsh is so plainly visible during one fight sequence, Pertwee had to overdub some grunts in the vain hope viewers would believe their ears over their eyes, and the death of the mythical beast Aggedor is somewhat undermined by his furry boots coming away from his furry trousers in his dying moments – *The Monster of Peladon* is utterly lacking in wit, imagination, passion or inspiration. At one point, the Doctor goes into a comatose state described as "complete sensory shutdown". And, frankly, who can blame him?

In the months they'd been working together, Lis Sladen had gradually started to get a better handle on her co-star, and the two had begun to develop a warm working relationship – even if it hadn't *quite* rid her of her occasional violent urges: "His heart was in the right place," the actress wrote in her autobiography. "But I could have throttled him sometimes."[26] In fact, it was probably only the thought of him doing that ridiculous boss-eyed thing that stopped her.

As filming continued on his swansong, *Planet of the Spiders*, Sladen sensed Pertwee now had serious regrets about his decision to give up the role. As a consequence of the recent shake-up in recording patterns, the actor ended up filming his "death scene" on one of the story's first studio days. Having completed his part in what the script refers to, for the first time, as a "regeneration", Pertwee apparently got up off the floor and walked out of the studio without saying a word.

As originally envisaged, the story would have revealed the Doctor and the Master to be two parts of the same person (the Id and the Ego – and it says something about the nature of this particular Doctor that the crazed, megalomaniacal supervillain *wouldn't* have been the Ego), with the Master eventually sacrificing himself to save the Doctor. Though human tragedy put paid to that, the Doctor's ego still takes a hammering in the broadcast story, as he is forced to atone for his sins (arrogance and – one presumes – excessive use of bad karate) and confront his darkest demons, even though he knows it will result in his death. "I had to face my fear," he tells Sarah at the end. "That was more important than just going on."

If that sounds a bit out of character – for this Doctor above all others – it's because, as producer, director and co-writer (with Robert Sloman again), Barry Letts had finally decided to indulge himself, as opposed to just his leading man. And, as we know, Letts was drawn to somewhat higher concerns than how fast he could make a souped-up jalopy go down the A40: "At that time I was obsessed by Buddhism, especially Zen Buddhism," he admitted, "so I was very keen we should get it into the show in some way."[27]

As well as the face-off between the Doctor's Id and Ego, "in some way" included an appearance by the Time Lord's childhood hermit friend – first referenced in *The Time Monster* – now rejuvenated into a wise Buddhist monk. "The whole show is absolutely riddled, if that's the word, with Buddhist theology and philosophy,"[27] said Terrance Dicks. Letts would probably have thought it *wasn't* the word, but we take his point.

Not that *Doctor Who* was suddenly operating entirely on an astral plane: this was Jon Pertwee's final story, after all, so when Letts asked if he had any last requests, he shouldn't have been too surprised to find himself at the Earl's Court Boat Show checking out a mini-hovercraft his star had got excited about.

"All through the season, we'd been promising Jon the use of autogyros, speedboats and other fast modes of transport in the programme," said Letts, "and I suddenly realised that we were getting perilously near the end of the season, and the promise had not been kept."[31]

His solution to this little man-management problem was to devote more than half an episode of *Planet of the Spiders* to an extended chase involving Bessie, the Whomobile – which could now fly, natch – a gyrocopter, a hovercraft, a police car and a speedboat. At one point, the hovercraft drives right over the top of a tramp, who reacts with a comedy double-take: with its combination of pointless gadgetry and amusing local yokel, this is perhaps the definitive Pertwee-era scene.

And just when BBC licence payers were starting to wonder if a gold watch or a carriage clock might not have been a cheaper retirement present, the entire sequence is rendered utterly pointless when, after 12 long minutes of high speed, low thrills pursuit, the villain the Doctor is chasing is magically teleported to safety by his spider paymasters. If they'd done that in the first place, it would have saved everyone a lot of time and effort; we can only assume the spiders had chipped in for Pertwee's leaving present, too.

About those spiders: according to the plot, the giant arachnids of Metebelis 3 – the blue planet that had so spectacularly failed to live up to the brochure in *The Green Death* – were originally transported there from Earth by human settlers. Having now grown very large and very aggressive, they are planning to return to their homeworld as rulers. But the Great One – the mummy of all spiders, roughly the size of an aircraft hangar (or just slightly smaller than Jon Pertwee's towering silver "do") – has even bigger ambitions: she wants to use the power of the blue crystal that the Doctor nicked on his last visit to rule the entire universe. (I know – get her.) The Doctor, incidentally, had given this stolen crystal to Jo as a wedding present – plainly ignoring everything on the gift list at John Lewis – but she sends it back at the start of this story, along with a note saying she and Cliff are still up the Amazon looking for their fungus. Weirdly, that's not even a euphemism.

The visual effects team had originally designed a spider which Letts deemed too convincing – he probably didn't want it showing up the rest of the cast – so a less terrifying version (nicknamed Boris by the fx team) was made. Though the props themselves are pretty good, the problem with the spiders is they can't really *do* anything – they just stand there, rooted to the spot, quivering a bit and shouting in excitable voices. (The Queen Spider was voiced by Roger Delgado's widow, Kismet; because Delgado had died in an unlicensed cab, there were serious issues surrounding his life insurance payout, so Letts arranged for Kismet to get an Equity card in order for her to earn some money to tide her over. He was like that, was Barry.)

The production is also dogged by some truly appalling CSO – Letts remaining a cheerleader for the still shaky technology to the end – so we can only marvel out how bad the sequence they cut after deciding it was unfit for broadcast must have looked.

Static spiders and dodgy bluescreen work aren't the least convincing things about the story, though: that honour has to go to Jenny Laird who, as Metebelis colonist Leska, is widely regarded to give Doctor Who's all-time worst performance, delivering the line "No I shan't... you shan't take him. Sabor, my husband, my love, why did you do it, why? I shan't let you take him, I shan't, I shan't" with the distracted air of a woman contemplating a new shade of blue for her hallway carpet. Bizarrely, there is a Jenny Laird Prize for acting given out at RADA each year – though it's possible it's meant ironically, I suppose.

You'll be pleased to know that the former Captain Mike Yates gets a chance to redeem himself here – which is fair enough because, apart from that "attempting to wipe out the entire human race" incident, he had an unblemished military record. According to Richard Franklin, plans to kill his character off were scrapped after the production team realised there'd be "a national outcry". Or a couple of letters to the Radio Times, anyway.

And so, having faced his fears – manifested in the form of a very big, slightly wobbly spider – on Saturday, August 8th, 1974, the third Doctor, his body wasted by radiation, stumbled out of the TARDIS, collapsed to the floor, and died.

For a generation of viewers who had never known any other Doctor, this was quite the most heartbreaking thing they'd ever seen. But no sooner had the Time Lord breathed his final words – "A tear, Sarah Jane? Don't cry. While there's life, there's... hope" – than he was reborn as a new man, and a new journey, perhaps the most extraordinary journey of all, was about to begin.

The man Who

Jon Pertwee went straight from Doctor Who to a part in the West End farce The Bedwinner. That summer, he also took over from Edward Woodward as host of the ITV panel show Whodunnit? – he'd previously impressed as a panellist, so wasn't just employed because it made for a good gag – while continuing to record episodes of The Navy Lark. He remained in both these jobs for several years and then, in 1979, took on the role many consider he was born to play: Worzel Gummidge. Based on the novels by Barbara Euphan Todd, and adapted for television by Keith Waterhouse and Willis Hall, it starred Pertwee as a walking, talking and, let's be honest, tiny bit terrifying scarecrow with a different head for every occasion. Hugely popular in its day, it ran for four seasons until Southern TV lost its franchise; a late 80s revival, Worzel Gummidge Down Under, saw the show relocated to New Zealand for two further series, until being cancelled by Channel 4 boss Michael Grade. Keep reading to find out why this is significant. Despite his success as Worzel – and there's no doubt the role came to define him as much as Doctor Who – Pertwee claimed to have spent the rest of his career struggling to shake off the Time Lord, stating as late as 1992 that "as far as one's career is concerned, Doctor Who is death".[29]

Despite – or perhaps because of – this, he remained an energetic, larger-than-life presence at Doctor Who conventions and events and, as we'll see, returned to the role several times over the years. (He also had an attic full of "borrowed" props to remind him of his time on the show – mostly things he'd brought home to give to his son; on one memorable occasion, he'd given a prop to young Sean that they hadn't actually finished using, and had had to buy it back off him.) In 1974, though, it's difficult to know who was the most upset by his departure from Doctor Who: the fans, or the Doctor himself.

The following year, the Season Eleven production team's efforts were rewarded when Doctor Who was presented with an award for Best Children's Drama Script by the Writer's Guild of Great Britain. (Somewhat gallingly for Terrance Dicks and Barry Letts, the names on the citation were Robert Holmes, Malcolm

Hulke, Terry Nation, Brian Hayles and Robert Sloman. You can bet Nation insisted on keeping it at his house.)

But their ultimate legacy would be far longer lived. Perhaps more than anyone else in the show's history, we owe the team of Letts, Dicks and Pertwee a huge debt for taking a programme that many considered had had its day – and was teetering permanently on the brink of cancellation – and turning it into such a reliably popular favourite, its place in BBC1's Saturday night schedule had quickly started to look like a birthright.

And while it's easy to mock certain aspects of Jon Pertwee's character, it's clear the people who worked with him held him in huge affection. It's also clear that, for all his showbiz excesses – the peacock clothes, the tall stories, the ridiculous gadgets, the insatiable need to be the centre of everyone's attention – he was a warm, generous performer who delighted in taking entire casts under his voluminous cloak (whether they wanted him to or not). What's more, he cared deeply, *passionately* about *Doctor Who*.

Lis Sladen recalled one incident that seemed to crystallise her co-star's often misunderstood attitude: during location filming for *Planet of the Spiders*, Pertwee was sitting in a corset (for his bad back) and curlers (after getting his hair wet) when a journalist from the local press arrived early for an interview. "Send him over," said Pertwee cheerfully, without so much as batting an eyelid.

"People who say Jon was vain really didn't get it," said Sladen. "The truth is, his vanity was all for the programme: he wanted his Doctor to look a certain way and he was very protective of that. Behind the scenes, or off-duty, he was as laid-back as anyone."[26]

Most people who had the privilege of working on the show in the early 1970s tell a similar story: for Jon Pertwee, *Doctor Who* mattered more than anything else in the world – even Jon Pertwee.

4 The Rocky Horror Show

"Dear Sir or Madam, I am writing to ask if you have any vacancies for a Doctor Who on your staff"

If Jon Pertwee was fond of tall stories, the man chosen as his successor *is* a tall story.

At the time, appointing a builder's labourer who'd sent a begging letter to the BBC might have seemed a perverse way of casting one of the biggest roles on TV. But it quickly became clear that the man they'd chosen was – perhaps above all others – born to be Doctor Who: eccentric, unpredictable, funny, mercurial, unknowable, alien... the only role Tom Baker has never convincingly been able to play is an ordinary human being.

Born in Liverpool in 1934, Baker was raised in extreme poverty, largely by his mother Mary Jane, a cleaner and barmaid, while his sailor father Stewart was away at sea. During the war, their compact family home sheltered up to 14 people (many more, if you counted the cockroaches). According to his 1997 autobiography, as dementedly brilliant a showbiz memoir as you will ever read – sample quote: "I shall never forget the expression on my father's face as with scolded balls he tried to find the budgie in the coal scuttle" – they were so poor that Baker used to fantasise about his mother being killed by a German bomb, so that her orphan child might be lifted out of the Liverpool slums to a better life. Or at least a slightly nicer slum.

Though his father was Jewish, Baker was raised as a strict Roman Catholic and, at 17, entered a monastery on Jersey. He spent six years there – praying silently, banned from talking to or even looking at his fellow apprentice monks – before a crisis of faith led to him being expelled for questioning the monastic vows of poverty, chastity and obedience. Especially the chastity.

He struggled to adjust in the outside world, and found forming relationships with women especially difficult – hardly surprising when you've just spent half a decade in a place where one man's allotted role was to bite your dick if you got an erection. (The monastery, I mean, not Jersey.)

While doing his national service with the Royal Army Medical Corps, Baker took up acting and, after being demobbed, went to study at the Rose Bruford College of Speech and Drama in Kent. It was there he met Anna Wheatcroft, a well-to-do girl from the famous Wheatcroft rose-growing dynasty: the couple married in 1960 and had two sons, Daniel and Piers – but Anna's sadistic parents, Alfred and Constance, made no secret of their contempt for the working class boy from Liverpool, and dedicated much of their energies to making their son-in-law's life a living hell. When Alfred suffered a stroke, Baker was forced to nurse his tormentor around the clock – a situation that drove him into a deep depression, including a failed suicide attempt when he swallowed 24 of his father-in-law's anti-depressants. "I felt completely isolated and alone," Baker told the *Daily Mail* in 1997. "I couldn't bear to look at my wife because she looked like her mother. And finally I couldn't look at my own children because they reminded me of their mother."[1]

After Alfred's death, Baker worked in the family's rose-beds until, one day, he heard Constance being so monstrous to some fellow workers that something in him snapped and, in a murderous rage, he began throwing garden hoes at her (forget delicate English roses – at Wheatcrofts it was bitches and hoes all the way). If his marriage to Anna had already been in crisis, trying to kill her mother can hardly have helped the situation, so Baker fled, leaving his wife and his children behind. "I don't know if I had a nervous breakdown," he recalled. "But I thought my children were possessed by them, the Wheatcrofts. I don't even think I said goodbye to them."[1]

After a spell working as a driver in Coventry, Baker went to London to try his luck as an actor. He managed to impress Laurence Olivier enough to be invited to join his National

Theatre Company and, in 1972, Lord O recommended him for the role of the Mad Monk Rasputin in the film *Nicholas and Alexandra*. (If your grasp of the fall of Russia's Romanov dynasty is shaky, suffice to say the situation is pithily summed up in Boney M's insightful socio-political analysis of the situation, and its inescapable conclusion that "it was a shame how he carried on".)

The following year, he was cast in Pier Paolo Pasolini's film of *The Canterbury Tales* – a fact *Doctor Who* fans often cite with some pride, despite not knowing who the hell Pier Paolo Pasolini is. (Wikipedia describes him as a "journalist, philosopher, linguist, novelist, playwright, filmmaker, newspaper columnist, actor, painter and political figure" – but he didn't like to boast.) In 1974, Baker appeared as the evil magician Koura in stop-motion legend Ray Harryhausen's *The Golden Voyage of Sinbad* (and *everybody* knows who Ray Harryhausen is – even if his poetry did leave something to be desired).

Despite these successes, work was sporadic and, even as Baker was fighting Sinbad on cinema screens across the world, the 40-year-old was living in a one-room flat in Pimlico, and working as a drill operator and hod carrier on a building site in Ebury Street.

On the evening of February 3rd, 1974, Baker wrote a letter to Bill Slater, who had directed him in a television play a couple of years earlier, and had just been made Head of Drama Serials at the BBC. At the same time, Barry Letts was having a spot of difficulty finding a replacement for Jon Pertwee in *Doctor Who*. His first choice had been our old friend Ron Moody, who continued to live up to his name by turning it down again. David Warner similarly felt the part beneath him – which is saying something from someone whose most recent credit was a man called Dennis Nipple. Pertwee's former Carry On co-star Jim Dale was tempted, but was tied up for the next year, while Richard Hearne – the man behind TV's slapstick geriatric Mr Pastry – got his wires crossed and thought they wanted to hire Pastry for the role, even though he didn't exist. (Letts had initially envisaged the new Doctor being older and less of an action man – possibly to cut down on annoying requests to include ridiculous vehicles in the show – hence

approaching Hearne, who was 71 when he died four years later; Bernard Cribbins, who was also interviewed, withdrew his application after learning the type of Doctor they were envisaging meant he'd probably get to do more stunts voicing *The Wombles*.)

Former Goon Michael Bentine was interested, but insisted on major script input which, for a generation raised on *Michael Bentine's Potty Time*, certainly conjures an interesting mental picture. Scottish actor Graham Crowden was also briefly in the frame, but admitted he'd probably want to return to the theatre after a year (unusual, as television actors usually only claim that theatre is their first love when they can't get any telly work). Favourite for the part, though, was another Scot, Fulton Mackay – but he ended up going to prison instead. (*Space Helmet*'s laywers have asked us to point out this is a reference to Mackay's role in the much-loved comedy *Porridge*, in which he played flinty prison warden Mr Mackay. He also played a lawyer called Mackay in the Morecambe and Wise film *Night Train to Murder*; if they'd changed the name of *Doctor Who* to *Doctor Mackay*, he'd probably have been in like a shot.)

Bill Slater was still considering Letts' shortlist – and it really was a short list by this stage – when, getting into bed at night, he spotted Baker's unopened letter. He read it aloud to his wife Mary – he had a way with pillow talk, the old devil – and they both agreed he'd be a good choice to play Doctor Who. Even though it was nearly midnight, Slater phoned Baker – tossing on his mattress three-and-a-half miles away in Pimlico – and invited him for a meeting at 6.30 the following evening.

The next day, having been tipped off by Slater, Letts and Terrance Dicks went along to the Victoria Cinema to watch Baker in action in *The Golden Voyage of Sinbad*. ("Are you sure you wouldn't prefer the Pasolini?" asked Slater. "No thanks," said Letts, "I've already had lunch.")

When Baker arrived at Television Centre that evening, he was ushered into a room with Slater, Head of Drama Shaun Sutton and Barry Letts. After about an hour of convivial chat, Slater told Baker they "had an idea", and invited him to come back the next day. Baker agreed, and went home none the wiser.

After another shift on the building site, Baker took himself back up to White City, where Barry Letts popped the question: "Tom," he said. "We'd like you to be the next Doctor Who. What do you think?"

Baker thought it was the best idea he'd ever heard, and accepted on the spot – though he did have a big building job on, so probably couldn't get to them until Tuesday week at the earliest.

Charged with keeping his appointment a secret, the actor returned to Ebury Street; just over a week later, he was given the day off to go to the BBC, telling his colleagues it was about "that little job" he'd been in to see them about. In fact, the "little job" was for his official unveiling as the fourth Doctor before the gentlemen of the press; posing in the BBC bar with Lis Sladen and a Cyberman (who was quite annoyed, as he'd only popped in for a quiet drink), Baker was delighted to see a photographer from *The Evening Standard* – the paper that was always read by his friends on the building site. The next day, he astounded them all by turning up for work as normal, and putting in the best part of a day's shift, before everyone knocked off early to help celebrate his good fortune. The following morning, a man from the *Daily Express* arrived to take pictures of the new Doctor Who and his soon-to-be former colleagues. "That lunchtime," said Baker, "I shook hands and swore eternal friendship with everyone and, full of tears and good resolution, I tottered off. I never saw them again. I was Doctor Who now. I was an alien."[2]

Is Begonia Pope a Catholic?

In the days that followed his appointment, Baker admitted he was "bursting" with his "promotion from general labourer to Time Lord".[2] Then came a "ghastly" lunch where his new bosses wanted to discuss how he might actually play the part. "I was so daunted," he admitted. "I thought, 'Jon has been doing this for five years. To everyone, he *is* the Doctor'. He was well known before he did the series, whereas I wasn't known by anybody. I think it was a brave decision for them to make but, at the time, I really didn't know how I was going to approach it, or whether I could follow Jon's act".[3]

If he was hoping the scripts might provide a clue... there weren't any. A four-part storyline set on a space station – the imaginatively titled *Space Station* – had been commissioned from a writer called Christopher Langley, and Terrance Dicks had secured himself a commission by citing the tradition of the outgoing script editor writing the new Doctor's debut – a tradition he had, in fact, just invented. But that was it. To help provide some continuity for viewers, it had been agreed the season opener would be a UNIT story – a *King Kong* homage in which the new Doctor would help the Brigadier and company tackle a giant robot. It would also introduce a new companion in the form of Harry Sullivan, a Naval surgeon on attachment – surgically attached, if you will – to UNIT. The character had originally been devised for handling the action sequences if, as intended, an older actor had been cast in the lead; when the relatively sprightly Baker was cast, Harry was re-tooled to handle the important Being Terribly English in a Smart Blazer duties instead.

Another new boy was incoming producer Philip Hinchliffe. A former script editor at Associated Television, Hinchcliffe had been set to earn his production stripes on an adaptation of Muriel Spark's *The Girls of Slender Means*, but, when that fell foul of industrial action, he moved straight on to *Doctor Who* instead. By the time he began trailing Letts in mid-March, the new season was beginning to take shape, with Robert Holmes commissioning a story about the Loch Ness Monster from his former colleague Robert Banks Stewart, and Terry Nation agreeing to deliver his annual Dalek story, which Letts had suggested should be about the creatures' creation. Nation had originally suggested something less innovative, until Letts pointed out he'd sold them that script several times already. ("No no no," said Nation. "That was about a space plague, set in a jungle. This one's about a star virus, set in a rainforest. It's *completely* different.")

The Doctor's new look was also coming together: inspired by two posters of the nineteenth-century French cabaret singer and comedian Aristide Bruant by Henri Toulouse-Latrec, costume designer James Acheson accessorised this season's Time Lord with a battered fedora and a long scarf. A *very* long scarf, as it turned out: according to legend, Acheson had a mountain of wool delivered to a lady called Begonia Pope, who misunderstood the instruction and worked the whole lot into a multicoloured muffler in excess of 12 feet long. According to Baker, "she was so impressed to be working with the BBC that she knitted up all the wool – and, because the wool was on the taxpayer, a whole lorry-load was delivered. When we went to her little house, we could only talk through the letterbox because we couldn't get in – the scarf filled the hall."[4]

If this seems an unlikely scenario, it's probably worth pausing at this juncture to consider, if you will, The Gospel According to Tom Baker. Because, if Jon Pertwee had a reputation for embroidering stories to sharpen the punchline, Tom Baker has practised a lifelong aversion to anything as crushingly dull and predictable as a mere anecdote; instead, he favours a kind of freewheeling, stream-of-conscious monologue peppered with quixotic asides, conversational blind alleys and an arsenal of reliably familiar themes and motifs – often involving God, sex and grannies, though rarely, thank goodness, at the same time – apparently designed to obscure and obfuscate the boring old facts as much as possible. When Baker opens his mouth, he seeks neither to inform nor enlighten, merely to amuse.

She really was called Begonia Pope, though.

In late April, less than a month after his fleeting appearance in studio to film the regeneration, Baker recorded his first proper scenes at the BBC's Wood Norton training centre in Evesham – the very location where Jon Pertwee had made his debut five years earlier. Whereas *Spearhead from Space* had broken new ground by being shot entirely on film, the exterior scenes on what was now called *Robot* were recorded on outside broadcast videotape in order to facilitate the extensive CSO work director Chris Barry knew would be necessary to turn the titular tin tyrant into a giant of Kong proportions.

With *Planet of the Spiders* being taped in London, Lis Sladen found herself working on two serials – with two separate Doctors – at the same time. Arriving on set in Evesham, she was relieved to find Baker a more relaxed and

unobtrusive presence than his predecessor. "I don't have to walk over and doff my cap with this one," she realised. "I don't have to pay my respects."[5] As it happened, the new leading man wasn't quite as relaxed as he seemed: for all his larger than life persona, Baker actually suffered badly with nerves, and would be seized by terrible stomach cramps shortly before the recording of each scene. (And you thought all those squelching sounds were added by the Radiophonic Workshop.)

With *Space Station* now delivered, former story editor Gerry Davis was commissioned to write a story re-using the same sets. Davis submitted a draft script called *Revenge of the Cybermen*, set aboard a casino in space (Cybermen have impeccable poker faces). This prompted a firm letter from Robert Holmes, who wrote: "We all feel much the same way – that you have written it only for children. It's too straightforward (particularly the characterisation). The audience these days is sixty per cent adult and so we need a level of interest behind the 'front' action... *Doctor Who* has probably changed considerably since your connection with it and, these days, we find our audience is ready to accept quite sophisticated concepts." What, even more sophisticated than a robot King Kong?

As he settled into his new role, Philip Hinchcliffe was increasingly dissatisfied with the cards he had been dealt for the upcoming season; he felt Letts and Holmes had played it "too safe", and wanted to inject a change of direction sooner rather than later.

As rehearsals for *Robot*'s studio sessions got under way, Baker struck up an easy friendship with Lis Sladen and Ian Marter, the 39-year-old former stage manager of the Bristol Old Vic who, as Harry Sullivan, was getting a second bite at the *Doctor Who* cherry, having previously been forced to turn down the part of Mike Yates. He also bonded with Nick Courtney over their shared love of a liquid lunch, and their firm belief these shouldn't necessarily be confined to lunchtimes.

"At the end of most rehearsals, Tom made a simple gesture in my direction, of pouring a drink down his throat," recalled Courtney. "Often we would move on to other watering holes. My wife and I were going through a rough patch, so staying out late with Tom was

space helmet for a cow

more agreeable than going straight home."[7] After one particularly heavy session, Courtney invited his new drinking buddy back to his house where, in the morning, his children ran into the bathroom to be confronted by the sight of a wet, glistening Baker emerging naked from the bath. Most children find it difficult coming to terms with a new Doctor Who when he's fully clothed, so you could hardly have blamed Courtney's kids if they'd chosen to watch ITV on Saturday nights from now on.

On May 21st, Baker's first day in the studio was written off by a scene shifter's strike (could it *be* any more 1974?). When they did finally start recording, they had to work around a stepladder that had been left in the middle of the set, which no-one had the authority to move. (That stepladder appears so often, it's probably still receiving repeat fees. Also, because the *Doctor Who* scenery couldn't be struck, that week's *Blue Peter* ended up being presented from the set of *Robot*. Let's hope none of the pets left a little gift behind, otherwise they'd have been filming around it for weeks.)

With time rapidly running out, there was one scene left that could only be completed by moving a chair – which would have caused the rest of the crew to down tools immediately. In the end, an exasperated Lis Sladen feigned a coughing fit and fell theatrically back onto the chair, which miraculously ended up on its mark. It's good to know those years at drama school weren't wasted.

Back at HQ, Robert Holmes commissioned a two-part story – the first since 1965's *The Rescue* – from Bob Baker and Dave Martin, to be made entirely as an outside broadcast as part of the same production block as *Space Station*. He also received a pitch from a young writer called Douglas Adams, about an ark in space full of wealthy but ultimately useless humans. The idea was rejected, possibly because they already had a story about a space station – albeit not a very good one. In fact, it had now become clear that Langley's story just wasn't working, so he was paid off and, in his place, Holmes commissioned a four-part serial from 60s scripter John Lucarotti called *The Ark in Space*. There has never been any suggestion this was in any way nicked from Douglas

Adams' idea – I guess arks in space were just all the rage in 1974.

After shooting wrapped on *Robot* on June 7th – the day before Jon Pertwee took his on-screen bow – Baker went into rehearsals for a TV adaptation of Henry James' *The Author of Beltraffio*. The actor didn't think much of the production, but was rather more taken with a fellow cast member, Marianne Ford; by now, Baker had long overcome his monastic shyness with the opposite sex and, according to those who knew him at the time, was considered curiously attractive – in a gangly, toothy, pop-eyed sort of a way – by women, and it wasn't long before Ford moved him into her house in Notting Hill Gate.

Sadly, the only banging going on in the *Doctor Who* office was Robert Holmes' head against the wall, as Robert Banks Stewart's Loch Ness script, which had been inked in to close the twelfth season, ran into choppy waters, and John Lucarotti's *Ark in Space* turned out to be way off the mark – a problem compounded by the scripts' late arrival, as Lucarotti had posted them from his boat off Corsica. During a postal strike. Holmes had no choice but to set to work rewriting them from scratch, shortly followed by similarly drastic emergency surgery on *Revenge of the Cybermen*. If Baker had asked him, he'd probably have had a crack at the Henry James, too.

Even as he disappeared behind a mountain of balled-up paper, Holmes also had half an eye on the future. He and Philip Hinchcliffe had quickly established a solid rapport, and both men were keen to push *Doctor Who* in a darker, more adult direction. "What I tried to do with Bob Holmes was to create a sort of power within the stories, which was a mixture of good acting and well written parts and create a very strong sense of atmosphere through the lighting and the sets and the scripts and the direction," said Hinchcliffe. "And create a very strong sense of place – I spent a lot of time thinking about how we can create a convincing world that our story takes place in."[6]

In a bid to inject more atmosphere into the programme, the producer deliberately shied away from using light entertainment lighting designers in favour of those who could create "mood". He also challenged the set designers to raise their game. "The set design was almost paramount, because it creates the atmosphere – it creates the world of the story. If the lighting's too high or you just don't believe the sets, it just won't be compelling."[6]

Hinchcliffe saw his relationship with his script editor as "a marriage of youth and experience". "Bob also wanted to take the show a bit in his direction, which was a bit more towards the macabre, and black humour."[6]

The pair were emboldened in their approach by research showing that 56% of *Doctor Who*'s audience was now aged 16 or above, and that the show had an increasingly loyal following among university students. And this was the 1970s, don't forget – before students started only liking things ironically, and before most universities replaced boring stuff like physics and maths with media studies, so you couldn't get extra marks just for watching telly.

Sex lives of the potato men

When production on Season Twelve resumed in September, cast and crew boarded the bus to Dartmoor to record Bob Baker and Dave Martin's *The Sontaran Experiment*. Lugging the heavy, studio-style outside broadcast cameras across the remote, rugged moorland proved a challenge – especially as they were all umbilically attached by cables running back to a vision mixing desk rigged up in a van. It was also perishingly cold, and the plumbing at the hotel was so ancient, there was only enough hot water for one bath per night. "I came home shivering and almost cried when I ran an ice-cold bath the first night," Lis Sladen recalled. "The second night I was cleverer. As soon as the closing scenes for the day were set up, my dresser offered to scoot back and hit the hot tap. What a treasure! She dived in first, which was fair, then I leapt in as soon as I made it back."[5] (Her dresser thought she could at least have waited for her to get out first, but didn't like to make a fuss.)

After a couple of days, the team moved to the exposed, craggy outcrop of Hound Tor to film the climactic fight sequence between the Doctor and the eponymous Sontaran, Field Marshal Styre. In a bid to give the scene as much authenticity as possible, Tom Baker declined the offer of Terry Walsh as a stand-in

– and promptly broke his collarbone. As their leading man was shipped off to hospital, everyone assumed the shoot would have to be abandoned – but Baker was back on set the next day, his neck brace handily hidden beneath that huge, stripey scarf. Begonia Pope had saved the day.

The decision to bring back the Sontarans was largely financial: as long as Kevin Lindsay was available, they wouldn't need to make a new costume. As it turned out, Lindsay *was* available but, unfortunately, wasn't in the best of health, so a new, more lightweight costume was made to ease his discomfort – which ended up costing more than the actor's fee. The new head didn't bear much resemblance to Linx – and he appeared to have two extra fingers on each hand; for any other monster, this wouldn't really have been a problem, but the Sontarans were meant to be a clone race (which must have been a nightmare at parties: "Oh hello, how lovely so see you again. Linx, isn't it? No? Terribly sorry – my mistake. I say, isn't that old Linxy over there?").

Bob Baker and Dave Martin were happy to incorporate Holmes' creation in their script – but perhaps didn't need *quite* as much backstory as he gave them. "Bob Holmes was the greatest script editor of all time – a genuine weirdo, but very helpful, and a good writer," said Martin. "He couldn't stop thinking about *Doctor Who*. He used to invent sex lives for his creatures! It never made it into the script, but he knew them inside out. The Sontarans had sex through the backs of their necks."[8] This might sound impractical, but actually makes a great deal of sense if your wife has got the exact same face as you – and, indeed, your brother, your boss and your great Aunt Violet. Hence the most popular position in the Sontaran Kama Sutra being the 96.

By now, both producer and star were starting to get more of a handle on how they saw the new Doctor developing. Hinchcliffe, in particular, was keen to make the character more aloof, unpredictable and... well, alien, and advised Baker to play it with "Olympian detachment".

According to Rodney Bennett, the director assigned to *The Sontaran Experiment* and *The Ark in Space*, Baker was already starting to riff on the character, looking for ways to develop his Doctor beyond the words on the page. "Tom was a very instinctive actor, as opposed to a thoughtful one," he said. "Occasionally, he would do something really wild, and look at me, expecting me to say it wasn't right. In those cases, there's always a boring person called a director who says, 'Sorry Tom, I really think you ought to pull back a bit!'."[9]

"Naturalism isn't my strong point," conceded Baker. "I'm not even good at coming through doors convincingly. But never mind – even if you can't come through a door convincingly, perhaps you can come through a door interestingly or, dare one say, amusingly."[10]

The actor could already count one fan in Lis Sladen: "Tom hit his stride far quicker than I did," she admitted. "He walked into the Doctor's role and I think even he was surprised at how well it fitted him. He never had to reach for it – it's the part he was born to play."[5] And his door work was just masterful.

But Sladen almost didn't live to see her co-star in action on screen: no sooner had she arrived on-set for *Revenge of the Cybermen* in the sprawling underground Wookey Hole caves in Somerset, than a suspicious local pointed at stalagmite resembling an old crone and declared, "The Witch doesn't like you – she doesn't want you here." Shortly afterwards, she and Ian Marter confided they were both having trouble memorising the same scene in their scripts – no matter how hard they stared at it, it just didn't make any sense. Later, it became apparent there was no such scene – and neither actor could find any trace of it in their scripts. (Insert your own *Twilight Zone* music here...)

Things got a bit weird for director Michael Briant, too: granted access to an after-hours recce, he was down in the caves at midnight when a man walked past, whistling and carrying an air tank. But no-one but Briant ever emerged from the caves that night – and he later discovered a diver had drowned down there five years earlier. As filming continued, crew members started falling ill, and an electrician fell and broke his leg and had to be stretchered out. It was all too much for the assistant floor manager, who had to be replaced after having what Briant described as a "nervous breakdown" and refusing to go back into the caves because of the "things".

And then, on November 20th, Sladen was shooting a scene in which she had to ride a small boat – actually more like a motorised surfboard – across a river running through the cave system. But the current was so fast, it started sweeping her downriver instead – directly towards an underground waterfall. "Ahead, all I could see was darkness," she recalled. "The sound, booming around that black cavern, was louder than in the cable car over Niagara Falls... I truly thought, *This is it. It's over.*"[5]

At the last minute, she managed to throw herself onto a rock emerging from the water in front of her, before Terry Walsh – in full frogman's outfit – dived in and pulled her to safety. The boat vanished into the blackness, and was never seen again.

By the end of the shoot, many were convinced the Witch of Wookey Hole was doing everything in her power to wreck the production. Perhaps she was just a Pertwee fan who was having trouble letting go.

While viewers waited to see what the new Doctor would be like, a couple of alternative models popped up to fill the gap. In London, Trevor Martin – who had played one of the Time Lords in *The War Games* – essayed an alternative fourth Doctor (dressed, somewhat confusingly, like William Hartnell) in snappily-titled stage play *Doctor Who and the Daleks in The Seven Keys to Doomsday* at the Adelphi Theatre. Accompanied by new companions Jimmy and Jenny (the latter played, with extreme canon-bothering implications, by Wendy Padbury), the Doctor had to prevent the Daleks and their crab-like slaves the Clawrantulas – yes, really – finding the seven crystals of Karn which would enable them to control the universe. Perhaps we should give scripter Terrance Dicks the benefit of the doubt and assume it was intended as a loving tribute to the work of Terry Nation. Poor box office takings forced the play to close after less than a month, and a planned transfer to Blackpool was scrapped. Trevor Martin continued to work regularly but, for the Daleks, it was back to waiting tables and trying to persuade sceptical directors to give them a crack at a Pinter.

Meanwhile, on Christmas Eve, the third Doctor was back in action – with leggy *Top of* the *Pops* hoofers Pan's People as his companions, the sly old dog – helping Aladdin escape from the Daleks in the *Crackerjack* Christmas panto. In the absence of the real thing, Terry Walsh donned the Pertwee bouffant one last time, giving viewers the chance to get a good, long look at the Time Lord's stunt double. So no change there then.

Then, on Saturday, December 28th, 1974, Britain finally got the chance to see the new-look *Doctor Who* for themselves. Except they didn't, because *Robot* is so clearly the last gasp of the old regime, it's a surprise there's no cameo for Katy Manning's knickers. The story of a peaceful robot re-programmed to steal nuclear codes, it's everything you'd expect from a UNIT caper, save for the disappointing omission of a country bumpkin with a comedy West Country accent. Oh, my mistake – it's got Benton in it.

The robot itself is a typically brilliant piece of design work from James Acheson. Unfortunately, the creature's transformation into a towering giant is one of the most unfortunately realised sequences in the programme's history. You could say there's something almost nobly appropriate about Barry Letts bowing out on a hopelessly over-ambitious CSO sequence – but by the time the robot picks up a Sarah Jane doll (think Barbie accessorised with a frumpy blue frock) and *an actual Action Man tank* rolls into shot, it starts to look like a bit like *Toy Story*, 20 years before they had the technology to actually make it.

With the Doctor in a state of post-regenerative mania, Tom Baker hits the ground jabbering with a hyperactive performance, chopping bricks with his bare hands and tossing out non-sequiturs such as "If the sum of the hypotenuse is equal to the sum of the square on the other two sides, why is a mouse when it spins?" with machine gun velocity. He also gets to run riot in the dressing-up box, appearing as a Viking, the King of Hearts and a clown, before settling on his trademark scarf and floppy hat combo, and even manages a dig at his predecessor's nose.

Aside from marking Baker's debut, *Robot* is unique to the *Doctor Who* canon in having a main villain called Hilda – Patricia Maynard donning a pair of enormous Deirdre Barlow specs as a mad technocrat with designs on taking over the earth (Dicks' script takes a weirdly dim view of scientific progress). Her deputy, Arnold Jellicoe, was played by Alec Linstead – though Chris Barry's first choice had been his brother's flatmate, an actor called Colin Baker. In the event, Baker was unavailable, but perhaps that's just as well, or he might have ended up labouring in the shadow of his more imposing namesake. And I'm afraid I'm going to have to ask you to wait another 91 pages or so for the payoff to that joke.

Though *Robot*'s ratings were impressive (only the final episode dipped below the ten million mark), reaction to Baker's Doctor was mixed. According to the BBC's audience research report, "some considered the new personality too clownish" – though this may have been a veiled reference to the scene where he was *dressed as a clown* – "an eccentric (occasionally 'too stupid for words') or too unlike the previous Doctor... On the other hand, a small group seem to have been instantly attracted, or won over by the end of the episode. The acting and production in general were mostly considered competent." Hey, let's not get carried away here. The most insightful comment, though, was from a viewer who "liked that tin thing with the clippy hands". Clive James' TV reviews really had gone downhill lately.

If *Robot* was a tepid start to the new era, *The Ark in Space* telegraphed the new regime's MO in spectacular style, as the Doctor, Sarah and Harry arrive on a deserted space station where the frozen remains of humanity are sheltering from devastating solar flares – only to find a race of giant insects have been laying their larvae inside the hibernating bodies. I know – eeeuw. Clearly, this required a strong stomach for kids tucking into their Saturday tea – even if the humans' transformation into the arthropodic Wirrn *is* achieved with generous amounts of bubblewrap (hey, this was space-age stuff in 1975).

Despite being the third writer to take a pass at it, Robert Holmes gets sole credit for the story, in the process proving that a Bob Holmes script dashed out in a hurry is still preferable to 90% of more considered offerings by his peers. The first episode, in particular, is a tour de force of taut, economical scripting – a highly atmospheric three-hander featuring just the regular cast exploring the deathly quiet station. It is here we first start to see the measure of Baker's Doctor – never more so than when he delivers an impassioned soliloquy to the silent ranks of hibernating humans: "Homo sapiens! What an inventive, invincible species! It's only been a few million years since they crawled up out of the mud and learned to walk. Puny, defenceless bipeds. They've survived flood, famine and plague. They've survived cosmic wars and holocausts. And now, here they are, out among the stars, waiting to begin a new life. Ready to outsit eternity. They're indomitable."

Delivered in Baker's rich, velvet-dipped-in-chocolate tones, an already fine piece of writing is transformed into a spine-shivering manifesto for *Doctor Who*'s new, boundless frontier. Though traditionalists will be pleased to know not *everything* from the previous era has been abandoned, as Sarah Jane accidentally gives us a flash of her undies.

Wardrobe malfunctions aside, Lis Sladen is as reliable as ever, and Baker's dominance shouldn't be allowed to eclipse Ian Marter's contribution – he excels as the slightly bumbling Harry, who gets a telling-off from the Doctor for fiddling with his helmic regulator (quite right too – they've only just met). Though the quality of the regulars only serves to expose the stilted performances of the guest cast, most of whom do their best work while still in suspended animation.

Designer Roger Murray-Leach's stark white sets provide an effectively sterile contrast to the story's parasitic body-horror (a full four years before Ridley Scott would achieve similar results in *Alien*), while Barbara Kidd's costumes also reflect the pharmaceutical theme – and, indeed, the theme of people being terrorised by massive flares.

Averaging 11 million viewers across the serial, episode two of *The Ark in Space* was watched by a colossal 13.6 million people – a new personal best for *Doctor Who*, smashing the previous record set a decade earlier by the first instalment of *The Web Planet*. And it would have had even more, if Tom Baker hadn't refused to watch himself on screen; instead, he got Marianne Ford to watch the episodes for him. As their relationship was still in its early days, this probably guaranteed rea-sonably good reviews – a few years further down the line and she'd have told him he was putting on weight, his hair was a mess and would it kill him to smile once in a while? Her mother would be watching, you know.

Mary, Mary, sodding contrary

It was fast becoming clear that *Doctor Who*'s latest relaunch was a hit – but the BBC were taking no chances. When word reached them that ITV were planning to network Gerry Anderson's lavish new sci-fi series *Space: 1999* that autumn, the decision was taken to bring *Doctor Who*'s next series forward to head the newcomer off at the pass. That would mean holding the planned current season finale, *Loch Ness*, over until September – but also ploughing straight into production for the rest of the thirteenth season, without a summer break. An exhausted Lis Sladen, who'd been planning a holiday to Tangiers with her husband, seriously considered quitting, but in the end both she and Baker signed on for the new run. Sadly, there was no such offer on the table for Ian Marter – Philip Hinchcliffe had decided that, now there was no need for extra muscle aboard the TARDIS, Harry was something of a fifth wheel, so *Terror of the Zygons*, as *Loch Ness* had become, would see him written out. Both Marter's co-stars were upset, and Hinchcliffe himself later came to regret the decision but, for now, it was a done deal.

Also feeling unloved by the new producer was Keith Miller of the Doctor Who Fan Club, who found Hinchcliffe less willing to share production nuggets than his predecessor. Miller was also struggling to meet the costs of distributing the fan club magazine, but was cheered during a studio set visit to find Tom Baker extremely enthusiastic – so much so, he even paid for the mailing labels to be printed. Baker was thrilled by the reaction he was already receiving from fans and the general public – especially younger viewers; he took his responsibilities as a hero very seriously, travelling all over the country to make personal appearances at everything from hospitals to fetes. He also made sure children never saw him drinking or smoking – mainly by doing both to excess in Soho clubs and pubs where no children were allowed.

The Rocky Horror Show

Continuing the series' ratings high, *The Sontaran Experiment* is possibly the cheapest Earth invasion movie ever made, as there's only one invader – and no-one left on the planet to be invaded.

Field Major Styre of the G3 Military Assessment Survey has come to Dartmoor – actually central London (probably), but they've let the grass grow a bit – to conduct a series of experiments on humans in advance of a planned full-scale incursion. But as there isn't actually anyone left there (most of them are on the Ark, waiting for solar flares to go out of fashion), he's reduced to using a crew of human colonists from the planet Galsec – who only came back to Earth in the first place to find out what he's up to. Add in the fact his experiments don't amount to much more than "if you kill people, they die", and you have to wonder how he got the funding in the first place. Possibly it came from the same person who put up the money for the videophone Styre uses to report back to his superiors. ("Do you think a clone race really *needs* video? Couldn't we just stick a picture on it? Or a mirror?")

The first 15 minutes or so unfolds largely without music which, combined with the videotape footage of all the lovely scenery, makes you half suspect Bill Oddie is about to pop up and introduce a family of nesting thrushes. It's not long before we're back on more familiar *Doctor Who* territory, though, as a monster with a wobbly head fights Terry Walsh in a dodgy wig.

Baker and Martin's script revisits some of the colonial themes of *The Mutants*, which is why all the Galsec colonists (including Glyn Jones, the writer of 1965's *The Space Museum*) have South African accents. But it all just feels a bit flimsy and inconsequential: a perfectly serviceable runaround that's as short and direct as its villain. (Kevin Lindsay sadly died from heart failure, aged just 51, seven months after recording the story. Though his swansong isn't anywhere near as strong as *The Time Warrior*, it's to Lindsay's credit that, even today, the Sontarans remain one of *Doctor Who's* Premier League monsters – and that we know how to pronounce their name properly.)

Back in the twentieth century, Robert Holmes was probably wondering if there

wasn't a way of cloning *himself*, as he sat down to fix yet another broken script. The previous summer, Holmes had commissioned a story from another former ATV colleague, Lewis Greifer, intended for Baker's sophomore season. Mixing Egyptology with astrophysics and robotics, *Pyramids of Mars* was the first example of what would become the defining trope of Holmes and Hinchliffe's tenure on the show: taking the "seed of ideas"[6] from a ragbag of genre fiction, and giving them a unique *Doctor Who* twist. "It seemed to be there was a poverty of genuine science fiction within the series – I mean of the literary kind," said Hinchliffe. "We had a deliberate plan to raid the whole genre of science fiction in all its manifestations, from sword and sorcery to the Gothic strain, but avoiding the earthbound setting of a present-day Doctor fighting an invasion from space."[11] In effect, the two men were rejecting the twentieth-century American tradition of "pulp" sci-fi in favour of a nineteenth-century British literary sensibility, where Frankenstein and Arthur Conan Doyle were more of a lodestone than Frank Herbert and Arthur C Clarke.

One of the problems with Greifer's script was that, ironically, he had researched his theme rather too well: authenticity was all very well – up to a point. "Egyptology, to our audience, means stone coffins, mysterious and eerie happenings and, above all, giant mummies wrapped in decaying bandages stalking through the studio fog," Holmes wrote in a letter to Greifer. "If this is their expectation, I think they are going to feel cheated when it isn't fulfilled."

Above all else, it was the "Gothic strain" cited by Hinchliffe that would go on to define this era of *Doctor Who* – for good and ill. "People do talk about the horror influence in my period as producer," he said. "The old sort of Hollywood horror – the Hammer Horror side of it – came from Bob, because he liked the humour and the darkness and the sort of sardonic side of it. Perhaps I let him get away with things he hadn't been able to get away with before. But he always wrapped them up in such intriguing stories."[6]

It is simply impossible to underestimate the contribution made by Robert Holmes to this period of *Doctor Who*: Hinchliffe actively encouraged his script editor to write his own stories, and makes no bones about the fact the best serials of his tenure were "either written by Bob Holmes from scratch, or page one rewrites".[6]

And so it was that, in early 1975, Holmes found himself sitting down to do his latest "page one rewrite" on *Pyramids of Mars*, junking Greifer's contemporary UNIT setting in favour of a period story set in 1911.

Holmes' fingerprints are all over the next televised story, *Genesis of the Daleks*, too. Unless there's another explanation as to why Terry Nation's six-parter – which has regularly been voted among the greatest *Doctor Who* stories of all time – should be so utterly unrecognisable from his previous efforts. Journeying back to Skaro at the time of the Daleks' creation, the Doctor, Sarah and Harry find themselves in a post-holocaust no-man's land filled with trenches, irradiated mutants and soldiers in gas masks being gunned down by machine gun fire. No wonder Mary Whitehouse – the Midlands housewife-turned-self-appointed guardian of the nation's Christian moral values, whose National Viewers and Listeners' Association pressure group campaigned against violence, profanity, sex, homosexuality, blasphemy and anything else that sounded like fun – nearly choked on her crucifix, claiming "*Doctor Who* has turned into teatime brutality for tots". There was solid support for the show, though, in the form of a rebuttal from Shaun Sutton, who claimed that, far from being terrifying, the charm of *Doctor Who* lay in the fact it was "tatty" and "repetitive". (Maybe a bit less solid support in the future wouldn't go amiss.)

On top of the violence, *Genesis* is at pains to make the Nazi parallels – always implicit from the Daleks' very first appearance 12 years earlier – very much *explicit*: most of the action takes place in a bunker, where a crippled, genocidal scientist called Davros is given to launching into Führer-style rants at his jackbooted henchmen. Peter Miles, as the Himmler-like security chief Nyder, even sneaked an Iron Cross onto his tunic for some scenes until director David Maloney told him to take it off. Imagine *Downfall* crossed with *Threads* and you'll have some idea just what a laugh-riot it is.

As Davros – the half-man, half-Dalek creator of what at this stage he's still calling a "Mark III Travel Machine" – Michael Wisher is electric: the actor had just finished filming *Revenge of the Cybermen* when he was hurriedly cast as a late replacement for the original actor earmarked for the role. Whoever that was, we owe him a debt of thanks, as Wisher totally makes the part his own – never more so than during two extraordinary speeches in which he contemplates the nature of power versus responsibility. Wisher was cast as Richard III on the strength of his performance, and it's not difficult to see why. John Friedlander's Davros mask is also one of the series' great pieces of design work – combined with Wisher's acting chops, the character is so instantly memorable, you barely notice that the Daleks are hardly in the story.

Davros doesn't get all the Shakespearean soliloquies, though: Tom Baker is simply brilliant in the scene where he questions his right to avert the Daleks' creation, claiming that some good must surely come from the Daleks (well, they'd helped keep *Doctor Who* on the air for all these years, for starters).

Genesis of the Daleks is far from perfect, though. At times, it really labours to fill its running time, with an awful lot of capture-escape padding, and a truly hilarious cameo by a killer clam. For something so highly regarded, the story's central premise is also one of the most ridiculous ever: basically, we're asked to believe in a thousand year war of attrition between two cities several hundred feet apart, into which enemy combatants can stroll in and out seemingly at will – even Davros, and he's not really the strolling type. For the modern viewer, it's also hard to watch a uniformed Guy Siner, as Ravon, without thinking of Lieutenant Gruber, the Nazi who put the camp in aid-de-camp in '*Allo 'Allo*.

But, for all its faults, this is a powerful, mythic reinvention of the Daleks, with Robert Holmes inspiring Terry Nation to his best work in years. With its muted pallete of greys and blacks, and its prologue and coda lovingly ripped from Bergman's *The Seventh Seal*, this is *Doctor Who* with the kid gloves off. For a generation – particularly those who grew up with the abridged audio LP released a few years later – *Genesis of the Daleks* is as iconic as it gets.

March 1975 also saw the re-launch of the

Target book range, now owned by WH Allen, with the publication of *Doctor Who and the Giant Robot*, the first of five titles knocked out – sorry, lovingly crafted – by Terrance Dicks that year alone. Meanwhile, Weetabix issued a collectable card series called *Doctor Who and His Enemies*. "It's breakfast-time brutality for tots," protested Mary Whitehouse. Or she probably would have done, if she hadn't been busy petitioning the BBC to commission "independent research into the effect of *Doctor Who* on the under-fives". As *Doctor Who* was never intended to be watched by under-fives, it's difficult to see what recommendations such a report could have made, beyond: more responsible parenting?

Despite – or perhaps encouraged by – Mrs W's protestations, Hinchcliffe and Holmes pressed ahead with their Gothic new take on the show, commissioning a Frankenstein-inspired story called *The Brain of Morbius* from Terrance Dicks – he only had four Target books on the go, so should be free by the weekend – and a sci-fi spin on Dr Jekyll and Mr Hyde from Louis Marks. Not the toy manufacturer. Are we all clear on that by now?

Coming straight off the back of six weeks of Dalek action, *Revenge of the Cybermen* plunged the audience straight into the first colour adventure with the show's second most enduring enemies. "You're really spoiling us," said the viewers when they read the *Radio Times*. "You're really spoiling *us*," said the Cybermen, when they read the script. Because, even after its Robert Holmes re-spray, Gerry Davis' story isn't exactly the silver giants' finest hour. For a start, they've gone *very* camp: as the Cyberleader, Christopher Robbie spends so much time with his hands on his hips, he must have "The Time Warp" playing in his helmet. This is also the first time the Cyber actors use their own voices, as opposed to the vocoder-style electronic burr of the 60s. As Robbie's day job was as an in-vision continuity announcer on Southern Television, the effect was rather peculiar – as if the Cyberleader were constantly on the verge of breaking off from threatening the Doctor to introduce a round-up of the day's regional news.

It doesn't help that the Doctor can't stop taking the piss, complementing the Cybermen on their "nice sense of irony" and dismissing them

as nothing more than "a pathetic bunch of tin soldiers, skulking about the galaxy in an ancient spaceship". You may be picking up a slight hint by now that Robert Holmes didn't really like the Cybermen – though at least one put-down, when the Doctor scoffs at their use of the word "fragmentise", was an ad-lib by Tom Baker.

Set thousands of years before *The Ark in Space* – when the ark was still a navigational beacon – the plot revolves around the Cybes' attempt to fragmentise Voga, a small planet made entirely of gold. (Gold, it turns out, is lethal to Cybermen, which is one of the reasons they've never really got into hip-hop.) But the Vogans are preparing to strike back with their own missile – at least they *claim* it's their own missile: suspiciously, it has UNITED STATES written up the side in big letters. ("Our only interest is in bringing stability to the region," said a Pentagon spokesman. "It has nothing whatsoever to do with all the gold.")

The chief Vogans are played by three of *Who's* finest supporting players – Kevin Stoney (*The Daleks' Master Plan / The Invasion*) as Tyrum, David Collings (making the first of three memorable appearances) as Vorus, and Michael Wisher (this was the gig that won him Davros) as Magrik. Unfortunately, Collings' mask serves to slightly muffle his voice, so that all his conversations with Wisher appear to be addressed to "Margaret". ("Of course, it's a big plan, but it will work – you and I together, Margaret, will make it work!") And the fact Margaret... sorry, Magrik, is permanently clutching a snotty hankie hardly helps. Maybe she's... I mean he's allergic to the planet of bling, too.

Despite its flaws, *Revenge of the Cybermen* delivered another impressive audience, cementing the fourth Doctor's first season as one of the strongest performing since the first wave of Dalekmania a decade earlier.

Tom Baker, it was clear, was a hit with everyone from children to students to grannies. And women – he was quite a hit with them, too. "The attention that came with the success of the programme brought temptation after temptation from curious girls who were enthusiastic to lay a Time Lord," Baker admitted (or possibly boasted, it's hard to tell). "It had very little to do with me. How could it? They were strangers. But I didn't spot it. I thought that I was genuinely irresistible and gave in to most of the time travellers."[2]

And yes, before you ask, more than one of them did insist on wearing the scarf. If Begonia Pope had known there was going to be any of that sort of carry on, she'd have used an itchier wool.

You take the (Bognor) high road

Summer may have been cancelled, but the three stars of *Doctor Who* did get a day out in Marlow as guests of honour at the town's annual fayre. Okay, so it's not quite Tangiers – but they did get as many goes on the hook-a-duck as they wanted. The trio also popped up on various TV shows during the short gap between seasons – including a rare appearance on The Other Side (what non-UK folks would call ITV) as part of slapstick Saturday morning foam-fest *Tiswas*.

For anyone who didn't grow up in Britain in the 70s – or lived in an area too posh for the local ITV station to broadcast it – *Tiswas* was basically *Swap Shop*'s naughty kid brother, where the juvenile audience was locked in cages and everyone spent the whole morning having plates full of shaving foam shoved in their faces by a miscreant calling himself the Phantom Flan Flinger. Hosted from Birmingham by Chris Tarrant and foxy first-crush magnet Sally James, it proved an early showcase for the likes of Lenny Henry, Jasper Carrott and someone calling himself Sylveste McCoy – a Scottish cabaret performer whose act included shoving ferrets down his trousers and banging six-inch nails up his nose. During a Q&A, one young audience member asked Baker how he'd got the job, and was no doubt incredulous to learn he'd been working on a building site at the time. At this rate, they'd be asking the ferret guy to be Doctor Who!

Not long afterwards, Baker returned to Birmingham to record a guest spot on Terry Wogan's Radio 4 show *Wogan's World* during a break in filming on the Louis Marks story, now called *Planet of Evil*. ("Let me get this straight – are you suggesting *a whole planet* could be possessed by a terrifying and malevolent force?" "Don't be silly – *Wogan's World* is just a name.")

Also that summer, Baker could be seen, in character, presenting the BBC's *Disney Time* clips show, the Doctor having apparently taken time out from saving the universe to watch cartoons in a London cinema. Meanwhile, the Daleks made an appearance on new kids' show *Jim'll Fix It*, in which posthumously disgraced medallion man Jimmy Savile made viewers' wildest dreams come true (so long as their wildest dreams were within BBC budget) from the comfort of his computer-controlled "magic chair". The item was met with a stiff letter from Terry Nation's ever-litigious agent, Roger Hancock (brother of Nation's erstwhile muse, Tony), who wrote: "Dear Jim, please could you fix it for my client to receive appropriate remuneration for unauthorised use of his intellectual property." On the plus side, at least they didn't use Davros – just as well, as one creepy, wizened old man in an electric chair was more than enough for anyone.

Shortly afterwards, Hancock refused Spike Milligan permission to use the Daleks in a skit for his *Q6* sketch show. Milligan went ahead and recorded it anyway. Later, the comedian wrote to Nation, reminding him that, 20 years earlier, he had been happy to accept a £10 charitable cheque from Milligan and his colleagues at Associated London Scripts. Hancock subsequently agreed Milligan could use the Daleks for free, as a "personal favour" from Nation. Which would be a lovely story, if the actual sketch – in which a Pakistani Dalek exterminates his family and puts them in a curry – wasn't so appallingly racist.

In late August, Tom Baker and Lis Sladen were finally allowed three weeks' holiday. There was no such luck for Robert Holmes, though: when financial constraints forced a rethink of *The Brain of Morbius*, and with Terrance Dicks off the radar on holiday, the script editor had no choice but to sit down and start unpicking his predecessor's work. Bob Baker and Dave Martin's latest, *The Hand of Fear*, was also causing headaches – so when Holmes was offered the chance to write the pilot for a new radio sci-fi drama called *Aliens in the Blood*, there was simply no way he could possibly find the time. Naturally, he said yes.

Bringing the curtain up on *Doctor Who*'s

thirteenth season on August 30th, *Terror of the Zygons* – formerly Loch Ness – is a tartan riot of kilts, haggis, ginger beards, bagpipes and superstitious inn-keepers called Angus. It could barely be more Scottish if they'd filmed it in Scotland (instead of near Bognor Regis). That the Zygons managed to achieve iconic status with just one appearance in *Doctor Who*'s original run is largely down to the brilliant design work by – who else? – James Acheson and John Friedlander; taking their cue from the script's depiction of the aliens as aquatic mammals who live on lactic fluid, the duo realised the creatures as giant barnacled embryos, somewhere between a human foetus and a seahorse. Nessie herself – actually a Zygon-controlled cyborg creature – is, it's fair to say, a less successful creation. But then, any *Doctor Who* story that requires the Loch Ness Monster to swim up the Thames and terrorise central London is clearly on a hiding to nothing: had they learned nothing from *Invasion of the Dinosaurs*?

The plot – which had eventually emerged from numerous rewrites – is a bit fuzzy around the edges, too (look out for the bit where Sarah accidentally stumbles on the library book that triggers the entrance to a secret passageway – because the person trying to keep it hidden has helpfully just lent her a stepladder). But it would take more than some wonky logic and a dodgy CSO monster to derail a story this rich in mood and atmosphere (beautifully directed by Dougie Camfield, who had been tempted out of retirement for a late Highland fling). The sock puppet Nessie gives it a bloody good go, though.

The Doctor himself – rather brilliantly described by Angus as "a man who might see around a few corners" – is here at his most brittle and remote, snapping at the Brigadier and barely acknowledging poor old Benton's existence. Though no-one realised it at the time, this really was the last gasp of the UNIT era – there's even a world energy conference, just for old times' sake – and this particular Doctor wasn't about to get sentimental about it.

The relationship between the Brig and his former scientific adviser was distinctly cooler off-screen, too. "On the whole, I found Tom much less easy to work with than he had been

previously," said Nick Courtney. "He was less congenial, and hyper-sensitive to criticism. I think he was off on his own plane, and the rest of us had to scramble to keep up with him." According to Courtney, "the tension turned ugly only once", when Baker was handed some uncomplimentary notes and lashed out: "He'd had the part for a year and didn't take kindly to being treated like an incompetent neophyte."[7] Well, who does?

Terror of the Zygons also marked the end of poor old Harry Sullivan's travels – though Ian Marter donned the blazer again when the *Doctor Who* gang switched on the world famous Blackpool illuminations in early September. Determined to use her short break to finally make it to Tangiers, Lis Sladen had initially refused to go to Blackpool – until some sneaky sod from BBC Enterprises' Emotional Blackmail Dept phoned her parents and invited them along for the weekend. The actual switch-on was to be achieved during a bit of business with the sonic screwdriver – prompting a last-minute panic when they realised they'd left it back at the hotel. Baker and company eventually lit up the Golden Mile in front of a crowd of 20,000, joining a prestigious roll call of switch-on celebrities that includes Jayne Mansfield, George Formby, Gracie Fields, Kermit the Frog and Red Rum (who had terrible trouble pressing the button – though, on the plus side, he only requested a very small rider).

Discussing criticism of the show in the press around this time, Baker revealed he had invited Mary Whitehouse out for lunch – something told him he wouldn't be needing the scarf for this one – but she had turned him down. Seems he wasn't as irresistible to women as he thought. Meanwhile, with *The Hand of Fear* still giving Holmes and Hinchcliffe the finger – metaphorically speaking – the producer asked Bill Slater if they could lose a couple of episodes from the next series; Slater refused, so Hinchcliffe hastily commissioned a back-up script about killer plants from Robert Banks Stewart.

After a tentative start in its late summer timeslot, the second story of the new season saw the ratings gathering momentum, helped by ITV's inability to get its act together and properly network *Space: 1999*. (How Lis Sladen laughed when she realised she could have spent the summer in Morocco after all.) Set on the edge of the known universe (but filmed more locally, including a stunning alien jungle set constructed by Roger Murray-Leach on a sound stage at Ealing), *Planet of Evil* follows the misfortunes of a human scientific expedition being menaced by a creature made of pure antimatter energy. Borrowing liberally from *Forbidden Planet* – itself nicked from *The Tempest* – as well as *Doctor Jekyll and Mr Hyde*, it's genuinely terrifying at times, the claustrophobic set and lighting helping disguise the lack of a real, coherent threat (as a monster, the anti-matter creature may have lacked substance – I thank you – but still managed to scare the screaming bejaysus out of a generation of children).

Louis Marks' script is serviceable at best, with drab characters spouting drab dialogue. Drably. And, as we've come to expect from this show, the so-called "science" is all over the shop – the story is set on a world where the matter and anti-matter universes "overlap", apparently, and chief boffin Sorenson develops a vaccine that turns him into Anti-Man (as in man made of anti-matter – he doesn't become a radical feminist). Despite this little setback, Sorenson still has more about him than ship's commander Salamar, thanks to a sopping wet performance from – oh hello – *Space: 1999*'s Prentis Hancock.

Like its predecessor, this story is more than the sum of its parts, thanks largely to Philip Hinchcliffe's decision to put more emphasis on areas like design and lighting: it's notable that, once the action moves from Murray-Leach's breathtaking alien jungle into a standard-issue boring spaceship, interest wanes rapidly.

Closer to home, two students at Westfield College, London – Stephen Payne and Jan Vincent Rudzki – formed a new organisation called the Doctor Who Appreciation Society; it was like the Doctor Who Fan Club, but with considerably more syllables. Its creation was perfectly timed, as rarely has there been more to appreciate in a *Doctor Who* story than that month's *Pyramids of Mars*. Writing under the pseudonym Stephen Harris, Robert Holmes takes the germ of Lewis Greifer's original idea and fashions perhaps the ultimate expression of this era's synthesis of science fiction and Gothic romance: "Egyptians mummies building rockets?" says an incredulous Sarah. "But that's crazy!" Crazy, but brilliant. This being *Doctor Who*, of course, they're not really mummies – they're service robots wrapped in bandages. And the story's Big Bad, Sutekh the Destroyer, Last of the Osirians, may look like your average jackal-headed Egyptian God, but is actually a powerful – if paralysed – alien holed up in a pyramid, waiting for his robot mummy slaves to fire their rocket at another pyramid – on Mars, keep up – thus destroying the signal holding him prisoner and freeing him to ravage the universe. Luckily for Sutekh, his captors saw fit – for reasons best known to themselves – to bury a load of rocket components alongside him. ("What do you *mean* the parts are still in the pyramid? No, don't bother going back for them – we've put all the stones back now. Just leave it, I'm sure it will be fine.")

In other words, it's another totally nutzoid plot carried off with such style that you barely notice. As Sutekh, Gabriel Woolf is utterly chilling, barely raising his voice above a whisper as he issues apocalyptic threats from his tomb such as "Where I tread, I leave nothing but dust and darkness. I find that good." It's just a pity that, when he does finally break free of his bonds and rises triumphantly to his feet, the viewer is somewhat distracted by the hand of a stage tech that appears around the back of the throne to stop his cushion falling off. (Nice of his jailers to give him something comfy to sit on for eternity. They really did think of everything.)

Holmes' eminently quotable script is also the perfect showcase for Baker's increasingly otherworldly Time Lord. "I'm not a human being," he tells Sarah. "I walk in eternity." Later, Sarah is sickened by the casual way the Doctor rolls a dead body away from him (the story is notable in that barely a single guest character survives), forcing him to explain that he hasn't got time to worry about one dead man when the whole of civilisation is at stake – a lovely grace note, beautifully played by Baker and Sladen. There are also flashes of Holmes' wickedly black sense of humour: "Deactivating a generator loop without the correct key is like repairing a watch with a hammer and chisel," says the Doctor. "One false move and you'll never tell the time again."

Appropriately, most of the serial was filmed at Stargroves Manor in Hampshire – the former home of the Fifth Earl or Carnarvon, who had famously discovered the tomb of Tutankhamun along with Howard Carter. By the time *Pyramids* was made, though, the house was the country retreat of Mick Jagger – but, apart from the 12 naked blondes in the bedroom, the Rolls in the swimming pool and the roadies passed out on the pool table, it had barley changed since the Earl's day.[1] The scenes in the Manor's grounds, with the Doctor and Sarah being pursued through woodland by the mummified robots, are infused with such an atmosphere of clammy tension, things can't help but take a handbrake turn for the worse in the final reel, when most of the action moves to Mars (i.e. into the studio) and the Doctor is reduced to solving logic puzzles in a blatant re-tread of *Death to the Daleks*. By then, though, *Pyramids of Mars* has already done enough to qualify as one of *Doctor Who*'s all-time greats, keeping almost 11 million viewers hooked across four weeks. The story can also claim a more interesting afterlife than most of its contemporaries as, 25 years later, scenes from the serial were intercut with the strongest gay sex ever seen on British television as part of Russell T Davies' drama *Queer as Folk*. Which was a shame, as Mrs Whitehouse had been really enjoying the programme until that point.

Sorry for the bland Robin

With the best part of two seasons under his belt, Tom Baker felt increasingly confident of his handle on the character, and the programme. As such, he grew progressively more vocal about how he thought the show should be made – and progressively more scornful when it fell short of his expectations. It didn't help that many of his script suggestions bordered on the fanciful – that's being polite – to say the least: during rehearsals for *Revenge of the Cybermen*, he had tried to persuade Robert Holmes to add a scene in which the Cybes ask the Doctor and Sarah to teach them how to dance like Fred Astaire and Ginger Rogers. According to Baker, Bob Holmes laughed and

"filled his pipe so that he could create a smoke-screen between us while he turned the idea down. I didn't really mind. Most of my ideas were rejected, and I got used to it. One can get used to almost anything – even rejection."[2]

Finding he was getting nowhere with his TV bosses, Baker roped Ian Marter into helping him write a script for a putative Doctor Who feature film. With Philip Hinchcliffe's approval, the pair, plus director James Hill, were granted an 18-month option on the movie rights to the franchise, as no-one called these things back then.

If Baker and Marter wanted a masterclass on how to write *Doctor Who*, they only had to tune in to BBC1 on Saturday evenings from late November – and then make sure they kept their eyes firmly shut and their fingers in their ears. Because, even by Terry Nation's less-than-rigorous standards, *The Android Invasion* is an unholy mess.

For a start, it's supposed to be a mystery story, building up to the shocking revelation that – gasp – all the human characters are really... androids! A pity, then, that no-one could be bothered to come up with a more enigmatic title: thank God that Terry Nation didn't write *The Sixth Sense*, otherwise it would probably have been called *Bruce Willis is Actually Dead*.

The plot, if you can call it that, involves a bunch of rhino-headed aliens called the Kraals recreating an entire English village on their own planet, for reasons no-one ever bothers to explain (maybe they're just big fans of *The Archers*). Later, they decide to blow it up, for similarly unfathomable reasons (maybe they're big fans of *Emmerdale*, too).

Another major plot beat is built around the moment Milton Johns, as British astronaut Guy Crayford, removes his eyepatch and discovers the Kraals have been lying to him because he does, in fact, have two perfectly good eyes, suggesting he has *never* taken his eyepatch off before. Let's hope he changes his underpants more often.

Any shred of credibility the story may have had left is shattered when, after three episodes of running about dodging androids, the Doctor suddenly whips out his "robot detector" (a box with a red light on it). For all we know, he's got a gaydar stashed away in the TARDIS, too.

Finally, the resolution to the whole shebang sees the Doctor using his android double to trick the Kraals, who can't defend themselves because all the android doubles have been, um, neutralised. ("Terry, I think this idea might need some wor... Oh forget it.")

Nation clearly thought he was still writing for a children's programme, so it's perhaps no surprise this would turn out to be one of his last contributions to *Doctor Who* (the fact that Holmes hated the Daleks was probably also a factor). *The Android Invasion* would also prove to be the final UNIT story for many years and sadly, they had to make do without Nick Courtney; according to the actor, the BBC flip-flopped so much over whether they wanted him or not, he ended up taking another job (a pity, as he loved a good eyepatch story). John Levene did return for a lap of honour as Benton, but it proved to be an unhappy experience: "By the time I got to that last story, I was very sad," Levene admitted. "Nick had gone, Pertwee had gone, Katy had gone, Roger was dead, and there I was, lonely Sergeant Benton. I found that a very hard story – sad, lonely and difficult."[12] And as if that wasn't bad enough, they'd taken his favourite pudding off the canteen menu.

The story also provides a wholly unsatisfactory coda for Ian Marter, here making a brief return as Harry Sullivan. "I didn't care for *The Android Invasion* one bit," said Marter. "There was no reason for Harry to be in it at all – I couldn't see the point of it. My last scene was particularly frustrating, as Harry just sort of fizzled out, tied up on the floor in the corner of a room."[13]

Barry Letts was also back on the payroll, and his direction – particularly during the atmospheric early scenes of the Doctor and Sarah exploring the eerily deserted village – almost manages to distract from the crunching plot gears. Almost, but not quite. After watching *The Android Invasion*, Carry On stalwart Kenneth Williams was moved to note in his diaries that "*Doctor Who* gets more and more silly". Coming from a man whose roles included Dr Kenneth Tinkle, Citizen Camambert, W.C. Boggs and The Khasi of Kalabar, that was really saying something.

In contrast to her co-star, Lis Sladen made a point of watching every episode of *Doctor Who*

as it went out. But when Douglas Camfield scheduled a weekend location shoot in Reigate – doubling, for obvious reasons, as Antarctica – for *The Seeds of Doom*, the actress was resigned to missing the third part of *The Android Invasion*. When she mentioned this to Tom Baker, he promptly stopped the coach in the middle of a suburban Surrey street, and marched a small party of cast and crew up to the nearest front door. "Hello, my dear," he beamed at the woman who answered. "I'm the Doctor and this is Sarah. We wondered if we might be able to watch ourselves on your television tonight?"

"Oh come in, Doctor!" replied the woman. And so they squeezed into her small living room and watched the entire episode, as the astonished homeowner looked from screen to sofa and back again. While no doubt wondering: "Is it always this shit?"

As the programme took a short Christmas break, Tom Baker told *The Guardian* he had turned down an offer to do panto because he didn't want to "rip off our *Doctor Who* audience". Also, his ad-libs would have been a nightmare. ("Have you seen my flying carpet, boys and girls? It's stiffer than an abbot's dick.") Instead, he appeared during Christmas week in an omnibus repeat of that feelgood festive fairytale, *Genesis of the Daleks*.

Doctor Who entered 1976 with our hero facing off against one of his own people – or what was left of him – in *The Brain of Morbius*. Executed by the Time Lords, arch criminal Morbius survives only as a brain in a jar – not ideal, but he kept telling himself some women cared more about brains than looks. In Terrance Dicks' original script, Morbius is patched back together by his faithful robot servant using body parts salvaged from the wreckage of crashed spaceships. In Holmes' rewrite, the robot is replaced by mad surgeon Mehendri Solon, who ends up trying to chop the Doctor's head off so he can stick it on top of the mishmash Frankenstein-style monster he's created in his lab. Dicks thought this was ludicrous, questioning why Solon wouldn't just put Morbius' brain straight into the Doctor instead, and asked for his name to be removed from the end product. "I was certainly miffed," he said. "It was the only time I'd ever been rewritten to that extent. Bob had actually gone too far."[14] When Holmes asked who he should credit it to, Dicks told him to come up with "some bland pseudonym" – so he couldn't help but smile when he saw the story credited to "Robin Bland". Especially as he still got to cash all of Robin's royalty cheques.

With its ruined castles, craggy outcrops and lightning storms (Barry Newbery only had a month to design and build the impressive sets for the studio-bound story), *The Brain of Morbius* is the most visually gothic story of *Doctor Who*'s most gothic period. It is also among its most violent, Holmes indulging his love of the Grand-Guignol to take the show into uncharted territory: when Solon shoots his manservant (that's not a euphemism – it's graphic, but it's not *that* graphic), blood geysers from his stomach like an early Tarantino movie. But that's nothing compared to the bit where Morbius' brain gets knocked over – and slops out of its case onto the floor with a wet slapping sound. One viewer wrote to complain that "*Doctor Who* has been changed in a nasty way because it's become more like a horror film that is shown at 11 o'clock at night"; this was Bob Holmes' idea of fan mail.

Some of the dialogue is pretty ripe, too: Solon calls said manservant "a chicken-brained biological disaster" – which is surely in breach of the Dignity at Work Act – while Morbius laments, rather brilliantly, that "even a sponge has more life than I" and rants about being "reduced to this... the condition where I envy a vegetable!" Vegetable envy is such an unbecoming trait. As Solon, Philip Madoc gives one of the programme's greatest guest performances – though, not to be outdone, Stuart Fell does some pretty good "hand acting", expressing all Morbius' impotent range with the only human body part on show.

At the climax, the Doctor defeats the Morbius creature in a mental battle of wills in which the combatants' thoughts are projected onto a video screen; as Morbius pushes the Doctor back into his own past, the faces of Jon Pertwee, Patrick Troughton and William Hartnell are followed by numerous members of the production team – including Hinchcliffe and Holmes, alongside director Chris Barry, production unit manager George Gallaccio, production assistant Graeme Harper, Douglas Camfield and Robert Banks Stewart – as what

appear to be earlier incarnations of the Doctor. This rather throws a grenade under established continuity, so it's since been decided the faces are either earlier incarnations of Morbius, younger versions of the Hartnell Doctor, or someone in the gallery just flashing up pictures of the *Doctor Who* office Christmas party by accident. None of which are *entirely* convincing – but if you think I'm going back and starting this book again, you've got another thing coming. (On the subject of continuity, the Doctor also gives his age in this story as 749, which indicates he's aged around 300 years since the Troughton era. No wonder Jon Pertwee's back was killing him.)

Doctor Who meets Scratchman, blames fleas

With Pertwee, Barry Letts, Terrance Dicks and the UNIT gang all gone, Elisabeth Sladen realised she was the last woman standing from the Who Class of 74 – and decided it was time to make her own excuses and leave. "I'd never been happier on *Doctor Who*," she admitted. "Tom was amazing, the show was reaching audience heights not seen since the 60s; there was a real buzz about it... But it was time to go."[5]

According to Sladen, Philip Hinchcliffe was surprised – shocked even – but didn't try to change her mind, beyond asking her to stay long enough to give her "a proper send-off". That particular job was to fall to Douglas Camfield, who Hinchcliffe had agreed to let write as well as direct a story about the Foreign Legion – *Beau Geste* with aliens, basically – which would climax with Sarah being shot, before dying in the Doctor's arms and being burned on a funeral pyre. If she'd been the paranoid type, Sladen might have thought they were trying to make sure she didn't come back.

Before that, though, there were several more adventures to be had – and few came more action-packed than Season Thirteen finale *The Seeds of Doom*. Banged out in less than a month, Robert Banks Stewart's six-parter spends the first third in the frozen Antarctic tundra – where a scientific expedition has hacked some alien seedpods out of the permafrost – before relocating to the English stately pile of Harrison Chase, an eccentric millionaire who has assembled the world's largest collection of plants, and will stop at nothing to get his hands on this prized new specimen. Unfortunately, the pod turns out to contain a "galactic weed" called a Krynoid, which infects everyone it touches by gradually turning them into a rampaging plant monster. Most people would find this inconvenient, at best, but Chase – who cherishes plant life over humanity – thinks it's all rather a hoot. Then again, what do you expect from a man who composes organ music for his flowerbeds, and tells the Doctor "I could play all day in my green cathedral". He's like a more homicidal version of Prince Charles.

In one sense, the story is perfectly in tune with this iteration of *Doctor Who*, its scenes of innocent victims slowly being transformed into writhing, tentacled mutants (actually a spray-painted Axon, fact fans) pushing the body horror factor even further than *The Brain of Morbius*. In others, though, it's like Banks Stewart has never even seen *Doctor Who*: our hero has never been more of an action man – even during the Pertwee era – running about with a gun and duffing up henchmen like James Bond. He even gets tied up and left to meet his fate in a giant composting machine. ("No, Mr Who, I expect you to fertilise the herbaceous borders.")

Or possibly John Steed is a more appropriate reference: there's a distinct *Avengers* vibe to the whole thing, from the theatrical villain to the fact the Doctor suddenly starts calling Sarah "Miss Smith". In one particularly dashing incident, Baker comes crashing through a skylight, flattens Chase's chief grunt Scorby, and rescues Sarah. "What do you do for an encore, Doctor?" asks Scorby. "I win," says our hero, flashing his trademark grin.

Okay, so it's not really *Doctor Who* – but it's still rather brilliant. Dougie Camfield – directing what would turn out to be his final *Who* – is the happiest kid in the sandbox choreographing all the shooting and fistiscuffs, the regulars have never been better and Tony Beckley (AKA *The Italian Job*'s Camp Freddie) and John Challis (later to gain immortality as Boycie, the used car salesman with the Gatling gun laugh in *Only Fools and Horses*) turn in two of the series' most delicious guest performances.

The story is only let down by its appalling cop-out ending, in which UNIT – minus any familiar faces – are clumsily reprised to join forces with the RAF and bomb the hell out of everything. Perhaps that's why Baker – who was becoming increasingly strident in his criticisms – proposed the script itself ought to be "composted". A few of his suggested ad-libs – such as when he tells the heavies "Get our hands up – that's right, grab us, we're very dangerous" – made the final cut, and the line about the Doctor having his toothbrush was a veiled reference to the fact Baker carried his everywhere. The old rascal.

It can't have helped the star's mood that filming was even more fraught than usual: rehearsal time was at a premium, and the later scripts arrived barely half-a-week before shooting began. On top of that, the serial was beset by bad luck: actor Michael McStay was involved in a car crash, and ended up playing his part with a false beard to cover his scars; half the cast went down with the flu; and Kenneth Gilbert, playing World Ecology Bureau chief Dunbar, decided to participate in that year's Bring Your Daughter's Chickenpox to Work scheme. Then, just prior to transmission of episode one, the BBC managed to lose the tape, and Hinchcliffe had to hastily edit it together again from the raw footage. Finally, the TARDIS prop that had been in constant service since 1963 took this opportunity to give up the ghost, and collapsed in protest on Baker and Sladen's heads.

On the plus side, they got to spend time filming in the grounds of the splendid Athelhampton House in Dorset. The house was owned by Tory MP Robert Cooke, and its annihilation by an RAF air strike was the second such disaster to befall it in a matter of weeks. At Christmas, it had been demolished by a giant Dougal – possibly as an act of class war – during *The Goodies'* Christmas special. The *Who* version, frankly, is less convincing.

The story's horrific transmutations prompted Mary Whitehouse to saddle up her high horse again, and the BBC received several letters of complaint. (Just wait until Mrs W and her Christian fellowship heard about the story that had just been commissioned from writer Chris Boucher under the in-no-way provocative title *The Day God Went Mad*.) But the programme received support from an unlikely source in a *Sunday Times* article titled "Doctor Who's Value: Morality and Integrity", in which Alan Thompson, Professor of Economics of Government at Herriott-Watt University, said the show set a fine example both to children and adults about not taking yourself too seriously, and concluded: "In Tom Baker, the BBC has the perfect Dr Who." Presumably the paper's TV critic was busy lecturing on Keynsian stimulus versus supply-side monetarism.

Hinchcliffe, for his part, insisted in a memo to Shaun Sutton that Whitehouse was "making a lot of fuss about nothing", and that it was parents' responsibility to make sure young children didn't watch anything unsuitable. ("Isn't that right, Shaun?" he added. "Shaun – I said isn't that right? Shaun? Hello?")

After shooting had wrapped on *The Seeds of Doom*, Tom Baker took advantage of his first proper break from *Doctor Who* to... work on his script for the Doctor Who movie. He and Ian Marter – accompanied by Marianne Ford, Ford's daughter Harriet and David Maloney's daughter Sophie – flew to Italy for a working holiday in a villa they had use of near Sienna. For a few days, they made good progress on their script for *Doctor Who Meets Scratchman* – in which the Doctor, Sarah and Harry would lock horns with the Devil himself, as well as an army of animated scarecrows, plus appearances by the Daleks and the Cybermen. It was envisaged the finale would take place on a giant pinball table. Yes, really.

Unfortunately, the old house was infested with fleas, which began enthusiastically feeding on the party – especially Marter, who was in agony. He tried to take his mind off it with work, but it didn't help when Baker kept talking about bloody Scratchman.

Then the holiday took an even worse turn while Baker was being given a swimming lesson in the villa's pool by the two young girls – and started drowning. To compound his distress, the actor could hear Marter insisting to the girls he was only acting – "and very badly, too" – which wounded his professional pride, even as he gasped for air. Eventually, the girls were convinced enough it was real to stage a rescue, after which Marter was able to thump a breath out of him. The following day,

the flea-bitten, half-drowned group decided to cut short their holiday, and flew home. "I've never been near deep water since," said Baker many years later, "and at home I only have showers."[2]

With Sladen working her notice, attention turned to her successor. Baker was petitioning to ditch the idea of a companion altogether and have the Doctor travel alone. And, while they were at it, perhaps they should consider changing the name from *Doctor Who* to *The Tom Baker Variety Half Hour*? Robert Holmes was keen to do a take on Jack the Ripper – because what could be more suitable for a teatime family fantasy serial than the real-life murder and disembowelling of prostitutes? – and suggested it could be used to introduce a Victorian Eliza Doolittle-type character. But Hinchcliffe's eye had been drawn to one of the minor characters in *The Day God Went Mad* – a savage female warrior called Leela – and he asked Chris Boucher to bump up the part with a view to her possibly becoming a regular.

Before starting work on the new series, Baker and Sladen lent their voices to a BBC Schools Radio programme, *Exploration Earth*, which used a 20-minute *Doctor Who* adventure as a framing device to tell the story of the planet's formation. ("Thanks for the script suggestions Tom, but I'm not sure there's much of a scientific consensus for the Earth having been fired out of a giant pinball machine.") Shortly afterwards, the pair recorded a less factually rigorous adventure about shark-like aliens invading the planet for an LP and cassette release called *Doctor Who and the Pescatons*, written by Troughton-era script regular Victor Pemberton.

On April 29th, the Doctor Who Appreciation Society (DWAS) hosted a gathering at Westfield College, with Terrance Dicks as special guest. Having taken over an existing fanzine called *TARDIS*, the society also began producing a monthly newsletter under the name *Celestial Toyroom*. Honestly, who in their right minds would think of naming their publication after an obscure detail from the Hartnell era after so many years?

A few days later, location filming began for *Doctor Who*'s fourteenth season: before signing up for a final eight episodes, Lis Sladen had heard a whisper they might be going to film in

Italy. Instead, she found herself boarding the bus for Portmeirion where, for reasons best known to himself, the architect Sir Clough William-Ellis had decided to built an entire Italian village on the North Welsh coast. (Perhaps it had started as part of an ambitious twinning scheme, in which the Italians promised to build a replica of Swansea on the shores of Lake Garda.) The village had previously been used as the location for *The Prisoner*, Patrick McGoohan's incomprehensible 60s counterculture thriller about identity and alienation and... all that stuff... but was being used by the *Doctor Who* crew to double for Renaissance Italy in Louis Marks' *The Masque of Mandragora*.

Sladen's imminent departure was announced to the world on May 13th, with the actress giving interviews to *Nationwide* and Radio 1's *Newsbeat*. Baker could also be heard on "the nation's favourite" that month, being interviewed by Dave Lee Travis – AKA The Hairy Cornflake (note to non-UK readers: ...actually, never mind) – on the Radio 1 Roadshow in Blackpool as part of the city's centenary celebrations. While he was there, he recorded an in-character (as the Doctor, that is – though all Tom Baker's appearances are, after a fashion, in character) appearance on TV end-of-the-pier variety showcase *Summertime Special*, this time chatting to another Radio 1 stalwart, Tony Blackburn. Whatever they were paying him, it wasn't enough.

As the cameras rolled on Sladen's final story – a new take on the troubled *Hand of Fear*, which had been revived to replace Dougie Camfield's clearly-not-going-to-happen Foreign Legion story – the rest of the season was taking shape. The Doctor was scheduled to fly solo for one adventure – a Gallifrey-set tale from Bob Holmes called *The Deadly Assassin* (other types of assassin are available, but they don't get much work), followed by Boucher's "God goes postal" story, plus a second serial from the same writer, provisionally – and, indeed, rubbishly – titled *Planet of the Robots*. Finally, Robert Banks Stewart had been commissioned to write the Jack the Ripper story, currently trading under the name *The Foe from the Future*.

Sladen taped Sarah's leaving scene during one of *The Hand of Fear*'s first recording blocks.

Initially, she'd been appalled at the off-hand – so to speak – way Bob Baker and Dave Martin had handled her departure, until she realised they'd sketched only a vague outline for someone else to shade in. And Holmes and Hinchcliffe insisted that job should fall to the two people who knew the characters best: Sladen and Baker. "Oh no, I couldn't possibly get involved in that side of things – I am but a humble player," is what Baker didn't say, whipping out the typewriter he kept in his pocket for emergencies.

Towards the end of her final day in the studio on Tuesday, July 20th, Sladen slipped over, and she and Baker got an attack of the giggles. Every subsequent take they tried to do, she slipped again, and the two of them became more and more hysterical. Director Lennie Mayne began to lose patience, while guest star Judith Paris – looking surprisingly sexy for a 150 million-year-old lump of rock – told them to get on with it so she could go for a fag. "But we couldn't help it," said Sladen. "It was quite uncontrollable. And, you know what? I'm glad we couldn't. If I have to remember anything of my time on *Who*, it would be just having a blast with Tom. Me and him, Doctor and companion – us against the universe."[5]

Change was in the air behind the scenes, too, with both Hinchcliffe and Holmes looking to leave at the end of the current season. Together, they pitched a new adult science fiction show called *Lituvin 40* to incoming Head of Serials Graeme McDonald. While he considered the idea, Holmes embarked on a rare holiday to Italy. Near Munich, however, his wife suffered a perforated stomach ulcer, forcing the family to remain in Germany for several weeks. By the time he got back to Britain, there was an apology from Robert Banks Stewart saying he'd got another job and couldn't write the season finale, while the producer of the *Aliens in the Blood* radio serial was spitting at least one of those things, forcing Holmes to hand over his outline for another writer to complete. Meanwhile, he sat down to bash out a new six-part story to conclude the current series. And somehow it was *his wife* who had the ulcer.

By now it had been decided that the character of Leela would continue for two more stories beyond *The Face of Evil* – the new, less inflammatory name for *The Day God Flipped His Lid* – and, in late August, former Royal Shakespeare Company actress Louise Jameson was booked to record 14 episodes between September and February. The same month saw the formation of a new fan club called the Friends of Tom Baker. Keep reading for why Louise Jameson was unlikely to become a member.

Talk to the hand

On Saturday, September 4th, *Doctor Who* returned to screens with the opening instalment of *The Masque of Mandragora*, in which a bundle of alien energy – accidentally carried to fifteenth-century Italy by the Doctor – tries to ruin the Rennaissance for everybody. Louis Marks was an obvious choice for this affectionate *Masque of the Red Death* pastiche, as he had previously lectured in Rennaissance history, and had written a postgraduate thesis called *The Development of the Institutions of Public Finance in Florence During the Last Sixty Years of the Republic c.1470-1539*. Which wasn't the snappiest title, but it was still better than *The Deadly Assassin*.

With extensive filming in Portmeirion, and costumes borrowed from the 1954 film of *Romeo and Juliet*, it's a sumptuous affair, the verisimilitude only slightly spoiled by some distinctly non-local accents: "I ain't goin' in there, Giovanni," grumbles one Cockney guard.

The story itself is a cri de coeur – or whatever the Italian equivalent is – for the valuing of science over superstition. It's a shame, then, that the science itself is a bit vague. But that's not really the point: it's not a science lesson, it's a history lesson about the importance of science. And rather handsome it is too.

The story also sees the introduction of a new "secondary" TARDIS control room. Sympatico with the literary influences of the era, Barry Newbery designed this smaller space with a distinctly Jules Verne-ish vibe, all polished brass and dark wood panelling. "I thought of a Victorian sailing ship, and tried to move the whole thing away from bright panels and flicking switches," explained Newbery.[15]

There was change of a less subtle stripe to be found in the pages of *TV Comic*, which was still religiously churning out Doctor Who adventure strips after more than a decade. The first issue of the rebranded title – from now on, it would be blowing its own trumpet as *Mighty TV Comic* – came with a free mini-issue featuring an old third Doctor strip in which Jon Pertwee's head had been crudely replaced with Tom Baker's. ("That's absolutely fine – I mean, the character is bigger than all of us, isn't he? There's no room for egos here," said Pertwee. Possibly.)

September 20th was a big day for Louise Jameson, as she made her debut on set at Ealing Film Studios as Leela. She'd already been shown her costume – a skimpy set of animal skins that left little to the imagination. Still, it could have been much worse – early test shots show they originally planned to black her up with bootpolish, which would have helped her set back the women's *and* race movements several decades at the same time.

"I remember that first day of filming on the jungle set," the actress recalled. "I hugged my dressing gown around me for as long as possible. I felt very naked, really, in that costume."[16] And was it her imagination, or were there more people than strictly necessary on that set? Surely the guys from TV Licensing didn't need to be there?

Still, at least she could count on her co-star's support. Right? In fact, Baker's behaviour towards Jameson was – by his own admission today – unforgivable. Sulking at not being allowed to go solo, his mood was worsened by the fact he thought the "noble savage" character was completely wrong for the show. "I remember being *appalled* at her aggression, without having the ammunition to put my side of the argument forward," he said. "There was a moral dimension, an ethical dilemma, because she *killed* things. I was furious at the beginning... Louise was very good, and hugely successful. But I was rattled by it."[17] Well, as long as it was a *moral* crusade – and not just Baker getting pissed off because everyone was now looking at the hot girl in the leather bikini.

However naked Jameson might have felt, she could take some comfort in Katy Manning choosing this particular moment to show solidarity by getting *all* her kit off and straddling that Dalek in *Girl Illustrated*. At the next meet-

space helmet for a cow

ing of the DWAS, members' eyes were out on stalks. ("Welcome to my world," said the Dalek. "Cor," they replied. "Is that an original 1973 refurbished gold casing from *Day of the Daleks*?" "I don't know – there's some stupid naked woman getting in the way.") Robert Holmes opened his postbag, meanwhile, to find Douglas Camfield's scripts for the appropriately titled *The Lost Legion* had finally arrived, less than a fortnight before its replacement began broadcasting.

Given its difficult birth – being bumped out of the schedules for *The Seeds of Doom*, before being bumped back in to replace Camfield's AWOL effort – it is perhaps no surprise *The Hand of Fear* is all fingers and thumbs at times. Loosely inspired by the 1924 Austrian expressionist film *The Hands of Orlac*, the story foregrounds Lis Sladen in her final fling by having Sarah possessed by the eponymous fossilised extremity, which uses the genetic code contained in its (frankly rather vulgar) ring to rebuild itself into Eldrad, the founder of the planet Kastria who was subsequently executed by his own people for war crimes. Eldrad's plan involves turning a nuclear reactor critical in an "un-explosion" (a bit like an implosion, but a bit more total bollocks). Luckily, the RAF are on hand to bomb the hell out of it (yes, again) allowing Bob Baker and Dave Martin to repeat their trick from *The Claws of Axos* of blowing up a nuclear power station and having our heroes shield themselves from the blast by driving down the road a bit and ducking down behind a jeep. I think it's fair to say Baker and Martin hadn't previously written a postdoctoral thesis on nuclear physics.

Eldrad is very much a villain of two halves: as played by Judith Paris, she's rattling good fun, but Stephen Thorne – who takes over as a sort of regenerated post-op version in episode four – simply rehashes his shouty shtick from *The Daemons* and *The Three Doctors*. "I quite liked her," says Sarah. "But I couldn't stand him." Well quite. Other memorable guest performances include Glyn Houston as a nuclear scientist who bids an emotional farewell to his wife on the phone, and a persistent studio fly that tries its best to ruin Houston's big moment, before being swallowed by Lis Sladen.

The 70s were a golden period for cool cars in action shows, and when *The Hand of Fear*

went out, British viewers were newly in thrall to Starsky and Hutch's iconic tomato-red Torino. Not to be outdone, the story features the Doctor racing to save the day in a... mustard yellow Austin Allegro, perhaps the most ironically-named vehicle in the sorry history of postwar British car manufacturing. He was lucky to get there before the end credits, frankly. The serial also introduces the concept of the TARDIS being in a state of "temporal grace", meaning no weapons can be used in anger within its confines – which might come in handy for Tom Baker if he kept winding up the new girl with the big knife.

The Hand of Fear, though, is all about saying goodbye to the *old* girl, and it has to be said that the leaving scene thrashed out by Baker and Sladen totally eclipses anything by Martin and the other Baker. "I must be mad," says Sarah, unsuccessfully trying to get the Doctor's attention as he tinkers with the TARDIS. "I'm sick of being cold and wet, and hypnotised left right and centre. I'm sick of being shot at, savaged by bug-eyed monsters, never knowing if I'm coming or going or been... I want a bath. I want my hair washed. I just want to feel human again." Getting no reaction, she stomps off to pack her bags – at the exact moment the Doctor receives a summons back to Gallifrey; a trip he must make alone.

The pair's final exchange still packs a punch, even after all these years. "Don't forget me," says Sarah. "Oh, Sarah. Don't you forget me." "Bye, Doctor. You know, travel *does* broaden the mind." "Yes. 'Till we meet again, Sarah." And then, after three years, two Doctors, 18 adventures and countless acts of bravery and heroism, she is gone, and a few million hearts are just that tiny bit more broken.

Obscene vegetable matters

On the Monday after Sarah Jane Smith's departure, Louise Jameson was revealed – in every sense of the word – to the gentlemen of the press at a photocall in the car park of Television Centre. ("Don't get the wrong idea – it won't always be this glamorous.")

By now, Hinchcliffe had been asked by Bill Slater to reconsider his decision to leave, and agreed to stay on for another season. Together with Holmes and his design team, the producer was already dreaming up ideas for future adventures – including stories inspired by H Rider Haggard and Joseph Conrad – when the BBC executed a sudden 180° turn, and decided he should go after all. During recording sessions for Chris Boucher's robots story, Hinchcliffe and Baker were stunned when a young former *Z-Cars* script editor was brought into the studio and introduced to them as Graham Williams – the new producer of *Doctor Who*.

Williams, who had been producing a programme called *The Zodiac Factor* until the American co-production money fell through, had been earmarked to launch *Target*, the Beeb's tough new response to ITV's hit cop show *The Sweeney*. But, almost certainly influenced by the thorn Mary Whitehouse was continuing to jab in their side, the Beeb's Sixth Floor decided a job swap might be in order, with Hinchcliffe more suited to the gritty, hard-hitting *Target* and Williams – a self-professed sci-fi fan – a natural fit for the TARDIS.

Maybe they'd already seen the edit of *The Deadly Assassin* – the longest resignation note in *Doctor Who* history. Transplanting *Manchurian Candidate*-style conspiracy theories (currently enjoying a new lease of life in the post-JFK era through films like 1974's political assassination thriller *The Parallax View*) to Gallifrey, Robert Holmes takes a gleeful pleasure in demolishing the reputation of the Time Lords, reducing them from immortal gods to squabbling monsters (a shady black ops outfit set up to interfere in other peoples and planets' business, against the official code of the Time Lords, is given the name Celestial Intervention Agency – see what he did there?). The Doctor is framed for the murder of the President, but the real culprit is eventually revealed to be none other than the Master, now reduced to a cadaverous nightmare of charred, rotting flesh, nearing the end of his final regeneration. Even he had to admit he'd looked better.

The concept of Time Lords having 13 lives is just one of the many significant additions to *Doctor Who* lore Holmes chucks in here: others include the Doctor's TARDIS being identified as an obsolete Type 40 model – it was so old, it didn't even have a CD player – a reference to "Artron energy" being the source of the Time

Lords' power, and the first mention of Rassilon, the founding father of Time Lord society.

The Deadly Assassin is certainly a game-changer – "Like it or not," says the Doctor, "Gallifrey's involved, and I'm afraid things will never be quite the same again" – and it caused uproar among fans at the time. Reviewing the story in *TARDIS* magazine, DWAS president Jan Vincent-Rudzki declared "as a *Doctor Who* story, *The Deadly Assassin* isn't even worth considering," before going on to consider it with such howls of anguish as: "Once, Time Lords were all-powerful, awe-inspiring beings, capable of imprisoning planets forever in force fields, defenders of truth and good (when called in). Now, they are petty, squabbling, feeble-minded, doddering old fools. WHAT HAS HAPPENED TO THE MAGIC OF DOCTOR WHO?" Fandom had well and truly arrived.

Bizarrely, it was contradictions to relatively minor continuity points that really upset the hardcore faithful, as opposed to the story's more obvious shortcomings. The stagey, studio-bound final episode, for example, is well below David Maloney's usual par, and only serves to highlight the utterly ludicrous plotting, like the fact the Great Key to unlock the dangerous black hole energy that powers Gallifrey is located a couple of yards away from the Great Keyhole in the middle of the Time Lords' main assembly chamber – and no-one's ever noticed it before.

It also appears that there are no women on Gallifrey – in fact there isn't a single woman in the whole story – so how the Time Lords ever get anything done is a mystery. Surely even Rassilon needed someone to say: "Are you going to harness the power of that black hole, or just sit on the sofa all day?"

But the real legacy of *The Deadly Assassin* wasn't to be its tinkering with continuity trivia, but Holmes and Hinchcliffe's bold – some may say stupid – attempt to see how far they could push at the edges of what they could get away with at 5.30 on a Saturday evening. We are talking, specifically, about the hallucinogenic nightmare of a third episode, in which the Doctor's consciousness undertakes a virtual reality journey into the Matrix, the repository of all Time Lord knowledge – sort of like a Gallifreyan version of Wikipedia, if Wikipedia was filled with terrifying visions of Samurai warriors, sinister clowns, spiders, syringe-wielding surgeons and gas-masked First World War soldiers, instead of nerds arguing about Jesus and *Star Trek*.

Hinchcliffe is on record as saying he wanted to see how much the Doctor could suffer – surely a few notes at his next appraisal would have sufficed? – but, in the end, it wasn't the Time Lord it pushed over the edge, but Mary Whitehouse. (Though, if we're keeping score, we should also mention James Acheson, who quit halfway through, saying the programme was asking for more than he could deliver on the budget). Whitehouse was particularly apoplectic about the episode three cliffhanger – a freeze-frame of the Doctor's head under water, apparently drowning.

"I write, in anger and despair," she wrote to Hinchcliffe, in anger and despair. "The programme contains some of the sickest and most horrific material ever seen on children's television," she added in a later public broadside. "My personal reaction to the sight of the Doctor being viciously throttled underwater is unimportant. What's important is the effect of such material upon the very young children still likely to be watching. Strangulation – by hand, by claw, by obscene vegetable matter – is the latest gimmick, sufficiently close-up so that they get the point. So what are we to do? Sit back and say nothing when – after panning to the contorted visage of the demented murderer – the final shot of this particular episode was a close-up shot of the Doctor's apparently drowned face lying still beneath the water? Nothing said – a new barrier broken."

("Right," said Hinchcliffe. "Shall I just put you down as 'undecided'?")

A few weeks later, Whitehouse received a response from the BBC's Director General, Sir Charles Curran, who wrote: "The television service was not totally satisfied with the way *The Deadly Assassin* developed. With hindsight, the service does accept that one or two viewers may have imagined that Dr. Who's dreams were reality. What actually happened was that the head of the department felt, before these episodes were transmitted, that some of the sequences were a little too realistic for a science-fiction series. Accordingly, several of them were edited out before transmission.

The result was what you saw on the screen, and which I myself think was reasonably acceptable. However, with hindsight, the head of the department responsible would have liked to have cut just a few more frames of the action than he did."

Which was BBC speak for: the head of department would like to cut the producer's head off, if he could.

In his defence, Hinchcliffe only had to point to the show's continued ratings success, with *The Deadly Assassin*'s contentious dream sequence instalment, for example, watched by 13 million viewers. One of them was a certain T Baker, who – in an echo of the previous year's impromptu *Android Invasion* viewing – watched the episode with a dumbfounded young family in Preston, having knocked on the door of their house while travelling home from the Doctor Who exhibition in Blackpool. Seems like someone would do anything to avoid buying a TV licence. It's probably just as well he hadn't been watching the previous evening, when Rod Hull and his notorious puppet irritant Emu had premiered the first in a series of Doctor Who spoofs, this time taking on the Deadly Dustbins. Then again, maybe Baker would have been pleased to know he wasn't the only Time Lord lumbered with an aggressive bird as a sidekick that season.

"We should have greased the rat"

It's a measure of how completely Tom Baker had imprinted himself on the role of the Doctor – and, in particular, his popularity with the undergraduate audience – that, in November 1976, the actor was invited to become the rector at St Andrew's University in Scotland. He declined, but it was obviously a huge honour to be asked. Or at least, it would have been if it hadn't later emerged their first choice had been Basil Brush. Students, eh?

With the rest of the season deferred until the New Year, compilation repeats of *Pyramids of Mars* and *The Brain of Morbius* were scheduled, the former attracting a staggering 13.7 million viewers – a new record for the show. No pressure, then, thought Graham Williams as he set about lining up scripts for the next series.

In December, the new producer joined the

cast and crew on location for Holmes' replacement season finale, *The Talons of Greel*, where he held discussions with Louise Jameson about staying on as Leela. The actress admitted she was finding her co-star's attitude hard to bear, but agreed to sign for a further 26 episodes on one condition: that she be allowed to kick Baker in the bollo... sorry, that she be allowed to ditch the brown contact lenses that were causing her agony, and revert to her natural blue eyes. Williams also persuaded Robert Holmes to stay for another six months to help him get the following year's scripts in shape. The producer had an idea about doing a season of linked stories under the umbrella title of *The Key to Time*, but abandoned the idea after running out of... well, time.

By now, it was becoming clear the new producer wouldn't be enjoying anything like the same freedoms as his predecessor. Graeme McDonald insisted on reading all scripts prior to production, and gave Williams explicit instructions to tone down the horror and violence and introduce more humour. While Williams broadly agreed his predecessor had gone too far, he was concerned his bosses wanted to take things to the other extreme, and argued for a compromise. "In the end, I was told, 'Okay, you can keep the fantastic violence, but anything else is verboten. Getting kids to watch from behind the sofa is fine, as long as it's not going to keep them awake at night."[18]

As Mary Whitehouse crowed about her triumph over the forces of evil in a victory address to *The Daily Telegraph*, *Doctor Who* also found itself under fire from none other than Terry Nation, who told the *Daily Express* it had lost its sense of excitement and was "taking itself a little too seriously". Or, to put it another way, was no longer accepting any old phoned-in tosh from Terry Nation.

The Face of Evil being a case in point: premiering on New Year's Day 1977, Chris Boucher's *Doctor Who* debut is one of the most sci-fi literate stories the series had ever attempted. Inspired by the works of hardcore SF scribblers Frank Herbert and Harry Harrison, it's packed full of intriguing ideas, particularly about the nature of religion and the Chinese whispers that allow faiths to flourish. Arriving on a jungle planet, the Doctor meets a savage tribe called the Sevateem, whose god Xoanon bears a startling resemblance to himself (or it does if the giant, Mt Rushmore-style visage carved into a mountain is anything to go by). The Doctor eventually discovers that Xoanon is a spaceship's computer that he had previously tried to fix, but ended up sending mad with a multiple personality disorder (that's the last time they let *him* man the IT helpdesk).

Over the centuries, elements of the crashed ship and its crew have become woven into local religious rites: the name Sevateem itself is a corruption of "survey team" and the Tesh who tend Xoanon are descendants of the original technicians, while the tribe's hand gestures originated as a way of checking the seal on a spacesuit.

It's all clever stuff, in a vaguely *Star Trek*-y way, peppered with dialogue that is both snappy and meaningful: "Never be certain of anything – it's a sign of weakness," says the Doctor. And when a Tesh drops to his knees in front of him, he asks, "Have you dropped something?" – classic Tom Baker flippancy reinvented as heresy in a story that delights in demolishing faith-based convictions.

It's not perfect, by any means: most of the guest characters are dull ciphers, and it lacks the atmospheric, chills-down-the-spine appeal of most of the stories of this era. But as a rare foray into "hard" (well, firm, anyway) sci-fi, it's extremely effective, and Louise Jameson gives an excellent account of herself in clearly trying circumstances.

In for a penny, in for a pound, Boucher also supplied the next four weeks of *Doctor Who* action. And, again, it's an unusually sci-fi premise for this period, taking inspiration from Isaac Asimov's three laws of robotics and *R.U.R.*, the 1920 play by Karel Capek that first coined the word robot, and feeding them into an Agatha Christie-style drawing room murder mystery.

On an unnamed desert world, the indolent human crew of a sandminer – a giant vehicle used for sifting precious metals from the raging sandstorms – find themselves under attack from their menial robot servants, who have somehow overridden the prime directive that – in theory at least – stops them killing.

In contrast to his previous script, here

Boucher ensures all the characters are well drawn, with the lazy, bitching, sarcastic (in other words, British) crew quick to turn on each other when it becomes clear one of them is in league with the robots. Leela is also fundamental to the plot, which makes good use of the fact she's uneducated but smart and therefore, despite what Tom Baker might have thought, the perfect *Doctor Who* companion. There's a wonderful moment in which the Doctor makes a – surprisingly convincing – attempt finally to explain how the TARDIS can be bigger on the inside. "That's silly," says Leela when he's finished. "That's transdimensional engineering," he shrugs.

The real trump card, though, is the design: instead of the usual boring silver ship and boring silver robots, designer Kenneth Sharp and costume designer Elizabeth Waller collaborated to bring a decadent art deco feel to the production, reasoning that, if humans were stuck in a metal box in the middle of an inhospitable desert for months on end, they'd probably do their best to make it more aesthetically bearable. The robots, with their elegantly sculpted faces, crimped metallic hair (somebody obviously left the Frizz-ese at home) and soft, slightly questioning voices, are a particular triumph: beautiful yet incredibly creepy, with the exception of the permanently puzzled undercover agent D84 – most memorable line: "Please do not throw hands at me" – who is actually rather adorable.

Okay, so any plot resolution that revolves around giving someone helium to affect their voice is bound to feel a *bit* silly. And it's an odd sort of whodunit that reveals the killer in episode three – but then carries on as if it hasn't. But those quibbles aside, this is a fitting testament to Philip Hinchcliffe's forensic attention to detail across all aspects of his productions, with script, acting, direction, design, costume and lighting all singing in perfect harmony.

Then again, Hinchcliffe had the money to do it. And even if he didn't, he was going to spend it anyway, apparently telling his teams not to worry about budgets and do whatever it took to make his final few stories look spectacular. For a BBC producer, there is no more cardinal sin than going over budget: he could have shown a 25-minute freeze frame of Leela embedding her knife in the Doctor's head and

got into less trouble. The punishment for such behaviour usually involved having the following year's budget capped and everybody involved shot – or at least moved on to a sitcom. So, depending on your point of view, Hinchcliffe was either heroically putting the programme's reputation over his own future career prospects – or selfishly going out in a blaze of glory and leaving Graham Williams to pick up the pieces.

Whichever version you choose to believe, there is little doubt that Hinchcliffe's parting gift to *Doctor Who* remains one of the crowning glories of the programme's 50-year reign. Graham Williams once recalled that "Bob [Holmes] had a good saying: 'We only ever use original ideas on *Doctor Who*, but not necessarily our own original ideas'."[18] This was never more true than in *The Talons of Weng-Chiang* (as it had now become) – a heady brew of popular Victoriana mixing elements of Sherlock Holmes, Fu Manchu, *The Phantom of the Opera*, Jack the Ripper and *Pygmalion*.

The plot – a hideously disfigured fifty-first century war criminal stranded in Victorian London is draining the life force of young girls to sustain him while he looks for his missing "time cabinet" – is beyond insane and, not surprisingly given how quickly Holmes had to turn it around, the logic often strains at the seams. But, honestly, who cares when everyone's having this much fun?

On the one hand, it's probably Holmes' most laugh-out-loud funny script, the writer clearly relishing the period's potential for florid dialogue: "On my oath," mutters a toothless old crone watching a body being fished from the Thames, "you wouldn't want that served with onions. Never seen anything like it in all my puff. Oh, make an 'orse sick, that would." Theatrical impresario Henry Gordon Jago, meanwhile, tips a knowing titfer to the magniloquent excesses of long-running TV music hall nostalgia-fest *The Good Old Days*: "Some paperwork commands my presence yet awhile," he bloviates, "but I shall doubtless descry those lugubrious liniments at the crepuscular hour." And the Doctor telling Leela that "Eureka's Greek for 'this bath is too hot'" is surely the sort of line *Doctor Who* was invented for.

At other times, the story is frankly terrifying,

most notably whenever Mr Sin is on screen. Originally given as a toy for the children of the Commissioner of the Icelandic Alliance, this pigtailed "Peking homunculus" is actually a robot with the cerebral cortex of a pig, now stalking the wings of London's theatreland as a knife-wielding, homicidal ventriloquist's dummy. Sin's origins are emblematic of the lashings of teasing backstory Holmes casually tosses into the script – Magnus Greel, we learn, was known as the Butcher of Brisbane, and prowled the fifty-first century death camps left by the victorious Icelandic armies, until the Filipino forces closed in on Rekjavic and... well, you get the idea.

With Greel preying on East End prostitutes, Louise Jameson sloshing about in the sewers in transparent, sopping wet underwear and a Chinaman with his leg chewed off tripping off his nut on opium, you can't help wondering if Holmes hadn't been indulging in the "pipe of poppy" himself. Or, as the unflappable pathologist Professor George Litefoot (whose team-up with Jago results in perhaps the finest example of the classic Robert Holmes comedy double act) so pithily puts it: "I may have had a bash on the head, but this is a dashed queer story."

Ah yes, about those Chinamen. If there's one thing that lets *The Talons of Weng-Chiang* down – actually, there are two things, but we'll come to the other in a moment – it's the fact that it's, well, basically quite racist. For a start, the main Chinese role – part-time stage conjurer and full-time servant of Weng Chiang, Li H'sen Chang – is played (admittedly rather brilliantly) by English actor John Bennett, while the actual Chinese actors are pigtailed "coolies" bundling bodies into laundry baskets and generally getting up to no good on behalf of a criminal gang called the Tong of the Black Scorpion. Of course, this depiction of the "yellow peril" is entirely in keeping with the story's origins in Victorian penny dreadfuls, and with exchanges like Doctor: "I've seen you somewhere before," Chang: "I understand we all look the same," you *could* argue it's a satirical swipe at contemporary British imperial attitudes. Let us know how you get on with that.

The other major blot on the story's copybook is the rat. Or, at least, the script insists it's a rat – a filthy, disease-carrying sewer-dweller

swollen to gigantic proportions as a by-product of Greel's experiments. Unfortunately, what appears on screen looks more like a very large, very fluffy and unfortunately rather cute pet hamster.

"We tried to cope, but we couldn't really," admitted a rather defeated David Maloney, who otherwise went out on a high on what was also his final story. "We should have greased the rat. The rat was good physically, and had the right shape, but it was too fluffy. It looked as though it had just had a shampoo and blow-dry."[19]

For Louise Jameson, being chewed by a giant gerbil was just another miserable day's work on a miserable shoot: the actress contracted glandular fever mid-way through recording the episode, but had no choice to come in and be filmed thrashing about in cold water, in the company of some real rats that had been added in a doomed attempt to distract from the fake one.

Production unit manager Chris D'Oyly-John was so appalled by the amount of money being thrown at the story, he resigned halfway through, and was replaced by a young buck called John Nathan-Turner. "David Maloney was a man who liked to go for broke. With it being Philip's final story as well, it just grew and grew," said D'Oyly-John. "It became a monster, but we were so over the top budget-wise at that point, it wasn't going to make a lot of difference anyway. I couldn't believe they were carrying on like this... It seemed, by the end of the season, that they thought they had carte blanche. People were just beyond caring what Philip was doing with *Doctor Who*... I don't know how he got away with it."[20]

However he got away with it, perhaps we should just be grateful that he did. Not that *The Talons of Weng-Chiang* is flawless – as well as the rat and the racism, it suffers from that common *Doctor Who* malaise of a weak final episode, and there's the occasional production slip-up, like a 1970s newspaper with a headline about Denis Healy in a laundry basket. (The newspaper is in the laundry basket, I mean, not Denis Healy – that would have been mental, even for this story. In most other aspects, incidentally, the team went to great lengths to ensure period accuracy: when one owner failed to respond to a request to remove all cars from a residential street, the set dressers had no choice but to bury the offending vehicle in a giant heap of hay. Given that it was a Porsche, he's lucky they didn't cover it in horse-shit instead.) Nevertheless, there is a strong argument to be made for *The Talons of Weng-Chiang* being one of, if not *the*, greatest – and certainly most dashed queer – *Doctor Who* stories ever made.

The day after the final episode of the show's fourteenth season had aired, the first "serious" documentary study of the *Doctor Who* phenomenon was broadcast as part of BBC2's *The Lively Arts* strand. Fronted by luxuriantly coiffed TV arts guru Melvyn Bragg – whose hair required even more taming than the fluffy rat – *Whose Doctor Who* combined a potted history of the series with behind-the-scenes footage from *Talons*, plus an attempt to examine the impact of *Doctor Who* on its audience with the help of children, parents and expert witnesses. A true portrait of Britain in the 70s – the fashions and dentistry are even scarier than Mr Sin – the programme features memorable contributions from such eminent authorities as Kenneth Bailey, educationalist (retired); a small child called Caspar dressed in a pinstripe suit; and, best of all, Dr Eric Sherwood Jones, consultant physician at a Merseyside hospital, who is such an avid *Doctor Who* fan he makes his entire intensive care staff watch it with him. "*Doctor Who* is an important part of our working lives," he tells Bragg. "We're delighted and relieved that, like ourselves, he makes mistakes and errors." Which is perhaps not the most reassuring statement from the man in charge of the ICU. Other memorable moments include the world's most sinister teacher insisting it's good to be scared, while his family mutter in nervous agreement, special sound boffin Dick Mills doing unspeakable things with Swarfega, and Tom Baker describing Jon Pertwee as "a tall lightbulb". It is also the first recorded occasion of Baker insisting "Doctor Who is not an acting part" – a line he continues to trot out on at least a weekly basis to this day.

The general conclusion from all parties is that, essentially, *Doctor Who* is A Good Thing – though some are more effusive than others, with one schoolboy declaring "If there's nothing good coming on, I'll watch it." Yeah, don't put yourself out, mate.

To promote the documentary, Philip Hinchcliffe submitted himself to trial by lunchtime television with an appearance on *Pebble Mill at One*. Presented with the notorious *Deadly Assassin* cliffhanger that had resulted in an official censure, he was unrepentant, claiming: "No, I'm not worried, because I thought about it carefully and took the decision at the time, and I stand by the decision." Her majesty's press, unfortunately, continued to take a different line, with Jean Rook of the *Daily Express* stitching up Bob Holmes in an interview headed Who Do You Think You Are, Scaring My Child? and the *Daily Mail* claiming "*Doctor Who* is Too Terrifying for Europe", in which BBC Enterprises explained why they were having trouble flogging the show on the continent. (A story taking a pop at the BBC *and* Europe? The *Mail*'s editor must have cartwheeled into the office that morning.)

A more surprising newspaper item was a quote from Tom Baker musing that he might only do one more season as the Doctor. The actor was increasingly frustrated at his lack of input into the scripts, so may just have been having a bad day. In less forlorn moments, though, he continued to view the role as a privilege, and was making more personal appearances than ever. He was particularly humbled by his frequent visits to hospital wards, and deeply moved by the notion that he could bring joy to sick and dying children. "I began to be like 'Uncle Tom'," said Baker. "A kind of children's entertainer, with my silly long scarf, and my thyroid eyes, and my long hair... Because I'm pathetic in some ways, it made me feel more important. It was simply wonderful to be famous, to be recognised and well-treated. I adored being adored."[4]

Whatever Uncle Tom's plans were, one thing was certain: Philip Hinchcliffe's tenure as producer, which had seen *Doctor Who* scale new heights of popularity – but also endure a new ferocity of criticism – was over. To many, the stories produced during Tom Baker's first three seasons remain the show's creative high watermark. To others, like Mary Whitehouse, they were the years when *Doctor Who* crossed a line, the consequences of which would be long and hard-felt.

"The three years that I produced *Doctor Who* were not an unqualified success," Hinchcliffe stated recently. "But there were a lot of stories that worked very well and they have remained popular. Why? I think Tom is a big factor in that. And the attention Bob Holmes and myself paid to the imaginative concepts behind the stories, and our attention to very good story-telling."[6]

"A lot of things came together," David Maloney concurred. "There were a lot of good designers who just happened to want to work on the show. There were some good direc-tors... I think that was the golden period. But then I would, wouldn't I?"[6]

You don't have to be a mental giant to work here...

"When Bill Sutton asked me to start on *Doctor Who*, I didn't think I knew it all by any means, but I had done every kind of television drama that it was possible to do," recalled Graham Williams in a 1984 interview. "So it was with absolute confidence that I went along to my first *Doctor Who* studio recording. I came out feeling like I was coming out of the Stone Age. I felt utterly shell-shocked. I was trem-bling, thinking 'What am I letting myself in for?'"[21]

What he was letting himself in for was per-haps the greatest uphill struggle faced by any *Doctor Who* producer since Verity Lambert. Williams was fighting on two fronts – one financial, one political. In the mid 1970s, inflation was running at a record high in Britain – it had reached an astonishing 27% in 1975, largely as a consequence of the Yom Kippur War's impact on oil prices, and the rate stayed north of 15% for another couple of years after that. On top of that, the *Doctor Who* budget was slashed by 8%, possibly as a pun-ishment for Philip Hinchcliffe's final year spending splurge. "You don't have to be a mental giant," said Williams, "to work out that's a reduction in budget."[22]

And then there was the auld enemy, Mrs Mary Whitehouse. "The day I was offered the job was the day Mary Whitehouse got cross about *The Deadly Assassin*," said Williams. "And I suppose, as a reaction against all that, I was told very firmly that what they saw as sad-ism and violence had to come out."[22] Spoilsports.

And, just to add an extra splash of piss on his chips, Williams was ordered to scrap his very first story, Terrance Dicks' *The Witch Lords*, because Graeme McDonald thought there was a conflict of interests with a big-budget Christmas adaptation of *Dracula* the BBC was planning. With "minus one script" on the table for the new season, a replacement opener called *Horror of Fang Rock* was hastily commissioned from Dicks, by which time the serial had lost its studio slot, and had to be relocated to Pebble Mill in Birmingham. ("Birmingham, really?" colleagues in the Television Centre bar commiserated. "How awful for you.")

The first story into production, though, would be Bob Baker and Dave Martin's *The Invisible Invader*, the script for which included a major part for a robot dog, which had provi-sionally been called FIDO – for Phenomenal Indication Data Observation, apparently, which would be rubbish even if *did* spell FIDO – but was now answering to the name K-9 (see what they did there?).

Bob Baker claimed the idea was born after Dave Martin lost three Springer Spaniels in road accidents in short succession, and wist-fully wondered whether he could get "a mechanical dog that wouldn't get run over". (Or, as a cheaper option, why not just keep it on a lead?)

Initial designs had favoured an armour-plated Doberman pincher or wolfhound, large enough for an actor to get inside, but Williams insisted on a smaller, less savage-looking remote controlled prop instead. (Bear in mind this was early 1977, when no-one had heard of R2-D2, C3PO, Muffet the Daggit, Twiki, Metal Mickey or any of the other cute/gay robots that would be clogging up the film and TV sched-ules for the rest of the decade. In that sense, *Doctor Who* was ahead of the curve – which is just as well, as the crew were about to learn the hard way that K-9 couldn't cope with curves.)

Away from the show, Tom Baker was still living with Marianne Ford – or at least that's where he slept most nights; his evenings were generally spent in various Soho drinking dens such as the Colony Room, the French House, the Swiss Tavern and the Coach and Horses, where he was part of a dipsomaniac coterie that also included the painter Francis Bacon, the novelist Frank Norman and the journalist-turned-dedicated liver-punisher Jeffrey Bernard. "These new companions became important to me over the next few years," Baker recalled in his autobiography. "It didn't matter where I was working or what I was working at, I always wanted to get down to Soho."[2]

It probably helped that most of his friends were so drunk they'd laugh at anything – which was decidedly not the case in the studio. "I used to see Graham Williams struggling to contain himself as I developed my notions about how it all should be," said Baker. "But he never did lose his rag with me. And I never stopped insisting that if the TARDIS was bigger on the inside than it was on the outside, then it could be very big. I could not understand why my potting shed should not be the interior or Wells Cathedral or, indeed, why I should not sometimes get lost there. I suspected that Graham Williams was longing for me just to get lost anywhere."[2]

In later years, Baker admitted his judgment may have been "a bit wonky": "As the part took hold of me, I began to think the entire BBC was colonised with hostile aliens who were slyly spreading a hideous and incurable virus of ordinariness. This could not have been the case, but it was the way I was seeing things."[2]

During the studio sessions for what was now *The Invisible Enemy*, it became clear K-9 was almost as unmanageable as Baker. "It was a bloody nightmare," said director Derrick Goodwin. "I remember the remote control going berserk, and the tin dog going in all the wrong directions in rehearsal. When we got to the studio, with all the lighting, sound and cameras, that seemed to send it berserk as well. I thought we were going to blow up the *Top of the Pops* studio!"[23]

Despite these technical hitches, Williams decided the tin dog would be enough of a hit with the kids to be worth keeping on beyond the end of the story. Bob Baker and Dave Martin were offered 50% ownership of the character and, according to Martin, the BBC also asked them to stump up half the money to build the thing, as they were £2,000 short. He must have had one hell of a pedigree.

To voice the character, Goodwin approached an old colleague from his rep days, John Leeson. "My agent phoned up and said, the BBC wants you to play a virus and a tin dog in an episode of *Doctor Who*,"[24] recalled Leeson. Well everyone has to specialise in something, I suppose. Undaunted, the actor quickly won the respect of his colleagues by spending every rehearsal crawling about on his hands and knees. A former crossword setter (that's someone who compiles crosswords, not another breed of dog), he also bonded with Baker by helping him tackle *The Times* head-scratcher most mornings. Leeson thought this Time Lord's-best-friend chemistry also translated well onto the screen. "It was one of those lovely relationships where the servant knows almost more than the master does," he said. "King Lear and his Fool, if you like."[24] If you like.

Word of the new creation soon got round the BBC, and an appearance was requested by *Blue Peter*. The visual effects team cautioned against it, claiming it "might be embarrassing". Given they were talking about a show in which an elephant had famously evacuated its bowels all over the studio floor – then dragged its keeper through the mess – that was really saying something.

As recording began on *Horror of Fang Rock* in Birmingham, director Paddy Russell was struck by the marked change in the show's leading man since their last encounter on *Pyramids of Mars*. "The difference between the two stories that I did with him was quite astounding. Eighteen months was all it took. In rehearsals, he was uncontainable, quite prone to walk out the door and get a cup of tea. He was utterly convinced that he was the programme – and, to give him his due, he *was* popular."[25]

Russell claims Baker so infuriated the crew, they tried to swing a pair of mole cranes at his head, until she saw what was happening and ordered them to stop. "Louise Jameson went through hell on that show," added the director. "I found her excellent to work with, but Tom hardly spoke to her. When he did, it was usually something nasty."[26]

Despite the tension with her co-star, Jameson cites *Fang Rock* as the story where she started to find her confidence – not least by repeatedly challenging a piece of direction, which she believes earned her Baker's grudging respect. "Tom is an exceedingly complex character," said the actress. "One of the most generous and most selfish people that I've ever met, encapsulated in one human being. I think his attitude to almost everything is ambivalent, including his job. One day he'd be charming, the next he'd ignore you. I just used to retreat, go home, and have the conversations that I should have had with him in my head."[27]

Jameson was impressed by Baker's commitment to good causes – he gave most of his personal appearance fees to charity – and his continued dedication to visiting sick children in hospital. On one occasion, she recalled, he became incensed that, having given all his earnings from a motor show event to a charity for children with mental health problems, his agent still insisted on taking 10% off the top. Furious, Baker sat down and wrote a cheque to cover the missing 10% himself. "Deep down, he's one of the kindest men I've ever met," Jameson concluded. "He's just a genuine eccentric."[28]

These days, Baker is the first to admit that his attitude to Jameson was unforgivable, and the two have a good relationship. But, for the most part, he believes it was directors, not his fellow actors, who bore the brunt of his temper. "Most directors have tears in their eyes after they've worked with me," he admitted in a 1997 Doctor Who Magazine interview. "Indeed, some of them die in agony not long afterwards... But I love being with actors most of the time. I like to think that the actors who worked with me on Doctor Who enjoyed it. Not many of them said that, when I look back. Hmmm, not many actors ring me up, come to think of it."[29]

"Who ordered the jacket potato with dog vomit?"

As he prepared to leave Doctor Who behind, Robert Holmes was offered the script editor's job on a new BBC science fiction series called Blake's 7. ("Sounds interesting," said Holmes. "Tell me more about it."

"Well, it's about a bunch of rebels on the run from an evil galactic federation – sort of like The Dirty Dozen in space."

"Sounds interesting. Who's written it?"
"Terry Nation."
"Actually I'm busy. I've been meaning to sort out the cupboard under the stairs for years. Good luck, though.")

In his place, Holmes recommended Chris Boucher, whose job it would become to collect all Nation's fag packets and try to translate the notes on them.

Holmes' replacement in the Doctor Who office was Anthony Read, a hugely experienced writer, producer and editor who had spent much of the 60s working on oil industry drama The Troubleshooters. Read was sceptical, but agreed to do the job for a year until a more permanent replacement could be found.

Tom Baker spent the early summer of 1977 juggling personal appearances with guest slots on TV shows like Pebble Mill at One and long-running game show Call My Bluff (he was particularly well suited to the latter, as it involved trying to convince people to believe a load of absolute bullshit). He also attended a miner's gala in Rotherham – that's 1970s showbiz for you.

Back on the day job, Baker was up to his old tricks – this time with writers. Before the readthrough for the next story to go into production, Image of the Fendahl, director George Spenton-Foster thought it would be a good idea to take everyone out to lunch and "relax" them. Unfortunately, Baker was so "relaxed" he spent the afternoon ripping Chris Boucher's script to shreds in front of his eyes. "I have never been so embarrassed in all my life," said Boucher. "Tom Baker was a very charismatic character – but a monster, as most charismatic characters are. I was so furious. For a long time, one of my ambitions was to see Tom Baker die in a cellar full of rats."[30]

"I was shamefully badly behaved with the scripts," admitted Baker. "I maltreated our writers' reputations in rehearsal more than anything else. I found it so frustrating. It's not that they were terrible scripts, but they weren't great either. They weren't so much deficient as dull."[3]

And that was Baker being polite: his favourite description for scripts he didn't like was "whippet shit", though, on more creative days, he could stretch to "Spud-U-Like with dog vomit". Perhaps if he'd approached the briefly popular carb-based fast food chain, they might have let him create a signature dish for them.

In July, there was bad publicity for the fledgling DWAS when member Clarence Atkinson from Burnley appeared in court accused of stealing *Doctor Who*-related pages of the *Radio Times* from Manchester Central Library. The public recoiled in horror at this heinous crime, and there were calls for the immediate return of capital punishment – or, at the very least, taking his library card off him.

The Society's organisers also found Graham Williams even less keen to share information than his predecessor, though he did throw his support behind the first Doctor Who convention, held at Broomwood Church Hall in Battersea on Saturday, August 6th, attended by 230 fans. Guests included Baker and Jameson – who arrived by limousine – as well as Jon Pertwee, Terrance Dicks, effects designer Mat Irvine and Williams himself. Questions from the floor included "What's your favourite monster?" and "What's your favourite story?" (And, from the tall, white-haired man in the frilly shirt, "How come he gets a fucking limo?")

Four weeks later, Graham Williams unleashed his bold new vision of *Doctor Who* on the world with the first episode of *Horror of Fang Rock* – a story which couldn't feel more like a Philip Hinchcliffe production if it came with a free severed limb. A tense, claustrophobic horror story in which literally *everybody* except the Doctor and Leela dies (even *Pyramids of Mars* had spared a couple of extras), it's like a last, two-fingered salute to Mary Whitehouse before the show is forced to settle down and start playing nicely in the BBC sandpit.

Despite being written in a frantic hurry, Terrance Dicks takes Robert Holmes' brief to "do a story set in a lighthouse (and do it cheaply)" as the basis for a richly atmospheric murder mystery in which the occupants of a remote, fogbound island are gradually picked off by an unknown assailant.

Taking inspiration from Wilfrid Wilson Gibson's poem *Flannan Isle*, which relates the true story of three lighthouse keepers who disappeared without trace in 1900, Dicks assembles a cast of well-drawn Edwardian archetypes: as well as the trio of keepers, there's a wealthy industrialist and his loyal

secretary, the salty sea dog bosun of his luxury yacht and a shifty MP trying to stave off a Parliamentary scandal.

The fourth Doctor, naturally, instinctively sides with the masses against the classes (if this had been a Pertwee story, he'd have been breaking out the port and cigars with the nobs before you could say "Salisbury, I said..."). Not that you could ever accuse this incarnation of the Time Lord of being predictable: he seems positively energised by the wholesale slaughter around him, and there's great sport to be had watching Baker visibly throwing the rest of the cast with his frequent off-the-cuff extemporising. Leela, meanwhile, reaffirms one of the unshakable tenets of the series when she states: "I, too, used to believe in magic, but the Doctor has taught me to believe in science. It is better to believe in science." You go, girlfriend.

Of course, it wouldn't be *Doctor Who* without a dodgy monster to spoil the party, so step – or rather slither – forward the Rutan Host, the mortal enemies of the Sontarans making their only on-screen appearance in the form of an amorphous blob of radioactive green jelly. The creatures were made from frozen Swarfega, and whenever one started to look a bit soggy under the studio lights, a technician would dash out and replace it with one from the freezer. ("No, the *other* freezer," said Paddy Russell, as the Doctor found himself being menaced by a packet of fish fingers.)

With an average audience of 8.4 million, the story saw *Doctor Who* dropping out of the TV Top 20, where it had been getting rather comfortable in recent years. But it was still a decent figure, and there was further good news when an influential report, *Television Violence and the Adolescent Boy*, gave the show the all-clear, claiming its fantasy violence was less likely to have an impact on impressionable young minds than such famously gritty dramas as *The Saint* and *Hawaii Five-O*. Graham Williams explained that he was happy to let his two-year-old son watch the show, while Baker would probably have been happy to let him have a crack at writing it.

Around the same time, adolescent boys everywhere received a treat when Denys Fisher released a range of action figures including the Doctor, Leela, a Dalek, a Cyberman and the

Giant Robot. If the Doctor didn't appear quite himself, it was because the mould of Tom Baker's head had been damaged, and replaced at the last-minute with a grinning Gareth Hunt from *The New Avengers*. Not that the adolescent boys cared about that – they'd been locked in their bedroom with the Leela doll ever since they'd got back from the shops.

The range would soon be expanded to include K-9, who received his official press launch in the first week of October, to coincide with the start of *The Invisible Enemy*. The metal mutt received a huge amount of media attention, including that belated *Blue Peter* appearance, where his canine credentials were proved beyond doubt when Shep, John Noakes' faithful border collie, ran straight up to him and started sniffing his rear end.

Tom Baker, inevitably, was less than happy with the latest addition to his crew, complaining because it never did what it was supposed to do on set, which was a bit bloody rich. ("I ++ do ++ not ++ think ++ my ++ master ++ likes ++ me ++ very ++ much," said K-9 as he drowned his sorrows in the BBC bar. "Don't worry, he's exactly like that with me too," Louise Jameson assured him. "Another oil for the road?")

Rushed into production a month early, *The Invisible Enemy* is an inauspicious start to the Graham William era proper. It's the first story to really get inside the Doctor's head – not, sadly, through any penetrating psychoanalytical insight, but by making mini Doctor and Leela clones and having them literally wander about inside his brain, and sundry other parts of his surprisingly roomy physiognomy, like day-trippers tramping round a Damien Hirst exhibition. You've seen *Fantastic Voyage*? Welcome to *Slightly Underwhelming Voyage*.

With the Doctor laid low by a deadly virus that feeds on intellectual activity – so at least the scriptwriters were immune – it's down to the teeny Time Lord clone and his itsy-bitsy sidekick (and you thought Leela's costume couldn't possibly get any smaller) to get in there and sort the problem out. As the pair cross from the rational half ("the brain") to the imaginative half ("the mind") of the Doctor's bonce, it becomes painfully clear that Bob Baker and Dave Martin flunked elementary biology as well as physics. But it's okay,

because the Time Lord does eventually get the virus out of his system – at which point it grows to the size of a human. A human dressed, inexplicably, as a giant shrimp. *The Invisible Enemy*? If only.

Even without the time constraints, it should have been obvious to everyone the whole idea was way too ambitious for *Doctor Who* – at any time, let alone this financial year. As such, the telltale signs of under-funding are everywhere, from the make-do, functional sets to the clearly pre-cut hole in the wall just waiting to be blasted out by K-9. John Leeson does a good job of breathing life into the tin dog, affecting a finicky, fusspot persona apparently based on Bertrand Russell, (not the most flattering tribute, but I'm sure he'd have been philosophical about it). The story also sees the re-introduction of the original TARDIS control room, the wooden panels of the Season Fourteen model having warped in storage – though they'd have looked a bit out of place anyway in Williams' noticeably more space age, post-Gothic iteration of the show.

Having missed the boat this year, Williams was determined to introduce his Key to Time story arc for his sophomore season and, together with Anthony Read, began briefing potential writers about the basic structure, which would see the Doctor charged by a god-like being called the White Guardian with tracking down the six scattered segments of a perfect cube which maintains the equilibrium of the entire universe. At least that's what it said on the box (batteries not included).

Part of Williams' reasoning was a determination to give the Doctor a sense of purpose. "He seemed to wander through [the universe] more and more with absolutely authority, but no responsibility to anybody," said the producer. "He'd just please himself and do what he liked."[22] ("Are we talking about the Doctor here, Graham, or the bloke who plays him?")

The first story commissioned for the series was *The Pirate Planet* by Douglas Adams. The Cambridge graduate had been sending in script ideas for several years, to no avail, so it was ironic his first story ended up being green-lit at exactly the same time Radio 4 asked him for a full series of a sci-fi comedy pilot he'd written called *The Hitchhiker's Guide to the Galaxy*. Undaunted – actually, scratch that, he was pretty bloody daunted indeed – Adams set to work on both projects simultaneously, labouring day and night to get the scripts finished on time. Except on Thursdays – he never could get the hang of Thursdays.

Other writers lined up for next year's run included newcomers David Fisher and Ted Lewis – whose novel *Jack's Return Home* had been adapted for the screen as *Get Carter* – as well as old hands Robert Holmes and Bob Baker and Dave Martin. By now, it was common knowledge that the next series would also introduce a new companion, following an announcement in *The Times* on October 7th that Louise Jameson was quitting to return to the theatre. A horrified *Sun* immediately launched a "Save Leela" campaign – possibly more as an excuse to print regular pictures of Jameson in her chamois leathers than a genuine attempt to influence her future career.

Another significant departure was marked by *Image of the Fendahl* – the last story to be script-edited by Robert Holmes. So it's appropriate we should find ourselves back in balls-out horror mode – haunted house, occult rituals, human sacrifices, squelchy slug monster and all. In some ways, this is unusual territory for the science fiction-literate Chris Boucher, though he's still at pains to sell us a Big Idea, even if the notion of aliens influencing human evolution had already been well-rehearsed in numerous sci-fi texts such as *Chariots of the Gods* and *Quatermass and the Pit*.

The story opens with the Doctor and Leela fetching up at Fetch Priory (actually Mick Jagger's old Stargroves pad again), where a bunch of scientists experimenting on a primeval skull inadvertently revive the Fendahl – an ancient telepathic gestalt entity that has been lying dormant for around 12 million years (so even older than Jagger, then). Revealed as the guiding hand behind the dark side of human nature, the riddle the Doctor must solve is: how do you kill death itself? (The slightly disappointing answer? Salt.)

Wanda Ventham – who had made her name in ITV actioners like *The Saint* and *UFO* – makes for an unusually attractive giant slug as the Fendahl's chosen host body, though painting the creature's eyes on her closed eyelids was never going to fool anyone. Apart from maybe Wanda Ventham, who had her eyes

shut.[II] Louise Jameson holds her own, too, in a new set of skins made from chamois leather (they really were trying hard to make her the ultimate dads' fantasy – a semi-naked Amazonian who could put a lovely polish on your Volvo into the bargain).

The typically shonky "science" moved one physicist to write in asking how a direct continuum implosion could occur without contravening the Second Law of Thermodynamics. An Open University boffin was wheeled out to explain that one, but even he was stumped by the head-scratcher posed by a *Nationwide* viewer – namely, why are the jelly babies the fourth Doctor is apparently so fond of actually liquorice allsorts? (Graham Williams' probable answer: Shut up, smartarse.)

Physics/confectionary-based conundrums aside, *Image of the Fendahl* – a spooky creature feature seasoned with typically Holmesian pitch-black humour like "What sort of corpse?" "A dead one, what other sort is there?" – serves as a fitting swansong for the series' best, and most controversial, script editor.

Not that Graeme McDonald saw it that way. In one of his increasingly choleric memos prior to recording, the serials boss told Graham Williams: "I find the incident on page 13 in episode four, where Stael raises a gun to his mouth, unacceptable. May we discuss an alternative please. It could cause a lot of concern for children, adults *and* me."

This level of micro-management from senior executives would dog Williams throughout his time in charge – if that is indeed what he was – on *Doctor Who*. For his part, the producer had his own concerns about the script for the *Doctor Who Meets Scratchman* film, which didn't overly endear him to his leading man. Despite problems securing funding (the British Board of Film Finance had offered half the proposed £500,000 budget, but that still left them... well, scratching around for the rest), Tom Baker, Ian Marter and James Hill were still confident the project had legs, while 60s icon Twiggy and horror legend Vincent Price had expressed interest in playing the companion and Scratchman respectively.

But they had received word of a big budget new sci-fi film from America that everyone was talking about as a game-changer for movie blockbusters, so Baker, Marter and Hill arranged to attend a press showing of *Star Wars* at the Dominion Theatre. All three emerged from the screening looking considerably paler than when they went in, as they realised their proposed *Scratchman* budget would barely have covered Chewbacca's vets bills.

Robert Holmes also had money on his mind, using his first freelance contribution of the Baker era for a protracted whinge about the hefty tax bill he'd just received. Just as George Harrison's self-serving "Taxman" is a black mark on The Beatles' *Revolver*, so *The Sun Makers* succeeds in making Robert Holmes – whose kaleidoscopic imagination was second to none – look unusually small and petty.

Some take the view that *The Sun Makers* – in which the population of Pluto's Megropolis One are literally being taxed to death by the merciless plutocrats of the Company – is one of *Doctor Who*'s great satires. But it's a pretty blunt instrument, with concepts like the elite guardsmen of the "Inner Retinue" and a chase down corridor P45 perhaps better suited to a sixth-form revue. Or maybe the jokes would work better if the plotting wasn't so uncharacteristically weak, Pennant Roberts' direction wasn't so characteristically dull, the sets weren't so cheap and overlit and the supporting characters weren't all faceless dullards running about in their pyjamas. (Henry Woolf's wonderfully oleaginous Collector is a notable exception, as is, for less admirable reasons, the appalling Jewish stereotype implicit in Richard Leech's grasping Gatherer Hade.)

Location filming took place on the rooftop car park of the Wills Tobacco factory in Bristol – look closely and you can see the signs; Roberts apparently advised the actors playing the downtrodden company employees to observe how miserable the Wills staff appeared to be with their lot (though, on the plus side, they were encouraged to take as many fag breaks as they liked). The story ends with the Plutonian workers rising up and literally overthrowing one of their oppressors from the roof of said car park, to much cheering and general rejoicing, which must have brought a few middle managers out in a sweat that Saturday evening.

Holmes' script had started life as a revolutionary, anti-colonialist polemic – until that whopping tax bill landed on his doormat – and, at heart, the story still feels like it's trying to say something meaningful about workers' rights, which just makes the whiff of Taxpayers' Alliance-style bluster feel that bit more unfortunate. But I guess that's what happens when you write television stories based on the contents of your morning post: let's just be grateful he didn't have any overdue library books as well.

Doctor Who took a two-week break over Christmas. On January 7th, 1978, the show returned to a changed world, as the British public had finally had the chance to see *Star Wars* for themselves. And the one thing they couldn't help but notice, among all the impossibly cool villains, impressive alien vistas and eye-popping space battles, was a distinct absence of giant hamsters, malevolent Swarfega or men dressed as prawns.

US Immigration officials alarmed by rise in illegal aliens

The world may have been dazzled by George Lucas' all-conquering space saga, but *Doctor Who*'s visual effects guys weren't so easily impressed. For them, it was all about the cash.

"We all went back saying, 'We can do this, but we can't do it with the budget',"[22] said Colin Mapson, fx designer on *The Hand of Fear* and *Image of the Fendahl*, among others. "You were stuck," added his colleague Mat Irvine. "You were trying to please your producer or your director by going 'Here's your *Star Wars* effect', for literally tea money. You can get the look for one or two shots – what you can't do is keep it going all the way through."[22]

Just to twist the knife, *Star Wars* exploded onto British cinema screens in the same week *Doctor Who*'s cheapest, most underfunded story yet limped apologetically into living rooms. Depending on how you look at it, *Underworld* is either a testament to the *Doctor Who* production team's resourcefulness, tenacity and sheer British stiff upper lip – or it's a salutary reminder that, sometimes, you have to know when to quit.

Returning from holiday – and it's fair to say he wouldn't be making *that* mistake again – Graham Williams found Bob Baker and Dave Martin's sci-fi take on Jason and the Golden

Fleece was going to cost around 200% more than he could afford (by *Space Helmet*'s calculation, that's probably around £200). The producer was under pressure from Graeme McDonald to drop the story entirely, but knew that would have a disastrous impact on next year's already laughable budget. Instead, he decided that, instead of building sets or going on location, they would shoot the majority of the episode against a green screen and add the sets in later. Luckily – from a production, if not a storytelling point of view – most of the "action" takes place underground, which is why, after a decent first episode taped on a surprisingly good spaceship set, the rest of the story is largely made up of slightly fuzzy actors running about in front of back-projections of some caves. (At home in London, Barry Letts let out a long, contented sigh: after four years, it seemed the show was finally getting back on track.)

We can only imagine how director Norman Stewart, making his *Doctor Who* debut, reacted when he was shown a four-foot model of one of the sets in the studio: "Oh yes – that will look wonderful. When do we start building them?" "Er, no – these *are* the sets." In fairness, it could have been a lot worse: some scenes look almost convincing, if you squint a bit (or a lot), and some viewers may have been fooled for no other reason than they'd never believe a futuristic sci-fi series would blow all its fx budget producing something as boring as caves.

The Greek myth parallels aren't subtle: the Minyans, of Minyos, are searching for the lost spaceship P7E (geddit?), which now forms the core of a new planet, ruled over by a ship's computer with a god complex (yes, another one – except this one's called the Oracle, naturally). But that doesn't stop the Doctor taking time to laboriously point them all out at the story's end for the hard-of-thinking.

Devoid of memorable dialogue or interesting plot twists – and with Baker and Martin adding cosmology and, indeed, gravity, to the growing list of things they were keen to demonstrate their total ignorance of – there is nothing to distract from the shabbiness of the visuals. Under-developed, under-funded and under-achieving, *Underworld* is ultimately underwhelming. Graham Williams likened

making the story to "being kicked to death by spiders" – which, let's be honest, would have been much more exciting telly.

For all its shortcomings, though, the serial actually did pretty good business in the ratings, benefiting from a new 6.25pm timeslot to average 9.7 million viewers. It just goes to show, thought Baker, that people will watch anything as long as I'm in it – as Williams desperately tried to cover up the bags full of fanmail for K-9, whose growing popularity saw him taking tea with a young fan on *Jim'll Fix It*, and making a personal appearance at that year's *Crufts*, where he walked off with the rosette in the closely-fought Best Robot Sidekick category.

The same weekend, K-9 joined his master and a menagerie of monsters, including a Dalek, a Zygon, a Wirrn and a Sontaran, at the United States Embassy, where they queued up for a visa in order to promote the sale of 98 Tom Baker episodes to North America. It must have made for some eye-opening interviews:

Officer: "What is the purpose of your trip to the United States?"

Zygon: "We shall wipe out the American people and become rulers of... I mean, erm, for a holiday."

Officer: "How long are you intending to stay in the country?"

Zygon: "Forever! Our own world was destroyed, so now we must take yours by... erm, I mean, two weeks."

Officer: "Have you travelled to any other countries in the last three years?"

Zygon: "I went to Scotland for a bit. That's in Sussex."

Officer: "Are you planning to take any foodstuffs into the country?"

Zygon: "We might have to take the lactic fluid of the Skarasen – it depends what they serve on the flight, I suppose."

There was also a bit of a kerfuffle when it came to checking the Sontaran's passport ("What do you *mean* it looks nothing like me?").

Meanwhile, the fifteenth season ended as it had begun, with a hurried replacement for another story – in this case, David Weir's *Killers in the Dark*, the shopping list of requirements for which included a scene with Wembley Stadium filled with cats. At night. (And in this in a year when they couldn't afford *caves*.) But whereas *Horror of Fang Rock* had shown Terrance Dicks' mettle under pressure, *The Invasion of Time* only demonstrates that Anthony Read and Graham Williams – writing under the pseudonym David Agnew – were spreading themselves way too thinly.

A Gallifrey invasion story, in which the Doctor finally takes office as President, only to appear to betray his people by allowing an aggressive alien race called the Vardans to stage a hostile assault on the planet, the material is stretched to breaking point across four episodes – at which point the Sontarans are revealed as the real villains, and the entire plot is re-set for another 50 long minutes.

This wouldn't be so bad if the last two episodes weren't, in themselves, hopelessly padded, with much of the running – and I do mean running – time eaten up with an interminable chase around the TARDIS. And what should be a landmark moment – the chance finally to explore the Doctor's ship beyond its control rooms – is rendered beyond absurd by the lack of money to build any new sets, and the added complication of two studio days lost through industrial action. Graeme McDonald was itching to bump the whole thing over until the following season by this point, but Williams had his heart set on the Key to Time concept, so found himself fighting to save another story from the axe. The result of all this is that the Doctor's infinite alien timeship looks suspiciously like a disused mental hospital in Redhill, Surrey – complete with brick walls and echoing concrete stairwells – and a municipal swimming pool.

The Sontarans fare little better, saddled with ill-fitting masks and an extraordinary performance from former window cleaner Derek Deadman, who plays Commander Stor with such a broad cockney accent you half expect him to gather everyone round the old Joanna for a few verses of "The Old Bull and Bush". But even he looks good next to the Vardans – one of a vanishingly small number of *Doctor Who* aliens made out of what people who don't watch *Doctor Who* think *all* the aliens are made out of: tinfoil.

After six episodes of this nonsense, the plot is "resolved" by the Doctor shooting the enemy with a big gun – surely a betrayal of the show's very ethos – while the waiting Sontaran invasion force simply disappears, possibly through sheer embarrassment. Then, to really put the tinfoil lid on it, Leela decides to stay behind on Gallifrey, having apparently fallen in love with a drippy guard she's barely spoken two words to in the whole story.

According to Louise Jameson, Graham Williams had been so sure she'd change her mind and stay on he hadn't bothered to write her out until the very last minute. "Even the day before we recorded the very last scene, Graham – very flatteringly – said, 'Come on, we could easily have you dive into the TARDIS. You don't have to go off and marry him. Please stay.' It was sweet of him, but I'd accepted the part of Portia down in Bristol, so I was already on my way."[16]

When she eventually saw the script for the final episode, the actress was horrified, and she and Christopher Tranchell, who played her blind date-cum-husband, did their best to at least add a few meaningful looks in their scenes together. (Having failed to retain Jameson, Williams asked Elisabeth Sladen to return as Sarah Jane instead, but she declined.)

K-9 also departs, staying behind with Leela – at which point the Doctor simply unpacks a near-identical Mark II model. (It's a genuine new build, with a quieter motor, but hardly different enough to warrant an on-screen explanation. Maybe the original K-9 was upset at not having his contract renewed, and insisted on a proper send-off.)

The Invasion of Time is not a complete write-off: Tom Baker is on great form, almost managing to convince the viewer that our hero really has gone rogue – though his to-camera ad-lib of "even the sonic screwdriver won't get me out of this one" probably didn't go down as well with his bosses as it did with the kids. John Arnatt is also excellent as a new incarnation of *The Deadly Assassin*'s Cardinal Borusa, now promoted to Lord Chancellor. (The script assumes a surprising amount of knowledge of the former story, and Time Lord history in general. I'm sure the Director General was delighted to be reminded of it.) But it's a sloppy end to a frequently sloppy season: beset by strikes, budget crises and unhelpful, often contradictory diktats from above, Williams had attempted to forge his own path, reinventing the show as a space-faring sci-fi adventure, with occasional forays into fairytale fantasy. But it can't have escaped many people's attention that the year's two most successful serials were the ones that stuck most closely to the Goth-lit template of his predecessor. With money so tight, there probably wasn't a worse time to stop doing everything the BBC was good at – costume drama, country houses, claustrophobic horror – in favour of everything they were bad at, like spaceships, alien planets and viral infections represented through the medium of seafood.

Ground control to major Tom

If Tom Baker had been less than enthusiastic about sharing the TARDIS with a savage – and I think we can say that was true, in the same way Churchill was "less than enthusiastic" about Hitler's foreign policy – Graham Williams was hopeful of a better reception for his new companion, a bit of posh from the Doctor's own planet, assigned by the Time Lords to assist him on his season-long quest. ("Sounds great," said Baker. "What's her name?" "Romanadvoratrelundar." "On second thoughts, Leela has a certain ring to it, don't you think?")

In truth, Baker had been pressing for something far more radical, with his "helpful" suggestions for the new companion including a parrot, a frog, a fox and a badger. ("I'll get on to central casting and see who might be available," said Williams. "Or, failing that, I'll try the pet shop.")

And so it was that, on Valentine's Day 1978, Baker helped audition – and no, that's not a euphemism – the six actresses shortlisted to play the new Time Lady in his life. The candidate favoured by the team – including George Spenton-Foster, who was slated to direct the season opener – was Mary Tamm, the Bradford-born daughter of Estonian immigrants who had featured in several notable projects, including a leading role the 1974 film adaptation of Frederick Forsyth's *The Odessa File*.

Tamm, however, was sceptical. "I wasn't very keen," she admitted, "because I had had a very high-profile career so far. But because my agent knew George, she was very insistent –

she kept saying, 'It's going to be a new character, she's not going to be a little screaming girl'.

"So I said I'd go and then... I was just kind of caught up in it. The audition went fine, and the scripts looked good, and it was fun doing my screen tests with Tom."[31]

The latter is perhaps surprising, as Tamm was an old friend of Louise Jameson from their RADA days. But if Jameson was tempted to intervene – by, for example, bundling her friend into the back of a Transit van and driving her back to Estonia – she appears to have kept her counsel, and Tamm was introduced to the press at a hastily arranged photocall just three days after the initial casting session.

Just before departing for a short family holiday in Madeira, Williams was summoned to a meeting with Graeme McDonald to discuss the future direction of the series. Having previously told the producer to cut out the horror and violence, McDonald was now concerned that too much comedy was creeping into the show, and a memo was drafted instructing directors not to let the humour be overplayed. Which was easy for him to say, as he wasn't the one left to wrangle Tom Baker back towards the script.

McDonald had particular concerns about Douglas Adams' script for *The Pirate Planet*. "This won't do," he wrote in a memo. "We're doing science fiction, remember, not comic cuts. The captain with the parrot is a cod figure out of *Treasure Island* with jokey lines which will inevitably lead Tom to stop taking himself seriously again."

This suggested Baker had at some point *started* taking himself seriously again, which was probably news to many on the production team. According to Anthony Read, "[Tom] got bigger and bigger and became more difficult to control as he became utterly established in the role, and a national institution. It's very hard to control a national institution."[22]

Starting work on the series at the end of March, Tamm was in little doubt where the programme's power base lay. "I got the impression that it was very much Tom's show," she said. "Tom ran it, and told the producers and directors what he wanted, and they were all a bit frightened of him."[32]

Around this time, according to Tamm, Baker was also in the habit of dressing like the

Doctor off-screen. "He'd walk down the street wearing his *Doctor Who* scarf and shouting, so you couldn't help but notice him,"[32] Well it's cheaper than hiring a publicist.

Despite some early tension caused by Baker's dislike of the white dress Tamm wore in her first story, which the actress had helped design, the two new co-stars got on well, with John Leeson completing a happier team than the show had been used to lately – though Baker still hated "the tin dog" as a concept.

The tin variety was the least of his worries, however, when a mutt belonging to Paul Seed, a guest actor on season opener *The Ribos Operation*, took a chunk out of Baker's top lip in the pub one lunchtime during rehearsals. Apparently, Seed had warned the party that using your finger to "pop" your cheek was guaranteed to aggravate the dog, and Baker had insisted on repeating the trick three times to see what would happen. What happened was a trip to A&E at Middlesex County Hospital, followed by a new season press photocall featuring the Time Lord sporting a huge plaster across his lip.

Doctor Who merchandise was still doing brisk business in the shops, though some of that summer's product smacked of desperation, such as the TARDIS Tuner – a transistor radio rendered more TARDIS-like by having the words "TARDIS Tuner" written on the side. *The Dr Who Sound Effects LP*, meanwhile, featured such timeless tracks as Gallifreyan Staser Gun (3 Blasts), Dematerializer Gun (Switch On And Fire), Kraal Disorientation Chamber and the all-time classic TARDIS Observation Screen Operates. ("It's not bad," said the head of BBC Records. "But I'm not sure I'm hearing a single.") There was also a *Dalek Colouring Book*, which is silly, as everyone knows Daleks are useless at colouring.

In mid August, 400 fans gathered at Imperial College in London for the Panopticon 78 convention, where guests included Tom Baker, John Leeson, Graham Williams and Anthony Read. The event – and the growing phenomenon of Doctor Who "fandom" – attracted acres of press coverage, from *The Times Higher Education Supplement* to *The Sun*, which ran a series of TV adverts featuring DWAS historian Jeremy Bentham dressed as a Robot of Death. "Find out all my filthy Super-Voc secrets in Saturday's super soaraway *Sun*!", he probably didn't say. In Joe Steeples' feature, Terry Nation claimed he didn't entirely approve of fans and conventions. But that was probably just because he hadn't been invited.

Meanwhile, in America, veteran actor Howard da Silva recorded opening and closing narrations to all 98 Baker episodes bought by Time Life, despite never having seen an episode in his life. ("Previously on *Doctor Who*... the English guy with the teeth and the funny clothes was really pissed with the ugly dude in the wheelchair, and basically told him to stop being such an asshole.") A former Broadway and movie actor, da Silva had been blacklisted in the 50s by the House Committee on Un-American Activities. Just wait until they heard about *this*.

Kicking off *Doctor Who*'s sixteenth season on September 2nd, *The Ribos Operation* is one of the series' true hidden gems, as sparkly and irresistible as the crown jewels the Doctor and Romana arrive on the titular planet to steal. Don't worry, they haven't gone rogue – they're actually after the first segment of the Key to Time, which happens to be disguised as a lump of rare mineral a galactic conman has just planted in the crown jewels in order to jack up the price of the planet, which he's hoping to flog to a deposed tyrant.

As you might have gathered, Robert Holmes is having rather a lot of fun with this one and, happily, the realisation largely does his imagination justice. Designer Ken Ledsham made use of sets from a recent BBC/Time Life co-production of *Anna Karenina*, and the Tsarist trappings – suggesting a society that exists in a permanent Russian winter – are so much more persuasive than just another planet full of boring white corridors. It's also a sign of things to come: this particular era loves to plunder the dressing-up box of Earth history and mythology for inspiration (without, oddly, ever actually doing a genuine period piece – *Horror of Fang Rock* is the first, and last, "historical" adventure of Graham Williams' tenure).

The characters are vividly drawn, Holmes serving up another of his patented classic double acts in the form of smooth-talking confidence trickster Garron and his less than fully committed accomplice Unstoffe. Iain Cuthbertson shines as the former – and Tom

Baker noticeably raises his game in their scenes together – while, as Unstoffe, Nigel Plaskitt gives a sympathetic performance a world away from his most famous role as the voice of mangy, flea-bitten puppet Hartley Hare in pre-school classic *Pipkins*. Special mention, too, for Timothy Bateson as Binro the Heretic, Ribos' own Galileo who, cast out for daring to suggest the stars are not, in fact, the crystals of the sky gods, finds redemption in his final moments when Unstoffe tells him he was right all along.

Having said that, for a story that goes out of its way to rubbish primitive superstitions, the White Guardian (played by Cyril Luckham – now there's a name that's crying out for a dirty limerick) is basically God – albeit a god who dresses like a pimp, and has a thing for wicker garden furniture. The idea of the Key to Time as a perfect cube that "maintains the equilibrium of time itself", meanwhile, strays perilously close to outright magic, and is as much of a semi-mystical maguffin as *Star Wars*' all-powerful Force.

Mary Tamm's reading of Romana is perfect from the get-go: part haughty, imperious ice-maiden, part gauche ingénue, her banter with the Doctor breathes new life into the TARDIS scenes, never more so than when she's flaunting her Triple First from the Time Lord Academy – our man, it turns out, scraped through with 51% on the second attempt. And, it has to be said, she looks pretty damn good for 140.

There isn't much in the way of monster action for the kids – if, indeed, any kids were still expecting monster action by this stage: the komodo-like shrivenzale looks like one of the Muppets after a road accident, and doesn't do much with its limited screen time. For everyone else, though, *The Ribos Operation* is an absolute blast.

With an average of 8.1 million viewers, ratings for the serial were slightly down on recent years, but nothing to suggest the show had been holed below the water line by the *Star Wars* effect. Its star, meanwhile, remained much in demand – as, much to Tom Baker's chagrin, did the tin dog: in late 1978, for example, Baker was joined by K-9 and a Dalek to launch a new computerised booking system at London's Penta Hotel. As one of the biggest stars in Britain, Baker could command a high

fee for such appearances – though still not quite enough to afford a night in a London hotel.

Back at the Beeb, however, trouble was brewing. Wearying of trying to control his wayward star, Graham Williams was considering re-casting the Doctor, while a frustrated Baker told Graeme McDonald and BBC1 Controller Bill Cotton over lunch that he would happily continue in the role if "certain changes" were made to the quality of the scripts and the way they were produced.

Baker was equally outspoken in a feature written for *The Sunday Times Magazine* by his drinking buddy Jeffrey Bernard, in which he talked about everything from his attempted suicide to his evenings spent in Soho necking "booze and valium", and described the BBC's Acton rehearsal rooms as "Kafkaville". Though technically still living with Marianne Ford, he was increasingly wont to make his home wherever he lay his hat – and that *is* a euphemism – and, realising he may have said too much on this subject, resorted to ripping the offending article from the magazine before Ford could see it. Life really was much simpler for wayward philanderers in the days before Google.

The same weekend saw Douglas Adams receive his first on-screen writers' credit for episode one of *The Pirate Planet*. For a man famous for enjoying the "whoosh" of passing deadlines, juggling the script with his other commitments had proved somewhat problematic, and may explain why this tale of a mad cyborg who materialises his hollow planet around other worlds in order to drain them of their energy has a distinctly *Hitchhiker*-ish hue: "magnifactoid eccentricolometer", anyone?

Despite Graeme McDonald's earlier caution over potential flashpoints where Tom Baker might lose all control, Baker actually plays the material largely straight – as Adams often suggested was the only way it *could* be played. The OTT hamming is mostly left to Bruce Purchase as the Captain, whose shouty, one-note performance makes the Daleks look positively nuanced. The character has clear echoes of Captain Hook – with cybernetic appendages in place of the hook and wooden leg – which must make the Doctor Peter Pan (Tom Baker certainly refused to grow up on occasion). There's also more than a hint of *Tintin*'s Captain

Haddock in the Captain's bombastic bluster: "by the frontal lobe of the Sky Demon!" etc.

He's accompanied, naturally, by a pet robot parrot, the Polyphase Avatron, who went missing from the set one day and later turned up in a skip. ("Some notes on my performance would have sufficed," it grumbled to the director.) In the continued absence of any monsters, K-9 fighting a robot parrot is probably as exciting as *The Pirate Planet* gets for younger viewers – though the flying space cars are also fun, if you can ignore the less-than special effects. Adams later admitted he should probably have written the flying cars and crashing spaceships for radio and used the people standing about talking in corridors on TV, instead of the other way round. McDonald had also tried to veto the script on the grounds it was too ambitious but, predictably, there was nothing else to replace it with.

Being Douglas Adams, it goes without saying the jokes are good, though it's surprising how clunking the plot-driven dialogue is; in one notorious scene, David Warwick, as rebel idealist Kimus, vows "Brandaginus Five, by every last breath in my body you'll be avenged!" – which is hard to say with a straight face even if you're *not* addressing it to a small lump of rock.

Graham Williams fell ill during transmission of the story, but was called in from his sick bed to discuss the latest twist in the Tom Baker saga. Graeme McDonald told him Baker had now demanded casting, director and story approval as a condition of signing for another year. At around the same time, Baker also slid a note under Williams' office door, offering his resignation. Williams was ready to call his bluff, so the conversation probably went something like this:

GW: "I mean, who's actually in charge of this show?"

GM (after an awkward pause): "Oh sorry, I thought it was a rhetorical question. Tom is."

Indeed, such was Baker's star wattage, McDonald decided that, if one of them had to go, it ought to be Williams. When Shaun Sutton returned from holiday, however, he reversed the decision, ordering Williams to sack Baker – which the ever-emollient Williams refused to do, insisting Baker would come to his senses given time.

One man who *was* clearing his desk was Anthony Read. Having honoured his one-year commitment, Read had been offered a major book deal, and there was nothing Williams or McDonald could do to persuade him to stay. Which was odd as, apart from the constant script crises, the impossible demands of the BBC sixth floor, the incredible shrinking budget and the endless stand-up rows between the production office and the leading man, it had been an absolute blast. Instead, Williams offered the job to Douglas Adams, who accepted, despite a punishing workload that also included writing a Hitchhiker's novel, second radio series and an LP adaptation, and producing a radio comedy called *Black Cinderella Two Goes East*.

The previous Doctor was also getting in on the publishing act: in October, Methuen published *The Jon Pertwee Book of Monsters*, a short story anthology for which Pertwee had, in fact, only written the preface. Or signed it, at least.

It's only rolling rocks, but I like it

On BBC1, *Doctor Who* reached a milestone with the transmission of its 100th story. Or perhaps that should be stories, as *The Stones of Blood* is such a game of two halves, you can't help wondering if David Fisher blacked out while writing it and forgot everything he'd already done. The first two-and-a-half episodes present a deliciously Hammer-esque tale of occult shenanigans and druidic rituals centred around a Cornish megalithic stone circle. Granted, having giant lumps of rock (actually a blood-sucking silicone-based alien lifeform called the Ogri) as your monster-of-the-week isn't exactly a *brilliant* idea – the chase sequences leave a lot to be desired – but the combination of good location work and extensive night filming (along with some less successful day-for-night filming) brings a shiver to the spine that's been sadly missing in recent stories.

Then, with a screech of brakes, everyone piles off the coach and back into a cheap-looking studio set for an extended skit in which the Doctor must defend himself in a trial presided over by a pair of bickering fairy lights – a joke which Baker further flogs to death by whipping a barrister's wig out of his pocket. Oh save our sides, do.

Still, at least the cast is consistent, with the women coming out firmly on top: Susan Engel is deliciously arch as an alien war criminal who's spent hundreds of years hanging out around the stone circle – for reasons the script never bothers to go into – and theatrical grand dame Beatrix Lehmann is simply wonderful as sharp-tongued archaeologist Amelia Rumford. (Baker, predictably, was so besotted he wanted her to stay on as a companion.) Faced with such competition, Mary Tamm still manages to shine as Romana – her puzzled reaction when Engel tells her she used to be a brown owl ("Really?") is priceless.

While cast and crew were filming near Oxford, a bunch of students stole the TARDIS prop and left it in a quarry (maybe there was a shortage of traffic cones that year). Whether this was a situationist prank designed as a comment on the over-reliance of quarry locations in *Doctor Who*, or merely too much strong cider, isn't known. Legend also has it that a school party visiting the Rollright Stones near Chipping Norton were suspicious that there appeared to be rather too many – especially when one of the ancient monoliths, which had stood unmoved since the Neolithic age, suddenly toppled over in a stiff breeze. Then Tom Baker turned up, and all suddenly became clear. One final production nugget: the visual of a wrecked spaceship was created by effects designer Mat Irvine smashing up a model of an Eagle transporter from *Space: 1999*. That'll learn 'em.

To celebrate the show making its century, Tom Baker, Mary Tamm and John Leeson devised an extra scene in which Romana and K-9 bring out a cake to celebrate the Doctor's birthday. The director, Darrol Blake, claims this wheeze might even have been his idea, but Graham Williams put his foot down and refused to let them record it, arguing it was silly and self-indulgent. ("Yes," said Baker. "What's your point?")

Despite this further deterioration in the relationship between producer and star, Baker did agree to suspend his resignation until Graeme McDonald returned from a trip to the US. Mary Tamm was equally undecided about staying, with Williams still hoping to persuade her to stay even as the cameras rolled on season finale *The Armageddon Factor*. But he certainly wasn't going to get down on his knees and beg her – he did have *some* pride, you know. And, besides, he'd tried that last year, and look where it had got him.

During taping of the story, the regulars took time out to record two spoof scenes for the BBC's "Christmas tape" – a long-standing tradition in which programme-makers would perform sketches for an in-house gag reel compiled by the Beeb's technical staff. One sketch features Baker asking K-9 a question and, when he fails to compute a satisfactory response, replying "Yeah, you never fucking know the answer when it's important". (At least, we assume it's a sketch – it probably looked very similar to a lot of studio outtakes around this time.) Another sees Baker and Tamm slumped by the TARDIS console, apparently caught in the middle of a passionate clinch, while K-9 balances a bottle of rum on his head.

On November 22nd, Baker and Tamm were joined by Carole Ann Ford for an edition of the BBC's early evening magazine programme *Nationwide* celebrating *Doctor Who*'s 15th anniversary. As a truly magisterial example of Tom Baker at the height of imperial phase, the show is hard to beat. It starts with our hero looking positively aghast as presenter Frank Bough introduces him, and there's an exquisitely awkward moment when Bough asks Tamm what Baker is like to work with. "Very funny, actually – we spend most of the time falling around laughing," says Tamm, as the camera cuts to Baker with the look of a man attending his own funeral.

Bough is curiously fixated on the idea of Baker and the Doctor being the same man, a point he refuses to let drop until Baker snaps back: "Well I don't have to be Doctor Who any more than you have to be Frank Bough." "Yes but I *am* Frank Bough," says the host. "I don't have a fictional image." "Of course you do," scoffs Baker. "People don't really believe you exist, they only see you on the television.

"The point is," he continues, "whenever I meet anyone who's interested in *Doctor Who*, there's no point being Tom Baker, because they'd find Tom Baker very dreary. Such is the gullibility of the public, and the potency of television, they ascribe to me all the virtues of Doctor Who – for example, I don't need anything boring like a bank card. I don't even need money. They make an assumption that my probity is beyond question."

"So if you're not very nice as Tom Baker," says Bough provocatively, "you have to work very hard at being Doctor Who when the occasion demands it."

"Yeah, it's not difficult," growls Baker. "I get on alright with people. Superficially."

Bough concludes with a closing comment that "Doctor Who is clearly something of a cult". At least I think that's what he says.

The fourth story in the Key to Time arc is perhaps the most straight-up Doctor Who pitch of them all: it's The Prisoner of Zenda – with robots! Forget stories "loosely based" on classic novels: here, David Fisher literally takes Anthony Hope's Victorian adventure about the struggle for the throne of a fictional kingdom, adds a few gags and circuit boards, and off we go. The result is one of the series' most effortlessly entertaining confections, a winning blend of adventure, comedy and romance filmed in the hazy sunshine of an English country summer. The production wisely retains the Ruritanian aesthetic of Hope's original (for a story about androids, it's surprisingly low-tech – and refreshingly technobabble free), which plays to the BBC's design strengths, while the castles, palaces and handsome princes are a further demonstration of the era's fondness for fairytales.

As the villainous Count Grendel, Peter Jeffrey steals every scene he can from under Tom Baker's nose: even when he's been thoroughly routed, the Count makes his escape with a defiant parting shot of "Next time, I shall not be so lenient!" Baker is no slouch, though, clearly having fun with the high gag rate, whether tossing out surrealist quips like, "Would you mind not standing on my chest? My hat's on fire," or noting dryly, "They always want you to go alone when you're walking into a trap – have you noticed that?" Mary Tamm holds her own, too, playing no fewer than four characters (if you include the two robot doubles). The only mild disappointment is that the big battle planned for the climax had to be abandoned after the main location, Leeds Castle in Kent, found itself playing host to an

Arab-Israeli peace summit attended by Anwar Sadat, Menachem Begin and Henry Kissinger, and it was decided a full-scale assault on the ramparts might not be such a good idea. As an aside, in 1986 Target Books published a guide to Doctor Who locations written by two American fans, who advised the best way to get to Leeds Castle was by taxi from Leeds City Station – a round trip of some 496 miles. (Probably best to agree a price before you set off.)

Fisher had been commissioned at short notice to provide a replacement for Ted Lewis' story, after Lewis turned up to a script meeting somewhat worse for wear. So we can probably forgive him for ripping off a literary classic so shamelessly – especially when he does it with such panache. Okay, so the ending – in which K-9 spins about in a boat while Tom Baker laughs like a loon – is pure Scooby Doo. And there's a deeply unfortunate cameo from a man in a gorilla suit pretending to be a "Taran wood beast" (you can't helping thinking the show's heart really wasn't in the monsters by this point). But overall this is a fresh, funny, swashbuckling pastiche with charm to spare.

The same month saw the Time Lord staging a raid on the pop charts, in a roundabout sort of way, when a bunch of sessions musicians calling themselves Mankind reached No. 2 with a disco take on the Doctor Who theme. Emerging from the African American, Latino and gay communities of New York and Philadelphia, the disco craze was an obvious fit for Doctor Who, a show produced by pipe-smoking middle-aged white men in Shepherd's Bush. There's no denying it's an undeniably groovy take on Ron Grainer's theme, though – even if the bunch of blokes who turned up to play it on Top of the Pops looked more like prog throwbacks than dancefloor divas, complete with keyboard player in standard-issue prog rock cape.

In the Doctor Who office, things remained distinctly un-groovy as Graham Williams found himself fighting a war on several fronts, the latest of which came in the form of Mary Tamm's agent, Irene Dawkins, who was demanding a better deal for her client, in terms of script and character development, if she was to remain with the show. "Unless some way can be found of ensuring that more use is made of her talent and ability," wrote Dawkins, "I fear we must set your offer aside."

Tamm was pregnant by this point – but even if she hadn't been, her enthusiasm was on the wane. "I think by about the beginning of *The Armageddon Factor*, I had realised that there was a certain repetition to it", she said. "There's a kind of lack of initiative which then starts happening, and I think I could then see that the character had really gone as far as it ever would be possible to go with it. And that's when I thought, I don't really want to do another year of very very hard work, just playing the same character who's never going to change."[31]

Tamm is particularly badly served by her penultimate story, *The Power of Kroll* – a cautionary tale of what happens when a good writer receives rotten advice. Anthony Read's brief to Robert Holmes was to write a story featuring "*Doctor Who*'s biggest ever monster". It's a mystery why he thought this would be a good idea, this year of all years – write a story featuring *Doctor Who*'s *cheapest* ever monster we could have understood (though maybe they felt they'd covered that with *The Androids of Tara*) – and even more of a mystery why a man with Holmes' backroom experience went along with it. But he did, turning in a tale in which the indigenous swamp-dwellers of a distant moon battle human colonists, with occasional interruptions from a mile-wide squid.

The model of the mighty (it says here) Kroll is actually pretty good – but any attempts to place it in the same frame as anyone else are frankly pitiful, and the scene in which a gas refinery comes under attack from a giant rubber tentacle represents a whole new low for the programme. And, let's not forget, that's a programme that not so long ago had featured our hero being menaced by a clam.

Graeme McDonald was so contemptuous of the sets, he instructed Graham Williams never to hire the designer again. "I really feel I must tell you how disappointed I have been with the design work on the currently transmitting Dr Who serial", wrote McDonald in one of his many memos. "A control room set which has run for four weeks has an unprofessional look. A countdown clock pokes through an unfinished hole in the wall; in another set the door

to the rocket launch pad is laughably wooden and a ladder above it is wavering near an equally insecure flat.

"As you know I am normally full of admiration for the contribution design make to this show, often against apparently insuperable odds. It's when you see such a duff effort as this you realise how much more impressive the normal contribution really is. You will understand, therefore I hope, if we do not ask for the services of Don Giles again." Whether Don Giles was equally understanding, we can't say.

To add insult to ignominy, Holmes – one of *Doctor Who*'s funniest writers – was told to "keep it serious", which means it's not only very silly, it's boring as well. (In retrospect, perhaps letting Tom Baker fill the gaps in the budget by clowning about wasn't such a bad idea after all, if this is what happens when he doesn't.)

Baker is visibly bored by the material (though there's a marvellous moment when someone hands him a drink and he casually drops it into his pocket), and Mary Tamm gets nothing to do – it's disappointing to see the man who wrote *The Ribos Operation* reducing Romana to little more than a Fay Wray-style damsel in distress.

The only people not phoning it in are John Abineri and the ever-reliable Philip Madoc – though Madoc was annoyed to find himself playing a different part to the one he'd signed up for. Original director Alan Browning had cast him as Thawn; then Browning fell ill and George Baker, cast as Fenner, pulled out, so incoming director Norman Stewart – he really did know how to pick 'em – re-cast Madoc in that role. Martin Jarvis, who was down to play Dugeen, also dropped out, giving John Leeson the chance finally to get his face on screen.

The one real success of *The Power of Kroll* is the location: the swamp moon of Delta Magna makes a nice change from the usual quarries and sandpits, and the scenes filmed at Iken Marsh in Suffolk are unusually striking. Pity about the swampies, though: what should have been vaguely amphibious marsh creatures are represented by a bunch of very bored-looking extras and stuntmen in green paint. Because of the wetland environment, the paint had to be water-resistant – and it was. So resistant, in fact, that the actors couldn't get it off, and had to be taken to a local RAF base and scrubbed with Swarfega (liquid Rutan, to you and me). A coach load of green men being bussed into a military base? This is exactly how Roswell-style conspiracy theories start.

By now, the Mexican stand-off between Baker and Williams had reached a new low. When Baker again refused to sign a new contract, Graeme McDonald took over the negotiations with the actor's agent, Jean Diamond, asking for a final decision by January 4th. For Baker, having some input into casting the new companion was a deal-breaker over which he and Williams had exchanged views, according to the producer, in the "frankest manner".

Baker then wrote to McDonald, stating: "I expected that I could go quietly and without rancour. I offered two extreme character suggestions for [Mary Tamm's] replacement – the outrageous and the strange. I understood these were to be discussed. Then at the end of December by taxi from Graham Williams I receive a 'within seven days' letter. What does it mean? Am I not to be in on the casting of the new girl? I don't want to cast her, I want to be involved. The letter made me wince... It suggests a lack of flair, my main reservation at our earlier meetings. Do let's resolve it with more style. Yours ever, Tom Baker."

The "outrageous and the strange" suggestion Baker refers to were a grossly overweight woman who would be forced to to "wheeze" around after him, and a talking cabbage. Unfortunately (or fortunately, for anyone who isn't Tom Baker), Williams couldn't find a cabbage with an Equity card – though it's possible he hadn't tried the northern club circuit.

An exasperated McDonald eventually summoned Baker and Williams to his office so they could have it out mano-a-mano. This helped clear the air, but it was obvious the two weren't about to embark on a hill-walking holiday together any time soon. "Graham was a very fragile soul," said Baker in later years. "He was so nice – he hated head-on confrontation, whereas sometimes I liked it, I liked some creative tension."[22]

"Some creative tension" was putting it mildly. Nevertheless, the companion situation resolved itself in an unlikely manner when Mary Tamm recruited her own replacement in the BBC bar. Lalla Ward had just finished playing an alien

princess in *The Armageddon Factor* (born the Honourable Sarah Ward, daughter of the 7th Viscount Bangor, she was clearly never going to be cast as the cleaner). Both Baker and Tamm had enjoyed working with the actress, and Tamm suggested she should take over as a regenerated Romana – an idea Baker was happy to run with.

"I think Tom and I hatched a plan, really, that it would be quite fun to do," recalled Ward. "He thought it was a good idea, and talked to Graham Williams, who took me out to lunch and offered me the job."[33]

On January 15th, Tom Baker signed for another year of *Doctor Who*, without having received the casting, script or director approval he'd asked for. On the plus side, he had found a new companion. And, as it would turn out, a wife.

The Key to Time: Time not actually locked, experts discover

Douglas Adams had joined *Doctor Who* with big ideas about reinvigorating the show's writing team with fresh blood. But his attempts to get workable scripts from talent as diverse as his Cambridge contemporary (and *Hitchhiker's* co-writer) John Lloyd, respected science fiction novelists John Brunner and Christopher Priest and even Tom Stoppard had proved stillborn. A script from Philip Hinchcliffe called *Valley of the Lost* had also been rejected on the grounds it would be too expensive (which must have come as a surprise to Hinchcliffe, who hadn't let such trivialities get in the way in *his* day).

In the end, as he lined up stories for the upcoming seventeenth season, Adams was forced to fall back on a familiar line-up of reliable warhorses including David Fisher, Bob Baker and even Terry Nation, who was commissioned to write his first Dalek story in five years.

Before that, though, Adams had to do a hasty repair job on the final story of the current run – which, in a year with more milestones than the A1, opened with *Doctor Who's* 500th episode. After an unprecedented season-long build-up, *The Armageddon Factor* had its work cut out to deliver a satisfactory pay-off to the Key to Time saga. Sadly, it struggles to carry the weight of its own story, let alone the whole series. An inter-planetary space war made entirely in-studio was always going to be a tall order and, strung out over six long weeks, with the budget for the year already spent, it's not for the faint-hearted.

It's Bob 'n' Dave's last outing together but, at times, it feels like they've already started working separately, as large chunks of the story bear absolutely no relation to each other: people forget things they already know, other people know stuff they haven't been told, and the incoherent denouement appears to suggest the whole Key to Time quest has been a colossal waste of the Doctor's – and our – time. Cheers for that. Douglas Adams drastically re-wrote the ending which, by all accounts, was even worse beforehand.

The production is as sloppy as the scripting: the TARDIS appears in the background of one scene, despite having already left the planet several minutes earlier, K-9 is variously sporting the wrong panels at the wrong time, and the Mutes – inhuman drones of the mysterious Shadow – wear Clark's lace-ups. Which wouldn't be so bad if the script didn't require their feet to be shown in *extreme close-up* while a miniaturised Doctor (yes, another one) runs around them like a badly CSO'd mouse.

The Shadow, it turns out, is really a puppet of the Black Guardian. (A Shadow puppet? Please yourselves.) Valentine Dyall – famous as radio's Man in Black (or at least they *said* he was in black) makes for a suitably stentorian villain, but his cosmic oppo is a no-show after Cyril Luckham proved unavailable. ("There once was an actor called Luckham, who when asked to return, said 'no...'" Well, you get the point.) You might have thought they'd have checked the schedule of the central player in the whole Key to Time shebang before employing him in the first place. But you'd be wrong.

The Black Guardian / Shadow's plan involves prolonging a war between the worlds of Atrios and Zeos. As the Marshall of Atrios, John Woodvine brings some much-needed gravity to the party; Zeos, by contrast, is run by a mad computer called Mentalis. That's right, Mentalis. The mental computer.

In rather a neat twist, the sixth segment of the Key is revealed to be a living, breathing person, the Princess Astra (the Honourable Sarah Ward). In a less neat twist, we meet another renegade Time Lord, Drax, played by Barry Jackson – whose stage name, imaginatively, was Jack Barry – with a cockney accent so strong, he could be a Sontaran. A former inmate of Brixton prison, Drax was forced by the Shadow to build and maintain Mentalis, ensuring the supercomputer continued to wage total war by switching it off and switching it on again occasionally. An old school chum of the Doctor's, Drax reveals our hero used to be known as Theta Sigma; it appears this may have been a genuine attempt to answer the series' enigmatic title question through the medium of some knockabout throwaway banter. Fortunately, everyone chose to ignore this and assume it must have been a jokey nickname. And besides, we've already established that the Doctor's real name is Donald.

On top of its other shortcomings, *The Armageddon Factor* contains probably the single worst example of Tom Baker's increasingly "experimental" approach to the role: as he finally holds the complete Key to Time in his hands, the Doctor rolls his eyes back into his skull and rants about how he now has absolute power over the entire universe. Even Kroll had to conclude it was probably "a bit large".

In retrospect, Graham Williams conceded he'd made a bit of a rod for his own back with the Key to Time shebang, not least because he'd robbed himself of the usual get-out clause of swapping the running order. Overall, though, he believed concept had worked well – even if Tom Baker and Mary Tamm weren't falling over themselves to agree.

In February 1978, Tom Baker departed to Australia for a *Doctor Who* publicity tour, throwing himself into a round of personal appearances – including lending his name to a Keep Australia Beautiful campaign. According to the gossip columns of the *Daily Mail*, the BBC were unhappy with the fact Marianne Ford had joined him for part of the trip, claiming the Corporation didn't look kindly on Doctor Who being seen to have a girlfriend in tow. Whether there was any truth in this we can't be sure, but it didn't exactly help the couple's already strained relationship, which Ford terminated not long afterwards.

It was around this time Baker was also forced to give up on another long-term relationship: the star was still talking up the *Doctor Who Meets Scratchman* movie during his Australian trip, saying he hoped it would be filmed in Lanzarote the following year. But it was probably little more than wishful thinking by this point, the project having failed to secure any significant funding. In an early example of crowd-sourcing, Baker had idly suggested the public might like to chip in to the project, and ended up having to return hundreds of pound notes sent in by children.

Sadly, that meant Ian Marter was denied his well-deserved encore as Harry Sullivan, though he did continue his association with *Doctor Who* by writing for the Target books range, where he achieved a certain notoriety for including the word "bastard" in his novelisation of *The Enemy of the World*. (Perhaps it's just as well they didn't let him do *The Android Invasion*.) In 1986, Marter died suddenly on his 42nd birthday after suffering a heart attack brought on by complications of diabetes.

It's perhaps ironic that Tom Baker's long-cherished *Doctor Who* film should have been scrapped just as the show was taking off in America – albeit it a modest, cult fashion. The syndicated screenings across PBS channels were successful enough for a US publisher to strike a deal to reprint selected Target novels, which were adapted for the American market ("The Master – I swear to God I'm gonna pop a cap in that blowhard's ass!" the Doctor didn't exclaim, while pulling out his sonic six-shooter) with a foreword by the prolific SF author Harlan Ellison explaining who the Sam Heck this Doctor Who guy was anyway. "The pleasure is all mine – and all yours, kiddo," he wrote, possibly while wearing a ten gallon hat and chomping on a cheroot.

Back in London, auditions were held for a new K-9 actor, John Leeson having decided to pursue other roles. He wasn't asking to play Lear – just something where he could stand up would do. ("If you could just read this short piece for us," the casting director told the new hopefuls. "That's wonderful. Now if you could just roll over onto your tummy. That's excellent, really great. Now sit up and beg – that's it. Who's a clever boy, then? You are! Yes you are! Thank you, we'll be in touch.") The gig even-tually went to David Brierley, whose previous roles had included Ken Barlow's lodger in *Coronation Street* – so at least they knew he was house trained.

Ooh Lalla!

As Douglas Adams wrangled with the scripts for the new series, the team had a change of heart about the direction of David Fisher's story, *A Gamble with Time*. The original draft would have seen the TARDIS team on the trail of a time-travelling alien cardsharp in 1920s Monte Carlo – until production unit manager John Nathan-Turner did his sums and worked out it would be just as cheap to film in actual Paris as mock up 20s Monaco. Fisher was too busy with other commitments – not least of them a messy divorce – to do the rewrites so, with production due to start the following Monday morning, Douglas Adams and Graham Williams locked themselves in Williams' spare room – "with a typewriter and a bottle of whiskey", according to legend – emerging three days later with four completed scripts and a pounding hangover. Michael Hayes, the director assigned to the serial, spent the weekend pacing around an upstairs room, like an expectant father, and taking Williams' young son out for walks.

"They rang me and said, 'We've done something awful – we've had Douglas rewrite this'," recalled Fisher. 'They offered to keep my name on it, and let me have all the money, but I didn't think it was fair that I had the credit or the money. They wouldn't hear of me turning down the money, so we reached an arrangement. I think I got something very generous like 70%."[34]

As filming on Season Seventeen began in March, Baker was delighted to find he and Lalla Ward were on the same page – i.e. any page not in the script. Ward shared her co-star's view that *Doctor Who* was for children, and colluded with him on rewriting scenes in a way the kids might find more amusing.

They're lucky there were any scenes *to* rewrite: around the same time, Douglas Adams sent a memo to Graeme McDonald lamenting the problems he had had trying to find new blood for the show, concluding that, having wasted "too much time and energy" on writers who hadn't worked out, he was resigned to falling back on old hands. Meanwhile, Tom Baker and *Doctor Who* were shortlisted for best children's TV star and best children's TV programme at the 1979 Multi-Coloured Swap Shop Awards, eventually losing out to avuncular painter Tony Hart and upstart comprehensive school drama *Grange Hill* respectively. Baker took his defeat gracefully – but Morph was livid.

In fact, Baker was busy starring in his own personal re-make of *April in Paris*, with Lalla Ward as his Doris Day. During *Doctor Who's* first ever overseas shoot, romance bloomed among the spring blossoms of the French capital and, not long after returning home, Baker had practically moved into Ward's apartment. And it's not like she didn't know what she was letting herself in for: footage from the studio sessions for the story shows Baker stalking menacingly about and instructing the director to "get this intolerable scene in before I have a bloody stroke", while Ward sits frozen in porcelain terror.

Douglas Adams, on the other hand, had practically moved into his office: he was already behind schedule with the next Hitchhiker's radio series, to the extent that several studio days had to be scrapped. He was also working on the novel and LP of the first series and, in May, was commissioned to write a pilot for a BBC TV adaptation. So we can only imagine how delighted he was when, all other options having fallen through, he realised he'd have to write the six-part *Doctor Who* season finale himself as well. After working day and night to bash out the story, and with the rest of the office having decamped to Paris, Adams let off steam with an epic international pub crawl, during which he and director Ken Grieve checked into – and got thrown out of – the same Paris hotel as the *Who* crew, before moving on to Berlin and eventually arriving back at Television Centre, somewhat worse for wear, minutes before Williams, Baker and company.

Adams' workload meant Williams inevitably shouldered more of the script burden than most of his predecessors. The producer was also in demand from BBC Enterprises to give more of his time to areas like overseas sales, merchandise and the show's increasingly

organised global fanbase. Williams was growing particularly irritated with the number of fans attending studio recordings. He had enough on his hands trying to keep Tom Baker under control, without people wandering about rustling Forbidden Planet carrier bags all over the shop. And so, in August, Williams told Graeme McDonald he was leaving *Doctor Who*. The head of serials tried to persuade him to stay for a fourth year, but Williams was adamant he'd had enough.

Fans in the studio were the least of anyone's problems, however, as recording sessions for *Nightmare of Eden*, the fourth serial of the new series, rapidly unravelled into the Nightmare of Television Centre. By now, most regular directors knew what to expect with Tom Baker, and could adjust accordingly – by, for example, turning up for work in full riot gear. But Alan Bromly – whose only previous *Doctor Who* credit had been *The Time Warrior* six years earlier – was a director of the old school, with more of the manner of a retired headmaster than a visionary auteur, and it was clear from the start he and Baker were on a collision course. Lalla Ward recalls one incident in which Bromly repeated the same instruction seven times from the gallery, after which Baker grabbed the boom mic and shouted: "Can someone tell me what's going on? I'm getting psittacosis listening to that parrot!" "One of them had to go," said Colin Mapson, the story's visual effects designer. "And it wasn't going to be Tom."[22]

Sure enough, Bromly walked out halfway through recording, leaving Graham Williams to step in and complete the story himself. ("No, honestly, I don't mind – I wasn't busy.")

As Williams' successor, Graeme McDonald initially approached former production unit manager George Gallaccio. When he turned it down, McDonald agreed to promote Williams' own preferred candidate, current incumbent John Nathan-Turner. As a precaution, he also asked Barry Letts to take an executive producer credit in return for keeping an eye on the new boy.

Launching *Doctor Who's* seventeenth season on Saturday, September 1st, *Destiny of the Daleks* is a sequel to *Genesis of the Daleks*, in so much as it's set on Skaro ("many centuries" after the events of the first story) and includes the words "of the Daleks" in its title. Beyond that, it's hard to find much shared DNA between the two serials: where *Genesis* presented an unremittingly bleak vision of an oppressive, post-Holocaust dystopia, *Destiny* just feels like a bunch of people dicking about in a quarry.

The tone is set from the start with a ridiculous sequence in which Romana tries out various different bodies while regenerating, apparently on a whim. You could forgive the way it casually cocks a snook at one of the central tenets of *Doctor Who* mythology if the result – This one's very short! Now she's really tall! – was in any way funny. But it isn't. Later, the Doctor gets trapped under some rubble, and whiles away the time reading *Origins of the Universe* by Oolon Colluphid (an in-joke for Hitchhiker's fans, almost) and, by the time he's slaughtered the elephant in the room by pointing out Daleks are too useless even to climb out of a hole – a joke manfully resisted for 17 years – you know we're in something of a hole ourselves.

Terry Nation was apparently unhappy with Douglas Adams sending up his creations – though he did gratefully adopt Adams and Graham Williams' central conceit of the Daleks digging up Davros to help them break the stalemate in their endless war with the robotic Movellans. A galactic game of chicken between two totally logical races would just about make sense – *if the Daleks were robots*. But then how was Nation supposed to know they weren't? He's only the guy who'd created them.

With their white spandex jumpsuits and silver dreadlocks, the Movellans couldn't be more disco if they broke out into a choreographed routine to "I Lost My Heart to a Starship Trooper". They're also pathetically easy to beat, thanks to the fashion for carrying their power-packs around on their belts (a design flaw, yes, but where else were they going to fit them in those skintight suits?), and are so easily re-programmed to betray their comrades a bright 12-year-old could probably do it on his Commodore Vic 20. (He could probably have written a better script, too.) How the Daleks have been unable to defeat these Studio 54 rejects is a mystery – until you see the shabby state of the Daleks themselves: the budget would only stretch to four badly

battered casings, all with various bits missing, so the numbers were bulked out with vacuum-formed dummy props. And they don't put up much of a fight themselves – the Doctor attaches a bomb to one then sends it into a panicked tailspin by hanging his hat on its eyestalk. Maybe they're just not hat people.

Davros, sadly, fares even worse: with Michael Wisher touring a play in Australia, actor David Gooderson was cast, less for his commanding presence and more for the fact he fit into Wisher's old costume. Or sort of fit: the mask's a bit wobbly, so he looks more like Davros after a mild stroke. Gooderson's interpretation of the megalomaniacal Dalek creator is less "homicidal rage", more "slightly annoyed". But then, with Tom Baker goofing about refusing to take anything seriously, who can blame him? Speaking of which, Baker is unwittingly responsible for the story's most memorable moment when, unable to decide between telling a Dalek to "stay back" or "back off", he heads down the middle and orders it to "spack off!" – much to the delight of snickering children everywhere.

There are a couple of saving graces, most notably Lalla Ward, whose Romana is less of an ice queen and more of a knowing, sassy female version of the Doctor (with her long scarf and coat, she even dresses like him). The production also benefits from the use of a steadicam, which the BBC had been offered on a free trial, and decided to experiment with on *Doctor Who*, as opposed to something they actually cared about. Director Ken Grieve puts it to good use, shooting the Daleks from below in an effort to give them a looming, powerful presence, and injecting those scenes with a kinetic energy sadly absent from the rest of this dull, plodding, painfully unfunny nonsense.

Destiny of the Daleks would prove to be Terry Nation's final contribution to *Doctor Who*. In the 1980s, he relocated to Los Angeles, where he co-wrote several episodes of *MacGyver* – an action/adventure series embedded in the minds of Generation X, in which Richard Dean Anderson's mulleted Vietnam vet foiled various dastardly plots armed only with a Swiss Army Knife and a roll of duct tape. Nation was trying to launch a *Blake's 7* revival when he died from emphysema in 1997. This book hasn't exactly fallen over itself to extol Nation's virtues, but it's fair to say that without his contribution, *Doctor Who* would probably have run for a few weeks in late 1963/early 1964, then sunk without trace.

City of Death: worst civic slogan ever

According to the Doctor in *City of Death* – as *A Gamble with Time* had become by the time it reached TV screens – 1979 is less a vintage year and "more of a table wine". That's certainly true of the year's *Doctor Who* output – with one very conspicuous exception. As our hero tells Romana as they survey the city from the top of the Eiffel Tower, Paris has "a life, an ethos, a bouquet". He might well be describing *City of Death* itself.

What's striking about this story – credited to David Agnew to reflect the input of David Fisher and Graham Williams alongside Douglas Adams – is that, while so many of the serials around it seem to pull in different directions, with Baker in particular often working against the material, here everyone appears to be tuned in to the same frequency. The result is a wonderful, effervescent comic caper bursting with wit, invention and romance.

This being *Doctor Who*'s first overseas adventure, there's no stinting on the cultural tourism, with endless shots of the Doctor and Romana in every picture postcard Paris location you can imagine. It's shameless padding, of course, but for viewers stuck in broke, strike-bound Britain, what could be more charming than watching the Time Lord and his Time Lady skipping hand-in-hand down the Avenue des Champs Elysees in springtime, accompanied by Dudley Simpson's really rather lovely musical motif?

The plot is both audacious and elegant: Scaroth, last of the linguini-headed Jagaroth, is splintered throughout history in various disguises, including the urbane Count Scarlioni, who is using the profits from his career as an art thief and forger to fund the time travel experiments that will allow him to go back and save his people. (That's a problem for the human race, as the explosion that scattered him through time also triggered life on Earth. And for the French chickens, who don't come out of the experiments at all well.) As well a

Gainsborough, several Guttenberg Bibles and a first draft of *Hamlet*, Scarlioni has no fewer than seven copies of the Mona Lisa – all of them genuine. What he doesn't know is that six of them have "This is a Fake" written on the canvas, which the Doctor helpfully scrawled there before Leonardo started painting them. It's that sort of story.

Julian Glover – in his first *Who* appearance since his 1965 turn as Richard the Lionheart – is perfect as the suave Scarlioni, and he's well matched by Catherine Schell's purring Countess. The couple's first encounter with the Doctor is surely a contender for *Doctor Who*'s funniest ever scene: "What a wonderful butler", grins the Time Lord as he's shoved into the room. "He's so violent!" Later, he flatters the Countess with "Well, you're a beautiful woman, probably". "My dear, I don't think he's as stupid as he seems", she observes. "My dear", replies her husband, "Nobody could be as stupid as *he* seems."

The final piece of the puzzle is Tom Chadbon's Duggan, the two-fisted Bulldog Drummond-style private eye that inspired Fisher's original treatment. The Doctor spends most of the story trying to stop Duggan thumping people – or, in one memorable instance, trying to attack Scarlioni's henchman with a priceless Louis Quinze chair – until finally allowing him to save the day with "the most important punch in history".

Adams tosses out great gags and whip-smart dialogue at every turn, from the Doctor being tortured with thumbscrews in sixteenth-century Florence – "Aaaagh!" "I haven't started yet." "I know, it's just his hands are cold." – to Kerensky, the Count's pet scientist, struggling to comprehend the true nature of his work: "It's the Jagaroth who need all the chickens, is it?".

And that's before the hastily-written cameo by Eleanor Bron and John Cleese – who was at a loose end while strike action disrupted the recording of *Fawlty Towers* – as a couple of pretentious art enthusiasts trying to deconstruct the meaning of the TARDIS when it's parked in an art gallery. "Divorced from its function and seen purely as a piece of art, its structure of line and colour is curiously counterpointed by the redundant vestiges of its function," says Cleese. The Doctor, Romana and Duggan then pile into the police box and it disappears. "Exquisite," sighs Bron in wonderment. "Absolutely exquisite." And so it is.

As well as being one of *Doctor Who*'s finest achievements, *City of Death* also attracted the show's largest ever audience, with an unprecedented 16.1 million tuning in for the final episode – admittedly with a little help from ITV, which was kept off air by an industrial dispute for more than ten weeks between August and October (*Destiny of the Daleks* had also averaged an impressive 13 million viewers). It might also have helped that Lalla Ward spent the entire story dressed as a schoolgirl. "I thought it would be fun to wear something little girls probably hated wearing," she explained. "I got loads of letters saying, 'I don't mind wearing my school uniform any more.' I didn't bank on the fact I'd also get loads of letters from their fathers... It simply hadn't crossed my mind that school uniform was a kind of turn-on for some people."[33]

As filming continued, John Nathan-Turner – or JN-T, as he would come to be known by friends and enemies alike – was already looking ahead to the next season, and sent copies of French keyboard wizard Jean Michael Jarre's trippy instrumental albums *Oxygène* and *Équinoxe* to Graeme McDonald, suggesting that something similar could be used for the show's incidental music. ("Yeah, that's cosmic, man," said McDonald after giving them a spin. "Hey, do you think I should get rid of my desk and chair and replace them with some cool bean bags and a lava lamp and shit? This place is, like, squaresville.") Equally groovy – to a generation of *Doctor Who* fans raised in the pre-video age, at least – was an abridged soundtrack LP of *Genesis of the Daleks*, which was released at the end of September, with linking narration by Tom Baker. Wisely, they never tried following it up with a record of *Destiny of the Daleks*, which would surely have qualified as the ultimate Difficult Second Album.

As if *that* wasn't exciting enough, after years of bunking in with the likes of Noddy and Lenny the Lion, Thursday, October 17th saw the Time Lord finally starring in his own comic with the launch of Marvel's *Doctor Who Weekly*. Promising Comic Strips! Features! and Pin-Ups! (don't worry, they weren't the Katy Manning sort), the cover of the Fantastic First Issue also boasted Free Transfers! And Free Transfers! (hey, if it's worth mentioning...) a "prize-winning competition" (always the best sort) and the exciting news that The Daleks Are Back! (or, at least, they had been about six weeks earlier). In "A Letter from the Doctor", our man told us to watch out for issue 879 – "it really was a beauty" – while "The Story of Dr Who" covered the entire history of the programme in less than 500 words. (Pipe down whoever just said they wish they'd read that version instead.)

Under the guidance of founding editor Dez Skinn – despite sounding like the singer with a punk band, Skinn was a big noise in UK comics, often described as "the British Stan Lee" – *Doctor Who Weekly* (a snip at 12p) was aimed squarely at children, though the quality of the comic strips proved appealing to older fans, too. Certainly something like Pat Mills and John Wagner's "The Iron Legion" – an epic adventure set in an alternate galaxy ruled by the Roman Empire, with artwork by a pre-*Watchmen* Dave Gibbons – seemed a lot more exciting and imaginative than many of the stories being turned out on TV at the time. Though, to be fair, vast armies of robot legionaries are easier to pull off in pen and ink than in BBC Television Centre during a period of hyperinflation.

It's a measure of Tom Baker's unwavering commitment to *Doctor Who* that he embarked on a UK tour to promote the new comic at his own expense, considering it both a favour to Skinn and an investment in his livelihood. After 43 issues, *Doctor Who Weekly* switched to become a monthly title, with at least one eye on the show's adult fanbase. More than 35 years on, *Doctor Who Magazine* is still going strong, holding the Guinness World Record for the longest-running TV tie-in magazine. Even a cursory glance at this book's endnotes will tell you it remains unrivalled as the programme's journal of record; over the years, it has also developed a wit and panache that means, for many fans – this one included – that monthly thud on the doormat is as welcome as a new episode of *Doctor Who* itself. And I sincerely hope that's enough brownnosing to persuade them not to sue us for nicking so many great quotes.

Shada woulda coulda

His tour of the provinces completed, Baker headed to Cambridge to start work on Douglas Adams' hastily-written (was there any other sort?) season finale, *Shada*. Despite his punishing workload, this time Adams partly had only himself to blame for the rushed nature of the scripts: since Philip Hinchcliffe and Robert Holmes' curatorship, he had been trying to pitch a story about an android race called the Krikkitmen, whose plan to spring their race from a Time Lord prison involved stealing the Ashes during a test match at Lords. Williams had repeatedly turned the idea down, but Adams figured that, if he left writing the six-part finale until the last possible minute, the producer would be forced to relent and go with the only thing left in the cupboard. Unluckily for Adams, Williams wouldn't budge – so it was out with the whisky and the black coffee again as the script editor settled in for another romantic weekend with his typewriter, eventually completing the scripts in six days.

In desperation, he turned to his home town: a lifelong science enthusiast, whose middle name was Noel, Adams was always immensely proud of having been born in Cambridge with the initials DNA, less than a year before Crick and Watson mapped the model of the double helix about a mile down the road. After moving to Brentwood, he had returned to Cambridge to read English at St John's College, and it was this picture-postcard view of the city – all punts, bicycles, cloisters and choristers – that informed *Shada*.

Re-using the concept of a Time Lord prison from his Krikkitmen story, *Shada* sees criminal genius Skagra on the hunt for a Time Lord who is living out his retirement as a Professor at a Cambridge college (the only place on Earth where you can exist for centuries without anyone noticing, according to Adams; that B minus had obviously really stung).

The story was allocated a full week's location filming – which Tom Baker recalls as a "terribly happy time". "I saw myself as some kind of Jude the Obscure," he said. "Being in Cambridge, with lots of money and being very famous, felt wonderful. I became very fond of the young students there. I told them some of my old jokes – it is most unseemly to be an old man telling young jokes – and so the whole experience was very happy. They made me an honorary fellow of St John's College. Another simply marvellous thing was that all the girls found me irresistibly attractive at that time, which was nice. I liked being irresistible."[35]

Lalla Ward's thoughts on this aren't known – though she did find the script irresistible, hailing it as "the epitome of Douglasness".[22] The writer himself was less enamoured with his efforts, though, describing it as "a mediocre four-parter stretched over six parts".[36]

That remained to be seen, as *Shada* was still several months away from broadcast. But "mediocre" isn't a term anyone would apply lightly to the next televised story. Unless they were feeling *very* generous. Or drunk. Like *City of Death*, *The Creature from the Pit* is an example of what can be achieved when everyone – from the writer to the actors to the designers to the director – pulls in the same direction. In this case, the wrong direction.

For starters, David Fisher's script can't decide if it wants to be sci-fi or comedy, so settles on being neither. It opens with the Doctor reading *The Tales of Peter Rabbit* to K-9, and goes steadily downhill from there, as the TARDIS arrives on the jungle planet of Chloris, where a giant alien called Erato is being kept prisoner at the bottom of a big hole by the Lady Adrasta as part of a wicked scheme to protect her monopoly on the planet's metal mines. Or something like that. When the Doctor finds himself stuck half way down the pit, he produces a book from his pocket called *Everest in Easy Stages*. When that turns out to be in Tibetan, he whips out another book called *Teach Yourself Tibetan*. It's good to know comedy isn't dead. Just very unwell.

Reading the script, Graeme McDonald could feel another memo/migraine coming on. "At first sight this serial hardly evidences the increased calibre of writing I expected this year," he wrote, betraying something of a talent for dry understatement. "It's littered with schoolboy humour that will reduce Tom's authority and credibility hopelessly... If we allow Tom to get his hands on material like this, surely it's an open invitation to him to be even more flippant and unmanageable." ("Since when had Tom needed an invitation to be flippant and unmanageable?", wondered Graham Williams darkly.)

The story's dialogue is priceless. "Why do you call it the place of death?" "Because anyone found here is automatically sentenced to death." Fair enough, stupid question really. At least the script is gracious enough to apologise for the clunking lines: "What's that?" asks Romana, staring into the pit. "We call it... The Pit," replies Adrasta. "Ah, you have such a way with words," grins the Doctor. Filming her first story, Lalla Ward realised exactly what she'd let herself in for when Adrasta ordered her to neutralise K-9 with the immortal line "Point the dog against the rock!" – which rendered both Ward and guest star Myra Frances helpless with laughter.

The story was also David Brierley's debut as K-9; whereas John Leeson had scampered about on all fours during rehearsals, Brierley preferred to sit in a chair while a toy pram stood in for the tin dog. (He should have realised he'd struggle to live up to his predecessor's more method approach: it wouldn't have surprised anyone if John Leeson had asked the lady in the BBC canteen put his lunch in a bowl on the floor.)

The final episode, meanwhile, collapses into a technobabble overload of junk science that would make even Bob Baker and Dave Martin blush. Sample quote: "A thin shell of aluminium wrapped around a neutron star will minimise its gravitational pull and we can yank it back out of the sun's field." David Fisher claimed this was a suggestion from someone he phoned up at the Cambridge Institute of Astronomy. The cleaner, presumably.

None of which matters a jot, at the end of the day, because *The Creature from the Pit* could have been written by Dennis Potter (it wasn't, I checked) and still the only thing anyone would remember about it is the fact that Erato looks like... how to put this delicately?... is the fact that Erato looks like nothing less than a 15-ft, bright green cock and balls.

With the already tight budget further squeezed by Graham Williams' decision to plough some of the money from the third, fourth and fifth serials into the spectacular season finale, Mat Irvine didn't have a lot to play with when designing the luckless Tythonian ambassador. His eventual solution

– the third attempt, so God knows what the first two must have been like – was to cover some weather balloons in latex, and add a tumescent green stalk onto the front. The result is... unfortunate, to say the least, and not helped by the Doctor trying to communicate with the creature by blowing into the end of its quivering proboscis. The fact no-one ran screaming onto the studio floor to insist this couldn't possibly be broadcast on actual television, in front of actual viewers, is frankly staggering. And so millions of children and their innocent parents settled down on a Saturday evening to see their hero wrap his laughing gear around the end of a long green shaft attached to a giant ballbag, all in the name of family entertainment.

(The Doctor does eventually find a way to communicate with the creature, incidentally: he lends it his own voice. Which is kind of appropriate, 'cos if there's one thing Tom Baker specialised in, it was talking bollocks.)

Adding to the genital vibe, Lalla Ward admitted to making "a complete balls-up" of her first story in front of the cameras. "I was trying to be like Mary, which was a mistake," she said. "I was desperately trying to be glamorous. I can't really do glamour. I looked pathetic, with my hair all swooped back and neat, and make-up on. It was through that... I didn't work out how to play it, I worked out how *not* to play it. I quickly reverted to something rather nearer myself."[33]

Surprisingly, it wasn't the giant bollock-monster that resulted in an urgent BBC post-mortem, but the quality of the model work, which Graham Williams judged so poor, he signed off on a costly re-shoot. This led to a bitter row with the Visual Effects Department, resulting in all parties being forced to sit round a table and have it out. The conclusion, according to director Christopher Barry – who described the whole *Creature from the Pit* experience as "the nadir" of his career – was that no-one was to blame, it was just one of those things. Dry sherry anyone?

While planning the future of *Doctor Who*, John Nathan-Turner had started to look to the show's past, having been introduced to Ian Levine, a former Northern Soul DJ turned hi-NRG record producer whose output would go on to include artists as, um, diverse as

Bananarama, Big Fun, Hazell Dean and an early incarnation of Take That ("the whipped cream years"). Levine was also a *Who* superfan who had been instrumental in stopping many old episodes being junked by the BBC. (On one of his first visits to the Beeb's archives, he had discovered the entire first Dalek story wrapped in parcel tape and marked "Withdrawn, De-accessioned and Junked"; a few hours later, and a hugely important piece of TV history would have been lost. He also managed to save *The Keys of Marinus* and *The Web Planet*, among many others, but let's not hold that against him.) Watching old episodes supplied by his new dealer, Nathan-Turner became increasingly enthusiastic about the idea of tapping into the show's history, which he thought would prove popular with the fans. Like his new mentor Barry Letts almost a decade earlier, the new producer was also keen to drop six-part stories, and persuaded BBC1 Controller Bill Cotton to allocate extra funding for a run of seven four-part stories the following year. ("That's great," said Graham Williams, through gritted teeth, when he heard. "I don't suppose there's any chance I could have a few extra... no, thought not. Forget I mentioned it. Oh, you already have.") By now, Nathan-Turner had also "invited" Lalla Ward to leave mid-way through the next series, with the producer expressing his desire for a more "vulnerable" TARDIS team than two Time Lords and their super-powered dog, so the actress was only contracted for the first 20 episodes.

On November 7th, the cast and crew of *Shada* returned from lunch to find themselves locked out of the studio, following a walk out by technical managers. The source of the latest industrial action was a long-running dispute between the studio electricians and the props department, which had come to a head over a row about whose job it was to set the hands on the *Play School* clock – the distinctly low-tech timepiece used by Humpty, Hamble, Big Ted and company to tell the time in the long-running rugrat favourite. As producer, Graham Williams had no choice but to send everybody home (he'd probably have gone home himself, too, if only he could remember where it was).

By the time Television Centre became available again, BBC bosses had decided to prioritise "prestige" shows such as *Fawlty Towers* and

the *Morecambe and Wise Christmas Special* – which didn't leave any room for you know Who. Williams protested that a whole week's worth of location filming and a studio session were already in the can – amounting to more than half the serial – not to mention the fact they'd scrimped and saved from numerous other stories in order to throw more money at the series finale. For a while, it seemed like they might be able to remount the production in the New Year but, when that idea was nixed too, Williams reluctantly had to accept that, for *Shada*, it was game over.

Still, chin up, eh? Because, while he might not have been ending his tenure on the high he'd been planning, Williams still had two stories left to broadcast – and I'm sure they were pretty great in their own way, right Graham? Graham?

Sex and drugs and rock & roll (one out of three ain't bad)

There's a serious story struggling to escape from *Nightmare of Eden*, which dared to introduce the concept of drugs to children a good six years before Zammo became a smackhead in *Grange Hill*. The narcotic in question is Vraxoin – "Vrax" for short – and its debilitating effects are obvious from the early scene in which we see the navigator of a spaceship whacked off his nut on the stuff. Actually, it looks like quite good fun – which is perhaps why the name was changed at the last minute from "Zip", which Lalla Ward thought sounded too appealing to youngsters. (Fair enough, but where did she think they were actually going to *buy* it?)

If this sounds like it's all suddenly gone a bit *Play for Today*, you'll be relieved to know said drug is actually made from powdered space monster – the non-granulated version being the Mandrels: fish-faced beasties in giant flares who lumber about a crashed space liner attempting, largely without success, to look menacing (never mind the *Star Wars* comparisons – it's sobering to think *this* was broadcast at the same time as *Alien* was in cinemas).

It's not a *bad* script, as such – just a bit dull and, once again, sorely let down by unforgivably sloppy production: a step visibly gives way beneath Tom Baker's foot, a stick holds up a spaceship, the Mandrels keep coming unzipped at the back and, when K-9 seals up a wall panel, a hand emerges to hold it in place. Classy.

But the problem isn't just the things that went *wrong* – the whole production has a make-do feel about it, from the boring sets to the rubbish visual effects and the slow, unconvincing, overlit monsters. Lewis Finader, as drug-trafficking scientist Tryst, performs the whole thing with a comedy German accent – apparently the result of a rehearsal room gag that somehow made the final cut – while Geoffrey Hinsliff, as Fisk, addresses Tryst as Fisk, and either no-one noticed or they didn't have time for a re-take. *Nightmare of Eden* does contain one genuinely powerful moment, as Tryst – or is it Fisk? – pleads for his sorry skin, only to be dismissed by the Doctor with a contemptuous "Go away". Hell hath no fury like the righteous anger of a Time Lord. Overall, though, it's a measure of how dull things are that it's a welcome diversion when Baker slips into default "flippant and unmanageable" mode, screaming "Oh my fingers! My arms! My legs! My everything!" while being grabbed by the Mandrels (ouch).

According to the script, Vrax is known to induce "warm complacency and total apathy". Take out the warm, and it's bang on the money.

Drowning their *Shada* sorrows in the BBC bar, Graham Williams and Tom Baker happened to bump into Terrance Dicks, who told them he was about to depart for Los Angeles as a guest at the USA's first major Doctor Who convention. Williams recalled having to turn down a similar invitation because it clashed with filming schedules, but, now that producer and star were unexpectedly at a loose end, it wasn't long before they found themselves checking into the event at the Sunset Hyatt Hotel on Sunset Boulevard. This is officially one of the most glamorous locations for anything associated with *Doctor Who* – though, being *Doctor Who* fans, most of the attendees would probably have preferred to spend the weekend in a gravel pit in Gerrard's Cross.

Both Baker and Williams – who, perhaps more than any production team since the 60s, viewed the show as essentially a children's programme – were taken aback to find the convention populated largely by adults. "I

could hardly keep my face straight," Baker admitted. "There were only a few children there, mostly young adults taking it extremely seriously and reading all sorts into the stories or into my character that I'd never thought of. Of course I couldn't say, 'Look here, you know it's a load of bullshit!' I was doing a job. I couldn't really disappoint them or disenchant them, but I was surprised at their obsession with it."[36]

Back in London, John Nathan-Turner was frantically going through the office cupboards looking for next year's scripts, but found them emptier than a student fridge. Reaching as far as he could down the back of the sofa, he pulled out a crumpled copy of Terrance Dicks' partially completed vampire story – the one that had got it in the neck from the BBC's *Dracula* production – and promptly commissioned a new version from the former script editor. Otherwise, like Douglas Adams before him, Nathan-Turner was keen to encourage greater input from new writers and directors who hadn't worked on the show before. All he had to do was find them – and then make sure they never spoke to anyone who had worked with Tom Baker before he'd got them to sign. The producer had also privately decided he wanted to axe K-9 from the show, but knew it would be a controversial decision, especially among younger viewers. "Children loved K-9," said Lalla Ward. "Teenage nerds thought less of him, quite naturally."[22] None taken.

On Christmas Saturday 1979, ITV's offering for younger viewers was *Digby, the Biggest Dog in the World*. But BBC1 managed to hit back with an even bigger dog in the form of *The Horns of Nimon*.

You have to feel sorry for Anthony Read, who clearly had good intentions for the story – the latest of *Doctor Who*'s sci-fi spins on Greek mythology, and its third pass at the legend of the Minotaur (after *The Mind Robber* and *The Time Monster*). Unfortunately, with yet more money being stashed away for the season's grand finale, the programme was running on air by this time – and it shows. Why, when the piggy bank was already lying in pieces on the production office floor, they kept trying to pretend they could play *Star Wars* at its own game is a mystery, but, coming right off the back of the previous story's hyperspace crash between two ships, this attempts a sequence in which the TARDIS runs into an asteroid field and crashes into a planet. "Attempts" being the operative word.

Whatever serious points Read was trying to make are lost in the usual mishmash of misjudged gags (the Doctor gives K-9 mouth-to-mouth, the TARDIS console makes a comedy "boooiinnggg!" sound, etc etc) and actors getting carried away with themselves. As Soldeed – a fawning scientist who sacrifices fresh young meat to the parasitic Nimon, while apparently dressed as a pantomime wicked queen – Graham Crowden is the worst offender: his performance is so over the top it's got snow on it, while his death scene makes Tom Baker's power trip from *The Armageddon Factor* look like a masterclass in minimalism. Crowden – a brilliant actor when he puts his mind to it – was apparently fully aware they only had time for one take, so decided to milk it for all it was worth. You can see what a hoot he thought this was by the fact he starts laughing in the middle of it. Considering how close he came to being cast as the fourth Doctor, you can't help thinking the show dodged a bullet there.

One of Soldeed's intended sacrifices, incidentally, was Janet Ellis, who would go on to cause a very British scandal by getting pregnant – out of wedlock! – while presenting *Blue Peter*. (Not *literally* while presenting *Blue Peter*, of course – that *would* have been a scandal. And I'm not sure Simon Groom had it in him.)

Baker, unusually, is sidelined to a supporting player in his own show: he's wheeled on every so often to do some comic business – "Later you will be questioned, tortured and killed." "Well, I hope you get it in the right order." – while Lalla Ward takes on the hero's role, doing everything the Doctor would do – and rather well, too, playing it admirably straight, even if no-one else is bothering to. By now, Ward was becoming quite an in-demand actress, and had just been cast as Ophelia to Derek Jacobi's Prince of Denmark and Patrick Stewart's Claudius in a BBC production of *Hamlet*. She also lent her talents to illustrating a book of astrology – for pets (surely the dumbest idea since... well, astrology for humans).

The Nimon themselves are prancing bull-

men in leather skirts (the leather was imported from Germany, so I guess we should at least be grateful they're not in full lederhosen) and 12-inch platforms that suggest they either suffer from small bull syndrome, or their planet is still very much in thrall to glam rock.

The final episode of *The Horns of Nimon* was broadcast on January 12th, 1980 – not the most auspicious start to the new decade, and hardly the most fitting end to the previous one, which still ranks as the most successful in *Doctor Who*'s 50-year history. With *Shada* officially canned, the story is also charged with bringing the curtain down on Graham Williams' tenure as producer (not to mention waving off Douglas Adams, David Brierley, the "time tunnel" opening titles, the diamond logo and Delia Derbyshire's original arrangement of the theme – none of which would survive the new broom that was about to sweep through the production office).

A joint leaving party was held for Williams and Adams – in a BBC basement. ("Honestly, you shouldn't have gone to so much trouble.") With *Shada* having just formally been written off, there wasn't exactly a party atmosphere, but both men were relieved to be moving on. Adams would go on to make millions from various iterations of *The Hitchhiker's Guide to the Galaxy* and its sequels (in which he finally found a home for his Krikkitmen story; large parts of the *Shada* script, meanwhile, were self-cannibalised for his 1987 novel *Dirk Gently's Holistic Detective Agency*). In an interview with *Doctor Who Magazine* some years later, the former script editor said: "In science fiction, death is not a hindrance to anything. I realise that not everything I want to do, I'm going to get to do. I shouldn't think I'd work for *Doctor Who* again – I've got too much of my own stuff to do now – but I hesitate to say 'never again', because look what happened to Sean Connery... On the whole, I have quite an optimistic view of the future."[37] Douglas Adams died of a heart attack at a gym in California in May 2001. He was 49.

For his part, Williams admitted he'd "run out of ingenuity" in the middle of his third year. "The budgetary limitations were phenomenal. Hyperinflation was really biting in 1979. In real terms, we made the third season for half the cost of the first. I'm not bitching, but Phil Hinchcliffe was making shows with three times the money that I had. I said, 'We can't do it,' and they said, 'Alright, we'll stop making the programme'. After that, you've not got much to say. I remember sitting up through an awful lot of midnights trying to devise ways in which we could save money on the scripts."[21]

Not surprisingly, the producer was physically exhausted, having barely taken any days off in the past three years. "The BBC had invented a 57-week year especially for *Doctor Who*," said Williams, "They must have thought, being a programme about time travel, it didn't matter how many weeks in the year. You actually stopped making *Doctor Who* 57 weeks after you started in any particular season – which meant technical phrases like holidays and days off never got used much."

Speaking in the mid-80s, Williams was of the opinion that "it all went wrong right from the start, when I was told to make the show more funny, and less violent. Unfortunately, this would have required a lot of money, of which we had practically sod all.

"Tom Baker, however, thought it was a splendid idea, and kept putting in all these bad puns and terrible jokes, which didn't get any better when I brought Dougie Adams in."[22]

Louise Jameson concurred with Tom Baker's assertion that Williams was "a fragile soul". "He took things to his own heart," she said. "He didn't protect himself sometimes from the pressures that go with the job."[22]

Williams left the BBC to produce the ITV anthology series *Tales of the Unexpected* and, after that, the children's comedy adventure *Supergran*. Later, he ran a computer hire company and, in the late 1980s, moved to the West Country to run a hotel in Devon, where he died in a shooting accident in 1990, age 45. He left a widow, Jacqueline, and three children.

Yes! Harder! Harder!

On the night of December 31st, 1979, John Nathan-Turner waited patiently for the old decade to expire. As the chimes of Big Ben sounded midnight, he carefully piled the whole of the 1970s onto a bonfire in his garden, lit a metaphorical match (trickier than you might think), and stood back to bask in the glow of history going up in metaphorical flames: the future had arrived – and he was ready. This was not a world in which people could afford to stand still: right now, scientists were working on computing machines with a processing power of up to 16 kilobytes of RAM. Others, meanwhile, would have the power to speak *and* spell. And didn't he hear they'd finally found a way of adding fizz to fruit cordials?

Impatient to make his mark on the new decade, Nathan-Turner's plans for the upcoming season involved changing just about everything short of the lead actor ('cos that would be madness, right?). He wanted new music, new titles, a new logo, new companions, new costumes, a new TARDIS, more science, less silliness... but apart from that, he didn't want to mess with a successful formula.

Graphic designer Sid Sutton was tasked with creating the new title sequence, which dispensed with the mysterious swirling time vortices of old in favour of a nakedly *Star Wars*-inspired journey through space, with Tom Baker's face forming out of the celestial bodies like some sort of god (which, to a certain generation, I suppose he was).

The new arrangement of Ron Grainer's theme fell to the Radiophonic Workshop's Peter Howell, who used "virtually everything the Workshop had"[38], including his own voice (don't worry, he put it through a sound manipulator – it isn't just him going "Woo-ee-ooo, doo-de-doo"; that would have been rubbish) to create a big, bombastic slab of noise that's actually quite brilliant, in a flashy, pyrotechnic ten-minute guitar solo sort of way.

Nathan-Turner was also keen for the Workshop to handle all the incidental music for the show, which he thought would give it a modern sound, while also saving money. As a test run – and to avoid a repeat of Malcolm Clarke's *Sea Devils* disaster from seven years earlier – the Workshop's composers were asked to re-score parts of *The Horns of Nimon*. ("You've made it very loud in places," the producer must have said, when he heard the results. "I can't hear a word Graham Crowden is saying. You're hired.")

Nathan-Turner took long-serving composer Dudley Simpson out to lunch, and told him his services would no longer be required – at which point the composer whipped out a trumpet to play a sad, parping lament. Possibly.

Most radically, the producer wanted to completely overhaul the Doctor's look – possibly even dispensing with the trademark scarf. Costume designer June Hudson thought this was a step too far, and persuaded him to keep the same basic silhouette, but smarten it up a bit. The new ensemble was very much more of a "uniform", with a burgundy Russian great coat, burgundy waistcoat and trousers, burgundy socks (from Prince Charles' personal sock-makers – let's hope they kept a spare pair for HRH), a burgundy hat and even the famous multi-cloured scarf now rendered in shades of maroon and purple. And burgundy. To this day, *Doctor Who* fans can't hear the word "burgundy" without having a flashback to 1980. (It's also a wine-producing region of France, apparently – who knew?)

Nathan-Turner also wanted a shirt that could be "marketed" as merchandise, which caused Hudson some headaches as, short of giving it three arms, there's only so much you can do with a shirt. In the end, she proposed putting question marks on the collars, which the producer loved, but no-one else did. Why not go the whole hog and give him a badge saying "Ooh, I'm dead mysterious, me"?

More significantly, Nathan-Turner was determined to cleanse the show of its streak of "undergraduate" humour, feeling it had a tendency to infect the whole production. "If the show was jokey, then I felt that the sets, too, became almost cartoon strip in style, and the costumes adopted a sort of operatic humour to them," he said. "To me, the humour of Tom's Doctor started to be reflected in the production values of the show, and I wanted to change these to bring them much more in line with the 1980s' more sophisticated style of television."[11] (To be fair, this was before *Hi-de-Hi!* started.)

To help shape his vision for the show, Nathan-Turner initially approached Johnny Byrne, a writer he had worked with on popular Yorkshire vet saga *All Creatures Great and Small*. When he declined, the producer followed up a recommendation from former *Who* scripter Robert Banks Stewart to see Christopher Hamilton Bidmead, a former journalist who had written scripts for Thames

Television but was now working as a journalist specialising in computers.

"I went in to see Barry Letts and John Nathan-Turner and said, 'Very nice of you to ask me, but I don't really want to do this, because I think the programme is – if I may say so – silly'," explained Bidmead. "They said, 'So do we – we want to make it un-silly'." That chimed with Bidmead's own feelings about the show, and the world in general. "I'd studied science at school, and got diverted into the arts world, and I'd just come to the realisation, at the age of 36, that I was getting a bit fed up with the arty people, and wanted the discipline of science back."[39]

So Christopher "H" Bidmead – he'd wanted the on-screen credit Christopher Hamilton Bidmead, but it wouldn't fit on the small tellies they had back then – was on board, and his first act was to renew the office subscription to *New Scientist*. He also issued a new writers' bible for the show, which said: "Without inhibiting creative ideas, we'd prefer writers to work in a way that acknowledges the appropriate disciplines. Charged Particle Physics (to pick a topic at random) is mapped territory accessible to many of our viewers (there are Doctor Who Appreciation Societies at universities all over the world), and writers who want to bring the topic into the story should at least glance at the relevant pages of the encyclopedia."

The new script editor's dream was attracting writers of the calibre of Nigel Kneale. It was destined to remain a dream: attending a meeting of the London Science Fiction Society, he made a request for "hard" SF stories, resulting in author John Brosnan submitting an idea about the Doctor landing in the car park of BBC Television Centre and teaming up with Tom Baker. ("Yeah, cheers for that," said Bidmead.) He also resurrected a story from novelist Christopher Priest – originally developed during Douglas Adams' tenure – called *Sealed Orders*. Set on Gallifrey, and featuring various time-hopping shenanigans involving numerous TARDISes and at least one additional Doctor, the end result was deemed unworkable by Bidmead, and it was eventually written off after he and Priest failed to come to an agreement on the way forward.

Bidmead also had his doubts about some of the stories that *were* going ahead: he was unhappy with David Fisher's submission for a story called *Avalon*, which had clearly been written to fit the jokier template of recent seasons, and he felt Terrance Dicks' scripts for *The Vampire Mutations* – his updated version of *The Witch Lords* – lacked the requisite hard science. Because it was about vampires. He had also developed a plan for a series of linked stories set in an alternative "anti-universe", which he shared with potential new recruits Stephen Gallagher, an established science fiction novelist, and 18-year-old *Doctor Who* fan Andrew Smith, who had been sending in story ideas on a regular basis since the age of 15.

Tom Baker and Lalla Ward, meanwhile, were getting into the spirit of the new regime by filming a series of Australian TV ads for Prime Computers – slogan: "Step into the 1980s". The couple had recently called off their office romance, though you'd never guess it from their flirtatious behaviour in the ads, which pack a surprising amount of sexual tension into a discussion about computer languages and protocols. Baker spent the first two months of the New Year filming TV movie *The Curse of King Tutankhamun's Tomb* in Wiltshire and Egypt, after which he departed for another promotional tour of Australia. In London, David Brierley went to see John Nathan-Turner to ask if he could show his face on-screen during the new season. ("Won't that look a bit weird?" asked the producer. "You're supposed to be a metal dog.") When he failed to receive a guarantee of a guest role, Brierley dropped the bombshell that he wouldn't be returning, throwing the entire future of *Doctor Who* into chaos for at least 15 seconds, until Nathan-Turner phoned up John Leeson and asked him to come back.

Also spending an increasing amount of time in the production office was Ian Levine, who Nathan-Turner had installed as a semi-official – i.e. unpaid – continuity adviser, with a brief to make sure stories didn't contravene established *Who* history, and also to suggest lines and references that could be dropped in to keep the die-hard fans happy. So instead of just saying, for example, "Look at that spaceship, Doctor!", they could say, "Look at that spaceship, Doctor! In a funny way, it reminds me of that one that crashed on the planet Desparus – you know, the penal planet where prisoners

were left to fend for themselves, and one of the convicts managed to get aboard the ship and held Katarina hostage so she had to sacrifice herself to save your life? Except I think that one was a slightly darker grey."

In March, John Nathan-Turner threw a party for the *Doctor Who* team at his home in Brighton, where filming for the new series was scheduled to begin on the beach the following day. Arriving straight off the flight from Sydney, Tom Baker was both jet-lagged and ill, with a metabolic disorder that had blighted his trip Down Under. His mood was not helped when it became clear that, rather than picking up their on-off romance as he'd expected, Lalla Ward wanted to keep things purely professional – or as professional as things got with those two. As such, recording of *The Leisure Hive* – as David Fisher's *Avalon* was now called – was a strained affair. The two leads were barely speaking, and Nathan-Turner had to persuade the gaunt, unwell-looking Baker to wear make-up, while rollers were needed to restore his lank hair to its trademark curls. Footage of the actor in the studio shows his impatience, with him protesting about having to throw "this fucking dreary prop" and snapping at the crew to "get on with it". On the plus side, Baker must have been delighted to know his face was now adorning the groins of small boys across Britain as British Home Stores released a pair of fetching Doctor Who underpants. Say what you like about the acting talents of Olivier, Gielgud, Richardson and company – but I don't remember *them* being immortalised on a pair of undercrackers, do you?

Lalla Ward wasn't in the best of moods around this time, either: she'd been offered another TV series, but Nathan-Turner refused to release her early, despite the fact it had been his idea to axe Romana. For her replacement, the producer was keen to introduce a young "cosmic Artful Dodger" type character and, between them, he and Bidmead devised the character of Adric (the name was an anagram of the Nobel prize-winning English theoretical physicist and mathematician Paul Dirac – no prizes for guess whose idea *that* was). To play him, Nathan-Turner cast a 17-year-old BBC filing clerk, who had recently filmed a part in period drama *To Serve Them All My Days*. What the producer didn't know was the teenager was a massive *Doctor Who* fan and had, in fact, had the very first letter published in *Doctor Who Weekly*. "Thanks for being an innovative publisher in these days when most comics are grossly plagiaristic", wrote the little suck-up.

Spring also saw a brief, late flurry of Dalekmania, with the pepperpots appearing on James Burke's science programme *The Real Thing* (which resulted in – you guessed it – a stiff letter from Roger Hancock) and David Jason and Sheila Steafel playing a married Dalek couple in a sketch on *The Jason Explanation*, while Liverpool synthpop outfit Dalek I Love You also released a self-titled single. (Okay, so maybe not Dalekmania as such – more Dalekmildlyexcitable.) Hancock also wrote to the BBC asking if they wanted to relinquish their share of the Dalek rights. "No," they wrote back. "We don't."

As filming commenced on Terrance Dicks' vampire tale – now called *State of Decay* – Tom Baker and Lalla Ward were less than happy (so what's new?) to be presented with Matthew Waterhouse as their new co-star. Baker, who had nearly gone to the wall over his lack of input over companion castings, made his feelings clear by ignoring the new boy altogether.

"I was really on a high after being offered the part but, after about three hours work on the first day of rehearsal, I felt suicidal," recalled Waterhouse. "It was all so different from how I'd imagined, and it was pretty tough-going. For me, it was a horrible time. Hell, in fact."[40]

At lunchtime, the youngster sidled over to Baker in the pub, but he still didn't speak to him. "By 4 o'clock, I thought it was getting silly, so I went over and said hello to him. He told me to piss off!"[41] Undaunted, the precocious teenager developed a habit of "suggesting" ways Baker might play scenes differently, which obviously endeared him even more to the star. There was no love lost between Waterhouse and Ward, either: the actress has variously described him as "obnoxious", "rude", "a little brat" and incapable of "acting his way out of a cardboard box". It wasn't the reference he'd been hoping for, but he supposed it was better than nothing. (On one occasion, when she overheard him being rude to a costume designer, Ward grabbed Waterhouse by the collar and dragged him into

his dressing room for a dressing down. Maybe that's why they call them dressing rooms.) To add to the youngster's woes, the actors' union Equity later complained about the casting of a non-member in a prominent role (and that was *before* they'd seen him in action).

In the studio, Baker and Ward's relationship was at a new low. "They would finish a scene, and walk as far away from each other as they could," remembered *State of Decay*'s director, Peter Moffatt. "When the Doctor and Romana were exploring the vampire spaceship, they had to jump down a ladder. On recording, I sent a message down to the floor saying it'd be nice if Tom helped Lalla down. Tom turned round and said, 'Why, is she a bloody cripple?'"[42] Moffatt had started his directing career in a prisoner of war camp: there were times during the making of *State of Decay* when he must have looked back on those days fondly. Soon afterwards, Ward decided she couldn't take any more, and agreed to get back together with her leading man, who was apparently so ill she had to spoon-feed him baby food.

While his co-stars fought like cats and... well, anyway, K-9 was keeping his head down, making appearances at trade shows and being taught how to do a three-point turn by Barbara Woodhouse, the matronly dog trainer who became insanely famous for a period in the late 70s and early 80s, on Terry Wogan's latest TV show. On June 7th, however, *The Sun* got wind of the dog's possible demise, and launched its own Save K-9 campaign (since the Save Leela one had been so successful).

John Nathan-Turner didn't have time to worry about all that, though. He had much bigger fish to fry, like firing off a letter to WH Allen complaining about the colour of the TARDIS on the cover of *The Keys of Marinus* novelisation. ("What about Tom?" asked his team. "He's becoming absolutely impossible to work with." "I know," said the producer. "But *look* – it's barely even blue. If anything it's more a sort of green.")

In fact, with his bosses indicating they would like him to stay on for at least another season, Nathan-Turner was acutely aware of the problems with his star. As, to be fair, was his star. "Maybe I'd stayed too long," Baker admitted later. "I don't know. I'd certainly become more proprietorial about *Doctor*

Who."[29] "[I'd say] 'Don't tell me how to pick up a glass of water or how to come through a door'. In other words, I became impossible. I thought to myself, 'I can't go on like this, disagreeing with people and thinking I know more than they do'."[43]

"The difficulties of working with Tom were becoming quite clear," agreed Christopher Bidmead. "When Tom did this thing of saying, 'Well I'm getting a bit long in the tooth for this and think I should leave', my recollection is we simply sat there in silence, nodding quietly to ourselves, and that really was the point we realised we were looking for a new Doctor."[43]

"Certainly, I think I detected a sigh of relief," laughed Baker. "No-one said, 'Oh Tom, are you sure?' I think they were glad to see the back of me, and quite right too."[43]

In an echo of his predecessor's departure, Baker figured he had nothing to lose by asking for a pay rise. When his request was turned down, the die was cast: the longest-serving, most popular Doctor Who to date was hanging up his scarf, and nothing would ever be quite the same again.

Why not visit the Leisure Hive? Now 45% less radioactive!

Though John Nathan-Turner had established a cautious friendship with Tom Baker – the pair would occasionally drink socially together – the producer was enthusiastic about being able to put the ultimate stamp on the programme, and cast his own star. But he was also aware what an upheaval it would be for the audience – especially younger viewers, who had never known any other Doctor but Baker. To this end, he sounded out Elisabeth Sladen and then Louise Jameson about returning to ease the transition.

"John Nathan-Turner rang me up and said, would I come and meet him?" said Jameson. "I thought, 'Ooh, I'm going to head my own TV series – finally!'. I hadn't been at the BBC for 18 months, and I swanned around the bar going, 'Hello, darling!' to everyone. And then a cameraman tapped me on the shoulder and said, 'Did you know your dress was tucked into your knickers?' It'd been there... well, I don't know how long! Anyway, John wanted Leela to come back for the episode in which

Tom left, and to go through the next series with the new Doctor. I said I'd come in for one story, then probably two of the next season, but I didn't want to do a whole year.

"Also, he asked Lis Sladen first!"[16/27]

Instead, Nathan-Turner hit on a different wheeze: if he couldn't bring back an old companion, why not bring back the Doctor's arch enemy? And so it was decided that the fourth Doctor's final adventure would see him engaged in a duel to the death with the Master. Plus the story would also introduce a new Australian companion called Tegan, whose inclusion was in-no-way part of an ongoing bid to attract Australian co-funding for the show. If you believed *The Sun* – and why would you? – there had also been a reprieve for K-9, as the tabloid trumpeted its success in guaranteeing the dog's inclusion in 20 more episodes, i.e. exactly the same number already planned.

Also in the departure lounge was Christopher Bidmead. Like his predecessors, Bidmead was finding the endless rewrites and script doctoring exhausting. He had had several stand-up rows with Nathan-Turner – who he thought lacked expertise when it came to script issues – and also felt the job was undervalued by the BBC, so requested a 30% pay rise to stay on. If they weren't going to give a rise to Tom Baker, you can imagine how the request from the computer magazine guy went down (though he did get some help with the workload from in-house script editor Antony Root, who was seconded to *Doctor Who* for a few months to help develop stories for the next series). Baker himself, meanwhile, took pride of place in a new Doctor Who exhibition at Madame Tussauds in London – or at least a waxwork copy of him did. And if you think *he* had a rictus grin, just wait 'til the bloke who had spent hundreds of hours making him found out he was leaving the show.

There may have been less than nine months separating the end of *The Horns of Nimon* and the start of *The Leisure Hive* on Saturday, August 30th, but, from the moment a vivid starburst announces the dynamic new title sequence, accompanied by the first sting of Peter Howell's muscular new theme arrangement, it's clear that everything is new. New, and so very shiny. With *The Leisure Hive* also introducing the new logo – a joined-up neon affair that's part *Star Wars*, part strip club – June Hudson's radical make-over of the fourth Doctor's trademark duds and even a new police box prop, John Nathan-Turner could barely have done more to mark his territory if he'd taken a piss on Graham Williams' desk.

In other ways, though, *The Leisure Hive* proves something of a false dawn. David Fisher's script, in particular, is an uneasy hybrid of the new and old regimes: when Nathan-Turner and Barry Letts outlined their idea for a race of reptilian aliens acting like the Mafia, Fisher imagined having great fun with giant lizard-men in dark glasses. Then they told him he had to take the Mafia lizards seriously, which is probably why the tone of the story is so uncertain. The basic premise of the Foamasi (Foamasi – Mafiosa, geddit?) staging a hostile takeover of the leisure and recreation planet run by their historic enemies the Argolins was apparently inspired by *The Godfather*, but you'd have to look really hard to see it. The Argolins are also experimenting with reduplication through the theoretical notion of tachyonics – Christopher Bidmead making good use of that *New Scientist* subscription – having been rendered infertile during a 20-minute nuclear holocaust some years earlier. (That's right – they've built a massive leisure complex for galactic tourists on an irradiated, post-nuclear wasteland. I'd love to have seen the bank manager's face when they presented *that* business plan.)

The Foamasi infiltrate the Leisure Hive by dressing up as humanoids – even though they're about twice as bulky in the raw (I don't know where they get their control pants from, but they could make a fortune selling them on QVC), which is a bit silly, but at least distracts from the endless blether about tachyonics.

Visually, the show takes its biggest leap forward since the switch to colour ten years earlier (*Doctor Who* does like to make an impression on a new decade), with massive improvements in almost all areas of production design. Director Lovett Bickford also gets a new toybox of video effects to play with, as the story is the first to experiment with the Quantel 5000 image processing software which, among other things, allows the TARDIS to materialise into a moving shot. "Wow," said the nation's children.

"That's amazing – that static, roll back and mix technique was getting so old. Can we go see *The Empire Strikes Back* again now?"

And that's *The Leisure Hive's* problem in a nutshell: Bickford and Nathan-Turner were shameless about going for style over substance; according to David Fisher, the director's instruction was "don't give me plot, just give me visuals", while the producer told him the series had become "too story-bound" (whatever that means). But the technical advances the production is desperate to show off are hardly the sort of spectacle to get young hearts racing; while George Lucas was sending his mammoth Imperial Walkers into battle on the ice plains of Hoth, Lovett Bickford was desperately trying to prove his auteur credentials by opening the new series of *Doctor Who* with a showboating, full minute-and-a-half panning shot of the Doctor fast asleep in a deckchair – a level of enthusiasm the strikingly subdued Tom Baker will maintain throughout all four episodes – while kids' favourite K-9 rolls into the sea and blows up. As a symbol of where they were going wrong, it could hardly have been more potent.

As it turned out, though, *Star Wars* wasn't the problem – or at least not directly. The all-conquering success of the movie had resulted in a sudden rush of sci-fi films and TV series being greenlit, and it was against one of these that *Doctor Who* now found itself directly scheduled. *Buck Rogers in the 25th Century* was one of American TV producer Glen A Larson's two rapid responses to R2-D2, Darth Vader and company (the other being the original *Battlestar Galactica*). Starring Gil Gerard as a NASA shuttle pilot who accidentally gets put into suspended animation before being defrosted 500 years into the future, it was dumb, derivative and destined only to run for two seasons. But in September 1980, its combination of glossy visuals, cute comedy robots and actress Erin Gray in a sprayed-on spandex jumpsuit was enough to send *Doctor Who* reeling, with *The Leisure Hive* averaging a paltry 5.1 million viewers – less than half the number who had tuned in for the final part of *The Horns of Nimon* in January.

If the opener had been a false start, the second story of the season sees John Nathan-Turner and Christopher Hamilton Bidmead trying to sell their new, serious, scientifically rigorous vision of *Doctor Who* – with a story about an evil cactus. Meglos – the malevolent pot plant in question – spends half the story impersonating the Doctor, which means Tom Baker spent much of the studio time being extremely prickly. (Honestly, this stuff writes itself sometimes, doesn't it?) Spiky's plan is to steal the Dodecahedron – the mysterious power source of the Tigellans, whose high priestess is played by original 60s companion Jacqueline Hill (shades of *The Aztecs* there – maybe she just had one of those faces?). He also forms an alliance with a bunch of grizzled space raiders led by TV veteran Bill Fraser – who apparently only took the job on condition he be allowed to kick the tin dog. Though he'd have to get in line behind the show's star and producer.

Director Terence Dudley had offered to write for *Doctor Who* way back in 1963; this was his last directing job before retirement but, proving it's never too late to learn, he was let loose with the latest bit of kit the BBC had on a sale or return basis: a revolutionary(ish) motion control process for improving CSO images called Scene Synch. (It was never used on *Doctor Who* again, but the BBC did buy it following its successful use in a 1982 adaptation of *Gulliver in Lilliput*, directed by – who else? – Barry Letts. Either that, or the 30-day free trial had expired and they'd forgotten to send it back.)

Meglos was John Flanagan and Andrew McCulloch's first TV credit, and was a bit pulpy for Chris Bidmead's liking; his method of trying to fix it was changing terms like "time loop" to "chronic hysteresis", which is equally meaningless, while also sounding like an unpleasant medical condition. The script does contain one notable pearl, though, when Tigellan leader Zastor says of the Doctor: "He sees the threads that join the universe together, and mends them when they break." Which is as good a job description as any, really.

Baker is on fine form as Meglos, clearly relishing the chance to do something different (and you have to admit, a psychotic cactus is different) despite his ill-health – though his Doctor, by contrast, is even more subdued.

Sadly, the new regime continues to heap indignities upon K-9, as it's revealed the advanced supercomputer needs re-charging every two hours. Who made him, Apple?

Romana, meanwhile, receives a message recalling her to Gallifrey, signalling her time by the Doctor's side is drawing to an end. Lalla Ward, to her credit, does her best to make this look like bad news.

The bride wore a look of mild surprise

In September, 48-year-old small screen veteran Anthony Ainley – who Nathan-Turner had previously worked with on a BBC adaptation of Anthony Trollope's *The Pallisers* – signed on to play the Master in *Doctor Who*'s big season finale. That's assuming there was anyone left standing to *make* the season finale. Before that, there was the small matter of getting through the shoot for the fifth story, Stephen Gallagher's *Warriors' Gate*, without any blood being spilled.

The problems had started at script stage, after Gallagher delivered what Christopher Bidmead described as "a wonderful novel" – but a lousy TV show, forcing Bidmead to perform a top-down rewrite in collaboration with the story's assigned director, Paul Joyce. Then, when rehearsals began, it became clear that Joyce – whose background was in photography and documentary-making – didn't have a clue how the BBC made television; his idea of prepping for the shoot was to arrange screenings of films like Alan Resnais' *L'Annee Derniere* and Jean Cocteau's *Orphée* – when what he should have been doing is blocking the camera shots. Joyce wanted to cover the action with a single camera, movie-style, which would have been impossible in the time available, so production assistant Graeme Harper stayed up all night writing the camera scripts himself.

And then there was the small matter of The Les Dawson Door Incident – one of the more celebrated stories from the heyday of BBC industrial unrest, in which the lugubrious northern comic walked through a glass door that was supposed to have been provided by two separate departments (for the sake of argument, let's call them The Door Dept and The Glass Dept), but ended up being handled by a single team – resulting in a walk-out and lost studio time for numerous shows, including *Warriors' Gate*'s entire first filming block.

With the recording falling into chaos, Nathan-Turner briefly sacked Joyce[III] and, along with Harper, took on some of the directing work himself, before Joyce was reinstated to finish the job. Tom Baker also stepped up to the plate to offer some advice on how best to get the story in the can and, for once, his suggestions were taken on board. At the eleventh hour, it seemed somebody was finally admitting what he'd been telling them all along – he really did know more about how to make this show than the directors.

With Romana and K-9 both departing at the end of the story, John Leeson and John Nathan-Turner went on BBC Radio 4's *Today* programme to sombrely confirm the robot dog's imminent departure to a shell-shocked nation. ("Erm, I am actually leaving as well, if anyone cares," said Lalla Ward.) Given how everything with Matthew Waterhouse was going so well, Nathan-Turner also decided that a teenage character in Johnny Byrne's penultimate story of the season might be worth retaining, so 18-year-old Sarah Sutton – who had played the lead in a 1978 BBC adaptation of Ice Warriors creator Brian Hayles' *The Moon Stallion* – was invited to join the TARDIS crèche. Meanwhile, Australian actress Janet Fielding, a veritable veteran at 27, was cast as air stewardess Tegan, having lied in her interview about a) her age and b) the minimum height requirement for Australian cabin crew (it's 163cm on Qantas, for anyone considering a career change).

Two days before his debut on screen, Matthew Waterhouse popped up on *Top of the Pops* to promote the BBC Records' single of Peter Howell's new theme tune. The sleeve had a portrait of a grinning Tom Baker, but Waterhouse was sure it would only be a matter of time before he was replaced with Adric.

Sadly, it would take a better PR stunt than that to rescue John Nathan-Turner's rapidly sinking ship. With *Meglos* averaging just 4.7 million viewers, the new producer's dream of relaunching *Doctor Who* as a glossy rival for *Star Wars* fans' affections was clearly in trouble.

For those who *were* still watching, however, *Full Circle* is where the John Nathan-Turner era of *Doctor Who* begins in earnest. In the first of the "E-Space Trilogy", the TARDIS falls through a Charged Vacuum Emboitment (always a bugger, that) into a mini-universe that exists outside our own. Here they pitch up on the planet Alzarius – beautifully realised as a lush, wetland alien landscape (they even went to the effort of dusting the tropical plants with powder paints) that does a brilliant job of disguising the fact it's really a country park just off the Slough Road.

At the time of Mistfall, amphibian creatures rise from the swamps to terrorise the local humanoid population, who have built their society in the crashed spaceship they hope will one day return them to their homeworld. In an intriguing twist, however, it turns out they're actually native Alzarians descended from the Marshmen – who in turn evolved from the planet's marsh spiders – and the Starliner has, in fact, been flight-ready for centuries. It's just no-one knows how to fly it.

Andrew Smith's script is full of these clever little notions. It also provides us with the most full-blooded moment of "real" drama in a long time, as a young Marsh-child, terrified by being subjected to experiments in the ship's lab, dies while trying to smash through a video screen because it's seen an image of the Doctor – the only person to have shown it any kindness. It's a genuinely upsetting scene, and Baker's righteous anger is all the more powerful for having spent the previous two stories moping about in a sulk. The Marshmen themselves – which owe more than a passing debt to the Creature from the Black Lagoon – are also the first decent monster in an age, with flaps of wet, leathery skin and snuffling, porcine grunts (recorded by the Radiophonic Workshop's Dick Mills on an actual pig farm; you have to admire his dedication, even if his colleague at the next desk probably didn't). The spiders are rubbish, though.

Peter Grimwade, making his directorial debut, had cut his *Who* teeth as far back as *The Robots of Death* – when, as production assistant, he had inspired Tom Baker to change the scripted name of the illness "Grimwold's syndrome" to "Grimwade's syndrome". He works hard to give the location work a luscious, cinematic quality, using coloured filters to subtly alter the lighting, while the Mistfall sequences conjure the most atmospheric alien environment since *Planet of Evil*.

The only real weak link – apart from the spiders – is Adric, who is less galactic artful dodger, more whiny brat in space pyjamas, while Matthew Waterhouse struggles even to walk convincingly. K-9, naturally, fares even worse – for those keeping score, in this one he gets his head knocked off by a Marshman with a big stick. He was starting to get the hint.

Andrew Smith was invited to the location shoot at Black Park in Buckinghamshire and, either through over-excitement or over-indulgence, managed to throw up on some of the costumes (maybe that's why Adric had to wear his jim-jams). Whether it was this, or the amount of work Bidmead had to put in finessing the scripts, Smith never worked for the show again, and later joined the Metropolitan Police. On the evidence of his one shot – the first truly successful *Doctor Who* story since *City of Death* – that's a shame. It's also unfortunate that Smith's story should have set an unwelcome new record: with a meagre 3.7 million viewers, episode two of *Full Circle* was the lowest-rated *Doctor Who* episode to date, ranking an astonishing 170th in that week's most-watched programmes. (Were there even 170 *programmes* a week in 1980 – or was it even beaten by that test card with the girl and the clown?) To the eternal shame of many fans – your correspondent included – we'd all convinced ourselves we were getting more bang for our Buck on ITV, and it was poor old *Doctor Who* that got Rogered.

Full Circle was also the first story viewers – or those that were left, anyway – watched in the knowledge that Tom Baker was leaving. On the day before the first episode went out, Baker had been due to open the new Tussaud's *Doctor Who* Experience, when John Nathan-Turner got wind that news of his departure had been leaked to the papers. A press conference was hurriedly arranged at the BBC's Cavendish Place, in which Baker announced his retirement from the role, and mischievously suggested his successor might be a woman. He and Nathan-Turner had apparently concocted this headline-grabbing wheeze on the way – as if news of Tom Baker quitting *Doctor Who* wasn't enough of a story in itself.

A muted Baker appeared on that evening's *Nationwide*, slouching against the TARDIS while fielding a series of baffling questions from Sue Cook such as "It must have been fun working with all that machinery" and concluding, of his future career, "I'm going into oblivion, I suppose."

The *News of the World* was quick to suggest candidates for the role, including John Cleese, Larry Grayson and Margaret Thatcher. Ho and, indeed, ho. The *Daily Mirror*, meanwhile, joined Baker for a boozy crawl around London, where he spoke frankly – and not entirely soberly – about his fears for the future. Recording his penultimate story, Johnny Byrne's *The Keeper of Traken*, Baker was more fractious than ever, with colleagues getting the impression things with Ward weren't great. At least he didn't tell Sarah Sutton, who was joining the cast for the first time, to piss off – though he did insist on calling her "Miss Basingstoke" (in reference to her birthplace), which many might say is worse. As if that wasn't bad enough, she also had to contend with Matthew Waterhouse trying to hug her – I don't *think* that's a euphemism – whenever he got the chance. "I suspect that Adric got lucky with Nyssa between episodes,"[41] said Waterhouse. Who needs fans to write slash fiction when the actors can do it themselves?

State of Decay is Season Eighteen's fish out of water: or, more accurately, its bat out of hell. Originally conceived at the fag end of Philip Hinchcliffe's reign, it has "1977" running through it like a stick of Blackpool rock. In fact, Terrance Dicks delivered such a blatant Hammer Horror pastiche, Christopher Bidmead insisted on rewriting it to make it less gothic and more hi-tech. Fortunately, sense prevailed and the story retains its cod-medieval setting, while the script is at pains to eulogise the potential of science for progress and emancipation, which seems a happy compromise in anybody's book.

At the heart of the story are Zargo, Camilla and Aukon – three vampires on a mission to revive the Great One, an old enemy of the Time Lords, on an un-named planet in E-space. In a – presumably coincidental – reversal of the previous story's big reveal, the Doctor discovers the Three Who Rule started out as Earth astronauts, and their castle is their cargo ship. There's some lovely stuff about the evolution of language here, so that Captain Sharky becomes Zargo, navigation officer Lauren MacMillan becomes Camilla and science officer Anthony O'Connor becomes Aukon. It's an old trick – Chris Boucher did it four years earlier in *The Face of Evil* – but a good one.

Being a hangover of a previous era, it's striking how much scarier this tries to be than the stories around it. The classic Hammer trope of a peasant village under curfew is well used to invoke a fear of the dark: the twilight scenes of gathering dusk in the forest are particularly atmospheric, helped in no small part by Paddy Kingsland's haunting score – possibly the finest of the programme's original run. Terrance Dicks provides plenty of mood music of his own, meanwhile, in a script that's not afraid to stop for a spooky ghost story – there are vampire legends on every planet, says the Doctor: "Creatures that stalk the night and feast on the blood of the living". And, once again, there's a worthy attempt to distil the essence of *Doctor Who* into a single soundbite: "The Doctor is not weaponless," says Camilla. "He has the greatest weapon of all – knowledge."

Of course, any *Doctor Who* story that racks up the tension by building towards the appearance of a giant vampire is just storing up trouble and, sure enough, the climax here is woeful. The bats are more of a qualified success – the footage of real ones superimposed over Aukons' operatic threats looks fab; the ones on strings being flung at the Doctor and Romana considerably less so. Look out, too, for the gag reel moment that made the final cut, when a door smashes Tom Baker in the face; he appears slightly stunned throughout the ensuing scene and misses his cue. Matthew Waterhouse also managed to take a lump out of his own leg when misusing a prop knife: there really was no beginning to his acting skills.

Given the tension between Baker and Ward that had beset the story's production, Peter Moffatt was as flabbergasted as anyone when it was suddenly announced that the pair were to marry before Christmas. The news broke on November 19th after Baker reluctantly agreed to another press call at Cavendish Place. When the happy couple arrived at the evening event, it was clear they'd already been – ahem – celebrating, and it turned into quite a party by all

accounts. The couple were married at Chelsea Registry Office on Saturday, December 13th, accompanied by a throng of journalists and photographers (but not the bride's parents).

A second set of Prime Computer commercials, filmed around this time, cashed in on the celebrations by upping the will-they-won't-they flirtation of the earlier ads: as the Doctor chunters on about how brilliant Prime Computers are, Romana nuzzles his ear and tells him to "ask it how to handle a woman". The computer's response? MARRY THE GIRL, DOCTOR. Which is probably as good an explanation for this unlikely union as any.

La Belle et la Bête et la Tin Dog

In Christmas week, K-9 made an appearance at that year's BBC Careers Conference – presumably looking for ideas about what to do next. For all we know, he could be answering the phones in accounts to this day.

Opinion on *Warriors' Gate*, which resumed Season Eighteen's run in the New Year, is divided into three camps: those who love it, those who think it's a load of pretentious old nonsense, and those who worked on it and were just grateful to finish the bloody thing.

Paul Joyce may have been wildly overambitious, and would clearly have come unstuck without wiser, more experienced hands to bail him out, but you could argue the pain was worth it because – let's cut to the chase here – *Warriors' Gate* is pretty bloody awesome: strange, oblique, frequently impenetrable and, yes, maybe a *teensy* bit pretentious. But awesome nonetheless.

Set in a sort-of galactic no-man's land between Exo-space and our own universe, most of the action takes place against a white void, which is both cheap and highly effective (in contrast to, say, *Underworld*). The Doctor and company run into the crew of a privateer ship who are using a captive Tharil – one of a noble race of leonine, time-sensitive aliens – to help them navigate the time vortex. Demonstrating an unusually complex morality, these wounded beasts are themselves later shown to have been slave-traders, plundering N-space from their castle in the gateway between universes.

Jean Cocteau casts a long shadow over the production, from the design of the Tharils to the use of mirrors as portals (a la *Orphée*) to the abandoned, crumbling fairytale castle, where cobwebbed skeletons sit out eternity around the table of the abandoned banqueting hall. (If Cocteau had directed the video for Adam Ant's "Stand and Deliver", this is how it would have looked. In fact there's a New Romantic feel to the production design generally – quite bleeding edge for *Doctor Who*, considering that, in 1980, the movement was still largely confined to a small clique of hipsters wearing eyeshadow and teatowels at the Blitz club.) Beyond the mirror, meanwhile, the Tharils' world is represented through the highly stylised use of black and white photographs – possibly the show's first use of CSO that's *meant* to look fake.

In satisfying contrast to the art-house imagery and meditations on philosophy (even K-9 starts quoting the I Ching – though you won't be surprised to hear that Barry Letts added that bit), the trader ship's crew are a realistically feckless bunch, more worried about missing lunch or having to lug heavy equipment about than the fact the void is shrinking around them. The *Waiting for Godot*-style duologues of below stairs skivvies Royce and Aldo are worthy of Robert Holmes himself.

Warriors' Gate also serves as a fitting valedictory turn for Lalla Ward's wonderful Romana who, once again, gets to take on most of the "Doctor" duties – and gets most of the best jokes – while Tom Baker wanders about looking magisterial. When she decides to stay behind and help free the Tharils from slavery, the Doctor tells her she was "the noblest Romana of them all". It's hard to disagree.

And it's farewell, too, to K-9: after four years of loyal service keeping the kids entertained, the tin dog trundles off into TV quarantine with the Mistress Romana, causing teenage nerds everywhere to sigh with relief that they've finally got rid of that pesky, irritating, squeaky little sod of a sidekick. Now it's just the Doctor and... oh, bugger it.

Scheduled at the earlier time of 5.10pm, *Warriors' Gate* benefited from weaker ITV opposition to win an average of 7.5 million viewers, at least 7.5 of whom claimed to have understood it.

On January 11th, the 7th Viscount and Lady Bangor posed for pictures with their new son-in-law, Liverpool seaman's boy Tommy Baker. One imagines conversation over dinner was strained. Two days earlier, Baker had laid down on a patch of fake grass in BBC Television Centre to record the fourth Doctor's dying moments – the subject of a disagreement, naturally, with the actor arguing it looked "unheroic" – though he continued working on the story for another fortnight, filming his final scenes on Saturday, January 24th.

"It was quite a sad moment for all of us in the studio," admitted Christopher Bidmead. "It finally came home to us that this was the last time we were going to be working with Tom. For all the ups and downs we'd had with Tom, it was a sad moment to see him go."[43] Afterwards, a party was held in the Television Centre bar, from which the outgoing star excused himself early.

For viewers, though, the fourth Doctor was still alive and, if not exactly kicking, then at least breaking into a purposeful stride now and again. But any kids frustrated by the lack of monster action in *Warriors' Gate* won't have found much succour in *The Keeper of Traken*. Set in the groves and palaces of a pseudo-Jacobean planet, it's *Doctor Who* at its most studio-bound and stately. There's very little in the way of action, and the closest thing to a traditional monster is the Melkur, a "living statue" which designer Tony Burrough based on Italian Futurist artist Umberto Boccioni's 1913 sculpture *Unique Forms of Continuity in Space* – which probably didn't give Terry Nation too many sleepless nights. For grown-ups of a certain inclination, though, *The Keeper of Traken* is a rather charming, if slight, chamber piece: a fairytale of good and evil in the night garden, it combines a lyrical script with future Oscar nominee Burrough's beautiful, deliberately theatrical, Gaudi-esque sets to winning effect.

Johnny Byrne was a former Beat poet who once shared digs with The Beatles – though John Nathan-Turner met him while they were both working on *All Creatures Great and Small*. (What next – Allen Ginsberg writing for *Emmerdale*?) His initial interpretation of *Doctor Who* falls somewhere between *A Midsummer Night's Dream* and Ursula K Le Guin, so we can thank/blame Christopher Bidmead for adding the thick layer of technobabble, examples of which include "recursive integrator", "gamma mode-encryption", "binary induction system", "fold back flow inducer" and "deep-filled flange boggler" (okay, I made that last one up).

According to the Doctor, Traken is an empire "held together by people being terribly nice to each other" – so a bit like the Church of England – although this turns out not to be strictly true (they're awfully quick to hand down to death penalty, for one thing). The Keeper is the "organising principle" of the Traken hivemind – a bit like Microsoft Outlook, but with a big white beard – who draws his power from the Source, a bioelectronic Maguffin used to keep the peace throughout the Traken union that the Master has his eye on as a way of prolonging his life.

Yes, he's back – and so are his over-complicated schemes, the latest of which involves disguising his TARDIS as a statue, hiding inside it for years on end while a young girl falls in love with it and then persuading her to... well, anyway, let's just say it all ends in disaster, naturally, but not before he gets to possess the body of Anthony Ainley's Consular Tremas. That's right, Tremas: no doubt the Master had come across hundreds of other suitable bodies in the years since we last saw him, but was holding out to satisfy his well-known love of a good anagram.

When we first meet him, the Master (Geoffrey Beevers – AKA Mr Caroline John) is still rocking his cadaverous look from *The Deadly Assassin*. The original costume was about to be thrown away before someone found it mouldering in a cardboard box in a warehouse. ("What condition is it in?" "It's rotted away to a pile of old rags." "Perfect – send it over.") Right at the end, the Master slips into Tremas' body – oh stop it – and thereby grows younger-looking and acquires a neatly trimmed, Satanic goatee and a black velveteen pantsuit. You can laugh, but all the megalomaniacs were wearing them that season.

Oh, we should mention Nyssa. Nyssa is Tremas' daughter. She has curly hair.

Back on Earth, there was panic in the streets of Britain when the Writer's Guild of Great Britain, embroiled in a row with WH Allen about contracts, tried to bring down the country by laying down their pens and refusing to write any more Doctor Who novelisations. Thankfully, the dispute was resolved before the bodies started piling up in the streets. Helping to fill the void, electro-pop pioneers the Human League penned their own tribute to the outgoing Time Lord in the form of "Tom Baker", the b-side to their single "Boys and Girls". The sleeve featured the fourth Doctor caught in one of his more enigmatic stares, while the vinyl itself was engraved with the message "Thanks Tom". The track is an instrumental, but it is possible to sing "his name is Tom Baker and he played Doctor Who-oo-oo" along to it if you've had a few too many to drink. Apparently.

Your number's up

And so, after seven years and 40 thrilling adventures in time and space (aw c'mon – even *The Power of Kroll* had nice scenery), it was, as the Doctor says in *Logopolis*, "the end... but the moment has been prepared for."

Specifically, the end had been prepared by Christopher Bidmead, who decided that the fourth Doctor, monster-vanquishing hero to millions, should bow out with... quadruple maths. Yes, Tom Baker's swansong sees Bidmead turning his educational remit up to 11 – then dividing it by the square root of 7, as the TARDIS takes a trip to the titular planet of mathematicians for a lesson in block transfer computation via the Second Law of Thermodynamics. "Structure is the essence of matter, and the essence of matter is mathematics," explains the Logopolitans' chief poindexter, thrillingly. (Bidmead later admitted to basing the entire story on the inner workings of his favourite new toy at the time, the Vectorgraphic MZ System B microcomputer. If you ever run into him, I'm sure he'd be happy to explain why at some length.)

But wait, come back because, you know what? It's actually pretty great, Peter Grimwade's direction capturing the melancholy, funereal mood as the Doctor marches inexorably towards his destiny. In a break with tradition, our hero is beckoned silently to his fate by the Watcher – a ghostly, half-formed manifestation of his future self (played by ballet dancer Adrian Gibbs, who puts all his training to good use by... standing completely still and waving occasionally). Janet Fielding debuts as mouthy Australian air stewardess Tegan Jovanka (and before you ask: no, it's not cockney rhyming slang), while Sarah Sutton joins proper as the now orphaned Nyssa – the first time since 1967 there have been three companions in the TARDIS. (Unless you count K-9 – though these three would be a lot harder to write out for episodes at a time by chopping their heads off or rolling them into the sea to explode.) As the Master, meanwhile, Anthony Ainley is a little, let's say, *fruitier* than Roger Delgado, veering just the right side of camp in a way that shouldn't work but, again, sort of does.

Logopolis also has the highest body count of any *Doctor Who* story, with the loss of countless billions of lives – albeit most of them represented by some fairly underwhelming computer graphics on the TARDIS monitor. Those mathematicians on Logopolis, it turns out, haven't just been counting for the fun of it – they're literally holding reality together through pure mathematics, and when the Master interferes (possibly by shouting out random numbers to put them off), great swathes of the universe just blink out of existence. Oh, and it's kinda sorta the Doctor's fault. Oops – butterfingers!

Our hero's last stand takes place at the Joddrell Bank (now that *is* cockney rhyming slang) Observatory, shortly after the Master has broadcast a tape-recorded message to the entire universe (not available to listeners on long-wave). If that seems silly, it's nothing compared to the story's dumbest moment, when the Doctor resolves to flush the Master out of his TARDIS – with astonishing literalness – by landing in the Thames and erm, opening the doors. "I've had a fair amount of flak [for that]," admitted Bidmead. "I wanted the Master to show himself, then he'd have a physical problem to deal with, rather than the rather metaphysical problem of the Master lurking somewhere in his TARDIS unknown."[43] Which is surely the first case of answering a metaphysical question by dropping it in a river.

As usual, Bidmead gets carried away with the pseudo-scientific bafflegab. When his plan goes tits up, as it inevitably does, and he's forced to forge an alliance with the Doctor, as

he inevitably must, the Master suggests "we reconfigure our two TARDISes into time-cone inverters [to] create a stable safe zone by applying temporal inversion isometry to as much of space-time as we can isolate." That's easy for him to say.

And yet... and yet... there's an operatic grandeur to *Logopolis* that feels entirely appropriate for such a significant story. Despite Baker's reservations about the "unheroic" final scenes (which are actually rather splendid, thanks in large part to Grimwade's direction and Paddy Kingsland's elegiac score) – and that small business of accidentally wiping out half the universe – the impending death in the family casts a sepulchral pall over the fourth Doctor's final stand, which is only right and proper.

Absurdly, only 6.1 million people tuned in to pay their respects – exactly ten million fewer than had watched the final part of *City of Death* a year earlier. Overall, Season Eighteen remains one of *Doctor Who*'s lowest-rated series, with 17 of its 28 episodes failing to dent the Top 100 – ironic, as there's a convincing argument for these being the strongest set of stories in some years. With dramatically improved production values and a serious – if occasionally po-faced – reinstatement of the series' founding scientific principles, Tom Baker's final run is the solid, dependable wife the nation ignored in favour of a brief, meaningless and ultimately grubby fling with the showy floozy flaunting her wares on ITV. Sorry about that, Tom – you really did deserve better.

Shortly after leaving *Doctor Who*, Baker went into a hairdressers' in Chelsea and had his famous curls lopped off. "As I strolled out, nobody recognised me," he wrote in his autobiography. "It was a great shock. I felt as if I were invisible, as if I were dead. But I tried to make the best of it and hoped new work would come to distract me from the death of the Doctor."[2]

Baker's marriage to Lalla Ward lasted barely more than a year. "One day, he came back and said, 'I think I'm bored with being married'," Ward recalled some 23 years later. "I thought, ah right – well if he still says that tomorrow, it's probably not that he's been in the pub too long. So I asked him again the next day. I said, 'What you said yesterday evening, is that what you still think?' He said, 'Yeah, I'm bored of being married. Off you go.' And I said, 'Okay, fine', and I went. That was the last time that I ever saw Tom. I've never seen him since. Not since that minute."[44] / IIII

"We were happy for a while," was Baker's take. "It was great. Things don't have to last a long, long time. We were okay for a while, and there was absolutely no hostility when it ended, none at all. A year of happiness."[43]

Though one side of the double life he had lived throughout the 70s was gone, Baker continued to haunt the drinking dens of Soho. "There's something terribly beguiling and thrilling about low-life," he said in a 2011 interview. "These people who are careless and hedonistic, lies and drunkenness and singing stories from the past. Some of them were very distinguished and they held down quite important jobs. I look back on it now and I think, of the group we're talking about, maybe I'm the only survivor. When I look in those old pubs, especially the French House, it's like going to a grave."[45]

Baker's first jobs after leaving *Doctor Who* were playing Oscar Wilde on stage at Chichester and Sherlock Holmes in a new BBC version of *The Hound of the Baskervilles*. But, while he was rarely out of work – and remained one of the country's most in-demand voiceover artists – he found it difficult to step out from the long shadow of *Doctor Who*. In the early 1990s, he took a regular role in ITV hospital drama *Medics*, and later joined Vic Reeves and Bob Mortimer in the BBC remake of supernatural crime caper *Randall and Hopkirk (Deceased)*. But it was as the deliriously deranged narrator of Matt Lucas and David Walliams' hit comedy *Little Britain*, first shown on TV in 2003, that he really found a new audience, leading to engagements as diverse as presenting the topical panel show *Have I Got News For You* and acting as the voice of BT's landline text service.

In 1986, Baker married Sue Jerrard, who had been an assistant editor on *Doctor Who*. They moved to Kent, close to the churchyard where the famously morbid Baker had his own headstone erected; the simple inscription reads "Tom Baker, 1934 – ". After a period in France, the couple returned to England, and currently live in the countryside in East Sussex.

In 2010, Tom Baker returned to the role of the Doctor for a series of audio dramas, in which he was reunited with, among others, Louise Jameson's Leela. They got on a lot better the second time round.

He remains, for many, the definitive Doctor Who, and his ill-temper and, by his own admission, "irrational behaviour" in later years shouldn't be allowed to detract from his hypnotic, otherworldly, utterly compelling performance as a truly alien Time Lord.

"Tom is really one of a kind," said Douglas Adams. "What you get at the end of it is an extraordinary characterisation that nobody else could have pulled off."[37] "I saw it as him caring passionately about the programme, and fighting for something that mattered," said Lalla Ward of Baker's reputation for tyranny. "I can see that other people saw it often as just a temperamental, difficult, pain in the backside actor who should have kept his trap shut more often. I don't agree with that – I think his energy, and because of his energy his difficulties sometimes, kept the programme going through an era when it could have folded."[22]

Graham Williams, the man whose backside felt more of that pain than anyone, agreed: "He was a terrific guy to work with. We had furious rows, but a lot of good times together. He felt very deeply about the series. We both felt quite strongly about what we were doing. He, more than anybody else I think I've ever met, devoted himself to *Doctor Who*. And I include myself in that – he worked for *Doctor Who* a lot harder than I did, or anybody else."[22]

Talk to Tom Baker long enough and he will inevitably bring up the subject of grannies' bosoms – about how they would tingle with pleasure whenever he walked past them, in memory of the times when their grandchildren had buried their heads there during his more frightening encounters with Daleks and Cybermen, Krynoids and Kraals. This, for Baker, was what it was all about – the sheer, guileless pleasure of being a hero to millions upon millions of children.

"Playing Doctor Who... yes, it was the happiest time of my life," he said. "I never just wanted to be liked. I don't even want to be loved. I want to be adored. When I played Doctor Who, I was adored. It will never happen again. But I was adored, once."[46]

It Shouldn't Happen to a Bloody Vet

5

"At least buy me dinner first" (reprise)

After seven years of the same face, a new Doctor Who was big news, even making the BBC's main evening bulletin – albeit in the "and finally" slot normally reserved for skateboarding parrots or the Welsh.

According to Peter Davison, when his face appeared on screen, friends who were watching with the sound down were concerned that he'd died. Though clearly not concerned enough to turn the volume up. (Well, it was in the days before remote controls, I suppose. Plus, being actors, most of his friends were watching in the pub.)

Born Peter Moffett in April 1951, as a young man Davison had held down various odd jobs – including a stint as a mortuary attendant, which would come in handy when working with Matthew Waterhouse – before training at the Central School of Speech and Drama. On graduating, he changed his name to avoid confusion with the actor and director Peter Moffatt, who would later help to ruin several of his *Doctor Who*s.

He made his TV debut in ITV's kiddie sci-fi saga *The Tomorrow People* – a sort of juvenile X-Men about a bunch of teenagers who "broke out" into the next stage of human evolution, called Homo superior. (Amazingly, none of this was intended to be an allegory.) It was here Davison met his future wife, helium-voiced American actress Sandra Dickinson, with whom he had a daughter who would subsequently help establish her father as the head of the nearest thing to a genuine *Doctor Who* dynasty. But that's a long way off yet.

In 1978, Davison had achieved instant fame as Tristan Farnon, the impetuous younger brother of Robert Hardy's Siegfried in *All Creatures Great and Small*, the BBC's hit adaptation of the popular memoirs *If Only They Could Talk* and *It Shouldn't Happen to a Vet*, written by Yorkshire veterinary surgeon Alf Wright under the name James Herriot. All of which paled in comparison to Davison's most momentous contribution to the sum of human achievement: co-writing, along with Dickinson, the theme to *Button Moon*, a charmingly makeshift pre-school show with a cast almost entirely made up of kitchen utensils, including Mr and Mrs Spoon and their daughter, Tina Tea-Spoon. (It's not clear why she had a different surname – I guess modern spoon families are complicated.)

John Nathan-Turner had initially sounded out gravel-voiced Scot Iain Cuthbertson (last seen stealing *The Ribos Operation* from under Tom Baker's nose) for the fifth Doctor, and had also met with Richard Griffiths (later to gain immortality as *Withnail and I*'s flamboyantly predatory Uncle Monty) on the set of his ITV sitcom *Nobody's Perfect*. When he'd subsequently phoned Davison to offer him the job in October 1980, his erstwhile *All Creatures Great and Small* colleague hadn't believed him, claiming it was only when the producer invited him to lunch that he knew he must be serious. (Actors love to make this sort of joke, especially about the BBC. In fact they're a curiously dinner-obsessed breed generally – let's not forget Jon Pertwee literally dining out for weeks on his initial invitation to join the show – regularly citing a good table in a restaurant as the best perk of being famous, even though the tables in most restaurants are identical.)

"The prospect of taking over from Tom was incredibly daunting," Davison admitted. "I thought, I'm probably going to turn this down. And then I remember thinking, if I turned it down, whenever whoever took over took over, I wouldn't be able to say 'I was offered that, you know'. It's just not a gentlemanly thing to do. So it was almost that ridiculous reason.

"It was a fantastic thing to be offered, *Doctor Who*, I was aware of that. It was just simply in terms of, you know, your career – whether it was a sensible thing to do. So I just sort of took the plunge."[1]

The actor signed a contract that paid him £600 per episode, plus a royalty on repeat fees and overseas sales. It was hardly Hollywood money, but it was enough to allow him to buy a house and a car, even in London.

With their leading man secured, Nathan-Turner and Antony Root issued a revised Writer's Guide, in which they were at pains to contrast the new Doctor with Tom Baker's invincible superhero, describing the new iteration as "fallible and vulnerable and only too conscious that life largely consists of things going wrong for well intentioned people like himself". Still, cheer up, eh? It might never happen.

In January 1981, Davison made his debut in the studio to record the regeneration scene at the end of *Logopolis*. He was called in around 5pm and, during the 7pm supper break, repaired to the bar (only two hours in, and already drinking on the job), where he met Tom Baker. He recalled that his predecessor said something to him, but he couldn't hear a word of it over the noise in the bar, so he just said, "Right, okay". "To this day," insisted Davison "I've no idea what he said."[1]

"It's very likely I was telling him to get the next round and make mine a large one," said Baker.[1] This is almost certainly not a joke.

The new leading man's overriding impression of his new workplace was "chaos" with "lots of people screaming at each other". But he'd signed the contract, so there was no backing out now.

After a tense few hours of trying to get all the shots in the can, at ten minutes past 10 on the evening of January 9th, television history was finally made as one Doctor Who got up from the studio floor, and another took his place. The assembled BBC technicians treated the moment with due reverence in the only way they knew how – by looking at their watches, shaking their heads and simultaneously filling in an overtime form and composing a letter to their union.

For his part, Davison was instructed to "sit up and pull some kind of expression". He opted, in his own words, for "mild surprise and bemusement, which was quite genuine."[1]

As is traditional, one of the new Doctor's first engagements was an appearance on *Blue Peter*. On his way to the studio, Davison met Patrick Troughton in the BBC car park (as the current TARDIS incumbent, Davison was allocated a space at Television Centre, while Troughton had to fend for himself). It was here that the veteran actor cautioned the younger man to do "three years and get out" – which Davison took to be good career advice from his favourite of his predecessors. (Though it's possible Troughton was just after his parking space.)

There was plenty more advice on offer for the new Doctor – whether he wanted it or not – when he visited a different BBC studio for an appearance on lunchtime chinwag session *Pebble Mill at One*.

With the co-operation of the *Doctor Who* production office, viewers had been invited to suggest how he might play the role. If Davison was wondering why the RSC never thought it necessary to seek the counsel of students, housewives and the long-term unemployable on how Ralph Richardson or John Gielgud should play Lear, he didn't let it show. In fact he took the process so seriously that, when a viewer called Stuart suggested his Doctor should be like "Tristan Farnon but with bravery and intellect", Davison pretty much chose to run with it, and has continued to quote it as a source of inspiration ever since. (It may also explain Tom Baker's comment – in so much as anything *can* explain a Tom Baker comment – that "it was very odd because I came back not as Peter Davison, but as a bloody vet".[1])

Another *Pebble Mill* viewer, Michael Cookston, suggested Davison "make Doctor Who more vulnerable, thus there'd be more drama in the character" – and vulnerability did indeed become a touchstone of this incarnation of the Doctor. In retrospect, perhaps the show had a lucky escape: if Stuart and Michael had suggested he play it like a Harlem pimp or a wife-beating drunk, the next three years could have been *very* interesting.

The best contribution of that particular show, though, was from a terribly posh girl called Justine Preston, who thought the Doctor looked "a bit common" and needed smartening up. She then went on to suggest he should dress as a waiter and his companion should be a chimpanzee in a sailor suit. Whether Justine had been hanging around Tom Baker too much, we can't be sure – but *Chimpanzee in a*

Sailor Suit was so very nearly the title of this book.

Producer plays hardball in celery negotiations

Having already delivered on mild surprise and bemusement, Davison's next task was to adopt a suitably ambiguous expression for the title sequence (wisely, the sequence's designer, Sid Sutton, chose to crop out the actor's hideous maroon Christmas jumper, which might have spoiled the futuristic vibe somewhat). And then, finally, he discovered there was more to being Doctor Who than just pulling faces when, in March 1981, rehearsals got under way for his first full season (though not *quite* as full as his predecessor's, as it turned out, as Nathan-Turner had already creamed off two episodes for a little pet project he was developing; more on *that* later).

Scripts in the frame for the fifth Doctor's debut run were a mix of bespoke commissions and leftovers from Christopher Bidmead's work on the previous season. These included *The Enemy Within* – a new story from Christopher Priest, who was hoping for a smoother passage than the *Sealed Orders* debacle – a story submitted on spec by Gerry Davis with the vaguely familiar title *Genesis of the Cybermen*, and an Earth invasion story from *Meglos* director Terence Dudley. That serial's writers, John Flanagan and Andrew McCulloch, were tasked with launching the new Doctor in a nuclear disarmament parable called *Project Zeta-Sigma*. However, concerns about the viability of the story saw it pushed back in the production schedule, with Dudley's script, *Four to Doomsday*, going before the cameras first. (The official reason given for this was that it would give the new boy time to find his feet before being exposed to the harsh glare of public scrutiny in his potentially make-or-break first story. Which is a very sensible strategy, in no way related to Dudley's script being the only one ready.)

In February, *Project Zeta-Sigma* was abandoned altogether, and Christopher Bidmead commissioned to write a new debut serial for the Doctor on a freelance basis. With Bidmead racing to get the scripts in shape in time for filming in August, the shooting order of the

first half of the season would now see the second story followed by the fourth, the third and then the first. Consequently, the Doctor's hair is all over the place during this year: it's long, then short, then a bit longer and then a bit shorter again. (At least we assume that's the reason for all the chopping and changing – maybe Time Lord hair is just dry and temporally unmanageable.)

On April 15th, the first day of recording on *Four to Doomsday*, Davison's costume was revealed to the world for the first time at a press call. And, in keeping with Nathan-Turner's ideas about Tom Baker's wardrobe in his final season, it was very much a Costume: a heavily stylised ensemble of cricketing whites, pyjama-striped slacks and a three-quarter length beige jacket with red piping. Unlike earlier Doctors' rag-bag efforts, this was not the sort of outfit you could imagine anybody wearing in real life – unless they were a *Doctor Who* fan humiliating themselves for the local press, of course.

As if this didn't quite get the Hey Everyone Look How Adorably Eccentric I Am message across strongly enough, the ensemble was soon completed by a stick of celery on the jacket lapel. Yes, you read that right – celery. Davison, not surprisingly, was "profoundly unconvinced" by this. "I said to John, okay fine, if you want me to wear a piece of celery, I'll wear a piece of celery, as long as you explain it before I leave the show."[2] Nathan-Turner, for his part, was as good as his word: an explanation was eventually given during Davison's final story three years later.

The celery was nothing, however, compared to being saddled with the wet lettuce that was Adric. According to Davison, Matthew Waterhouse wasted no time in informing his new leading man that he'd never be able to follow Tom Baker's act and, later in the run, took it upon himself to try to tell the Hollywood veteran Richard Todd – nominated for an Oscar for 1949's *The Hasty Heart* – how to act.

"Bless his little wooden socks," said Janet Fielding in a 2005 interview. "He had no humility – none. Absolutely zero."[4]

Peter Davison was even more forthright: "He was a twat," he declared. "But only because he was put in that situation. If you take someone out of the postal room or wherever they got him from, and put him in a successful series, it's going to go to his head."[5]

It probably didn't help that, while out and about filming for Season Nineteen, Waterhouse was the member of the cast children most recognised and wanted to meet. And *Doctor Who* really did have a regular ensemble cast again: the first time since 1967, there were four people on the TARDIS. Davison felt it was too many, and was particularly unhappy with the abrasive nature of Tegan – a frustration he admits he may have inadvertently taken out on Janet Fielding. "Janet said I was really horrible to her," he revealed in later years. "I don't remember being horrible to Janet at all, but Sarah Sutton also says I was horrible to Janet, so I don't think she was making it up."[5] Fielding herself wasn't much more enamoured with her character, feeling she was "one-dimensional" and describing her as *"Peanuts'* Lucy in space." And the salary was peanuts, too, now she came to think about it.

Nathan-Turner wanted to launch his new Doctor in the autumn, but the BBC were keen for Davison to meet his commitments on *Sink or Swim* – the hit sitcom about two mismatched northern brothers living together in London, which the actor would rehearse in the mornings before recording *Doctor Who* in the afternoons. Somehow, he also found time to tape his leading role in the ITV role-reversal comedy *Holding the Fort*, in which he played a stay-at-home husband and father. It's often been said that the fifth Doctor is less assured than his predecessors, but if Davison looks panic-stricken at times, it's probably because he's trying to remember whether he's supposed to be saving the planet or warming a bottle (with Adric on board, it's possibly both).[1] His currency as a go-to guy for TV commercial directors, meanwhile, led his *Who* colleagues to nickname him Chocolate Chip Cookie, because he was flavour of the month. And possibly because he was flogging a lot of chocolate chip cookies at the time.

Partly to help Davison juggle this schedule, it had now been decided that the fifth Doctor would make his screen debut in January 1982. More controversially, for the first time in its 19-year history, *Doctor Who* would be leaving its traditional Saturday home for a twice-weekly evening slot on Mondays and Tuesdays.

One possible reason for this is that the BBC were floating the idea of a new soap opera – what would eventually become *EastEnders* – and wanted to see how a drama would fly in that slot. (Though a teenage pregnancy plot in which Nyssa gets knocked-up by the pub landlord would probably have been going too far.)

Alas, there would be no place on Mondays, Tuesdays or a month of Sundays for *The Enemy Within*, as Christopher Priest found his *Doctor Who* script bunkered in the sand for the second time in as many years. Citing a lack of communication from the production office, the novelist refused to undertake major rewrites, and the project subsequently went the same way as *Sealed Orders*.

One of the requirements of Priest's story had been to write out Adric, John Nathan-Turner having decided to replace his "cosmic Artful Dodger" with an "unscrupulous alien youth". He was nothing if not radical. Sadly, no-one saw fit to inform Matthew Waterhouse of this decision, with the teenager only learning of his imminent departure when Peter Davison casually dropped it into conversation with him at the BBC's Acton rehearsal rooms.

By now, a new script editor had been found in the form of Eric Saward, an experienced radio dramatist whose first *Doctor Who* submission – about alien shenanigans being the true cause of the Great Fire of London – had not only been greenlit, but had impressed John Nathan-Turner enough to hire him as a permanent replacement for Antony Root. With Christopher Priest's script disappearing off the radar, and a gaping hole in the schedule, Saward was initiated into that well-worn story editor's ritual of rolling up your sleeves and writing the bloody thing yourself.

In July, the new head of series and serials, David Reid, told Nathan-Turner he'd earned enough trust to have the stabilisers taken off, and Barry Letts was stood down as executive producer. The following month, Peter Davison was one of the stars of the BBC's autumn season press launch, wearing his *Doctor Who* outfit while *Not the Nine O'Clock News* bombshell Pamela Stephenson perched on his knee in a barely-there leopard print skirt. The publicity shots were so successful, it would have been churlish to point out *Doctor Who* wasn't actually going to be *on* in the Autumn, and Davison was supposed to be promoting *Sink or Swim*. Either this was an early example of 360° multi-platform brand synergy – or someone had left the wrong costume out in his dressing room.

Somehow, Davison's schedule also allowed him to attend his first US *Doctor Who* convention in Tulsa, Oklahoma – where an audience member helped put him at his ease by asking if he was worried about being assassinated "like John Lennon". Davison replied that he hadn't been – until now.

To help keep the show in the public eye during its longest ever break between series, John Nathan-Turner had a couple of aces up his sleeve. Or one ace and a joker, anyway. For starters, he persuaded the BBC to schedule the first ever proper retrospective of vintage stories under the banner *The Five Faces of Doctor Who*. And so it was that, as the show came of age in November 1981, BBC2 viewers were transported back 18 years to the night when a curious policeman emerged from the fog in the opening seconds of *An Unearthly Child* – the first time *Doctor Who*'s debut episode had been seen on British television since its hastily-scheduled repeat showing on November 30th, 1963. The rest of the story played out over consecutive nights, followed over the next few weeks by *The Krotons*, *Carnival of Monsters*, *The Three Doctors* and, finally, a repeat showing of *Logopolis* – chosen, to the disappointment of some fans hoping for Tom Baker action of a more vintage stripe, because Davison's brief appearance at the end was needed to justify the "Five Faces" tag. Despite how creaking and primitive some of the stories must have seemed to sophisticated 80s viewers with their Soda Streams, BBC Micros, Breville sandwich toasters and high-speed dubbing cassettes, the series was a huge hit – with one episode of *Logopolis* actually attracting a bigger audience than its first run on the main channel earlier in the year.

With a renewed appetite for all things *Who* among the viewing public, all Nathan-Turner had to do now was hit them with something to prove the show's golden age was far from over. Or, failing that, *K-9 and Company*.

Does exactly what it says on the tin dog

Don't be fooled by the title: *Doctor Who*'s first ever spin-off is not, in fact, a boardroom drama in which the Time Lord's faithful metallic mutt sets up his own pet supplies business. The company in question is none other than Elisabeth Sladen as Sarah Jane Smith – which was news to the actress as, according to her, she had been lured back by Nathan-Turner on the second attempt with the promise of star billing in her own show, *Sarah and K-9*.

In the 50-minute pilot episode, *A Girl's Best Friend*, Sarah decamps to her Aunt Lavinia's house in the village of Morton Harwood, where she discovers that the Doctor has sent her a present in the form of a robot dog – who comes in very handy when the village turns out to be a hotbed of witchcraft and ritual human sacrifice.

The result is an uneasy mix of genuinely atmospheric occult shenanigans and knockabout children's telly adventure – a sort of teatime *The Wicker Man*, with Britt Ekland's naked dance number replaced by K-9 singing "We Wish You a Merry Christmas" (don't worry, he keeps his collar on).

Writer Terence Dudley clearly set out with the intention of writing a mystery story; the only problem is, it's painfully obvious from the start who the villain is: not so much a Whodunnit as a Ohthatswhodunnit. And the kids must have been disappointed by K-9's limited screen time, especially when the alternative is an exciting investigation into the pH balance of the local soil. Oh, and we're also asked to believe that Aunt Lavinia is a virologist with her own literary agent, and that Sarah was raised on the colossal profits of her book *Teleological Response to the Virus*, which seems highly unlikely (unless it was *Harry Potter and the Teleological Response to the Virus*).

Production on the episode was fraught – not helped by Nathan-Turner getting the hump with Sladen (who hated the script and its depiction of her character) over some office politics, and refusing to talk to her for half the shoot. But if *K-9 and Company* is remembered for one thing above all, it's its legendary title sequence and theme music.

Nathan-Turner had made it clear he wanted

to base the opening credits on glossy US crime caper *Hart to Hart*. But instead of Robert Wagner and Stefanie Powers sipping Champagne in the jacuzzi or racing their convertible Mercs through the LA sunshine, we get Lis Sladen steering an open-top Mini Metro (did they really even make such a thing? Or had she just taken it under a very low railway bridge?) through the mizzling Gloucestershire countryside, peeking enigmatically over the top of *The Guardian* in the middle of a muddy field and trying (and failing) not to look embarrassed as both she and, most memorably, K-9 are shown perching atop a dry stone wall. Little wonder that, in 2011, *K-9 and Company* had the honour of being named telly's worst ever title sequence in an episode of David Walliams' *Awfully Good TV*.

The theme music, meanwhile, was written by Ian Levine and one Fiachra Trench, who sounds like a cabaret drag act, but is in fact an Irish songwriter of some repute. Levine claimed it had been intended to be an orchestral score, but was arranged instead from his electronic demo, while John Leeson provided the immortal chorus of "K-9! K-9!" (lyric sheets are available for those who want them).

Broadcast three days after Christmas 1981, *K-9 and Company* was watched by an impressive 8.4 million viewers – a triumph by any standards. Nathan-Turner was confident the show would go to a full series but, unfortunately, since commissioning the pilot, BBC One boss Bill Cotton had been replaced by a new controller, Alan Hart, who simply didn't like it. Or, if you prefer, Hart had no heart for a half-hearted *Hart to Hart*, and so K-9 was put back into storage until further notice. It would be two years until we heard from him again – probably the approximate time it took him to get down off that bloody wall.

Barthesian semiotics craze sweeps nation's playgrounds

And so, more than a year after he'd first set foot in the *Doctor Who* studio, viewers finally got to see Peter Davison in action when, on Monday, January 4th, 1982, the fifth Doctor climbed to his feet, looked around... then wobbled a bit, fell over and spent the next couple of episodes being carried around in a sealed box. (At least we're led to believe he's in the box – he was probably off slipping in a couple more episodes of *Sink or Swim*[II].)

Despite the lengthy gap between stories, Davison's debut serial, *Castrovalva*, is very much a continuation of *Logopolis*, both literally (or as literally as they could manage – the TARDIS has somehow moved itself into a different field, the Doctor's boots have mysteriously been replaced shoes and knee-socks, and all the security guards appear to have got in on the regeneration game too) and spiritually: there's lashings more block-transfer computation for the kids and, for good measure, a liberal dose of recursive occlusion and telebiogenesis thrown in too.

Both the title and the central concept of an illusory, Renaissance-style citadel (created by the Master using Adric's head for figures) literally folding in on itself are inspired by every maths geek's favourite artist, MC Escher. And yet, for all that, it's a pleasingly lyrical piece – as much about poetry as algorithms. Whether the concept of the new Doctor fighting to establish himself was intended as a commentary on the task facing the production team we can't be sure, but there's a lovely moment in which Davison literally unravels Baker's iconic scarf – possibly as a symbolic gesture of renewal, like a snake shedding its skin, or possibly just to make sure the bugger couldn't come back. (It's significant that Baker is not included as one of Davison's – rather good – impersonations of his former selves.)

The location filming for *Castrovalva* was undertaken at Buckhurst Park in Sussex, where owner Lord De La Warr invited cast and crew up to the house for evening drinks. Matthew Waterhouse rather took advantage of his Lordship's hospitality and, in scenes filmed the following day, is the only alien in *Doctor Who*'s history to appear green without the aid of make-up. At one point, he disappears from shot altogether to throw up behind a tree, while his colleagues just carry on acting. They're lovely at that age, aren't they?

Any doubts Davison may have felt about stepping into Baker's shoes – apart from the obvious "Are you sure these aren't supposed to be boots?" – would have been assuaged by the news that a whopping 9.1 million had tuned in for episode one of *Castrovalva*, rising to an astonishing 10.4 million by the final instalment – more than four million more than had watched Tom Baker's swansong, and a ringing endorsement both for the new man and the decision to move to a weekday slot. Not all viewers were convinced on the latter point, though: on Radio 4's *Feedback*, listeners railed against the "cavalier treatment of a national institution", describing the BBC's decision to wrench the show from its Saturday heartland as "at best a callous disregard for the audience and at worst an utter contempt for them", while the *Daily Mail* accused BBC Director General Alasdair Milne of "having no soul". So business as usual there, then.

But the most worrying criticism came from the Beeb's own head of drama, Graeme MacDonald, who, having viewed the first episode, wrote a letter to David Reid protesting that "Dr Who is too valuable a show to us to let its standard slip so dramatically", lamenting the "unimaginative" script and dismissing the performances of "the two girls" as "bad". He has a point on that score, at least: during the lengthy scenes where the Doctor is incapacitated, it's painfully apparent that his companions struggle to carry both him and the story.

If, for all its charms, *Castrovalva* is a bit on the slow side, *Four to Doomsday* is positively glacial. Davison's first recorded adventure – if that's not overstating the case – tells the story of an amphibious alien who wants to travel back to the beginning of the universe to meet God, but ends up meeting Adric instead.

Unfolding at its own, stately pace, the story is actually rather good, with Terence Dudley's intelligent script well served by strong production values and slick direction from John Black, not to mention a commanding guest turn from Stratford Johns, who brings as much dignity to the part as any man dressed as a giant frog can reasonably be expected to. But it's an extreme example of this era of *Doctor Who*'s bid to appeal to a more grown-up audience, and you do wonder what The Kids must have made of all the weighty discussions of physics, classical antiquity and democracy, not to mention the frequent musical interludes. In case you think that sounds a bit *Glee!*, you'll be disappointed to hear the TARDIS crew don't actually break out into song, but rather are forced to sit through several demonstrations of traditional dance from different eras of Earth history, courtesy of the various ethnic groups Froggy has collected aboard his spaceship[III]. Yes, instead of trying to compete with *Star Wars*, *Doctor Who* chose to win children's hearts and minds with something closely resembling an end-of-term assembly. As for sci-fi spectacle, in the year that Eliot and ET rode a bicycle across the moon, the best *Four to Doomsday* could manage was a brief space walk achieved by pushing Peter Davison round TVC Studio 8 on an office chair. (They edited the office chair out, obviously, otherwise it would have looked ridiculous. As opposed to just very silly.)

Four to Doomsday was kid's stuff, though, compared to what came next. Depending on your point of view, *Kinda* is either *Doctor Who*'s most daring excursion into the realms of philosophy, spirituality and sexual discovery – or it's the really pretentious one with the massive pink rubber snake.

Newcomer Christopher Bailey's script is built from a grab-bag of religious symbols and iconography – mainly Buddhist, but with strong Christian and Celtic influences. The planet of Deva Loka, for example, is named in honour of the Therevada Buddhist word for "heaven", while the story's big bad, the Mara, means "temptation" – but as the latter takes the form of a serpent in the former's paradise garden, you don't need to shave your head and live up a mountain to appreciate the allusion. The story, heavily influenced by Ursula K le Guin's 1976 novel *The Word for World is Forest*, is also something of a meditation on colonialism, sexual politics (significantly, only the women have voice) and the nature of wisdom and the subconscious – none of which presented BBC Enterprises with any obvious ideas for new action figures.

Kinda boasts a no-nonsense approach to dealing with the problem of overcrowding in the TARDIS: while Tegan gets possessed by the Mara and disappears into a New Romantic pop video, Nyssa flakes out at the start of episode one and doesn't wake up again until the end of episode four. "They put me in a cupboard so Janet could have a decent story,"[6] recalled Sarah Sutton, who spends the serial in the TARDIS hooked up to a "delta wave augmentor", which the Doctor says is designed to cure her headaches, but sounds like it might well double as a home perming kit.

That leaves more room for the top-rank guest cast, led by former Hollywood leading man Richard Todd and Simon Rouse as members of a rapidly-diminishing Earth survey team who the Mara is using the native population to repel. These pith-helmeted bumblers aren't the most subtle depiction of British Empire-building, but Rouse's Hindle slowly losing his mind – "You can't mend *people*," he screams when the Doctor steps on the cardboard cut-outs he's made of his missing colleagues – is perhaps the most powerful depiction of madness *Doctor Who* has ever attempted.

About that snake: spiritual and sexual subtext is all very well but, this being *Doctor Who*, there also needs to be a money shot, so to speak; or, in this case, a no-money shot, as the climax – oh stop it – of the show sees the Mara finally made manifest in the form of an enormous pink rubber monstrosity that looks a bit like Rod Hull's Emu has forgotten to get dressed.

The studio-bound story is served well by the theatrical script, and the designer actually does a brilliant job of creating a jungle Eden in BBC Television Centre, though Chris Bailey didn't agree: as well as being horrified by Eric Saward's rewrites, he complained the result looked like "paradise in a garden centre – you could see the pot plants".[7]

Kinda is also notable for being one of the few twentieth-century *Doctor Who* stories in which our hero gets to indulge in some outrageous flirting (the lucky girl in question is Dr Todd, played by Nerys Hughes who, contrary to Half Man Half Biscuit's shouty 1985 hatchet job, the Doctor appears to really quite like). It's equally notable for being one of 159 (out of a possible 159) twentieth-century *Doctor Who* stories not written by Kate Bush (though that didn't stop the rumour that it had been – and, if not her, then Tom Stoppard – doing the rounds for a good 15 years).

While this story was being recorded, the studio was visited by two academics, John Tulloch and Manuel Alvarado, as part of their research for their forthcoming book, *Doctor Who: The Unfolding Text*. The first of many "serious" scholarly analyses of *Doctor Who*,

Tulloch and Alvarado's book was eventually published in December 1983 – just in time to disappoint thousands of children who were hoping for exciting pictures of Daleks and Cybermen, but instead opened their stockings to find a doorstop tome full of ponderous passages on Barthesian semiotics, Bertolt Brecht's theories of engagement and, for an encore, a whole final chapter devoted to *Kinda's* Conditions of Production and Performance. Thanks for nothing, Santa.

It was lucky for the authors their studio visit happened to coincide with one of *Doctor Who's* most thoughtful and allegorical productions – even a pair as windy as this might have struggled to find much to say about the next broadcast story. (In fact the production of *The Visitation* was the subject of a book, *Doctor Who: The Making of a Television Series*, but it distinguished itself from *The Unfolding Text* by being aimed and children and focusing on stuff that actually existed, like cameras and make-up artists and TV's Peter Davison.)

A historical runaround in which the Doctor accidentally starts the Great Fire of London (d'oh!), *The Visitation* is a decent – some may say refreshingly straightforward – adventure, in which fishlike warmongers the Terileptils crash land in Restoration England and hatch a plan to cull the natives using plague rats. The problem is the direction: it takes a special kind of skill, for example, to make an android disguised as the Grim Reaper stalking through the woods not even remotely scary, but in Peter Moffatt's hands, the result looks like a particularly restful episode of *Countryfile*.

The story opens with the Doctor promising to return Tegan to Heathrow, but arriving 300 years early. With possibly unnecessary attention to detail, the location filming really did take place in the Heathrow area – in Black Park, near Slough – which would have been a nice touch if it weren't for the peace and tranquility of Restoration England being shattered by the sound of a passenger jet passing overhead at an average rate of one-per-minute. Luckily, this being the early days of the Thatcher administration, all the filming managed to be achieved during an air traffic controller's strike. So maybe it was worth those three million jobless after all.

On the Buses star Michael Robins gives an

It Shouldn't Happen to a Bloody Vet

enjoyably theatrical – in every sense of the word – performance as Richard Mace, an actor-turned-highwayman who is just about the only human non-regular afforded a name, let alone any lines. And future Queen Vic landlord Michael Melia gives it a good go as the slightly singed-about-the-edges Terileptil leader (Melia sweated so much under the latex, his socks changed colour), who books his place in *Who* history by destroying the Doctor's trusty sonic screwdriver. (John Nathan-Turner wanted rid of it because he thought, like K-9, it provided the Doctor with an overly convenient get-out-of-jail card, and he wanted the scriptwriters to come up with more ingenious solutions like, for example, forgetting to lock the door.)

The first historical adventure in seven years, *The Visitation* is an enjoyable enough runaround, elements of its plot recalling 1973's *The Time Warrior* – though, sadly, without an ounce of that story's inventive wit.

You wait ages for a historical story, then two come along at once. Two-parter *Black Orchid* is not only the first *Doctor Who* story since 1975 to clock in at under an hour, it's also the first since the 60s not to feature any science fiction elements (bar the TARDIS) at all. Instead, writer Terence Dudley delivers a whimsical, Margery Allingham-style 1920s country house murder mystery that's as flimsy as a flapper's hemline, and no less charming for it. Even if it is predicated on a ludicrous number of coincidences, chief among them Nyssa arriving at a house on the very day when the family's deranged son – lost his mind during some bad business up the Orinocco, don'tcha know – breaks out of his confinement with designs on a plucky young gel who just happens to be her exact double. (John Tulloch and Manuel Alvarado would no doubt argue this use of doppelgangers subscribes to Tzvetan Todorov's theories of the Fantastic Uncanny; for the rest of us, it just looks like lazy writing and a chance to save on the wage bill.)

Unlike *Four to Doomsday*, here the regular cast *do* get to shake a bit of a tail-feather in several dance sequences, with Tegan in particular demonstrating a mean Charleston. Unfortunately, as a dancer, Matthew Waterhouse makes a good actor – and that's saying something – which is why he spends

most of those scenes hanging round the buffet table stuffing his face.

A fine cast of British character actors are clearly having a ball as the various lords and ladies of the manor, and Peter Davison's permanently bewildered Doctor – on the back foot at the best of times – fits the role of exasperated murder suspect perfectly. The fifth Doctor also gets to play some actual cricket (in another of the script's many contrivances, the family just happen to have been expecting a cricketing doctor when our man turns up in his whites) and Davison showed his prowess by bowling out the batsman for real, on camera.

Despite being filmed in chilly October, *Black Orchid* succeeds in evoking a languid, summer spritzer vibe – though look closely and you might see a few tell-tale goosebumps revealed by those dinky flapper frocks – that saw the show continuing to ride high in the ratings, with ten million people tuning in to both episodes. That's not that many less than had watched ITV's slightly more expensive period drama, *Brideshead Revisited*, a few months earlier: factor in the recent success of *Chariots and Fire* and it's clear the fifth Doctor, with his white cricketing pullover and preppy demeanor, was perfectly in tune with the early 80s nostalgic yearning for clean-limbed English public schoolboys peering prettily through their golden fringes at the endless Oxbridge summers of a more innocent age.

"I didn't realise that when I was being cast, I was sort of being turned into a gay icon," Davison reflected 30 years later. "That's why John insisted on highlights in my hair."[8] (Clearly, in Nathan-Turner's mind, a case of gentlemen prefer blondes.) They probably could have cashed in on this a bit more – with further pre-war adventures, perhaps, or the Doctor trying to get off with Adric. Instead, the nineteenth season took a sudden handbrake turn into balls-out blockbuster mode with an ambitious attempt to match the sci-fi spectacle of *Star Wars* or *Alien* – albeit with Sigourney Weaver replaced by 63-year-old Brummie character actress Beryl Reid. (Let's just be grateful that, unlike Ripley, she didn't feel the need to strip down to her pants.)

Adric dies; end title theme replaced with ~~laughter track~~ dignified silence

Apart from Reid as the only ship's captain in the cosmos sporting a henna rinse, *Earthshock* is chiefly remembered for two reasons: the return of the Cybermen after an absence of seven years, and the death of Adric – the first regular TARDIS crew member to meet a sticky end in the show's history. (See Chapter One for the thrilling debate about whether short-lived Hartnell sidekicks Katarina and Sarah Kingdom should also count – suffice to say the UN is *still* maintaining a shameful silence on the issue.)

At the time, both came as a massive shock: John Nathan-Turner had succeeded in keeping the Cybes' return a secret right up until the first cliffhanger (he even turned down the offer of a *Radio Times* cover) while Adric carking it in episode four left viewers stunned into silence – literally. Instead of the end theme, the titles rolled mutely over an image of the Alazarian's broken badge for mathematical excellence. With the benefit of hindsight, it's easy to mock Adric – that's why I've spent much of the last two chapters doing exactly that – but, if you were 12 in 1982, his death was just about the most upsetting thing to happen on TV since they axed *Magpie*[IV].

Looked at objectively, *Earthshock* is a bit of a dog's breakfast: the plot – in which the silver cyborgs make two attempts to destroy the Earth during an anti-Cyber conference – is hard to comprehend, the dialogue is leaden and there are numerous, *Acorn Antiques*-style blunders, including one shot in which a member of the production team can clearly be seen sitting in a corner reading the script. Also, if we're honest, this sort of macho, gung-ho action caper is not really what *Doctor Who* is supposed to be about. But after several years of cheap comedies followed by dusty science lectures, this interstellar epic – thrillingly scored by Malcolm Clarke – proved a real shot in the arm for the series. The new-look Cybermen were also a huge hit – not even their spray-painted moon boots could detract from their impact (though the helmets were so constrictive the actors suffered from an acute case of "Cyber-nose"). There's a terrific scene in which the Doctor taunts David Banks'

Cyberleader for his inability to comprehend that "for some people, small, beautiful events are what life is all about". It's a powerful denunciation of the Cybermen's assertion that emotion is a weakness – a point of view only slightly compromised by their evident delight in acts of revenge and wanton cruelty, and the fact their leader keeps shouting "excellent!" while literally punching the air (at one point, you swear he's going to high-five his lieutenant). It also stretches credibility when two of these apparently emotionless cyborgs are pictured animatedly gossiping away like old ladies over the garden fence. ("So I said to him, if you think you're walking over my nice clean floor in those muddy moon boots, you've got another thing coming, Kettlehead...")

By now, it was clear the public were loving this latest iteration of *Doctor Who* – all that remained to complete the triumph was a spectacular final story to see the series out with a bang. And to really seal the deal, Nathan-Turner had become the first drama producer in television history to secure the use of an actual working Concorde, so it was a simple case of commissioning an action-packed adventure to showcase the world's most famous supersonic passenger airliner in all its glory. The only *slight* problem was that, by this point in the season, all the money had run out.

In the end, *Time-Flight* director Ron Jones was forced to record scenes of the 200-foot-long, £23 million aircraft crash-landing on Prehistoric heathland in the corner of a studio more suited to hosting quiz shows and *Top of the Pops*. Imagine someone placing an Airfix model in the middle of a shop window display, and you'll get some idea of just how convincing the finished result looked.

They did get to do some location filming, of course – climbing aboard a stationary Concorde as it stood on the tarmac in British Airways' maintenance area at Heathrow. Woop and, indeed, de-doo. Writer Peter Grimwade had been forced to submit his script to BA's PR team, who suggested a few tweaks ("Dear Mr Grimwade, instead of shouting 'What is that hideous creature?', we thought it might be more dramatic at this point if Nyssa asked, 'But Doctor, how *does* BA remain so competitive on price without compromising its impeccable safety record?' We look forward to hearing your thoughts.")

Having scored such a coup with the Cybermen, this serial also saw the surprise return of the Master after an absence of, ooh, almost ten weeks. And in the new spirit of hush-hush, need-to-know secrecy, he spends the first two episodes wearing what appears to be a mudpack and talking in a comedy oriental accent for no readily apparent reason – a pretence he keeps up even when he's totally alone. To further deepen the mystery, *Time-Flight* continues the tradition started with *Castrovalva* of disguising Anthony Ainley's name in the credits and pre-publicity with cunning anagrams. The first time it was the vaguely plausible Neil Tornay; here it's frankly ridiculous Leon Ny Taiy (Tony Ainley); the next time he appears, he'll be listed as James Stoker (Master's Joke) and, the time after that, AA Hitching Rhino Most (Oh Christ Not Him Again). Okay, I made that last one up.

The Master's latest experiment from his Bumper Book of Hopeless Plans for Boys involves using the Nucleus – the hivemind of a race of aliens called the Xeraphin – to repair his broken TARDIS and help him attain... you know, unlimited power and suchlike. He's also using another branch of the Xeraphin gestalt called the Plasmatons (made by pouring polyurethane liquid over mail sacks, fx fans) as slaves, as part of a plot so convoluted it apparently can't be achieved without dragging a supersonic passenger jet 140 million years back in time, and wearing a fat suit.

Despite bowing out on this unmitigated disaster, the consensus was that Peter Davison's first run as the Doctor had been a resounding success, further establishing its leading man as one of the biggest stars of the day. In March 1982, Davison became an unusually youthful "victim" of long-running gush-fest *This is Your Life*, Eamonn Andrews surprising him with the famous red book before subjecting him to half-an-hour of friends, family and colleagues being terribly nice about him (to his face, anyway). Davison was under the impression he was filming a promo for Australian TV when Andrews doorstepped the TARDIS – either that, or he just made a habit of hanging out in Trafalgar Square in his full *Doctor Who* costume of an evening.

The following month, Davison capped off a triumphant year by being named Best Man on TV at the Swap Shop Awards: note the award wasn't for mere best actor – in the eyes of *Swap Shop* viewers, he was nothing less than the pinnacle of human masculinity. Larry Grayson was gutted.

Recording on *Doctor Who*'s landmark twentieth season began the day after the final episode of *Time-Flight* was broadcast. Once again, the second story was taped first, this time because Nathan-Turner had managed to secure an overseas location shoot for the season opener – the series' first foreign jaunt since 1979's *City of Death*. Amsterdam was chosen largely because of the links the BBC had established while filming notorious shipboard soap *Triangle* (imagine, if you will, *The Love Boat* set aboard a North Sea ferry pounding the slate grey waves between Felixtowe, Gothenburg and the Dutch capital) and the team wanted to wait until later in the spring to take advantage of the better weather. For dramatic purposes, obviously. Not because anyone was looking upon it as a free holiday. That would be unprofessional. (Though they *would* find enough time to go for a walk around the red light district, where Sarah Sutton asked if she could sit in one of the windows – it's possible she hadn't realised there was a bit more to it than that – and Janet Fielding got propositioned. Whether the unfortunate would-be punter survived the incident is not recorded.)

As well as added tulip/windmill/clog value, *Arc of Infinity* was designed to set a suitably nostalgic tone for the 20th anniversary by reintroducing two classic characters from the show's past. One was Omega, the legendary Time Lord temporal engineer who last appeared in previous birthday shindig *The Three Doctors* ten years earlier (you'll always find him in the matter universe at parties). And the other was Tegan Jovanka, who last appeared at the end of *Time-Flight*, broadcast a few weeks ago. Janet Fielding was never in the frame to be written out, so we can only assume her brief departure was designed as some sort of tease.

And they weren't the only ones staging a comeback that year. More by accident than design (apparently no-one realised until Ian Levine, in his role as unofficial continuity adviser, pointed it out to a BBC press officer), there was to be something from the show's past in every story of the twenieth season. And the biggest of those somethings was the Daleks – following the success of *Earthshock*, Eric Saward planned to bring back the show's public enemy No. 1 in similarly blockbusting fashion in a story called *The Return*. Though, as it turned out, the pepperpots would be back sooner than that: when NBC's *Bret Maverick* – a faltering revival of 50s cowboy caper *Maverick*, starring James Garner – was unceremoniously cancelled mid-run, BBC1 found itself with a Stetson-shaped hole in its summer schedules. Never one to miss a trick, John Nathan-Turner suggested another run of classic *Doctor Who* serials in the vein of *The Five Faces* season. This time, the theme was *Doctor Who and the Monsters*, with an average of five million people tuning in to see Jon Pertwee face off against the Ice Warriors in *The Curse of Peladon*, followed by a cut-down version of *Genesis of the Daleks* and a repeat showing of *Earthshock*. (The Beeb also re-ran an old episode of *Star Trek* in the slot, but you can't have everything.)

By this point Nathan-Turner was looking to the future as well as the past: deciding it was time to get a new job, he explored what would be the first of many *Who* exit strategies by attempting to re-mount *Compact*, the vintage BBC soap set in the glamorous world of magazine publishing. He wanted to call the revived version *Impact*, but, clearly, the idea failed to have any.

One person who *was* moving on was Sarah Sutton. In July, it was announced she would be leaving mid-way through the next series, shortly after most of her clothes. Don't worry, we'll come to that. Nathan-Turner had written to the actress a few months earlier, explaining he wasn't going to renew her contract. "This is no reflection on your portrayal," he added, "which I must say has been super, but merely that I feel the companions should change every couple of years". Peter Davison was unhappy with this move, having grown close to Sutton – whose character he felt was a better foil for his Doctor than the more strident Tegan – but the producer was adamant.

Recording on Sutton's final story – the appropriately named *Terminus* – was dogged by industrial action by the electricians' union,

unravelling director Mary Ridge's shooting schedule beyond repair. When it became obvious an extra day would be needed to finish the job, a less-than sympathetic John Nathan-Turner threw a tantrum and bawled Ridge out. "He did upset her greatly," said Peter Davison, "because she didn't finish, and that was sort of a crime."[8]

Sarah Sutton's leaving party on October 27th went ahead as planned but was, by all accounts, a muted affair – especially as she was now going to have to come back a few weeks later for another day's work.

In November, filming on the next story, *Enlightenment*, got under way at Ealing, but when the industrial action was stepped up, it became clear the recording sessions planned for Television Centre later that month would have to be scrapped. Suddenly, *Doctor Who* found itself staring down the barrel of a *Shada* situation. Determined to salvage the story, John Nathan-Turner took the controversial decision to scrap the anniversary season's explosive Dalek finale – the scripts for which had already been given the Royal assent by Terry Nation – and re-allocate its studio time to the completion of *Enlightenment*.

Peter Grimwade had been assigned to direct *The Return*, and had done a fair bit of preparatory work on the serial. When the news broke that the production was being scuttled, Grimwade took some of his team out to lunch to commiserate. It was to prove a very expensive lunch, with hidden extras including a 10% service charge and the loss of Grimwade's entire career as a director on *Doctor Who*.

According to Eric Saward, John Nathan-Turner went ballistic when he heard about the lunch, "shouting and screaming about why he hadn't been invited".[12] Nathan-Turner's partner, sometime production manager Gary Downie, later dismissed this account as "total lies"[13], but it's certainly true that Grimwade – one of the better directors of the era – never got behind the cameras on the show again (though Saward did commission one further script from him).

As a somewhat sour coda to the incident, Grimwade later wrote and directed an episode of the children's anthology series *Dramarama* called "The Come-Uppance of Captain Katt" – about the travails of a low-budget TV sci-fi series and its megalomaniacal producer. You know those disclaimers they sometimes put at the end of programmes declaring, "All characters appearing in this work are fictitious. Any resemblance to real persons, living or dead, is purely coincidental"? This didn't have one of those.

Bringing what had been a rollercoaster year to a close, Peter Davison cashed in on his current star wattage and jetted off to Hollywood at Christmas to film a role in a forthcoming Hollywood blockbuster. Not really: he was appearing in John Nathan-Turner's production of *Cinderella* in Tunbridge Wells with his wife and Anthony Ainley.

"It wasn't part of the deal to do a panto," said Davison. "I think he [Nathan-Turner] just sold us very cleverly because he was good at that kind of thing. 'It's going to be fantastic.' But the location was terrible – it wasn't even a proper theatre. Outrageously, we would often spend *Doctor Who* rehearsal time rehearsing for the pantomime. I wasn't mad about that."[8]

Gary Downie – a professional hoofer who had been known to shake a clog alongside Pan's People – was hired as choreographer, and was so horrible to the dancers, Davison stormed off. "That was one of the few tantrums of my professional career," he said. "Gary I really didn't like. It was baffling as to why they were together."[8]

On December 30th, *The Sun* broke the news that *Doctor Who*'s 20th anniversary would be marked with a special feature-length adventure called – you guessed it – *The Five Doctors*. It wasn't always going to be quite so obvious, though: for quite a while, the story went under the radically different title of *The Six Doctors*, for reasons that will become clear as we don our party hats and plunge headlong into the brave new world of 1983. There will be cake.

Omega: "What do you mean I'm not an Alpha male?"

Peter Cushing, Patrick Stewart, Pierce Brosnan and Honor Blackman: these are just four of the distinguished stars of stage and screen who don't appear in *Arc of Infinity* (though all were approached). Instead, it's down to a pre-*Batman* Michael Gough (making his first *Who* appearance since 1966's *The*

Celestial Toymaker) to bring some heavyweight thesping to the story, which also features Leonard Sachs (best known for marshalling mass "Daisy Day" sing-a-longs on bafflingly enduring music hall throwback *The Good Old Days*) and a bloke called Colin Baker. The latter's approach to playing Gallifreyan security commander Maxil was so arch (Baker even tried to effect a sort of comedy double act with his guard's helmet), John Nathan-Turner took to calling him Archie, and at one point intervened to ask him to tone it down. So you can be pretty sure it's the last we'll hear of *him*.

Though all the elements were in place for a classic tale (Omega, a return to Gallifrey, glamorous overseas filming), *Arc of Infinity* manages to smash all these plates spectacularly. The villain himself, who's after the Doctor's body (so to speak), is not so much anti-matter as doesn't-matter – and he's not helped by having the most ludicrous outsize chicken since *The Time Monster* on the payroll. Meanwhile, the Doctor's home planet – where his people have thoughtfully laid on a welcome back execution – appears to have been furnished entirely from Habitat, and the traitor in the midst is not so much hidden in plain sight as just... well, in plain sight.

And Tegan's sudden return is just baffling, as there's no attempt at a "ta-daaa!" moment of surprise: she just saunters on like a regular character and then, somewhat improbably, casually bumps into Omega – the very being the Doctor is currently engaged in tracking down several million light years away – in the crypt of an Amsterdam mansion. What are the odds? (Incalculable, since you ask.)

Things pick up in the final episode, when Omega transforms himself into a degenerating version of the Doctor (Peter Davison with green gunk and actual Rice Krispies stuck to his face) for a lively chase around the Dutch capital. (Apparently no-one batted an eyelid at the sight of a green man covered in breakfast cereal running around the place. But then, half the population of Amsterdam wouldn't be surprised to see a talking horse driving a tram, if you know what I mean.) *Arc of Infinity* is also the only *Doctor Who* story to feature an on-screen appearance by John Nathan-Turner – sporting a natty football manager's sheepskin coat, no less – though apparently this was accidental and he was "just trying to keep bystanders out of shot". Yeah, whatever.

Snakedance is Chris Bailey's sequel to *Kinda*. It's a good example of how the "something from the series' past in every story" line might have been over-sold, unless some viewers were feeling particularly nostalgic for the good old days of 11 months ago. In every other sense, though, it's an absolute triumph: a beautifully written origin story that places the Mara at the centre of an epic mythology, full of lyrical writing and memorable characters. It's so good, you can even forgive the somewhat wishy-washy pseudo-science (on the planet Manussa, the Mara plots to return on the 500th anniversary of its exile, using the power of thought amplified through a, um, crystal) that just about manages to avoid wobbling over the line into trippy New Age occultism.

For all its many qualities, though, *Snakedance* is chiefly remembered for guest-starring a young Martin Clunes in a dress. And rather fabulous he is too, in the role of an indolent prince regent who causes mayhem not so much from wickedness as sheer boredom. Now that Clunes is one of Britain's most bankable TV stars, clips from *Snakedance* are a regular feature on those before-they-were-famous type shows, where everyone always laughs at the daft clothes, while rarely commenting on the brilliant dialogue, design and direction; or the story's intelligent mix of Zen philosophy, Hinduism, Native American rituals, colonial hypocrisy, Evelyn Waugh and TS Eliot. Perhaps it's just as well no-one told them some of the sets were recycled from the previous year's *A Song for Europe* – they might get the idea that *Doctor Who* is somehow camp.

Mawdryn Undead marks the start of a trilogy of stories featuring the Black Guardian, last seen bothering Tom Baker's Doctor in the similarly-linked Key to Time season four years earlier. For those keeping a close eye on the returning characters scoreboard, yes, it is cheating to have the *same* classic villain across three stories. But *Mawdryn Undead* throws us a bonus ball in the form of another old soldier: no less than Brigadier Alistair Gordon Lethbridge-Stewart.

Welcome though it is to see Nick Courtney back in action, the original, even more fan-pleasing plan was to reach all the way back into *Doctor Who's* roots and bring in William Russell as Ian Chesterton. When Russell (and then Ian Marter, approached to revive his role as Harry Sullivan) proved unavailable, Peter Grimwade rewrote his script to make the Brigadier a school teacher instead. If the idea of the Brig quitting UNIT to teach maths to public schoolboys seems unlikely, that's nothing compared to the fact that he was doing it in 1983 – thus chucking a HAVOC-style hand grenade into the centre of the whole UNIT dating hoo-ha.

To really drive the point home, the script also required Courtney to play another version of himself from 1977. According to director Peter Moffatt: "We were careful to work in subtle differences between the Brigadiers. It wasn't easy to do, but I tried to get some of that into the dialogue, little mannerisms and so forth."[9] And, if you didn't pick up on that, there was always the big stick-on moustache.

Mawdryn, played by the ever-reliable David Collings, is one of a group of alien scientists whose bungled experiment with stolen Time Lord technology has doomed them to a life of perpetual mutation aboard an opulent spaceship. It's an intriguing sci-fi spin on the Flying Dutchman myth, if somewhat weighed down by technobabble and assumed *Doctor Who* scholarship. (Though the latter, to be fair, works more like a bonus loyalty reward scheme than a precondition to understanding the story. For newcomers, it's not so difficult to work out that the Brigaider is one of the Doctor's best friends, or on which side of the "goodie vs. baddie" equation the scheming Black Guardian falls.)

Janet Fielding and Sarah Sutton, meanwhile, had to endure hours in the make-up chair to create aged versions of Tegan and Nyssa. Fielding got married shortly afterwards, and a picture of her was taken in her wedding dress, complete with the old-age make-up. At least her husband-to-be[V] *hoped* it was make-up, or he was going to be in for a shock first thing in the morning. (For the scene in which the two companions reverted back to childhood, the characters were played by Lucy Benjamin and Sian Pattenden, a future *EastEnders* star and *Smash Hits* journalist respectively.)

Valentine Dyall dials it up to 11 as the Black Guardian who, for reasons that aren't clear, now sports a dead crow on his head (perhaps it just nested there and he hasn't noticed). His diabolical scheme this time around is to persuade an English schoolboy called Turlough that the Doctor is a wrong 'un and that it's his duty to bump him off. This is certainly an eccentric modus operandi for one of the most powerful beings in the universe – and he doesn't help himself in his plan to convince the kid he's one of the good guys by constantly dropping in tell-tale phrases like "in the name of all that is evil", followed by a megalomaniacal laugh.

The actor chosen to play this unlikely juvenile assassin was 23-year-old newcomer Mark Strickson, who had recently made his TV debut in the nursing soap *Angels*. That show's producer, Julia Smith – of *The Underwater Menace* infamy – apparently told Strickson he could stay with her and do "real acting", or earn more money on *Doctor Who*, to which John Nathan-Turner countered that he could either be one of a large ensemble cast, or one of the leads. He took the money... I mean, the better part.

Having secured his services, Nathan-Turner then decided Strickson's blonde hair made him look too similar to Davison, and tried to get him to shave his head. The actor's agent argued this might cost him other work, so it was decided instead to dye his hair ginger. Suddenly, being bald didn't sound so bad. For the scenes in which Turlough communicated with the Black Guardian, Strickson also had to hold a small glowing cube, which used to get so hot it burned his hands. But apart from the bright red hair and blisters, he was totally loving his new job.

Lost in space: one series finale, one ladies' skirt

The middle part of the Black Guardian trilogy, *Terminus*, has a reputation for being a bit slow and boring – at least until Nyssa's clothes fall off. It's certainly light on *Earthshock*-style whizzes and bangs and, being set aboard what is effectively a leper colony – the use of the word prompted a complaint on behalf of the Leprosy Mission – it's not exactly a laugh-riot. But, like writer Stephen Gallagher's previous story, *Warriors' Gate*, *Terminus* treats its audi-

ence with intelligence, and rewards their patience with a script full of interesting ideas and rich dialogue.

The eponymous space station is a fake hospital-cum-internment camp for people suffering from Lazar's disease. It also happens to be at the exact centre of the universe, and when a time-travelling spaceship jettisoned its fuel there, it accidentally triggered the Big Bang – quite an event in a story with a reputation for nothing much happening.

The unusually sombre tone is expertly reflected in the Memento mori outfits of the Vanir (the second nod to Norse mythology in as many stories), slave guards clad in radiation amour that appears to be fashioned from clanking bones. It's somewhat less expertly reflected in the story's token "monster" (though he's really a nice guy): Gallagher envisioned the Garm as "a sort of shape in the darkness" and was dismayed to find he'd ended up as "a giant talking dog". The costume was so hot that the actor inside, RJ Bell, kept fainting – possibly because they kept leaving him in the car without opening a window.

Mark Strickson was also continuing to have fun, losing the skin off his already blistered hands and the knees from his trousers during the many scenes he and Janet Fielding spend crawling about in the underfloor ducting.

Director Mary Ridge had helped found the Open University[VI], so the "science" on display here – including the entire universe being saved by a dog pushing a big red handle – must have been a bit hard to swallow. But, while far from perfect, *Terminus* deserves re-evaluating as one of the series' overlooked gems – not least for Peter Benson's wonderful performance as the Vanir Bor: switching between lugubrious cynicism and irradiated derangement, it's one of the show's all-time great guest turns.[VII]

That's all very well, you say – but what about Nyssa and those missing clothes? Both Sarah Sutton and Janet Fielding's costumes had been gradually falling prey to the law of diminishing returns – originally Nyssa had been buttoned-up to the chin in a velveteen trouser suit, while Tegan had stayed in her stewardess' uniform, possibly while serving tiny packets of vacuum-packed peanuts aboard the TARDIS. By the start of Season Twenty, Sutton had slipped into something more comfortable while Fielding looked distinctly *un*comfortable in a white boob tube that she kept popping out of – not least when a mischievous Peter Davison asked her to raise her hands in the air. (Actors can get away with this sort of thing – or at least they could in the 80s – but I wouldn't recommend trying it with Carol in accounts.)

By the time of her last story, Sarah Sutton is wearing a costume that already looks a bit like underwear, even before she strips down to her *actual* underwear. "Nysaa's outfit for the previous season had included a brooch that secured her costume around her neck," explained Gallagher. "I had intended for her to remove the brooch in order to breathe properly, and drop it so as it would point the Doctor in the right direction. Unbeknownst to me, Tegan and Nyssa's costumes were both completely revamped, leaving her without a brooch. Eric was left to find something else for her to drop, and the only thing that was detachable was her skirt."[10] Oh well since you put it like *that*, it sounds entirely reasonable.

In fact, the writer needn't have felt compelled to come up with such a convoluted excuse because, according to Sarah Sutton: "It was my idea... It was my parting gesture to all those fans who wanted to see the real Nyssa."[11] Blimey, is it me or has it suddenly got hot in here? Thankfully, she also spends some quality time synthesising enzymes, so isn't *entirely* out of character.

Possibly to prevent a march on Television Centre by radical feminists incensed by all this boob-poppin', skirt-droppin' shenanigans, the next story was scripted by a woman, Barbara Clegg. Yes, just 20 years after Verity Lambert struck a blow for equal opportunities in television, it was decided to let a lady have a go at actually writing a story.

Clegg rose to the challenge with *Enlightenment*, an enchanting lyrical fantasy based around a wonderful central motif of solar winds propelling sailing ships from different periods of Earth history in a race through space (beautifully realised on 35mm film at Ealing). The Doctor and company land on an Edwardian clipper crewed by a race of beings called the Eternals, one of whom has a massive crush on Tegan. "You're not like any

Ephemeral I've ever met," he moons. (It's probably the boob tube.)

The prize in the race is literally something called Enlightenment – either transcending to a higher spiritual plane, or a big lump of perspex (it's hard to tell). A rival Eternal, Captain Wrack – a statuesque lady pirate played with gusto by Lynda Baron – has entered into an unholy bargain with the Black Guardian that will allow him to "invade time" and unleash merry hell, but his plans are scuppered when Turlough chooses to save the Doctor over collecting the trophy. (See? Just because he's ginger, it doesn't make him a bad person.)

The dialogue is excellent – when the Doctor tells the Eternal ship's captain he's a Time Lord, he replies: "Are there lords in such a small domain?" – and the ambitious concept is brilliantly served by director Fiona Cumming and her team. Yes, it was written *and* directed by a woman. Imagine the head-patting that must have gone on when they saw the result.

One effect of the serial's delayed production was the loss of guest star Peter Sallis – last seen in *The Ice Warriors*, but by this time more famous for his hillside bathtub antics in *Last of the Summer Wine* – as the ironically named Captain Striker; sitcom stalwart Keith Barron stepped in to do the honours instead, and is rather good. Pop star Leee John – frontman of briefly fashionable 80s soul-poppers Imagination – is also among the cast, for no immediately obvious reeeason.

Enlightenment brings the Black Guardian trilogy to a close with a return appearance by his opposite number, still being forced to ride out eternity in white – black is so much more slimming – and now sporting his own avian millinery in the form of what appears to be a dead pigeon.

With *The Return* returned to sender before it had even arrived, the penultimate story – a timid little two-parter called *The King's Demons* – was pushed blinking into the spotlight and told to get on with the job of bringing the curtain down on the season as best it could. Despite the handsome location work at Bodiam Castle in East Sussex (handy for the nearby panto rehearsals in Tunbridge Wells), this primary school history lesson struggles to fill 50 minutes, and the cliffhanger – in which King John's champion, Sir Gilles Estram (Estram –

see what they did there?), is revealed to be the Master – somewhat lacks shock value after 25 minutes of what is very clearly Anthony Ainley smirking through a ginger beard and talking in zees truly terreeble Fraunch aczent (correspondents to the following week's *Points of View* were particularly unimpressed). Even the Doctor tells the Master that the plot – some business about mucking about with Magna Carta – is "small time villainy by your standards". (The Master insists it's part of a much wider plan to undermine the key civilisations of the universe. Could take a while.)

But not to worry, because the production still had an ace up its sleeve in the form of a brand new companion. And not just *any* companion: this was to be *Doctor Who*'s first fully-automated, fully-articulated, genuine (as opposed to a motorised box on wheels) robot companion.

The production office had been approached by the robot's creators, and John Nathan-Turner and Eric Saward had driven to Oxford to see it put through its paces. Suitably impressed, they decided to write it into the show as a new character called Kamelion. Sadly, one of the software designers was killed in a motorboat accident before the first studio session, where it very quickly became clear the thing just didn't work. "We'd go over to a Kamelion scene," recalled Mark Strickson, "and there would be a couple of legs there with wires hanging out. So we'd cancel that, and go onto another scene, and then we'd go back and they'd have managed to get half the body on, but by that time a leg had fallen off... It was a complete disaster. Laughable. Hysterical."[14]

A decision was taken to write Kamelion – voiced by Gerald Flood, who's actually pretty faultless as a rather camp King John – out at the first opportunity. Until then, he would be consigned to a TARDIS store-room and never mentioned again. How come no-one ever had that idea with Adric?

Broadcast on Tuesdays and Wednesdays instead of Mondays and Tuesdays, and facing stiffer competition from big-hitting ITV soaps *Crossroads* and *Emmerdale Farm*, ratings for the 1983 series had averaged around seven million: pretty respectable, but a long way short of the previous year's skyscraping figures. Peter Davison was also unhappy with the quality of

some of the season's stories, which strengthened his resolve to quit after three years – though he admits he wobbled and almost signed on for a fourth run.

"It was a difficult decision, really," he said, "especially as Season Three got under way and I rather liked it, much more than I'd liked Season Two. Had the third season been the second season, I might well have done a fourth season."[15]

In particular, though he had a good working relationship with John Nathan-Turner, they fundamentally disagreed about the direction the show should be taking. "He had this vision of *Doctor Who* as a wonderfully camp show," said Davison. "I would have made it an altogether darker experience."[15]

In an eye-wateringly forthright interview with *Doctor Who Magazine* shortly after Nathan-Turner's death, Gary Downie once again saw things differently, dismissing the camp allegation as "totally wrong", adding: "Maybe Peter Davison wanted his character to be darker, but then would he be capable of playing a darker character? Peter Davison, with all due respect, is boring. All the characters he plays on television are wet."[13] And that was with all due respect.

For all Davison's dismissal of it, the twentieth season actually stands up rather well. Weak start and finish aside, the bedrock of the series is four strong, conceptually-driven stories on the trot – an unusually consistent run by *Doctor Who*'s bungee-ing quality control standards. Maybe it was not so much the scripts as the endless production headaches caused by the year's rolling industrial action that eventually wore Davison down. Or maybe he just really, really couldn't stand the sight of celery any longer.

I saw the queues at Longleat

Mere hours after the broadcast of episode two of *The King's Demons* – and with the nation still reeling with shock over the Master's dastardly plan to... what was it again? – Peter Davison was back in costume for a very special photocall, lining up alongside all his predecessors to promote the forthcoming anniversary special.

Okay, not quite *all* his predecessors. In place

of the late William Hartnell, veteran actor Richard Hurndall had been contracted to provide locum cover for the first Doctor. And the fixed grin on Tom Baker's face isn't just because he's having to share the limelight with Jon Pertwee and company: it's because he's a waxwork dummy on loan from Madame Tussauds.

To understand how we got here, let's rewind to the previous summer when, having been given the green light for the 90-minute special, Eric Saward had approached the venerable Robert Holmes about writing the script. John Nathan-Turner had initially resisted the idea, leading many to surmise he felt threatened by the likes of Holmes, who might have represented a challenge to his own status as the presiding authority on all matters *Who*. Certainly, it's hard to think of any other reason why he would have looked such a gift horse in the pipe.

The producer eventually relented, and Holmes took the commission. But relations quickly soured, with even Saward – a huge admirer and, later, friend of Holmes – admitting his predecessor acted like "a prat"[12] by refusing to submit a story breakdown ("I don't do storylines," Holmes is reputed to have said). For his part, Holmes claimed the production team didn't know what they wanted, and changed the brief on an almost daily basis.

Seeing the way the wind was blowing, Saward solicited Terrance Dicks to write an alternative script, the intention being to choose the best of the two. Dicks was furious about being played off against Holmes, and refused to have anything to do with it, claiming, "That's no way to treat a writer of Bob's status or, for that matter, mine".[16]

It was eventually agreed by all parties that Holmes' script for *The Six Doctors* (the supernumerary Time Lord being a robot duplicate of the first Doctor) wasn't working, and the writer withdrew from the project. Re-enter Terrance Dicks, stage left, who by January 1983 had submitted a script that just about managed to juggle all the various characters and elements demanded by the production office.

And that's when Tom Baker pulled out.

Having initially agreed to take part, Baker had eventually decided it was too soon to go back to *Doctor Who* – in retrospect, an understandable decision, though it's unlikely Dicks saw it that way when he took the call from Saward.

Baker's other selves weren't overly impressed either, which is why the publicity pictures you *didn't* see from that photocall include Troughton, Pertwee and Davison using the fourth Doctor as a battering ram, and attempting to dump him in a rubbish bin. It's hard to know whose grin was the most frozen – Baker's or the luckless BBC PR man's.

Baker, incidentally, wasn't the only one who declined to appear: John Levene turned down a cameo as Sergeant Benton, apparently on the advice of his daughter, who "didn't want him to belittle the character". Of what was basically a glorified extra. Ho-hum. Meanwhile, Colin Baker had been approached about reprising his role as *Arc of Infinity*'s Commander Maxil, but was unavailable – and his helmet didn't feel ready to go it alone.

Filming on *The Five Doctors* wrapped at Easter, when all four surviving Doctors – including a living, breathing, fully poseable Tom Baker, no less – repaired to the country for a nice quiet bank holiday weekend with a few friends and colleagues, the odd old enemy... and 56,000 very cross *Doctor Who* fans.

Longleat House in Wiltshire had been home to a permanent Doctor Who exhibition since 1973. A decade later, the estate's notoriously roistering owner, the Marquess of Bath – AKA the Loins of Longleat, a sort of aristo Hugh Heffner, famous for squiring more than 70 mistresses in between writing some very bad novels – invited the BBC to host *Doctor Who*'s official 20th birthday party in the grounds of his six-acre pile. Billed as "The Doctor Who Celebration: 20 Years of a Time Lord", the event over Easter Sunday and Monday was expected to attract around 13,000 visitors. Instead – thanks in part to Mark Strickson announcing on the previous weekend's *Saturday Superstore* that you didn't need to bother booking and should "just turn up" – closer to 56,000 decamped to Wiltshire, bringing large parts of the county to a standstill.

The traffic gridlock made the evening news while, on Radio 2, Ed Stewart made panicked pleas for people to stay away, as if a great humanitarian crisis were unfolding in the

It Shouldn't Happen to a Bloody Vet

beseiged Tudor estate. ("Send help – we're down to our last three Target novelisations!") The site itself must have looked like the world's worst-dressed refugee camp ("Through the heat and the dust they came, carrying their TARDIS rucksacks on their backs..."), as thousands swarmed – if you *can* swarm while standing in a 12-hour queue – all over the grounds in the futile hope of actually getting in to see anything. Spend long enough on the British motorway system and you're bound to see a bumper sticker claiming "We've seen the lions at Longleat Safari Park". But it's a rare hunter indeed who caught a glimpse of Tom Baker or Jon Pertwee over that Easter weekend.

If they held a similar event today, there'd be a corporate hospitality area sponsored by Virgin handing out free vodka shots and mobile phones. In 1983, there wasn't so much as a backstage toilet for the VIP guests – the stars had to take their chances in the public portaloos along with everyone else. Lis Sladen – who likened the weekend to being in "a castle besieged by angry villagers" – recalled enjoying a brief moment to herself, so to speak, when the person in the next cubicle asked whether she'd mind signing a photo if they slipped it under the door.

A victim of its own success it may have been, but "The Doctor Who Celebration: 20 Hours of Queueing for a Burger" was at least confirmation of the nation's enduring affection for the series, and the publicity before, during and after the event – even Patrick Troughton turned up on breakfast telly to talk it up – proved the show was still considered "good copy".

There was also a brisk trade in merchandise around this time: Peter Davison lent his name to two sci-fi anthology collections, while *The Doctor Who Technical Manual* – a kind of Haynes' guide to the Whoniverse – finally put fans out of their misery by revealing such vital information as the height of a Quark's arm (80cms from its feet, if you're interested) and, to quote the cover blurb, "the inner workings of the Doctor's tool-kit". Cheers for that. But perhaps the finest tie-in product from this era was a Doctor Who Easter Egg which, when the front flap of the TARDIS packaging was opened, appeared to reveal Peter Davison pro-

jecting a Dalek death ray directly from his groin. No wonder he didn't need the sonic screwdriver any more.

The Three-And-A-Bit Doctors (and a man who looks a bit like another Doctor)

Recording on *Doctor Who*'s twenty-first season commenced in late June, with Davison's departure made public a month later. The actor explained his decision in numerous TV and press interviews, and speculation quickly turned to who might succeed him, with some tabloids suggesting the new Doctor might be a woman, based largely on the fact that particular wheeze had gone down well three years earlier.

There was shocking news for the cast and crew on August 1st when the actor Peter Arne – a veteran of more than 50 films, including *Ice Cold in Alex* and *A Conspiracy of Hearts* – was found beaten to death in his Knightsbridge apartment, shortly before he had been due to begin rehearsals on upcoming story *Frontios*. Arne had just returned from a costume fitting for the serial when he is thought to have become involved in an argument with a homeless Italian schoolteacher who he had been providing with food. The teacher's body was found in the Thames four days later, with police concluding the man had murdered Arne before taking his own life. William Lucas, well known for his role in TV's *The Adventures of Black Beauty*, took on the role at short notice.

In the autumn, *Doctor Who* took its first baby steps into a shiny new future when it made its debut on two cutting-edge new technology platforms. *The Mines of Terror* was the first official Doctor Who computer game; written by a 17-year-old fan – so a bit over-the-hill by programmer standards – it featured the fifth Doctor (in so much as the tiny blob of pixels was vaguely beige in colour) in *Who*-themed variations on arcade classics *Pac-Man*, *Frogger*, *Space Invaders* and *Battleship*. As a visual spectacle, it was slightly less exciting than typing 20 GOTO 10 RUN and watching the words DOCTOR WHO scroll across the screen.

Meanwhile, October saw the release of the very first *Doctor Who* story on video. To ensure this potentially lucrative new merchandising

193

opportunity got off to the best possible start, the marketing whizzkids at BBC Enterprises did a quick calculation: Most popular Doctor (Tom Baker) + Most popular monster (Daleks) = guaranteed payola. Unfortunately, they couldn't get the rights to use the Daleks, so opted for the next best thing – without stopping to check if Baker's only encounter with the next best thing was actually any good. And that's how middling, unloved 1975 series grout *Revenge of the Cybermen* came to blaze the trail for *Doctor Who* on home video. (For the record, it was released on four formats – VHS, Betamax, Laserdisc and Video 2000. Remember that? Me neither.)

Nevertheless, vintage *Who*-on-demand was still a pretty exciting concept for most fans: all they had to do now was save up six months' worth of pocket money to be able to afford the hefty £40 price tag (around £115 in today's money). And even then, they still had to fork out for a stamp to write and complain that they'd used the wrong logo, the wrong type of Cyberman and the wrong picture of Tom Baker on the cover. Hey, this stuff matters.

Target publisher WH Allen's contribution to the 20th anniversary was the lavish hardback *Doctor Who: A Celebration* by Peter Haining. This handsome volume was the first book to attempt to tell the complete history of the series, with exclusive contributions from Verity Lambert, Barry Letts and Terrance Dicks, among others, plus a mix of bespoke and recycled interviews with all five Doctors. (Tom Baker's recollections were headed "I like *Doctor Who* because it was all Fun, Fun, Fun!". No doubt many of his directors would beg to differ.)

The book proved something of a publishing sensation, selling more than 100,000 copies and running to three reprints in its first year. (Haining would subsequently attempt to bottle lightning several more times, to ever-diminishing returns, over the next five years.) The *Radio Times*, for its part, updated its much-loved 10th anniversary special with a – wait for it – 20th anniversary special, which featured an exclusive short story, "Birth of a Renegade", in which Eric Saward decided to sketch in some of the Doctor's backstory, including the controversial revelation that Susan wasn't actually his granddaughter. And no, it's not canon.

The National Film Theatre paid its own birthday tribute with a two-day restrospective in October called "Doctor Who: The Developing Art". They probably had to call it that to get a grant or something, but, with screenings of more than 80 episodes plus various panel interviews with cast and creatives, it was basically a very posh *Doctor Who* convention – and something of a testament to how seriously this Saturday teatime filler-turned-British institution was being taken these days.

The *Radio Times* published on Thursday, November 17th came wrapped in an exclusive *Five Doctors* illustration by Target books artist Andrew Skilleter – *Doctor Who*'s first *RT* cover for ten years (amazingly, Tom Baker's mug never made the front page) – while the show's stars gave the story the hard-sell on everything from Pebble Mill to a special, *Who*-themed edition of *Blue Peter*, in which the first and fifth Doctors drove a mini-bus and pretended to have an argument.

And then, on November 23rd, the waiting was finally over as fans got the chance to see the eagerly-awaited anniversary special in all its glory. Well, at least they did if they lived in America. In the States, *The Five Doctors* was broadcast on the 20th anniversary itself, but British viewers had to wait an extra two days – the first time an episode of *Doctor Who* had ever premiered outside the UK[VIII]. Today, of course, everyone outside the US would have downloaded it off the internet – or got their kids to download it – within ten minutes of the credits rolling. But these were more innocent days, and UK fans had to make do with picking up what small clues they could – like reading the entire Target novel, which had accidentally been distributed to bookshops in advance of the broadcast. (John Nathan-Turner was so cross, he threatened to revoke WH Allen's licence and move publication of the novelisations in-house.)

The reason for the transatlantic time-lag was because the BBC wanted to broadcast *The Five Doctors* as part of its annual *Children in Need* charity telethon. For most viewers, this just meant a twinkly-eyed Terry Wogan topping and tailing the show. But in some regions, the viewing experience was somewhat spoiled by the constant *Children in Need* messages scrolling across the screen: you'd be surprised how distracting it can be when the historic first meeting of the fifth Doctor and his predecessors is accompanied by a caption thanking the staff at Asda in Keighley for raising £80 through a sponsored three-legged race.

Given the straitjacket he was placed in, Terrance Dicks does a fair job of marshalling all the required elements of *The Five Doctors* into something approaching a coherent narrative. His central conceit of having a mysterious power manipulating the players in a war game (wonder where he got that idea from?) saves an awful lot of time by allowing him to plonk everyone down exactly where they need to be. Drawing inspiration from Robert Browning's poem "Childe Roland to the Dark Tower Came", Dicks sends our heroes on a mission through Gallifrey's notorious Death Zone (the name does nothing for the house prices there) and into the legendary Tomb of Rassilon – the daddy of all Time Lords – himself.

Of course, since said mysterious power's plan hinges on the Doctors all making it to the final rendezvous point and solving all the problems for him, you might well ask why he goes to the effort of throwing so many obstacles in their path; director Peter Moffatt certainly did – and no-one could give him a plausible answer.

But it hardly matters: *The Five Doctors* is all about the journey, not the destination. And from the opening scenes in which the (newly-pimped) TARDIS visits the fabled Eye of Orion – pre-sold to us as the most tranquil place in the universe, but looking an awful lot like a wet weekend in Wales – to the re-set button at the end where the Doctor is forced on the run from his own people all over again, it's a hoot.

With a solitary – and highly excitable – Dalek making little more than a cameo (Nathan-Turner and Saward were keeping their powder dry for the following year's re-mount of *The Return*), primary menacing duties are undertaken by the Cybermen – though they wouldn't have been if Dicks had had his way. "Eric had an obsession with the Cybermen to a sinister extent," said the writer. "I noticed he had a Cyber helmet and boots hanging on the back of the office door. I said, you dress up in them when you're alone, don't you Eric?"[17]

The story introduces a new innovation for the Mondasian meanies: Cyber vomit. In one infamous sequence (actually directed by Nathan-Turner), a platoon of Cybermen line up – quite politely, it has to be said – to be massacred by a sharp-shootin' silver droid called the Raston Warrior Robot. And promptly start throwing up as if they've had a particularly heavy night on the WD40. (You could forgive stuntman Stuart Fell for *actually* throwing up, though: his Cyber helmet filled up with smoke and he nearly choked to death.)

Taken at face value, as a sugar-rush hit straight to the nostalgia neurons, *The Five Doctors* is a great success. Troughton, Pertwee and Davison are all in fine fettle, Richard Hundall gives a respectable account of the first Doctor, and even Tom Baker makes his presence felt courtesy of some deftly inserted footage from the unbroadcast *Shada*.

It's no classic, though, let down by Moffatt's flatlining direction (both Waris Hussein and Douglas Camfield had turned it down) and some badly misjudged performances. The scenes in the Time Lord citadel are particularly clunking: Anthony Ainley appears to think he's still in that Tunbridge Wells panto, and guest actor Paul Jericho's reading of the immortal line "No, not the mind probe!" would quickly pass into fan lore, even inspiring the title of a fanzine. Jericho claimed Nathan-Turner had told him to stress the *mind*, while Moffatt thought the emphasis should be on *probe* – so he went down the middle, with a spectacular lack of success.

Even that, though, is not as notorious as the scene in which the third Doctor rescues Sarah from the Slight Incline of Doom. As scripted, Sarah is supposed to get lost in the fog and pitch headlong over the edge of a treacherous ravine. But, having apparently failed to find a treacherous ravine (despite the fact there are clearly loads more suitable locations in later scenes), the sequence as shot shows Pertwee using Bessie and a tow-rope to drag poor Lis Sladen up a glorified grass verge so shallow even K-9 could have trundled up it without too much trouble.

After all the hype and pre-publicity, *The Five Doctors*' audience of 7.7 million was something of a disappointment – not a disaster by any means, but it's sobering to think it was watched almost a million fewer people than *K-9 and*

Company. Then again, maybe the British audience wasn't quite so important any more: having been the first to see *The Five Doctors*, America was also the place the stars of *Doctor Who* flocked in their dozens that November to celebrate the 20th anniversary at a huge convention in Chicago. A planned British event, to be staged by the Doctor Who Appreciation Society, had to be cancelled as organisers conceded they couldn't compete with the big bucks being offered by their US counterparts, and would probably have had to make do with an extra from *The Keys of Marinus*. Or John Levene.

By this time, it had also been announced that the Doctor's next companion would be played by an American. An uneasy Peter Davison complained to John Nathan-Turner that *Doctor Who* was in danger of "losing its Britishness". Quite which exact moment he chose to make this protest isn't known – possibly it was on the plane to Chicago.

"A panto horse walks into a seabase..."

With the sound of party poppers fading and the last of the cake crumbs swept away, it was back home and back to business for the current *Who* production team. Which, naturally, meant teetering on the brink of disaster, as recording on Peter Davison's final story was beset by a scene shifter's strike, and the scripts for his successor's debut – to be shown, in a break with tradition, as the final story of the current season[IX] – had proved unworkable, forcing Saward to perform some fairly drastic surgery.

The twenty-first series of *Doctor Who* lumbered out of the traps in the first week of January 1984 with the much-anticpiated *Warriors of the Deep.* On paper, this looked like a winner: a return to the Troughton era staple of a base under siege – in this case, a futuristic undersea base at the centre of a Cold War spy game – featuring a Marvel Comics-style team-up between 70s amphibian antagonists the Silurians and the Sea Devils. What's not to love?

Just about everything, as it turns out. Actually, the sets are pretty good – which is just as well, as the whole thing is lit more like

a supermarket than a sea-base (director Pennant Roberts claimed he wasn't allowed to hit the dimmer switch owing to an arcane BBC directive about picture quality). But there's precious little else to recommend this soggy mess of a story: the Sea Devils are so slow and cumbersome, and their heads so wobbly, they look more like an *It's A Knockout* team than a crack fighting unit (you half expect the humans to start throwing wet sponges at them); Johnny Byrne's script, clearly an attempt to "do an *Earthshock*" for another returning villain, rides roughshod over established continuity (not that the majority of the audience watching cared two hoots about that, of course); and the ending is so clunkingly telegraphed (hexachromite gas is "lethal to marine and reptile life", the Doctor helpfully informs us in episode one), it's not so much Chekhov showing the gun in the first act as waving it about and going "hey everybody, look at this gun".

The human villains of the piece, meanwhile, are the world's two most obvious double agents, and the Doctor's idea of creating a diversion is to deliberately overload a nuclear reactor (he should have just tried the old boob-tube trick). As the reptile invaders stage their merciless onslaught (it says here), the giant steel doors of the sea base flop over like mattresses – possibly that's what they were – creating one of those unfortunate moments which certain bar-room wags think *all Doctor Who* was like, even though it rarely was.

But if there's one reason anyone remembers *Warriors of the Deep* – or *Warriors on the Cheap*, as it was dubbed by fans – it's the Myrka. Alarm bells should clearly have rung somewhere when Byrne handed in a script in which a giant, Loch Ness-style sea monster goes on the rampage in TVC 6. Today, this would be be achieved with a bit of CGO jiggery-pokery; in 1983, they got a pantomime horse and painted it green.

Or as good as, anyway: the Myrka was operated by the same guys who worked Dobbin, the panto nag in zero-budget kids' sitcom *Rentaghost*. But even these professional horse-wranglers struggled to inject life into what looked like a half-deflated bouncy castle covered in green paint. And the paint wasn't even dry – by the end of the first recording session, Janet Fielding was covered in the stuff, while guest star Ingrid Pitt, as the treacherous Dr Solow, insisted on adding a scene where she takes the unfortunate beast on with a karate kick. If there's a sillier scene in *Doctor Who*, *Space Helmet* has yet to see it.

In their defence, the visual effects team were supposed to have had a month to make the creature, but ended up with just nine days after the studio dates were rescheduled owing to a snap general election. In other words, as with so much in Britain in the early 80s, blame Thatcher.

After *Black Orchid* and *The King's Demons*, this year's brief historical skirmish came with a twist: *The Awakening* is actually set in 1984, but a series of Civil War games brings a threat from Tudor England back to life – no, not dysentery, it's a giant alien face walled up in the church. The Malus, a cyborg which feeds off the psychic energy created by human pain and misery, is planning to gorge itself by recreating Little Hodcombe's decisive Roundhead-Cavalier smackdown for real (it was either that, or invent *EastEnders* a year early).

The Doctor teams up with a village school teacher (Polly James – Peter Davison flirting outrageously with his second Liver Bird in almost as many years; all he needs now is Molly Sugden and he's got the set) – to stop a local magistrate (the excellent Denis Lill) doing the Malus' bidding. He also finds time to help a seventeenth-century urchin who has somehow slipped forward in time several centuries (you can tell he's from the past, because he speaks in a Mummerset accent, even though the story is clearly set in the Home Counties) and meets Tegan's grandfather – the third member of her family to casually wander into the middle of an alien invasion in recent times.

A small but perfectly-formed tale – like a mini-*Daemons*, blending history, science and magic – *The Awakening* is most famous for an incident in which a horse accidentally demolishes a lych gate. In fact, it's the only reason *Doctor Who* fans know what a lych gate is. This clip has been seen so often on TV outtake shows, it comes as something of a surprise that the episode itself doesn't have a laughter track. Maybe they should have used the guys from *Rentaghost* again.

Frontios is the first story written by Christopher Bidmead since Peter Davison's

debut. As such, it sees the fifth Doctor returning to first principles as an old man in a young man's body. Davison loved this bookish approach – he felt the other writers could have made more of it, too – and rises to the challenge with one of his best performances, in an effective and atmospheric story of frontier folk battling for survival at the very edge of the universe.

The titular planet is home to one of the last surviving Earth colonies, an embattled bunch living on the brink of extinction from constant meteor bombardments, not to mention the large alien grubs tunnelling about under the soil as part of a plan to turn the planet into an enormous spaceship. (If that sounds vaguely familiar, it's because it was the plot of *The Dalek Invasion of Earth*, way back in 1964.)

Despite this bonkers premise, it's an intellectually satisfying piece, with Bidmead clearly enjoying riffing on his favourite theme of civilisations which have lost their scientific heritage. It also boasts some memorable (and gruesome) images, not least the exploded TARDIS scattered across the planet.

Bidmead says the script was based on the Beirut crisis – though you'd have to look really hard to see it: certainly, I don't recall giant woodlice dragging corpses underground being cited as a prominent causal factor in most anaylses of the Middle East situation. The crustaceans in question, the Tractators, were actually inspired by the woodlice in Bidmead's flat. (Who knows what else we might have had if he'd continued writing for the show – the Iran-Contra scandal acted out by the hairy bathplug monsters?)

Director Ron Jones is on unusually good form, making effective use of the all-studio setting, though the less said about the Tractators the better. Bidmead was certainly miffed with the finished result but, as a former script editor, he really ought to have known better what was achievable on a *Doctor Who* budget.

Better late than never – or possibly not – Eric Saward's *The Return* finally made it to the screen in February 1984, under the new title *Resurrection of the Daleks*. Like *Earthshock*, it sees an auld enemy embarking on a preposterously complicated plan that involves duplicates of human beings, temporal corridors, an entirely unnecessary invasion of London's

Docklands (maybe they were just trying to get a toe-hold in the property market) and an incidental scheme to assassinate the High Council of Time Lords. Also like *Earthshock*, it's a whizz-bang, gung-ho sort of affair, all sound and fury – except this time it really does signify nothing. In fact, it's an almost uniquely unpleasant story in *Doctor Who* terms – scarcely any of the guest cast survive, and several characters are horribly disfigured before they die. A couple of them are even seen smoking cigarettes, which obviously upset middle class parents a lot more than all the death and mutilation.

Eric Saward later admitted that "in many ways, it's probably the worst script ever written for *Doctor Who*".[12] (After which there was a long, awkward pause until someone blurted out, "Oh sorry Eric, no, of course it isn't, don't be silly".)

Had the story been made as part of Season Twenty, it would have seen Michael Wisher recreating his role as the original Davros. As it was, he was unavailable and the job went to Terry Molloy, a veteran of radio soap *The Archers*, where he has played milkman and farm labourer Mike Tucker since 1973. Molloy acquits himself well, despite a new mask with a mouth like a dog's bottom that makes the Dalek creator look like he's got a permanent bad smell under his nose. (Though, to be fair, that commode probably hasn't been emptied in a while.)

The headline guest stars at the time were flame-haired Polish beauty Rula Lenska, Maurice Colbourne – star of gritty 70s thriller *Gangsters* and, later, the decidely less gritty marina soap *Howards' Way* – and "Mr Rodney" Bewes, erstwhile Likely Lad and consort to Basil Brush. (In the last act, Bewes' robot duplicate character manages to override his programming and blow up the Dalek spaceship. Boom boom!) In retrospect, though, the serial is more notable for marking the TV debut of Leslie Grantham, a convicted murderer who had been encouraged to go into acting by Louise Jameson during a visit to Leyhill Prison. (Jameson had been running a series of workshops with hardcore criminals and killers, presumably as a bit of light relief after working with Tom Baker.) Grantham, of course, would go on to find notoriety the fol-

lowing year as "Dirty" Den Watts in *EastEnders* and, a couple of decades later, even more notoriety on his dressing room webcam. Let's move on, shall we?

Resurrection of the Daleks was broadcast as two 45-minute episodes to make way for coverage of the Winter Olympics from Sarajevo. While Torvill and Dean skated their way into the history books with their record-breaking Arabesques and choctaw turns, *Resurrection's* death spiral – it has the highest on-screen body count of any *Doctor Who* story – saw Tegan leave the TARDIS (for good this time) because she was "sick" of all the violence and bloodshed. After this brutal, macho, militaristic corspe-fest, it's hard not to disagree.

By contrast, the following week's *Planet of Fire* brought a welcome splash of Mediterranean sunshine to proceedings, as the show took its latest foreign holiday on the volcanic island of Lanzarote (doubling, confusingly, for the volcanic planet of Sarn and, erm, Lanzarote).

As you can imagine, Janet Fielding wasn't best pleased. "Three years on that show and I'm written out just before they go swanning off to Lanzarote! Isn't that great?"[18] She even tried to convince the production team the flights had been cancelled – but no-one believed her, which says a lot about how convincing she had been playing an air stewardess for the past four seasons.

Surrey seems to be the hardest word

The location for *Planet of Fire* had actually been suggested by director Fiona Cumming after she'd taken a holiday there. But she and Nathan-Turner went back to the island on a further two recces – just, you know, to be absolutely sure. Writer Peter Grimwade, perhaps unsurprisingly, wasn't invited on either trip. "I was given the director's holiday snaps to look at," he grumbled[19].

Grimwade's shopping list brief for the story had included using both Lanzarote and the Master, writing out Turlough and writing in the new companion. Perpugilliam "Peri" Brown was to be the Doctor's first American fellow traveller; Nathan-Turner was keen to exploit the show's popularity in the States and thought giving them one of their own as a regular character would help boost its profile even further, so step forward Nicola Bryant, a perky 22-year-old drama school graduate from... Guildford.

Bryant had dual citizenship through her marriage to an American drama coach. But as she'd be playing an American in a series filmed largely in north London, that wouldn't really be any help. On the advice of her agent, Bryant – who, having been offered the role, had to sing in nightclubs in order to earn her Equity card – kept up the pretence of being from the States, and thus found herself effectively living a double life, pretending to be American, even to her co-stars. And, just to add to the cloak and dagger vibe, John Nathan-Turner also asked her to play down the fact she was married.

"She was speaking in a kind of weird voice," recalled Peter Davison, who wasn't officially in on the secret. "You could obviously tell that her accent wasn't very good and it was clear to me as, at the time, I was married to an American."[8]

To make matters worse, the Lanzarote crew were accompanied by a group of British press reporters and photographers, which meant Bryant had to be on her guard at all times. (It must have been quite exhausting: "Hey can you hold the lift... I mean the *elevator*" ... "I'm just off the loo... as, erm, I believe you charming English people call it" ... "Can you pass me some of that aubergine... eggplant, I meant eggplant!".[X])

So why *was* she cast? "I sat in the auditions for Peri, and Nicola Bryant was by far and away the best," recalled Eric Saward. "She came in wearing shorts, she was tanned, I think she had the blouse tied under her breasts – she looked very sexy, all of it working for her. And she read the part beautifully; it wasn't just a matter of a woman with a big chest and a – as it turned out – phoney American accent."[12] I'm sure she'd be very flattered to know that.

They may not have employed her for her chest, but they certainly made full use of it on location. Firstly, Nathan-Turner arranged a photocall with Bryant in a white bikini and a clearly uncomfortable Davison, complete with tux and handgun, as the world's least convincing James Bond (with a licence to kill his producer).

Bryant's first episode also sees her sporting a different bikini (pink this time) in some of *Doctor Who*'s most freeze-framed moments. Or, ahem, so I'm told, anyway. In one of these scenes, Peri jumps off a boat and has to be rescued by Turlough (Mark Strickson gamely doing his bit for equality by stripping down to a pair of skimpy trunks: this was the closest *Doctor Who* would ever come to *Baywatch*). In fact, Bryant's drowning acting was so convincing, it attracted the attention of a German nudist on a nearby beach, who swam out to rescue her. Whether she managed to keep up her American accent while being manhandled by a naked German isn't known, but the naturist himself wasn't best pleased, and later tried to ruin another shot by running into the background. The show hadn't seen anything quite so obscene since *The Creature from the Pit*.

Planet of Fire doesn't have much in the way of a story (the Master has managed to shrink himself to the size of an Action Man, and needs the gas in an alien volcano to restore him to size), but it *does* have an awful lot of backstory, as well as being the series' most overt piece of anti-religious polemic since Leela dismissed all people of faith as idiots. This mix of Biblical set-dressing and fabulous location work gives the enterprise an unusually glossy, expensive sheen, while Bryant – accent notwithstanding – makes a very promising start and Grimwade provides a decent exit for Turlough, who is revealed to have been exiled to Earth after ending up on the losing side of a civil war on his native Trion. Oh, and he also writes out Kamelion – in so much as you *can* write out a character who was never really written *in*.

If Nathan-Turner's colleagues were surprised to see Peter Grimwade back on the payroll, it must have been an even bigger shock when Eric Saward persuaded the producer to relax his year zero approach to scriptwriters and let Robert Holmes pen Davison's final story. (The commission, for which Holmes was given the simple brief "Kill the Doctor", was partly Saward's way of mending fences after *The Six Doctors* fallout.) As if to compensate for being lumbered with such a safe pair of hands, Nathan-Turner offered the director's gig to a young rookie called Graeme Harper, whose only previous credits included some episodes of *Angels*, and salvaging massive parts of

Warriors' Gate after the official director's little meltdown.

Harper's approach was quite unlike anything seen in the programme before: despite the risks involved, he chose to shoot single camera – or as close an approximation as he could get away with in the studio – using cross fades, focus pulls and all the other tricks of the trade his colleagues thought were a bit fancy-pants in order bring the story alive on screen. [XI] With the lights finally turned down, and a menacing, snake-rattle of a score by Roger Limb, the result feels like the show has suddenly leapt forward 15 years in time.

With Harper's direction allied to Holmes' script – a pitch-black revenge tragedy borrowing liberally from *The Phantom of the Opera*, with the opulence of early twentieth-century Paris replaced by grimy gun-runners' dens on a backwater planet at the arse-end of nowhere – *The Caves of Androzani* is a triumph. In a 2009 series-wide poll conducted by *Doctor Who Magazine*, the serial was voted the greatest *Doctor Who* story of all time. And it's a definite contender for that title although, weirdly, it's also one of the least *Doctor Who*-like stories of all time. For a series that derives so much of its appeal from its oddball humour and English eccentricity, *The Caves of Androzani* is unusually dark and gritty: right from the get-go, the fifth Doctor is locked into an inevitable slide towards a grim death brought about by nothing more than his own stupid curiosity and desire to protect Peri from the same fate – not to mention the clutches of disfigured drugs and arms dealer Sharaz Jek. The latter, beautifully played by the late dancer Christopher Gable, is one of *Who*'s most fully realised villains, and his insane lust for Peri another example of the story's unusually adult themes.

Jek's mortal enemy is Morgus, head of a business conglomerate who purports to be trying to seize back control of the planet's supply of Spectrox – a life-prolonging elixir found in nests in the caves controlled by Jek – but who is secretly prolonging the war for his own ends. Morgus is a classic Holmes' bureaucrat reinvented as a vicious 80s City trader, brilliantly brought to life by John Normington "Tut tut, how sad," he deadpans on hearing of a mining disaster that has solved his little "over-production problem". At one point,

Normington glowers through the fourth wall by turning in his office chair and speaking a line straight down the camera lens. Apparently this was due to his misunderstanding Harper's note, but it's thrilling nonetheless.

Though Holmes later admitted, not having seen the show lately, to having written the script with Tom Baker in mind, Peter Davison has rarely been better served, as his Doctor slowly succumbs to the effects of Spectrox poisoning (that'll teach him to go poking about in alien nests); the actor was in no doubt this was the best story of his tenure, and was delighted to be going out on a high. But then, everyone suddenly feels well-disposed to their job in their last week at work, don't they?

The location filming took place in a Devon quarry. Unfortunately for Nicola Bryant, she was still dressed for the Canaries: her legs turned blue, and she got frostbite and pneumonia. Then Peter Davison dropped her from a height while fumbling for the TARDIS key. On the plus side, at least the quarry workers kept their clothes on.

The regeneration sequence itself was inspired by the rising crescendo in the middle of The Beatles' "A Day in the Life". Rather than simply recycle old clips, all the fifth Doctor's companions were brought back for a small cameo as disembodied heads circling Davison's face (well, it was a small cameo for most – for Kamelion, it was one of his biggest scenes yet).

It's an extremely effective device – although it does mean that the final word ever spoken by the fifth Doctor is "Adric", which is perhaps not the most dignified way to go. (Matthew Waterhouse admitted he was "slightly narked" not to have been able to turn the scene down: "I would have liked to have been able to say that I just couldn't fit it in because I was too busy. In fact, I was wretchedly out of work.")[20] Davison has since pointed out that his heroic last moments are also somewhat overshadowed by having Nicola Bryant leaning over him while spilling out of her bikini top – so the fifth Doctor's final soliloquy could have been the lyrics to *Button Moon* for all anyone was paying attention.

Nevertheless, Davison admitted to a lump in the throat (at least I *think* he said throat) during the delayed recording of his final scenes on the evening of Thursday, January 12th. "It was a

It Shouldn't Happen to a Bloody Vet

weird feeling, knowing that I'd never do *Doctor Who* again," said the actor. "But I never really regretted leaving. I was just glad that the third season was so much better than the second."[21]

Broadcast on Thursdays and Fridays, the twenty-first season's batting average remained around seven million, with Thursdays generally faring better as the show's fanbase opted to spend Friday evenings out drinking, dancing and getting off with each other. Or maybe it was Cubs that night.

The day after completing his *Who* duties, Davison travelled to Birmingham to play the male lead in a BBC adaptation of Arnold Bennett's *Anna of the Five Towns*. From there, he never looked back, managing to shuck off the ghost of *Doctor Who* more successfully than any actor before him, with starring roles in Andrew Davies' deliciously dark campus comedy *A Very Peculiar Practice* and two series of films based on Margery Allingham's 20s detective Campion among his more high-profile successes. He also reprised his role as Tristan Farnham in four more series of *All Creatures Great and Small* broadcast from 1988 to 1990.

After a minor dry spell in the late 90s, Davison returned to prominence in Sally Wainwright's 2000 comedy drama *At Home with the Braithwaites*, which he followed with four series as DC "Dangerous" Davies in ITV's *The Last Detective*. In recent years, the actor – as much to his surprise as anyone else's – has carved out something of a niche in musical theatre, playing King Arthur in *Monty Python's Spamalot* and spending two years in the West End in *Legally Blonde*. In addition to regular TV guest spots – including, somewhat improbably, playing Denis Thatcher in a film for Channel 4 – in 2011, he also took on a leading role in ITV's cops and courts procedural *Law and Order: UK*. In 2013, he rather heroically wrote and directed *The Five(ish) Doctors Reboot* (the "ish" came about when Tom Baker – after some prevaricating – declined to participate), a next-to-no budget celebration of *Doctor Who*'s 50th anniversary featuring Davison, Colin Baker and Sylvester McCoy, that was later nominated for a Hugo Award.

Davison got into a spot of bother in the 90s when he described certain aspects of his time on *Doctor Who* as "crap" – but this was clearly just his salty sense of humour (check out his

hilariously waspish DVD commentaries for further proof). In fact, he has remained engaged with the programme and its fans, despite his often heavy workload, and has so far starred in more than 50 *Doctor Who* audio plays (see Chapter Eight) since the turn of the century.

In the great sweep of *Doctor Who* history, it's perhaps easy to overlook the fifth Doctor's short-ish tenure, coming as it did at the end Tom Baker's Imperial reign. But Davison is never less than compelling in the role, and his part in reinvigorating the show after the disastrous ratings slide in Baker's final year can't be overestimated.

If Davison *had* signed for that fourth year, it's interesting to imagine how differently *Doctor Who*'s future might have played out. But it wasn't to be. "John did try to persuade me to stay on," Davison recalled. "But, being John, he quite quickly got excited about who to get next. He saw it as another opportunity."[22]

Around this time, Davison heard the man who Nathan-Turner had got next talking on the radio about "all the marvellous things" he was going to do with the part. "And I thought, yeah, you haven't started it yet – you don't know what you're up against. You were always battling."[5]

As it turned out, his successor was about to wade into the biggest – and bloodiest – battle in *Doctor Who*'s history.

201

6 Hex and Violence

"Just because you've had a drink, there's no need to show off"

In the 1980s, John Nathan-Turner was a man permanently on the rebound. At the dawn of the decade, he had cast Peter Davison for all the qualities that marked him out as distinct from his predecessor: youth, blonde hair, reputation for not telling directors how to do their job, or trying to hire a talking cabbage. So when Davison handed in his notice three years later, Nathan-Turner simply threw the process into reverse – and went looking for a 40-year-old, curly-haired, larger-than-life bloke called Baker.

Actually, that would have made a lot more sense than the *actual* reason Nathan-Turner cast Colin Baker as the sixth Doctor – because he had made him laugh at a wedding.

The blushing bride at said nuptials was Lynn Richards, who had been assistant floor manager on *Arc of Infinity*, during which Baker had dramatically expressed an interest in the lead role by shooting his predecessor in the chest. Whatever happened to sending in a CV? (This raises the question, incidentally, of just how many friends Richards and her fiancé actually had, if they were reduced to inviting colleagues they'd worked with for a couple of weeks a few months earlier. Isn't that what the evening do is supposed to be for?)

Anyway, Baker, being an actor, wasn't busy, so rocked up with his wife Marion and, glass in hand, proceeded to entertain the assembled guests in his inimitable, shy and retiring fashion.

"One day in a thousand you're on song," the actor recalled later. "Though I can't help thinking what a terrible bore I must have been, clearly liking the sound of my own voice."[1]

In the car on the way home, Nathan-Turner turned to Gary Downie and declared: "I've found my new Doctor."

Many have subsequently questioned the wisdom of this method of casting. But Nathan-Turner remained unrepentant, telling one interviewer: "I said to the last three Doctors, the key to how to play it is 'you at a party'. It's you one notch up."[2] Besides, even Baker's most vociferous critics had to admit it could have been worse – who knows who else was at the wedding? They could have ended up with one of Lynn Edwards' drunken uncles as the Doctor, and seen the theme tune reworked by Dave, of Dave's Mobile Disco.

Born in London in 1943, but raised in Rochdale, Colin Baker had made his name in the mid-70s in the BBC's hit Sunday night trucking saga *The Brothers*, playing the villainous merchant banker (that's not just rhyming slang, he really was a merchant banker) Paul Merroney – a sort of cross between JR Ewing and Eddie Stobart.[1] The programme was so insanely popular with Dutch viewers, for some reason, that the cast even recorded a Christmas album for them.

When Nathan-Turner contacted Baker during a theatre engagement in Richmond and invited him in for a chat, the actor assumed he was going to be asked to open a fete or appear in a charity show. So he was staggered when, on June 10th, 1983 – just two days after his 40th birthday – he was formally offered the part of the Doctor. In the weeks that followed, he admitted, he was "ridiculously excited" about his new job, waking up in the mornings in a state of extreme exhilaration, which is perhaps not a mental image to dwell upon. He also insisted his wife address him as "the Doctor", and kept disappearing into the wardrobe for hours at a time. Okay, I made that last bit up – but he was pretty damn psyched.

Though Baker was asked to keep the news a secret, he was rumbled by his predecessor when Peter Davison and Sandra Dickinson bumped into him and Nathan-Turner having a drink together in the Bush Hotel near Television Centre. His casting was officially announced on August 19th – three weeks after the *Telegraph* and the *Express* had already told everyone the new Doctor was to be Brian Blessed. (The truth is that the blusterous *Flash*

Gordon shouter was in frame, but Nathan-Turner had clearly decided he was a bit reserved for the sixth Doctor he had in mind.)

Baker was interviewed on Radio 4's *PM*, and discussed his thoughts on the role on BBC1's *Breakfast Time* the following Monday. He also gave an exclusive interview to BBC Radio Derbyshire, because that's the way things worked back then. With his contract including options on his services up until 1988, it was around this time that the actor announced his intention to try to beat his namesake's seven-year-record in the role. Isn't hindsight a marvellous thing?

Sadly, between his appointment and his first day's filming in the role, Baker and his wife were to suffer a devastating personal tragedy when, on November 13th, their baby son Jack was found dead in his cot, aged just seven weeks. Baker would go on to use his newly increased profile to campaign energetically for the Foundation for the Study of Infant Deaths, with *Doctor Who* fans raising thousands for the charity over the years.

Making his debut in the studio a month later, Baker was nonetheless on ebullient form – in contrast to Peter Davison, who was feeling subdued and, he later admitted, not a little put out to see how easily life would go on without him. Baker mooning Davison's wife on-set probably didn't help – though the outgoing Time Lord had the last laugh when the more, ahem, fuller figured Baker couldn't do up his predecessor's trousers.

According to Nicola Bryant, Davison had spent his last few weeks in the job winding her up about how difficult Baker would be to work with, to the point where she started out being a bit stand-offish with her new, perfectly agreeable co-star. In a spectacularly wrong-headed attempt to cement their relationship, Baker took it upon himself to bite Bryant on the backside during the filming of their first full story together. "It broke the ice,"[3] he said. He's lucky that wasn't all that got broken.

When Baker was presented with his costume for the show, fitting into the trousers was the least of his worries. John Nathan-Turner had asked costume designer Pat Godfrey to come up with something in "extremely bad taste", but she kept coming back with concepts the producer decreed "not tasteless enough".

Legend has it she produced the final design as a joke, thinking Nathan-Turner would laugh her out of his office. One look at his own penchant for candy-coloured Hawaiian shirts should have told her he'd have loved it. "Cruel people – and I wasn't one of them," Eric Sward was keen to point out in later years, "said that what he wanted to do was reflect his own style of dress in the Doctor."[1]

Whatever the thinking behind the resulting explosion in a fabric factory – think clown costume made from carpet offcuts – you have to admit that the sixth Doctor's costume was at least a product of its time: all it needed was a pair of deely boppers and a The Doctor Says Relax T-shirt and the ensemble would have been complete.

The show's title sequence was also given a slight makeover, with some disco lights added to the starfield and the *Doctor Who* logo now rendered in 3D – albeit the fuzzy, unreadable 3D effect you get when you've lost the little cardboard glasses.

To complete this clean sweep[II], it was also decided that, in a break from tradition, the new Doctor would be less of a courageous hero and more of a... well, more of a nob, really. Saward described the character as "gruffer, rougher and tougher," while Baker and Nathan-Turner discussed the Doctor having "a secret" that would be gradually revealed to have been making him such a grump. Baker described it as "a bit like Mr Darcy". No-one else did. The actor also said the character should have layers, that the audience would discover over time "like peeling an onion". Well, it certainly made people cry.

Another innovation was introducing the new Doctor – who enthusiastically talked up his role with costumed appearances on the likes of *Blue Peter*, *Breakfast Time* and *Saturday Superstore*, as well as sharing a sofa with Peter Davison for a slightly awkward grilling by Russell Harty – in the penultimate story of the season. Nathan-Turner thought that nine months was too long a wait to see the new man in action, and was worried that, in Eric Saward's words, "the audience wouldn't come back". So he tacked *The Twin Dilemma* on to the end of Season Twenty-One, to make damn sure they wouldn't.

Colin Baker recently described his debut

adventure as "not a classic story". This is true, in the same way that Ann Widdecombe is not a classic beauty. For a story about maths, virtually nothing about it adds up: a perfect storm of florid, over-ambitious scripting, rotten acting, Play School production design and phoned-in direction, *The Twin Dilemma* is regularly voted the worst story in *Doctor Who's* history. And *Doctor Who's* history includes *The Time Monster*.

It's difficult to know where to begin the post-mortem on such a heroically bad piece of television, but the titular twins, Romulus and Remus – a pair of twerpish adolescents we are asked to believe have the power to change the orbit of planets just by thinking really hard about stuff – probably just about edge it over Mestor, a despotic, boss-eyed slug who really *did* sport a pair of deely boppers, presumably to distract from the fact his body was made from a roll of loft insulation. (The twins were played by Paul and Andrew Conrad, one of whom apparently went on to be a Shakespearean actor of some repute. Paul Conrad also changed his name, possibly from sheer shame.) And then there's Kevin McNally, who plays permanently bewildered space policeman Hugo Lang in the manner of someone who's just woken up and found himself in a television studio; at one point, having clearly had enough of being the only one who didn't get the fancy dress invite, Lt Lang promptly swaps his copper's uniform for a rainbow-coloured tinfoil number that appears to have fallen off the back of Bjorn Again's tour bus.

Writer Anthony Steven was best known in BBC circles for his adaptations of classic novels like *Swallows and Amazons* and *Fanny by Gaslight*, which may explain why everyone declaims in such an absurdly theatrical manner – "That is a direct order from the Minister," says space police chief Fabian. "And may my bones rot for obeying it!" Her futuristic intergalactic incident room, incidentally, appears to have been kitted out from a fire sale at Office World, or possibly it's the furniture Juliet Bravo threw out of her provincial cop shop for looking a bit dated.

Perhaps the story's biggest problem, though, is that the Doctor spends the whole thing in a post-regenerative derangement that sees him, by turns, trying to strangle Peri to death, cry-

ing like a girl and generally acting like a bit of a bell-end. As Baker himself so neatly put it: "They'd decided to regenerate during a series, so the 'Who's going to be the new Doctor?' cliffhanger became the 'My God, is he really going to be that awful?' cliffhanger."[1]

And thus the new Doctor was not so much launched as shoved off a cliff and left to sink or swim. To be fair to Baker, he is the best thing about *The Twin Dilemma* by a country mile: whatever the logic of reinventing one of TV's most iconic heroes as a boorish lout – or a loutish bore, if you prefer – there's no denying Baker gives it his all. And possibly a bit of someone else's, too.

On the plus side, there was fresh evidence it wasn't just new *Doctor Who* that was rubbish when the final part of long-lost presumed classic *The Celestial Toymaker* turned up in Australia around the time of *The Twin Dilemma's* broadcast and, if anything, proved to be even worse. Of course, it's unfair to compare a story made in 1966 with one made nearly 20 years later – though it's interesting to note that both feature actors dressed as scary clowns. Sadly, in *The Twin Dilemma*, it's the leading man.

Outrage as *Doctor Who* wrenched from traditional midweek slot

Incredible as it may seem to today's armies of expertly-drilled media and screenwriting graduates, when you can't order a latte in White City without the waiter thrusting a script in your hand at the same time, the biggest problem faced by Eric Saward, as with so many of his predecessors, was that no-one was sending in scripts – or certainly not usable ones with more sophisticated titles than *Doctor Who Fights the Killer Robots from Space*.

Ideas briefly in the fray for the twenty-second season included *The Macro Men*, a story about microscopic alien invaders from Ingrid Pitt – last seen busting chop socky moves on the Myrka in *Warriors of the Deep* – and Tony Rudlin; something about bee-hives from *Crossroads* creators Hazel Adair and Peter (*The Mind Robber*) Ling; *Children of Seth*, from *Kinda* and *Snakedance* author Christopher Bailey; untitled breakdowns from Chrises Bidmead and Boucher; and *Strange Encounter*, a submission from former TARDIS traveller Ian Marter that appears to have been based around the thrilling sci-fi concept of hospital overcrowding. It also proved to be the last gasp for *The Space Whale*, an ambitious story about a group of castaways living in the belly of a giant... well, you work it out... that had been stuck in Development Hell since the last Baker was in office. Writer Pat Mills – co-scripter of classic *Doctor Who Weekly* comic strips such as "The Iron Legion" – had originally pitched it for the fourth Doctor's final run, and it had eventually been commissioned for Season Twenty, before being deferred for another couple of years and finally given the last rites in the spring of 1984.

In desperation, the production team resorted to putting the word out on the industry bush telegraph and, by Nathan-Turner's own admission, taking whatever they could find – a situation not helped by the producer's continued wariness about anyone who might turn out to know more about this *Doctor Who* lark than he did.

One "new talent" nurtured by the producer was husband-and-wife writing team Pip and Jane Baker – though they weren't exactly what you'd call rookies, having been knocking scripts out since the early 60s. Nathan-Turner unearthed a submission that had been left in the office by Graham Williams, which impressed him enough to commission a storyline about a renegade Time Lady meddling with Earth history. The story's working title was *Too Clever By Far*, which was just one word away from being a well-known saying. A script was also greenlit from Philip Martin, creator of *Gangsters* – the aforementioned Maurcie Cobourne-starring gritty BBC thriller, which is best remembered for its often violent depiction of multi-racial 70s Birmingham and its truly insane theme song, enthusiastically attacked by blues growler Chris Farlowe, despite the fact parts of it were at least two octaves too high for him.

And so the sixth Doctor's debut series slowly began to take shape – and a radically different shape at that. As well as a new leading man, Season Twenty-Two would see *Doctor Who* abandoning the 25-minute episodes that had sustained it since 1963 in favour of a new 45-minute format. (The BBC had wanted 50-minute episodes, but Nathan-Turner

argued this would cumulatively amount to an extra hour of material he hadn't budgeted for – a victory he came to regret when many of the stories ended up overrunning.)

It wasn't all shiny and new, though – to the delight of many fans, the twenty-second season would also see *Doctor Who* returning to the bosom of its traditional Saturday evening slot. And if you think the use of the word "bosom" there is a smutty joke at the expense of one of the regular cast, you're right – but once you've seen Colin Baker with his top off, it's a hard image to shake.

Returning from a European tour of *The Mousetrap* in late May, Baker joined Nicola Bryant for location filming on the first story of the new season, *Attack of the Cybermen* (in retrospect, *Doctor Who Fights the Killer Robots from Space* wasn't that wide of the mark, was it?). The sixth Doctor also made his debut in *Doctor Who Magazine*'s long-running comic strip, accompanied by a new companion called Frobisher who, in theory at least, was a shape-changing alien Whifferdill but who chose, for reasons best known to himself, to stay as a penguin. I guess if you're going to hang around with a man dressed like the BBC test card, there's no point trying to look inconspicuous.

In August, the cast and crew flew to Spain to spend a week filming in an around Seville for a three-part story that would feature the return of Patrick Troughton's second Doctor, along with Frazer Hines as Jamie. After years of playing down his association with the programme, Troughton had enjoyed making *The Five Doctors* so much he'd let it be known he'd be up for another go, and had also become a regular on the convention circuit.

The original plan had been to shoot the story in New Orleans: John Nathan-Turner was spending increasing amounts of time shuttling back and forth across the Atlantic to conventions, and was keen to make a story in the US as part of his charm offensive on the nation's expanding *Doctor Who* fanbase. He chose New Orleans largely because he'd had such a good time at the city's legendary Mardi Gras a few years earlier, and commissioned a breakdown for a story called *Way Down Yonder* from London-based American writer Lesley Elizabeth Thomas. When that didn't work out, it was Robert Holmes who ended up being presented with a shopping list of requirements for the story which, as well as the second Doctor, Jamie and the Big Easy, included the return of his 70s creations the Sontarans. When the BBC's bean counters put the kibosh on that excursion, Spain was suggested as an alternative, and Gary Downie was despatched to Andalusia to scout possible locations. It was a tough job, but someone had to do it. And that someone was the producer's boyfriend.

By all accounts, the cast and crew had a riotous old time, with Troughton and Colin Baker – old friends since the 70s, when Baker shared a flat with Troughton's son David – getting on like a hacienda on fire. Troughton had a habit of referring to his co-star as Miss Piggy, and the pair of them were ringmasters at rehearsals filled with practical jokes. In one scene, Baker was supposed to splash cold water on Nicola Bryant's face, and ended up chucking the whole jug over her – only for the arachnophobic actor to get his comeuppance when he found his dressing room filled with fake spiders. But apart from that and the free Spanish holiday, everyone was working really hard.

The second Doctor and Jamie weren't the only blasts from the pasts that month: at the Edinburgh Festival, Richard Franklin premiered his play *Recall UNIT: The Great T-Bag Mystery*, in which he reprised his role as Captain Mike Yates alongside John Levene's Sergeant Benton. Nicholas Courtney had originally been scheduled to appear as the Brigadier, but in the end could only make a pre-recorded vocal contribution. The story was a satire on the Falklands war – which would have been highly topical two years earlier – featuring a race of aliens called the Dragoids, who bore an uncanny resemblance to Margaret Thatcher. At one point, Yates and Benton had to stage a pantomime – which involved dragging up as the Ugly Sisters – while Franklin also appeared as a schoolboy singing "Daddy Wouldn't Buy Me a Bow-Wow". Maybe you had to be there. A short time later, Franklin offered to novelise the story for Target books. He's still waiting for them to get back to him.

In late August, Colin Baker went to Blackpool to open the new Space Invader ride at the Lancashire resort's famous Please Beach – planting a seed in John Nathan-Turner's mind about setting a story there. (So what if

they couldn't afford New Orleans? Blackpool was even better – they don't give you gravy on your chips in Louisiana, for one thing.) Over the Bank Holiday weekend, Baker joined Elisabeth Sladen for an appearance at the Kenilworth Agricultural Show, the line-up for which also included Jon Pertwee and Janet Fielding. Farmers in Warwickshire must really love *Doctor Who*.

Meanwhile, September brought mixed fortunes for the show: on the plus side, Ian Levine managed to recover all the missing episodes of lost Hartnell stories *The Time Meddler* and *The War Machines* from a Nigerian TV station. Less happily, the new controller of BBC1 was announced as Michael Grade, the flamboyant, cigar-chewing nephew of flamboyant, cigar-chewing impresarios Lew Grade and Bernard Delfont. Keep reading for why this is significant – but let's just say the new man at the top wasn't in a hurry to renew his DWAS membership.

A break in production allowed Colin Baker to take a holiday in Majorca – and he had to pay for it himself this time – while Nicola Bryant took a trip to America... sorry, I mean *flew home* to America. John Nathan-Turner and Gary Downie, meanwhile, jetted off on another production recce for the following season, this time as guests of the Singapore Tourist Board. On their return, Nathan-Turner made Eric Saward and Robert Holmes watch 40 minutes of their holiday video footage to help give them some story ideas. ("Maybe the Doctor could stop for a Singapore Sling at Raffles Hotel? Look, here's Gary trying one out for you. And here's me having a go. Honestly, it was exhausting!")

Returning to work, the team decamped to rainy Shropshire to film Pip and Jane Baker's *The Mark of the Rani* at Blists Hill Victorian Town, part of the Ironbridge Gorge Industrial Heritage Museum – which is a much better day out than it sounds. It was a trying shoot for all involved: firstly, Nathan-Turner had successfully bid for the services of a BBC film crew that, owing to some administrative cock-up, was going spare for a week – but hadn't bargained on having to fork out for their food and accommodation. Then Colin Baker managed to dislocate his finger during a stunt sequence, while filming was delayed by a recalcitrant horse that was pining for its recently-sacked handler (who was subsequently re-hired at the BBC's expense) – and a donkey pressed into service as an extra managed to knock a tourist into the River Severn. Three days of Biblical rain forced a re-mount in a country park in Hampshire, where Baker insists he was left tied to a pole while the rest of the cast and crew went to lunch and, to add insult to injury, the star accidentally had dog shit smeared all over his face (at least they *said* it was an accident). And some actors complain about the size of their trailer.

As Christmas approached, fans had no shortage of merchandise to put on their lists to Santa (indeed, The Who Shop – an entire emporium dedicated to the show – opened in Wapping in December), although, increasingly, this was targeted at adult collectors (particularly in America) with a notable lack of anything you might call an actual *toy*. Pick of the bunch had to be *The Doctor Who Pattern Book*, in which the delightfully-named Joy Gammon showed you how to knit everything from a K-9 shoulder bag to Adric's tunic, complete with memorable pictures of moustachioed "models" striking classic catalogue poses in the middle of a quarry.

John Nathan-Turner also had a busy December, juggling recording of the upcoming season with rehearsals for his latest panto at the Gaumont Theatre in Southampton (though, naturally, he still managed to slot in another US convention trip). *Cinderella* was billed as an all-*Who* affair, with Colin Baker's Buttons and Nicola Bryant's Cinders joined by Anthony Ainley, Mary Tamm and upcoming *Two Doctors* guest star Jacqueline Pearce (AKA evil space dominatrix Servalan off of *Blake's 7*). Baker had let it be known he'd rather have Christmas off, but was talked round by his producer, and offered 2% of the box office takings. Unfortunately, the production ended up making a loss, leaving its knackered star with... well, buttons.

Previously, on *Doctor Who*...

On the morning of the new season's January 5th debut, Colin Baker and Nicola Bryant returned to the *Saturday Superstore* studio, accompanied by Jacqueline Pearce. Viewer

questions were almost exclusively directed at Baker, leaving Bryant and Pearce feeling even more self-conscious than usual as they sat holding the pretend-phones to their ears. "Is it true you're going to get a robot cat?", one youngster asked the Time Lord, hopefully. He did his best to let him down gently.

Baker has described this period as one of the happiest times of his life as an actor. And with just shy of nine million people tuning in to watch the first part of *Attack of the Cybermen* (despite the disappointingly early 5.20pm timeslot), the omens were good.

Which is more than can be said for the story itself. To be fair, it starts well: the early scenes of a bunch of lags casing a bank job have a gritty, naturalistic quality more familiar from Euston Films fare such as *Minder* and *The Sweeney* than the stagey, studio-bound space opera of the preceding few years. As it progresses, though, the serial begins to collapse beneath the combined weight of muddled writing and an avalanche of continuity porn.

This latter aspect is perhaps not surprising when you learn that one of several people claiming authorship of *Attack of the Cybermen* is Ian Levine, who was still dutifully providing his services as the show's unofficial continuity consultant. Known by the production team as "Evil Annie", Levine was always available at the end of a phone to answer pressing questions about Venum Grub breeding cycles or the correct number of spikes on a Zolfa-Thuran. Continuity was increasingly important to John Nathan-Turner, who seemed to enjoy his own celebrity status among fans – particularly fans in the US – and, according to his critics at least, increasingly pandered to the hardcore faithful at the expense of the wider audience.

That said, you don't *need* an in-depth knowledge of Cyber history to understand the basic plot of *Attack of the Cybermen*. To be fair to... whoever wrote it (we'll come to that), it's all pretty much laid out there on screen for newcomers, and the central threat – the Cybermen's homeworld of Mondas has been destroyed, and they want to retroactively undo that defeat – is clear-cut enough. Instead, the continuity references are tossed out like doggy treats to reward "proper" fans (or casual viewers who just happen to have photographic memories). Which only makes the production designer's lack of attention to detail all the more baffling: clearly no-one bothered to take so much as a cursory glance at what the catacombs in *Tomb of the Cybermen* actually looked like, which is why they're re-imagined here as a cross between a supermarket freezer section and a spray-tan salon. (Though they did go to the effort of filming in the same Gerrard's Cross quarry as Patrick Troughton and company had used 20 years earlier.)

In one spectacularly wrongheaded sop to the past, it was decided to hire Michael Kilgarriff to reprise his role as the Cyber Controller from 18 years earlier. Unfortunately, Kilgarriff had – how to put this? – let himself go a bit by this time, the results of which appeared to contradict the fifth Doctor's *Earthshock* speech about the Cybermen not appreciating the value of a well-prepared meal. Imagine re-making *The Karate Kid* with a 51-year-old Ralph Macchio, and you'll have some idea of just how preposterous the Fat Controller[III] looks waddling around on Telos – or was it Mondas? – like a Teletubby on work experience at NASA.

The story features further low-rent stunt casting in the form of impressionist Faith Brown – whose career effectively ended the day Margaret Thatcher resigned – and ex-*Blue Peter* presenter Sarah Greene. Greene's role was originally taken by Koo Stark – who had appeared in some soft-core erotica before finding fleeting tabloid currency as the squeeze of HRH Prince Andrew – but she is alleged to have walked out during rehearsals. It hardly mattered though, as the actresses had been cast as members of an alien race called the Cryons, and were so heavily disguised beneath elaborate perspex headpieces they could have been played by Cannon and Ball, for all anyone knew.

Attack of the Cybermen is credited to Paula Moore – a pen-name for Paula Wolsey, who was Eric Saward's girlfriend at the time. Arguments about who *actually* wrote it still rage to this day – with the various claimants actually appearing to *want* the credit for it, bizarrely enough – but the best guess is that Saward wrote the script from a rough (possibly *very* rough) story outline supplied by Levine. Either that, or Saward genuinely did sit back and let his girlfriend hammer away at the key-

board producing any old rubbish – the Linda McCartney of *Doctor Who*, effectively.

Given Levine's specific remit was to advise on continuity, it's remarkable how the story he had the biggest hand in drives a coach and horses through established events. The Cybermen's big plan here is to destroy the Earth with Halley's Comet in order to save their home planet – except that *The Tenth Planet* was at pains to stress that Mondas *needs* the Earth in order to survive, so clearly that little escapade was never going to end well. And, just to add an extra frisson of tension, the Cybes have also decided to mine their adopted home world of Telos and blow it up, apparently for no other reason than they think it's a cool thing to do.

The story also came under fire for its level of violence – most controversially, a scene in which the space mercenary Lytton literally has blood on his hands after a particularly firm Cyber handshake. Again, much of the aggression comes from the Doctor himself: he blasts the Cybercontroller with a massive gun, stabs another kettlehead in the chest with his "sonic lance" (nothing as mimsy as a screwdriver for *this* guy) and blithely tells Peri to shoot a policeman. Whether he is still supposed to be suffering a post-regenerative fugue, or is basically now just a bit of a headcase, isn't obvious. But it's clear from the next serial that he's only just getting started...

Sun, sex and sadism

Vengeance on Varos is a gloomy parable set on a dystopian world in which bored, desensitised television viewers vote to inflict torture and humiliation on the luckless stooges on the screen. Yeah, like *that* would ever happen.

It's ironic that such a thoughtful critique of the medium – and the then-current boom in "video nasties"[IV] – should end up attracting flak for its own lapses in taste, but Philip Martin's script certainly doesn't stint on the macabre imagery, from acid bath deaths to facial disfiguration to reptilian transmogrification and, worst of all, the sight of two old men running around in nappies (I believe there are specialist clubs for that sort of thing). One correspondent to the *Radio Times* described the story as "exceeding the atrocities of World War II," which Philip Martin found so amusing he pinned up a copy in his downstairs loo, while the *Telegraph* railed against the serial's "unaccustomed crudity, sex and sadism" (which makes it sound way more exciting than it really is).

Certainly, the sixth Doctor is at his most sadistic here, rigging up a deadly trap for the (quite clearly mentally disturbed) nappy men and responding to the sight of two guards dissolving in sulphuric acid with a Bondian quip. He also continues to act like a petulant child, uncharacteristically chucking the towel in when the TARDIS runs out of power and dismissing Peri's distress at this with a withering "You'll die soon enough". Even Jo Grant never had to put up with this much shit.

Despite this, the story's use of a Greek chorus device, in which two bored viewers watch everything unfold with glassy-eyed ennui, is brave and innovative, Martin Jarvis is reliably good as the weak and compromised Governor, and Nabil Shaban is simply glorious as the oleaginous corporate hustler Sil, arguably the one great villain of the Colin Baker era. (Shaban, who was born with the genetic bone disorder osteogenesis imperfecta, spent the entire story squeezed in to what was effectively a slug costume, while a constant diet of peaches – serving as an alien delicacy called marsh minnows – gave him the runs. You do the math.)

The main thrust of the plot – a thinly-veiled allegory for oil cartels in which Sil conspires to artificially rig the price of Varos' most precious mineral commodity – *feels* grown up, but then flunks it by misunderstanding the nature of supply-side economics that would be obvious to any GCSE student. Ron Jones' direction is flat and uninspired, and the less said about Jason Connery's excruciating performance as an over-earnest freedom fighter the better. (When your dad's James Bond, acting must seem like a very tempting career choice. Perhaps he should have given it a try.)

And yet, despite all this, there are enough interesting ideas here – the cliffhanger, in which Varosian viewers apparently witness the Doctor's protracted death throes until the Governor orders "And cut it... now", is an enjoyably postmodern touch – to qualify

Vengeance on Varos as one of the more successful experiments of the period.

The Mark of the Rani is notable for featuring the debut of Kate O'Mara as the titular renegade Time Lady (the Rani, not Mark) and, perhaps more significantly, Pip and Jane Baker. More – oh so much more – on them later. The story itself is a pretty-looking piece of historical fluff combining elements of Catherine Cookson (cloth-capped, salt-of-the-earth Geordie pitmen), *Dynasty* (O'Mara's campy space bitch), *Last of the Summer Wine* (the Doctor races downhill strapped to a trolley, with hilarious consequences) and a very low budget school production of *The Lord of the Rings* (Peri is groped by a rubber tree).

The Rani's diabolical scheme involves extracting the brain chemicals of miners, thus robbing them of sleep and leaving them running around like half-crazed coke fiends, intent on smashing up the nearest non-condensing steam engine (or finding the nearest all-night garage – whichever is easier). Unfortunately for her, old school chum the Master is also in town with his latest bonkers plan to harness the geniuses of the Industrial Revolution in order to turn the Earth into the seat of a galactic empire (or something like that). But mainly he's preoccupied with annoying the Doctor, going to a lot of effort to drag the TARDIS off course so the Time Lord can basically ruin all his plans. Will he *never* learn?

Director Sarah Hellings extracts maximum value from the fabulous heritage location to deliver the most visually sumptuous *Doctor Who* story in years, Kate O'Mara is deliciously arch, and there's a pleasingly simple, almost languorous charm to the story, so long as you don't poke about in its internal logic too vigorously. (Sydney Newman, for one, would be pleased to see the show rediscovering its educational remit, with the likes of George Stephenson, Thomas Telford and Humphrey Davy breathlessly promoted as among these islands' greatest heroes.)

If anything lets *The Mark of the Rani* down – apart from that tree, which really does have to be seen to be believed – it's the writers' alarming propensity for an overly baroque turn of phrase. "Unfortunate? Fortuitous would be a more apposite epithet," bibbles the Master – shortly before threatening to have the TARDIS thrown down t'pit: "All the way down," he gloats, "to the bottom!"

With a script by Robert Holmes and guest turns by Patrick Troughton and Frazer Hines – not to mention the long-awaited return of spud-headed faves the Sontarans, and all filmed on location in sunny Spain – *The Two Doctors* should have been the season's tentpole event story. But the serial has ended up being remembered for all the wrong reasons. Firstly, Holmes' script is all over the place: ostensibly a story about the Sontarans wanting to crack the secret of time travel by dissecting the Doctor, it ends up getting weirdly sidetracked into an extended piece of vegetarian propaganda, full of over-ripe dialogue – "I have a desire to taste one of these human beasts; the meat looks so white and roundsomely layered on the bone" – and humour so black, it sucks all Holmes' usual lightness of touch into its pitiless grip; the sequence in which resting actor-turned-restaurateur Oscar milks his death scene after being brutally stabbed tries to walk a perilous tightrope between funny and touching, but just ends up being *horribly* tasteless. Left stranded alone on a space station, meanwhile, Jamie's natural response is to start crawling about the infrastructure life a feral beastie, wrapping himself in dirty rags and protecting his pile of animal bones by fending off interlopers with an inhuman growl. At least until the Doctor and Peri turn up, anyway, after which he has a wash and is basically fine.

Peter Moffatt directs as if he missed the flight from Gatwick, not least when he chooses to introduce the Sontarans – an A-list *Doctor Who* monster making their first appearance for seven years – in long shot, ambling about the Spanish countryside like British tourists who've gone a bit crispy in the sun.

If the Sontarans are badly served – and the new costumes are hopeless; less "nasty, brutish and short" than "clumsy, ill-fitting and surprisingly tall" – that's nothing compared to the indignities heaped upon poor Patrick Troughton, who spends most of the three-hour running time either strapped to a bed or staring out from beneath two orange caterpillars as he slowly morphs into Russ Abbot's See You Jimmy (actually an Androgum – a gluttonous race of warty barbarians with the permanent

munchies). This means we see get to see very little of the classic, impish Troughton we all know and love – and there's a disappointing lack of Doctor-on-Doctor action (so to speak), to boot – which, given that was the reason Troughton was hired in the first place, is nothing short of baffling. (Also, we'd expect Robert Holmes, of all people, to know that the second Doctor couldn't have been sent on a mission for the Time Lords prior to the events of *The War Games*. Presumably, Ian Levine was too busy cross-checking the number of spots on his hankie or something.)

By the time the third episode ramps up the cultural tourism – the leisurely strolls around Seville come complete with flamenco guitar soundtrack and, at one point, a señorita tossing a rose from a balcony – the whole thing starts to feel a bit like one of those feature-length sitcom episodes where the cast all go to the Costa del Sol. Except this one's a lot harder to take seriously.

And as if the main event wasn't indigestible enough, the edition of *Jim'll Fix It* broadcast immediately after the second instalment saw Colin Baker and Janet Fielding (standing in for a holidaying Nicola Bryant) starring in a mini *Doctor Who* adventure, *A Fix With Sontarans*, in which one excitable chap fulfils his dream of dressing up as the Doctor and playing with the TARDIS controls. Some kid called Gareth Jenkins got to join in, too.

But perhaps the main reason *The Two Doctors* is imprinted on the minds of every fan of a certain vintage is because it was during the broadcast of this story that The Bomb Dropped. Not *the* bomb, obviously – though even the none-more-80s prospect of a nuclear winter would have been preferable in some *Doctor Who* fans' eyes to what actually happened on February 27th, 1985, when Sue Lawley soberly announced on the *BBC Six O'Clock News* that *Doctor Who* had been cancelled. Until next year, anyway.

Dr Who is not axed
in BBC plot

Even now, almost 30 years on, no-one seems quite sure of the exact sequence of events that led to production of *Doctor Who's* twenty-third season being put on hold in 1985. According to Sue Lawley on that news bulletin, *Doctor Who* was "to take a rest": "The Time Lord, who's been on our screens for some 22 years now," intoned Sue, with funereal solemnity, "will be off the air for 18 months. The Doctor Who Appreciation Society is up in arms – they've called the decision 'horrifying and staggering'."

That's a bit strong, clearly. But many believed the 18-month thing was a red herring. *The Sun* certainly did: its front page splash screamed "Dr Who is Axed in Plot by BBC", and it was one of several tabloids to launch its own Save Dr Who campaign (the *Daily Star* even had button badges).

Years later, Jonathan Powell, who was the BBC's head of series and serials at the time, went on record to concede that, yes, the original plan had been much more drastic than a nine-month delay to the start of the next series. "We did try to cancel it," he admitted. "Bill Cotton, the Managing Director, Michael Grade and myself. But the reaction was so severe, the *Doctor Who* fans at one point threatened to picket the House of Commons with Daleks."[1]

"I was summoned to a meeting," Powell told John Nathan-Turner's biographer, Richard Marson, "after we'd cancelled it. Keith Samuels, who was head of press, said, 'If they take the Daleks to the House of Commons, that photograph will be on the front page of every newspaper in the entire world'. At which point we said, 'Okay, maybe we haven't cancelled it – maybe it will come back in a year's time'." The BBC running scared of tabloid headlines? Unthinkable today, of course. "It was hard," added Powell, "because the *Doctor Who* lobby was quite a fearsome lobby, actually. Though why we couldn't all fucking stand up and say, 'Look, this programme has come to an end, it's run its course', I don't quite know."[4]

Michael Grade was the target of most of the tabloid fury, and had to endure a rash of bad newspaper cartoons depicting him as a Dalek

– John Nathan-Turner even claimed to have received a call from the US asking if he'd like Grade "wiped out", presumably by the paramilitary wing of the North American Doctor Who Fan Club. This may explain why, when he appeared on the BBC comedy *Room 101* a couple of decades later, *Doctor Who* was one of the things Grade chose to consign to the show's repository of nightmares. "I thought it was pathetic," he said. "I'd seen *Star Wars* and *Close Encounters* and then I had to watch these cardboard things clonking across the floor trying to scare kids. You'd just sit and laugh at it." Not that he's a man to hold a grudge or anything.

If anything, Jonathan Powell showed even more antipathy towards the show – and its producer. "If one would have loved *Doctor Who*, one would have found a way of doing it," he admitted. "Nobody loved it. Nobody loved *him* [Nathan-Turner]. Well they might have loved him down on the studio floor but up at my level he didn't have any allies. I didn't really want to help him, that's the truth of the matter and, in any case, he didn't have any intelligent views on the thing. In the end, in everybody's mind, if we couldn't cancel it because of the bloody *Doctor Who* society, we just wanted it to die, and sadly he became part of that process."[4]

Not that Powell or the people at "his level" were able to offer any "intelligent views" of their own: in sharp contrast to his predecessor David Reid's detailed script notes, Powell had passed all the scripts for Season Twenty-Two with minimal – and generally positive – comment (he'd described *The Two Doctors* script as "excellent" – then monstered the finished result). If we didn't know better, we might think he hadn't bothered reading them at all. ("Enjoyed the bit where the guy said the thing about the thing. Needs more K-9, though.") Also, *Doctor Who* was, in fact, still doing pretty brisk business for the Beeb. Their own news bulletin had talked of it attracting "over seven million viewers" in the UK (the 1985 series average was 7.12 million – perfectly respectable, though only half the number tuning in to see *The A-Team's* BA, Hannibal and company do a bit of impromptu spot-welding on what was still known back then as "the other side") and "110 million worldwide". Perhaps the "lack of institutional willpower" really boiled down to a few people in key positions not liking it. Eric Saward certainly thinks so – he recalls Powell actually nodding off during one producer's playback. Though, to be fair, it may well have been *Arc of Infinity*.

Despite these enemies in high places, the "BBC plot" referred to by *The Sun* was, in fact, a bit of counter-spin dreamed up by a distraught John Nathan-Turner and Ian Levine, who between them had hatched a plan to leak the cancellation story to the press, with the faintly ludicrous cover story that the Beeb was effectively holding *Doctor Who* hostage in order to extract a better licence fee settlement from the Government. Whether they went as far as chaining Colin Baker to a radiator isn't known, but, as the frontman of this top-secret BBC black ops unit, Levine did at least get to use the Corporation's own cool, super-spy tabloid codename. It was Snowball.

Nicola Bryant was out of the country at the time of the announcement – possibly pretending to visit her folks in America – and, on her return, was phoned up by a reporter who asked her: "What do you think about the death of Doctor Who?" She recalled putting the phone down in shock, thinking Colin Baker had died. If true, it certainly wasn't the most sensitive way of phrasing the question – though it is a nostalgic reminder of the days when journalists actually bothered to phone you up, instead of just listening to your voicemails.

As the media storm built, at one point DWAS co-ordinator David Saunders[V] was scheduled for a smackdown on breakfast telly with Michael Grade himself – until the channel controller decided he'd prefer to keep his head down on a skiing holiday in the French Alps. (No such luck – the paparazzi just followed him there.) Patrick Troughton also reported for duty at the *Doctor Who* production office, manning the phones to anguished fans. ("Hello, I'm not sure if I've got the right office – is that *Doctor Who*?" "Speaking.")

At what exact point *Doctor Who* was spared the axe remains moot. Was the 18-month hiatus – and hiatus was *the* buzzword among Whovians in 1985, despite some people making a late bid for "interregnum" – a cover story to soften the public up for the show's eventual cancellation? (In retrospect, it does seem odd that a small delay between seasons of a TV show was considered worthy of the main evening news, especially a show the BBC seemed to be suggesting no-one gave a toss about any more anyway.) Or had Powell, Grade and company, the distant thunder of tabloid sound and fury rumbling in their ears, already rowed back by the time of that initial announcement?

Whatever the chronology, it's clear the series had already won a reprieve by the time 20-odd – and I do mean odd – people gathered in a London recording studio for what surely still stands as one of the most ill-conceived enterprises in *Doctor Who*'s long history.

In November 1984, Bob Geldof, the famously dishevelled singer with Irish punk outfit the Boomtown Rats, had organised the Band Aid charity single "Do They Know It's Christmas?" in response to the devastating famine threatening millions of lives in the Horn of Africa. Using their contacts within the industry, Geldof and his co-conspirator Midge Ure marshalled an impressive line-up of reigning rock and pop aristocracy, including George Michael, Sting, U2, Paul Weller, Culture Club, Duran Duran, Spandau Ballet, Simple Minds, Tears for Fears, Status Quo and Paul McCartney.

In March 1985, Gary Downie, unfamously bearded former hoofer with Pan's People-turned BBC production manager, organised the Who Cares charity single "Doctor in Distress" in response to the slight delay in transmission of the next series of *Doctor Who*. Using their contacts within the industry, Downie and his co-conspirator Ian Levine marshalled a line-up of... well, let's just say they marshalled a line-up, including Faith Brown, Hazell Dean, Floyd Pearce from Hot Gossip, Bobby G from Bucks Fizz, John Rocca from Freeez, David Van Day from Dollar, two members of Matt Bianco and Sally Thomsett off of *Man About the House*.

Early reports suggesting Elton John, Holly Johnson and the Village People would be taking part proved unfounded (perhaps they weren't considered camp enough), but the stellar chorus was complemented by the inclusion of Colin Baker, Nicola Bryant and those famed hi-NRG disco divas Nicholas Courtney and Anthony Ainley.

The song itself, co-written by Levine and

our old friend Fiachra Trench, was a doomed attempt to tell the entire history of *Doctor Who* in three verses, which inevitably ended up running out of road mid-way through the Troughton era. Though they did find room for the immortal couplet: "There was the Brigadier and the Master and a canine computer / Each screaming girl just hoped that a Yeti wouldn't shoot her". The chorus meanwhile, was a revolutionary call to arms that declared: "Eighteen months is too long to wait / Bring back the Doctor, don't hesitate!"

Perhaps realising that the scheduling of a TV show wasn't quite as emotive an issue as a Biblical famine, it was decided that all profits from the single would go to Cancer Research. Suffice to say, there *were* no profits – Levine estimates the record sold less than a thousand copies, while thousands more had to be melted down. "It was an absolute balls-up fiasco," he said later. "It was pathetic and bad and stupid. It almost ruined me."[5] Someone who did escape with his reputation intact, though, was Hans Zimmer: the man who knocked out that grating tune on a Fairlight II went on to become one of Hollywood's leading film composers, winning an Academy Award for *The Lion King*.

Though they were soon to fall out spectacularly, to this day Ian Levine maintains fighting for the show's survival in 1985 was John Nathan-Turner's finest hour. "If he hadn't done that, they would have cancelled the show," he said. "The BBC said they were going to rest it for a while and bring it back. They had no intention of doing that. It was a lie."[4]

Richard III wannabe told to stop being a dick

Meanwhile, all those people who had been up in arms about the proposed cancellation of this classic British institution tuned in to see what it was they loved so much about it – and were greeted with *Timelash*.

Like *The Twin Dilemma*, *Timelash* – or *Lame Shit*, as it is more commonly known among anagram enthusiasts – has since become short-hand for *Doctor Who* at its most enervated, not least because of the Timelash itself, which is sold to us as "a fate worse than death" but is, in fact, a large room with a gaudy climbing

wall, from which hangs a few limp strands of tinsel. Yes, actual tinsel. Middle-class viewers were appalled. ("I mean, *tinsel*? What's wrong with a nice sprig of holly?")

The tinsel is positively tasteful, however, compared with Paul Darrow's gobsmacking performance as the villainous Maylin Tekker – puppet ruler of the planet Karfel – which, astonishingly, the *Blake's 7* actor was allowed to get away with playing as a showboating pastiche of Olivier's Richard III (apparently he even suggested a hump at one point). Legend has it Darrow had decided to get his own back on Colin Baker for the latter's similarly restrained guest turn in *Blake's 7* (Baker had played an assassin called Bayban the Butcher, whose prime cut was a hefty side of ham). As far as we know, Olivier never saw fit to return the compliment by playing Lear in the style of Avon off *Blake's 7*.

Karfel's despotic ruler is the Borad, who became hideously disfigured (there's a lot of it about in *Doctor Who* in this era) when his experiments saw him biologically merged with indigenous giant worms the Morlox. (It's probably best not to dwell on how.) The Borad envisages the same fate for Peri (will people never stop groping the poor girl?), while forcing the Doctor to enter the Timelash to retrieve the amulet that gives him the source of his power. At the end of this tinsel time corridor, the Doctor meets a young HG Wells, who feverishly makes notes of everything the Time Lord does – an idea so clunkingly obvious, you can see why everyone had wisely resisted it for the past 22 years.

The script, by Glen McCoy – whose previous writing credits included the classic 1981 tome *Jobs in the Ambulance Service and Hospitals* – is iffy, but might have been rescued by good performances and direction. Sadly, it gets neither: Pennant Roberts seems to think it's enough to make sure the camera is pointing the right way (which, to be fair, it generally is), while the guest actors are almost universally dire, with the notable exception of Robert Ashby's quietly menacing Borad. (Rumour has it Eric Saward wrote the character this way as a direct challenge to Colin Baker's assertion that there had been no other way to play Bayban the Butcher.)

The drab sets display more acres of white

than a Scottish nudist beach – a shortcoming not helped by being lit like an episode of *Blankety Blank* – and, for a story apparently set more than 20,000 years in our future, the costumes all appear to have been stolen from Spandau Ballet's dressing room.

The whole sorry saga ends with an appearance by the ambassador of planetary rivals the Bandrils, who is not so much a puppet ruler as an *actual* glove puppet. You half expect him to ask, "What do you think of it so far, boys and girls?" To which the answer, of course, would have been: rubbish.

Colin Baker's debut season concluded with Eric Saward's *Revelation of the Daleks*, a black comedy inspired in part by Evelyn Waugh's *The Loved Ones* that majors on death, with a side serving of sex, incest, alcoholism and at least one proper nob gag, as well as lashings of violence and body horror (including Peri battering a poor mutant[VI] to death with a tree branch) and a truly grotesque Dalek-human hybrid with its internal organs growing on the outside of his head, begging for a merciful death. And all before *Jim'll Fix It*.

What it didn't have, though, was flying Daleks: this was supposed to be the serial that finally put paid to all those lame jokes about stairs, but the mechanics of firing two full-size Dalek props from a spring-loaded platform proved too costly. (If you're confused, kids, this was in the days before CGI – ask your parents.) And this despite the fact they'd managed to save some money by re-using sets from other series like *The Little and Large Show*.

Saward is clearly on a mission to best even his great hero Robert Holmes in the macabre humour stakes: Davros is now running a funeral parlour-cum-cryogenic suspension facility, earning the soubriquet the Great Healer for eradicating hunger in the galaxy by recycling his clients into food, while at the same time harvesting their organs to create a new race of Daleks. Oh, and he's also hired a DJ (Alexei Sayle) to keep the stiffs happy with classic Earth rock and roll hits. Meanwhile, preening, toupee-d funeral director Jobel (an extraordinary performance from Clive Swift) takes sadistic pleasure in rebuffing the affections of smitten student Tasambeker (an even more – ahem – extraordinary performance from Jenny Tomasin), to the point where she

stabs him with a hypodermic syringe and he slumps to the floor, losing his life and his wig in that order. Throw in a pair of bodysnatchers and a noble assassin (William Gaunt) with a faulty hydraulic leg, and there's little room for either the Doctor or the Daleks. (This is nothing new: Saward leaves the sixth Doctor on the sidelines so often during this era, many have speculated he was doing it deliberately in protest at what he saw as Baker's mis-casting. But it reaches critical mass here, with the Doctor and Peri not arriving at the scene of the action until what, in old money, would have been the third episode.)

Back in the director's chair (not that he sat in it much), Graeme Harper proves the flourish he'd brought to the fifth Doctor's swansong was no fluke: kinetic camera work and an empathetic understanding of the script's sepulchral mood and pace lift this light years above anyone else's work on the series at the time (though he struck lucky with the weather: heavy snow during the location shoot in Hampshire lends the planet Necros a distinctive aesthetic quality and, as a bonus, means Colin Baker gets to cover up that bloody coat).

Though *Revelation of the Daleks* is probably not what *Doctor Who* ought to be – and especially not at twenty past five in the afternoon – its combination of morbid wit and directorial flair stacks up as probably the single most successful serial of the Colin Baker era. Sadly, few were in a mood to look beyond the surface detail, and the story's adult themes and massive body count only added succour to the claim that *Doctor Who* had become too violent. In reality, this argument was as specious as it had been every other time it had reared its blue-rinsed head, which it was wont to do at least once every decade. The difference was, this time it was the BBC itself that was making it, the show's enemies on the Corporation's sixth floor seizing upon it as another excuse to put the boot in. At the time, Mary Whitehouse was actually more concerned with what ITV was putting out in opposition to *Doctor Who*: the fantasy series *Robin of Sherwood*, a fantastical re-telling of the Robin Hood legend, had already raised Christian hackles with its pagan poster boy hero – spiritual son of the tree god Herne the Hunter. By the time Rula Lenska and a cabal of half-naked nuns summoned the

Devil himself into existence, like a Ken Russell movie shown at teatime, Whitehouse was apoplectic. By contrast, a couple of bloody fists in *Attack of the Cybermen* – which made Lytton look like he'd been pruning a particularly tricksy rose bush – seemed very tame.

Revelation was supposed to end with the Doctor promising to take Peri on that trip to Blackpool. In the event, the frame was frozen before Baker could namecheck the greasy own-brand Vegas – not because Hampstead-dwelling BBC execs were too squeamish to hear the word, but because plans for the next series were already being torn up as production on *Doctor Who* was wound down.

The Blackpool jaunt would have seen the Doctor and Peri facing off against Michael Gough's Celestial Toymaker – last seen on screen in 1966 – and Graham Williams' script for *The Nightmare Fair* was well advanced by the time the axe fell. Two other stories were also in development: *The Ultimate Evil*, by Wally K Daly (no relation to Wile E Coyote, as far as we know), was based around an evil arms-dealing dwarf, while *Mission to Magnus* envisaged a team-up between Sil (so wheeler-dealers of restricted height very much the theme with that year's villains) and, back after an absence of more than a decade, the Ice Warriors. Like Colin Baker and Nicola Bryant (along with Nabil Shaban, who had already been contracted), most of the writers for this lost season were paid in full, with the total write-off amounting to £89,471 (more than £200,000 in today's money).

Despite production grinding to a halt, Nathan-Turner and Saward still had to turn up for work, spending the next three months rattling around Television Centre like lost souls. "When you're a staff producer, there's nothing more degrading than sitting round in an office not making programmes,"[2] said Nathan-Turner. Which isn't strictly true – he could have been sitting around making *The Tripods*. (The BBC's adaptation of John Christopher's sci-fi novels was launched with great fanfare in 1984, and some at the BBC clearly saw it as the shiny new alternative to wheezy old *Doctor Who*. Unfortunately, budget restrictions limited the screen time available to the titular three-legged tyrants, and the result was so boring it was pulled after just two seasons. Not even

Matt Bianco could be bothered to record a protest song about that one.)

Jonathan Powell later admitted that he had originally wanted to put a new production team in place for *Doctor Who*'s re-launch but "couldn't find anybody else to do it". Well it's not like BBC's Head of Series and Serials just has a load of TV producers he can call up out of the blue, is it? "If I'd loved the programme," he conceded, "I would have gone and somehow found a producer. I didn't know what to do. I had no ideas. Also, what was I going to do with fucking John Nathan-Turner? What was he going to do? I didn't want him doing anything else because I didn't think he was good enough. You didn't want to give him stuff because you didn't trust him. I wanted him to fuck off and solve it – or die, really."[4] (Nathan-Turner had to admit, it wasn't the *best* annual appraisal he'd ever had.)

Colin Baker, meanwhile, had decided to make the best of the situation: his wife had just given birth to a baby daughter, so the actor looked upon the hiatus as paid paternity leave. He was technically free to undertake other work, so long as he phoned the BBC every day to check his services weren't required. ("Hello, it's Colin Baker here. Will you be needing a Doctor Who today? No? Okay, fine. Anything else you'd like me to do? Quiz show? Voiceover? Bit of plastering? Someone to run the hoover round?")

In between changing nappies and sterilising bottles, the star's public engagements – much of which was dedicated to raising money for cot death research – included switching on British Telecom's new speaking clock ("the time until the next episode of *Doctor Who* will be 13,147 hours precisely") and opening a supermarket in Reading and a Texas Homecare store in Preston. (He'd have preferred a Preston Homecare store in Texas, but you took the work where you could find it.)

Less is less

What Colin Baker didn't know was that, behind the scenes, John Nathan-Turner was fighting for his leading man's job. In April, the producer met with Michael Grade and Jonathan Powell to discuss the way forward for *Doctor Who*, during which Grade argued Baker ought to be replaced. Despite the BBC's Audience Research Report for the twenty-second season concluding Baker's performance had been "not highly regarded", Nathan-Turner succeeded in convincing his bosses the actor deserved more time.

That summer, Baker did make room in his diary for one outing as the Time Lord, when he and Bryant recorded a *Doctor Who* radio serial, *Slipback*. The story was broadcast in frustratingly random ten-minute chunks during the school holidays as part of a magazine programme called *Pirate Radio 4* – a doomed, Reithian attempt to attract a younger audience to Middle England's favourite radio station, presumably in the hope they'd stay on to listen to *Money Box* and *The World at One*. They might as well have plonked *Gardener's Question Time* in the middle of *Swap Shop*.

The serial itself was written by Eric Saward who, perhaps inspired by the medium, delivered a noisily unfunny Douglas Adams pastiche about a spaceship under threat from a computer with a split personality and a deranged captain deliberately incubating contagious spores with which to infect his crew. It also saw Saward pushing his vision of a, shall we say, less heroic leading man by opening with the Doctor nursing a pounding hangover after a heavy night on the sauce. Among its many shortcomings, *Slipback* would prove an ignominious valedictory turn for radio legend Valentine Dyall, who died shortly before it was broadcast. Though, on the plus side, the sixth Doctor's costume had never looked better.

After all the hand-wringing and soul-searching of the previous months, in late 1985, the BBC execs finally unveiled their masterplan to re-launch *Doctor Who* as a reinvigorated brand fit for the post-*Star Wars* paradigm. Their big idea? Make less of it.

Having publicly savaged the production team for their lack of inspiration and imagination, Grade, Powell and company eventually went back to the very same people and simply told them to get on with it, offering no more guidance or instructions beyond toning down the violence and reverting to the traditional 25-minute format. They also hit on the genius idea that, if they made roughly the same number of episodes, but made them roughly half as long... well, that ought to free up a bit of cash

for that exciting new Bobby Davro vehicle light ents had mentioned.

Rumours that *Who* fans might be about to be served a short-measure first surfaced as early as April 1985, when Ian Levine told a convention audience the next series was likely to be reduced to twenty 25-minute episodes. Levine was followed on stage, somewhat awkwardly, by John Nathan-Turner and Colin Baker, where the producer wasted no time in denouncing his former collaborator's claims as "rabble-rousing". The following month's issue of the Doctor Who Appreciation Society newsletter ran an article on the convention, under the headline "Who Do You Believe?", in which it compared Levine's performance to "a Hitler rally". And the name of this rancorous, ill-tempered event? DWASocial 5.

To help fans fill the long gap between seasons – or 15 minutes of it, anyway – Nathan-Turner published a book, *The TARDIS Inside Out*. Claiming to offer "fresh insight" into the history of the show, it was little more than a few sketchy anecdotes about the producer's dealings with the six actors who had played the Doctor – *very* sketchy, in William Hartnell's case, as Nathan-Turner had never actually met him. The pictures were nice, though. And *The TARDIS Inside Out* was Booker Prize material compared with the other non-fiction title published in the spring of 1985, as Nathan-Turner's other half, Gary Downie, got in on the act with *The Doctor Who Cookbook*, in which cast and crew were strongarmed into providing their favourite recipes. Or, failing that, any recipe that could be given an amusing *Doctor Who* name – hence Patrick Troughton's Vegetable Soup with Dalek Krotons and Johnny Byrne's (wait for it) Kipper of Traken. Other mouthwatering treats included Janet Fielding's Ocker Balls (don't ask, or you might get kicked in them) – and if you've ever wanted a full-page picture of Fiona Cumming tucking into a slice of gateau, this is the place. Barry Letts, meanwhile, took a more whimsical approach with an unnamed dish from Venus, the ingredients for which included Grated Snadge. And he always seemed like such a gentleman.

The row over the number of episodes allocated for the forthcoming season continued to simmer over the summer until, in September, the BBC sent a fax to *Doctor Who*'s US distributors, Lionheart, confirming the next series would actually consist of just 14 25-minute episodes. Or at least, they *meant* to send it to Lionheart – with the professionalism and competence we've come to expect from this particular era of BBC management, they actually faxed it to the president of the American Doctor Who fan club. I think the word you're looking for is "d'oh!".

Still, it was 14 more episodes than the current production team had been expecting. When John Nathan-Turner and Eric Saward discovered, much to their surprise, that they would be the men charged with making the next series of *Doctor Who* after all, they probably wished they'd spent more time in recent months thinking up story ideas and less time trying to get scrunched-up balls of paper into the waste basket.

In desperation, Saward called up his good friend Bob Holmes. ("Whatever you do," Holmes must have suggested, "you're going to have to come up with something pretty special because, in many ways, this is your last chance. It's like you're on trial for your life... like the Doctor himself is *on trial for his very life*." At which point Saward asked: "I know – any ideas?")

In truth, Saward and Holmes had cooked up the concept of reflecting the show's behind-the-scenes travails in the on-screen drama fairly early on in the "cancellation crisis". A story in which a bearded man in a Hawaiian shirt spends 14 weeks sobbing into a polystyrene cup would have been a bit close to the bone, so they hit on the idea of a season-long trial scenario instead, with Nathan-Turner chipping in with a *Christmas Carol*-style "past, present and future" element.

The plan was to top and tail the season with stories by Holmes, with the other segments made up of a revised Sil re-match by Philip Martin – which would see the departure of Nicola Bryant, who had indicated her wish to move on – and a pair of two-parters from celebrated *Play for Today* writers David Halliwell and Jack Trevor Story. (The latter's effort – the Story story, if you will – had the in-no-way over-confident title *The Second Coming* and, from what we can gather, featured a man playing a saxophone inside a gasometer. Halliwell's

Attack of the Mind, meanwhile, concerned a conflict between the rat-like Freds and the sophisticated Penelopeans. Both scripts were eventually abandoned. Play for Today? Not today, thank you.)

In August, the Doctor regenerated into Lenny Henry for a sketch on the Brummie comic's hit BBC1 show. While not exactly laser-sharp satire – sample gag: "I'm the Doctor". "Great, 'cos I've got this really nasty rash on my back." – the skit was probably the first to mint the standard joke about running up and down corridors, and ended with the memorable image of a Cyberman complete with Margaret Thatcher's bouffant "do" and handbag. Not funny, but memorable.

The summer also saw the series parting company with two iconic features of every British *Doctor Who* fan's childhood: World Distributors' 1986 annual would prove to be the last gasp for the hardback tie-in that had reliably filled Christmas stockings every year since 1965 while, on the Golden Mile, the Doctor Who Exhibition closed its doors at the end of the season, never to re-open. Only two years after Longleat and the fanfare surrounding the 20th anniversary celebrations – not to mention the snowballing interest across the Atlantic – could Britain have been losing faith with *Doctor Who*? Or was it naïve to expect anything less when the BBC's own top brass had gone out of their way to tell everyone how shit it was?

In the face of all this, there was still something of a celebratory feel during November's *Children in Need* broadcast when no fewer than 22 cast members past and present filed out of the TARDIS to mark the show's 22nd birthday. Alongside Patrick Troughton, Jon Pertwee, Peter Davison and Colin Baker, the roll call included most of the companions from over the years, though eagle-eyed viewers may have noted the numbers being made up by a toy Dalek and a K-9 plushie. And Adrienne Hill.

And then, after months of rumours, denials and trash-talking, official public confirmation of the episode count for the new series finally came on December 18th – a good week to bury bad news under an avalanche of fake snow. Though, given that Eric Saward and company were currently struggling to fill even *that* many episodes, maybe it was a blessing in disguise.

Their disappointment at this latest setback notwithstanding, after the fractious, tumultuous events of the previous year, fans had every reason to look forward with optimism to 1986 – the year *Doctor Who* would put all the rows and recriminations behind it and return, refreshed and rejuvenated, to claim its rightful place at the heart of British family viewing. Oh, and did we mention Bonnie Langford was going to be in it?

In space, no-one can hear you thcream

Bonita Melody Lysette Langford had found fame as a child star – so, naturally, no-one could stand the sight of her. She had made her first appearance on stage aged just 15 months, and became a household name – whether those households liked it or not – when she won the talent show *Opportunity Knocks* with some juvenile song and dance business. She then went on to star in the BBC's 70s adpaptation of Richmal Crompton's *Just William* stories, playing a lisping, spoiled brat millionaire's daughter whose catchphrase was "I'll thcream and thcream 'till I'm thick". Seriously, what's not to love?

So we can only imagine Eric Saward's face when John Nathan-Turner collared him and said: "I was driving home last night and decided we needed a red-headed companion – what about Bonnie Langford?" There are two lessons we can take from this: one is that Nathan-Turner actually cast Langford's hair, and the rest of her came with it as a job lot. And the second is someone really ought to have taken his driving licence away from him by this point.

A despairing Saward persuaded Nathan-Turner she would have to be properly auditioned, and the producer reluctantly agreed. By his own admission, the script editor then set about writing an "incredibly complicated" audition piece to try to trip the actress up. Unfortunately for Saward, she made rather a good fist of it – which is just as well, as Nathan-Turner had already gone ahead and done the press call.

Langford was unveiled as the new compan-ion on Thursday, January 23rd, 1986. At the time, she was appearing as Peter Pan at London's Aldwych Theatre – so someone thought it would be a good wheeze to strap Colin Baker into a kirby harness and have him fly about alongside her. Baker would be the first to admit he is built for comfort, not flight, and the resulting image of him trussed up like a post-Christmas turkey must have brought tears to the eyes of even the most hardened tabloid hacks.

To her credit, Langford didn't lack self-awareness: she was the first to admit people were going to go "oh no" when she was announced as joining the show – which does make you wonder quite what Nathan-Turner was thinking. Ian Levine – to whom Nathan-Turner flatly denied he'd cast the actress – believes the producer hired her with one (or possibly both) eyes on his sideline career as a panto producer. But it's more likely Nathan-Turner cast her simply because he was a fan of musical theatre, and because he thought she'd generate publicity. Which, of course, she did – mainly from people saying "Bonnie Langford: are they bloody *mental*?"

Having dropped that little ginger bombshell, Nathan-Turner departed for one of his increasingly frequent US convention appearances – this time accompanying Patrick Troughton on a trip to Florida. Not that Eric Saward was bitter about being left to mind the shop while the boss swanned around in the sunshine again – why, the very idea. And his mood wasn't helped when Jonathan Powell passed judgement on the first seven scripts of the new season: in contrast to his previous give-a-damn approach, this time Powell "passed judgement" in the way a cat might pass judgement on a prized flower bed, forcing Saward to go back to Robert Holmes, a man he held in the highest esteem and who was not in the best of health, and demand rewrites.

By this time, replacement stories for the Jack Trevor Story story and the other one that's not as funny had been commissioned from Christopher H Bidmead and *Sapphire and Steel* creator PJ Hammond. Sadly, Bidmead's *Pinacotheca* was all Greek to Saward – much to the disgruntlement of his predecessor, who managed to secure payment in full for his troubles – while Hammond's *Paradise Five* quickly turned into Paradise Lost. In that sense, at least, it was pretty much business as usual.

In February, with production on the series just weeks away, John Nathan-Turner happened to bump into Pip and Jane Baker in a lift at Television Centre, and asked them to submit ideas for a four-part serial. The Bakers subsequent proposal was enough to win them the commission on the strength of its plot, ideas and did we mention they started filming the bloody thing in a few weeks' time? (And there is, we're assured, no truth to the rumour that Pip 'n' Jane had been up and down in the lift 155 times waiting for this "chance encounter" with the producer of *Doctor Who*.)

During March, Robert Holmes juggled rewrites on the season opener with his scripts for the two-part finale, *Time Inc*; by now, Eric Saward was largely working from home, the script editor having become increasingly estranged from his producer, and increasingly worried about the strain being placed on the unwell Holmes. Also, it meant he had less chance of running into Pip and Jane Baker in the lift.

On Friday, April 4th, Colin Baker and Nicola Bryant arrived on location at Queen Elizabeth Country Park in Hampshire and, four days later, the cameras finally turned again on *Doctor Who* – a mere 372 days later than originally scheduled. A press photocall saw the two stars camping it up with canes and straw boaters that was presumably designed to sell the message "the show must go on" – either that, or it was coming back as a musical.

A week or so later, Baker and Bryant were joined by Janet Fielding and John Nathan-Turner for another photo-op – this time, the launch of a travelling Doctor Who exhibition that was departing to tour the United States. And so it became clear that the long-running Blackpool exhibition hadn't closed through lack of interest – it had closed because they'd raided all the props, stuck them on the back of a 48-foot truck and sent it off to wow the unsuspecting denizens of Knoxville, Fargo and Baton Rouge. In total, the tour was scheduled to take in a whopping 185 cities – which was nearly as many as Nathan-Turner had visited recently – though it got off to a bad start when someone dropped it while loading it onto a ship at Liverpool. (With hundreds of original

Doctor Who props on board, the damage could have been as much as £15.)

Sadly, it wasn't the worst attempt at brand management that month: in a bid to crack down on unlicensed merchandise, Nathan-Turner arranged for a raid on a specialist store – only to find they'd been tipped off and offloaded the offending stock. The police immediately issued a warning for people to be aware of counterfeit Doctor Who cookbooks and a bad batch of Dalek baseball caps circulating in the area. Possibly.

There was even worse news back at the office, though, where the producer was informed that Eric Saward had handed his notice in – if you can call "I've left and I'm not coming back" notice. In a letter to Jonathan Powell, Saward wrote that "in order to keep *Doctor Who* afloat... I have put the best writer the series ever had in hospital and, out of sheer desperation, I am now working with two of the most talentless people who have ever had the nerve to set pen to paper". "What's more," he added, "I will be expected to 'fix' their appalling drivel so that it will appear less like the pile of trash it is – a task I fear beyond Jehovah himself". Jonathan Powell was quick to let Nathan-Turner know that no other script editors would be made available to him, but promised to talk to Saward to ~~bitch about Nathan-Turner behind his back~~ see if he could be persuaded to return. Meanwhile, Nathan-Turner undertook script-editing duties on Pip and Jane Bakers' latest story himself. What could *possibly* go wrong?

In Washington DC, the Big Doctor Who Lorry (may not be actual title) got its Stateside send-off from Peter Davison and – the bloody cheek of it – Michael Grade. Nathan-Turner was also in America on Saturday, May 24th – the day that Robert Holmes died from the chronic liver ailment that had troubled him for a number of years. The producer was told the news by a badly shaken Saward, who promised to honour his friend's intentions by completing Holmes' unfinished fourteenth episode.

Which is where things *really* started to go wrong.

The crux of the problem was the final scene of Saward's script – and thus the whole trial-themed season – which would have left viewers on a cliffhanger, with the Doctor locked in a desperate struggle for his life. Nathan-Turner hated it. "[Saward's] idea was to end with an enormous question mark over the future of the Doctor," the producer would later explain. "I was determined that, after 14 weeks, there had to be a very firm and very clear resolution."[1]

Saward, for his part, insisted Holmes' climax was sacred, and refused to provide the "pappy, pantomime sort of ending"[1] he felt Nathan-Turner wanted. When the two men failed to reach an agreement, Saward quit (again), withdrawing permission for his final episode to be used.

A blizzard of increasingly choleric correspondence then ensued between Saward, Nathan-Turner and Powell, lowlights of which included the script editor accusing the producer of defaming him in front of fans: "I have always been aware of your obsession with the fans – especially the American ones – but I had always put that down to the large amount of money you've told me you earn by attending their conventions... Little did I know that you also opened your mind to them before conferring with the people with whom you work." and Powell warning Saward to withdraw his "grossly defamatory statements".

With the cameras about to roll, Nathan-Turner desperately needed to come up with a script to conclude the epic story that was supposed to have served as Doctor Who's phoenix-from-the-flames rebirth. He turned to – who else? – his new BFs Pip and Jane, who were given just days to turn around the episode. To make things more complicated, for copyright reasons they weren't allowed to be told anything about Saward's script, and lawyers were present at all commissioning meetings. After several false starts – possibly involving a story in which the Doctor abandons his travels in time and space to set up a really happening copyright law firm ("Can you shut up and stick to the legal stuff, please?") – a workable, if not entirely intelligible, script was turned around in little more than a week.

Several months later, encouraged by Ian Levine, Saward would launch an acrimonious public attack on his former boss through the pages of Starburst magazine. According to Saward, the producer – who he labelled "the biggest prima donna on the show" – had lost all sense of perspective, spending more time going to US conventions or "piddling about with some crappy piece of merchandising"[6] than focusing on getting the programme made. It was all very exciting for Starburst readers, who weren't used to this kind of salacious kiss 'n' tell gossip: the magazine's stock-in-trade was usually very dry interviews with visual effects guys about how to make an animatronic spider; this month, it was like Heat for geeks.

Nathan-Turner sought legal advice, but Jonathan Powell advised him to let it go. "That was good advice," Powell reflected 25 years later. "But I probably thought, too, 'Oh, hooray, that's another nail in his coffin'."[4] But apart from all that, everyone at the BBC was like one big happy family.

As for Robert Holmes, his legacy was probably best summed up by the BAFTA-winning screenwriter Russell T Davies – and you might want to keep an eye on him – who said in a 2007 newspaper interview: "Watch episode one of The Talons of Weng-Chiang. It's the best dialogue ever written. It's up there with Dennis Potter. By a man called Robert Holmes. When the history of television drama comes to be written, Robert Holmes won't be remembered at all because he only wrote genre stuff. And that, I reckon, is a real tragedy."

Like Star Wars, only completely different

Despite the Doctor and Peri's trip to Blackpool being so rudely interrupted, the duo did make a belated appearance on the Pleasure Beach in the summer of 86 as part of that year's Hot Ice Show. (We can only imagine the conversation when they phoned up to request the rights: "Hi, is that John Nathan-Turner? We'd like to put Doctor Who on ice." "What, again?") The eight-minute routine (performed by David McGrouther and Julie Sharrock, for the completists among you) saw Peri searching for her missing brother, while being menaced by the Daleks, the Master and the Cyber, er, noids.

But Daleks on skates wasn't the strangest thing to happen to Doctor Who that summer. That came at the BBC's Autumn press launch in London, where Michael Grade sought out John Nathan-Turner and made a point of congratulating him on the first few episodes of the upcoming season. And then, on August 19th, the BBC blindsided everybody by announcing a twenty-fourth series of *Doctor Who* had already been confirmed for 1987. Nathan-Turner, for one, was delighted: it seemed all his efforts to secure the future of the show had paid off. Now all he needed to do was make sure they found some other poor bastard to actually make it.

But first, there was the small matter of the show's long-awaited reboot in the form of *The Trial of a Time Lord* – at 14 episodes, the longest story in *Doctor Who*'s history, though many would (and often do – they're *Doctor Who* fans after all) argue that it is actually four separate(ish) stories with an over-arching theme, not dissimilar to 1978's Key to Time season.

Given the media hoo-ha of the previous year, there wasn't exactly an avalanche of publicity to herald the new series. Several newspapers ran preview features, Bonnie Langford – not scheduled to make her debut for another two months – was a guest on the BBC's low-rent summer *Superstore* stand-in, *The Saturday Picture Show*, and Colin Baker appeared on *Wogan* to discuss his "lucky knickers". (He obviously hadn't been wearing them much lately. Indeed, he had more bad luck that very week when he appeared in court over a speeding offence. A trained lawyer, Baker decided to conduct his own defence. He was banned from driving for three months.) The *Radio Times*, meanwhile, continued to relegate the show to its kids' pages, while reserving its cover for madcap funnyman (it says here) Russ Abbot.

And then, at 5.45pm on Saturday, September 6th, 1986, the wait was finally over: *Doctor Who* was back – and with something of a bang, too, as the 23rd series hit the ground running with an impressive, 45-second motion-control sequence of the TARDIS being dragged towards a vast space station. At £8,000, this was the show's most expensive special effect to date, but it was worth it to show the naysayers that *Doctor Who* could punch its weight alongside the Lucases and Spielbergs of this world. And indeed it is highly reminiscent of the opening of *Star Wars* – or would have been, if that iconic shot of the Imperial Star Destroyer had

then cut straight to a videotaped 1980s hair salon.

At least, that's what it looks like. The set in question is actually supposed to be an antechamber to the ship-board courtroom, where the Doctor will spend the next three months being prosecuted by the Time Lords, as represented by the Inquisitor (Oxo mum Lynda Bellingham in a swimming cap) and the Valeyard (Michael Jayston in a tea-cosy).

Evidence takes the form of footage of the Doctor's adventures – supposedly demonstrating his culpability as "an incorrigible meddler in the affairs of other peoples and planets" – relayed to the court on a giant video screen (the Inquisitor had requested something a bit smaller and more tasteful, but you know what boys are like with their plasma tellies). The footage is all gleaned from the Matrix – nothing to do with Keanu Reeves dodging slo-mo bullets (which disappointed a few Time Lords who'd turned up and bought tickets, only to find themselves on jury service), but a mass computer system serving as a repository for all Time Lord knowledge (Wikipedia crossed with YouTube, basically). The Matrix, it turns out, records everything – and not just in the way that Ian Levine records everything: it literally records *everything* that ever happens in the observable universe. Told you it was like YouTube.

The Valeyard explains he is going to show a story from the defendant's past, present and future, at which point everyone gets very excited, thinking they might finally be about to see *The Tenth Planet* episode four. Instead, he starts with the Doctor's recent jaunt to the planet Ravalox, where we discover that the Matrix comes fitted with a multi-camera set-up as standard, but that they've skimped on the film stock a bit. (From this story until the end of the show's original run, all location footage would be recorded on electronic "outside broadcast" tape instead of 16mm film. To *Doctor Who* fans, it had a massive impact on the look and feel of the show – but try explaining it to your mum and she just won't be able to tell the difference.)

We also discover just how jarring it's going to be to keep cutting back to the trial room every time someone wants to make an objection, a legal point of order or, more often than not, a bad pun. If we wanted the action interrupted every ten minutes by a lot of pointless shouting, we'd watch ITV. At the very least they could have flashed up the little white square in the corner of the screen so we'd know when to put the kettle on.

The first episode also introduces a new version of the theme tune by freelance composer Dominic Glynn, John Nathan-Turner having decided to look beyond the BBC Radiophonic Workshop for the first time under his tenure. Apparently, after an 18-month delay between series, Glynn had eventually been given just five days to come up with the new arrangement – which is probably why it sounded like it was being played on a child's toy trumpet.

Colin Baker had noticeably put weight on during the series break, and had also acquired a frizzy, wet-look perm that meant his 80s ensemble was now complete. On the plus side, the Doctor's antagonistic relationship with Peri appears to have mellowed, and the early scenes of the time travellers exploring the forests of Ravolox have a refreshingly easy charm.

The Big Bad of the opening instalment (also known as *The Mysterious Planet*) is Drathro, a giant, anvil-headed robot tasked with guarding the mysterious "three sleepers" in his underground lair, apparently oblivious to the fact he's overslept himself, and his charges died centuries ago. He's voiced by "chartered accountant-cum-actor" (thanks Wikipedia) Roger Brierley, whose real name is David Brierley – not to be confused with the robot voice artist David Brierley, who played K9 in Season Seventeen. I'm glad we've cleared that one up.

At one point, the Valeyard beeps out a section of the dialogue because, he claims, it is for the Inquisitor's ears only. The Doctor is outraged by this act of censorship – unlike the viewers, who wonder if they couldn't have beeped out a bit more of it.

Actually, the story isn't bad – it's written by Robert Holmes, after all – but, given everything that was riding on it, it's a curiously lightweight[VII] affair: the revelation that Ravolox is, in fact, Earth after a devastating fireball is just one of the script's many intriguing ideas, and the atmospheric sequence in which the Doctor and Peri explore the subterranean ruins of Marble Arch tube station offers a tantalising

hint of what might have been. Elsewhere, though, director Nicholas Mallett chooses to keep things firmly on the brisk and breezy side – an approach that comes badly adrift in the scenes featuring the Tribe of the Free, where what Holmes' clearly envisioned as a feral, *Mad Max*-style post-apocalyptic society is reduced to a bunch of spear-carrying extras ambling about an Iron Age educational site under the command of the never-knowingly Boudicca-like Joan Sims. *Carry On Up the Thunderdome*, anyone?

In a less slight adventure, the classic Holmes double act of Glitz and Dibber – a pair of intergalactic confidence tricksters on a mission to steal the sleepers' secrets by blowing up Drathro's power source, which is currently being used by the Tribe of the Free as a totem pole – might offer welcome comic relief, but here they just feel like part of the wider problem (especially given Tony Selby and Glen Murphy's somewhat large reading of the roles). By the time our heroes stage an assault on the robot's underground lair – and are "gunged" with bright green, CBBC-style comedy slime for their troubles – you can't help wondering if Holmes and Saward are trying to make a deliberate point about the ridiculous constraints of the "no violence" diktat.

The real disaster, though, was the viewing figures: 18 months after being "rested" in a bid to halt what the BBC insisted was declining interest in the show, *Doctor Who* returned to an audience of just 4.9 million – almost three million less than the number of people who had tuned in to the previous episode. As re-launches went, it made New Coke look like a marketing triumph.

Fun with Pip and Jane

Unloved *The Mysterious Planet* may have been, but at least what was on screen was largely what the BBC had asked for, unlike the next segment of the Trial, which suggests someone had forgotten to copy writer Philip Martin in on the "less violence" memo: a notional sequel to *Vengeance on Varos*, *Mindwarp* – as it is commonly known – is a bleakly sadistic affair, highlights of which include the first full companion lobotomy (and no, before you ask, Adric doesn't qualify) and the Doctor torturing said companion, who is chained to a rock in the sea, in an early, enthusiastic example of waterboarding.

This lurch into an even more unsympathetic sixth Doctor is the result of our hero having had his brain fried by the demented local neurosurgeon. Or possibly it's the Valeyard tampering with the evidence. Or maybe the Doctor is just bluffing. Nobody seemed to know for sure – certainly not the lead actor or the guy running the show. At one point, Colin Baker asked director Ron Jones what his motivation was supposed to be, and was told to ask Eric Saward. Who didn't know either. Whatever the reason, it seems beyond perverse that, having taken a conscious decision to sand down the Doctor's more abrasive edges, they should turn him into a full-on cackling maniac after just one story.

As well as a typically restrained guest turn from Brian Blessed – think Flash Gordon's Prince Vultan cranked up a few notches for effect – as a rampaging warlord, the serial also features the return of Nabil Shaban as Sil. To coincide with the story, John Nathan-Turner tried to interest Trebor in marketing a marsh minnow sweet. ("You know, like Sil," he told their baffled marketing bods. "Sil! Surely you know Sil? The kids talk of little else!" There was an awkward pause, before someone said: "What about something from Airwolf?")

Set on Sil's homeworld of Thoros Beta – rendered with a lurid pink sea, green sky and purple rocks thanks to a new bit of Paintbox kit called HARRY – Martin's story concerns the efforts of a surgeon (played with gimlet-eyed relish by a slightly over-keen Patrick Ryecart) to transplant the brain (and/or "mind", depending on what page of the script you're on) of local bigwig Kiv into a new – and, if possible, less sluggish – body. There's also a side plot, bolted on by Eric Saward, concerning a milk-warm rebellion by a bunch of drippy slaves led by Gordon Warnecke, who attacks the role with all the enthusiasm of a trip to the out-of-hours dentist.

About that lobotomy. Nicola Bryant's resignation had prompted Nathan-Turner to declare: "Peri must die." (He wasn't threatening to have her killed for quitting – he was just trying to ensure she got a good send-off.) To this end, the final episode climaxes with one of

the most dramatic departures in Doctor Who's history, as Peri, her shaved head now home to Kiv's brain, issues a terrifying alien roar, before being blasted to bits by Brian Blessed. (Or so we thought... more on that later.) Meanwhile, if Bryant had any qualms about leaving, the news that the cost of hiring a piece of the set – a large round door that features prominently in the story – was more than her fee probably helped convince her she was doing the right thing. Though, to be fair, it is a lovely door.

As with Varos, Martin does a decent job of presenting Thoros Beta as a fully-realised world – helped by sterling work from designer Andrew Howe-Davies and unusually sympathetic lighting from Don Babbage. However, this only serves to highlight how artificial and increasingly bewildering the trial scenes have become. At the end of the story, the Time Lords intervene to lift the Doctor out of the action and drag him to the courtroom – so basically doing the very thing the defendant stands accused of – and then have the temerity to blame him for cutting and running. It's almost as if they're making this stuff up on the spot, eh readers?

The season's third story-within-a-story is supposed to represent the Doctor's defence, but the fact a) it takes place in the future and b) he's a bit rubbish in it, suggests the Time Lord is as effective at the Bar as the man who plays him. Terror of the Vervoids is infamous for many things, not least its titular plant monsters, whose heads look uncannily like genitals – though which genitals you choose to see depends on your brain, or possibly your sexuality. The fact their bodies are track suits with leaves stuck to them, and some of them talk in Scouse accents, hardly adds to their reputation.

Pip and Jane Baker's starting premise – Agatha Christie meets Day of the Triffids... on a spaceship – sounds like it has the makings of a classic. To say it didn't quite work out that way is the biggest understatement since Mrs Lincoln complained about someone ruining her trip to the theatre.

Firstly, as a murder mystery, it makes absolutely no sense whatsoever: everyone acts suspiciously simply because the conventions of these things decree they ought to, and the murderer is similarly going through the motions with such a lack of motivation, even Hercule Poirot would have to admit your guess was as good as his. (The guilty party, Doland, has a plan to sell the Vervoids as slaves, but that fails to explain a good 90% of his actions in this story.)

Then there's more of that deathless dialogue from Pip 'n' Jane, still refusing to use one word where 45 will do. "On the previous occasion that the Doctor's path crossed mine," declares Michael Craig's spaceship commodore improbably, "I found myself involved in a web of mayhem and intrigue!", before adding: "Whoever's been dumped in there has been pulverised into fragments and sent floating in space – and in my book, that's murder!"

If you're feeling generous, you might put at least some of this down to the fact it was a late replacement story, recorded last in the run, after the script editor had already made his excuses and left. But there's no excusing the shoddy production values, in which a thirtieth-century luxury spaceliner is presented as a cross between a 1980s municipal leisure centre and a rather sterile wine bar, everyone dresses like they're heading to aerobics class – which, to be fair, they often are, thanks to the script's bizarre obsession with regular gym workouts – and cast are so uniformly awful, you're actively cheering the killer on. Guest star of the week Honor Blackman gives it her all as a steely agronomist, but there's only so much you can do with lines like "You appalling dunderhead!" Don Babbage, meanwhile, appears to have broken – or possibly fixed – the dimmer switch he used on the previous story, so it's back to the full house lights for this one. Or maybe he's just trying to be simpatico with the setting, ensuring that, like deep space, this story has no atmosphere whatsoever.

By now, attempts to apply any kind of logic to the trial process have been given up as a bad job. For reasons best known to himself, the Doctor seems to have accepted his culpability in the first two adventures – despite being the victim of the most obvious show trial this side of Salem – and has resorted to arguing he gets better in future, suggesting that Gallifreyan law accepts "I'm terribly sorry, I won't do it again" as a valid defence. The fact he chooses to present his evidence in the form of an incident from his future does rather suggest he's going

to avoid execution or a long stretch at the end of the trial, *despite* having just happened to have chosen an escapade in which – whoops, silly me – he proves he's guilty of an even greater crime by sort of perhaps accidentally committing a little bit of genocide. (Wouldn't he have been better choosing something like, say, *Genesis of the Daleks*, in which the Time Lords send him on a genocidal mission, which he chooses not to complete? Maybe he couldn't afford Terry Nation's repeat fees.)

But if there's one reason *Terror of the Vervoids* is seared in the memory above all others, it is because this was the story that introduced Bonnie Langford as the Doctor's companion.

Langford is clearly a versatile and talented performer, but her hands-on-hips principal boy eagerness is woefully out of place, even in this new, bowdlerised version of *Doctor Who*. It didn't help that the Bakers, and several writers that followed, chose to write her character – computer programmer and fitness fanatic Melanie Bush – almost as a Bonnie Langford pastiche: for her first cliffhanger, she was even asked to thcream... sorry, scream in the key of F in order to match the end title music (and she did it as well, the old pro).

The story prompted a mini re-launch for the *Trial* season, with Langford chatting on the *Wogan* sofa and joining Colin Baker, John Nathan-Turner and, um, Pip and Jane Baker for a press call. But ratings for the season were still clinging stubbornly around the five million mark, and many of those five million didn't appear to actually *like* it: a memorable edition of the BBC viewer feedback programme *Open Air* saw a bewildered Pip 'n' Jane being handbagged by a bunch of irate fans, including a freckle-faced teenager called Chris Chibnall – sporting an outfit even more 80s than the Doctor's – who we haven't heard the last of in this story. Michael Grade also informed Nathan-Turner that, while the new series was an improvement, he still wasn't entirely happy, and suggested he had some plans up his sleeve. Better late than never, I suppose.

Meanwhile, *Doctor Who Bulletin* – a bellicose semi-professional magazine that had begun waging a high-profile campaign against Nathan-Turner – declared on its front page: "89% of fans want a new producer." Though the figure was probably a bit higher if you included the producer himself.

There's nothing you can do to prevent the catharsis of spurious morality, say experts

In November 1986, the BBC commemorated its 60th birthday with a season of classic programmes from the archives designed to celebrate the glorious heritage of the world's most respected broadcaster. At one point, this was to have included a repeat of first Doctor adventure *The Chase*, but the idea was canned – possibly because the likes of Jonathan Powell and Michael Grade couldn't see what *Doctor Who* had to do with *anyone's* glorious heritage, or possibly because someone was judicious enough to actually watch it beforehand. So it fell to the closing act of *The Trial of a Time Lord* to represent the good Doctor at the party – and suddenly those Daleks arsing about on the Empire State Building with Peter Purves didn't seem so bad.

Watched with the mute button on, *The Ultimate Foe* – as the last two episodes of the 1986 series are somewhat optimistically known – is quite impressive. After a very stagey, studio-bound season, the OB filming at the Gladstone Pottery Museum in Stoke feels like a breath of... well, fresh air. (I know, it's not exactly a Bond movie location, but anything's better than that sodding trial room.) Recording also took place at Camber Sands, where a large pit was dug for Colin Baker on the beach. (And was it his imagination, or did he just catch a glimpse of a cigar-chomping BBC1 controller standing on the sand shouting "keep going... bit deeper"?)

With the benefit – if that's the right word – of sound, however, the final episodes of *The Trial of a Time Lord* are an inchoate, utterly insane mess, in which the Master pops up to reveal the whole process has been a show trial cooked up between the Valeyard and the Time Lord High Council to pin the Ravalox affair on the Doctor, and bury the fact it was the Time Lords who incinerated the Earth in an attempt to torch stolen secrets from the Matrix.

Let's just rewind that, for a moment, shall we? The Time Lords' method of covering up their culpability in the Ravalox affair was to convene a court and replay the whole thing on a big screen, complete with bleeped-out sections in which, if your lip-reading skills were good enough, you could decipher Glitz explaining "it was the Time Lords wot done it"? We've heard of hiding in plain sight, but this is ridiculous.

Meanwhile, the Valeyard – who it transpires is actually an evil version of the Doctor himself, "somewhere between his twelfth and final incarnation" – has his own agenda to wipe out the High Court from within the Matrix using a Heath Robinson-esque contraption, complete with disco lights, which Mel identifies with boggle-eyed wonder as "a megabyte modem". That's right, the resident computer expert thinks the Valeyard is planning to blow a hole through the fabric of two realities and commit mass murder using the processing power required to generate a medium-sized jpeg. Also, he's apparently going to do it by exploding the screen in the trial room, suggesting Pip and Jane Baker believe the things they see on TV actually take place *inside* the television.

Fortunately, the Doctor rumbles the Valeyard's scheme after the latter invites him to "disseminate" the news, loading the word with such moustache-twiddling mischief our hero is able to work out the contraption is a particle disseminator. Even the Master had to admit this new guy's Evil Plans were a bit rubbish.

Episode fourteen also contains what is widely considered to be one of the most ludicrous lines of dialogue in the whole of the *Doctor Who* canon, as the Valeyard triumphantly tells our hero: "There's nothing you can do to prevent the catharsis of spurious morality!" (At which point, on a Paris sofa, Jacques Derrida must have turned to his wife and said: "Huh?") Oh, and it turns out Peri wasn't killed after all, but is now happily married to Brian Blessed, thus upgrading her status from "dead" to merely "deaf".

The effort taken to conjure a surreal world of sinister Victoriana inside the Matrix largely pays off – though it's nowhere near as nightmarish as the fourth Doctor's excursion into the mainframe in *The Deadly Assassin*, for obvious reasons – and Colin Baker is belatedly gifted at least one great grandstanding speech, railing against the Time Lords and the corrupting influence of their "ten million years of absolute power". But, overall, as a piece of television, *The Ultimate Foe* is a garbled mess. And as the conclusion to what had been sold as a 14-week epic, it's an unmitigated disaster, offering no resolution and no closure, and leaving what few loyal viewers were left with way more questions than answers – chiefly, the question of how they were going to get those six hours of their life back.

John Nathan-Turner, of course, got his way over the ending: instead of the Doctor and the Valeyard locked in mortal combat over a virtual reality version of the Reichenbach Falls, the season closes with the Inquisitor all but slapping her thigh and declaring "So, that's that" (while wilfully ignoring the fact that, according to the Keeper of the Matrix, insurrectionists are currently running amok on Gallifrey) before blithely assuring the Doctor all charges against him are dismissed. With everyone happy – though did we mention the whole running amok thing? – Mel and the Doctor make their excuses and depart together in the TARDIS (technically before she's actually met him, confusingly) for more thrilling adventures in time and space.

Fate apologises to actor over finger gesture

Except, for Colin Baker, there would be no more adventures, thrilling or otherwise. After several weeks of rumours, on Saturday, December 13th – one week after the conclusion of *The Trial of a Time Lord* – it was reported in *The Sun* that the actor had been sacked from the role he loved.

"That'll teach me for saying I'd like to beat Tom Baker's record," his namesake reflected many years later. "Every now and then you open your gob and say something the fickle finger of fate is going to tap you on the shoulder for quite smartly. And it did."[1]

In the event, the fickle finger of fate took the form of a phone call from John Nathan-Turner. "I've got some good news and some bad news," the producer told his leading man. The good news was that the series was being recommissioned: the bad news was he wouldn't be in it. "It's not quite the way I'd have framed what he was about to tell me," said Baker. "That was a body blow, that was."[1]

The official BBC line was that "Doctors do three years". Which would have been slightly more convincing if Jon Pertwee hadn't done five, Tom Baker seven and Colin Baker himself just two. The actor went to see Jonathan Powell who, with the courage and leadership we've come to expect, said Michael Grade had told him to do it. He also had the cheek to chastise the man he'd just fired for refusing to come back and film a regeneration scene. Baker said if he could do the whole of the next series, he'd go quietly at the end of it. Powell said he'd think about it and, naturally, Baker never heard from him again.

Ever the trouper, the actor – who took the bullet three days before the first part of the Vervoids story was broadcast – continued his promotional duties for the latter *Trial* episodes, including an in-character appearance on the *Tomorrow's World Christmas Quiz* and another interview – not in costume, significantly – on *Saturday Superstore*. Faced with a *Superstore* viewer posing the perennial chestnut of where he would travel if he had a real TARDIS, Baker's answer was – with hindsight – more than a little poignant. "I think I'd probably go back to the beginning and start all over again," he said, "because I've enjoyed doing *Doctor Who* so much." Sniff.

To further rub salt in the wound, Eric Saward went on record to say he'd never believed Baker had been right for the role in the first place: "He lacks that quality that I think the part demands," he told one interviewer. "Colin is a fair character actor, but not really a leading man."[1]

Baker, who had always got on well with the script editor, felt "betrayed", claiming Saward had often confided in him about his concerns over the show, but had never once indicated he thought he might be part of the problem. "I suppose it's a big ask to ask someone to be that obvious if that's what you thought," reflected Baker. "But, on the other hand, if I had any doubts about someone's contributions in the past and I hadn't said anything, I'd keep quiet about it."[1]

The two men's paths never crossed again. "I've always said the reason I don't want to meet him again is that I would hit him if I did," said the normally affable Baker. "I suppose I probably wouldn't. But I would certainly look at him and I might curl my lip."[4]

Nathan-Turner, for his part, went to his grave blaming the costume. This was one of very few things the producer would ever admit to a serious error of judgment over, but most people now agree that Colin Baker – whose humiliation was made public one week before Christmas – was caught in a perfect storm of poor scripts, production chaos and vehement antipathy from the BBC's own management. Go back and re-watch the sixth Doctor's era and it's hard to escape the conclusion that Baker's unfailing energy is the only thing keeping the show on the road.

Having started with such hope and optimism, Baker's *Doctor Who* dream ended in sourness and recrimination: even his parting interview with *The Sun* was blown up into headlines about how his sacking would hit his fundraising efforts for cot death research – a piece of spin that left the actor fuming.

And yet...

Whatever F Scott Fitzgerald might have thought, Baker went on to prove that, sometimes, there is indeed a second act. Despite everything that had happened, he has remained a loyal and enthusiastic ambassador for the show, regularly appearing on TV to bang the drum for it, while remaining a popular staple of the convention circuit. And when, at the turn of the century, he became one of several past Doctors to reprise his role for a popular series of audio CDs (see Chapter Eight), he showed exactly what he could do when served with better scripts, and was rewarded by being voted the best actor in the range by fans.

This incarnation of the Doctor, in fact, has always fared well in alternative media: even as the show was going through hell on – and off – TV in the mid-80s, the long-running comic strip in *Doctor Who Magazine* was enjoying a particular purple patch, pushing the boundaries of the form with fantastical, magical fairytale adventures that merely highlighted the paucity of what was being offered on screen. For many, these remain the definitive sixth Doctor stories.[VIII]

In 2011, Colin Baker's rehabilitation was completed when he was voted, by an overwhelming majority, to succeed such luminaries as Jon Pertwee and Nicholas Courtney as Honorary President of the Doctor Who Appreciation Society. As for the events of late 1986, Baker is still looking for answers: "I'd love to know the real truth," he said recently. "Or perhaps I wouldn't – perhaps I'd be deeply mortified. Perhaps they just thought I was a rubbish actor. It's not just optimism on my part that thinks that isn't the whole story."[1]

Gary Downie, in that now infamous *Doctor Who Magazine* interview, thought that wasn't the whole story either. "There's a history between Colin and Michael Grade," he said. "Liza Goddard was Colin's first wife, and she was Michael Grade's best friend. The divorce was acrimonious. She moved into Michael Grade's house while she was getting over the divorce – and I'll say no more. Michael Grade was determined: he did not want Colin Baker working for the BBC."[7]

Baker dismisses this, claiming Grade "wouldn't be so petty". He also cites a separate conspiracy theory – told to him by Peter Davison, no less – that Grade was actually trying to call Nathan-Turner's bluff, hoping to sack the producer when he refused to carry out his execution order. Whatever the truth of the matter, Baker admits he "still feels cheated" by what happened to him.

"I happened to be the Doctor when the programme was going through a tumultuous time, and I did get the blame pinned on me to a large extent by the fans who didn't rate my Doctor compared with others. Which they're perfectly entitled to do, but it's quite painful and hurtful.

"You can't help thinking: well, with different stories, and a different budget, and a different timeslot... I believe my Doctor could have, had he had the chance, had a wider appeal. I still do believe that."[8]

But perhaps we should leave the last word to the Time Lord himself: as the TARDIS dematerialised for the final time at the end of the twenty-third season, the sixth Doctor's parting shot was left hanging in the air – a fitting epitaph for a valiant hero, unfairly taken from us before his time:

"Carrot juice, carrot juice, carrot juice."

It was that sort of era.

The Greatest Show in the Galaxy! (cancelled)

"John, I think we've got just the job for you – what do you know about *Doctor Who*?"

Being forced to knife his leading man between the shoulder blades perhaps wasn't the ideal way for John Nathan-Turner to sign off from *Doctor Who* (he'd probably have preferred to finish with a musical number), but now that the deed was done, at least he was finally free to move on and put it all behind him. Or so he thought.

Returning to work in early December 1986, after a short holiday to prepare his annual Christmas panto, Nathan-Turner was summoned to Jonathan Powell's office to be told of his exciting new assignment: the long-running science fiction series *Doctor Who*.

"There was no choice in it," recalled the producer of the "stranglehold" the Corporation placed him in. "I was instructed to do it."[1]

"I couldn't find anyone else to do it," was the ever-resourceful Powell's excuse. Again. "And, actually, we'd lost the will to do so."[1]

In fact, some genuine effort to inject fresh blood into the series does appear to have been made around this time – if you can call Sydney Newman fresh blood. In 1986, Newman had written to the BBC requesting a creator's credit on the show. The Corporation declined, but Michael Grade did invite Newman – who described the current iteration of the programme as "largely socially valueless escapist schlock" – to pitch ideas for a *Doctor Who* reboot. Unfortunately, he seemed to have missed the memo that it was no longer 1967: his main suggestions were bringing back Patrick Troughton as the Doctor and stressing that "the important fact is that Dr Who does *not* know how to control his time-space machine! At a later stage," his proposal continued, "Dr Who would be metamorphosed into a woman" while, for the companion, he proposed a homesick girl of 12 wearing John Lennon type glasses, to whom the Doctor –

sorry, Dr Who – would address remarks like "Hush, child! You're addlepating me!" In other words, he wanted to recreate the William Hartnell era with Pat Troughton and, at some point further down the line, a sex change. ("That's terrific," said Grade as he leafed through the notes. "Really terrific. Sandra, can you get me John Nathan-Turner on the line, please.")

For his part, Nathan-Turner was so convinced he wasn't going to be doing *Doctor Who* any more, he hadn't bothered to commission any stories – either out of respect for his successor's vision for the show or, possibly, because he thought it was someone else's problem. By the time Powell dropped his bombshell, the producer found himself less than three months from production with no scripts, no script editor and no Doctor. Apart from that, though, he had it all under control.

Still, if he was addlepated (it's a real word – I looked it up), let's hope he wasn't tempted to phone up Colin Baker looking for sympathy: "Can you believe I'm still stuck on *Doctor Who*? It's a nightmare. Every day it's like, *Doctor Who* this, *Doctor Who* that. I sometimes think the BBC wants to keep me on *Doctor Who* forever! Can you imagine how that feels, Colin? Can you? Honestly, I wish they'd just sack me, I really do. But enough about me, how've you been? Colin? Hello?"

On December 18th, Nathan-Turner received a call from Clive Doig, a former *Doctor Who* vision mixer-turned-children's TV producer who'd heard he was hunting for a new Doctor and wanted to recommend a Scottish actor he'd done a lot of work with called Sylvester McCoy. By coincidence – or so everyone insists – the next call Nathan-Turner received was from McCoy's agent. (And straight after that he received one from S. McCoy Windows Ltd, asking if he'd considered the benefits of double-glazing?)

Despite Colin Baker's protestations to the contrary, Nathan-Turner was still convinced he'd be able to persuade his recently departed leading man to return for one final story, and to that end commissioned – you guessed it – Pip and Jane Baker to write the sixth Doctor's swansong: a rematch with Kate O'Mara's renegade Time Lady, the Rani. He also met with a young writer called Stephen Wyatt, while Nathan-Turner's own agent recommended another promising newcomer called Andrew Cartmel for the post of script editor on the basis of a phone sex thriller he'd written (not for *Doctor Who*, obviously).

When he wasn't attending BBC scriptwriting workshops, Cartmel was working for a computer software company in Cambridge. If he was surprised at being asked to go from this to masterminding *Doctor Who's* story output, he didn't show it: when Nathan-Turner asked him at his interview what one thing he'd like to achieve with *Doctor Who*, Cartmel responded coolly: "Overthrow the government." For a show whose boss hadn't even managed to overthrow himself, this was perhaps ambitious.

Next, Cartmel had to be vetted by Jonathan Powell. At the end of the interview, Powell asked him: "Who do you think *Doctor Who* is for?" "*Doctor Who* is for everyone," said Cartmel – at which point Powell shook his head and said firmly: "No, *Doctor Who* is for children." "I said that I agreed," recalled Cartmel. "But I was lying through my teeth. I already believed, with equal firmness, that it was an adult show with adult possibilities."[2] Blimey, maybe he really *was* thinking of doing a story about phone sex.

In the papers, speculation was rife about who Baker's replacement might be, with Pat Troughton and Jon Pertwee both apparently in the frame (they weren't) while the *Daily Mirror* ran a story headlined "600 Beg 'Make Me Doctor Who'" (they hadn't), claiming a quarter of the inquiries were from women (they weren't).

Names that appear to have been given genuine consideration include Andrew Sachs – then still more famous for being bashed about the head by John Cleese in *Fawlty Towers* than for his wayward granddaughter's unusual lifestyle choices – and the relatively unknown Chris Jury. But the frontrunners were McCoy and Ken Campbell – in whose experimental theatre troupe, by coincidence, McCoy had launched his career. In early January, Nathan-Turner and his partner Gary Downie went along to see McCoy playing the Pied Piper at the National Theatre – a role that had been specially created for him by Adrian Mitchell. "It was a very good audition piece for *Doctor Who*," said McCoy, who had previously applied for the job when Peter Davison had resigned. "I wore an extraordinary, wonderful, multi-coloured coat, which I think, visually, must have tingled something in John's mind."[3] Hopefully something like: "I must make sure I don't f*** *this* costume up as well".

While Downie was convinced they'd found their man, Nathan-Turner had reservations, but agreed McCoy was worthy of further investigation. Meanwhile, it had been decided the new season would be made up of two four-parters and two three-parters[I], the latter to be made as one production block, with one story made entirely on location and the other in the studio. Bonnie Langford had also indicated her intention to leave at the end of the year, though the producer was hopeful he could persuade her to stay, even if no-one else was.

Andrew Cartmel officially joined the team on January 16th and set about learning the office lingo – apparently, "barkers" was Nathan-Turner's less-than affectionate term for barking mad *Doctor Who* fans, while the third Doctor was commonly known as Mother Pertwee. Very early into his role, the new script ed was delighted to come in and find Pat Troughton perched pixie-like on top of a filing cabinet, swinging his legs and chatting to the office secretary, while duties not included in the job description included photocopying an advert for Dalek dildos for his boss (his interest was strictly from a licensing compliance point of view, you understand).

Cartmel was a huge fan of comics, which were currently enjoying something of a creative high watermark with the likes of Alan Moore's *Watchmen* and Frank Miller's *The Dark Knight Returns*. The script editor's recommended reading for prospective *Doctor Who* writers included Moore's *The Ballad of Halo Jones* strip from *2000AD* alongside, more worryingly, John Tulloch and Manuel Alvarado's media studies doorstop *Doctor Who: The Unfolding Text*. Moore was also top of Cartmel's writers' wish-list but, when his overtures fell on deaf ears, he turned instead to some of the people he'd met at the BBC's script workshops, including Malcolm Kohll and Ian Briggs.

Before that, though, he had to deal with the two-headed Hydra of Pip and Jane – and it wasn't exactly love at first sight. The Bakers carped about Cartmel's inexperience, while Cartmel found their approach running contrary to all his ideas about where the show should be going. "It was a script where characters say things like 'earthling' and 'radiation wave meter'," he grumbled. "They also say things like 'inaction is anathema' and 'egalitarian', 'inert', 'debilitating', 'indolent' (twice) and 'incompetent fool'."[2]

"We do occasionally receive complaints that the vocabulary we use in our scripts and our books isn't monosyllabic," conceded Pip. "Well I don't buy that." "They can always use a dictionary,"[4] suggested Jane. Later, the script editor admitted drunkenly filing drafts of the script with some laundry in a drawer labelled "Pip and Jane and Dirty Socks".

The first thing Cartmel actually wrote for *Doctor Who* was an audition piece for Ken Campbell and Sylvester McCoy, to be performed with John Nathan-Turner standing in as Mel. (What? I didn't say a word.) Convinced McCoy was the real... well, you get the idea, Nathan-Turner introduced him to Jonathan Powell.

"Normally you took a photo up and said, this is who I want to cast, and it then went up to the sixth floor just to get the kind of Papal nod," recalled the producer. "But this time, when I went up and said, this is Sylvester McCoy, here's the photo, Jonathan kept saying, 'Are you sure?'. He said, 'I think you ought to get a casting director in, just in case there might be somebody else just waiting around the corner'."[1]

Nathan-Turner had eventually ruled out Ken Campbell as "too scary" for the kids. Interestingly, the following year Campbell was cast as a mysterious time traveller accompanied by two young companions in ITV kids' show *Erasmus Microman* – a part originally written for Sil actor Nabil Shaban who, scandalously, the network had decided was even scarier than Campbell.

With Stephen Wyatt having being commissioned for a test script called *Paradise Tower*, and Malcolm Kohll working on the all-location story, which the team planned to shoot in Wales, Cartmel and Nathan-Turner outlined a possible replacement for Mel in the form of Alf, a streetwise London teenage girl now living on another planet after being swept up in a time storm. (Not to be confused with A.L.F, a streetwise Alien Life Form now living on another planet after crashing into the Tanner family's garage.)

Kate O'Mara's return as the Rani was announced in the press at the end of the month, by which time Colin Baker had committed to a production of Gerald Moon's play *Corpse!* in the West End, forcing Nathan-Turner to concede defeat in his battle to win him back for one last outing. Baker had also been due to attend a *Doctor Who* convention in America, but suddenly found his invitation withdrawn, seemingly at the request of the BBC. Which was nice.

In collaboration with casting director Marilyn Johnson, Nathan-Turner screen-tested three other actors – Dermot Crowley, David Fielder and another whose identity remains unknown – alongside McCoy. Each performed two scenes opposite Janet Fielding who, picking up on Cartmel's obvious inspiration for one of the scenes, opted to play the female villain as Margaret Thatcher – which was all the inspiration a 60s beatnik like McCoy needed to smash it out of the park. Johnson was immediately convinced McCoy was the right man for the job and, on viewing the tapes, Jonathan Powell and Michael Grade agreed. Nathan-Turner had found his new Doctor.

Ferret-trouserer brings shame on family by taking job in City

Percy James Patrick Kent-Smith was born in Dunoon, on the west coast of Scotland, in August 1943, one month after his English father had been killed in action during World War II. Raised by his Scottish mother and grandmother, at the age of 11 he entered a seminary to train to be a priest. Three or four years later, he changed his mind and decided, like Tom Baker before him, to become a monk – in this case, a Dominican Monk in South America (well, if you're going to live a life of chastity and penitence, you might at least go where it's warm). But his application was rejected because he was too young, and instead he found himself back at the local grammar school – where he discovered girls. "That was it," he recalled in a 2010 interview. "I decided during that year that, rather than wear a skirt, I'd rather chase it."[5]

Moving to London at the height of its 60s swing, Kent-Smith trained as an actuary for an insurance company, before jacking it in to work at the box office of the Roundhouse Theatre – where, as well as counting the ticket stubs, the 5' 5" "Scottish elf" (as Andrew Cartmel later labelled him) found himself standing in for a night as the Rolling Stones' least convincing bodyguard ever.

One day, Ken Campbell came in frantically searching for a replacement actor to appear in his experimental comedy *Roadshow*, and Brian Murphy – later to find fame as the henpecked, pickled onion-eating half of sitcom couple *George and Mildred* – recommended his box-office colleague on the basis he was "out of his head".

Kent-Smith's most popular contribution to the Roadshow was playing a stuntman called Sylveste (the "r" came later) McCoy, whose shtick included stuffing ferrets down his trousers, hammering six-inch nails up his nose and setting fire to his head – three skills they conspicuously fail to teach at RADA.

"It was quite mad," said McCoy, who adopted his alter-ego's name for his professional moniker soon afterwards. "My granny, who brought me up, she couldn't understand why I'd given up a job in insurance in the City to bang nails into my face."[5] This was in the days, it should be pointed out, when the City was still just about considered a more honourable calling than face-nailing.

Bob Hoskins was one of McCoy's contemporaries in the Roadshow, whose anarchic antics would occasionally result in landlords paying them off to stop performing. "From the very beginning, I was an eccentric," declared McCoy. "I wanted to stretch the envelope. Or balloon. Or whatever it was. I wasn't one of those actors who was internal and compact. I wanted to fly. I've never played a normal person in any of the acting that I've done. I wouldn't quite know how."[5]

By the mid-80s, McCoy had carved out a dual career combining regular work on children's TV shows like *Vision On*, *Tiswas* and *Jigsaw* (as one half of blundering superheroes The O-Men) with stage work ranging from portrayals of Buster Keaton and Stan Laurel to the more Puckish end of the Shakespeare repertoire. In 1986, he had appeared in a season of Shakespeare at the Theatre Royal, Haymarket alongside Vanessa Redgrave and Timothy Dalton, during which he and Dalton had discussed the scarcity of secure jobs in the business. Within a year, one of them was Doctor Who and the other was James Bond. ("Wanna swap?" asked McCoy, as he watched Dalton squiring another exotic beauty.)

Pip and Jane Baker were given a tape of McCoy's screen test to help them adapt their season opener, *Strange Matter*, from the sixth Doctor to the seventh. To launch the new era, Nathan-Turner also decided it was time to replace the starfield title sequence, variations of which had served the show since 1980, and the current theme arrangement, which had served the show since, ooh, about four months earlier. The former was assigned to graphic designer Oliver Elmes, who teamed up with Gareth Edwards of CAL Video to create *Doctor Who*'s first fully computer-generated titles (plus a new logo), while the new version of the theme was entrusted to Keff McCulloch, a musician and sound engineer who Nathan-Turner had met while directing his fiancée in panto. A brave choice, perhaps, given McCulloch's lack of television experience. And, indeed, lack of a synthesizer – he had to hire one to do the job. (It was either that, or do the theme using a paper and comb – which some may argue would have resulted in a better job.)

Having been formally offered the part of the Doctor at the second time of applying, McCoy did what any relatively unknown actor would do having been handed one of the biggest jobs on television: he said he'd think about it. "I went away to the country, and sat in a cottage somewhere, thinking, should I do this or not?" he remembered. "I suppose I was worried about typecasting, and knowing what I was going to be doing for the next three years. To me, that was an appalling thought. That's one of the things about the acting profession: it's very uncertain, but there's a sense of incredible adventure. I hate it when I don't know what's happening next. At the same time, once I do know, I hate that as well."[3] Bloody actors.

Having decided that, on balance, three years of *Doctor Who* was better than not knowing where the next ferret-trousering gig was coming from, McCoy signed on the dotted line – and within a week had been whisked off to America to join Jon Pertwee on the *Doctor Who* touring exhibition's latest pit-stop in Atlanta. How the fans lapped up his memories of his four days as the Doctor so far. ("There was this one time I was in Atlanta, talking to you lot...")

Back home, *The Sun* broke the news of the BBC's "shock choice" under the headline "New Doctor Who is the Unknown McCoy" and, two days later, the new man stepped out of the TARDIS at an official photocall, followed by a brief appearance on *Blue Peter* in which he did a convincing impression of a man who hadn't been told anything about anything.

Also on board the new *Who* was Ian Briggs, whose studio three-parter *The Pyramid's Treasure* would made as part of the same block as Malcolm Kohll's 50s-set Welsh escapade. Briggs had included the Alf character under the new name of Ace, while Kohll's story featured a Welsh girl called Ray, both of whom were being considered as potential new companions. (Memo to BBC Facilities Manager: someone seems to have nicked the *Doctor Who* office's book of girls' names.)

In late March, *Doctor Who* finally made it into space for real when the SuperChannel satellite TV station started broadcasting repeats of the Tom Baker serials – the first chance (a handful of) British viewers had had to see vintage *Who* since the repeat seasons of the early 80s. In the same week, disturbing husband-and-wife/schoolboy-and-"special-friend" combo the Krankies recorded a sketch as Dr Why and his wee assistant Jimmy What; let's just be thankful Nathan-Turner had already cast his own kids' telly star by the time this went out – otherwise who knows what light-bulbs might have started flashing above his head.

Sadly, on Saturday, March 28th, just two days before the new series was due to go into rehearsals, the *Doctor Who* office received news that Patrick Troughton had died after suffering

a heart attack in the early hours while attending a convention in Columbus, Georgia, USA. After a decade or so in which he had been reticent to talk about *Doctor Who*, *The Five Doctors* had reignited the actor's enthusiasm for the show: as well as requesting a third return appearance in *The Two Doctors*, he had become a popular figure on the convention circuit, where he was renowned for his friendly rivalry and increasingly elaborate games of one-upmanship with Jon Pertwee. By all accounts Troughton, who had just turned 67, was in high spirits during the Georgia event, and was looking forward to a birthday celebration at the convention on the Saturday, along with a screening of *The Dominators* he had personally requested.

Of all the actors to have played the role, Troughton remains the influence most often cited by his fellow Time Lords: the Doctor's Doctor, and a hero to millions more besides.

Free Doctor Who with every hat

As he entered rehearsals on March 30th, McCoy was still uncertain how he should play the part. Having studied tapes of some of his predecessors – including *The Three Doctors* – he had begun to formulate an idea for his Doctor incorporating elements of Troughton, Hartnell, Buster Keaton and windmill-armed TV boffin Magnus Pike. But he was unsettled by the fact *Strange Matter* had clearly been written for his predecessor, and by Nathan-Turner intervening to tell him to tone down the comedy a shade.

On Saturday, April 4th, the actor knew he had truly arrived as Doctor Who when he commenced filming in – where else? – a rainy quarry in Somerset, and a press call on the Monday gave the world its first look at the seventh Doctor's costume. Sporting Troughton-esque check trousers and braces, a cream-coloured baggy jacket and matching panama hat (model's own – McCoy had worn it to the interview, and has often claimed the hat got the job and he came with it), the new duds looked much less like a uniform than the previous couple of Doctors – though, having kept the question mark collars through two changes of Time Lord, Nathan-Turner now upped the ante with a retro golfing jumper positively covered in the sodding things. As a nod to the series' enigmatic title it was hardly subtle – he looked less like a mysterious alien and more like the Riddler on Christmas morning.

Interviewed on location for the local TV news, a soggy Kate O'Mara explained her reasons for returning to the show: "I actually did write to the producer and say, 'Hollywood's all very well, but the relentless sunshine is getting me down, and I just long to be back under the lowering skies up to my eyes in mud'." Although, on reflection, perhaps not quite *this* much mud.

At the hotel, McCoy made the mistake of showing Nathan-Turner his party piece of playing the spoons – little realising entire eras of the programme had been founded on less. "He came up to me and said, 'We've got to get those into *Doctor Who!*'" said McCoy. "I thought he was joking. I thought he was drunk." But it did have its upside. "I had to play them all over Kate O'Mara's front. What a privilege that was."[1]

Back at Television Centre, one of McCoy's first jobs was recording the regeneration. In the absence of his predecessor, he was forced to don Baker's costume and a curly blonde wig that made him look, by his own estimation, "like Harpo Marx". (You know things are bad when someone's wearing the sixth Doctor's costume and it *isn't* the most ridiculous thing about them.)

As he watched the new Doctor's debut unfold before the cameras with a heavy heart, Andrew Cartmel was determined to put his stamp on the rest of the season. Unfortunately, Malcolm Kohll's effort – working title *Flight of the Chimeron* – was currently receiving a roasting in Development Hell, with Nathan-Turner describing episode two as "the worst script I've ever read". With the clock ticking, the writer churned out a new episode in 48 hours – though Cartmel was still nervous, heading into the office on a Sunday evening in order to make sure the manuscript was fit to cross his boss's desk the next day. Still, at least he wasn't there alone: on top of his filing cabinet was a ridiculously large circular photograph of Sylvester McCoy's face that covered half the wall. The picture had been ordered for the Doctor Who Exhibition at Longleat but, in a

moment of *Spinal Tap*-style confusion, the manufacturer had interpreted the dimensions as inches instead of centimetres. ("I see this new Doctor Who's a bit of a big 'ead," grumbled the postman as he wrestled it through the door.)

In May, McCoy jetted back across the Atlantic for another stint on the Doctor Who Exhibition Tour, this time appearing in Boston alongside Janet Fielding, before returning to record his sophomore story, *Paradise Towers*. The actor was still jittery about his performance, and spoke to Cartmel about ways they might improve the Doctor's relationship with Mel, though Cartmel was somewhat distracted by the sudden influx of young ladies hired to play the Towers' feral female street gangs, the Kangs. So distracted, in fact, he ended up snogging one of them in a BBC lift. The Mel problem resolved itself shortly afterwards when, after much dithering, Bonnie Langford turned down Nathan-Turner's offer of eight more episodes, citing a lack of character development. "You keep thinking, people are going to be so sick of this loon with the red hair running around saying, 'Doctor!'"[6] said Langford. (After which there was an awkward silence until somebody said: "What? No – don't be ridiculous! You're just being paranoid.")

As thoughts turned to Mel's replacement, 24-year-old Sophie Aldred was offered the role of Ace in Ian Briggs' season finale, with an option of retaining her for a further 14 episodes. Aldred was appearing in a production of *Fiddler on the Roof* in Manchester at the time, alongside Topol and long-serving Dalek operator John Scott Martin (playing a different role, obviously – there aren't any Daleks in *Fiddler on the Roof*). When she received the call offering her the *Doctor Who* job, Martin handed her a Dalek postcard on which he'd written: "Earthling Sophie: Congratulations and welcome to the family." Later, Topol congratulated the actress and told her mother, who was visiting, "I knew she was going to be a star!" Frankly, it sounded like the cue for a song.

Recording *Flight of the Chimeron* in Wales, Sylvester McCoy unveiled the latest addition to his outfit – an umbrella with a handle fashioned into the shape of a bright red... full stop. Nah, just kidding – it was a question mark. (Seriously, it was only a matter of time until he

233

started walking around with a sandwich board with "Can You Guess Who I'm Supposed To Be?" written on it.) The main location for the shoot was the Majestic Holiday Camp on Barry Island – which wasn't exactly majestic (but was quite camp). When he'd innocently discussed the future with Timothy Dalton all those months ago, little did McCoy know that one of them would soon be filming in Tangiers, Vienna, Gibralta and California, while the other was holed up in a disused Butlin's in Glamorgan. Not that he was bitter, you understand.

For the part of motorbike-riding tomboy Ray – still in the frame as a potential companion – director Chris Clough had originally cast Lynn Gardner, but the actress had to be replaced by Sara Griffiths after breaking her arm while learning to ride a scooter in the BBC car park. And eyebrows were raised when the role of the Tollmaster, a sort of galactic ticket inspector, went to comedy veteran Ken Dodd. The job had originally been accepted by Bob Monkhouse, but he'd had to cancel in order to go into hospital for a throat operation. Nathan-Turner had then offered it to Christopher Biggins, whose agent apparently said he was too big a star for a glorified cameo. So the gig went to the self-styled Squire of Knotty Ash who – predictably – was tickled pink. "I was overjoyed," said Doddy, who claimed to have watched the show religiously from the beginning. "I was overjoyed. I was discomknockerated as a matter of fact. Yes, discomknockerated."[7] (Honestly, he really talks like that.)

According to McCoy, Dodd ended up playing the scene as himself because no-one else told him what to do. "I just went on and tried to be tattifilarious,"[7] said Doddy, inevitably. Though the part was relatively small, he managed to extend it considerably with a heroic contender for the longest death scene in *Who* history – and apparently it was even longer in the original edit.

In interviews to accompany a photocall with Doddy, McCoy and Langford, Nathan-Turner compared *Doctor Who* to *The Morecambe and Wise Show*, in so much as "everyone wants to be in it". Some fans took this at face value as yet further evidence that Nathan-Turner was more interested in making a light entertainment show than a science fantasy drama, and

there was more criticism for the producer at a convention in Bath that weekend, when he came under fire from some of his own former colleagues. Sylvester McCoy, meanwhile, was racking up more Air Miles with a flying visit to yet another US convention. But if he was working hard at building an international audience, he was about to get some serious competition as, in July, a production company called Coast to Coast announced they had bought the rights to a *Doctor Who* feature film – and, with £1.5 million backing still to be found for a project with global ambitions, the chances of it starring the ferret-wrangler from *Tiswas* were, it had to be said, pretty slim.

The real McKay

Around six weeks before the launch of the new series, John Nathan-Turner was told BBC bosses were once again planning to hoik *Doctor Who* out of its traditional Saturday home and back into a weekday slot. And this time, it would be going mano-a-mano with no less a rival than *Coronation Street*.

ITV's venerable Manchester soap had been churning out successive generations of hair-netted harridans and tragi-comic fag-ash matriarchs since 1960. So in one sense the scheduling was billed as a straight fight between two of Britain's most cherished television institutions. In reality, though, *Corrie* was still at the top of its game, with one 1986 episode (a fire at the Rovers Return) having pulled in just under 27 million viewers. To the conspiracy theorists, it seemed like a deliberate plot to let Hilda Ogden and company finish the job Michael Grade had bungled two years earlier. This was nonsense, according to Jonathan Powell, who insisted in a BBC statement: "We don't invest good money in a series just to throw it away." In later years, however, he came clean, admitting: "Moving it against *Coronation Street* was a way of throwing it away, really, because in those days nothing got an audience against it."[8] A case of giving them enough soap to hang themselves, if you will.

At the end of July, Sophie Aldred made her *Doctor Who* debut when she recorded her first scenes as Ace at Television Centre. That's when she'd eventually managed to find out where it was; the actress was embarrassed to ask in front of Bonnie Langford, "who must have been given directions on how to get there in the womb".[9] Having seen some of the hideous creations her predecessor was forced to wear (white trousers – *in a quarry?*), Aldred was delighted to be able to have an input into Ace's look. She was keen to emulate a picture she'd seen in hipster bible *The Face* of a young woman wearing a black bomber jacket, cycling shorts and stripey tights, and joined costume designer Richard Croft on a shopping spree down the King's Road in Chelsea. The pair of them covered the jacket in badges – including a *Blue Peter* badge, which caused a bit of a fuss as *BP*'s legendarily fierce editor, Biddy Baxter, wouldn't allow such a coveted item to be worn by someone who hadn't earned it. Nathan-Turner's production secretary was duly dispatched to check its provenance, and was able to confirm that, in 1970, said badge had been won fairly and squarely by 11-year-old Sophie Aldred, of Blackheath, for her brilliant design for a rocket launcher built using a washing-up liquid bottle and a length of garden hose. (Aldred had long dreamed of being a *Blue Peter* presenter and, at around the same time she was cast as Ace, also landed a job hosting a new BBC children's programme called *Corners*. On the new show, she would be accompanied by a funny little alien with a silly voice. And on *Corners*, her co-presenter was a green puppet.)

During taping for *Dragonfire*, as the season finale was now called, Aldred put her hands behind her head and revealed some stray wisps of underarm hair, forcing the scene to be re-shot as, according to an exasperated Andrew Cartmel, certain production personnel believed "the un-shaven armpits of a female companion could have brought down the nation".[10]

Personal grooming issues notwithstanding, at the end of her first day's filming, Aldred was approached by Nathan-Turner, who told her "we're on if you're on". She accepted the role of the Doctor's new companion on the spot (at least she assumed he was talking about the role of the Doctor's new companion – he didn't seem the type to be propositioning her for anything else), while Ian Briggs – who had based Ace on three girls he knew that he thought might fit the brief for "Alf" – agreed to sign over copyright of the character to the BBC. "I did need to sign a waiver saying I wouldn't make any financial claims or become a nuisance," he said. "But the alternative was, if I'd said, 'No, I'm not going to do that', she would just have gone down there and then. In monetary terms, I wasn't going to get anything either way, so I might as well have the satisfaction of seeing her have more adventures."[11] In other words, he was getting no money and no creative control, but hoped he would at least be able to impress people at parties by telling them he'd created Ace off of TV's *Doctor Who* ("Yes, it is still going").

In mid-August, Michael Grade hosted a press launch for BBC1's autumn season, including a trailer for the new *Doctor Who* series that promised "a galaxy of stars", followed by clips of such dazzling international A-listers as Hugh Lloyd, Brenda Bruce, Richard Briers, Bonnie Langford, Clive Merrison, Judy Cornwell, Ken Dodd, Don Henderson and Stubby Kaye. The new Doctor, meanwhile, was represented by a fleeting shot of Sylvester McCoy, spark out with his eyes shut. Grade, clearly dazzled by such stellar talent as Terry Scott's former sidekick in *Hugh and I* and "Angela Stacey" from the *Crown Court* episode "A Matter of Honour", got a bit carried away with himself and announced the series would continue "irrespective of viewing figures" if it demonstrated an upswing in quality. The press, however, seemed less interested in the likes of Judy Cornwell and Don Henderson than the show's forthcoming ratings showdown with Hilda, Bet and company, while the *Telegraph* introduced readers to the brand new Doctor, "Sylvester McKay".

But Michael Grade, it seemed, was as good as his word, as John Nathan-Turner was told the next season had been greenlit, even before the current one had started airing. This time, the prospect of overseeing the show's 25th anniversary celebrations – possibly combined with having sod all else to do – helped persuade the producer to stay on for one more year. But after that, he was finally, definitely leaving, and there was nothing anyone could say to change his mind. Apart from, possibly, "Will you stay another year?"

In fact, planning for the silver anniversary season was already well advanced, with a test script called *The Crooked Smile* commissioned from Graeme Curry; an Arthurian fable called

Storm Over Avallion was also on the cards, which Nathan-Turner suggested might see a return for Brigadier Lethbridge-Stewart and UNIT.

As launch week arrived, the *Radio Times* continued the understated promotional campaign by once again relegating the show to John Craven's Back Pages (which weren't on the back, and weren't written by John Craven) and, four days later, at 7.35pm on Monday, September 7th, television history was made as millions of children sat down to enjoy the seventh Doctor's TV debut – only to be told by their parents to clear off, as it was time for *Corrie*.

The Two Bonnies

Heralded by Oliver Elmes' impressive new title sequence – a kinetic tumble through swirling spiral galaxies that's only let down by Sylvester McCoy's daft wink, some extracted molars masquerading as asteroids and a truly hideous new logo that looks like it belongs on the side of an ice-cream van – *Time and the Rani* is the cautionary tale of what happens when a producer and his favourite writing team get to interpret their vision of *Doctor Who* straight on to the screen without the restraining hand of a script editor. Or, indeed, anyone else who might have been on hand to say: "Really – are you *sure*?"

The last time we met her, the Rani was disguised as an old Geordie hag. This time, she appears to have stepped straight off the plane from *Dynasty* – which, of course, Kate O'Mara had – complete with big hair, shoulder pads that could have your eye out and a TARDIS "disguised" as a giant pink pyramid. In the middle of a quarry. The Rani's first words on entering the TARDIS and encountering the unconscious Doctor (children's entertainer Sylvester McCoy in that Harpo wig) and Mel are: "Leave the girl – it's the man I want". And if you think *that's* camp, just wait until she starts dressing up as Bonnie Langford.

Yes, you read that right – in possibly the most woefully misconceived notion ever to make it beyond the BBC bar, Kate O'Mara spends a good portion of the first two episodes of this wearing a ginger wig and pink legwarmers and talking in a squeaky voice in an

attempt to fool a dazed and confused Doctor into believing she's Mel. And the fact she does it so well – even perfecting Langford's absurdly bouncy stage-school gait – just makes it all the more excruciating. Apparently the crew dubbed them the Two Bonnies – which is much funnier than anything in the actual script.

"It was alright when Bonnie wasn't on set," recalled a mortified O'Mara. "When she was on set, it was deeply embarrassing. Bonnie, I think, was quite flattered, as far as I know. Well, she's still speaking to me."[1]

The Rani's plan involves kidnapping a selection of history's most brilliant scientists, including Einstein, Louis Pasteur and Hypatia, and feeding their collective genius into the giant brain she keeps on the table in her laboratory, in an attempt to formulate a substitute for Strange Matter (hence the working title, which would have been far less of an insult to the memory of JB Priestley than the one they went with). She then intends to load said formula onto a rocket in order to explode a Strange Matter asteroid, which will then turn the giant brain into an all-powerful Time Manipulator. True story.

In the end, the whole thing is scuppered when the rocket misses the asteroid *because the Rani has forgotten to put a hinge on the launcher* (she should have drafted in the 11-year-old Sophie Aldred as a design consultant). Though chances are the plan would still have ended in failure anyway on account of being, you know, a crock of total shit.

While the script may have been the same old Pip and Jane nonsense, the serial does signal something of a fresh new look for the show. Sure, it's filmed in a quarry, but it's an unusually *good* quarry, and the series' first ever use of CGI – to create flying bubble traps that send their victims spinning through the air – is impressive (if you can tune out Bonnie Langford's screaming, which only selected breeds of dog are lucky enough to be able to do). It's just a pity the script's camp sensibility is allowed to infect so many other parts of the production: as well as the Rani's TARDIS, Quantel Paintbox is used to turn the sky a vivid shade of pink, while the designer has clearly decided the concrete tube that Mel hides in at one point is either a) not alien

enough or b) not gay enough. So he's hung a
bit of tinsel on it.

Mention should also be made of newcomer
Keff McCulloch's determination to drown everything out by apparently leaving his Emulator
synthesizer on demo mode – complete with
handclaps. But with a script this bad, perhaps
that's no bad thing. (McCulloch's interpretation of the theme, meanwhile, breaks with
tradition by not even *trying* to recreate Delia
Derbyshire's famed "woo-oo" sound – stop me
if I'm getting too technical – instead falling
back on a busy synth arrangement that would,
at best, make a pretty average Pet Shop Boys
b-side.)

As the Doctor, Sylvester McCoy doesn't so
much hit the ground running as smack head
first into it: his introductory scene is so frantic
and garbled, it makes Tom Baker's debut in
Robot look positively underplayed. It was also
clearly written for his predecessor – imagine
Colin Baker speaking these lines and it suddenly makes a lot more sense.

For anyone brave enough to watch all four
parts in one sitting – and *Space Helmet* would
recommend a very stiff drink before doing so
– *Time and the Rani* affords the opportunity to
see the new Doctor literally finding his feet
before your eyes: by the end, you may very
well be won over by this curious, quixotic little
man. But McCoy's extraordinary performance
in the opening instalment, matched by Bonnie
Langford at her worst and Kate O'Mara as
Bonnie Langford at her worst, conspire with
P&J's brutal assault on the English language to
create perhaps the most painful 25 minutes in
the entire *Doctor Who* corpus. Later, after half
an hour of scrambling across shale in white
ski-pants and a pink blouson, Mel appears to
have a sudden epiphany, and declares: "I've
had enough of this drivel." At home, four million heads nodded in unison.

With Tim Curry being touted as a possible
big screen Doctor, McCoy headed back to
America for yet another promotional tour.
Which is just as well as, back home, the reaction to the new series was mixed, to say the
least. *Today's* Janet Street-Porter claimed to be
charmed, and *The Stage* and *Television Today*
felt there was still some life in the old dog yet,
but *The Daily Telegraph* and the *Evening
Standard* were withering, while one corre-

spondent to the BBC's *Points of View* described
episode one as "25 minutes of the most appalling mindless drivel that would insult the intelligence of a five-year-old". Thank you Mr A
Cartmel, of London.

The most savage attack, however, came from
DWAS co-ordinator Andrew Beech, who
launched an eye-watering broadside against
the programme in the pages of the *Daily Mail*,
claiming many of his members believed "there
is something radically wrong with a show that,
24 years ago, had something indefinable but
sufficiently attractive to capture the hearts and
imaginations of the British public.

"Whether through the short-sighted inepti-
tude of the planners or the excesses of the
production team," he added, "*Doctor Who* (as a
popular television show) is slowly but surely
being killed." I bet he still watched the story at
least ten times, though.

Still, at least McCoy could comfort himself
with the fact the Controller of BBC1 was fully
behind him. According to Andrew Cartmel,
after watching episode one of *Time and the Rani*
in his office, Powell nodded and said: "Great
hat. I like the hat." Right now, that was looking
like a pretty good review.

More seriously, the ratings were utterly dis-
mal: averaging just 4.6 million across its four
episodes, against *Coronation Street's* heady 14
million, *Time and the Rani* languished in the
doldrums of the Top 100 like a Su Pollard
album in Woolworth's bargain bin. And, just to
add an extra bit of sand in his sandwich,
McCoy was crowned Wally of the Week by the
Express' TV critic, Nina Myskow. (Yeah, beat
that, Corrie!)

On September 29th, *Doctor Who* was once
again subjected to trial by morning television
in a repeat of the previous year's mauling on
viewer talkback show *Open Air*. This time, it
was McCoy, Langford and Nathan-Turner who
were forced to sit with fixed smiles as presenter Pattie Cauldwell dragged up every bad
review she could lay her hands on, including
reminding McCoy of his Wally of the Week
honour. In fact, many of the callers to the show
were broadly supportive, but this didn't seem
to deter Cauldwell, and a harangued Nathan-
Turner was forced to trot out his well-worn
"memory treats" defence, claiming: "I think
everybody who has ever watched the series has

an era that is their favourite... and I think that 20 years later, the appreciation of it is perhaps a little cloudy."

In later years, McCoy admitted to have been stung by the criticism. "You have to have a very thick skin," he told *Doctor Who Magazine* in 2010. "Anyone who says, 'He's the worst Doctor Who' – it's the stupidity of actors, listening to those people. We are stupid. But I got over it."[5]

A Clockwork Orange: the sitcom

As a new month dawned, there was no let-up in the series' bad publicity: on October 1st, Bonnie Langford was exposed in the tabloids as a thieving crack-whore caught selling drugs to schoolchildren (just kidding – though they did report she'd been fined for speeding on the way to rehearsals) and, the following day, *The Sun* ran a story headed "Beeb axe Dr Who after 24 years". The story was nonsense, of course, and was followed a week or so later by the inevitable follow-up, "Carry On Doctor", in which the paper took credit for the BBC reversing the decision it had never taken in the first place. How very clever of them.

In the real world, planning on the next season was picking up a gear, with Andrew Cartmel now convinced the series would benefit from being a shade darker in tone, while re-introducing an element of mystery and unpredictability around the Doctor. Both ideas found favour with Sylvester McCoy, who liked the idea of his character as a manipulative cosmic chess player. Cartmel was also keen to foreground Sophie Aldred's Ace in many of the stories – another notion that appealed to McCoy, as it meant he'd have fewer lines to learn.

As scripted, *Paradise Towers* might well have appeared as a portent of things to come. With its cavalcade of cannibals, fascists, savage street gangs, murdered teenagers and scenes of urban decay, the basic premise reads like an 18-rated cross between *A Clockwork Orange* and *Nineteen Eighty-Four*. Yet it's played and directed like children's telly – or somebody's unfortunate idea of children's telly – complete with comedy mugging and jokey production design (the homicidal robot cleaners, which should be ter-

rifying, are particularly rubbish – though the sets and lighting are a cut above what we've been used to lately.)

Stephen Wyatt's story also suffers from a fatal lapse of logic, which asks us to believe that, when the Towers' "great architect" Kroagnon went nuts, the tenants of the decaying apartment block removed his brain and stuck it in the basement – seemingly along with the necessary equipment to transfer it into a homicidal new body. ("Well does anyone have a *better* plan?" asked the chairman of the residents' committee defensively.) In other ways, though, the script demonstrates a renewed inventiveness, with real thought having gone into the evolution of the language – "brainquarters", "mayhaps", etc – and a delightful sequence in which the Doctor uses the skewey logic of the Towers' all-important rulebook to talk himself out of captivity, paving the way for many such confrontations with authority figures over the next few years. Andrew Cartmel's arrival on the scene is also signalled in other subtle but significant ways, including minimal TARDIS scenes (we're going to be seeing a *lot* less of those roundels than we did during the Davison and C. Baker years) and, tellingly, a total absence of continuity references.

For these reasons and more, *Paradise Towers* has the makings of a genuine relaunch. What a pity, then, that director Nicholas Mallett and his cast aren't on the same page as the writer and script editor. Keff McCulloch, of all people, came up with a hypothesis that this season's writers all thought they were scripting film noir, but the directors thought they were making screwball comedies. It's as good a theory as any.

As played, the Kangs feel less like a bunch of street-smart female savages than a stage school production of *Cats* while, as the fascistic Chief Caretaker, Richard Briers (complete with Hitler 'tache and "comedy" Nazi salute) soars so far over the top, he's in danger of needing oxygen. And that's *before* he's possessed by the brain of Kroagnon, after which he just takes the piss to a level that's insulting to everyone else involved. "The producer was worried that I wasn't taking the role seriously," said Briers. "He thought that *Doctor Who* was some kind of classic, which I suppose it was, but he considered it a

The Greatest Show in the Galaxy! (cancelled)

classic like one of Shakespeare's plays. He thought that I wanted to send up *Doctor Who*. I think he was frightened I would start overdoing it – so I did."[12] Yeah, cheers for that.

Sylvester McCoy, by contrast, is rather good. By now, the actor has started to settle into the role and is making a pretty decent fist of it. And it's almost despite himself: because he learned his craft banging nails up his nose as opposed to studying Stanislavski and vocal warm-ups, there's a wild, unpolished quality to McCoy's performance that is frequently ridiculous, but just as frequently compelling. Apparently lacking such basic skills as knowing which words and syllables to emphasise – something, to be fair, that applies as much to his diction off-screen as on – McCoy has a habit of coming unstuck at critical moments, especially when called upon to do voluble anger. But the same cavalier attitude to conventional speech also allows him to turn the most prosaic piece of plot exposition into something rather magical and strange, and he excels at scenes of quiet despair and world-weary contemplation. The result is the most genuinely odd Time Lord since Tom Baker and the sense that, while it would be a stretch to call McCoy a great actor, at his best, he's capable of being a great Doctor Who.

With *Paradise Towers* averaging 4.9 million viewers, ratings were still flatlining, but at least one man was impressed: after the final episode, Jonathan Powell took the unprecedented step of sending a memo to the production team congratulating them on a "first rate" job. Presumably he was in the loo during all Richard Briers' scenes. It turned out to be a good time to have Powell on-side, too, as, in mid-October, Michael Grade left the BBC to go to Channel 4; Powell took his place as Controller of BBC1, while producer Mark Shivas stepped up as Head of Drama.

In his memo, Powell had wondered if there wasn't mileage for a *Paradise Towers* sequel featuring the Daleks (he wasn't on the big bucks for nothing, you know). But, mindful of the upcoming anniversary, Nathan-Turner and Cartmel already had the Daleks pencilled in for the sequel to another story: 1963's *An Unearthly Child*.

To write it, Cartmel had commissioned a newcomer called Ben Aaronovitch, who had proposed the aforesaid Arthurian story, which the script editor likened to "hitting a seam of gold". The script had been passed to him by BBC producer Caroline Oulton, who described Aaronovitch as "a young fat guy whose mum answers the phone". Having failed to track down the fat guy's mum's number, Cartmel took a chance on a number in the phone book, and the call was answered by Aaronovitch's dad. With the unassuming modesty for which he would become famous, Cartmel said of Aaronovitch: "He had an educated and instinctive understanding of science fiction which was way beyond that of any other writer I knew. Not beyond mine, though."[2]

No sooner had he acceded to a reluctant Cartmel's request to abandon his original Arthurian proposal in order to incorporate Nathan-Turner's desire to bring back the Daleks, Aaronovitch's scripts hit a snag in the form of Terry Nation's ever-amenable agent Roger Hancock, who declared: "I read the first two scripts on Friday and my reaction was, frankly: Forget it."[2] Thankfully, the situation was soon remedied by a hasty rewrite – of the numbers on Nation's royalty cheque.

On October 31st, there was a Hallowe'en treat for TV trickster Sylvester McCoy when *The Sun* did an unexpected volt-face and hailed him as the show's saviour – though most positive press was still reserved for talking up the Doctor Who movie, which, depending on what paper you read, was slated to star either Tom Conti, John Cleese or Dudley Moore, with ex-Bond girl Caroline Munro rumoured to be playing a robot in charge of an intergalactic pirate radio station. Stranger things have happened, I guess – many of them in *Delta and the Bannermen*, which brought a welcome blast of sunshine to the long winter nights of November 1987. Say what you like about Malcolm Kohll's three-parter – and many have – it's not like any *Doctor Who* story we've seen before, or since. Filmed entirely on location during June and July, it's a fresh, summery musical comedy (yes, really) in which an alien queen arrives in a 1950s Welsh holiday camp – via a flying intergalactic tourbus that crash lands in the herbaceous borders – pursued by a bunch of leather-clad space mercenaries, who stop off to kill Ken Dodd on the way. "Now let me try and get this right," says the

239

camp's unflappable manager, Burton. "Now you are telling me you are not the Happy Hearts Holiday Club from Bolton, but instead are spacemen in fear of an attack from some other spacemen?"

And the madness doesn't end there. While the rest of the alien tour party arrive clutching toothbrushes and plastic suitcases, Delta, queen of the Chimeron, is carrying an unborn child around in an egg (best not to dwell on how it was produced). When said baby later hatches, it starts out as a mewling green hand-puppet, but is soon replaced by a real baby in a romper suit and green face paint. Meanwhile, local rock and roll heartthrob Billy is so smitten by Delta, he resolves to turn into one of her kind by eating some Chimeron baby food (interesting plan – if he ate some nuts, would he turn into a squirrel?). This is the cause of some distress for local biker chick Ray, who goes for a cry in the laundry room and runs into an alien hitman played by the lead singer of crepe-soled 80s a cappella group the Flying Pickets. Broadway and Hollywood musical star Stubby Kaye, 60s sitcom veteran Hugh Lloyd and Bulman star Don Henderson complete the world's most unlikely "all-star cast".

Frankly, it has about as much substance as a knobbly knees contest, and the plot is flimsier than a chalet party wall. But it's also terrific fun, and a real breath of fresh air after all the "standing around in the TARDIS arguing" longueurs of recent years. And Sylvester McCoy's Doctor looks just as at home jiving on the dancefloor and clutching a Stratocaster as he does fighting off an alien invasion. Even his harshest critics would surely find it hard to resist the bit of improvised business where he listens to an apple.

Hi-de-Hi meets Kurosawa via Star Wars and Back to the Future, Delta and the Bannermen is a genuinely fun romp that brings a whole new meaning to the term holiday camp.

"You know what was missing from *Citizen Kane*? A dragon."

If *Delta and the Bannermen* held out the vague but tantalising promise of better things to come, not many saw it that way at the time: several newspapers laid into the serial, with *The Times* dismissing it as "desperately antisep-

tic" and the *Sunday Express* declaring that "many former *Doctor Who* enthusiasts, including this one, now feel that events in the BBC gravel pit are of little interest." Ouch.

That was nothing, however, compared to the criticism from closer to home. In its November issue, rabble-rousing news mag *Doctor Who Bulletin* stepped up its personal hate crusade against John Nathan-Turner by launching Operation Who: a campaign to pressure the BBC into removing the "hopelessly inadequate producer" who was "sounding the series' death-knell". In a front page editorial under the banner headline "JN-T MUST GO NOW", "the historian and world's leading authority on *Doctor Who*", Ian Levine, explained the reasoning behind this "final desperate bid to restore *Doctor Who*'s credibility for its twenty-fifth anniversary season".

Many in the press were only happy to play along, resulting in a further slew of bad publicity. Furthermore, the magazine caught the eye of a researcher on *Did You See?*, BBC2's long-running television review show, which decided to scrap a planned birthday feature on the enduring appeal of *Doctor Who* in favour of giving airtime to some of its most disaffected fans. "It's become a mockery, pantomime version if its former self," railed Levine, sitting in his living room in front of his three – yes three – TVs.

According to Andrew Cartmel, Nathan-Turner was hugely "depressed" by all the vitriol. "I felt he'd made major mistakes during his term as producer," the script editor wrote in his diaries. "But now I couldn't help feeling sorry for him as he sat glumly in his office leafing through the personal attacks."[2] That same month, Cartmel had his own run-in with the producer when he went out for a working lunch with some of the writers, the production secretary and Sophie Aldred, without inviting the boss. Little realising Peter Grimwade's *Doctor Who* career had been terminated for less, he had to spend much of the afternoon talking Nathan-Turner out of a sulk. ("Honestly, I can't understand why you didn't get the invite, John – I put it inside this old copy of *Peter Davison's Book of Alien Planets* on your shelf so you wouldn't miss it.")

On top of all the rows and unpleasantness, there was still a job to do, and by now Cartmel

240

had commissioned the silver anniversary serial from another new writer, Kevin Clarke. *The Harbinger* was to feature the Cybermen in a story designed to throw a huge question mark over the Doctor's real identity. (Figuratively speaking, of course – though if Nathan-Turner got wind of the idea...)

On November 19th, Sylvester McCoy was contracted for another 14 episodes the following year. The reduced episode counts meant that, unlike his predecessors, the actor was only required for five months of the year – something he found highly appealing, often describing *Doctor Who* as his "summer job". Well, it beats working in McDonald's. Probably.

Kicking off on the show's twenty-fourth anniversary, season finale *Dragonfire* is another example of the disconnect between intention and execution that had dogged *Paradise Towers*. Ian Briggs clearly envisioned an Indiana Jones-style Saturday matinee adventure in which the Doctor and company search for a lost treasure in the frozen catacombs beneath a planet of ice. It's also something of a love letter to film itself, with most of the characters named after filmmakers or, rather indulgently, film theorists, like the Hungarian critic Béla Balázs, the German academic Siegfried Kracauer and André Bazin, founder of the French journal *Cahiers du cinema*. Meanwhile, Kane – the main villain of the piece – takes his name from what is widely regarded as the greatest achievement in motion picture history. No pressure, then.

All of which only makes it more acutely apparent that what appears on screen could barely be less cinematic – it's played like a light comedy, lit like a gameshow and directed like bog-standard kids' telly. But then, what did they expect from a cross between *King Solomon's Mines* and *Aliens* filmed entirely in TC1, large chunks of which take place in a freezer centre?

Yeah, about that: so ice man Kane – whose body temperature is so low he can kill humans just by touching them – is exiled by his own people to the dark side of the planet Svartos, along with a biomechanoid dragon jailer who, bizarrely, holds the means to his escape. (Yes, again – what is the *matter* with people?) To pass the time, Kane takes it upon himself to open his own space-port-cum-frozen food supermarket. Fair enough, everyone needs a

hobby, I suppose – but why stick at it for *three thousand years* before bothering to search for the dragon? Unless there was a *very* long queue at the 10 Items or Less till.

As well as all the Film Theory 101 stuff, the sense that the show has now been colonised by last year's graduating media studies class is compounded by a scene – added by Cartmel – in which a guard quotes a chunk of John Tulloch and Manuel Alvarado's *Doctor Who: The Unfolding Text* – some guff about the "semiotic thickness of auxhiliary performance codes" – at the Doctor, which is all very meta and everything. On the whole, though, Ian Briggs' dialogue is smart and peppy – "time for a quick adventure, then back for tea!" – while talk of such wonders as ice gardens and singing trees add a certain poetic quality.

The story marks a speedy return for Tony Selby's lovable rogue/homicidal maniac (delete as applicable) Sabalom Glitz, who co-opts the Doctor into his treasure hunt during a random encounter in a very low-rent recreation of *Star Wars*' famous cantina scene. Briggs had originally written a Han Solo-type character called Razorback instead; Harrison Ford probably wasn't in the frame for it.

As Ace, Sophie Aldred makes a winning debut, even if her supposedly realistic "street" argot – which includes "bilgebag" "doughnut" and, most bafflingly, "birdbath" – is as unconvincing as her backstory. (She was transported from Perivale to Iceworld after accidentally whipping up a time storm in the school chemistry lab. Apparently. And her real name turns out to be Dorothy. See what they did there?)

In her final story, Bonnie Langford gives probably her best performance in the role, suggesting she might finally have found a way to make Mel less nails-down-the-blackboard irritating (yes, as good as that). For her leaving scene, Sylvester McCoy had been adamant they should use one of the pieces Cartmel had provided for his audition. The script editor handed it over more to prove it wouldn't work than anything else, at which point he saw it being photocopied and added into the cast's scripts. Along with Ian Briggs, Cartmel ended up doing a hasty final rewrite on the back of some napkins in the BBC breakfast bar on the day it was recorded.

Turns out McCoy was right: like Sarah Jane's

departure a decade earlier, this is the best scene in the whole show – maybe they ought to write *all* the scripts on napkins in the bar. And McCoy plays it beautifully – "Think about me when you're living your life one day after another, all in a neat pattern – think about the homeless traveller and his old police box, his days like crazy paving" – even managing to distract the viewer from the fundamental absurdity of Mel choosing to travel the universe with Glitz instead of the Doctor. Maybe, deep down, squeaky clean Mel just really loves the bad boys.

Despite this, *Dragonfire* is probably best remembered for two particularly controversial moments. The first is Kane's rather graphic demise, another *Raiders of the Lost Ark* homage in which his face falls off after being exposed to direct sunlight – an effect achieved by melting a wax casting of actor Edward Peel's head while the visual effects team pumped extra goo through his nose and mouth. The sequence led to complaints in the press from "horrified" parents, which must have been strangely gratifying for the production team – it was a long time since *Doctor Who* had made headlines for being terrifying, as opposed to being terrible. And it could have been so much worse: the scene had originally intended to feature a shot of Kane's body withering away as well, which the fx crew hoped to achieve using a sex doll. Unfortunately, during recording the dummy deflated so much its trousers fell off – which really *would* have given the mums and dads something to write in about.

Even more memorable than that, though – for fans at least – is *Dragonfire*'s overly literal interpretation of the word "cliffhanger" when, at the end of episode one, Sylvester McCoy climbs over the side of a cliff and hangs there from his brolly, for no readily apparent reason. Given all the snickering film studies stuff, it wouldn't be a surprise to learn it was intended as a witty deconstruction of the language of episodic adventure serials. But apparently it was just a cock-up.

Cartmel recalled watching the finished broadcast with Ian Briggs and "aching at the cheapness and nastiness with which it had been shot"[2] but, for what it was worth, the story did enough to top most fan season polls, and prompted an unexpected outbreak of enthusiasm from *The Daily Telegraph*'s Charles Spencer, who declared: "Sylvester McCoy is an appealing Doctor with a genuine sense of wonder and a nice line in irony, though he could possibly do with a little less whimsy and a shade more authority.

"I find myself warming to the idea of *Doctor Who* as a slightly camp interstellar variety show," he added. "Indeed, I enjoyed the first episode of *Dragonfire* so much that I immediately re-ran the video." Crikey.

With ratings still stuck stubbornly around the five million mark, the BBC's annual audience research report gave McCoy a less than emphatic 46% approval rating – the same number of people who expressed a desire to see the show come back the following year – while Langford's performance rated a miserly 34%. BBC bigwigs, however, were surprisingly upbeat, congratulating Nathan-Turner on a job well done and bigging up the re-launch as a resounding success. But then, having made a point of sacking the leading man but keeping the producer in the harness, maybe there was nothing else they *could* say. And besides, it really *was* a very nice hat.

25 glorious years (apart from the rubbish ones)

In the first week of *Doctor Who*'s silver anniversary year, the BBC received a card from *Doctor Who Bulletin* publisher Gary Levy congratulating the Corporation on the show's continued success, and proposing a toast to 25 more glorious years. Although, on closer inspection, it actually turned out to be a letter to the Beeb's solicitors refusing to apologise for saying John Nathan-Turner couldn't produce his way out of a paper bag. Still, it's the thought that counts.

With all four of the year's stories commissioned, Andrew Cartmel arranged a get-together with the writers, Sylvester McCoy and Sophie Aldred to discuss how their characters might develop.

In fact, Cartmel and Ben Aaronovitch, who seemed to have been adopted as an unofficial assistant script editor, had already been working on a new mythology for the Doctor, in which he would be revealed to be the Third Man of ancient Gallifreyan lore, alongside

Rassilon and Omega, rather than, in Cartmel's words, "a mere chump of a Time Lord."[2]

The producers of the proposed Doctor Who movie, meanwhile, continued to prove they were better at making headlines than films, as more press stories appeared, suggesting John Cleese was on the verge of signing for three movies, with Caroline Munro now playing the companion. Ian Levine was also on board, not as the companion – that would have been disappointing for everyone – but in an advisory role. Around this time, Levine also appeared on Steve Allen's LBC London radio show, offering his views on the current TV iteration. Turns out he wasn't that keen. But not to worry because, in March, *DWB* proclaimed an end to hostilities with the triumphant news that victory was assured, and that John Nathan-Turner would be leaving *Doctor Who* at the end of the current series. ("Please God let it be true," said Nathan-Turner when he received his copy.)

Though there was still plenty of Doctor Who merchandise around during this period, it tended to be aimed at fans rather than the general consumer. But a company called Dapol did wade into the kids' toy market in 1988 by launching a range of Doctor Who action figures and playsets. Unfortunately, they seemed to have been produced without access to any photos of the things they were meant to be based on – hence Davros had two working arms, K-9 was painted green and the TARDIS console had five sides instead of six. On the plus side, collectors could get *two* different versions of Mel – perfect for recreating scenes from *Time and the Rani*, which is surely any child's dream.

Filming for the new series commenced in explosive style on April 4th, when a pyrotechnic effect for opener *Remembrance of the Daleks* succeeded in sparking a major security alert. The blast – in a tunnel beneath Waterloo East railway station on Easter Monday – was met by police cars, ambulances and a fire engine racing to the scene, fearing an IRA attack. "When the emergency services arrived," guest star George Sewell recalled, "their jaws dropped in disbelief as an army of Daleks emerged from the smoke, gliding towards them."[14] The station was temporarily closed, leaving angry commuters to contemplate British Rail's latest bizarre excuse of "Daleks under the line".

In their first story together as the new TARDIS team, McCoy and Aldred struck up an instant rapport. Unfortunately, relations between the new companion and her producer were proving distinctly cooler. According to Aldred, Nathan-Turner got upset when she complained about the quality of the Ace postcard the BBC had produced: "John lit a fag. He took a very long draw on it, and sort of looked down his nose at me. I felt like I was being frozen by this icy stare. 'Who do you think you are?', he said."[13]

Things got worse when, while recording an early scene for the Dalek story, Aldred asked if Nathan-Turner wouldn't mind putting his cigarette out. "John glared at me from across the room," she recalled. "He opened his jacket, took out his pack of fags, took one, and lit it very obviously in front of me.

"I was going home and crying to my boyfriend, because I didn't know what to do about John. I didn't know if he thought he'd made a mistake in casting me, or if he didn't like me. I remember being very upset about it. Maybe he was showing me who was boss."[13]

A photocall with McCoy, Aldred and the Daleks resulted in a fair amount of positive press coverage, but the taint of bad feeling was never very far away, with Ian Levine once again popping up on LBC, this time getting into a lengthy row with Janet Fielding on "whispering" Bob Harris' phone-in show. And the good news kept on coming: starved of enough regular new episodes to put into syndication, *Doctor Who*'s foothold in America began to slip, and plans for anniversary jaunt for the travelling tourbus exhibition were scrapped. (It was either that, or downgrade it to Jon Pertwee and a Cyberman on a tandem.)

Still, at least the weather was nice, as cast and crew decamped to Somerset to film Stephen Wyatt's circus-set *The Greatest Show in the Galaxy* in a baking hot quarry. It was in the nearby hotel one night that Sophie Aldred plucked up the courage to join John Nathan-Turner at the bar: "And we just talked," she recalled. "We got to know each other, and I think then he realised who I was. From that day on, we got on like a house on fire."[13]

The serial also continued the year's trend for unexpectedly big bangs. The original plan had been to set off an air mortar explosion that would ripple the fabric of a dummy circus tent entrance as Sylvester McCoy walked calmly away. But when the fx boys discovered they'd been supplied with the wrong fittings, they had no choice but to go for something with more wallop instead. Unfortunately, no-one saw fit to convey this to McCoy who, to his credit, barely flinched as a huge ball of dust and flame erupted behind him. Still, he couldn't help wonder if they were trying to tell him something: at least the last guy had just received a phone call...

Back in London, the BBC were approached by theatre producer Mark Furness about acquiring the rights to a Doctor Who stage show. Nathan-Turner was keen, and hoped to be able to direct it himself, with McCoy as star. And just because it was planned for a Christmas run, fans shouldn't go assuming the show would be "pantomime-esque" – though he might have McCoy measured up for a cow costume, just in case. (And those years on *Tiswas* were bound to come in handy for the scene in which he defeated the Daleks with a few well-placed custard pies.)

"I don't care if it *is* The Greatest Show in the Galaxy – where am I supposed to park?"

Amidst all the bitching, backbiting, negative headlines and dwindling public interest, there was one crumb of comfort for John Nathan-Turner in the spring of 1988: after several years of lurching from one crisis to another, actual production of the show was running unusually smoothly. Andrew Cartmel and his team of young Turks had the writing side of things under control (this was the first time for several years he hadn't had to pull the emergency Pip and Jane ripcord), and no-one in the office appeared to want to kill him. To signal a fresh start, he'd even shaved off his trademark beard (though it's possible, given all the criticism he'd been coming in for, that this was simply a poor attempt at a disguise).

Then, over the Spring Bank Holiday weekend at the end of May, maintenance workers discovered asbestos at Television Centre and, as a consequence, Nathan-Turner was told the

studio sessions for *The Greatest Show in the Galaxy* would have to be cancelled.

The producer was having none of it. "It just seemed criminal that all the costumes had been made, we'd done all the location work," he said. "I didn't want to see [the story] go down the pan in the way that *Shada* had done."[15]

In desperation, he rang up the serial's designer, David Laskey, and asked him if, given that the main set was a tent, they couldn't just put it up somewhere else. Laskey was sceptical, as what he'd built wasn't waterproof – and didn't have a roof. As a tent, frankly, it was rubbish. But then he had an idea. "I'd been working the previous year on the game show *Going for Gold* at Elstree, and I knew a lot of people up there," explained Laskey. "So I rang up the facilities assistant up there and I said, 'Look, you've got a big car park, what are the chances of us putting a tent on it?' So he said he'd look into it. In the meantime, I started ringing round tent contractors, and eventually I found one."[15]

And so it was that the fake studio tent came to be erected inside a real tent in the Elstree car park, and the whole thing was recorded as an OB shoot instead.

"The chance they happened to have a story all set in a circus tent is extraordinary," said visual effects assistant Mike Tucker. "Any other story in that season, presented with the same scenario, would probably have not been able to go ahead."[15] Maybe next year they ought to write a story set in the BBC car park, just to be on the safe side.

Unfortunately, the move brought its own problems – not least the lack of soundproofing from a makeshift studio in a busy car park on the Heathrow flight path. "We had planes going overhead, we had things like lorries delivering the beer barrels to the bar at Elstree, or other cast and crew from other programmes zooming into the car park," said Sophie Aldred. "And every time we'd have to stop and re-do it."[15]

On one occasion, they also had to cope with a fire alarm, trooping out of the tent and mingling with the Nazis and French Resistance fighters of *'Allo 'Allo*, who were recording next door. According to David Laskey, the *'Allo 'Allo* cast were far more interested in having their

The Greatest Show in the Galaxy! (cancelled)

picture taken with the firemen than with Doctor Who. Bloody cheek. (Still, it could have been worse – they could have had to talk to the cast of *EastEnders*.)

There were further problems when a cage door, being manually operated by members of the crew pulling on wires, crashed down on actor Ian Reddington's head, hard enough for him to need dental work to repair his smashed back teeth. According to Reddington, as he was led off set, he heard one of the wire operators say to the other: "I told you that would happen."

With so much recording time having been lost, director Alan Wareing and his team were under increasing pressure to get the job finished; the heat inside the tent was also becoming unbearable, and tempers started to fray. Production manager Gary Downie snapped at Sophie Aldred, who bit back her tears long enough to finish the scene, then dashed off to the toilets "for a quick cry". "Highly embarrassed by my over-sensitivity, I visited make-up for a repair job on my eyes, and Gary apologised profusely,"[9] said Aldred. Frankly, it was all getting a bit in-tents.

In the end, they got the story in the can – a feat Alan Wareing lays entirely at John Nathan-Turner's door: "If it hadn't been for his effort and his determination," he said, "we would never have completed the show."[15]

As the cast sweltered under canvas, something very odd was happening during that long, hot British summer: *Doctor Who* found itself at the top of the charts. Not the TV charts, obviously, but a duo calling themselves The Timelords did reach number one with their single "Doctorin' the Tardis", an infectious glam rock mash-up of Ron Grainer's *Doctor Who* theme, The Sweet's *Blockbuster* and Gary Glitter's *Rock and Roll (Part Two)*. Using the aliases Lord Rock and Time Boy, the project was just one of many guises adopted by pop chameleons Bill Drummond and Jimmy Cauty, formerly known as the Justified Ancients of Mu Mu and, later, the KLF. In 1991, the duo used the profits from "Doctorin' the Tardis" to fund the pioneering (and rather fabulous) "stadium house" album *The White Room*, which briefly saw them becoming the biggest-selling singles act in the world. The following year, the band signalled their retirement by firing

blanks from an automatic weapon over the heads of shocked industry suits at the 1992 BRIT Awards, before announcing "The KLF have now left the music business," and dumping a dead sheep in the entrance to a post-ceremony party. In 1994, Drummond and Cauty burned what was left of their earnings – a million pounds in cash – as an artistic statement or, quite possibly, an ironic comment on vacuous artistic statements. The fact that the vinyl for "Doctorin' the Tardis" was engraved with the message "probably the most nauseating record in the world" suggests the single was also intended as some sort of situationist prank – though, as novelty records go, it's actually pretty good. At the height of its success, Gary Glitter also got in on the act by releasing a 12" remix called "Gary in the Tardis". Let's not go there.

After all the problems on *Greatest Show*, Sylvester McCoy and Sophie Aldred were late joining the cast and crew of anniversary shindig *Silver Nemesis* (formerly *The Harbinger*). A photocall was held at Arundel Castle in Sussex – doubling for Windsor – featuring the regulars and Mary Reynolds, who was promoted as a lookalike for the Queen, though it's not entirely evident from the pictures which one. The royal connection was in honour of the show's silver jubilee – according to newspapers at the time, Prince Edward had turned down the offer of a cameo, for which he would have received the princely sum of £50, thus taking his life's legitimate earnings to £50.

By all accounts, the shoot was fairly rancorous and, when John Nathan-Turner monstered writer Kevin Clarke for no good reason, Andrew Cartmel jumped on the first train back to London to escape the "poisonous atmosphere".[2] Things got so bad, even the preternaturally genial McCoy lost his temper and snapped at Aldred. "I couldn't stop the tears rolling down my cheeks," said Aldred, who was clearly having one of those months. "Luckily, this broke the tension; Sylv gave me a big hug and we laughed at our bad tempers."[9]

Unfortunately, the tension wasn't the only thing that was broken: so much dried paint had been applied to the Cybermen's costumes that they started splitting at the crotch, which is the sort of wardrobe malfunction you could really do without when you're trying to terrorise the galaxy without a sense of humour.

Among the guest cast for the serial was Anton Diffring, who had made a career playing various Nazi officers in films like *The Heroes of Telemark* and *Where Eagles Dare*. Diffring made no secret of the fact he thought the script was terrible, and had only accepted the role so he could be in England during Wimbledon fortnight. The only *Doctor Who* story he had ever seen was the tape of *Dragonfire* Nathan-Turner had given him. According to Aldred, his only critique of her debut performance was: "Sophie, mein Got, you vere so *fat!*" The old charmer.

The story would also feature a cameo from Dolores Gray, a Broadway veteran whose voice was memorably described by one critic as "a freight-train slathered in honey", and who had famously won a Tony Award for a show that only lasted six performances. Gray was appearing on stage in London at the time and Nathan-Turner – who was not averse to a show tune himself – thought it was too good an opportunity to miss to get her onto *Doctor Who*, even though no-one else had much of a clue who she actually was. While the rest of the cast travelled to the location under their own steam, Ms Gray insisted on a chauffer-driven limo. It was only when they arrived in Arundel the driver realised he had left her cases on the roadside in Putney – one of which contained nearly £25,000 in diamonds. "She was in such a state," chortled Fiona Walker, who played one of the story's main guest roles. "She practically had to be given the smelling salts!"[16]

British jazz favourite Courtney Pine also put in a cameo appearance, claiming to be such a fan of the show he saw Cybermen in his dreams. "I think all the Doctors are jazz lovers," he declared. "It's because of the time continuum and all that; jazz allows you to think individually. Jazz and the Doctor are one and the same."[17] That's how jazz people talk.

Completing one of the downright oddest line-ups the show had ever fielded, *Silver Nemesis* also features two former drivers for the Kray Twins playing a pair of Cyber henchmen. (Presumably, director Chris Clough told them however they wanted to play it was fine with him – "just don't hurt me or my family".)

A few days after the shoot wrapped, Sylvester McCoy made his UK convention debut at an event in Bath, alongside Sophie Aldred and his two predecessors in the role. If Colin Baker bore his successor any ill will, he certainly didn't let it show – though you wouldn't have blamed McCoy for checking under his car, just in case. Later that month, the seventh Doctor – in full costume – could be found working behind the counter in a Covent Garden shop as part of an event to raise money for the Terrence Higgins Trust. Sure, it was a bit of a comedown after centuries spent saving the universe from evil, but the hours were good and there was a 10% staff discount on all stock.

At a US convention in early August, Terry Nation branded the previous season "a disgrace" and laid into McCoy's performance. The Dalek creator advocated a "back to basics" approach, which many in the audience were agreement with – though perhaps not *quite* as basic as some of Terry Nation's stories. And the list of people who had it in for John Nathan-Turner was expanded to include the Writers' Guild of Great Britain, who launched an investigation into screenings of episodes at US conventions following breach of copyright claims lodged by such former BFFs as Eric Saward, Peter Grimwade and Christopher Bidmead.

August also saw *Doctor Who* take a step into a parallel universe with the direct-to-video release of the first ever "official" fan-made spin-off, *Wartime*. Produced and directed by Keith Barnfather, whose Reeltime Pictures had released a number of video interviews with various *Who* alumni, the 35-minute drama starred John Levene – almost certainly the only time those three words have ever been used together – as Warrant Officer Benton, who returns to his childhood home to confront the ghosts of his past. With a gun. The production was made possible because Derrick Sherwin, who had created both Benton and UNIT, gave his permission for them to be used, as long as no mention was made of the Doctor. Well, who needs him anyway, when you've got the character who gave us such iconic *Doctor Who* images as a grown man in a nappy and, um, a soldier fetching some tea?

Producer's farewell party: nice vol-au-vents, shame about the farewell

As filming on another season concluded, John Nathan-Turner was confident his *Who* days were finally about to be behind him. No, really, he was. He had a number of possible irons in the fire – including a pilot script written by Ian Briggs which had attracted the attention of a star actor – and the *Doctor Who* team were *so* confident this was a "golden wrap" for the producer, they threw him a farewell party.

On August 16th, Sylvester McCoy was one of the stars who joined Jonathan Powell to launch BBC1's autumn season, where he posed for pictures with *'Allo 'Allo*'s Vicki Michelle (presumably no firemen were available). *Doctor Who*'s new run was scheduled to start in the first week of September, but, at the last minute, the decision was taken to delay transmission by a month to make way for coverage of the Olympic Games from Seoul. (Fair enough – I mean, it's not like they'd had much time to plan in the seven years since South Korea won the bid, was it?) Keen to ensure episode one of *Silver Nemesis* still fell on the 25th anniversary, Nathan-Turner opted to swap the running order so that *The Greatest Show in the Galaxy* would become the season finale. Not that it was really his problem any more, of course – it would soon be someone else's job to worry about *Doctor Who*, right? I said isn't that right, Jonathan? Jonathan?

In fact, the only candidate Powell and company had in their sights was Paul Stone, who had produced a string of children's drama hits for the BBC, including *Box of Delights* and *The Children of Green Knowe*. But he turned them down to "go freelance" (yeah right), and spent the next few years producing adaptations of *The Chronicles of Narnia* for the Corporation instead. And so Nathan-Turner was summoned before his boss and told he was being kept behind for another year. Again. A furious Amnesty International immediately added the producer to its list of Prisoners of Conscience, and issued a statement decrying his brutal treatment at the hands of oppressors who were forcing him to keep making a slightly silly sci-fi show against his wishes.

At their first script meeting to discuss the next series, Cartmel argued they should continue to take the show in a darker direction. (To his surprise, Nathan-Turner agreed – though he *was* rocking back and forth in his chair with a dead-eyed stare, muttering "the darkness, yes, the pitiless, pitiless darkness" at the time.) Cartmel was also keen to set more stories on Earth – while his boss still preferred alien planets – and so commissioned Ben Aaronovitch to revive his Arthurian/UNIT adventure, *Storm Over Avallion*. The series itself was confirmed on September 8th. ("Congratulations!" said Nathan-Turner's producer colleagues as they passed him in the corridor. "Thank you," he said. "If anyone needs me, I'll be sitting in my car.")

During September, the Doctor and Ace encountered a Cyberman running low on energy in a radio advert for Panasonic batteries, the BBC having granted a rare licence for Sylvester McCoy, Sophie Aldred and David Banks to appear in character for a commercial. The punchline saw the TARDIS conking out because the Doctor had failed to use the correct brand of battery – which is silly, as everyone knows the TARDIS is powered by temporal energy (otherwise known as members of the crew crouching out of sight and tugging on bits of string).

McCoy, Aldred and Banks were three of the guests at the DWAS' Panopticon IX convention at Imperial College, London later that month – as were would-be *Who* movie producers Peter Litten and George Dugdale, their writer Johnny Byrne and Caroline Munro, who announced she would now be playing a villain called Morgana. (By now, the only role she *hadn't* been linked with was the Doctor – but she was still in with more of a shout than Sylvester McCoy.)

The low rumble of fan dissension was in evidence during the occasionally fractious event – but it was nothing compared to what happened the following week when, during a lecture at the National Film Theatre, Sydney Newman gave the current production team both barrels, accusing them of "screwing [the show] up completely" and concluding: "It's a bore. They've killed a beautiful thing." "If anyone needs me," said John Nathan-Turner, "I'll be sitting in my car."

What Sydney Newman couldn't have known, though, was the beautiful thing he presumed dead was about to defy doctors' predictions in the most unexpected way...

Ask the man in the street to draw a cardiogram representing *Doctor Who*'s creative peaks and troughs, and he'd probably tell you to go away, you weirdo. But if you *could* persuade him to do it, the result would probably be characterised by massive spikes in the mid 60s and 70s, followed by a period of prolonged decline before – spoiler! – flatlining into oblivion in the mid-late 80s.

But anyone who was still bothering to keep faith with the show during those dying days knows it wasn't quite that simple. Because, while the Sylvester McCoy years would never scale the popular heights of William Hartnell, Tom Baker or even Peter Davison's tenures, even the show's most vociferous critics couldn't fail to notice a sudden, vertiginous climb in quality during McCoy's tenure. And *Remembrance of the Daleks*, ladies and gentlemen, is the tipping point – the moment when *Doctor Who* Starts Getting Good Again.

And it does it by going back to basics. Literally. For the first time in a quarter of a century, the Doctor returns to London in November 1963, to settle a little unfinished business. Because it turns out a big gap in Coal Hill School's teaching timetable wasn't all he left behind when he did a runner all those years ago: he also forgot to pick up the Hand of Omega, an ancient piece of Time Lord technology capable of rewriting stars that's now the prize of not one but two rival Dalek armies, who don't mind if London gets blown apart during their fight for it. Oops – careless!

With locations including said Coal Hill School and the Totters Lane junkyard, the story is one huge Proustian rush for anyone who had huddled round their Bakelite set to witness the birth of a TV legend on that distant November Saturday. But this is a world away from the excessive continuity porn of recent years: here, the trip down memory lane actually serves a useful plot purpose, and is never allowed to get in the way of a rattling good yarn. It's also as if the writers have suddenly remembered that, back in the day, *Doctor Who* used to be about Great Moments and, to add to such iconic scenes as the Autons breaking

out of a shop window on Ealing High Street, or the Yeti stalking the London Underground, here we get a spaceship landing in a school playground, Davros emerging from a bulbous, *TV Century 21*-style Emperor Dalek and, best of all, one pioneering pepperpot finally laying to rest 25 years of bad jokes about stairs by chasing the Doctor up a flight of the bloody things. Punch the air? I think we just might have. (It's probably just as well we didn't know at the time that this iconic feat had been achieved with the help of a Stannah stairlift. Their Skaro branch must have aced the Salesman of the Month competition every time.)

In many ways, it's the simple things that make the difference: after so many years spent stuck in studios, with the occasional foray into the local country park, it's wonderful to see *Doctor Who* back on the city streets again, inhabiting a real world with real buildings (some of them suspiciously modern-looking, granted) and real people. There's also an unusually strong sense of the passage of time – of people going to bed at night, and getting up in the morning. Which is refreshing, even if it does end up in a bit of a muddle: it's sunny in the evenings in late November and, in a bid to crowbar in a gag about the broadcast of the first episode, a TV announcer says it's 5.15pm mere minutes after the breakfast things have been cleared away.

Reality also intrudes on the Doctor's fantasy world, as Ben Aaronovitch dares to reference the fact that, alongside the Biba smocks and swinging Carnaby Street hipsters, the 60s also contained a lot of people not being terribly nice to each other. Ace's "dolly sergeant" – as Jo Grant would have called him – Mike turns out to be involved with a bunch of crypto-fascists (operating out of a builders' merchants, like you do), while his mum runs a boarding house with a "No coloureds" sign in the window. Yeah, so it's all a bit theatre-in-education – Aaronovitch was so right-on, he originally named the head of the fascist group after a member of the Thatcher cabinet – but, for a series that only a decade earlier was dressing up white actors up as sinister pigtailed Chinamen, this was surely progress. Andrew Cartmel recalled watching the episode in drama boss Mark Shivas' office, and proudly

The Greatest Show in the Galaxy! (cancelled)

anticipating the "No coloureds" scene. When Shivas broke off to take a phone call at the crucial moment, Cartmel insisted he rewind the tape and watch what he'd missed. All Shivas said was: "She should have ripped up the sign."

Race relations are also discussed in a truly lovely vignette in which the Doctor visits a late-night café to talk sugar, slavery and the nature of consequences with the Jamaican man behind the counter. It's not a scene that has any bearing on the plot, but rather is included simply as a moment to pause and reflect, and is all the more powerful for it.

Remembrance of the Daleks isn't perfect (would you really expect it to be?). The ending, in which the Doctor tricks Davros into using the Hand of Omega to destroy Skaro, is pat, and Sylvester McCoy and Terry Molloy play it less like an epic confrontation than a pub argument. The Daleks, which the fx crew equipped with wheelbarrow-style roller-balls, wobble alarmingly across the cobbled streets, and the scene where the Doctor sends one of them into a suicidal tailspin just by taunting it is very silly – though possibly preferable to the original option of just blowing it up with a bazooka, which McCoy insisted be rewritten. But there's so much that's good – from the grimy, tank-like Special Weapons Dalek blasting chunks out of its opponents, to Ace literally hiding behind the sofa (talk about back to basics) while a weaponised schoolgirl stalks her – that there's a persuasive case to be made for this being the best Dalek story of the lot.

Not that you'd get that impression reading the papers the morning after the first episode. By now, it seems, slagging off *Doctor Who* had become a reflex response in certain quarters of the British press, who seemed more interested in playing bad pun bingo than offering any sort of considered appraisal of the story. "Sorry Doc, you're not the Real McCoy", hooted the *Express*, while *The Sun* said the current incarnation should be "struck off" and that the Daleks "couldn't frighten a jelly baby." They even threatened to kickstart a Bring Back Blake's Seven campaign. You had to admit, the popular press really did have their finger firmly on the pulse of 1979.

"Nest of anti-Thatcherite subversives" attempts to bring down Government, fails

The Friday after the final episode of *Remembrance* went out, Sylvester McCoy and Sophie Aldred were joined by Jon Pertwee to discuss 25 years of *Doctor Who* on BBC1's *Daytime Live* (the spiritual successor to *Pebble Mill at One*). The sequence, rather charmingly, saw McCoy taking the Pat Troughton role as Pertwee's comedy sparring partner, while presenter Judi Spiers came straight out and asked: "Sylvester, you're a bit of a clown, aren't you?" Everyone's a critic (and I do mean *everyone*).

At the end of October, McCoy started a new job hosting *What's Your Story?*, a live interactive drama running four nights a week on BBC1, in which children had to phone in and suggest what happened next. What a pity they couldn't have tried the same thing with *Time and the Rani* ("Stuart from Birmingham called in to say he thinks the Rani should stop pricking about pretending to be Bonnie Langford, and the Doctor should turn back into the bloke with the curly hair").

Debuting the same week, *The Happiness Patrol* is another slightly tarnished example of this era's struggle to translate its writers' vision on to the screen. Which is not to say the writing is a work of genius – Graeme Curry's tale of a planet where being miserable is a capital offence is a satire of sorts, but not a very sharp one, labouring to make much of a point beyond: enforced jollity is annoying, and you can't have sunshine without a little shade. Well duh.

What it is, though, is packed full of great moments and concepts: the Kandyman, a homicidal scientist made entirely of sweets, is a fantastic creation straight out of Tim Burton's wildest dreams, while the scene in which the Doctor sticks him to the floor using a canister of lemonade is pure Roald Dahl. Curry originally envisaged the character as a more straightforward lab-coated scientist in edible candy specs, rather than the Bertie Bassett-style Liquorice Allsort creation we ended up with, but you can't help thinking that, on this occasion, the designer made the right call. Speaking of calls, you have to love the way he answers the phone – "Kandyman" – while his

249

bickering relationship with his lab partner Gilbert M – "What time do you call this?!" – hints at the planet's oddest married couple. Takes Allsorts, I guess.

Continuing the recent theme, the script once against casts the Doctor as a revolutionary firebrand, who succeeds in his mission of bringing down the Government in a night – "I can hear the sound of empires toppling", he says – without actually getting his hands very dirty. We also learn that he likes the blues and can croon a mean version of "As Time Goes By", while the seventh Doctor's Face-off of the Week sees him talking two snipers into taking up a less homicidal career. He could make a killing on the motivational speaking circuit.

The Happiness Patrol also has a cast to die for, stuffed to the rafters with dependable stage and screen veterans like Ronald Fraser, John Normington, Georgina Hale, Harold Innocent, Lesley Dunlop and, at the top of the tree, Sheila Hancock as Helen A, the planet's despotic ruler – who viewers might have found just a *tiny* bit familiar.

"I only accepted the part on the condition that I could play her like Margaret Thatcher," admitted Hancock. "I hate Margaret Thatcher with a passion, so I was allowed to slightly alter the part from how it was written to accommodate a Thatcherite theme."[18]

Helen A was normally to be found accompanied by her pet Stigorax – essentially a more ferocious version of those ridiculous little dogs Hollywood stars carry around with them. "[It] was actually a sort of glove puppet," said Hancock. "During fiming, I had a man in between my legs with his hand up my skirt, operating this ferocious creature."[18] For once, *Space Helmet* is lost for words.

With so much going for it, it's a pity *The Happiness Patrol* doesn't quite hang together in the way it should. The sense of the *Doctor Who* torch having been passed from the pipe-smoking BBC old guard to a bunch of trenchcoated *V For Vendetta* fans is palpable (even if Curry himself looked more like a young John Major), but director Chris Clough is very firmly of the old guard – though it's debatable if anyone could have done this justice, filmed entirely in the studio at the fag end of a budget year. As a world-building exercise, it's wholly unconvincing – especially the attempt to convey exterior

city streets, while an escape by a go-kart that could be outrun by a particularly nippy glacier is just mortifying for everyone involved.

With an average audience of just 5.1 million, you might have expected *The Happiness Patrol* to have sunk without trace; in fact, it went on to have perhaps the most unpredictable afterlife of any *Doctor Who* story. In the mid-noughties, the Kandyman was listed among a fatuous Channel 4 run-down of TV's most embarrassing moments. Then, a few years later, Sylvester McCoy blew the lid on Sheila Hancock's oh-so subtle Margaret Thatcher impression, claiming the production team had viewed Mrs T as "far more terrifying than any monster the Doctor had encountered." Never one to pass up an opportunity to accuse the BBC of left-wing bias, various tabloids ran with the story, leading to Andrew Cartmel being hauled onto *Newsnight* to answer the charge that the *Doctor Who* office of the late 1980s had been "a nest of anti-Thatcherite subversives". Recalling the job interview in which he'd professed his desire to bring down the government, Cartmel insisted John Nathan-Turner had told him "the most you can do is say that people with purple skin and green skin are all equal – which is what we proceeded to do."

Finally, in 2011, the then Archbishop of Canterbury, Rowan Williams, referenced the story in his Easter sermon on the subject of happiness and joy, completing the serial's unexpected journey from TV Hell to the Kingdom of Heaven in just a few short years.

We now return you to November 1988, where Ian Briggs has just been commissioned to write Season Twenty-Six opener *Wolf-Time* – *Doctor Who*'s first foray (surprisingly, given the enduring British obsession with the period) into the Second World War. Long-time fan Marc Platt, meanwhile, had developed a story called *Lungbarrow* that would delve feet first into the Doctor's past and reveal more about his origins (something to do with a genetic "loom" that had re-spun one of Gallifrey's godlike founding fathers into our favourite Time Lord, possibly with just enough left over for a question mark jumper). John Nathan-Turner deemed this "too much, too soon", but liked the concept of a surreal Gothic house, which Platt relocated to Victorian England in his revised treatment, *Life-Cycle*. For the final story of the season, Cartmel commissioned a script called *Cat Flap* – about man's struggle to control his animal instincts – from a young Scottish writer called Rona Munro.

That year's *Children in Need* fundraiser included a stunt in which the Daleks took over Radio 4's *Woman's Hour*, with most commentators agreeing their handling of the issue of sexual harassment in the workplace ("FEMALE ++ WORK ++ UNITS ++ WILL ++ CEASE ++ COMPLAINING") lacked sensitivity. The *News of the World* also reported that Liquorice Allsorts manufacturer Bassett's had complained to the BBC about the Kandyman, arguing it was bad PR to turn their cheery mascot, Bertie Bassett, into a homicidal maniac. Nathan-Turner was about to respond by telling them there was no such thing as bad publicity, until he remembered the fat cuttings file on his desk.

The Fourth Reich: like the Third Reich, only much, much smaller

On November 15th, *Doctor Who's* official 25th anniversary celebrations kicked off with a party at the newly-opened Space Adventure attraction in central London. As well as launching a temporary Doctor Who exhibition at the venue, Sylvester McCoy and Sophie Aldred posed for pictures cutting a TARDIS birthday cake, followed by a press screening of episode one of *Silver Nemesis*. Afterwards, McCoy and Nathan-Turner flew to America as guests on a six-day Caribbean cruise with a group of fans who had paid handsomely to be able to ignore the breathtaking scenery in order to watch a bunch of people talking about *Doctor Who*. One female fan was so convinced that nothing in her life could ever top the experience, she tried to jump overboard and had to be coaxed back to safety. The drama left everyone feeling shaken though, on the plus side, McCoy and Nathan-Turner had to admit it was the best review they'd had in some time. Back home, the *Sunday Sport* ran an interview with a woman who claimed to have been sharing her bed with a "red hot Dalek lover" for 12 years. DWAS co-ordinator Andrew Beech soberly told the paper he'd "never heard of this type of

thing before" – unless you counted the Dalek hot water bottle some fans cuddled up to at night.

During filming for *Silver Nemesis*, a special photoshoot with the Cybermen had been arranged for the *Radio Times*, for use on the cover during the anniversary week. To Nathan-Turner's disappointment, the magazine decided against using it in favour of a cover promoting *The Lion, The Witch and the Wardrobe*. Episode two. Yeah, we get the hint, thanks.

The start of the anniversary story was heavily trailed on BBC1, at least, with footage from *Silver Nemesis* preceded by a clip of William Hartnell in *The Web Planet*. Of course, to a generation raised on a diet of *Star Wars* and *ET*, it looked hopelessly cheap and outdated – and *The Web Planet* looked even worse.

At 75 minutes, *Silver Nemesis* is like a badly overstuffed cushion, splitting at the seams as it battles to accommodate three sets of villains – a seventeenth-century sorceress, some very shiny, suitably sterling new Cybermen and the world's least convincing neo-Nazi movement – while also attempting to push the re-set button on *Doctor Who* itself. Bafflingly, the response to this problem was to leave large chunks of vital exposition on the cutting room floor while still retaining at least one entirely unnecessary – and violently unfunny – piece of "comedy" padding per episode.

All the bad guys are in pursuit of the Nemesis statue, a Time Lord super-weapon previously launched into space by the Doctor, which crash lands in Berkshire on the sunniest November 23rd in history. That's right – this is about the Doctor returning to deal with the consequences of a powerful Gallifreyan maguffin from his own past; in other words – exactly the same story as the one from a few weeks earlier, except with Cybermen instead of Daleks.

As the witch and poisoner Lady Peinforte, Fiona Walker – last seen way back in 1964's *The Keys of Marinus* – is terrific value, though her black magic powers seem somewhat out of step with the programme's pseudo-scientific MO, and the scene where she materialises amidst a swirling time storm in the middle of a Windsor café, and none of the customers bat an eyelid, is among the series' daftest ever. The polished, chrome-domed Cybermen look great, but are now pathetically vulnerable to gold, to the extent that Ace wipes a squad of them out using a catapult and some coins. (For all we know, they might even be chocolate coins.) But the lamest villains have to be Anton Diffring and his motley crew of neo-Nazis, who are attempting to bring about the Fourth Reich from the back of a Transit van – think *The Boys from Brazil* meets *Auf Wiedersehen, Pet*. (At one point, they also appear to check into a hotel in full military uniform, complete with automatic weapons. Talk about service with discretion.)

The much-telegraphed "big reveal" about the Doctor, meanwhile, turns out to amount to little more than a vague threat by Peinforte to "tell [the Cybermen] of Gallifrey, tell them of the old time, the time of chaos". But then, if your idea is to reintroduce the idea of the Doctor as an intergalactic man of mystery, I guess you could argue that less is more. Kevin Clarke's view was that the Doctor is God, which may just have been verging on the controversial. According to the writer, Nathan-Turner and Cartmel told him, "You can do that, as long as you don't say it". Cartmel, for his part, claimed he saw the character as "a godlike being" – but not *that* godlike being.

On first viewing, *Silver Nemesis* moves fast enough (it has more locations than some entire seasons of the Peter Davison era) to distract you from the fact it makes absolutely zero sense, even by *Doctor Who*'s less-than rigorous standards. But let any daylight in on the plot, and it turns to dust in front of your eyes.

For the record, incidentally, that comedy padding in full: In episode one, there's some hideous mugging from Sylvester McCoy as the Doctor and Ace try to dodge the Queen unlookalike in the grounds of Windsor Castle. In episode two, Lady Peinforte and her man-servant are set upon by some skinheads who mistake them for social workers (full Jacobean dress clearly being all the rage among child protection services in the Winsdor area). And in episode three, there is the endless faffing about with "star" guest Dolores Gray. Laugh? No, since you ask.

The heavy promotion for the first episode paid off, with viewing figures breaking the six million barrier for the first time in several years. Almost a million had deserted by the

second instalment, though, and the story met with a mixed reaction from critics. *The News of the World* declared it "timeless twaddle", while the *New Statesman*'s Nicky Smith claimed to have been hooked, but added that, of a straw poll of 30-40 children she'd carried out, none were regular viewers. *The Mail on Sunday*'s Alan Coren, however, was effusive in his praise, concluding: "What's up, Doc? Everything, and a rattling good everything, too." And Mark Lawson, writing in the BBC's *The Listener* magazine, went one better, proclaiming the show to be in "splendid form" and declaring McCoy "the best actor in years".

McCoy himself offered a more qualified appraisal of the serial: "As a 25th anniversary story, *Silver Nemesis* was obviously a disappointment," he told *Doctor Who Magazine* some six years later. "But as an ordinary one, I thought it was quite good, really."[19] And that's literally the nicest thing there is to say about *Silver Nemesis*.

As a soundtrack to the silver jubilee celebrations, the BBC released the ultimate party record in the shape of *The Doctor Who 25th Anniversary Album*. The title proved somewhat misleading as, apart from the four official versions of the theme tune, all the tracks were taken from Keff McCulloch's recent scores for the series. (It's just a pity it wasn't TV advertised: "Now you too can enjoy such all-time classics as 'Drinksmat Dawning' and 'Newsreel Past'. And who could ever forget the timeless 'Burton's Escape'? Order now and get a free bonus album, Keff McCulloch Plays Mantovani, now with added handclaps.")

After a couple of mis-steps, the creative renewal signalled by *Remembrance of the Daleks* continues with *The Greatest Show in the Galaxy*, Stephen Wyatt's inventive, thoughtful, sad and sometimes scary tale of dread and circuses, which makes a far better fist of being a season finale than *Silly Nemesis* ever could have.

If it's about anything – and quite a lot of *Doctor Who* from this era tends to be "about" things – it's the death of 60s idealism, as represented by the Psychic Circus, an intergalactic travelling carnival that's run aground on the desert planet of Segonax, and from which no visitors ever return. While the hippies who founded the circus are gradually being picked off by the sinister Chief Clown – representing

The Man (probably) – the Doctor and Ace join a rag-bag collection of hopefuls who have come to try their luck at its famous open mic spot, including the Blimpish explorer Captain Cook and his werewolf sidekick Mags, Hell's Angel-style biker Nord the Vandal and a twer-pish teenage nerd called Whizzkid. The latter, played by Gian Sammarco of Adrian Mole fame, is a very obvious parody of a certain type of *Doctor Who* fan – sample quote: "Although I never got to see the early days, I know it's not as good as it used to be but I'm still terribly interested" – which is as unprofessional as it is unfunny. But we'll let it go, since everything else is so on-the-money. Again, it's the moments, the *images* that endure: the Chief Clown, in full undertaker's garb, gliding through the sand dunes in a silent black hearse; doomed idealist Bellboy committing suicide in a room full of robot clowns, and... well, lots of creepy stuff with clowns, basically.

This time, Wyatt's script is well served by a director who really gets it – it's tantalising to think what Alan Wareing might have done with *Paradise Towers* – and a fine cast: TP McKenna is perfect as the blustering captain, Christopher Guard gives the story heart as Bellboy, and Sylvester McCoy has rarely been more watchable. (But then, what story could better suit the seventh Doctor than one about sad clowns?) Best of all, though, is Ian Reddington as the Chief Clown, dispensing death with a maniacal laugh and a theatrical flourish that puts even the Joker to shame.

Usual plot fumbles aside, everything about *The Greatest Show in the Galaxy* screams of a series fired up with a renewed vigour, self-confidence and a positive surfeit of ideas (on top of which, it also has *Doctor Who's* best ever quarry). It's also horrifyingly prescient: the Psychic Circus' founding ideals turn out to have been corrupted by the Gods of Ragnarok, three ancient beings who sit in judgement while their luckless victims die humiliating deaths in the name of entertainment. Remind you of anyone? Give them a flat-top and a ludicrously high waistband and they'd start to look scarily familiar.

With the nation too stuffed with turkey to get out of its armchairs, the final episode of *The Greatest Show in the Galaxy* ended the series on a high of 6.6 million viewers – *Doctor*

Who's biggest audience since *Revelation of the Daleks*, way back before the so-called "hiatus" wreaked such havoc with viewers' loyalties.

"*Greatest Show* is an example of JN-T at his best," reckoned effects assistant Mike Tucker. "He allowed Andrew and Stephen Wyatt to go off and do something different and new and quirky and fresh, but he also had the experience and the knowledge of how the BBC worked to be able to take what could have been an absolute disaster and not only pull a competent show out of it, but pull a great show out of it. I think all of us really at that point started to realise quite what an asset John was to the programme."[15]

Some critics were impressed, too, with *The Scotsman* claiming "*Who* has gone imaginative and very stylish," and adding: "There's a lot of galactic go in the old police box yet."

It's a lovely sentiment. But by now the calendar on the wall was reading 1989 – and the Storm Over Avallion wasn't the only dark cloud on the horizon.

Dark side of Dunoon

Sylvester McCoy entered 1989 with a renewed resolve to turn his Doctor into a darker, more troubled figure: an ancient wanderer, heavy with the burden of centuries of death and destruction. He drew inspiration from his late grandmother who, having lived to 100 (in Dunoon, of all places), had told him how sad and lonely it was to have loved and lost so many people. ("Okay, whatever you say," said John Nathan-Turner. "But it's the last time I'm inviting you to one of my New Year's Eve parties.")

"Like all actors, you bring a lot of yourself to the Doctor," recalled McCoy some years later. "Life had made me kind of clown-like and comic. I see things in a comic way. But I'm also angry. Comedy does come from anger. It's the flipside of the coin, isn't it?"[5]

This, of course, chimed precisely with Andrew Cartmel's vision for the character. "The Doctor had become sort of a whipping boy," claimed the script editor. "He'd become a victim of his own show... he wasn't master of his own destiny. It was really crucial to turn the Doctor around and make him heroic and powerful, and a person who made things happen instead of things happening to him. Darker, more powerful, more mysterious – that's not a bad three word summary of what we wanted the character to be."[20] Maths wasn't his strong point.

Nathan-Turner didn't object to any of this, but stressed there should be no more specific revelations about the Doctor's background in the upcoming season, which had now been allocated a budget £1.6M, £530,000 of which was to come from BBC Enterprises.

As an article in *Sounds* (the long-running rock weekly no-one remembers as well as *Melody Maker* and the *NME*, probably on account of its dogged devotion to prog-rock) hailed *Doctor Who*'s "recent renaissance" in an article focusing heavily on Sophie Aldred, the actress did a stint on *Jackanory* before starting presenting duties on a new children's quiz show called *Knock Knock*. One of the guests on this was Sylvester McCoy; I bet they spent days thinking up a good joke they could use to introduce him.

On February 27th, at a press launch at the London Palladium, Jon Pertwee was unveiled as the star of *Doctor Who: The Ultimate Adventure*, which was due to open at Wimbledon in late March, followed by a tour of the UK and, hopefully, Australia. Producer Mark Furness had rejected Ben Aaronovitch and Andrew Cartmel's original script, *War World*, claiming it was too ambitious for the stage. Instead, he turned to Terrance Dicks – the writer he'd wanted in the first place, until John Nathan-Turner insisted he try the current team. The change of date from Christmas to spring meant Sylvester McCoy wouldn't be able to star, so Furness had initially approached Colin Baker. When he also proved unavailable, Dicks had suggested Pertwee, who had agreed to sign up for a limited run, after which the plan was for Baker to take over.

For Dicks, it was business as usual: "Mark phoned me up in a state and said, 'Jon's not happy about the script'. I said, 'Jon is *never* happy about the script'. What he was mainly worried about was the physical action, as he was getting on a bit. I told him that he'd just stroll through the action calmly and occasionally swat someone aside, at which point they would do three back-flips and crash through the scenery. Jon said, 'I like working with you,

Terrance. You listen.' That's practically the only compliment he ever paid me!"[21] Better late than never, I suppose.

Meanwhile, with fewer TV stories to keep feeding the beast, the new editor of the Target books range, Peter Darvill-Evans, entered discussions with John Nathan-Turner about issuing original Doctor Who fiction. There was also a discussion about novelising *The Ultimate Adventure*, which would have been interesting, as it was being sold as a "laser musical spectacular". In the end, this was kyboshed by our old friend Roger Hancock, who didn't want the Daleks appearing in just any old rubbish. Not for that money, anyway.

In mid-March, Sylvester McCoy was contracted for a further two series – which didn't mean they'd necessarily make two series, just that he'd have to star in them if they did. In fact, McCoy had always planned to stop after three years but, according to the actor, Nathan-Turner insisted he also agree to the fourth, or he wouldn't hire him for the third. (This seems a somewhat bizarre negotiating tactic: perhaps he thought it would be better for the programme's security to have someone signed up for two years – but was he *really* prepared to start from scratch with a new Doctor, *again*?)

The whole subject of BBC contracts was a surprisingly hot topic around this time. On his appointment as Director General in 1987, John Birt had been charged with a root-and-branch reform of the Corporation, introducing a sweeping Thatcherite revolution which, depending on who you believe, either saved the BBC from a government sell-off, or sacrificed its integrity and creative freedom on the altar of free market reform. His critics had a habit of couching their concerns in strangely Skaro-centric terms: on one BBC staff Christmas tape, the DG was presented as Davros, while veteran *Who* director David Maloney claimed Birt had "succeeded where Davros failed, and ruined the BBC"; most famously of all, Dennis Potter called him a "croak-voiced Dalek". Either way, by 1989 the Corporation had been tasked with commissioning a quarter of its output from external programme-makers – leading to much speculation about which independent production companies might be in the running to take on *Doctor Who*.

But that was the future. On March 27th, fans were more interested in taking a journey into the show's past as they gathered excitedly at the Wimbledon Theatre to see the third Doctor make his comeback on the opening night of *The Ultimate Adventure*. They *gasped* as the TARDIS materialised on stage before their very eyes, *cheered* as the doors were thrown open, and *whooped* as the Doctor stepped out into... a total blackout.

"Just as he let rip with 'I am the Doctor!', the whole stage was plunged into darkness," recalled Colin Baker, who was in the audience. "Knowing Jon as I did, he would have been livid, because he liked to make an entrance, and it was blown out of the water."[22]

Despite this unfortunate technical hitch, the reviews were generally good: a fun runaround featuring Daleks, Cybermen, laser effects, a flying sequence, a cameo from Margaret Thatcher and several musical numbers of varying quality, it was never going to win a Tony – though ballsy showstopper "Business is Business", belted out by "Madame Delilah" in the style of Shirley Bassey, might just scoop the award for the campest thing ever associated with *Doctor Who*. And that, let me tell you, is really saying something.

Brown is the new beige

By the time shooting on the new season started in April, the original recording schedule had been ripped up in order to accommodate Nicholas Courtney, who wasn't available during *Storm Over Avallion*'s original dates. Instead, it was Ian Briggs' *The Curse* (formerly *Wolves*) *of Fenric* that went first before the cameras. After a lot of persuasion, director Nicholas Mallett had convinced John Nathan-Turner to let him shoot the whole thing on location, the main unit base being the Crowborough Army Training Camp in East Sussex. In grand *Doctor Who* tradition, the filming was beset by bizarre weather, with heavy rain and even snow, forcing some dialogue to be hastily rewritten – including a saucy line about the heat making Ace's clothes stick to her body: instead, she had to make do with feeling the wind whipping up through her thermals, which wasn't *quite* as sexy. Less easy to fix was the loss of a day's worth of footage from a second camera

after the VT operator accidentally taped over it. How they laughed.

Sylvester McCoy was delighted to be sporting a new look for the new season: it had been agreed the best way to depict his new, "darker" interpretation of the Doctor would be through a combination of scripted dialogue and subtle shifts in his performance. But mainly by giving him a brown jacket. The actor was also visited on-set by his sons, Sam and Joe, who were pressed into service as a pair of blue aquatic vampire-zombies – pretty exciting, when you consider the best most kids can hope for on a visit to Dad's work is a spin in a swivel chair.

Meanwhile, Mother Pertwee continued her royal tour of the country, taking the opportunity to make personal appearances at everything from a Ford dealership in Liverpool to a coal merchants in Bristol (well, who doesn't do a little coke when they're on the road?). When the show arrived at the Alexandra Theatre in Birmingham, the born performer suffered a rare attack of stage fright, turned to the almost 3,000 strong audience and said, "I'm sorry ladies and gentlemen, I'm not feeling very well. I'm afraid I can't go on." David Banks stepped up to the plate and did two performances as a linen-suited alternative Doctor. Once he'd recovered his wits, Pertwee continued his enthusiastic promotions schedule, which included opening new rides at a Midlands theme park and signing Doctor Who videos at HMV in Oxford Street. (He even signed the ones starring the other fellas, though personally he couldn't really see the point of releasing them in the first place.)

Over the May Day bank holiday, various *Who* luminaries, including Sylvester McCoy, Sophie Aldred and Colin Baker, took part in a benefit show in Brighton organised by John Nathan-Turner to raise money for victims of the Hillsborough disaster. Shortly afterwards cast and crew headed up to Rutland Water for a week's filming on *Battlefield*, as Ben Aaronovitch's *Storm Over Avallion* had become. Because of strike action at Television Centre, the studio dates had to be rescheduled – and they also discovered that the TARDIS console set had been junked. ("But don't read anything into that," said Jonathan Powell, with a funny sort of smile on his face.) A single section of wall was hastily knocked up, and the lights turned so low McCoy had to squint to see the console.

Joining the production, Nick Courtney was delighted to see the cast also included Jean Marsh, who'd played his sister way back in his first *Doctor Who* appearance in *The Daleks' Master Plan*. "Twenty-four years had passed since we had last met, so it was hardly surprising that she had no recollection of me at all," said Courtney, "or the fact she had been responsible for my demise."[23]

The original plan to kill the Brigadier had been abandoned when the fanboy in Aaronovitch couldn't bring himself to do the deed – but there was still widespread speculation it might happen after Courtney himself started a rumour that they'd filmed several alternative endings. "It was tomfoolery, chicanery and calumny," he admitted, "and I thoroughly enjoyed my part in initiating it."[23]

A press call on location had seen some papers trailing the Brig's return, but the *News of the World* was more excited by the news that Nicholas Parsons – then best known for presenting cheesy game show *Sale of the Century* "live from Norwich" – was going to play a "parson" (talk about typecasting) in *The Curse of Fenric*.

Entering the *Battlefield* studio on June 1st, Sophie Aldred noticed some towels had been laid out on the floor, apparently soaking up leaks from a glass tank that, later that day, was scheduled to be filled with water – with her inside it. When the time came to record the sequence, with water rushing down onto her head and filling up around her, the actress spread her hands across the glass – which suddenly gave way with a loud crack. Instinctively, Aldred reached into the air and the crew, alerted by a cry of "Get her out of there!" from McCoy, hauled her to safety.

"For a second or two, no-one moved," she recalled, "and then suddenly there was a mad dash for the studio doors as the front of the tank buckled and bowed, and gallons of water gushed forth, spilling onto the studio floor and sending cameramen, actors and crew running for safety – water and electric power cables are not a good mix."[9]

It was only later Aldred realised how serious the incident could have been if the water had pushed her through the splintered glass. The

next morning, she received a call from her agent, who said the tabloids were planning to print a story about how her face had been "ripped to shreds", and that she was planning to sue the BBC for six million pounds. "Having been shown the clip, I realised that it was the heroic Mr McCoy who probably saved my life," said Aldred. "Or, at the very least, my six million pound face."[9] Some people may have questioned McCoy's suitability for the role – but how many Doctors could claim to have saved their companion's life for real?

The following week, Colin Baker shrugged his Technicolor Nightmare Coat back on and stepped out on stage to play the Doctor for the first time since being so unceremoniously dumped from the part three years earlier. If he was bitter about playing a matinee show to a hundred people in Northampton instead of millions of TV viewers, he remained stoically professional. "I never turn down scripts without good reason," Baker once remarked. "If I did, I would probably very seldom work. I dare say I would have declined to do *Yes, That's My Bum!* or a touring play of that ilk, but that aside..."[22]

His successor, meanwhile, had started work on *Survival*, Rona Munro's "cat flap" story which was scheduled to close the twenty-sixth season. A press call with comedy (it says here) double act Hale and Pace – cameo-ing as a pair of shopkeepers – only managed to pique the interest of one Sunday paper, which may have been a worrying indicator of public interest in *Doctor Who*. Or it might just have been because it was Hale and Pace.

For the alien planet scenes, Alan Wareing took his crew back to Warmwell Quarry in Somerset, where temperatures reached in excess of 100 degress. This proved a problem for the actors playing the indigenous Cheetah People (indigenous to the alien planet, not Somerset), who were dressed head-to-toe in fake leopard fur. When one girl had the audacity to complain about it, Gary Downie sacked her on the spot – and pretty grateful she was, too. "She just stripped off her costume and ran away towards the train station," recalled Sylvester McCoy. "Very pretty she was when she stripped off her costume..."[24] Down boy.

But even as *Doctor Who* was doing exactly what it had always done – torturing extras in a sandpit – BBC Enterprises received a phone call that was to have a profound effect on the future of the series. Philip Segal, a British-born, LA-based producer with Columbia Television Pictures, claimed to have interested ABC Television in launching *Doctor Who* in America as part of a co-production deal with the BBC. When they heard, Jonathan Powell and Head of Series Peter Cregeen were cock-a-hoop – not because they expected the series would ever come to anything but because, as long as someone else was talking about making *Doctor Who*, it meant they didn't have to.

As rehearsals for the final recording block of the season began in London, Sophie Aldred suffered a wardrobe malfunction when co-star Katharine Schlesinger accidentally wrestled her out of her crop top. According to Aldred, the rest of the cast were too engrossed in a crossword puzzle to notice – though there's many a fanboy who, despite not even being there, is able to picture the incident with strangely perfect clarity to this day.

On Thursday, August 3rd, recording of the final scenes of Marc Platt's *Ghost Light* brought production on the season to a close. At the end of the evening's wrap party, Sylvester McCoy turned to the regular cast and crew and said: "Well, see you next year." It was only when he got home it occurred to him that no-one had bothered replying.

Destroyer of Worlds in Shanghai knocking shop shame

With theatre audiences down across the board because of the unusually good summer, Colin Baker's run in *Yes, That's My Bum...* sorry, in *Doctor Who: The Ultimate Adventure* came to an end in late August, and plans for a tour Down Under were subsequently scrapped.

As Philip Segal flew in to London to meet senior BBC execs that month, he must have been encouraged to see the publicity machine for the upcoming season cranking into full gear. Which, as in recent years, meant a couple of cursory mentions during Jonathan Powell's BBC1 season launch, and the now standard half-page in the *Radio Times* – and who knows if they'd even have got that much, if Sophie Aldred hadn't agreed to write it herself?

Sylvester McCoy's appearance at the Space Adventure in London prompted some press interest, but there was a noticeable absence of buzz surrounding the new series – even compared to a year ago – when episode one of *Battlefield* kicked off *Doctor Who's* 26th run on Wednesday, September 6th.

On paper, Ben Aaronovitch's Arthurian parallel world fantasy – in which subtle variations on the usual cast of Camelot arrive from an alternative Britain in search of their once and future king – is one of the most irresistible *Doctor Who* pitches ever. And there are enough intriguing notions – not least the Doctor turning out to be Merlin, as much to his surprise as anyone else's – to offer a tantalising glimpse of what might have been. But by his own admission, Aaronovitch was juggling too many ideas, and badly fumbled the job of stitching a fourth episode on to what had been conceived as a three-parter – though not nearly as badly, it has to be said, as Michael Kerrigan fumbles the direction.

Kerrigan had recently helmed another futurist-medieval saga, *Knights of God*, so quite why he was so out of his depth is a mystery. The action sequences, in particular, are hopeless: the first battle between rival knights makes *Monty Python and the Holy Grail* look grittily realistic, while the episode one cliffhanger is a perfect storm of bad acting, editing, camerawork and visual effects. And who the hell thought it was a good idea to open *the entire season* with a leisurely shot of a couple of pensioners pottering round a garden centre? (The olds in question are the Brigadier and his good lady wife, Doris – first alluded to as far back as *Planet of the Spiders*, when the Brig wistfully reminisced about a dirty weekend in Brighton.)

If, as originally envisaged, this had proved to be the old soldier's last stand, it wouldn't have been too shabby a way to go: having ordered horned demon The Destroyer (also known as Lord of Darkness and Eater of Worlds, but he didn't like to boast) to "get off this world", our man dutifully accepts his role as the Earth's chosen champion with a stoic: "I just do the best I can."

The Destroyer himself – think Tim Curry's bull-headed beast in Legend on secondment to the Blue Man Group – is a fantastic creation, courtesy of model makers Sue Moore and

Stephen Mansfield. A pity, then, that he turns out to be all mouth and bondage trousers, constantly making threats about blowing up the world, but not actually doing anything about it. Still, at least he *looks* impressive, which is more than can be said for the rest of the production. According to Andrew Cartmel, he and the writers had got so fed up with being let down by poor design work, they started to put important details in the dialogue, on the assumption that, if someone mentioned it, you'd have to show it. "But this approach backfired spectacularly on *Battlefield*," he admitted. "The spaceship at the bottom of the lake was supposed to be an organic style of technology, and Ben's script makes this point repeatedly. Thus we have Ace saying to the Doctor, 'It's like being in some huge animal,' when in fact all we get is the two of them trotting up a spiral staircase with some Christmas tree lights on it...[II] And then there was the lamentable sparkly effect that was supposed to be the 'interstitial vortex' between dimensions, but which looks more like a twinkly bead curtain in a Shanghai knocking shop".[2]

With a handful of honourable exceptions – step forward Marcus Gilbert's flirtacious Ancelyn and Nick Courtney's unflappable Brig – no-one seems comfortable in their roles: Sylvester McCoy and Sophie Aldred seem to have forgotten how to play their characters, Jean Marsh and Christopher Bowen chew chunks out of their mother-and-son sword and sorcery shtick and Angela Bruce, as Brigadier Winifred Bambera, is one of *Doctor Who*'s all-time most misjudged performances – though, to be fair, there's only so much a Geordie actress can do with lines partly written in Jamaican patois.

Plenty of *Battlefield*'s other shortcomings, though, are right there in the script, such as the ludicrous ending in which, having talked her out of destroying the world with an atomic missile (an Arthurian anti-nuclear polemic – only in *Doctor Who*), the Doctor orders Morgaine of the Faye – Sorceress, Sun Killer, Battle Queen of the S'rax and Dominator of the 13 Worlds – to be locked up. As this is a woman who can teleport between dimensions and turn night into day, I think it's safe to assume she won't have much need for the old file-in-a-cake trick.

To this day, Ben Aaronovitch claims *Battlefield* is "too painful" to watch. It's hard not to agree. John Russell of the *Sunday Express* was one of the few critics who bothered to review the story. "I know it's not meant to be taken seriously," he said, "but in its present state I am afraid it's unlikely to be taken at all. I mean, what sort of intergalactic genius of a Time Lord schedules himself against *Coronation Street*?"

Sadly, though he may have lacked a basic understanding of the TV scheduling process, Russell was right about one thing: no-one seemed interested any more. With an audience of just 3.1 million, the opening instalment of *Battlefield* holds the lousy distinction of being the lowest-rated first-run episode of *Doctor Who* ever. And with the serial averaging just 3.7 million across its four weeks, clearly the game was up. Jonathan Powell knew it, Peter Cregeen knew it, even John Nathan-Turner and Andrew Cartmel knew it. In fact, come to think of it, it was probably time somebody called the Doctor...

"I didn't know anything about it until, one day at home, the phone rang," recalled Sylvester McCoy. "It was JN-T, phoning up to tell me he'd written me a letter, which seemed a strange thing. I said, 'Are you going to tell me what's in the letter?' And he told me that it was that it wasn't coming back."[20]

Sophie Aldred was rehearsing *Corners* in Acton at the time. "I got a phone call in the office and it was Sylvester, and he said, 'Are you sitting down?' I said, 'Well, I am now'. He said, 'Apparently, we're not doing any more *Doctor Who*'.

"I was shocked. It was the end of an era. It was history stopping. I just couldn't believe they'd finally pulled the plug on *Doctor Who*."[20] Aware that no new series was imminent, Andrew Cartmel had accepted the script editor's job on the popular medical drama *Casualty*. "Nobody said, 'this is going to be the last season, or anything like that'," said Cartmel. "It was just, as we got towards the end of it, John began to get the sense of things: that perhaps there'd been something said, but nothing specifically said to him or me."[20]

The script editor left *Doctor Who* following a surprise farewell party on September 15th. If he'd occasionally got carried away with a sense of his own brilliance, and that of his young scions, there's no denying Cartmel deserves huge credit for injecting a new vitality and urgency into *Doctor Who* as it fought for its life in those dying days. Two years earlier, the tank had been running on empty, with such a dearth of ideas someone actually thought *two* Bonnie Langfords would be a ratings winner. Cartmel and his eager apprentices had ideas to spare. They didn't always work, and it may have been too late for most people to care anyway but, for the first time in too long, *Doctor Who* had purpose, direction, momentum and, most importantly, imagination.

And the best was still to come. Take *Ghost Light*: trying to describe Marc Platt's enigmatic riddle of a three-parter is like trying to pin a cloud on a unicorn. Andrew Cartmel opted for "an unholy hybrid of Mervyn Peake and Agatha Christie", but that's not the half of it. Just explaining the plot gives you a headache. But here goes: The Doctor takes Ace back to Perivale in 1883 to spend some time in Gabriel Chase, a house she will burn down a century later, in order to exorcise some ghosts from her past. Or is it her future? The house is currently occupied by Josiah Samuel Smith, an alien who has evolved into a Victorian gentleman. As well has his large collection of stuffed animals, he keeps a Neanderthal as a butler, a police inspector in a chest of drawers, a spaceship in the basement and the domestic staff hidden in the walls. Following this so far? He's also kidnapped a famous explorer, who's going to help him assassinate Queen Victoria and take control of the Empire. Oh, and there's a vicar in the attic who's devolved into monkey, as punishment for not enjoying *On the Origin of Species*. That'll learn 'im.

None of which really scratches the surface of what this is actually *about*. In a script as densely packed as Gabriel Chase itself, Platt filters a magpie's nest of ideas from science, history, philosophy, horror and fantasy through a prism of pop-Victoriana taking in Darwin, Conrad, Bernard Shaw, Conan Doyle, Lewis Carroll and more. If you're looking for it, virtually every other line of dialogue contains an allusion to something else, while Platt gifts Sylvester McCoy some of the best lines any Doctor has had to work with – and he responds with one of his best performances in

the role. "Don't you have things you hate?", asks a furious Ace when she learns where he's brought her. "I can't stand burnt toast," admits the Doctor. "I loathe bus stations. Terrible places, full of lost luggage and lost souls... Then there's unrequited love, and tyranny, and cruelty."

There's also a rich thread of macabre humour running through the piece – "The cream of Scotland Yard," crows Josiah, when the luckless inspector has found his way out of the drawer and into the soup tureen – and, if that all sounds a bit clever for its own good, it's also *properly* scary: when A(li)ce disappears down the rabbit hole into the basement, she's confronted by a rasping voice whispering, "There's a new scent in the dark. There's warming, pulsing, racing blood!" And then two giant insects come out of the shadows, in full evening dress. It's little wonder guest star Sylvia Sims turned to Platt at the readthrough and asked: "What have you been sprinkling on your cornflakes, then?"

With assured direction from Alan Wareing, a beautiful musical score from Mark Ayres and electrifying performances from a prestige cast including Sims, Ian Hogg, Michael Cochrane, Sharon Duce, Frank Windsor, John Hallam and Katharine Schlesinger, and a historical setting that plays to the BBC's design strengths, it's no wonder *The Independent* – in a rare piece of positive press for the time – called this "quintessential *Doctor Who*", and hailed it as the best story in a decade. Though some have dismissed the story as wilfully oblique and impossible to follow, to these eyes *Ghost Light* is as fine a slice of Gothic horror as the show ever pulled off. For all the received wisdom about *Doctor Who* having shrivelled away to nothing at the end of its original run, it's heartening to know that the last story made is also one of the best they ever made.

The cast and crew were certainly impressed with the script – even if none of them could quite work out what it was about. "It really immersed itself in Darwinian theory," said Ian Hogg. "I evolved into a younger me. A philosophical doughnut – never ending, do you see?"[22] Er, sure, why not. Platt himself cites William Blake as his main influence, with the characters of Control and Josiah personifying Blake's concept of Innocence and Experience.

Sylvester McCoy was more direct: "It was well done," he said. "But God knows what it was about."[19]

Producer "excited" by new paperclip reorganisation challenge

While Philip Segal continued to court the BBC, and other independent production companies – including those run by former producer Verity Lambert and ex-story editor Victor Pemberton – expressed their interest in taking on the good Doctor, John Nathan-Turner once again found himself kept behind after school, swinging his legs on a chair outside the Controller's office while the BBC tried to find ~~someone to come and pick him up~~ something else for him to do. It had been bad enough when they'd kept making him stay on to make *Doctor Who* – now they were making him stay on and *not* make *Doctor Who*. "Nonsense," said Jonathan Powell. "There's loads of useful stuff you can be getting on with. Look, that pile of Doctor Who button badges is a bit untidy for a start. And those postcards of Colin Baker won't bin themselves."

"If anyone needs me," said the producer, "I'll be sitting in my car."

"Actually, we had to give your parking space to the producer of *Bob's Full House*. In fact, I think that's your car I can see being towed away now."

According to Andrew Cartmel, Nathan-Turner *had* been offered another job at one point – but had been scuppered by his own ego. "They offered him *Bergerac*," said Cartmel. "He came back to the office and said he would only do it if he could fire John Nettles and set it somewhere other than Jersey!"[20]

Still, at least there would soon be *some* new *Doctor Who* stories in the pipeline. With no new series imminent, Nathan-Turner had agreed that Target books editor Peter Darvill-Evans could proceed with his proposed series of original novels to continue the adventure of the seventh Doctor and Ace in print. If nothing else, thought Nathan-Turner, it would be nice to have some new cover art to complain about.

On October 19th, a mid-season press launch saw McCoy, Aldred and Nicholas Parsons joined by Peter Cregeen, who deflected questions about the show's lack of publicity, and guaranteed "more *Doctor Who* in the future". (Before adding: "A long, *long* time in the future – a-ha-ha-ha-ha-ha-ha-ha-ha! Er, sorry about that. Don't know what came over me.")

A couple of days later, McCoy, Aldred and Nathan-Turner attended a party to celebrate ten years of *Doctor Who Magazine* – on the very day *The Sun* ran a story claiming the BBC had axed the series. "*Doctor Who* is being exterminated... by CORONATION STREET," thundered the red-top. "The BBC show, telly's longest-running sci-fi drama, will be axed next month. The Doctor, played by Sylvester McCoy, 46, has plummeted out of TV's top 100. Last night, a member of the *Doctor Who* production team said: 'Our only hope is for an independent production company to step in and save it. It isn't popular any more. Only the *Doctor Who* fans have saved the show from the chop in the past."

("Er, still," said the editor of *Doctor Who Magazine* nervously as he took the mic. "I'm sure we're all still going to have a wonderful evening and, erm... yeah, anyway. Cheers.")

As McCoy began rehearsals for another run of *What's Your Story?*, several newspapers reported Hollywood hellraiser Donald Sutherland had been cast as Coast to Coast's movie Doctor. Sutherland would play a "beer-swilling, sex mad" version of the Time Lord, according to *The Sun*, whose correspondent was clearly having trouble grasping the concept of "acting". Meanwhile, despite claiming to have interested both ABC and Fox in a co-production deal, Philip Segal was given the cold shoulder by BBC Enterprises, who said they wanted to defer any decision until the following year. ("Honestly," said Segal. "Anyone would think you guys don't even *want* to make *Doctor Who*!" At which point everyone started looking at the floor and clearing their throats.)

On BBC1, *The Curse of Fenric* continued the series' creative resurgence in fine style with a convincing slice of Gothic horror combining vampires, chemical weapons, sea monsters, Nordic legends, World War II code-cracking and the Red Army with themes of faith, doubt, betrayal, sexual awakening and mother-daughter conflict. And all before *Brush Strokes*.

Again, you'd struggle to fit the plot into a

two-line *Radio Times* synopsis: Fenric – a force of "pure evil" that has existed "since the dawn of time" – was trapped by the Doctor in a magic flask many centuries ago, but is inadvertently freed when an Alan Turing-inspired decryption genius in wartime Whitby uses an Enigma-style cipher machine to unlock an ancient computer programme carved into the local runes. Meanwhile, toxins leaking into the sea have caused centuries of drowned sailors to mutate into aquatic vampires; the Russians have arrived to steal the cipher machine: Ace meets her mother, who she hates, as a baby, who she loves; and TV's Nicholas Parsons plays a vicar whose faith has been shaken by the war. Whatever Marc Platt was sprinkling on his cornflakes, there was clearly enough left over for Ian Briggs.

Like *Ghost Light*, *The Curse of Fenric* doesn't exactly go overboard on the explanations. This is mainly because, in common with the majority of stories under Andrew Cartmel's stewardship, the scripts were way over length, and a lot of vital exposition got lost in the edit. That said, the story actually benefits from this in one sense, as director Nicholas Mallett – making a good job of atoning for his sins on *Paradise Towers* – is forced to use overdubs and montages in order to compress the narrative, resulting in such highly atmospheric scenes as the Doctor reading a translation of the Viking inscriptions ("Black fog turned day into night, and the fingers of death reached out from the waters to reclaim the treasure we have stolen") as the camera prowls among sunken longboats and floating corpses beneath the waves. "It's very difficult to time a *Doctor Who* episode," was John Nathan-Turner's defence. "You can read a script from front to back endlessly and get 33 different timings."[25] (Funny how everyone else managed to do it, though.)

This is the seventh Doctor at his most manipulative, playing a long game for the highest of stakes. Realising Fenric feeds off faith, he pushes Ace to the limit in order to break her trust in the one thing she truly believes in: him. "She's an emotional cripple," he says dismissively. "I wouldn't waste my time on her, unless I had to use her somehow." It's powerful stuff, though the pop-Freudian coda, in which Ace dives into the sea in order to literally cleanse herself of her demons, is a bit

silly, as is the scene in which she distracts a soldier with the most surreal seduction technique ever: "Sometimes I travel so fast I don't exist," says Ace. Luckily for her, she's dealing with a squaddie whose response to such cod philosophy is to ask "Faster than the second hand on a watch?", rather than, "Okay, can I put my hand in your bra now?".

Briggs and Cartmel also take the opportunity to retcon a couple of the dafter ideas from recent years, revealing it was in fact Fenric, and not just a very powerful chemistry set, that whipped up the storm that took Ace to Iceworld, as well, presumably, as the one that brought Lady Peinforte to 1980s Windsor. Basically, if you want to go anywhere in a time storm, Fenric's your man – though it will cost you extra after midnight.

The script is well served by another top-drawer cast, including Dinsdale Landen, Anne Reid and Alfred Millington. Sylvester McCoy strays a bit off the map during his big emotional plea to Ace, but otherwise does a fairly solid job, but it's Nicholas Parsons who really shines as the conflicted Rev Wainwright: he's so good, it's no wonder two Norwegian tourists mistook him for a real vicar. (The dog collar also helped, to be fair.)

Andrew Cartmel has cited Alan Moore's *Swamp Thing* story "Still Waters", about a colony of underwater vampires in a flooded Midwestern town, as the inspiration for what became *The Curse of Fenric*. To the viewer, though, the story feels like a love letter to *Doctor Who*'s own Gothic horror heyday, with added emotional clout. Whatever the intention, the result is something rather wonderful – and it's nothing less than a tragedy that only four million people saw it.

In November, Sylvester McCoy started in a run of *I Miss My War*, a new play written specially for him, which premiered in Leicester before moving to London. He also appeared as part of that year's *Children in Need*, while John Nathan-Turner attended the Doctor Who Mega-Quiz 89 at Aston University. ("Question one is for John: Will there be a new series of *Doctor Who* next year? Question two, also for John: No, really, will there?")

On the series 26th anniversary, in response to a number of letters speculating over the show's cancellation, Peter Cregeen told *Radio*

Times: "I would like to reassure *Doctor Who* devotees there are no plans to axe *Doctor Who*. There may be a little longer between this series and the next than usual, but I very much hope that it will continue to be as successful in the 90s as it has been for the last 26 years." ("What do you mean, 'Why have I got my fingers crossed?'")

Behind the scenes, Cregeen held a meeting with former script editor Gerry Davis about a joint bid between him and Terry Nation to take on the series. ("We're excited by the infinite range of the show," said the pair. "For example, one week you might have, say, the Daleks, and the next week, say, the Cybermen, and the week after that the Daleks again, and then the Cybermen, and so on. So many possibilities.")

And let's not forget that Coast to Coast's *Doctor Who* movie was still very much a live project – in its producers' heads, if nowhere else. (Anyone eager to learn how this particular saga ends should consult Volume II, where it will reach a somewhat unexpected conclusion with a cast of characters including Bryan Ferry, the bass player from Dire Straits, and The French.)

Meanwhile, there was still one old-skool, in-house story left on the shelf. And so *Doctor Who* ends as it began, with a mysterious alien and a teenage girl making a hasty departure from modern-day London and finding themselves in a strange, savage landscape of blood, bone and sand. And yet, even at the death, *Survival* offers compelling evidence of a series still pushing forward, discovering new and exciting ways to tell stories.

Rona Munro was an award-winning playwright who went on to script a Ken Loach movie, so it's perhaps no surprise her shot at *Doctor Who* turned out to be a polemical attack on Thatcherism and the ruthless free market law of the jungle. It's also, in part, a treatise about feminism and, oh blimey, menstruation – but not in a way that would have raised any awkward questions over the dinner table.

What's striking from the start is how recognisably familiar the story's setting is to the average viewer – and therefore how *different* it feels to any *Doctor Who* that's gone before it. The last time the TARDIS touched down in suburbia was all the way back at the end of *The Hand of Fear*, and even that was a flying visit.

Survival, by contrast, opens with a leisurely tour of a boring Sunday in Perivale: "nothing but tin cans and stray cats," according to Ace – though admittedly she did arrive slightly too late to see the bloke washing his car being kidnapped by a cheetah on horseback. It even manages to do teenagers convincingly: "Oh hi Ace, I thought you were dead," says the wonderfully poker-faced Ange, listlessly shaking a Hunt Saboteurs tin on the Medway Parade. "That's what they said. Either you were dead, or you'd gone to Birmingham."

Our heroes are then whisked off to the planet of the Cheetah People, which is just as fully realised in its own way, the shimmering clay pits of Warmwell quarry once again doing the honours, augmented with some subtly effective CGI to suggest a planet on the brink of destruction. The native big cats have an unusually symbiotic relationship with their world: it has the power to heal them, but their natural aggression is also hastening its eventual demise. The message, in case you missed it kids, is: control your animal instincts, or we'll all end up toast.

The Cheetah People – possibly not their real name, but it's what everyone calls them – also possess the ability to change other species into their own kind, a process that is well advanced on one particular subject, who now has pointy fangs to match his pointy beard. Yes, the Master is back and, for once, his plan is nothing more complicated than finding a way to get the hell off the planet before it blows up or he turns into a big pussycat, whichever comes first. Surprisingly, Anthony Ainley gives one of his most restrained performances in the role, despite being a half feral creature who literally howls at the moon. By sheer good luck, the climactic scenes of the Doctor locked in a Reichenbach-style showdown with his arch nemesis makes for a fitting final act in what they didn't know at the time would be the last story – though an earlier confrontation, in which the Doctor plays a game of motorbike chicken with the Master's young stooge, and ends up draped over a sofa with his arse in the air, is perhaps less dignified. It's also rather lovely that the Cheetah planet's power to send people home delivers the Doctor not to Gallifrey, but a small corner of planet Earth, where a certain blue box is waiting for him...

The Greatest Show in the Galaxy! (cancelled)

Sylvester McCoy described working with Ainley as "very interesting": "He loves being the Master. He'd like to spend the rest of his life being the Master."[19] Gary Downie, typically, was less cryptic: "He's a big, dictatorial bully," said the production manager, recalling how Ainley had ranted about the lack of water on-set at Warmwell. "He stopped production to have a tirade, coming up face-to-face with me. I thought, you lay one hand on me and it'll be the most expensive punch of your life."[26] Thankfully, things calmed down before the situation could escalate into fully-fledged hair-pulling.

If anything let's Survival down, it's the cats: the Master's "kitling" is represented by an animatronic prop that looks like it ought to be sitting on Harry Hill's desk, while the Cheetah People themselves, as scripted, were supposed to look like humans with vaguely feline features, until John Nathan-Turner insisted the story needed some "proper" monsters. According to Rona Munro, Alan Wareing kept insisting "as long as we don't get Puss in Boots". Which, of course, is exactly what he did get.

Once it became clear the show wouldn't be returning the following year, Nathan-Turner asked Andrew Cartmel to write a closing monologue that would serve, if necessary, as a worthy coda for the entire run of Doctor Who. No pressure, then.

Sylvester McCoy went into the studio to record these words on November 23rd, 1989 – exactly 26 years to the day after William Hartnell had emerged from the London fog to transport viewers on a journey more extraordinary than even he, the programme's first true fanboy, could possibly have imagined.

EXTERIOR, DAY, HORSENDEN HILL:

The Doctor: Where to now, Ace?
Ace: Home.
The Doctor: Home?
Ace: The TARDIS.
The Doctor (smiling): Yes, the TARDIS.
(They walk off together, arm in arm, down Horsenden Hill.)
The Doctor (V/O): There are worlds out there where the sky is burning, where the sea's asleep, and the rivers dream. People made of smoke, and cities made of song. Somewhere there's danger, somewhere there's injustice, and somewhere else the tea's getting cold. Come on, Ace, we've got work to do.

And the menstruation bit? Eeeeuw, I don't know. Ask a girl.

"Just because we're not making it any more, it doesn't mean we've cancelled it"

At Christmas 1989, Sylvester McCoy could be seen in Aladdin in Manchester, while Sophie Aldred took the title role in Hull New Theatre's production of Cinderella, starring TV's Les Dennis as Buttons. The latter was to cause a bit of a scandal when the News of the World splashed with the front page headline "Les Dennis Quits Wife for Dr Who Girl Sophie". (In fact Aldred and Dennis remained an item for several years – after which his love life got really messy.)

As a new decade dawned, fans and programme makers alike were left to ponder the fate of their beloved show. "They killed us through scheduling," was Andrew Cartmel's verdict. "At that time, Coronation Street was the biggest hit on British television. It was the mountain. It was a monster. Moving us from Saturdays and putting us up against Coronation Street was like putting an infant on the M1 and leaving them to walk across. We were doomed. We were sent out on a suicide mission."[20]

"The BBC at the time was entirely run by people who hated science fiction," added Ben Aaronovitch. "That's why there was no science fiction on the BBC for, like, ten years afterwards. They didn't like it. They were mostly public school, Oxbridge educated people who fear more than anything else the embarrassment of their peers."[20]

In 2007, Peter Cregeen finally broke his silence on the events of the late 1980s. "The reason Doctor Who finished in 1989," he said, "was that we had really decided this wasn't the programme it had been and that, if it was to have any life again in the future, it needed a long rest.

"Michael Grade had actually tried to cancel the programme a few years beforehand when he'd been the controller of BBC1, so when

space helmet for a cow

Jonathan Powell and I talked about not renewing it the following year, I think initially he was probably quite cautious about it, and sort of said to me, 'Well Michael Grade couldn't do it...'

"However, I felt very strongly this was a programme that had been a great programme, a programme that could still be invaluable to the BBC. Had there been somebody around who was absolutely passionate about the programme – a producer, a writer, who had got a vision for that programme that would bring it into a new life and a new world, it could have been an option to push that forward at that stage. But we couldn't see anybody around – I think most people at that stage regarded it as a programme that had seen better days."[20]

For the then cast and crew, this unspoken DNR order proved a messy, unsatisfactory end to three years in which they had worked hard to restore the series' credibility in the face of declining public interest and rising management hostility. Sadly, John Nathan-Turner never did get that second line on his producer's CV. The last staff producer in the Series and Serials department, he finally left the BBC in August 1990 for a job with... BBC Enterprises. He remained nominal custodian of the Doctor Who brand for several more years, consulting on various special projects, most notably for BBC Video, and co-writing the 1993 charity special *Dimensions in Time* (see Volume II for more on that particular horror).

Sophie Aldred continued to work as a presenter and performer, mainly in children's television, and stayed close to fandom by appearing in various spin-off audio and video productions. These included her playing "Alice" to Sylvester McCoy's "the Professor" in one audio series, for which she appeared in a series of promotional shots wearing only a bedsheet. (McCoy, thankfully, remained fully clothed from the hat down.) She resurrected the role of Ace proper in Big Finish's series of officially licensed *Doctor Who* audios from 1999 onwards, and also juggled motherhood with lucrative voiceover work for the likes of Hovis and TravelSupermarket.com. On children's television, she has given voice to such iconic characters as Noddy and Dennis the Menace and, since 2012, has taken the title role in the popular CBeebies animation *Tree Fu Tom*,

alongside David Tennant, most famous for his role as TV's... well, all in good time.

Sylvester McCoy combined a solid stage career with various TV appearances in roles in which he was required to be not quite... normal. He was Rab C Nesbitt's's mentally ill brother, an injured ventriloquist on *Casualty* and a vicar who looked like a beaver in short-lived cop caper *Mayo*. In 2008, he also appeared in daytime soap *Doctors* playing the former star of children's time-travel drama *The Amazing Lollipop Man*, a part written especially for him, and whose resemblance to a certain other TV show was purely intentional. He was also one of the first Doctors to sign up to Big Finish's *Doctor Who* audio range, where he has so far clocked up more than 50 new adventures.

On stage, he toured the world with the Royal Shakespeare Company, playing the Fool to Sir Ian McKellen's King Lear. Several years earlier, McCoy had come close to playing Bilbo Baggins to McKellen's Gandalf in Peter Jackson's *The Lord of the Rings* trilogy, but had lost out to Ian Holm. Nevertheless, Jackson was such a fan of the seventh Doctor – he even kept an original version of his costume at his Wellington home – that he wrote the part of the wizard Radagast the Brown into his adaptation of *The Hobbit*, thus turning a somewhat surprised McCoy into a fully-fledged movie star at the grand age of 69.

It can't help but have felt like a moment of redemption for the man who, to the general public at least, had always been tarred with the stigma of having let *Doctor Who* die on his watch. In truth, of course, the seventh Doctor had always enjoyed the support of a devoted fanbase – in early 1990, he had beaten even the mighty Tom Baker into second place in *Doctor Who Magazine's* Best Doctor Ever poll, and even Terry Nation had overcome his initial condemnation at around that time to declare him "tremendously capable and very promising" – but even this didn't stop the barbs from coming. Presenting the comedy news quiz *Have I Got News For You* in 2008, a typically impish Tom Baker taunted the audience with "and if you think this is bad, wait until I turn into Sylvester McCoy", while most tests of public opinion continue to place the seventh

The Greatest Show in the Galaxy! (cancelled)

Doctor in the middle rankings of TV Time Lords.

There were times when McCoy admitted he allowed himself to listen to the negative voices – both real and imagined. But some steely inner resolve ensured they never got the better of him.

"I think in other jobs, other shows, I would have been really hurt," he said. "I don't like criticism, I don't think many people do. But I had an inner feeling – I don't know where it came from, some cockiness that I'd never had before – I knew I was right for this job. I knew I would get it right. I really believed it. I thought, I shall show you, given time – and I don't think I was given *quite* enough time – I'll prove to you I was okay to play Doctor Who."[1]

As it happened, fate would conspire to give him another chance to prove it – he'd just have to wait a little longer than he'd originally anticipated before encountering the Time Lord again. As, for that matter, would the rest of us.

Whatever the future might or might not bring, the fact remains that, in 1989, *Doctor Who* – the television institution that had kept generations of children and adults pinned behind the sofa as it pushed restlessly at the limits of human imagination and potential (while straining the BBC's budgets to breaking point) – was sentenced to die a quiet, unheralded death, sliding from the schedules with barely a whimper, let alone a bang. From its first baby steps as a runtish upstart battling against institutional indifference and snobbery, the show had faced down numerous threats of cancellation and, thanks to the heroic efforts of a succession of indefatigable stewards – who refused to buckle even when the odds were so stacked against them they were in danger of being crushed – had doggedly earned its place at the heart of the British cultural landscape. From Dalekmania to *The Daemons* to Tom Baker bestriding Saturday nights like a pop-eyed colossus in 13 feet of Begonia Pope's best yarn, *Doctor Who* had transcended its origins as 405 lines of flickering monochrome to turn its lead character into one of the most iconic heroes of the twentieth century. And now, it seemed, the time traveller had come full circle, seeing out his days as he'd begun them: unloved, unwanted, a ghost at the feast.

But, according to the man with his prints all over the smoking gun, Peter Cregeen, it was never really meant to end like this.

"I said, 'Let's give it a rest'. A lot of people saw that as a smokescreen to cancellation, but it really wasn't," Gregeen insisted. "I thought probably it would come back on the air again in three or four years' time. As it was, it took considerably longer than that."[20]

But that's a whole other story.

265

Sourcing Notations

1: Adventures in Time and Spain... in Space!

1 *Doctor Who: Origins* (BBC, 2006)
2 *Doctor Who Magazine (DWM)* #141
3 *DWM* #234
4 *DWM* #345
5 *DWM* #272
6 *DWM* #83
7 Most Terrance Dicks novelisations
8 "Continuity Errors" by Steven Moffat (*Decalog 3*, Virgin Publishing)
9 *DWM* #221
10 *DWM* #231
11 *DWM* #274
12 *Daleks Conquer and Destroy* (BBC, 2009)
13 *DWM* #105
14 *DWM* #314
15 *DWM* #235
16 *Daleks Beyond the Screen* (BBC, 2009)
17 *DWM* #201
18 *DWM* #98
19 *DWM* #93
20 *Last Stop White City* (BBC, 2009)
21 *DWM* #153
22 *DWM Winter Special 1983*
23 *DWM* #156
24 *End of the Line* (BBC, 2011)
25 *DWM* #322
26 *DWM* #180
27 *DWM* #275
28 *My Grandfather, The Doctor* (BBC, 2010)
29 *DWM* #191

2: Run for Your Wives

1 *DWM* #78
2 *Patrick Troughton* by Michael Troughton, Hirst Publishing, 2011
3 *DWM* #322
4 *DWM* #180
5 *DWM* #225
6 *DWM* #243
7 *DWM* #308
8 *DWM* #102
9 *DWM* #268
10 *Down to Earth: Filming Spearhead from Space* (BBC, 2011)
11 *DWM* #230
12 *DWM* #241
13 *War Zone: The End of an Era* (BBC, 2009)
14 *DWM* #272
15 *DWM* #458

3: Hai! My Name is...

1 *Down to Earth: Filming Spearhead from Space* (BBC, 2009)
2 *DWM* #181
3 BBV
4 *Who & Me* by Barry Letts
5 *Still Getting Away With It: The life and times of Nicholas Courtney* (scificollector.c.uk, 2005)
6 *Who & Me* (Fantom Publishing, 2009)
7 *DWM* #114
8 *DWM* #337
9 *DWM* #219
10 *DWM* #113
11 *DWM* #261
12 *Life on Earth*
13 *DWM Winter Special 1985*

14 *DWM* #187
15 *DWM* #256
16 *DWM* #312
17 *DWM* #235
18 *DWM* #199
19 *Happy Birthday to Who* (BBC, 2012)
20 *DWM* #83
21 *DWM* #198
22 *DWM* #168
23 *DWM* #57
24 *DWM* #145
25 *DWM* #97
26 *Elizabeth Sladen: The Autobiography* (Aaurum, 2011)
27 *The Final Curtain* (BBC, 2011)
28 *DWM* #288
29 *DWM* #183
30 *DWM* #264
31 *The Final Curtain*
32 *DWM* #52

4: The Rocky Horror Show

1 *Daily Mail*, September 20, 1997
2 *Who On Earth Is Tom Baker?* (HarperCollins, 1997)
3 *DWM* #92
4 *DWM* #290
5 *Elizabeth Sladen: The Autobiography*
6 *Serial Thrillers* (BBC, 2004)
7 *Still Getting Away With It: The life and times of Nicholas Courtney* (scificollector.c.uk, 2005)
8 *DWM* #235
9 *DWM* #268
10 *DWM* #179
11 *DWM Winter Special 1983/84*

12 *DWM* #230
13 *DWM* #93
14 *DWM* #172
15 *DWM* #161
16 *DWM* #215
17 *DWM* #180
18 1984 interview (repro-
duced *DWM* #278)
19 *DWM* #203
20 *DWM* #242
21 1984 interview by John
Heckford and Michael Stead,
reproduced in *DWM* #248
22 *A Matter of Time* (BBC,
2007)
23 *DWM* #271
24 *DWM* #228
25 *DWM* #266
26 *DWM* #127
27 *DWM* #136
28 *DWM* #85
29 *DWM* #258
30 *DWM* #261
31 *There's Something About
Mary* (BBC, 2007)
32 *DWM* #262
33 *DWM* #340
34 *DWM* #269
35 *DWM* #181
36 Interview with *Eye of
Horus* website
37 *DWM* #313
38 *DWM* #194
39 *DWM* #257
40 *DWM* #107
41 *DWM* #202
42 *DWM* #253
43 *A New Body At Last*
(BBC, 2007)
44 *DWM* #341
45 Interview with *The Fan
Can* website
46 *Myth Makers: Tom Baker*,
BBV Video

5: It Shouldn't Happen to a Bloody Vet

1 *A New Body At Last* (BBC, 2007)
2 *Being Doctor Who* (BBC, 2007)
3 *DWM* #346
4 *DWM* #353
5 *DWM* #313
6 *The Crowded TARDIS* (BBC, 2007)
7 *DWM* #327
8 *JN-T: The Life and Scandalous Times of John Nathan-Turner* by Richard Marson (Miwk, 2013)
9 *DWM* #253
10 *DWM* #295
11 *DWM* #110
12 *DWM* #347
13 *DWM* #339
14 *DWM* #227
15 *Being Doctor Who*
16 *Celebration* (BBC, 2008)
17 *DWM* #272
18 *DWM* #353
19 *DWM* #133
20 *DWM* #202
21 *DWM* #215
22 *Being Doctor Who*

6: Hex and Violence

1 *Trials and Tribulations* (BBC, 2008)
2 *The Doctors: 30 Years of Time Travel and Beyond* (BBV, 1995)
3 *DWM* #322
4 *JN-T: The Scandalous Life and Times of John Nathan-Turner*
5 *The Guardian*, October 22, 2005
7 *Starburst* #97
7 *DWM* #338
8 *DWM* #387

7: The Greatest Show in the Galaxy! (cancelled)

1 *Last Chance Saloon* (BBC, 2011)
2 *Script Doctor: The Inside Story of Doctor Who 1986-89* by Andrew Cartmel (Reynolds & Hearn, 2005)
3 *DWM* #216
4 *DWM* #301
5 *DWM* #425
6 *DWM* #131
7 *DWM* #301
8 *JN-T: The Life & Scandalous Times of John Nathan-Turner*
9 *Ace! The Inside Story of the End of an Era* by Sophie Aldred and Mike Tucker (Virgin, 1996)
10 *DWM* #224
11 *Fire and Ice* (BBC, 2012)
12 *DWM* #326
13 *DWM* #425
14 *DWM* #299
15 *The Show Must Go On* (BBC, 2012)
16 *DWM* #262
17 *DWM* #325
18 *DWM* #302
19 *DWM* #218
20 *Endgame* (BBC, 2007)
21 *DWM* #273
22 *DWM* #323
23 *Still Getting Away With It: The life and times of Nicholas Courtney*
24 *DWM* #217
25 *DWM* #153
26 *DWM* #339

End Notes

Chapter 1

I. For non-UK readers: Tony Hancock's lugubrious homespun philosophising – often delivered from beneath his trademark homburg hat – made him the biggest British comedy star of the late 50s and early 60s. He is best immortalised in Ray Galton and Alan Simpson's scripts for his BBC sitcom, *Hancock's Half Hour*.

II. A word on titles. From 1963 until 1966, *Doctor Who* serials didn't have overall titles, just individual episode names. So, for example, the four episodes of Anthony Coburn's debut story were presented to viewers as "An Unearthly Child" followed by "The Cave of Skulls", "The Forest of Fear" and "The Firemaker". But it was clearly necessary to have some sort of umbrella title for the purposes of paperwork and (in later years) commercial ventures such as book, video and DVD releases, and also to avoid fans having to have arguments like "I can't believe you think 'An Unearthly Child', 'The Cave of Skulls', 'The Forest of Fear' and 'The Firemaker' is a better story than 'A Land of Fear', 'Guests of Madame Guillotine', 'A Change of Identity', 'The Tyrant of France', 'A Bargain of Necessity' and 'Prisoners of Conciergerie'!"

But agreeing an "official" title for these early serials has been the cause of much heated debate – and possibly the occasional bit of hair-pulling – over the years. In the case of that debut story, for example, there are at least five contenders: *The Tribe of Gum* was the working title prior to recording (hence its use in this chapter so far); the first publicity release, as we've seen, referred to it as *100,000 BC*; Verity Lambert was known to call it *The Palelolithic Age*, while *The Stone Age* was a slightly dumbed-down version used in publicity material a couple of years after broadcast. But the most influential source of consensus for these early stories continues to be 1973's *Radio Times Tenth Anniversary Special*. In this instance, the magazine opted to call the whole shooting match *An Unearthly Child*: that's pretty much stuck ever since, and is the name to look for if you want to seek out the serial in any of its available formats. Apart from on DVD, where it actually appears as part of a box set called *The Beginning*. Told you it was confusing. Oh, and it was also issued as a script book in the late 80s under the title *The Tribe of Gum*, but they were just showing off.

III. Okay, so he might not have done the Troy McClure routine – but the examples from his CV are, believe it or not, all true.

IV. For those who still can't, it's a pun on *Prisoners of Conscience*. Told you it was rubbish.

V. For non-UK readers: Dick Emery was a comic actor whose self-titled sketch show ran on BBC1 from 1963 to 1981. A spiritual precursor to Matt Lucas and David Walliams' *Little Britain*, Emery was fond of dragging up, and his most famous catchphrase was "Oooh you are awful – but I like you." Maybe you had to be there.

Chapter 2

I. And nineteenth-century astronomers beat them both to it, using the name Vulcan for a "missing" planet they believed existed between Mercury and the Sun, but which turned out to be gravitational lensing caused by the mass of the sun and... you know, stuff like that. (Other physics textbooks are available.)

II. Drinks weren't all they stopped for. In a 2013 *Doctor Who Magazine* interview, Frazer Hines said of Patrick Troughton: "Sometimes he'd give me a lift home from work. We'd go to three different houses on the way. He'd knock on the door, give this woman some money, and then we'd drive off. I'd look the other way."[15]

III. For non-UK readers (and readers who like their music amped up to 11): Nick Drake was an English singer-songwriter and guitarist who died from an overdose at the age of 26, having produced three exquisitely beautiful but commercially disastrous albums of fragile acoustic folk-pop. Posthumously, his reputation grew over time to the point where is regularly cited as one of the most influential artists of his generation, and he was recently the subject of a documentary presented by überfan Brad Pitt.

IV. Hines later blamed his agent for badgering him to leave the show before he was ready – and claimed Patrick Troughton's wife had been instrumental in *his* decision to quit. "If we hadn't had those two blasted women nagging us," he said nearly 45 years later, "we'd still be there."[15]

V. A word on production codes (no wait, come back): Reflecting the order of recording – as opposed to transmission – the Hartnell serials started with a basic A-Z code (albeit without "I" or "O"). From *The Savages* until the end of the Troughton era, the stories were assigned double letters – AA, BB etc. The third Doctor rocked triple letters – starting, not unreasonably, with AAA – until the format switched to the simpler 4A, 4B etc when the next guy game in. He stayed so long he ate up most of the 5s as well, which meant the fifth Doctor's first broadcast serial was 5Z and most of his other stories were 6s. Nothing at all confusing about that. The sixth Doctor briefly got things back on track by taking 6S to 6Z, after which he and the seventh Doctor shared a bunch of 7s. If you want to know more about this subject, seek medical help.

VI. Or is it the 80s? For more on this, see Chapter 3...

Chapter 3

I. But *which* decade? Okay, buckle up, this gets complicated. Most of the evidence suggests the production team who devised the UNIT / Earthbound format intended the stories to be set in the "near future". And, certainly, some of the technology on display during the Pertwee era is vaguely futuristic – even if the fashions very noticeably aren't. If you've got a calculator, the scripts for *The Web of Fear*, *The Abominable Snowmen* and *The Invasion* and a little too much time on your hands, you can work out from various bits of dialogue that the latter story is set no earlier than 1979 – thus placing the third Doctor's stories firmly in the 80s. However, this is clearly contradicted later in the series' run, when much of the evidence – from the odd fan-pleasing continuity refer-

ence to fully-fledged guest appearances by former cast members – points to the UNIT stories being roughly contemporaneous to their 70s broadcast date. Later still, twenty-first century *Doctor Who* acknowledged the confusion with cheeky gags about the Doctor having worked for UNIT "in the 70s – or was it the 80s?", and the Brigadier's files being either "70s or 80s", depending on the dating protocol one uses. If you have a particularly long evening to fill, there are almost 5,000 words on this subject on Wikipedia's UNIT Dating Controversy page – all of them very disappointing to anyone who went there hoping to find out if the Brigadier ever got off with another member of staff at the Christmas party.

II. The idea of Camfield putting Levene through his paces in Richmond Park, of all places, has recently become even funnier thanks to a certain viral video sensation filmed there in 2011. If it somehow passed you by, look up "Jesus Christ in Richmond Park" on YouTube, and then see how impossible it is not to imagine Camfield shouting "Benton! Benton!" as Levene scampers around doing werewolf noises.

III. Camfield wouldn't return to *Doctor Who* until after Jon Pertwee had left, which may or may not have been related to the actor's avowed dislike of his military style of direction.

IV. For many years, *The Mind of Evil* only existed as a black and white print, which was somewhat more forgiving of the creature's shortcomings. Recently, though, the story has been restored to full colour, with Puff's appearance being greeted at one public screening with a memorable cry of "Awwww, soooo cute". Which is perhaps not *quite* what they were aiming for.

V. This sorry beast is also frequently dubbed "the Giant Testicle God." During a dinner that *Space Helmet*'s publisher enjoyed with Terrance Dicks and Barry Letts in 2004, the former was still testifying as to its testicular nature, while the latter insisted it was more squarish in appearance. The debate concluded with Letts good-naturedly telling Dicks: "Perhaps your testicles are square. Mine aren't."

VI. Richard Franklin actually coined this term. Not that he was bitter on behalf of the spurned Captain Yates, you understand.

Chapter 4

I. Actually, Jagger's parents were living there at the time – so cavorting of any sort was probably kept to a minimum.

II. It was probably the closest Ventham had come to a decent sleep for a while, having given birth to a baby boy the previous year. Using his father's family name of Cumberbatch, baby Benedict would grow up to be one of the biggest stars of his day, and help redefine Sir Arthur Conan Doyle's Sherlock Holmes for the twenty-first century. We'll be hearing from him again in Volume II.

III. Joyce later claimed to have been dismissed from the production no fewer than three times, before being re-hired "20 minutes later".

IV. In late 2013, it was announced that the fourth Doctor and Romana II would be reuniting for a series of audio plays – but with Tom Baker and Lalla Ward recording their lines separately.

Chapter 5

I. It wasn't quite this manic all the time: in fact, recording on *Doctor Who* was stood down for two months between the second and third production blocks to allow Davison to concentrate on *Sink or Swim*. The following year, the production break would be nearer three months: clearly the Beeb's hit new sitcom was considered the priority, while *Doctor Who* would just have to learn to... well, sink or swim.

II. During one rehearsal session for *Castrovalva*, the absent Davison's place was taken by none other than Patrick Troughton.

III. Only one Aboriginal dancer answered the production team's advert in *The Stage*, while the Chinese hoofers were recruited from a local Shepherd's Bush takeaway.

IV. In 2001, Matthew Waterhouse would be honoured – if that's the right word – in the name of a character in the first radio series of Matt Lucas and David Walliams' *Little Britain*. In their version, Matthew Waterhouse was a rubbish inventor whose ideas included Sugar Poofs – "real gay men frosted in sugar".

V. Fielding's husband Nicholas Davies, a former foreign editor at the *Daily Mirror*, was a close associate of Robert Maxwell, and was famously accused in a book of dealing arms on behalf of Mossad, the Israeli secret service – a claim he has always denied. He and Fielding divorced in 1991.

VI. For non-UK readers: The Open University (OU) is a distance-learning and research university with an open-entry policy. From 1971 until 2006, one of the OU's primary teaching methods was through BBC television broadcasts, which is why generously bearded men in kipper ties could often be found expounding in front of complicated-looking equations several decades after they'd retired, died or – at the very least – updated their wardrobes.

VII. Future national treasure Kathy Burke also appears as an extra, playing a disease-ridden Lazar. (She's the first to admit she's rarely cast for her looks.) The voice of Terminus, meanwhile, was provided by Martin Mulcaster – the man who did the "mind the gap" announcements on the London Underground.

VIII. Though America got first dibs, it was actually Australia's ABC network who'd put up some of the money for *The Five Doctors*, as part of the series' first international co-production deal. Sadly, that didn't buy any influence over the script, so we were denied the second Doctor greeting Jamie with a cry of "Strewth, that bloke's got no strides!", the Doctor addressing Susan as Sheila, and (*that's enough Australia gags – Ed*)

IX. Davison was a bit miffed about not getting to do a full season – but felt slightly less miffed when it was made clear he'd still be getting paid for it.

X. John Nathan-Turner also managed to smother a scandal concerning guest star Peter Wyngarde. After finding fame as proto-Austin Powers dandy detective Jason King, Wyngarde – known to his friends as Petunia Winegum – had struggled to revive his career after being convicted for an act of gross indecency in a bus station toilet. One of the reporters embedded on the *Who* location shoot was ready to file more lurid revelations about the star, but Nathan-Turner succeeded in "persuading" him otherwise – apparently by threatening to claim he'd slept with him. In later years, it emerged that Wyngarde had enjoyed a decade-long relationship with Brit screen legend Alan Bates.

XI. In recent years, Graeme Harper has claimed that he only shot *The Caves of Androzani* this way because he didn't know how things were *supposed* to be done at the BBC. Given his many years on the studio floor in the preceeding years, *Space Helmet* suspects this is more an attempt at modesty than a genuine confession.

Chapter 6

I. For non-UK readers: Eddie Stobart was the founder of a road haulage firm so famous in Britain it even had its own TV show – though episodes like the one in which "a new truck causes a bit of a stir" were unlikely to trouble *Dallas*' "Who shot JR?" cliffhanger in the iconic telly stakes.

II. Around the same time, Nathan-Turner also cheekily let it be known that the TARDIS' iconic exterior might be about to be scrapped. This led to even more publicity than the new Doctor received – first when the idea was originally mooted, and again when the police box shell was sensationally "saved". (The truth is it was never in danger in the first place, of course – it was just another example of Nathan-Turner the showman at his Barnum-like best.)

III. For non-UK readers: The Fat Controller is the strikingly un-PC name for the well-fed fellow who runs the railway in the Rev W V Awdry's Thomas the Tank Engine stories. In the US, the character is known, somewhat less provocatively, as Sir Topham Hatt. The name seems doubly apt in *Attack of the Cybermen*, in which the line "It is a fact, Controller" is frequently misheard as "It is a Fat Controller".

IV. We have our dear friend Mary Whitehouse to thank for this term: her National Viewers' and Listeners' Association coined the phrase to describe the glut of violent films such as *The Driller Killer, I Spit On Your Grave* and *Dude, Where's My Spleen?*+ that appeared on home video in the early 80s thanks to a loophole in the UK's film classification.

(+ Okay, I made that one up.)

V. Other superfans who *almost* made it to the screen included David J Howe, who was briefly in the frame for ITV's breakfast show, and Ian Levine – who, bizarrely, was lined up for a slot on primetime chat show *Wogan*. John Nathan-Turner also wanted Levine to smash his TV for a publicity stunt. He said he'd happily lose a limb for *Doctor Who*, but he drew the line at losing his telly. (Levine *did* once smash a vinyl copy of Sinitta's *So Macho* over Simon Cowell's head – but that's a whole other story.)

VI. The part of the mutant had been offered to Laurence Olivier. Despite letting it be known via his biographer, *Mark of the Rani* guest star Gawn Grainger, that he might entertain a small role on film, Lord Olivier eventually declined the offer. Possibly this was down to availability or possibly it was because, with the creature's "dialogue" largely made of of animalistic grunts, it wasn't exactly *King Lear*.

VII. Lightweight was also Jonathan Powell's verdict on the story – which was a bit bloody rich, since he was one of the people who'd ordered the production team to make it less violent and more humorous.

VIII. They also reached an unusually large audience, thanks to a promotion that saw mini-comics being given away in multi-packs of Golden Wonder crisps.

Chapter 7

I. John Nathan-Turner had originally budgeted for two four-parters and one six-parter, to be made half in studio, half on location, but rather cannily split the latter into three episodes in studio and three on location, in order to create a fourth story. Even the producer's most vociferous critics had to concede he was adept with a calculator.

II. To be fair, the spiral staircase only appears in a cut scene restored to the DVD version, which offers a new edit presumaby designed to make the story bearable for Ben Aaronovitch to watch.

Acknowledgements

It should be noted that most of the raw data – the facts, if you will – on these pages is drawn from secondary sources. To this end, I am grateful to all those *Who* scholars who, over the years, have done the real hard work, putting in hours of research for numerous books, documentaries and magazine articles. I am, of course, especially indebted to the good offices of *Doctor Who Magazine* which, particularly under the recent editorship of Gary Gillatt, Clayton Hickman and Tom Spilsbury, has managed to combine being the programme's official journal of record with being endlessly inventive and, crucially, laugh-out-loud funny. And also to *Doctor Who*'s pre-eminent historian – and that's not too grand a word – Andrew Pixley, whose forensic attention to detail is the reason we know so much of what we know about this show. Thanks, too, to all the talented documentary makers who have contributed to the *Doctor Who* DVD range, and to Benjamin Cook, for his astute work in wrangling 30 years of *Doctor Who Magazine* interviews into the fabulous *In Their Own Words* series, which saved me literally weeks of living in the attic – and possibly a messy divorce, too.

I thought of all the jokes myself though.

I owe a huge debt to Steve Manfred, whose encyclopaedic knowledge of the series helped me avoid the occasional howler that would have seen me pilloried in the street by right-thinking *Doctor Who* fans for evermore. Thanks also to Robert Aston, Simon Colenutt, David James, Ian Berriman, Neil Perryman, Steve O'Brien, Nick Setchfield, John Williams and Mark Wright for sharing my enduring love of this daft programme, and answering numerous ridiculous questions on Facebook.

But my biggest thanks must go to two people without whom none of this would have been possible in the first place: Firstly, to the great Lars Pearson, who took a gamble on some random hack from England, and subsequently proved to be a brilliant, insightful and sympathetic editor – and a deeply lovely man, to boot. And, finally, to my wonderful wife, Rachel, who sacrificed so much to allow me

scratch this particular itch – which, for reasons best known to myself, I decided to start writing in the same week our second son was born. How she laughed.

About the author

Paul Kirkley was born in Leeds approximately two-and-a-half hours before episode three of *The Daemons*, but they kept you in hospital for ages in those days, so he missed it. Four decades on, he works in Cambridge (a lovely city, though technically non-canonical thanks to a silly spat over the *Play School* clock – see Chapter 4), where he lives with his wife Rachel and their sons George and Thomas.

After 20 years in newspapers, most recently as deputy editor of the *Cambridge News*, Paul now works as a freelance writer and media consultant. He started his journalism career as a teenager, publishing his own *Doctor Who* fanzine called, imaginatively, *The Fanzine*. He writes regularly on the subject of *Doctor Who* for *SFX* magazine, and has been a frequent contributor to websites such as *Behind the Sofa* and *Tachyon TV*. In 2011, he beat off competition from literally some other journalists to win the coveted-ish title of Newspaper Columnist of the Year (East of England) for his column/blog, *About a Boy*, a trick he somehow managed to repeat in 2013 for his latest column, *Paul Kirkley's Newsround*. He never believes anyone who says they used to watch *Doctor Who* behind the sofa, because everyone he knows has their sofa against the wall.

Dedication

This book is dedicated to my mum and dad, Wendy and Adrian Kirkley, who gave me the sort of childhood where I felt safe enough to be scared by *Doctor Who*; to my sons, George and Thomas, the next generation of *Who* fans (else there'll be trouble…); and to my wife, Rachel, who has already given so much to the *Space Helmet* cause, I've promised not to ask her to read it.